PHILIP'S

STREET ATLAS
Dorset
Bournemouth and Poole

First published in 2002 by

Philip's, a division of
Octopus Publishing Group Ltd
2-4 Heron Quays, London E14 4JP

First edition 2002
Third impression with revisions 2004

ISBN 0-540-08119-1 (hardback)
ISBN 0-540-08120-5 (spiral)

© Philip's 2004

 Ordnance Survey®

This product includes mapping data licensed
from Ordnance Survey® with the permission of
the Controller of Her Majesty's Stationery Office.
© Crown copyright 2004. All rights reserved.
Licence number 100011710.

Printed and bound in Spain
by Cayfosa-Quebecor

Contents

III   **Key to map symbols**

IV   **Key to map pages**

VI   **Route planning**

VIII   **Administrative and Postcode boundaries**

1   **Street maps** at 3½ inches to 1 mile

188   **Street maps** at 1¾ inches to 1 mile

212   **Street map** at 3½ inches to 1 mile

213   **Town map of** Salisbury

214   **Index** of towns and villages

217   **Index** of streets, hospitals, industrial estates, railway
stations, schools, shopping centres, universities
and places of interest

Digital Data

The exceptionally high-quality mapping found in this atlas is available as digital data in TIFF format, which is easily convertible to other bitmapped (raster) image formats.

The index is also available in digital form as a standard database table. It contains all the details found in the printed index together with the National Grid reference for the map square in which each entry is named.

For further information and to discuss your requirements, please contact Philip's on 020 7644 6932 or james.mann@philips-maps.co.uk

22a	**Motorway** with junction number
	Primary route – dual/single carriageway
	A road – dual/single carriageway
	B road – dual/single carriageway
	Minor road – dual/single carriageway
	Other minor road – dual/single carriageway
	Road under construction
	Pedestrianised area
DY7	**Postcode boundaries**
	County and unitary authority boundaries
	Railway
	Railway under construction
	Tramway, miniature railway
	Rural track, private road or narrow road in urban area
	Gate or obstruction to traffic (restrictions may not apply at all times or to all vehicles)
	Path, bridleway, byway open to all traffic, road used as a public path

The representation in this atlas of a road, track or path is no evidence of the existence of a right of way

Adjoining page indicators
(The colour of the arrow indicates the scale of the adjoining page - see scales below)

214
168
72
217

The map area within the blue band is shown at a larger scale on the page, indicated by the blue block and arrow

Walsall	**Railway station**
	Private railway station
	Bus, coach station
	Ambulance station
	Coastguard station
	Fire station
	Police station
+	**Accident and Emergency entrance to hospital**
H	**Hospital**
+	**Place of worship**
i	**Information Centre** (open all year)
P	**Parking**
P&R	**Park and Ride**
PO	**Post Office**
Å	**Camping site**
	Caravan site
	Golf course
	Picnic site
Prim Sch	**Important buildings, schools, colleges, universities and hospitals**
River Medway	**Water name**
	River, stream
	Lock, weir
	Water
	Tidal water
	Woods
	Houses
Church	**Non-Roman antiquity**
ROMAN FORT	**Roman antiquity**

Abbr	Full	Abbr	Full
Acad	Academy	Mkt	Market
Allot Gdns	Allotments	Meml	Memorial
Cemy	Cemetery	Mon	Monument
C Ctr	Civic Centre	Mus	Museum
CH	Club House	Obsy	Observatory
Coll	College	Pal	Royal Palace
Crem	Crematorium	PH	Public House
Ent	Enterprise	Recn Gd	Recreation Ground
Ex H	Exhibition Hall	Resr	Reservoir
Ind Est	Industrial Estate	Ret Pk	Retail Park
IRB Sta	Inshore Rescue Boat Station	Sch	School
		Sh Ctr	Shopping Centre
Inst	Institute	TH	Town Hall/House
Ct	Law Court	Trad Est	Trading Estate
L Ctr	Leisure Centre	Univ	University
LC	Level Crossing	Wks	Works
Liby	Library	YH	Youth Hostel

■ The small numbers around the edges of the maps identify the 1 kilometre National Grid lines ■ The dark grey border on the inside edge of some pages indicates that the mapping does not continue onto the adjacent page

The scale of the maps on the pages numbered in blue is 5.52 cm to 1 km • 3½ inches to 1 mile • 1: 18103

0 ¼ ½ ¾ 1 mile
0 250m 500m 750m 1 kilometre

The scale of the maps on pages numbered in green is 2.76 cm to 1 km • 1¾ inches to 1 mile • 1: 36206

0 ¼ ½ ¾ 1 mile
0 250m 500m 750m 1kilometre

Key to map pages

| 212 | Map pages at 3½ inches to 1 mile | 190 | Map pages at 1¾ inches to 1 mile |

Frome

Wells

A371

A39

Shepton Mallet

Evercreech

A361

M5

A371

A37

A359

Bruton

Castle Cary

Penselwood 1 2 Zeals

Bourton

Wincanton

A303

Milton on Stour

4 5

Cucklington

Rodgrove

8 9 West 10 Stour

Kington Magna

Taunton

A378

A372

A359

A37

Rimpton 14 15 16 17 Yenston 18 19 Stour Provost 20 21

Mudford

Trent

Poyntington

Milborne Port

Henstridge

Pillwell

A303

A3088

Over Compton 28 A30 29 Sherborne 30 31 Stalbridge 32 33 Hinton St Mary 34 35

Brympton 26 27 Yeovil

Bradford Abbas

Alweston

Stourton Caundle

Sturminster Newton

South Petherton

Ilminster

Dinnington

Merriott

Hardington Mandeville

Barwick

Longburton

A3030

Bishop's Caundle

Okeford Fitzpaine

Yetminster 194 195 196 197

Chard

191 192 193

Crewkerne

North Perrott

Leigh

Pulham

Ibberton

A356

A352

Clapton

Halstock

Chetnole

Glanvilles Wootton

A30

Drimpton

Mosterton

Evershot

Buckland Newton

Hilton

Thorncombe

Broadwindsor

Rampisham

Batcombe

202 203 204 205 206 207 208 209

Hawkchurch

Netherbury

Beaminster

Hooke

Cerne Abbas

Piddletrenthide

Cheselbourne

A3066

A356

Toller Porcorum

Cattistock

Sydling St Nicholas

Dewlish

Axminster

A35

A358

Salway Ash

Powerstock

Maiden Newton

Godmanstone

Milborne St Andrew

64 65 Broad Oak 68 69 70 71 72 73 74 75 Piddlehinton 76 77 78 79

Wootton Fitzpaine 66 67 Bradpole West Compton Frampton Charlton Down Puddletown

Morcombelake

Charmouth

Chideock

Bridport

Askerswell

Compton Valence

Stratton

A35

Affpuddle

96 97 98 99 100 101 102 103 104 105 106 107 108 109 110 111

Lyme Regis Lower Eype Shipton Gorge Litton Cheney Winterborne Abbas Dorchester Stinsford Woodsford

Seaton

A3052

Burton Bradstock

Littlebredy

Martinstown

134 135

Crossways

Moreton

128 129 Puncknowle 132 133 Winterborne Monkton 136 137 138

130 131 Portesham West Knighton

Abbotsbury

Upwey

Owermoigne

A352

148 149 150 151 152 153 154 155 156

Langton Herring

Preston

Osmington

Chaldon Herring

A354

Chickerell

Osmington Mills

165 166 167 168 169 170 171

Weymouth

Wyke Regis

180 181

A354

Fortuneswell

186 187 Easton

Southwell

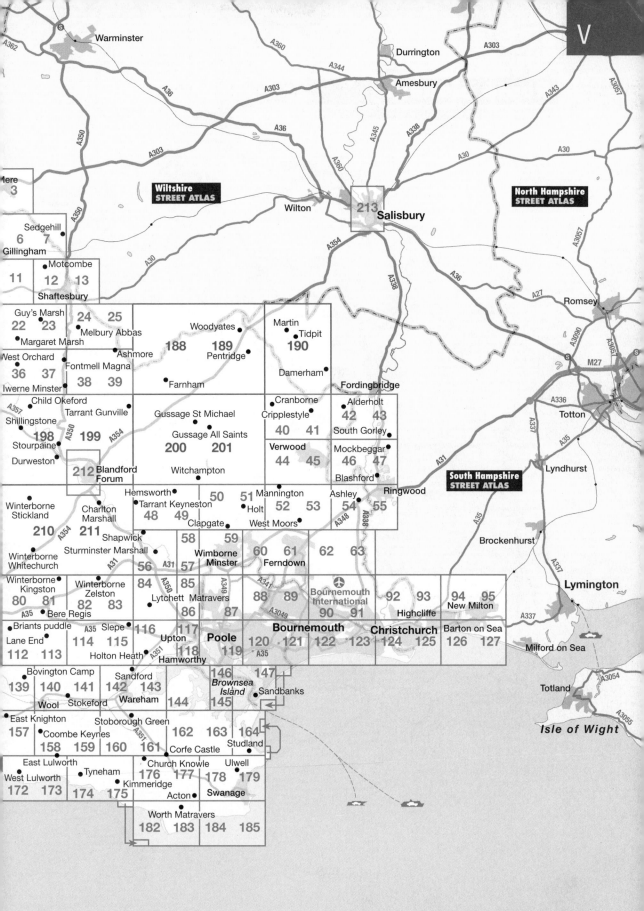

V

Warminster

Wiltshire
STREET ATLAS

Durrington

Amesbury

Wilton

213 Salisbury

North Hampshire
STREET ATLAS

Romsey

M27

Mere
3

Sedgehill
6   7
Gillingham

Motcombe
11   12   13
Shaftesbury

Guy's Marsh
22   23   24   25
Melbury Abbas
Margaret Marsh
Ashmore
West Orchard
36   37   Fontmell Magna
38   39
Iwerne Minster

Woodyates
188   189
Pentridge

Farnham

Martin
190   Tidpit

Damerham

Fordingbridge

Alderholt
42   43
South Gorley

Totton

Lyndhurst

Child Okeford
Tarrant Gunville
Shillingstone
198   199
Stourpaine
Durweston

Gussage St Michael
Gussage All Saints
200   201
Witchampton

Cranborne
Cripplestyle
40   41
Verwood
44   45

Mockbeggar
46   47
Blashford

Ringwood

South Hampshire
STREET ATLAS

Brockenhurst

Lymington

212 Blandford
Forum

Hemsworth
Winterborne
Stickland
Charlton
Marshall
210   211
Shapwick
Winterborne
Whitechurch
Sturminster Marshall
56   57

50
Tarrant Keyneston
48   49
Clapgate
58   59
Wimborne
Minster

51 Mannington
Holt
52   53
West Moors

Ashley
54   55

60   61   62   63
Ferndown

Winterborne
Kingston
80   81
Bere Regis

Winterborne
Zelston
82   83
Lytchett Matravers
84   85
86   87

Bournemouth
International
88   89
90   91

92   93
Highcliffe

94   95
New Milton

Barton on Sea
126   127

Milford on Sea

Briants puddle
Lane End
112   113
114   115
Holton Heath

Slepe
116   117
Upton
118   119
Hamworthy

Poole
120   121
A35

122   123
BOURNEMOUTH

Christchurch
124   125

Totland

Isle of Wight

Bovington Camp
139   140   141
Wool   Stokeford

Sandford
142   143
Wareham
144

146   147
Brownsea
Island
145   Sandbanks

East Knighton
157   Coombe Keynes
158   159   160   161
Corfe Castle

Stoborough Green
162   163   164
Studland

East Lulworth
West Lulworth
172   173   174   175
Tyneham
Kimmeridge
Acton

Church Knowle
176   177
178   179
Swanage
Ulwell

Worth Matravers
182   183   184   185

Scale
0   5   10   15   20 km
0   5   10 miles

Route planning

Scale

0	5	10	15	20 km
0		5		10 miles

Administrative and Postcode boundaries

Legend:
- County and unitary authority boundaries
- Postcode boundaries
- Area covered by this atlas

1 Bournemouth
2 Poole
3 Christchurch
4 Weymouth and Portland

Scale

0 5 10 15 20 25 30km
0 5 10 15 20 miles

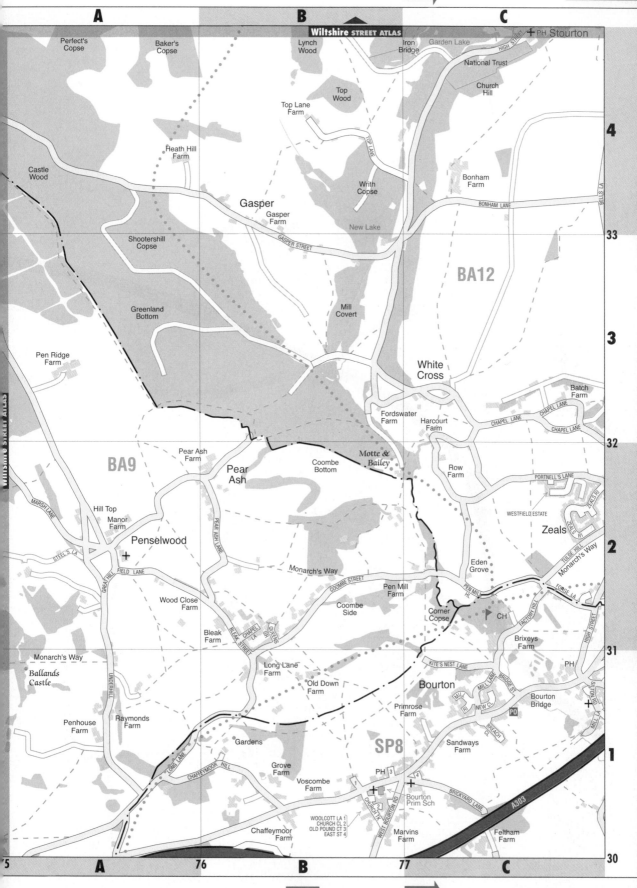

Wiltshire STREET ATLAS

Perfect's Copse
Baker's Copse
Lynch Wood
Iron Bridge
Garden Lake
PH Stourton
High Street
National Trust
Church Hill
Top Lane Farm
Top Wood
Bonham Farm
Heath Hill Farm
Writh Copse
Bells La
Castle Wood
Gasper
Bonham Lane
Gasper Farm
New Lake
BA12
Gasper Street
Shootershill Copse
Greenland Bottom
Mill Covert
White Cross
Pen Ridge Farm
Batch Farm
Fordswater Farm
Harcourt Farm
Chapel Lane
Chapel Lane
Chapel Lane
Pear Ash Farm
Motte & Bailey
BA9
Pear Ash
Coombe Bottom
Row Farm
Portnell's Lane
Zeals Rd
Westfield Estate
Zeals
Hill Top Manor Farm
Marsh Lane
Monarch's Way
Steel S La
Penselwood
Pear Ash Lane
Monarch's Way
Coombe Street
Pen Mill Farm
Eden Grove
Tulse Hill
Forge La
Great Hill
Field Lane
Wood Close Farm
Coombe Side
Pen Mill Hl
Corner Copse
CH
Factory Hill
High Street
Brixeys Farm
Bleak Farm
Chapel La
Bleak St
Queens Street
PH
Monarch's Way
Underhill
Kite's Nest Lane
Bourton
Mill Rd
New Cl
PO
Bourton Bridge
Knoll La
Mill La
Ballands Castle
Long Lane Farm
Old Down Farm
Primrose Farm
Breach Cl
Penhouse Farm
Raymonds Farm
Gardens
SP8
Sandways Farm
Longs Lane
Chaffeymoor Hill
Grove Farm
Voscombe Farm
PH 3
Brickyard Lane
A303
Bourton Prim Sch
West Bourton Rd
Church Tk
Chaffeymoor Farm
WOOLCOTT LA 1
CHURCH CL 2
OLD POUND CT 3
EAST ST 4
Marvins Farm
Feltham Farm

A   B   C

4

3

2

1

Rifle
Range

Great
Bottom

*Strip
Lynchets*

Mere
Down

Aucombe
Bottom

Ashfield
Bottom

Earthwork

B3095

East
Hill

Chetcombe
Bottom

Manor
Farm

A303 Andover

Castle
Plantation

Chetcombe
Farm

Mere Quarry
(limestone)

33

DOWNSIDE CL

CHETCOMBE RD

A303

JACK PAUL
CL

NORTH
ST

STEEP
ST

OLD HOLLOW

THE FIELDS

SPRINGFIELD SCH

HAZZARD'S HILL

WHITE ROAD

1 QUEENS RD
2 SPINNERS WY
3 NURSERY GDS
4 UPPER WATER ST
5 FENNEL RD

CASTLE HILL
CR

BISHOPS CL

DENES AV

THE
ROWS

NEW
CUT

Duchy Manor
Middle Sch

Tumulus

Wiltshire STREET ATLAS

CASTLE HILL LA

NORTH ST

SALISBURY
ST

First Sch

Burton

Burton Lane
Copse

3

CASTLE HILL
LA

BARTON
CL

Liby &
Mus

THE
SQ

P

IVY MEAD

Ashfield Water

Burton
Farm

MERE

P
CHURCH ST

DARK LANE

WATER ST

MILL LANE

Holwell

Chaddenwick
Wood

Charnage
Farm

Charnage

The Chantry

ANGEL LA

BARNES
PL

Cemy

PETTRIDGE LANE

LYNCH CL

BA12

Monarch's Way

32

Edge
Bridge

CLEMENT'S LANE

Southbrook

PH

Little
Wood

Charnage

Rook
Street

LORDSMEAD
RD

ROOK ST

Industrial
Estate

SHAFTESBURY ROAD

1 ASHGROVE
2 SOUTHBROOK GDS
3 WHITEMARSH
4 THE BARTLETTS
5 BALMOOR CL

SOUTHBROOK

Limpers
Hill

Sewage
Works

Shreen Water

*Woodlands
Manor*

The Causeway

Field
End

Causeway
Farm

BARROW STREET LANE

Woodlands
Farm

2

31

Swain's Ford
Bridge

WOODLANDS ROAD

White Hill
Wood

White
Hill

Church
Farm

Barrow
Street

West Swainsford
Farm

East Swainsford
Farm

Wet Lane
Farm

WET LANE

Lyemarsh
Farm

Barrow Street
Farm

Breaches
Farm

1

Homestead
Farm

SP8

Two Counties
Farm

Black House
Farm

PIMPERLEAZE ROAD

CUNNAGE LA

30

A   82   B   83   C

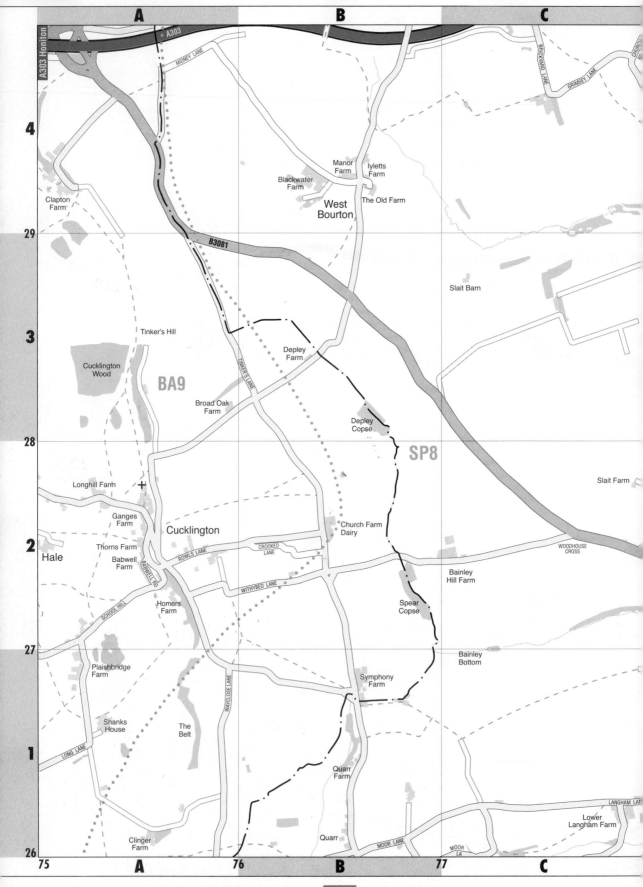

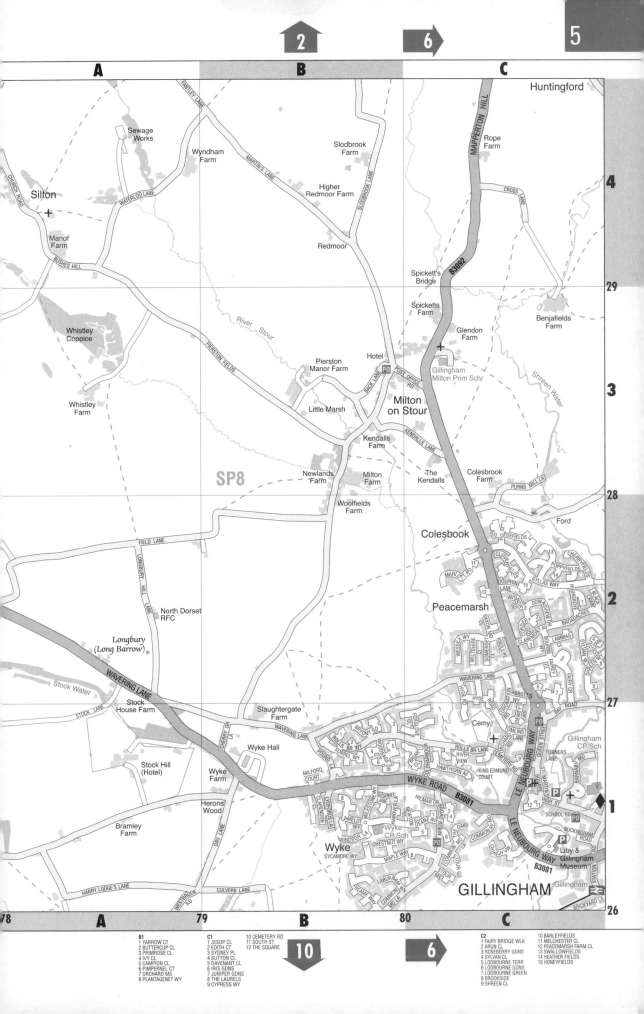

A   B   C

Huntingford

Sewage Works

Wyndham Farm

Slodbrook Farm

Higher Redmoor Farm

MAPPERTON HILL

Rope Farm

CROSS LANE

CHURCH ROAD

Silton

4

Manor Farm

BUSHES HILL

WATERLOO LANE

FANTLEY LANE

MARTIN'S LANE

SLODBROOK LANE

Redmoor

B3092

Spickett's Bridge

29

Whistley Coppice

River Stour

PIERSTON FIELDS

Spicketts Farm

Glendon Farm

Benjafields Farm

Shreen Water

Whistley Farm

Pierston Manor Farm

Hotel

PO

POST OFFICE RD

BACK LANE

Gillingham Milton Prim Sch

3

Little Marsh

Milton on Stour

KENDALLS LANE

SP8

Newlands Farm

Kendalls Farm

Milton Farm

The Kendalls

Colesbrook Farm

PURNS MILL LA

28

Woolfields Farm

Colesbook

Ford

FIELD LANE

CASEFIELDS

13

CHERRYFIELDS

POPPYFIELDS

14

MARLOT RD

CLOVERFIELDS

DOLPHIN LANE

15

GYLLAS WAY

HIGHGROVE

BLACK BRIDGE

North Dorset RFC

LONGBURY HILL LANE

Peacemarsh

12

AVON CL

CORFE CL

DOWNSVIEW DR

BROADACRES

MANSYLVAN

2

Longbury (Long Barrow)

WESSEX WY

WILTSHIRE

SOMERSET WAYS

KNOLL PL

CLARENDON AV

BOURNE CL

LAMMAS CL

FAIREY

SHREEN WY

Stock Water

WAVERING LANE

Stock House Farm

Stock Lane

Slaughtergate Farm

WAVERING LANE

Wavering Lane

HYDE RD

HYDE RD

ABBOTT'S

5

FAIRY CR

27

CHERRY DR

Wyke Hall

BRYONY GD

FOXGLOVE CL

WOODSAGE DR

CORONATION RD

Cemy

TOMLINS LANE

PO

Gillingham CP Sch

TURNERS LANE

BARNHILL RD

Stock Hill (Hotel)

Wyke Farm

MILFORD COURT

POUND

SORREL WY

ROLLS BR WY

HAWTHORN AV

RIVER VIEW

KING EDMUND COURT

QUEEN STREET

ST MARTINS

BARNHILL RD

Herons Wood

DRY LANE

CLAREDONI

LUVWARDS LA

WYKE ROAD

B3081

LE NEUBOURG WAY

High St

P

School Rd

PO

1

Bramley Farm

WINDSOR LA

CHESTNUT WY

MAPLE WAY

Wyke CP Sch

STUART LANE

NEWTON

DEANE AVE

HILMAR DR

BROAD ROBIN

THE OAKS

COMMON MD

COMMON AV

CHURCH

LE NEUBOURG WAY

Liby & Gillingham Museum

B3081

STATION RD

Wyke

SYCAMORE WY

LABURNUM WY

FREAME WAY

COMMON MD

GILLINGHAM

Gillingham

BRICKYARD LA

26

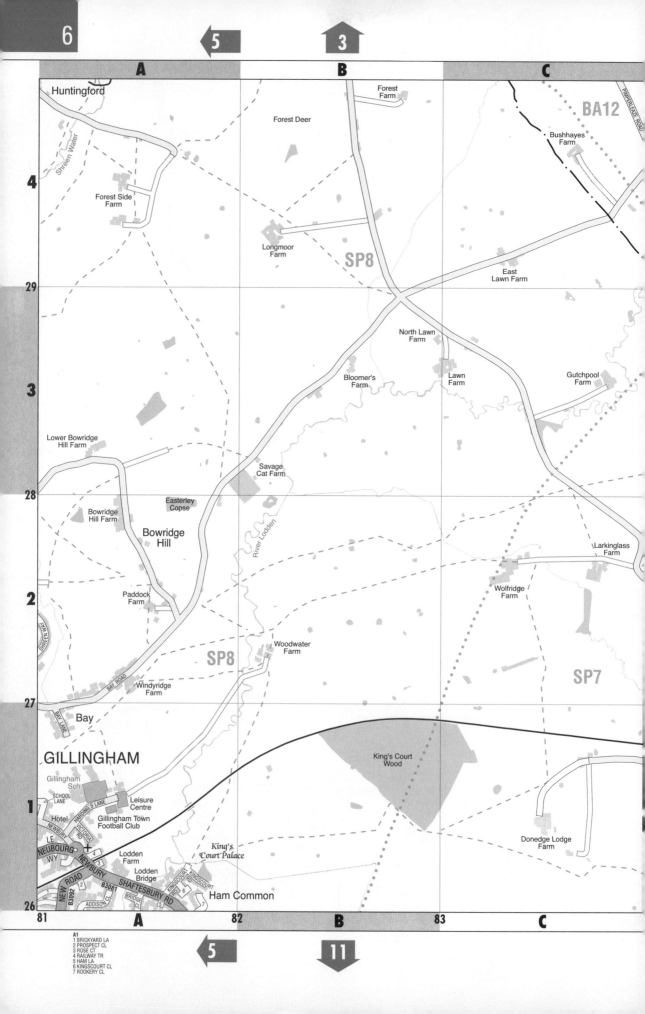

A B C

Huntingford
BA12

Forest Farm
Forest Deer
Bushhayes Farm

Shreen Water
Forest Side Farm

4

Longmoor Farm
SP8
East Lawn Farm

29

North Lawn Farm

3
Bloomer's Farm
Lawn Farm
Gutchpool Farm

Lower Bowridge Hill Farm

Savage Cat Farm

28
Easterley Copse

Bowridge Hill Farm
River Lodden
Larkinglass Farm

Bowridge Hill

2
Paddock Farm
Wolfridge Farm
SP7

Woodwater Farm
SP8

Windyridge Farm

27
Bay
Bay Lane

GILLINGHAM
King's Court Wood

Gillingham Sch
SCHOOL LANE
Leisure Centre

1
Hotel
Gillingham Town Football Club

LE NEUBOURG WY
Lodden Farm
King's Court Palace
King's Court Palace
Donedge Lodge Farm

NEW ROAD
SHAFTESBURY RD
Lodden Bridge

B3092
B3081
ADDISON

26
Ham Common

A1
1 BRICKYARD LA
2 PROSPECT CL
3 ROSE CT
4 RAILWAY TR
5 HAM LA
6 KINGSCOURT CL
7 ROOKERY CL

SP3

BA12

Park Pale

Higher Mere Park

River Lodden

New Leaze Farm

Snaggs Farm

Lower Park Farm

Forest Oaks

Grove Coppice

Westmarsh Farm

Pitts Farm

PITTS LANE

Sweetwell Farm

Church Farm

Sedgehill

CRATE LANE

Lower House Farm

SP7

Cowridge Copse

Withies Farm

Earthwork

Berrybrook Farm

BROADWELL LANE

Hull Copse

STREET LANE

North End Farm

Sedgehill Manor

Hayes Copse

Park Farm

North End

Guests Farm

Dewdown Copse

Butterstake Farm

Culver House Farm

Knapp Hill

Huggler's Hole

Stile End

West Coppleridge Farm

PH

CORNER LANE

The Corner

Elm Hill

ELM

HUNTERS MD

STAINERS MD

THE STREET

CORNER LANE

North Hayes Farm

Westley Copse

Motcombe Grange Preparatory Sch

Sewage Works

A350 Warminster

A350

4

29

3

28

2

27

1

26

A B C

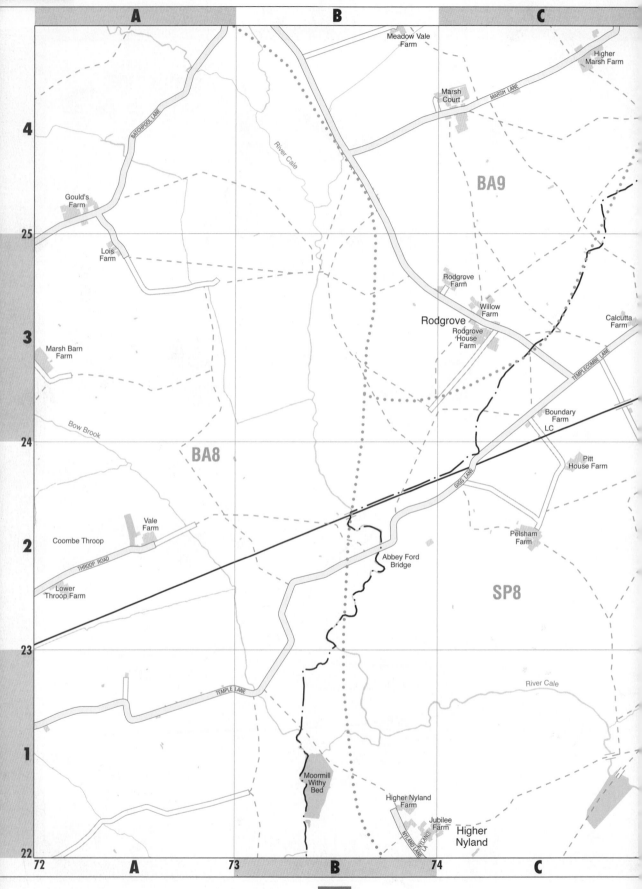

A B C

Meadow Vale Farm

Higher Marsh Farm

Marsh Court

MARSH LANE

BATCHPOOL LANE

River Cale

BA9

4

Gould's Farm

Rodgrove Farm

Willow Farm

Calcutta Farm

25

Lois Farm

Rodgrove

Rodgrove House Farm

TEMPLECOMBE LANE

3

Marsh Barn Farm

Boundary Farm

LC

Pitt House Farm

Bow Brook

24

BA8

GIGG LANE

Vale Farm

Pelsham Farm

2

Coombe Throop

THROOP ROAD

Abbey Ford Bridge

SP8

Lower Throop Farm

23

TEMPLE LANE

River Cale

1

Moormill Withy Bed

Higher Nyland Farm

NYLAND LANE

Jubilee Farm

Higher Nyland

22

72 A 73 B 74 C

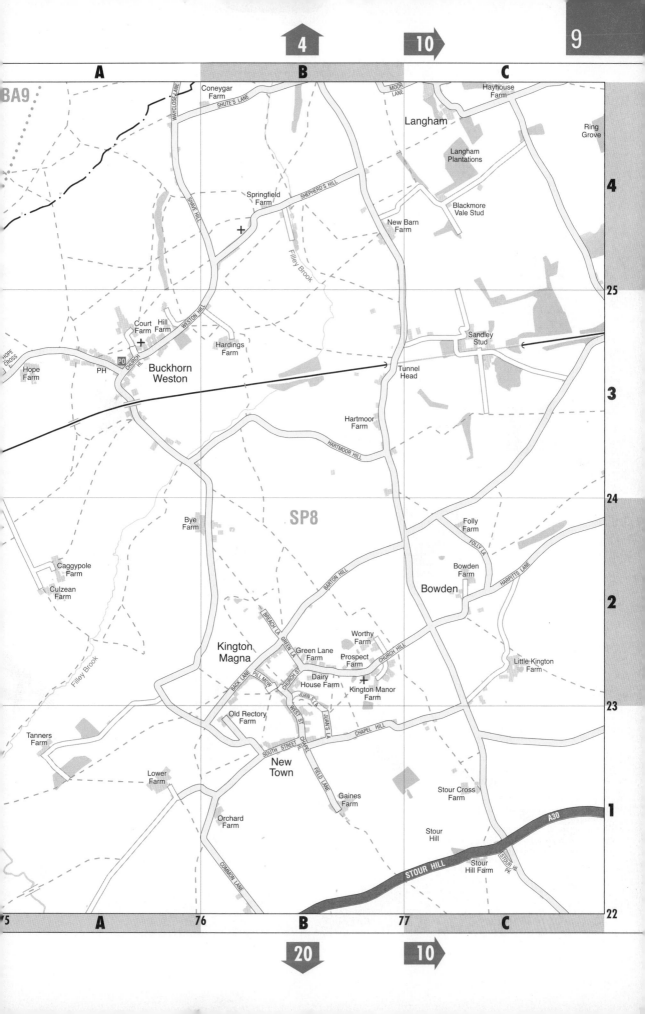

A | **B** | **C**

Ring Grove

Westbrook Farm

WESTBROOK ROAD

Culvers Farm

Thorngrove

COMMON MEAD LANE

Sewage Works

River Stour

BRICKYARD LN

Horkesley Hall Stud Farm

KINE BUSH LANE

Eccliffe

Presthayes Farm

Madjeston Farm

4

Bugley Court Farm

Walnut Tree Farm

Quarry Farm

Madjeston

Muddock's Copse

25

Pound Farm

B3092

Bugley Bridge

NATIONS ROAD

Bugley

BLEET LANE

STANDPITTS LANE

Hunger Hill

Woolhouse Farm

Hunger Hill Farm

3

River Stour

Bleet Farm

FOLLY LANE

Folly Farm

Dorey's Coppice

HARPITTS LANE

SP8

24

Primrose Farm

WITCH LANE

PH

2

Halletts Farm

Clay Hill House

BACK STREET

SANDLANDS

Hartgill Farm

WITCH CL

Needles Farm

WHITEFIELD DR

East Stour

Sunnylands Farm

BROWN'S LANE

HEAD LA

PO

THE FIELDINGS

Manor Farm

FRONT STREET

23

Church Farm

Highbridge Mill Farm

LOTMOOR HILL

A30

A30

CHURCH HILL

West Stour

High Bridge

Church Farm

STOUR CL 1
FORGE END 2

Butterwell Farm

Vanners Farm

CHURCH ST

CHURCH ST

Manor Farm

PH

Sewage Works

B3092

1

Townsend Farm

Terrace Farm

SCOTCHEY HILL

River Stour

Chequers Farm

SCOTCHEY LANE

ANGEL LANE

22

A | **B** | **C**

78 | 79 | 80

A
B
C

NEW ROAD
ADDISON CL
1 ADDISON CL
2 LODDEN VW
3 THE MS
4 MEADOWCROFT

ROOKERY CL
LOCKWOOD TR

Ham Farm

Park Farm

Rare Breeds Centre

Palemead Coppice

Lockwood Farm

SHAFTESBURY ROAD

Forest Lodge Farm

Lodden Lakes

Madjeston Bridge

Park Pale

Cole Street Farm

COLE STREET LANE

Meadow Brook Farm

Waterloo Farm

New House Farm

B3081

Shearstock Farm

Turnpike Wood

LINTERN LANE

SHAFTESBURY ROAD

Fernbrook Farm

SP8

High Grove Farm

Cowslip Farm

Lox Lane Covert

LOX LANE

SP7

Lox Lane Farm

Black Venn Farm

Lower Duncliffe Farm

A30

SHERBORNE CAUSEWAY

COMMON LANE

East Stour Common

PH

FERN HILL

Hunt's Farm

Causeway Farm

CHERRY ORCHARD LANE

Fry's Farm

Old Acres Farm

NEW LANE

Duncliffe Hill

Green's Farm

Duncliffe Wood

Nature Reserve

New Gate Farm

A   B   C

Shorts Green Farm
PH
New Lane
Shorts Green Lane
Willow Wy
The Limes
Valencia
PO
The Street
Glebe Cl
Grays Cl
Motcombe
Mole End

4

The Plantation

Avenue Farm
Frog Lane

Grant's Copse

Kingsettle Wood

Nature Reserve

Sheloes Copse

A350

P
Motcombe CE Sch
Church Wy

Church Farm

Little Grove

Bittles Green

25

Meaders Farm

Kingsettle Wood

Bittles Green Farm

Motcombe Road

Thanes Farm

North Heath

Manor Farm

Ryal's Plantation

Port Regis Sch

The Cliff

3

Motcombe House Plantations

Motcombe Park

Oates Plantation

Cowherd Shute Farm

Homefield

Tollgate Pk
Hicks Wy
Heathfields Wy
Woodmill
Maple Cl

B3081

Shaftesbury Road

SP7

Homefield

Littledown

Whitehouse Farm

24

Hawkers Hill Farm

Quoits Copse

Grosvenor Rd
Crookhays
Lane Side
St Lawrence Cr
Sweetmans Rd

Calves Lane

Old Brickyard Farm

Lady's Copse

SHAFTESBURY

The Venn
Longmead
Wincombe La

2

New Road

Motcombe Road

Long Cross

Grosvenor Road

Lt Content La
Christy's La

New Rd
Nettlebed Nursery
B3081

Bleke St
Mount
Barton St

A30

Long Cross Farm

Enmore Green

Sally Kings La
Yeatmans Close
Well La
Yeatmans
Tout Hl
The Knapp
Haimes La
Victoria Rd

Barton Hill House Sch

Sherborne Causeway

Church Hill
Horseponds
The Butts

Woolcotts Farm

23

Breach Lane

Umbers Hl 1
Langfords La 2
Laundry La 3

Bimport
TH
Mus
High St

Liby
PO
P
Bell St
Salisbury St

Football Club
Coppice Street

Grants Farm

Breach Lane

Abbey Mus
Westminster Meml
Love Lane

Gold La

Mus
B3091
Salisbury St
Rumbold's Rd
St George's
Belmont
Boundary

Shaftesbury Upp Sch

1

Alcester

Tanyard La
St James Street
St James
Ratcliffs Gd

Abbots Vale

St James

French Mill Ri

Hawkesdene Lane

St John's Hl
Kingsman La
Watery Lane

Church Farm

The Abbey CE First Sch

Brinscombe Farm

Cherry Orchard Farm

Foyle Hill

Edwards Farm

Cherry Or Lane
Coles La

B3091

Gascoigne Lane
French Mill Lane

Brinscombe La

22

84   A   85   B   86   C

C1
1 LWR BLANDFORD RD

C2
1 THE BEECHES
2 KINGS HL
3 PARSONS POOL
4 MUSTONS LA
5 ST EDWARDS
6 GRANVILLE GD
7 CHARLES GARRETT CL
8 JEANNEAU CL
9 CRANBORNE DR

10 WESTMINSTER CL
11 FOUNTAIN MD
12 OXENCROFT

A **B** **C**

Lyefield's Copse

Oysters Coppice
Oysters Farm

Harthill Farm

Benett's Copse

Froud's Copse

Stib Acre Copse

Westwood Farm

Knipes Farm

Gutch Common

Clift Farm

4

SP7

Hilldown Copse

Crates Wood

Tittle Path Hill

Donhead Clift

BRITMORE LANE

Hatts Farm

Aldermoor Copse

Castle Rings

25

Semley Hill

Lodge Wood

Bungalow Castle Farm

3

Nadder Head

Lower Wincombe Farm

Wincombe Business Park

Morgan's Copse

Wincombe Park

Ramshill Farm

Mullins' Copse

Wiltshire STREET ATLAS

24

Great Hanging

Step Cross Copse

Higher Wincombe Farm

BLACKMORE ROAD

Ivy Cross

King Alfred's Middle Sch

WINCOMBE LANE

SP7

WINDWHISTLE CORNER

2

Eastleaze Farm

Langdale Farm

Dockham Bottom

Mampits Farm

MELBURY WY

BURTON CL

HARDY THOMAS

23

Shaftesbury First Sch

MAMPITTS LANE

Cemy

St Marys Sch

Long Bottom

Ten Acre Copse

Hotel Old Cann Sch

Landsley Farm

Cave Copse

Coombe

Knights Barn Farm

A30 Salisbury

HIGHER BLANDFORD RD

Long Copse

The Rising Sun (PH)

A30

1

CHRISTY'S LA

A30

SALISBURY ROAD

White Close Farm

Mayo Farm

B3081 HIGHER BLANDFORD RD

NEW LANE

Hillside Farm

CHARLTON LANE

22

Boyne Hollow

LWR BLANDFORD RD A350

A1
1 BUTTS MD
2 LWR BLANDFORD RD
3 BRINSCOMBE LA

A2
1 HAWTHORN CL
2 SPRINGFIELD CL

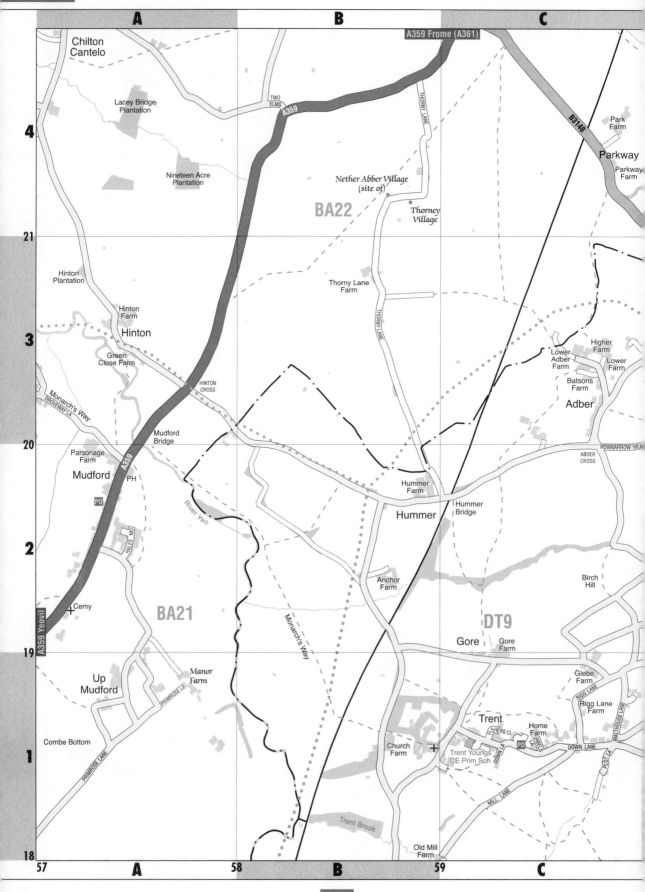

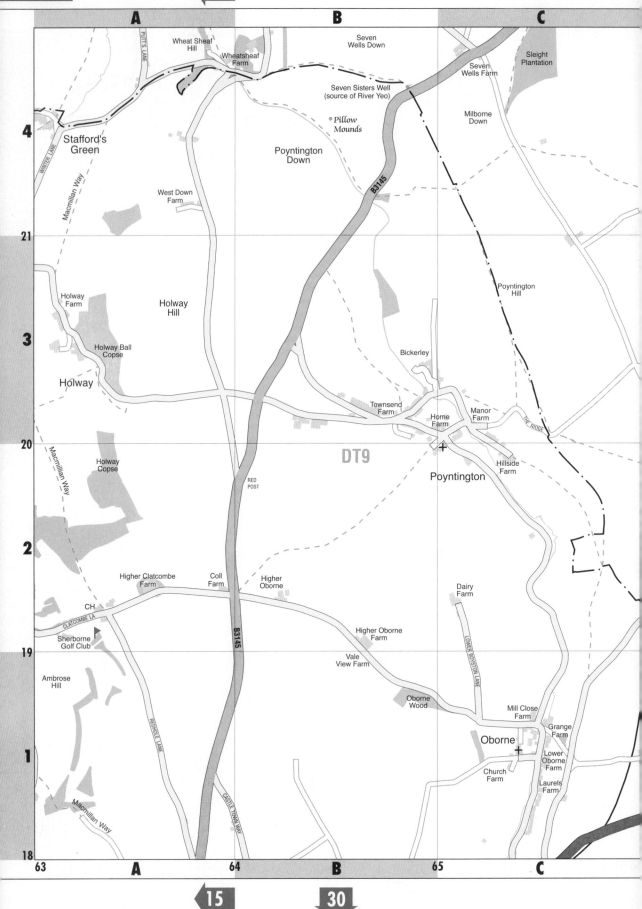

A B C

PUTT'S LANE

Wheat Sheaf
Hill

Wheatsheaf
Farm

Seven
Wells Down

Seven Wells Farm

Sleight
Plantation

Seven Sisters Well
(source of River Yeo)

Milborne
Down

4

WINTER LANE

Stafford's
Green

Pillow
Mounds

Poyntington
Down

Macmillan Way

West Down
Farm

B3145

21

Poyntington
Hill

Holway
Farm

Holway
Hill

3

Holway Ball
Copse

Bickerley

Holway

Townsend
Farm

Home
Farm

Manor
Farm

THE RIDGE

20

Macmillan Way

Holway
Copse

RED
POST

DT9

Poyntington

Hillside
Farm

2

Higher Clatcombe
Farm

Coll
Farm

Higher
Oborne

Dairy
Farm

CH

Clatcombe La

B3145

Higher Oborne
Farm

LOWER BOYSTON LANE

Sherborne
Golf Club

19

Vale
View Farm

Ambrose
Hill

Oborne
Wood

Mill Close
Farm

Grange
Farm

REDHOLE LANE

Oborne

Lower
Oborne
Farm

1

Church
Farm

Laurels
Farm

CASTLE TOWN WAY

Macmillan Way

18

63 A 64 B 65 C

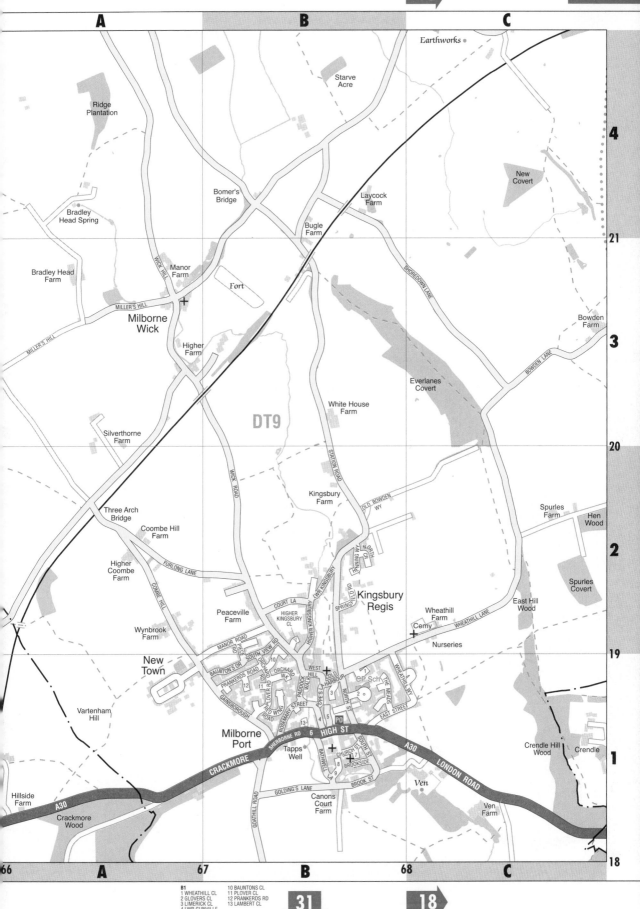

B1
1 WHEATHILL CL
2 GLOVERS CL
3 LIMERICK CL
4 LWR GUNVILLE
5 HIGHER GUNVILLE
6 SANSOME'S HL
7 CHAPEL LA
8 CANNON CT MS
9 PUD BROOK
10 BAUNTONS CL
11 PLOVER CL
12 PRANKERDS RD
13 LAMBERT CL

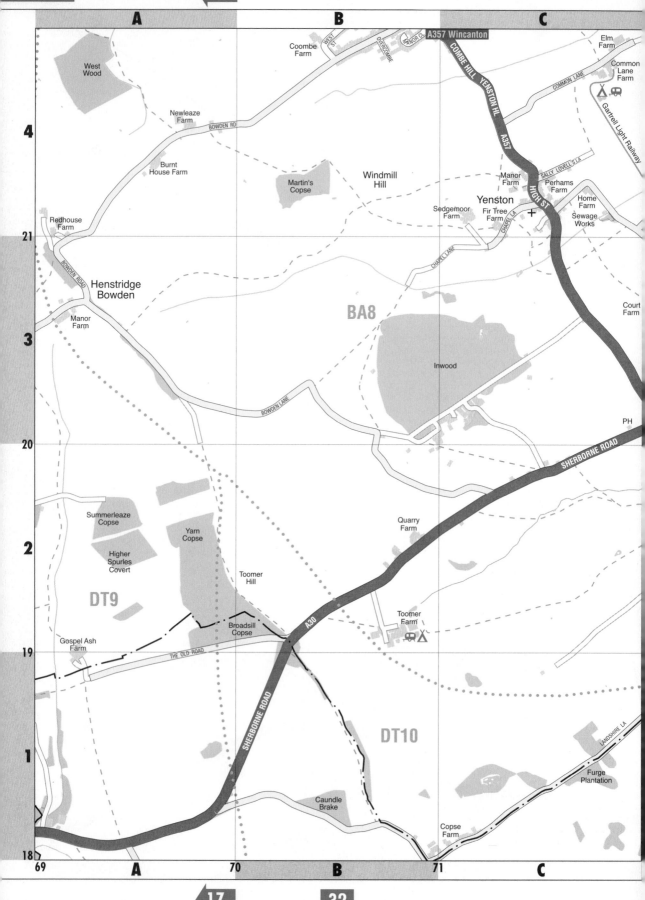

A | B | C

4

21

3

20

2

1

18

West Wood

Coombe Farm

WEST ST

OVERCOMBE

MANOR CL

A357 Wincanton

Elm Farm

Common Lane Farm

COMMON LANE

Gartrell Light Railway

Newleaze Farm

BOWDEN RD

Martin's Copse

Windmill Hill

COOMBE HILL

YENSTON HL

A357

Manor Farm

SALLY LOVELL'S LA

Perhams Farm

Home Farm

Burnt House Farm

Yenston

Sedgemoor Farm

Fir Tree Farm

CHAPEL LA

HIGH ST

Sewage Works

Redhouse Farm

BOWDEN ROAD

CHAPEL LANE

Court Farm

Henstridge Bowden

BA8

Manor Farm

BOWDEN LANE

Inwood

PH

SHERBORNE ROAD

Summerleaze Copse

Yarn Copse

Quarry Farm

Higher Spurles Covert

Toomer Hill

DT9

Broadsill Copse

A30

Toomer Farm

Gospel Ash Farm

THE OLD ROAD

SHERBORNE ROAD

DT10

LANDSHIRE LA

1

Furge Plantation

Caundle Brake

Copse Farm

69 | 70 | 71

A | B | C

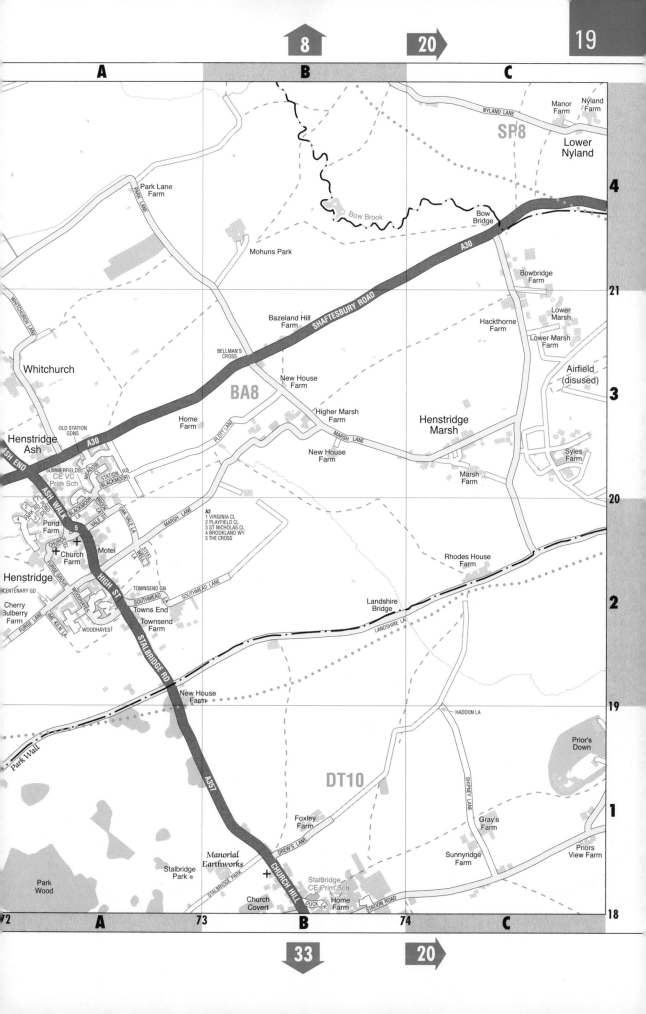

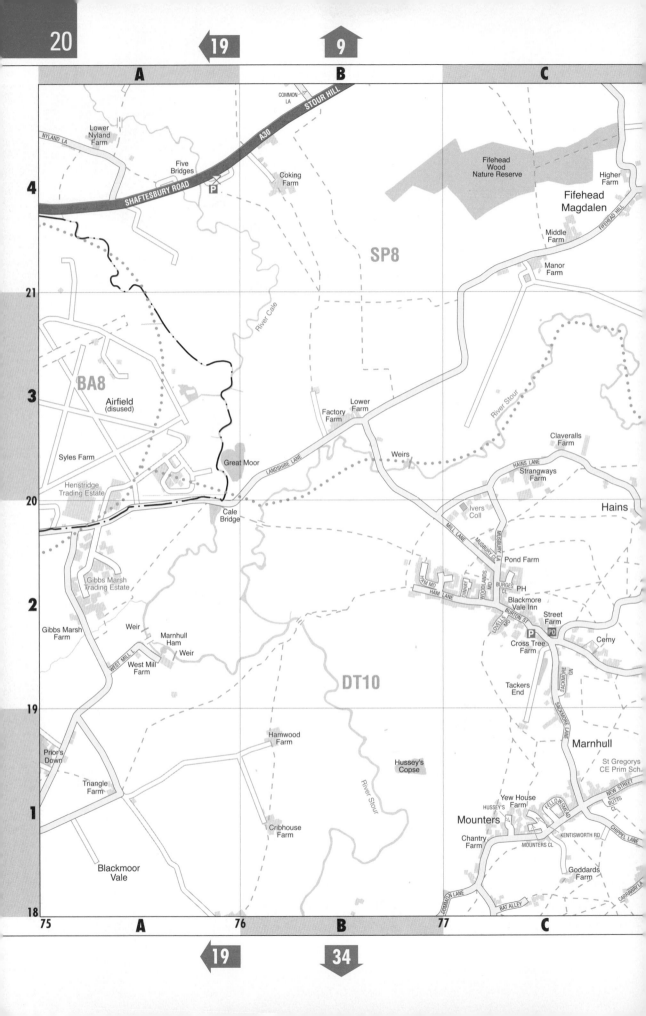

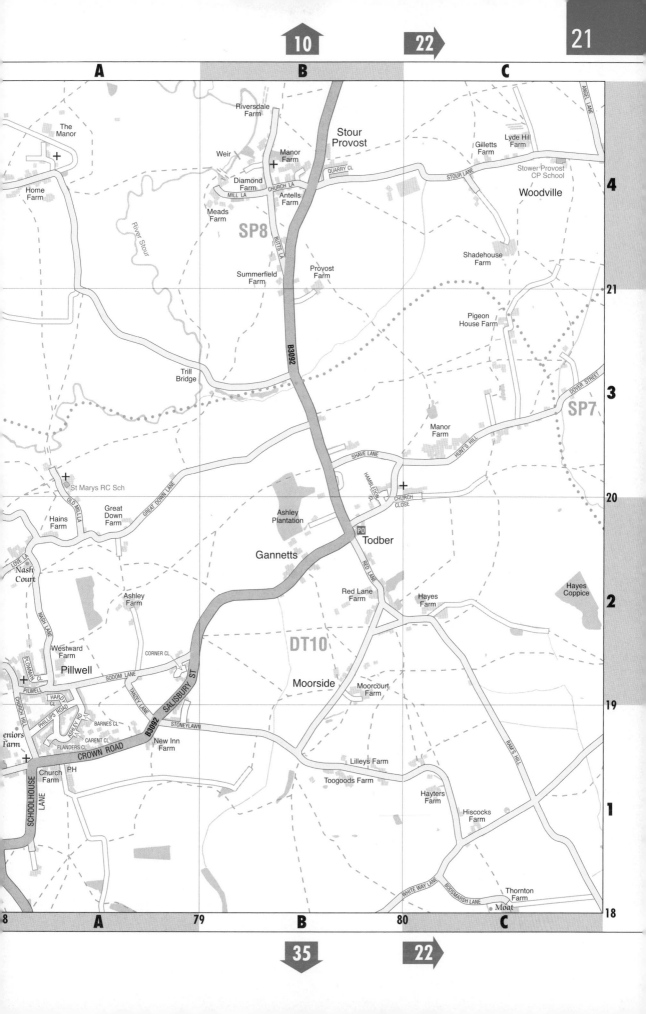

A   B   C

SP8

Hawkers Farm

Duncliffe Wood

Blynfield Farm

Jolliffes Farm

Thomas's Farm

Blakes Farm

STOUR LANE

HAWKER'S LA

4

Hill Farm

Duncliffe Home Farm

Stour Row

Yew Tree Farm

Paynthouse Farm

DOVER STREET

CHURCH CL

COLLEGE ARMS CR

Yeatmans Farm

21

Woodville Farm

Froghole Farm

Good's Farm

Great House Farm

Hunts Farm

Sweets Farm

Gore Farm

3

Tile House Farm

Doncliffe Hall Farm

Gupple's Copse

20

SP7

GREEN LANE

Wadmill Farm

Marsh Common

Jopps Farm

2

Black Ven Farm

Elm Farm

Jolliffes Farm

Lymburghs Farm

Green Farm

Venns Farm

Blackven Common

19

Marsh Farm

Lower Farm

New House Farm

B3091

Margaret Marsh

CHURCH LA

Lower Hartgrove Farm

Cherry Grove

DT10

Church Farm

Blackberry Farm

1

Cowgrove Farm

BLEAX CL

Bleax Hill

Hartgrove

CHURCH LA

18

RAM'S HL

81   A   82   B   83   C

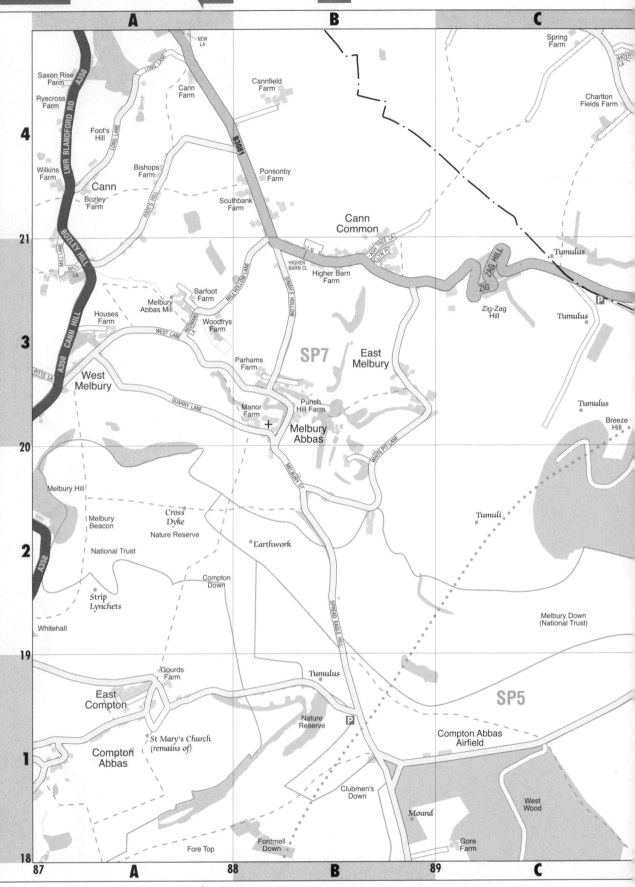

A

B

C

Wiltshire STREET ATLAS

Home Farm

BARTERS LANE

CHARLTON LANE

Manor Farm

Wessex Ridgeway

SP7

DONHEAD HOLLOW

Higher Berrycourt Farm

4

Beech Clump

21

Elliott's Shed

Tumulus

National Trust

Charlton Down

B3081

Tumulus

Win Green

3

Hawcombe Copse

Charlton Down

Cross Dyke

P

Wessex Ridgeway

20

Win Green Plantation

Quarry Bottom

Melbury Wood

Long Barrow

Melbury Down

SP5

2

Nature Reserve

Ashmore Down

Abbot's Copse

POSSESSIONS CORNER

19

Hatts Copse

NORTH ROAD

Ashgrove Farm

Hatts Barn

Cross Dyke

B3081

1

Boyne Bottom

Woodley Down

South Farm

Wessex Ridgeway

INAGE ST

PO

18

90

A

91

B

92

C

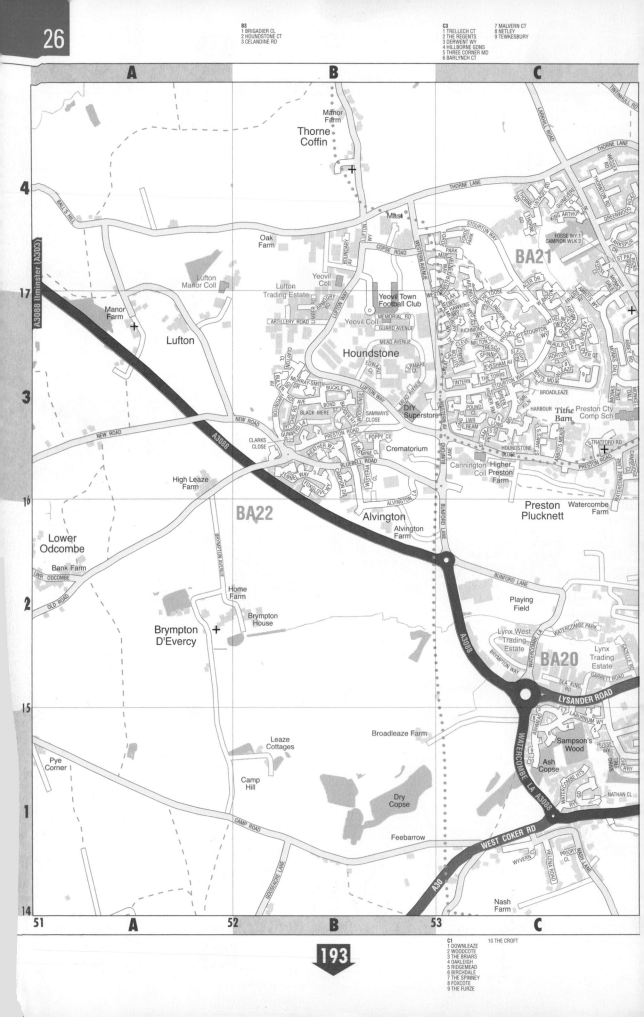

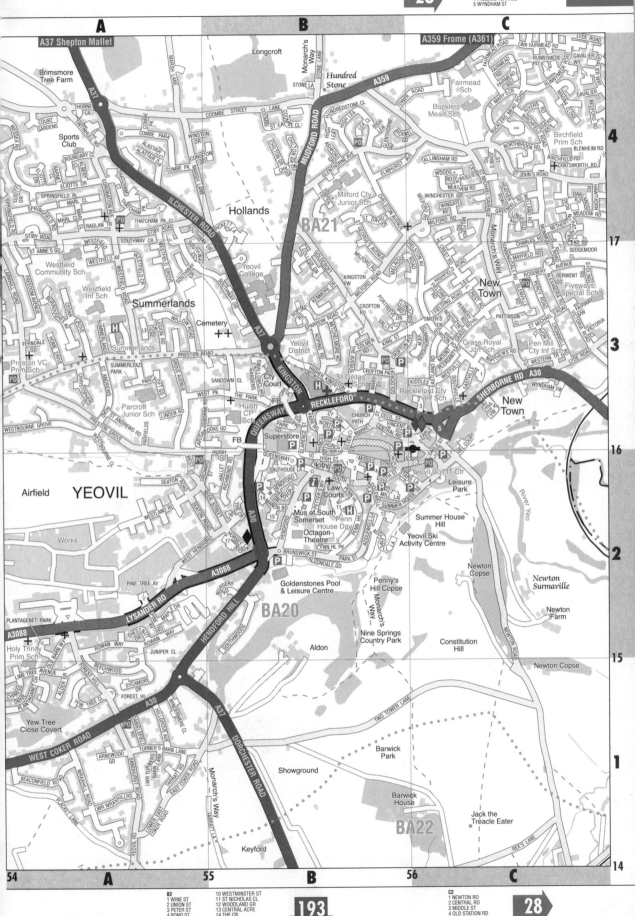

28 →

27

C3
1 ST THOMAS CROSS
2 DAMPIER PL
3 DAMPIER ST
4 HILLSIDE TERRACE
5 WYNDHAM ST

A37 Shepton Mallet

A359 Frome (A361)

Longcroft

Brimsmore
Tree Farm

Hundred
Stone

Fairmead
Sch

Bucklers
Mead Sch

Birchfield
Prim Sch

Sports
Club

4

Milford Cty
Junior Sch

Hollands

BA21

17

Westfield
Community Sch

Yeovil
College

New
Town

Summerlands

Cemetery

Fiveways
Special Sch

Westfield
Inf Sch

3

Preston VC
Prim Sch

Yeovil
District

Grass Royal
Jun Sch

Pen Mill
Cty Inf Sch

St Gildas
Sch

Reckleford Cty
Inf Sch

New
Town

SHERBORNE RD   A30

Parcroft
Junior Sch

Huish
CP Sch

Cty
Court

RECKLEFORD

16

Superstore

Yeovil Coll/IT Ctr

Airfield

YEOVIL

QUEENSWAY

Library

Leisure
Park

Law
Courts

Mus of South
Somerset

Summer House
Hill

Penn
Day

River Yeo

2

Works

Octagon
Theatre

Yeovil Ski
Activity Centre

Newton
Copse

Newton
Surmaville

LYSANDER RD

HENDFORD HILL

Goldenstones Pool
& Leisure Centre

BA20

Penny's
Hill Copse

Newton
Farm

Plantagenet Park

A3088

Holy Trinity
Prim Sch

Aldon

Nine Springs
Country Park

Constitution
Hill

Newton Copse

15

Yew Tree
Close Covert

WEST COKER ROAD

A37

DORCHESTER ROAD

Showground

Barwick
Park

1

Barwick
House

Jack the
Treacle Eater

BA22

Keyford

14

54   A   55   B   56   C

B2
1 WINE ST
2 UNION ST
3 PETER ST
4 BOND ST
5 CLOVERS WK
6 HENDFORD
7 KING GEORGE ST
8 TABERNACLE LA
9 VICARAGE ST
10 WESTMINSTER ST
11 ST NICHOLAS CL
12 WOODLAND GR
13 CENTRAL ACRE
14 THE CR
15 EVERTON RD
16 BERKELEY RD
17 MILLBROOK
18 YARN BARTON

C2
1 NEWTON RD
2 CENTRAL RD
3 MIDDLE ST
4 OLD STATION RD

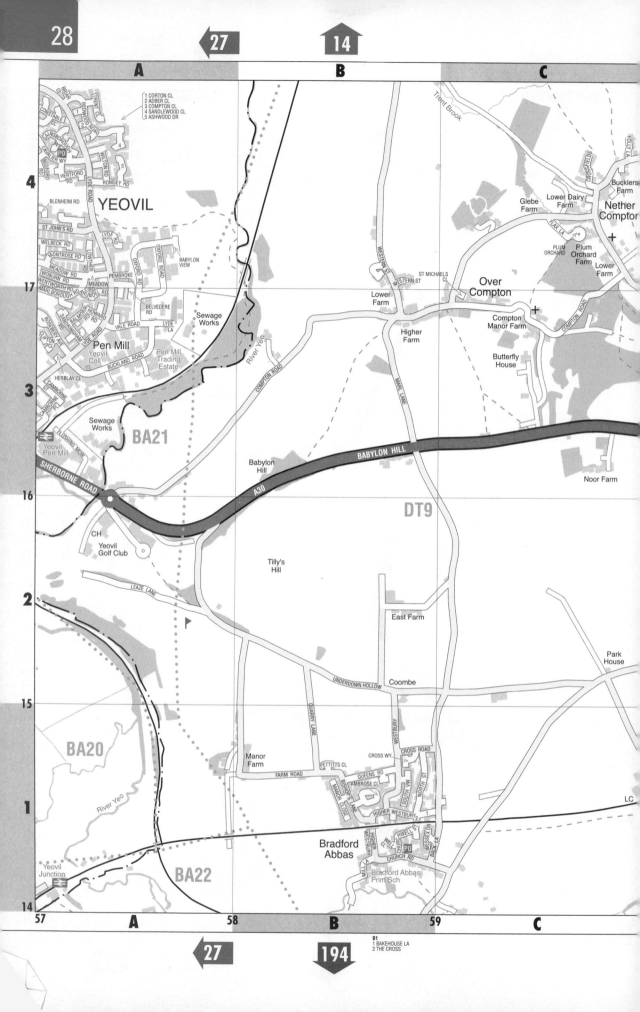

A B C

4

1 CORTON CL
2 ADBER CL
3 COMPTON CL
4 SANDLEWOOD CL
5 ASHWOOD DR

YEOVIL

BRIAR CL
CONSTABLE WY
GAINSBOROUGH
REDWOOD CL
TRENT RD
CAVALIER WY
BEDFORD
HERTFORD RD
WILTON RD
LYDE ROAD
ROMSEY RD

BLENHEIM RD

ST JOHN'S RD
WELBECK RD
MONTROSE RD
LOWTHER
OXFORD RD
OXFORD ROAD

MEADOW RD
WOBURN RD
WENTWORTH RD
MARLBOROUGH RD
PEMBROKE RD
MEADOW RD
ARUNDEL RD

BABYLON VIEW

17

Trent Brook

CROSSFIELDS
TOLLA LA

Glebe Farm
Lower Dairy Farm
Bucklers Farm
Nether Compton

FLAX LA

PLUM ORCHARD
Plum Orchard Farm
Lower Farm

WESTERN ST
WESTERN ST
St Michaels
ST MICHAELS CL

Lower Farm

Over Compton

Compton Manor Farm

Higher Farm

Butterfly House

BELVEDERE RD
VALE ROAD
LYDE LA

Sewage Works

River Yeo

COMPTON ROAD

Pen Mill
Yeovil Coll
HERBLAY CL
BUCKLAND ROAD
Pen Mill Trading Estate

ROSKERRY AVE
CAMBORNE
CAMBORNE PL
CLIFTON CL
SANDRINGHAM
BALMORAL
HOWARD RD

3

Sewage Works

BA21

MARL LANE

COMPTON ROAD

Noor Farm

FLUSHING MDW
Yeovil Pen Mill

SHERBORNE ROAD

BABYLON HILL

BABYLON HILL
A30

Babylon Hill

DT9

16

CH
Yeovil Golf Club

Tilly's Hill

2

LEAZE LANE

East Farm

Park House

BA20

UNDERDOWN HOLLOW
Coombe

River Yeo

QUARRY LANE

15

BURY LANE

CROSS ROAD

Manor Farm
FARM ROAD
PETTITTS CL
CROSS WY.
Queens RD
Ambrose Cl
SOUTH VW
NORTH ST
LC

1

MANOR CLOSE
BISHOPS LANE
HIGHER WESTBURY

HIGHER WESTBURY
WELL CHWELL
WESSEX DR
BACK LA
P.O

Bradford Abbas

Yeovil Junction

BA22

MILL LA
CHURCH ROAD
Bradford Abbas Prim Sch

14

B1
1 BAKEHOUSE LA
2 THE CROSS

30

A3
1 HORNCASTLES LA
2 ST CATHERINE'S CR
3 RIDGEWAY
4 WYNNES CL
5 SPRINGFIELD CR
6 WESTRIDGE

29   16

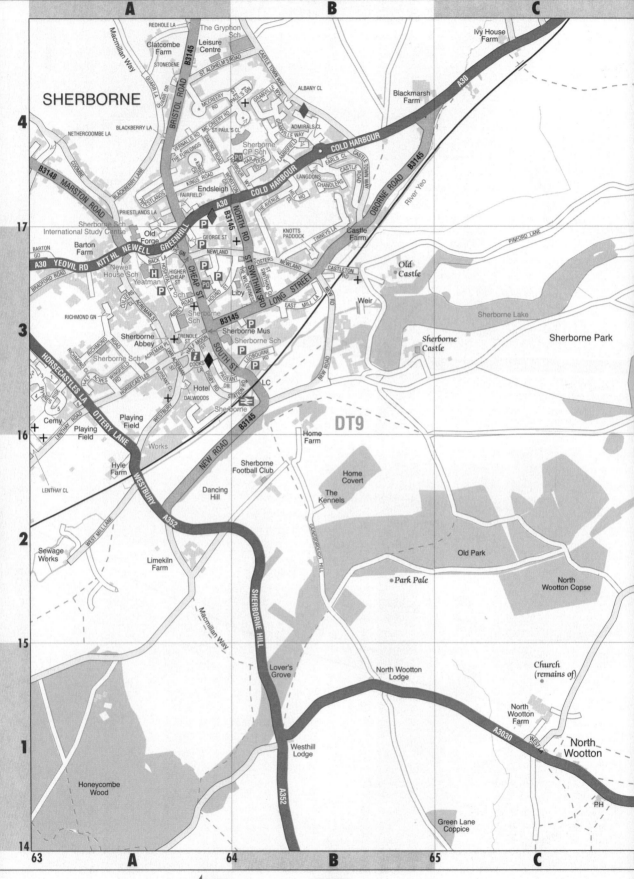

A
B
C

Home
Farm
Purse
Caundle
Manor House
Church
Farm
Court
Farm
Cemy
Manor
Farm
Frith
Wood
Frith
House
Dales
Covert
Frith
Farm
Park Wall

4

17

Clayhanger
West Coppice
Middle
Farm
Manor
Farm

Wood House
Covert
West
Wood
PILE LA

3

Cockhill
Farm
Haddon
Lodge
Cockhill Coppice
Rum
Coppice

Herridge
Coppice

DT9

16

Plumley Wood
New Leaze
Wood
DT10
Rockhill
Farm
Newlands
Farm
STABRIDGE ROAD

Woodrow
Farm
Woodclose
Farm
Woodclose
Poultry Farm
STOKES LANE

2

Bilcombe
Copse
Brunsell Knap
Farm
Brunsell
Farm
DROVE ROAD

Knoll Copse
Stourton Caundle

Manor
Farm
Chapel
PH
BARROW HILL

15

Holt Woods
HOLT LANE
HOLT LANE
GOLDEN HILL

1

CAUNDLE LANE
Caundle
Farm
RONPESY MILL LANE

Holtwood

Bishop's
Caundle Wood

14

69
A
70
B
71
C

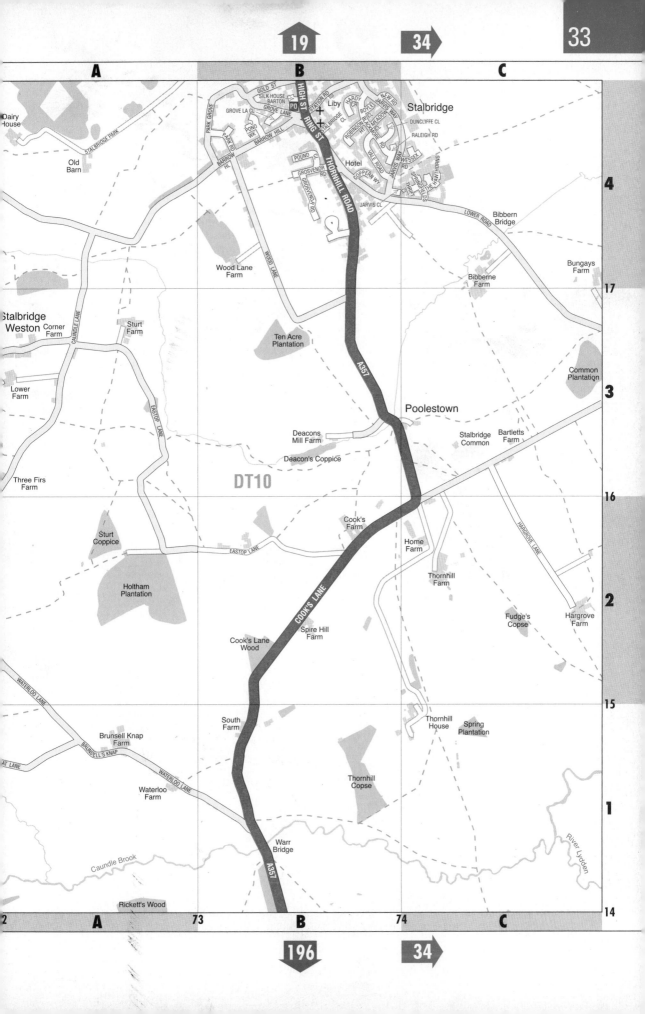

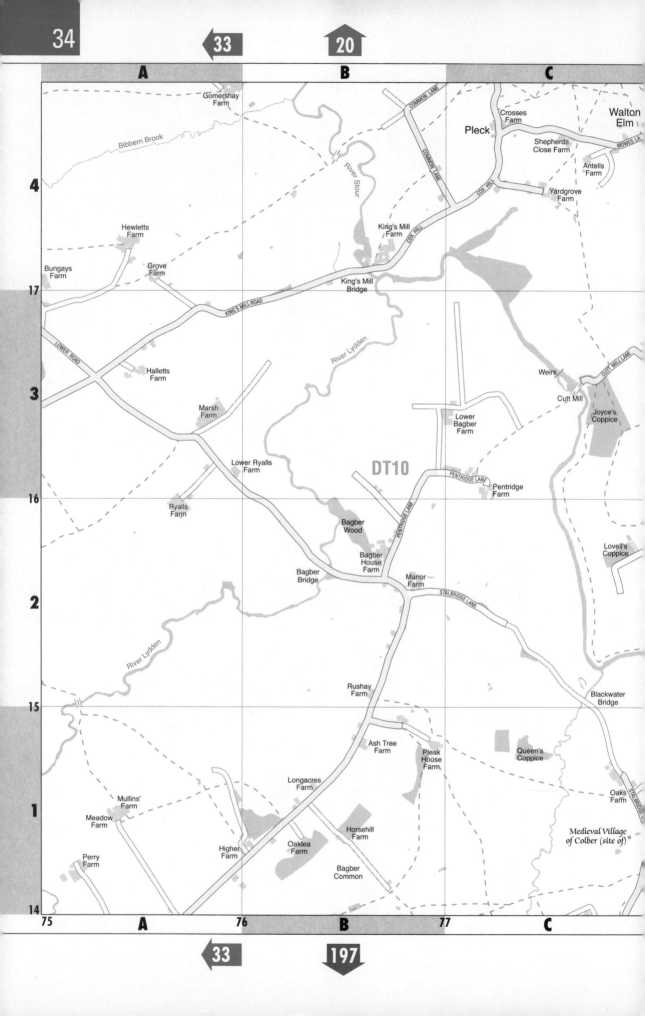

A B C

Gomershay Farm

Bibbern Brook

COMMON LANE

Crosses Farm

Walton Elm

Pleck

Shepherds Close Farm

MOWES LA.

Antells Farm

4

River Stour

COMMON LANE

COX HILL

Yardgrove Farm

King's Mill Farm

COX HILL

Hewletts Farm

Bungays Farm

Grove Farm

King's Mill Bridge

17

KING'S MILL ROAD

River Lydden

Weirs

CUTT MILL LANE

LOWER ROAD

Halletts Farm

Cutt Mill

Joyce's Coppice

3

Marsh Farm

Lower Bagber Farm

Lower Ryalls Farm

DT10

PENTRIDGE LANE

Pentridge Farm

16

Ryalls Farm

Lovell's Coppice

Bagber Wood

Bagber House Farm

PENTRIDGE LANE

Bagber Bridge

Manor Farm

STALBRIDGE LANE

2

River Lydden

Rushay Farm

Blackwater Bridge

15

Ash Tree Farm

Pleak House Farm

Queen's Coppice

Mullins' Farm

Longacres Farm

Oaks Farm

STALBRIDGE

1

Meadow Farm

Horsehill Farm

Medieval Village of Colber (site of)

Perry Farm

Higher Farm

Oaklea Farm

Bagber Common

14

A | B | C

4

Lushes Farm

Swainscombe Farm

CHURCH LANE

East Orchard

Trapdoor Farm

Breach Farm

Key Brook

Keybrook Farm

Higher Keybrook Farm

Henbury Farm

Bowling Green Farm

Lower Breach Farm

SP7

RAM'S HILL

17

Ramshill Farm

Manor Farm

Northwood Farm

Sch House Farm

DROVE LANE

Gullivers Farm

Meads Farm

B3091

3

Folly Farm

West Orchard

CHURCH LANE

Conegar Farm

FISHEY LANE

Winchells Farm

Manor Farm

PH

DT10

Naish's Farm

16

Manston Brook

Sewage Works

2

Middle Farm

Manston

Manston Farm

DT11

Lower Farm

15

Manston House

Fontmell Farm

Weir

Manor Farm

Cross

Fontmell Parva

Hammoon

LOWER COMMON ROAD

Porter's Hill

GALLOWS CORNER

Hazel Copse

1

Newbury Copse

Ridgeway Farm

14

81 | A | 82 | B | 83 | C

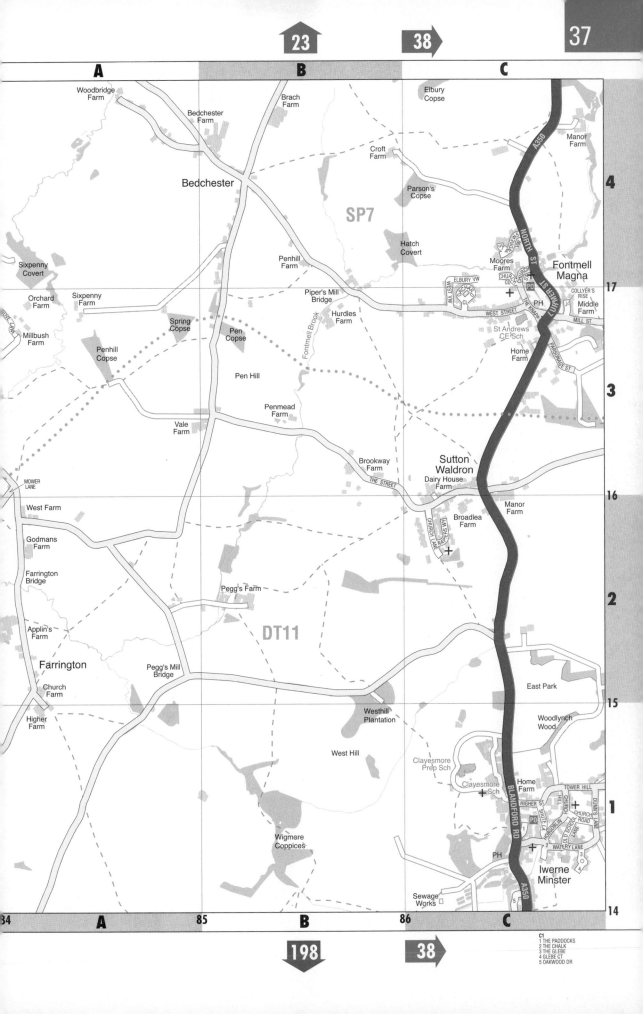

A

B

C

Woodbridge Farm

Brach Farm

Bedchester Farm

Elbury Copse

Manor Farm

A350

Croft Farm

Bedchester

Parson's Copse

SP7

4

Hatch Covert

Sixpenny Covert

Penhill Farm

Moores Farm

ELBURY VW

WEST ST

ANDREWS

CHURCH

NORTH ST

Fontmell Magna

CHURCH

COLLYER'S RISE

CL

CHURCH CL

Orchard Farm

Sixpenny Farm

Piper's Mill Bridge

ORCHARD CL

PH

THE KNAPP

TURNER ST

Middle Farm

17

Millbush Farm

Spring Copse

Pen Copse

Hurdles Farm

WEST STREET

St Andrews CE Sch

PH

MILL ST

Penhill Copse

Fontmell Brook

Home Farm

PARSONAGE ST

Pen Hill

3

Penmead Farm

Vale Farm

Brookway Farm

Sutton Waldron

Dairy House Farm

Manor Farm

MOWER LANE

THE STREET

16

West Farm

CHURCH LANE

NAPS MEAD

Broadlea Farm

Godmans Farm

Farrington Bridge

DT11

Manor Farm

Pegg's Farm

2

Applin's Farm

Farrington

East Park

Pegg's Mill Bridge

15

Church Farm

Westhill Plantation

Woodlynch Wood

Higher Farm

West Hill

Clayesmore Prep Sch

Home Farm

TOWER HILL

Clayesmore Sch

HIGHER ST

SHUTE LA

CHURCH HILL

CHURCH ROAD

DUNN'S LANE

1

PO

WATERY LANE

Wigmore Coppices

Iwerne Minster

PH

A350

BLANDFORD RD

Sewage Works

14

37
24

A   B   C

Fontmell Down

Fore Top

Longcombe Bottom

West Wood

SP5

Cross Dyke

Shepherd's Bottom

Fontmell Wood

4

SP7

Littlecombe Bottom

Fontmell Hill House

17

Springhead Farm

MILL STREET

Washers Pit

Balfour's Wood

Strip Lynchets

STUBHAMPTON BOTTOM

Washers Pit Coppice

Stubhamton Bottom

3

STUBHAMPTON BOTTOM

Enclosure

Combe Bottom

Sutton Hill Farm

16

Sutton Hill

West Lodge

DT11

Spinney Pits Coppice

Higher Barn Plantation

Folly Barrow

2

Higher Barn Plantation

Freak's Coppice

Lower Freaks Coppice

Bareden Down

Tumuli

15

Wales Wood

Bareden Wood

Tumuli

Payne Coppice

Common Bushes

Iwerne Hill

Great Peakey Coppice

TOWER HILL

1

TOWER HILL

Hill Farm

Brookman's Valley

BOYNE'S LANE

Heron Grove Coppice

14

Rolf's Wood

87   A   88   B   89   C

37
199

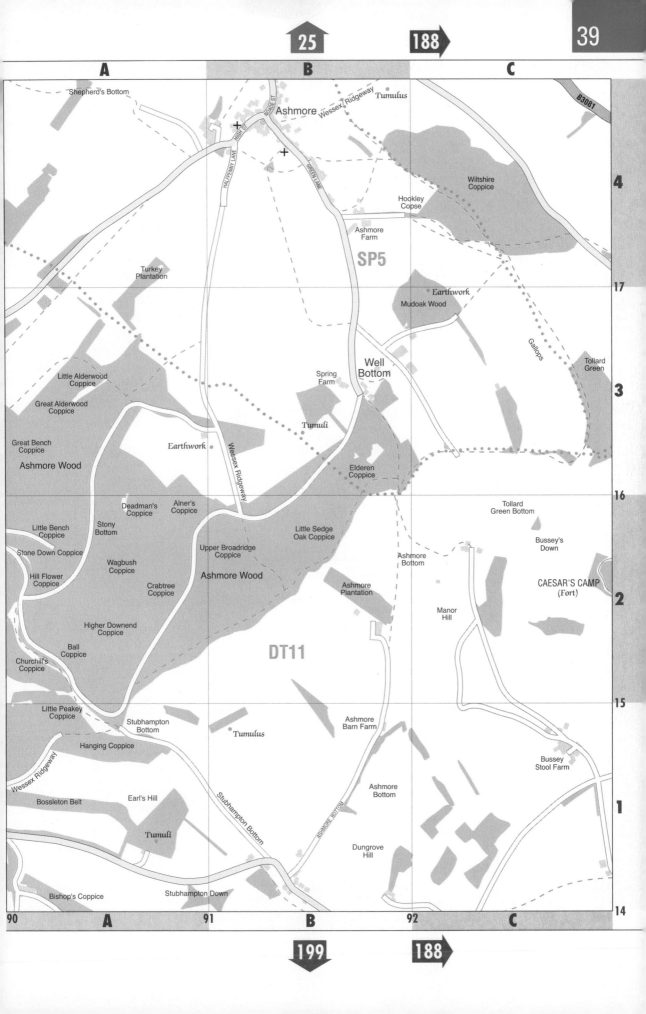

A B C

B3081

Shepherd's Bottom

Ashmore

Wessex Ridgeway

Tumulus

HIGH ST
MADE ST
HALFPENNY LANE
GREEN LANE

4

Wiltshire
Coppice

Hookley
Copse

Turkey
Plantation

Ashmore
Farm

SP5

17

Earthwork

Mudoak Wood

Gallops

Tollard
Green

Little Alderwood
Coppice

Great Alderwood
Coppice

Spring
Farm

Well
Bottom

3

Great Bench
Coppice

Earthwork

Tumuli

Wessex Ridgeway

Ashmore Wood

Elderen
Coppice

16

Deadman's
Coppice

Alner's
Coppice

Little Sedge
Oak Coppice

Tollard
Green Bottom

Little Bench
Coppice

Stony
Bottom

Bussey's
Down

Stone Down Coppice

Upper Broadridge
Coppice

Ashmore
Bottom

CAESAR'S CAMP
(Fort)

Wagbush
Coppice

Ashmore Wood

2

Hill Flower
Coppice

Crabtree
Coppice

Ashmore
Plantation

Manor
Hill

Higher Downend
Coppice

DT11

Ball
Coppice

Churchill's
Coppice

15

Little Peakey
Coppice

Stubhampton
Bottom

Tumulus

Ashmore
Barn Farm

Hanging Coppice

Bussey
Stool Farm

Wessex Ridgeway

Earl's Hill

Ashmore
Bottom

1

Bossleton Belt

Stubhampton Bottom

ASHMORE BOTTOM

Tumuli

Dungrove
Hill

Bishop's Coppice

Stubhampton Down

14

90 A 91 B 92 C

A **B** **C**

Burwood

BELLOWS CROSS

Long Copse

Pound Farm

Cranborne Cty Middle Sch

Paul's Copse

Ashes Farm

4

SALISBURY STREET

GRUGS LA

HIGH THE SQ CRANE ST

Cranborne

PENNY'S LANE

CRANE

Holwell Farm

Jordan Hill Plantation

Old Claygrounds

WATER ST

PENNY'S MD

FRIDAY'S HERON

SWAN ST

CHURCH ST

WIMBORNE

PH

Gardens

CASTLE ST

CHURCHILL DROVE

Cranborne CE First Sch

Higher Holwell Farm

Cranborne Lodge

CASTLE CT

HUBBARDS FIELD

B3078

13

CASTLE HL LA

CASTLE HL LA

River Crane

B3078

Castle Hill

Lower Holwell

Gilham's Copse

Hill Wood

Motte & Bailey

MILL LANE

3

Fir Copse

Mill Farm

HARE LANE

Cranborne Copse

Castle Hill Wood

Bottom Copse

Long Copse

Great Rhymes Copse

12

Lower Farm

Barnfield Farm

BH21

Little Rhymes Copse

Woodward's Copse

Edmondsham House

Furze Common Copse

Mill Copse

MILL LANE

2

Common Copse

Cook's Moor

Edmondsham

Wingsdown

Upper Farm

Pert Copse

Smallbridge Farm

11

Hobbys Copse

Chalybeate Spring

Bramble Farm

Heavy Horse Centre

Maldry Wood

Sandy's Hill

Smallbridge Copse

Pinnocks Moor Bridge

Pinnocks Moor

1

Deer Park Ponds

Sutton Copse

Pains Moor Copse

Westworth Farm

River Crane

B3081

Great Rough Copse

HORTON RD

Sutton Farm

Birches Copse

10

South Hampshire STREET ATLAS

Perry Copse

Lake
Farm

Hill
Farm

BOWERWOOD ROAD

Home
Farm

ASHFORD ROAD

Manor
Farm

New
Farm

4

Park
Farm
Alderholt
Park

Hill
Cottage
Farm

SANDLEHEATH ROAD

Midgham
Wood

High
Wood

Salisbury
Arms
Farm

FORDINGBRIDGE ROAD

Cross
Farm

HILLBURY RD

Bonfire
Hill

Wolvercrate
Copse

13

Wolvercroft
Spinney

High
Wood

B3078

Camel
Green

Hilbury
Wood

Alderholt

COPPERS CL

HAYTERS WAY

1 GREEN DR
2 SILVERDALE CR
3 CAMEL GN RD

LIME TREE CL

STATION ROAD

St James
CE First
School

Hillbury
Farm

DAGGONS ROAD

STATION RD

PH

PO

Charing
Cross

ALTWOOD CL

OAK ROAD

PINE ROAD

BROADFIELD DR

BROOMFIELD DR

Birchwood DR

SP6

HARBRIDGE DROVE

12

RINGWOOD ROAD

Alderholt
Sports Club

Cross Roads
Plantation

Sleepbrook
Farm

Marsh Lands

Oak Tree
Farm

Drove
End
Farm

LOMER LANE

NORTH END LANE

2

Warren
Park
Farm

Lomer
Copse

LOMER LA

Bleak
Hill Farm

Alderholt
Common

Whitefield
Bottom

Braemoor

Bleak
Hill

Fern Hi
Copse

Plumley
Wood

11

Sleep Brook

Sleep
Bottom

Whitefield
Bottom

BH31

Coble
Woo

1

Plumley
Wood

North
Plumley Farm

BH24

Hamer
Copse

Kent Hill

Wiggs Copse

Cootman's
Copse

10

A · B · C

4
13
3
12
2
11
1
10

A338 Salisbury

FORDINGBRIDGE

DIAMOND CL
CHURCH ST
MILBERRY RD
BROOK
CHURCH FARM
PADSTOW PL
B3078
Bushells Farm
BUSHELLS FARM
River Avon
B3078
A338
FROG LANE
Avon Valley Path
Redbrook Farm
Sewage Works
Aqueduct
Weir
Bickton
Beaverflow Fish Farm
HERN LANE

Rose Farm
The Merrie Thought
Broadhill Wood
BROADHILL LANE
Stuckton Farm
Seagers Farm
Hill Farm PH
Stuckton
STUCKTON RD
Brooklands Farm
Fir Tree Farm
Frogham
Flaxfields
FROGHAM HILL
Hyde Copse
HYDE LANE
PENTONS HL
Hyde
Hyde CE Prim Sch
BLISSFORD HILL
Hungerford Hill
Hungerford
GORLEY LYNCH
Hungerford Copse
Dairy Farm
GORLEY LYNCH

SP6

Long Copse
East Moor
RINGWOOD ROAD
Herne Gate Farm
PH
Green Farm
Little Brook Farm
BUDDLE HILL
Gorley Common
LAWRENCE LANE
Gorley Cross Farm
North Gorley
Gorley Hill
Furzehill Farm

North End
North End Farm
River Avon
Harbridge Green
BH24
CHURCHFIELD LANE
Avon Valley Path
Huckles Bridge
King's Copse
Ford
Gorley Wood
Hucklesbrook Farm
South Gorley
BROOKSIDE
Cuckoo Hill Railway
Cuckoo Copse
Little Chibden Bottom
SALISBURY ROAD
BLIND LA
New Farm
Hockeys Farm
Kent Lane
Harbridge
Weir
IBSLEY DROVE
NEWTOWN LANE
Copse Farm
Cottage Plantation
NEWTOWN LA
A338

4 · A · 15 · B · 16 · C

King's
Wood

Walnut
Farm

Sutton
Holms

Birches
Copse

Sutton
Hill Farm

B3081

Romford
Mill Farm

Ironmongers
Copse

Boys
Wood

Romford
East Farm

Romford
West
Farm

Romford
Bridge

B3081

STATION RD
PH

ALBION WAY

JESSICA AV
PINE TW RD
PINE TW CL

DEWLANDS
RD

Gravel Pits
Plantation

Jubilee
Farm

CH

Crane Valley
Golf Club

Dewlands
Woods

WEST CLOSE

STAGSWOOD

17 DEWLANDS

ALBION
WY

Rainbow's
End

Brook Farm

CHAPEL LA

BROOK LA

WHITMORE LA

CHURCH HILL

Hemmings
Farm

Ninney-
cox Wood

Dewlands
Common

Woodlands

Shirewood
Farm

Whitmore

HILLSIDE RD
NEW LA
BURGESS FIELD RD

Woodlands
Common

ALBION RD

Dewlands
Farm

Apple Tree
Farm

HAYWARD

PARK LANE

Brookfield
Martins Farm

Martins
Farm

Mount Pleasant
Farm

BH31

River Crane

Woodlands Park

Cranborne
Game Farm

HORTON WAY

Bridge
Farm

08

Wedgehill
Farm

BH21

Oakfield
Farm

Homer's
Wood

Knob's
Crook

Tumulus

Tumulus

Redman's Hill

Ford

SLOUGH LANE

Tumulus

Tumuli

Earthworks

Riverside
Farm

SLOUGH LANE

Monmouth
Ash Farm

Ford

Monmouth's
Ash

Bog
Farm

SLOUGH LA

Horton
Wood

Horton
Heath
Farm

Grixey
Farm

Horton
Common

Hart's
Bridge

Harts
Farm

Horton
Heath

HORTON RD

Hart's
Copse

Nettletree
Farm

Hope
Lodge Farm

Bramble
Farm

Clump Hill

Silverwood
Farm

CLUMP HILL

BURT LA

HORTON ROAD

Holt
Lodge
Farm

Chapel
Farm

Clump
Hill Farm

Rose Cottage Farm

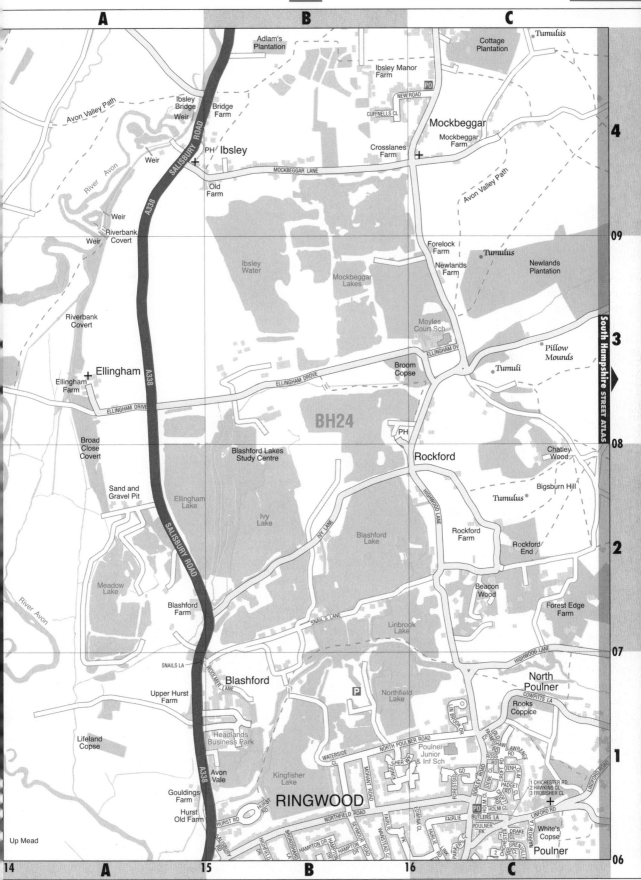

A
B
C

Adlam's Plantation

Cottage Plantation

Tumulus

Ibsley Manor Farm

PO
NEW ROAD

CUFFNELLS CL.

Mockbeggar

4

Mockbeggar Farm

Avon Valley Path

Ibsley Bridge Weir

Bridge Farm

PH Ibsley

Crosslanes Farm

Weir

Old Farm

MOCKBEGGAR LANE

River Avon

A338

SALISBURY ROAD

Weir

Weir

Riverbank Covert

Ibsley Water

Mockbeggar Lakes

Forelock Farm

Tumulus

Newlands Farm

Newlands Plantation

09

Riverbank Covert

Moyles Court Sch

ELLINGHAM DV.

Pillow Mounds

3

South Hampshire STREET ATLAS

Ellingham

A338

Broom Copse

Tumuli

Ellingham Farm

ELLINGHAM DRIVE

ELLINGHAM DRIVE

BH24

PH

Broad Close Covert

Blashford Lakes Study Centre

Rockford

Chatley Wood

08

Sand and Gravel Pit

Ellingham Lake

Ivy Lake

HIGHWOOD LANE

IVY LANE

Blashford Lake

Rockford Farm

Bigsburn Hill

Tumulus

Rockford End

2

Meadow Lake

Beacon Wood

Forest Edge Farm

River Avon

Blashford Farm

SNAIL'S LANE

Linbrook Lake

07

SNAILS LA

HIGHWOOD LANE

WOOLMER LANE

Blashford

North Poulner

Upper Hurst Farm

P

Northfield Lake

COWPITTS LA.

Rooks Coppice

Headlands Business Park

WATERSIDE CL

NORTH POULNER ROAD

Poulner Junior & Inf Sch

LN BROOK DR

LAWRENCE RD

1

Lifeland Copse

Kingfisher Lake

MORANT ROAD

KINGSLEY

FORESTSIDE GD

ROSS

1 CHICHESTER RD
2 HAWKINS CL
3 FROBISHER CL

Avon Vale

RINGWOOD

NORTHFIELD ROAD

SEYMOUR ROAD

FAIRLIE

EDWINA CL.

FAIRLIE PK

FAIRLIE

POULNER PK

PO

HOLM CL

LINFORD RD

White's Copse

Gouldings Farm

HURST RD

BROADSHARD

HAMPTON DR.

HAMPTON DR

WANSTEAD CL

PARKER CL

Poulner

Hurst Old Farm

A338

SALISBURY RD

HURST RD

HIGHFIELD

BUTLERS LA.

Up Mead

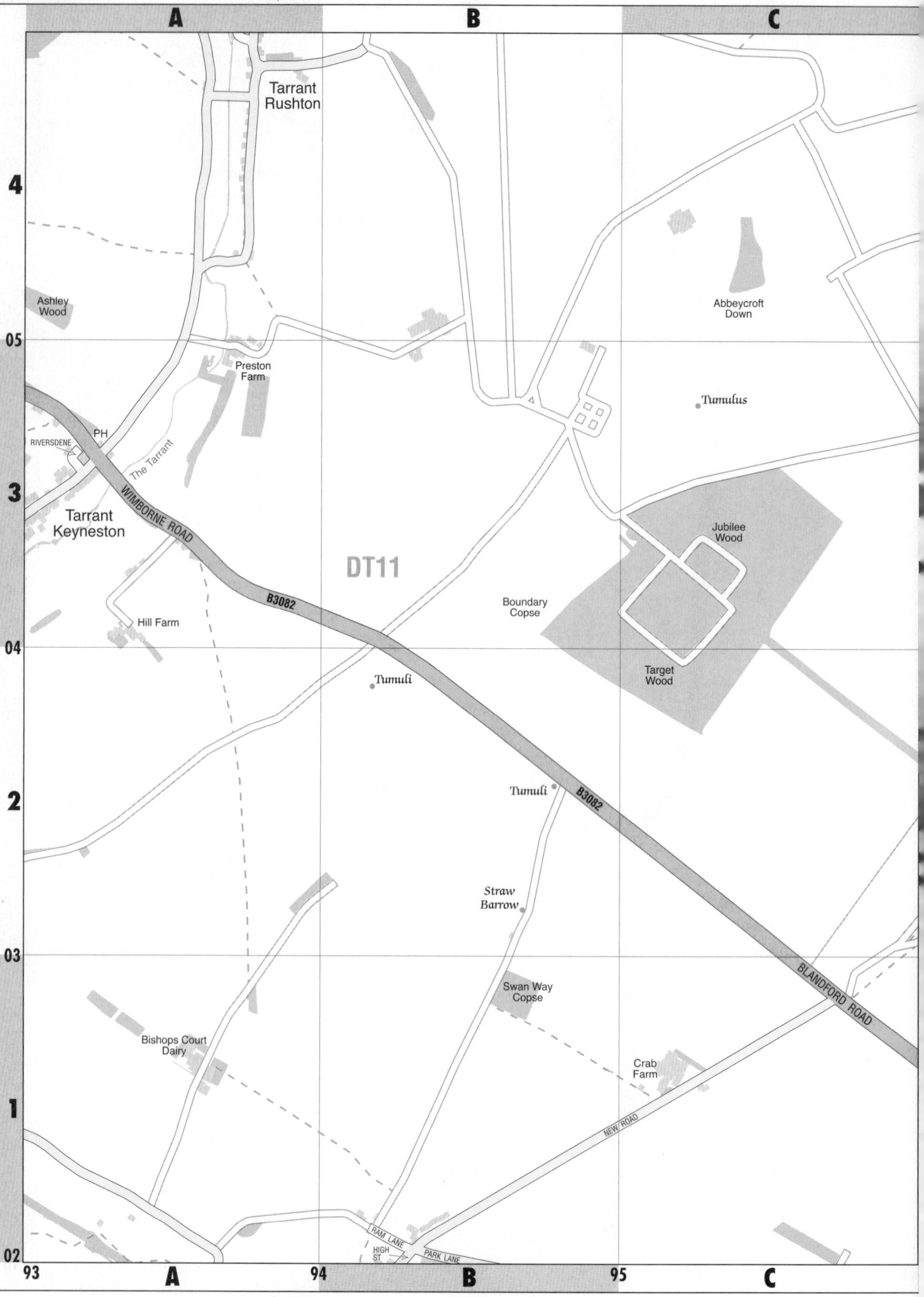

A　　　　**B**　　　　**C**

Tarrant
Rushton

4

Ashley
Wood

Abbeycroft
Down

05

Preston
Farm

Tumulus

PH

RIVERSDENE

The Tarrant

3

Tarrant
Keyneston

WIMBORNE ROAD

DT11

Jubilee
Wood

B3082

Boundary
Copse

Hill Farm

04

Target
Wood

Tumuli

2

Tumuli

B3082

Straw
Barrow

03

Swan Way
Copse

BLANDFORD ROAD

Bishops Court
Dairy

Crab
Farm

1

NEW ROAD

02

93　　　　**A**　　　　94　　　　**B**　　　　95　　　　**C**

RAM LANE

PARK LANE

HIGH
ST

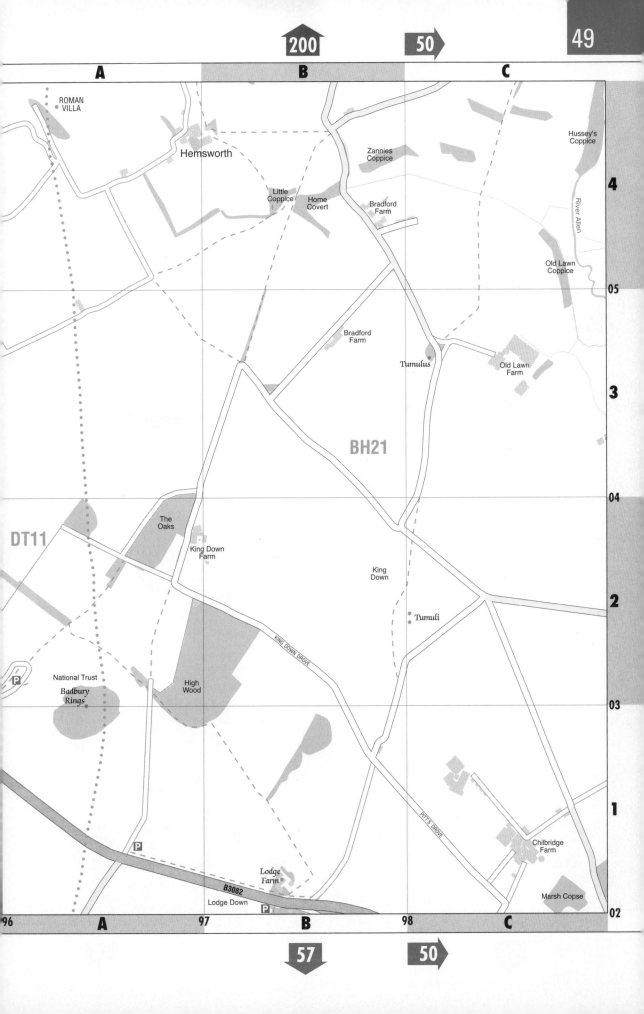

A
B
C

ROMAN VILLA

Hemsworth

Zannies Coppice

Hussey's Coppice

4

Little Coppice

Home Covert

Bradford Farm

River Allen

Old Lawn Coppice

05

Bradford Farm

Tumulus

Old Lawn Farm

3

BH21

04

The Oaks

DT11

King Down Farm

King Down

2

Tumuli

National Trust

Badbury Rings

KING DOWN DROVE

High Wood

03

PITT'S DROVE

1

Chilbridge Farm

Lodge Farm

B3082

Marsh Copse

Lodge Down

02

A **B** **C**

WITCHAMPTON LANE

High Lea
Farm

High Lea
Sch

EMLEY LANE

Clay
Hill

4

B3078

WOODCUTTS LANE

Underwood
Farm

05

Woodcutts
Farm

Gardens

Close
Copse

3

Hinton Mill
Farm

Hinton
Parva

River Allen

Ashton Wood

Sweet Apple
Copse

Gaunt's
House

CRANBORNE ROAD

Ashton
Farm

BH21

04

Stanbridge

+

Barnsley
Farm

Brach
Copse

Scriven's
Copse

The Barn
Copse

Green
Farm

2

BARNSLEY DROVE

High Hall
Copse

Lower
Barnsley Farm

03

Chapel
Copse

Honeybrook
Farm

High
Hall

Dog Kennel
Copse

Clapgate

GRANGE

Grange

1

Fitche's
Bridge

B3078

GRANGE

Grange
End

FURZEHILL

Stocks
Farm

Higher
Honeybrook
Farm

River Allen

PH

Honeybrook
Copse

Furzehill

SMUGGLERS LANE

Biddle's
Copse

PO

02

99 **A** **00** **B** **01** **C**

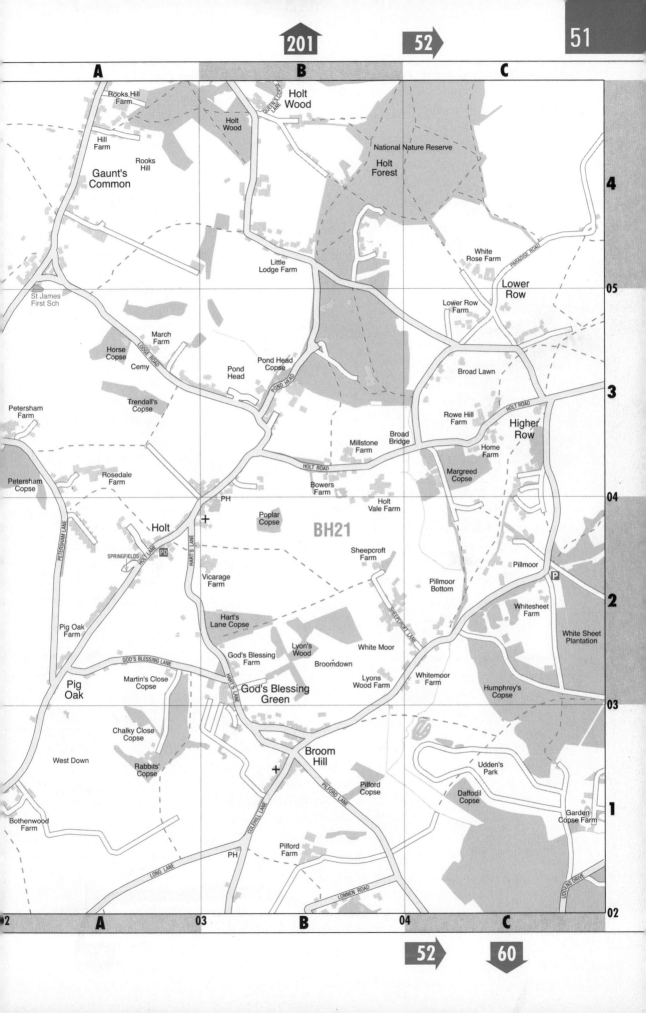

A   **B**   **C**

Earlys
Farm

Brooklands
Farm

Mannington

Skies
Farm

4

Crooked
Withies

Crooked Withies
Farm

Bulbarrow
Poultry Farm

Lower
Mannington

Jubilee
Farm

Mannington
Copse

Mannington
Farm

The
Copse

Haddons
Farm

05

Bull
Barrow

Mannington
Farm

Barewood Copse

PH

Summerlug Hill

Sturts
Farm

3

Holt
Heath

Newman's
Farm

Meadows
Farm

NEWMAN'S LANE

BH21

Enclosure

Gulliver's
Farm

Holt Heath
National
Nature Reserve

04

WEST MOORS ROAD

WOODSIDE
RD

DENEWOOD
RD

NEWMAN'S LANE

BOND AV

DENEWOOD
COPSE

2

White Sheet Plantation

RITCHIE
PL

B3072

Hatchard's
Copse

St Marys
First School

HESTON WY

Ferndown Stour and Forest Trail

03

Clayford
Farm

PO

RIVERSIDE ROAD

PULLMAN CT

MARY
LA

Park
Copse

Uddens Water

BH22

Liby

MANNINGTON WY

FARM RD

PARK RD

BIRCH GR

Pennington's
Copse

PENNINGTON RD

1

Red
Bridge

Ferndown   Forest

CH
Dolman's
Farm

Ferndown Forest
Golf Club

Castleman   Trailway

FOREST LINKS ROAD

AMEYSFORD RD

Ameysford

Broadmoor
Coppice

A31

02

COBHAM ROAD

AMEYSFORD RD

05   **A**   **06**   **B**   **07**   **C**

A   B   C

Three
Legged Cross

EVERGREEN CL

FURZELANDS ROAD

B3072

VERWOOD RD

CHURCH ROAD

JUNIPER CL

BAY CL

JOYS RD

RINGWOOD ROAD

WEST MOORS ROAD

B3072

THREE CROSS ROAD

+ PO
Stugan
Farm

PH

FERN BANK

DYMEWOOD RD

Homestead
Farm

RINGWOOD ROAD

SCHOOL LA

LOWER COMMON LA

SANDHURST DR

RINGWOOD ROAD

Gundrys
Farm

BH21

Homeland
Farm

Woolsbridge

PH

CRANE WY

VICTORY CL

LIBERTY CL

AZURA CL

CONDOR CL

OLD BARN FARM RD

Woolsbridge
Industrial
Estate

RINGWOOD ROAD

Woolsbridge
Manor Farm

Woolsbridge
Farm

Wools
Bridge

HORTON ROAD

HORTON RD

Moors River

Railway

Visitor Centre

Moors Valley
Country Park

4

05

Ashley
Heath

PINE MANOR RD

FOREST EDGE DRIVE

BURTON CL

WEBBS CL

3

Collingwood
Rd

NEWMANS CL

PAYNE CL

Cricket
Ground

Depot

JIMMY BROWN AVENUE

Little Lions
Farm

Lions
Hill

LIONS HILL WAY

GROSVENOR CLOSE

LIONS LANE

ST LEONARDS WAY

SHELLEY CL

BRACKEN CL

04

SARUM AVE

SARUM AV

BLACKFIELD LA

FIR CL

THE AVENUE

ASHHURST RD

ARNOLD CL

ARNOLD RD

NEWCOMBE RD

BRIDGES CL

HARRISON WY

MOORLANDS RD

BRESSÜE ROAD

FOREST RD

MOORLANDS ROAD

GLENWOOD

1 CHARNWOOD CL
2 GLENWOOD WY
3 GLENWOOD WY
4 SUMMERCROFT WY

BH22

West Moors Plantation

LIONS HILL WAY

BH24

Moors River

GARTH CL

WILLOW CL

HEATH CL

CONIFER CL

ROWAN CL

SYLVAN CL

GORSE CL

CRAGSIDE RD

IVY CL

OAKS DRIVE

BIRCH CL

C2
1 HOLLY CL
2 SPINNEY CL
3 CEDAR AV

Racecourse   Heath

OAKS DR

CHERRY TREE

2

West Moors

BELLE VUE GR

GLENWOOD WY

KINGFISHER

GLEN WD RD

GLENWOOD

FIR GLEN RD

MOORSIDE ROAD

GLENWOOD RD

SHIRLEY CL

PENNSIDE ROAD

OAKHURST CL

FIRS GLEN RD

OAKHURST LANE

MILFORD CL

UPLANDS RD

UPLANDS RD

UPLANDS RD

BOGEMOOR RD

East
Moors Farm

Hill Farm

FIR TREE CL

03

RAMBLE

GLEN WD RD

STATION RD

NGS

SPINNERS CL

WEAVERS CL

FIR TEASEL WY

WOOLSLOPE GD

WOOLSLOPE CL

SOUTHDOWN WY

CANTERBURY RD

MERINO WY

MALOREN WY

SHAFTESBURY CL

SHAFTESBURY RD

HARDY RD

HARDY CL

ELMHURST RD

ELMHURST WY

HEATHFIELD WAY

SOUTHERN AVENUE

BEECHMOOR RD

UPLANDS RD

UPLANDS RD

COMPTON CR

HEATHERDOWN ROAD

1 HEATHERDOWN RD
2 HEATHERDOWN WY

Hotel

RINGWOOD ROAD

A31

RINGWOOD ROAD

GRANGE RD

BOUNDARY LANE

WAYSIDE RD

P

H

St Leonards

1

02

West Moors
Middle School

PINEHURST ROAD

Woolslope
Coppice

8   A   09   B   10   C   02

A4
1 LINDEN GD
2 MANOR GD

B3
1 HARRY BARROW CL
2 CHARING CL
3 WATERLOO WY
4 SOUTHFIELD MS
5 CROW ARCH LA
6 JOYCE DICKSON CL

B4
1 BEECHCROFT LA
2 BEECHCROFT MS
3 WANSTEAD CL

C3
1 OLD STACKS GD
2 THE CLOISTERS
3 SANDERLINGS
4 HOLMWOOD GARTH
5 ASHBURN GARTH
6 FOREST CT HILLS

C4
1 WHITEHART FIELDS
2 PIPERS ASH
3 RALEIGH CL
4 CUNNINGHAM CL

South Hampshire STREET ATLAS

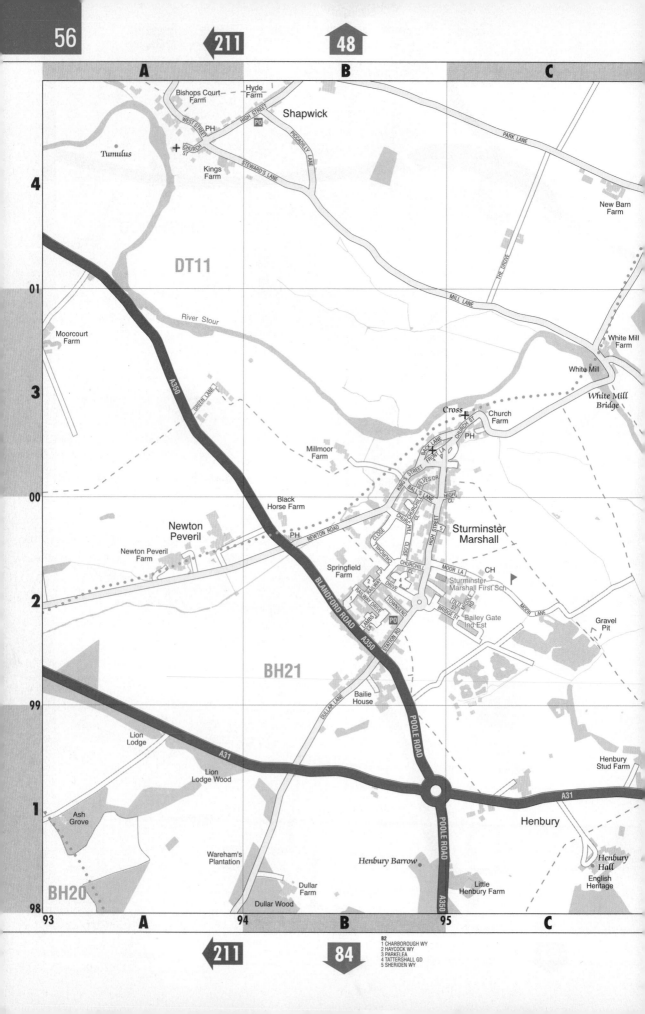

211
48

A   B   C

Bishops Court
Farm

Hyde
Farm

WEST STREET

HIGH STREET

PO

Shapwick

PH

PICCADILLY LANE

CHURCH ST

STEWARD'S LANE

PARK LANE

Tumulus

Kings
Farm

New Barn
Farm

4

DT11

THE DROVE

MILL LANE

01

River Stour

White Mill
Farm

Moorcourt
Farm

White Mill

White Mill
Bridge

3

A350

GREEN LANE

Cross

Church
Farm

PH

Millmoor
Farm

BLACK LANE

FRONT LA

CHURCH ST

KING'S STREET

REEVES DR

BALL'S LANE

HIGH
CL

Sturminster
Marshall

Black
Horse Farm

00

Newton
Peveril

PH

Newton Peveril
Farm

Newton Road

CLOSE

CHURCHILL

CHURCHILL CLOSE

HIGH STREET

TWICHURH

CHURCHILL
CL

MOOR LA

CH

Springfield
Farm

RAILWAY

RAILWAY DRIVE

TOWNSEND

DRIVE

Sturminster
Marshall First Sch

OLD MOOR RD

2

BLANDFORD ROAD

A350

LAMBS
CR

STATION RD

PO

BRIDGE ST

Bailey Gate
Ind Est

MOOR LANE

Gravel
Pit

BH21

99

Dullar Lane

Bailie
House

POOLE ROAD

Lion
Lodge

A31

Henbury
Stud Farm

Lion
Lodge Wood

A31

1

Ash
Grove

POOLE ROAD

Henbury

BH20

Wareham's
Plantation

Henbury Barrow

A350

Little
Henbury Farm

Henbury
Hall

English
Heritage

Dullar
Farm

Dullar Wood

98

93   A   94   B   95   C

211
84

B2
1 CHARBOROUGH WY
2 HAYCOCK WY
3 PARKELEA
4 TATTERSHALL GD
5 SHERIDEN WY

A   B   C

4

Locust Clump

Lodge Down

B3082

Kingston Plantation

BLANDFORD ROAD

PITTS DROVE

TADDON COTTS

Ralph Copse

Coneygar Copse

Kingston Lacy Park

Lodge

01

Kingston Lacy House
(National Trust)

Obelisks

ABBOTT STREET

Manor House

P

Barford Farm

Wynne Copse

P

Kingston Lacy Gardens

Kingston Lacy Home Farm

Stour Valley Wlk

All Fools Lane

Holly Lane

3

SANDY LANE

Poplar Farm

Firs Farm

BH21

Star Cottage Garden

Higher Dairy Farm

ROMAN WAY

COWGROVE ROAD

Cowgrove

00

Cowgrove Common

Cowgrove Farm

Lower Barford Farm

Chaw Meadow

River Stour

2

River Stour

99

Weir

Weir

Coventry Arms (PH)

Court House

Court Farm

A31

CANDYS LA

MILL STREET

Henbury Manor

Spring Coppice

Orchard Coppice

BRICKYARD LA

KNOLL LA

Mill Farm

Water Works

BLANDFORD ROAD

BROG ST

RECTORY AVE

Sleight

1

SLEIGHT LA

B3074

98

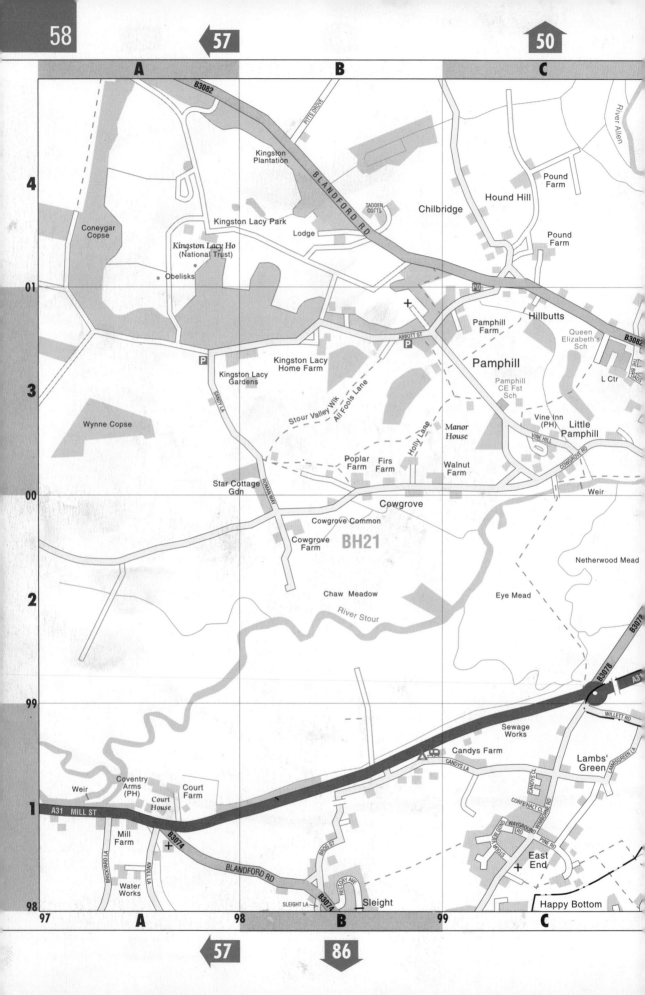

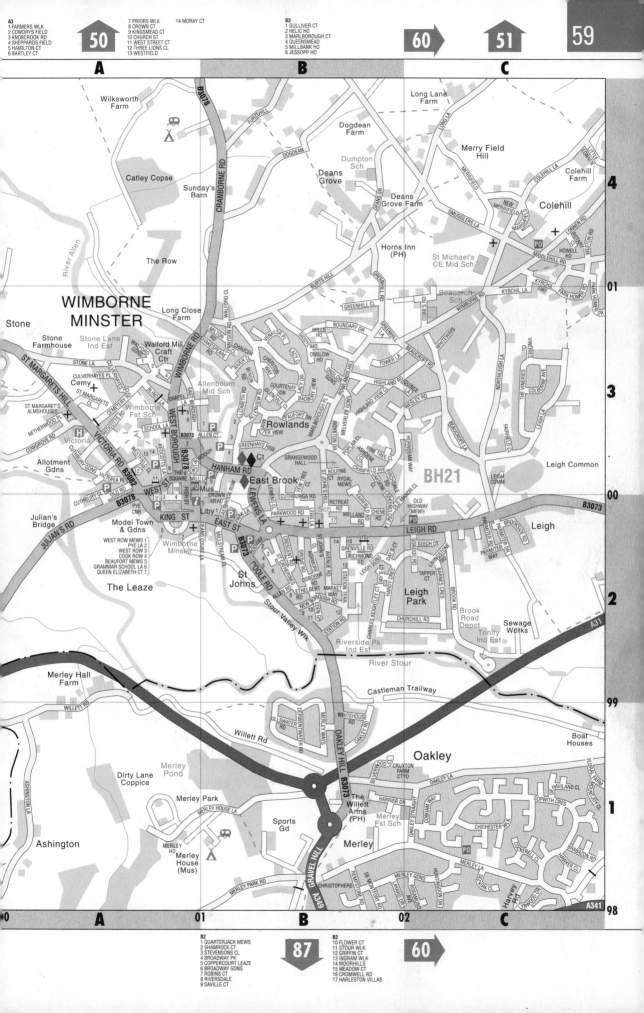

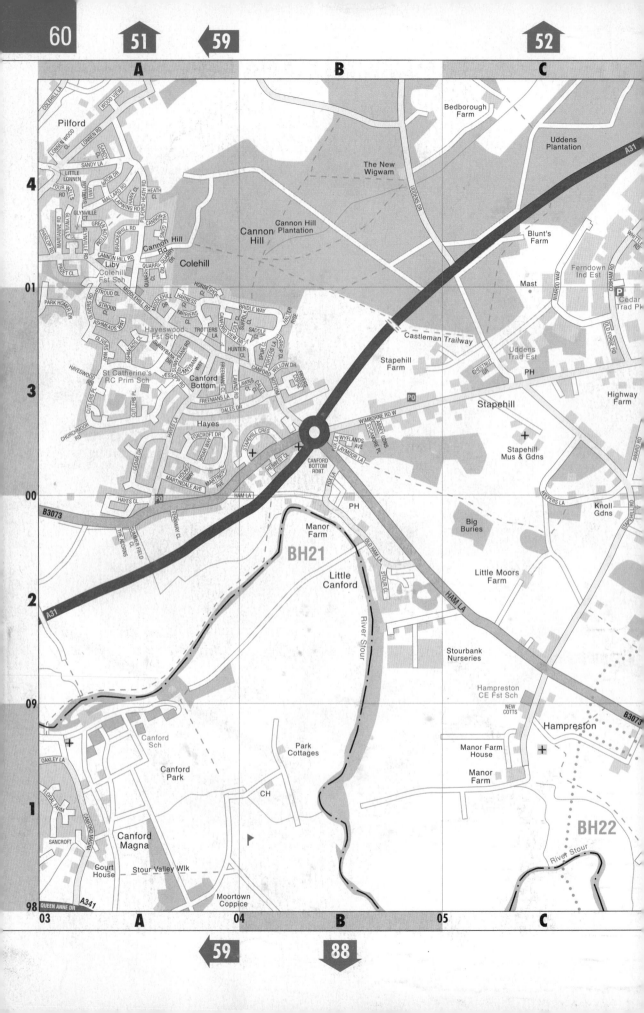

A   B   C

Pilford

Bedborough Farm

Uddens Plantation

The New Wigwam

Cannon Hill Plantation

Blunt's Farm

4

Cannon Hill

Mast

Ferndown Ind Est

Cannon Hill Rd

Colehill

Cedar Trad Pk

Liby

Colehill Fst Sch

01

Castleman Trailway

Uddens Trad Est

PH

Hayeswood Fst Sch

Stapehill Farm

Highway Farm

3

St Catherine's RC Prim Sch

Canford Bottom

Stapehill

Hayes

PO

Stapehill Mus & Gdns

Canford Bottom RDBT

Wimborne Rd W

00

PO

Knoll Gdns

B3073

Manor Farm

Big Buries

BH21

Little Canford

Little Moors Farm

2

A31

Stourbank Nurseries

River Stour

HAM LA

09

Hampreston CE Fst Sch

B3073

NEW COTTS

Hampreston

Canford Sch

Park Cottages

Manor Farm House

Canford Park

CH

Manor Farm

1

BH22

Canford Magna

River Stour

Sancroft

Court House

Stour Valley Wlk

98

A341

Moortown Coppice

Queen Anne Dr

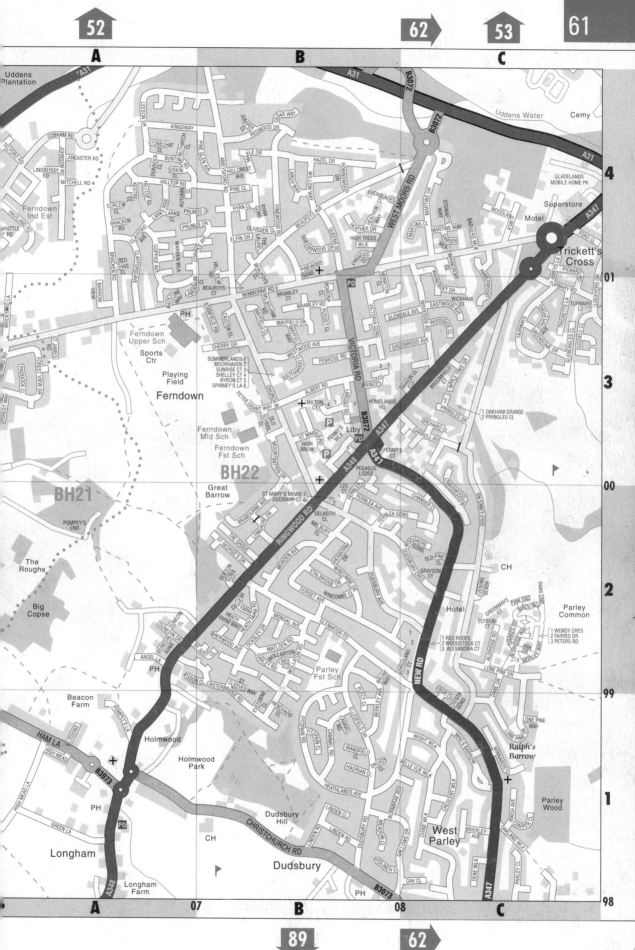

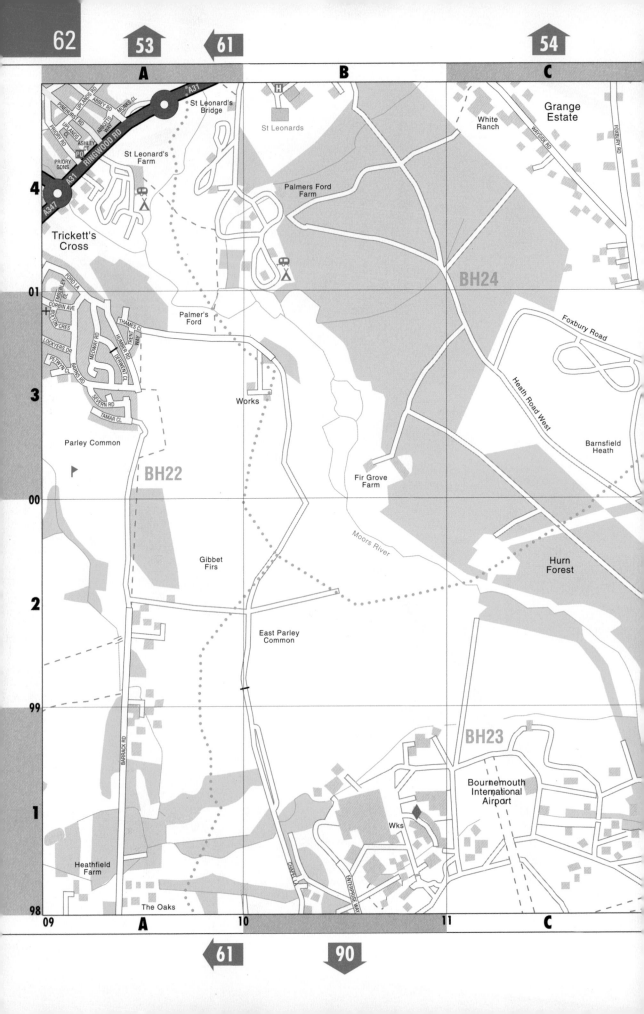

A   B   C

Avon Heath
Ctry Pk
(South Park)

Matchams
Farm

Kingston

Dean's
Farm

DRAGON LA

4

Matcham's
House

Wattons Ford
Common

Wattons Ford

Avon Valley Path

Matcham's
Park

Alder Bed
Copse

Parsonage
Wood

BH24

01

HURN RD

MATCHAMS CL

Stadium

The
Warren

Bisterne

Lower Side
Copse

River Avon

Ppg
Sta

Hill Road

Week
Wood

B3347

3

Foxbury Hill

Watermain Road

Week
Farm

North End
Copse

North End
Farm

00

Plantation Road

Bostwick
Farm

Week
Common

Watermeadows

Tyrrell's
Ford
(Hotel)

2

Heath Road East

MATCHAMS LA

Christchurch
Ski & Leisure
Centre

BH23

Watermeadows

Sabines
Farm

AVON FARM
COTTS

Avon Tyrrell
Farm

Fillybrook
Bottom

London
Farm

99

P

LONDON LA

COUNCIL
HOS

Furzy
Copse

New Queen
Inn
(PH)

Avon

Fillybrook

Coronation
Cottages

1

Avon
Common

Pithouse
Farm

Watermeadows

Valley
Farm

B3347

A   13   B   14   C   98

A338

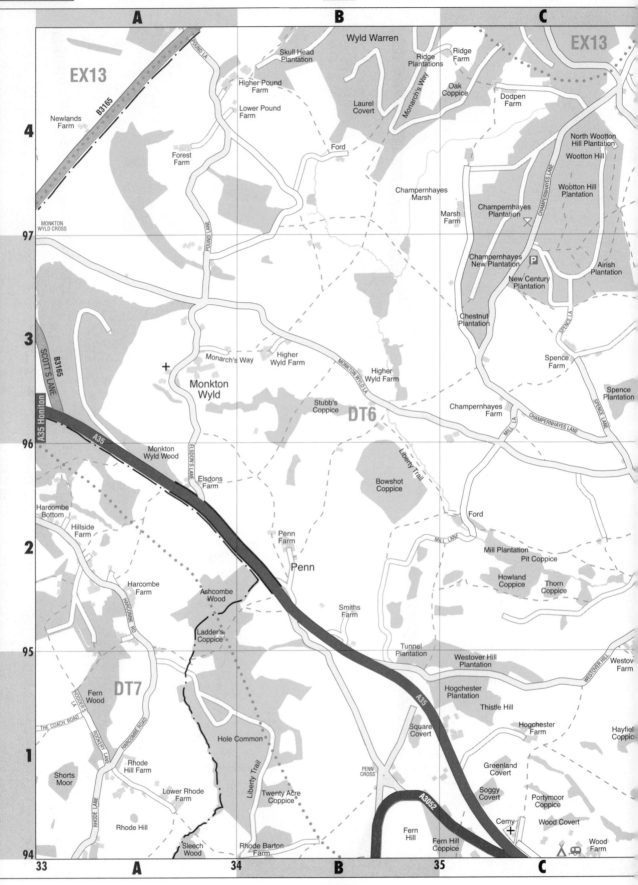

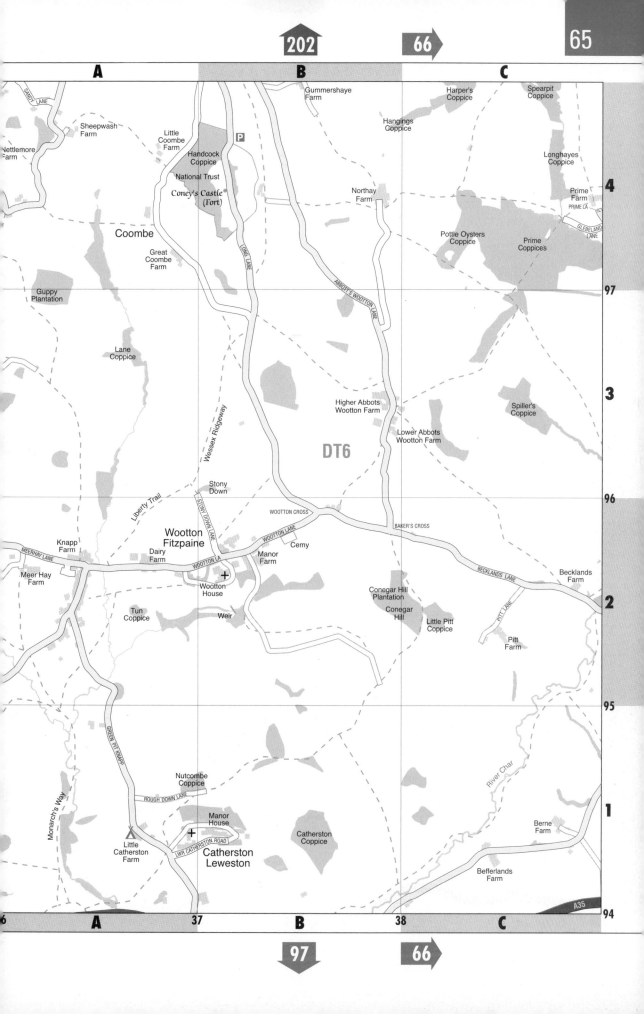

A B C

4

97

3

DT6

96

2

95

1

94

SANDY LANE

Nettlemore Farm

Sheepwash Farm

Little Coombe Farm

P

Handcock Coppice

National Trust

Coney's Castle (Fort)

Coombe

Great Coombe Farm

Guppy Plantation

LONG LANE

Lane Coppice

Wessex Ridgeway

Liberty Trail

Stony Down

STONY DOWN LANE

Wootton Fitzpaine

WOOTTON LA

Knapp Farm

MEERHAY LANE

Dairy Farm

Meer Hay Farm

+ Wootton House

Tun Coppice

Weir

Gummershaye Farm

Hangings Coppice

Northay Farm

ABBOTT'S WOOTTON LANE

Higher Abbots Wootton Farm

Lower Abbots Wootton Farm

WOOTTON CROSS

WOOTTON LANE

Cemy

Manor Farm

BAKER'S CROSS

Conegar Hill Plantation

Conegar Hill

Little Pitt Coppice

Harper's Coppice

Spearpit Coppice

Longhayes Coppice

Prime Farm

PRIME LA

GLEBELAND LANE

Pottle Oysters Coppice

Prime Coppices

Spiller's Coppice

BECKLANDS LANE

Becklands Farm

PITT LANE

Pitt Farm

GREEN PIT KNAPP

Monarch's Way

Nutcombe Coppice

ROUGH DOWN LANE

Little Catherston Farm

+

Manor House

LWR CATHERSTON ROAD

Catherston Leweston

Catherston Coppice

River Char

Berne Farm

Befferlands Farm

A35

A B C

6

37

38

A   **B**   **C**

Spinney Coppice

Taphouse Farm

POORHOUSE LA
TAPHOUSE LA

PH

Lower Park Farm

Bridge Farm

Castle

Lodgehouse Farm

Bluntshay Lane

4

SCADDEN'S CORNER

Shave Farm

Crabbs Bluntshay Farm

PRIME LANE

Valehouse Farm

CARDS MILL LANE

Great Bluntshay Farm

Bluntshay

Prime Coppices

Little Bluntshay Farm

MANDEVILLE STOKE LANE

Marshwood Vale

97

Mandeville Stoke Farm

Cards Mill Farm

Ossellhayes Farm

3

Cutty Stubbs

Blackmore Farm

Purcombe Farm

Lower Coppice

Higher Coppice

96

River Char

Peace Farm

DT6

Lower Beerland Farm

Coppet Hill

Plenty House

GASSINS LANE

Ryall Bottom

Monarch's Way

2

Whitchurch Canonicorum

+

Wakelys Farm

BECKLANDS LANE

Berehayes Farm

PH

Beerland Farm

Bonhays Farm

Greenway Farm

Hodders Farm

Ryall Farm

Crooch Farm

Dedley Farm

RYALL ROAD

Pothills Farm

BUTT LANE

Venn Farm

95

Cockwell Farm

Green Close Farm

LOSCOMBE'S WELL ROAD

Gates Farm

Ryall

VENN LANE

TAYLOR'S LANE

Butt Farm

BUTT LANE

TAYLOR'S LA

PITMAN'S LANE

Manscombe Abbey

National Trust

River Winniford

1

Mast

Tumuli

TIZARD'S KNAP

PITMAN'S LANE

LOVE'S LANE

Hardown Hill

Right Bottom

BUTT

Morcombelake

Barn Close Farm
PH

+

MERRIOTT'S LA

LOVE'S LANE

GIBBS LA

94

A35

SHIP KNAPP

39   **A**   40   **B**   41   **C**

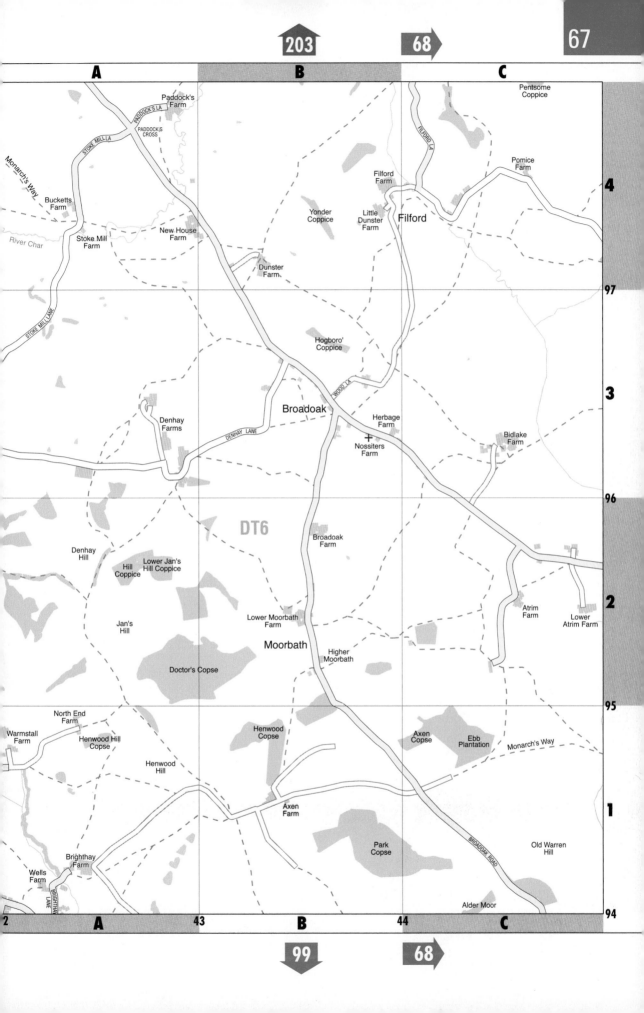

A
B
C

Pentsome Coppice

Monarch's Way

Paddock's Farm

PADDOCK'S LA

STOKE MILL LA

PADDOCK'S CROSS

FILFORD LA

Pomice Farm

4

Bucketts Farm

River Char

Stoke Mill Farm

New House Farm

Yonder Coppice

Filford Farm

Little Dunster Farm

Filford

97

STOKE MILL LANE

Dunster Farm

Hogboro' Coppice

WOOD LA

3

Broadoak

Herbage Farm

Denhay Farms

DENHAY LANE

Nossiters Farm

Bidlake Farm

96

DT6

Denhay Hill

Hill Coppice

Lower Jan's Hill Coppice

Broadoak Farm

Jan's Hill

Lower Moorbath Farm

Atrim Farm

Lower Atrim Farm

2

Doctor's Copse

Moorbath

Higher Moorbath

95

Warmstall Farm

North End Farm

Henwood Hill Copse

Henwood Copse

Axen Copse

Ebb Plantation

Monarch's Way

Henwood Hill

1

Axen Farm

Park Copse

BROADOAK ROAD

Old Warren Hill

Brighthay Farm

Wells Farm

BRIGHTHAY LANE

Alder Moor

94

2
A
43
B
44
C

A   B   C

Oxbridge

Higher
Kingsland Farm

Kershay
Farms

Long Bottom
Coppice

Perhay
Farm

Myrtle
Farm

Oxbridge
Farm

Nurserymead
Coppice

Waytown

Shatcombe
Coppice

B3162

Salwayash
Prim Sch

White House
Farm

4

Kingsland

Higher Kershay
Farm

Way Farm

WHITHAY LA

Lower
Kershay Farm

Marlis
Farm

Camesworth

STRONGATE
LA

Brinsham
Farm

Elwell
Lodge

STRONGATE LA

WHITHAY LANE

97

Strongate
Farm

Ash
Farm

FIR TREE
CL

PINEAPPLE LANE

Elwell
Farms

Higher
Elwell
Farm

Snailscroft
Farm

Foxmoor
Coppice

Church
Grounds

SALWAY DR

Pineapple
Farm

Higher Ford
Farm

Hill
Farm

PITCHE

PH

Salwayash

3

Lambrook

River Brit

B3162

Lambrook
Farm

Bingham's
Farm

Broadenham
Farm

Ash Lane
Farm

ASH LANE

Seaview
Farm

96

Ash

Higher
Ash Farm

Higher
Wooth Farm

Limbury

DT6

Ashleigh
Farm

Sewage
Works

Atrim

Wooth Old
Farm

2

Colly Farm

Wooth
Farm

Wooth

Dottery

Lower Ash
Farm

PYMORE LANE

Higher
Pymore Farm

WATFORD LANE

Watford
Farm

95

Bilshay
Farm

BILSHAY LANE

A3066

BLIND LANE

Middle
Pymore
Farm

PH

GORE
CROSS

GORE
LANE

River Simene

Monarch's Way

Factory

CORBIN WAY

RIDGEWAY

BEAMINSTER RD

HEMLETS

TOWNSEND WY

New Close
Farm

DOTTERY ROAD

Lower
Pymore
Farm

Pymore

PYMORE ROAD

HILLVIEW

DODHAMS

BSM CL

BEAMINSTER ROAD

COURT CL

1

Washingpool
Farm

QUEENWELL

Sir John
Colfox Sch

BANTON
SHARD

VILLAGE

River Brit

Seymour
Farm

B3162

GIPSY LANE

ST ANDREW'S
ROAD

KNIGHTSTONE R

TRINITY

94

45   A   46   B   47   C

C1
1 FISHWEIR FIELDS
2 ACER AV
3 WHITE CL
4 SPRING CL
5 GORE CROSS WY
6 BATH ORCHARD

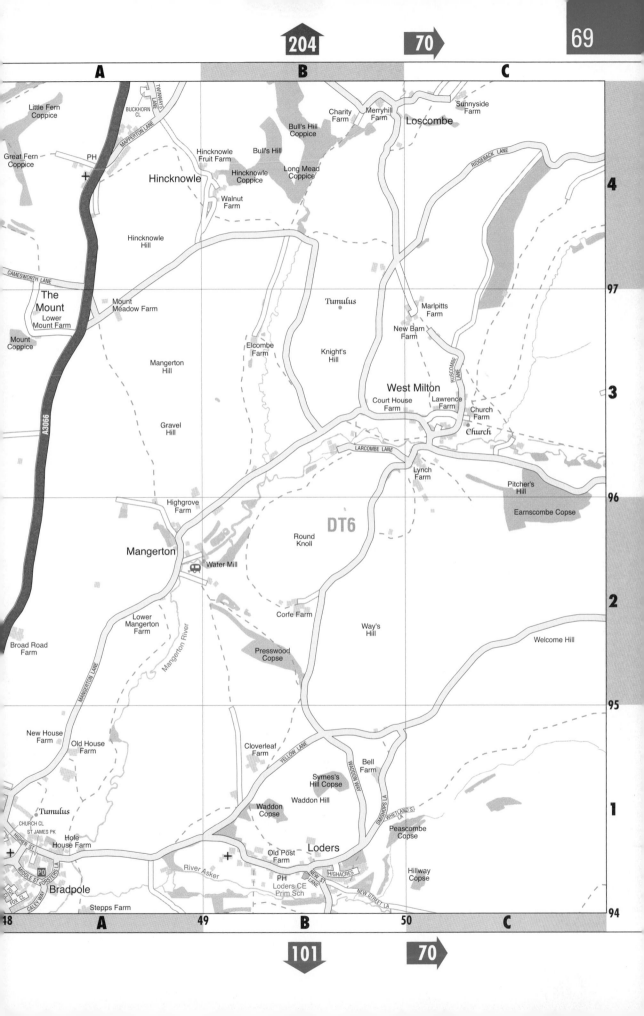

A   B   C

Regent's Coppice

RIDGEBACK LANE

South Poorton Farm

Spring Hill Farm

Bottom Farm

Leggland Farm

South Poorton

Lower Long Hay Coppice

Strap's Coppice

Caseley's Coppice

Elmside Coppice

4

Poorton Hill Farm

Hungry Hill

Wytherston Wood

LAKE HILL

Poorton Hill

Nature Reserve

Strip Lynchets

Swyre Hill

Wytherston Farm

97

Swyre Bottom

Swyre Coppice

DUGBERRY HILL

Broadfield Coppice

Quarry

Strip Lynchets

3

Lower Townsend Farm

Townsend Farm

DT6

Whetley

Strip Lynchets

Manor Farm

Glebe Farm

Whetley Farm

+**Powerstock**

SCHOOL HILL

PH

Eastwater Farm

KING'S LANE

96

Merriott

Motte & Bailey

Castle Mill Farm

King's Farm

PH

WELL LA.

Southmead Farm

THE SQUARE

2

Mappercombe Manor Farm

Nettlecombe

KING'S LANE

Browns Farm

Marsh Farm

Bell Stone

95

Mappercombe Manor

Ridge Copse

Belstone Covert

Warren Plantation

Sweed's Copse

Eggardor Hill

Marsh Copse

Chaffins Coppice

1

Whinhill Copse

Knowle Hill

Knowle Copse

Knowle Plantation

North Eggardon Farm

Shedbush Copse

94

51   A   52   B   53   C

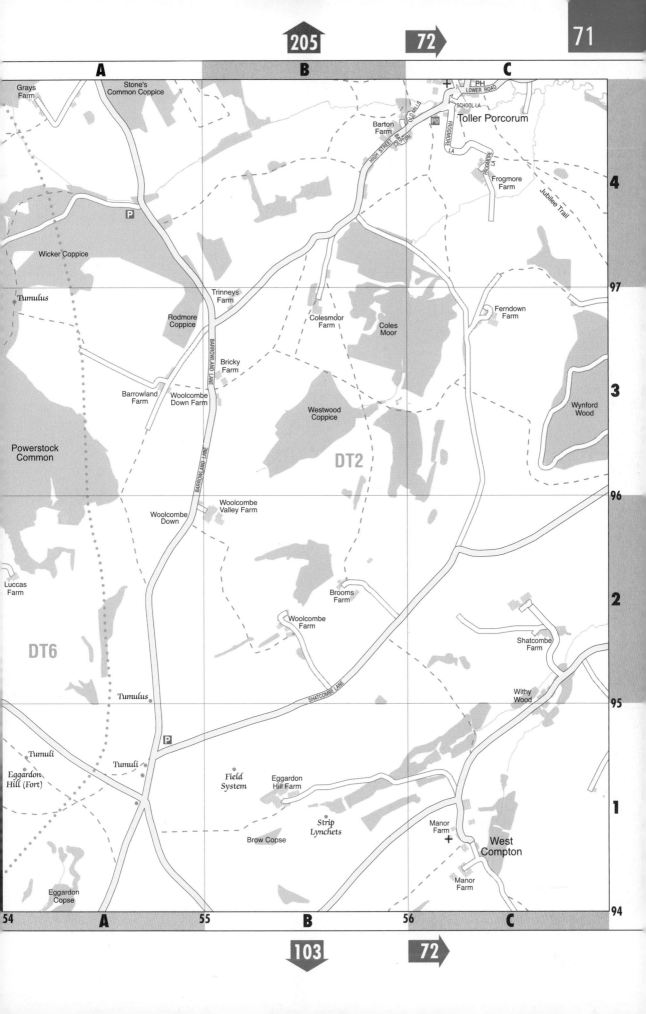

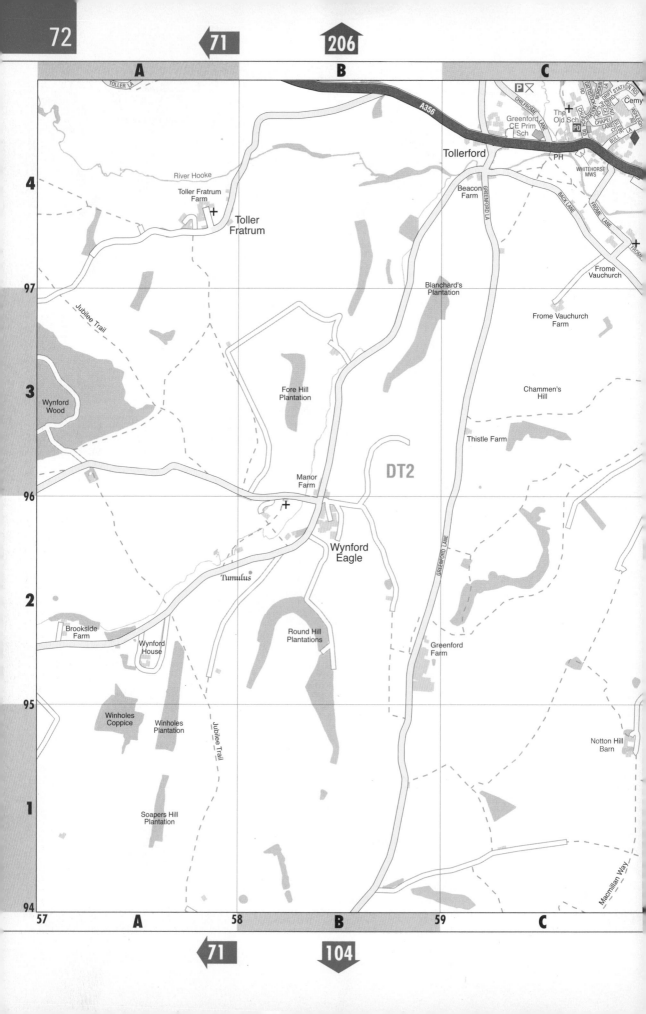

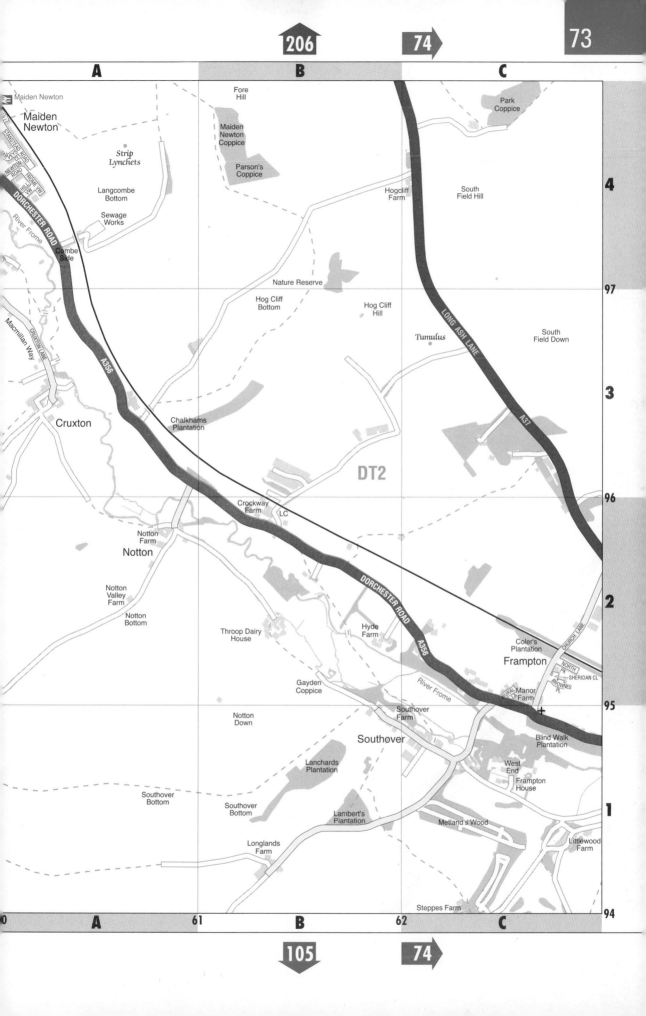

A

B

C

Maiden Newton

Maiden
Newton

Fore
Hill

Park
Coppice

Maiden
Newton
Coppice

4

Strip
Lynchets

Parson's
Coppice

Langcombe
Bottom

Hogcliff
Farm

South
Field Hill

Sewage
Works

DORCHESTER ROAD

River Frome

Combe
Side

Nature Reserve

97

Hog Cliff
Bottom

Hog Cliff
Hill

South
Field Down

Macmillan Way

CRUXTON LANE

A356

Tumulus

LONG ASH LANE

3

A37

Cruxton

Chalkhams
Plantation

DT2

Crockway
Farm

LC

96

Notton
Farm

Notton

Notton
Valley
Farm

DORCHESTER ROAD

A356

2

Notton
Bottom

Throop Dairy
House

Hyde
Farm

Coler's
Plantation

CHURCH LANE

Frampton

NORTH
PK
SHERIDAN CL
BROWNES
PL
RURAL
LA

Gayden
Coppice

River Frome

Manor
Farm

95

Notton
Down

Southover
Farm

Blind Walk
Plantation

Southover

West
End

Frampton
House

Southover
Bottom

Lanchards
Plantation

Southover
Bottom

Lambert's
Plantation

Metland's Wood

1

Littlewood
Farm

Longlands
Farm

Steppes Farm

94

61
62

A

B

C

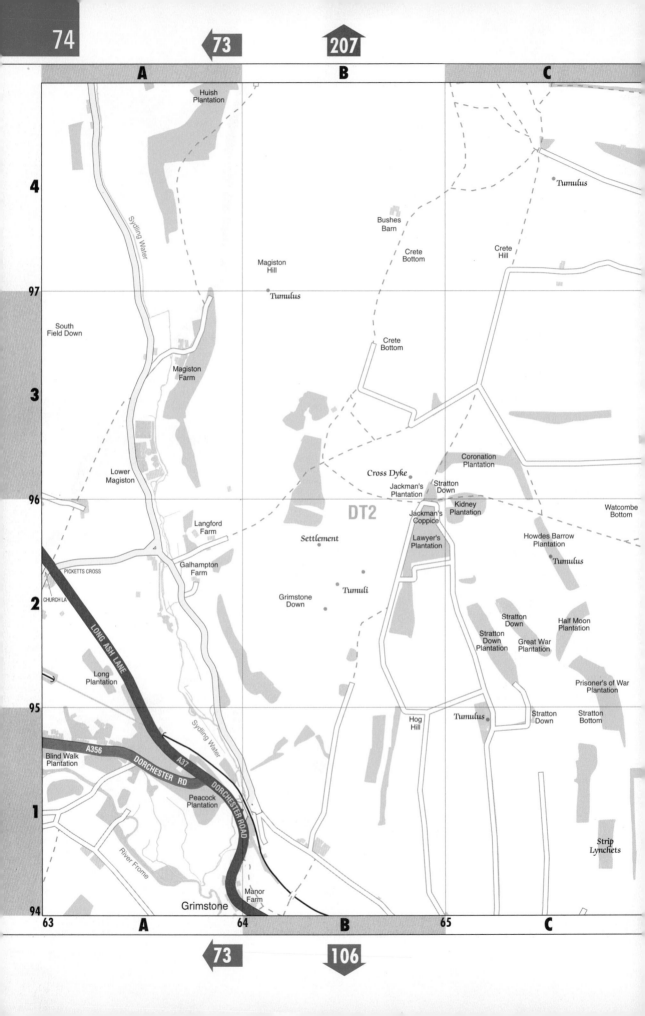

A   B   C

4

Huish
Plantation

Tumulus

Bushes
Barn

Crete
Bottom

Crete
Hill

Magiston
Hill

97

Tumulus

Sydling Water

South
Field Down

Crete
Bottom

3

Magiston
Farm

Coronation
Plantation

Lower
Magiston

Cross Dyke

Stratton
Down

Jackman's
Plantation

Kidney
Plantation

Watcombe
Bottom

96

DT2

Langford
Farm

Jackman's
Coppice

Galhampton
Farm

Settlement

Lawyer's
Plantation

Howdes Barrow
Plantation

Tumulus

PICKETTS CROSS

Tumuli

CHURCH LA

Grimstone
Down

Stratton
Down

Half Moon
Plantation

2

Stratton
Down
Plantation

Great War
Plantation

LONG ASH LANE

Long
Plantation

Prisoner's of War
Plantation

95

Sydling Water

Hog
Hill

Tumulus

Stratton
Down

Stratton
Bottom

A356

Blind Walk
Plantation

DORCHESTER RD

A37

DORCHESTER ROAD

Peacock
Plantation

1

Strip
Lynchets

River Frome

Manor
Farm

Grimstone

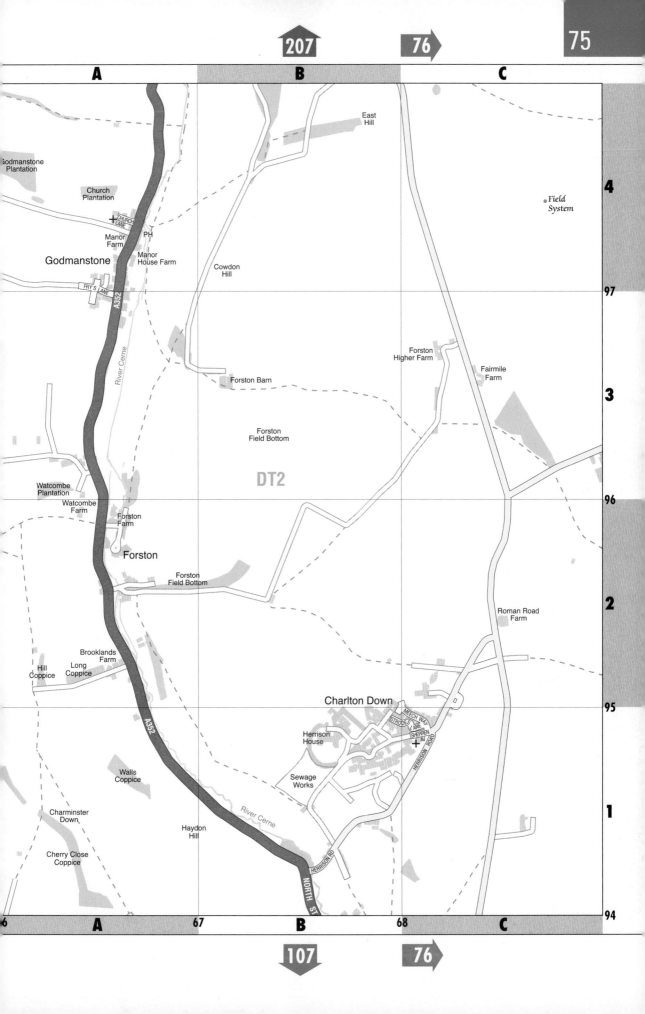

A
B
C

East
Hill

Godmanstone
Plantation

Church
Plantation

4

• Field
System

CHURCH
LANE
PH

Manor
Farm

Godmanstone

Manor
House Farm

Cowdon
Hill

FRY'S LANE

A352

97

Forston
Higher Farm

Fairmile
Farm

River Cerne

3

Forston Barn

Forston
Field Bottom

DT2

Watcombe
Plantation

96

Watcombe
Farm

Forston
Farm

Forston

Forston
Field Bottom

Roman Road
Farm

2

Brooklands
Farm

Hill
Coppice

Long
Coppice

Charlton Down

95

A352

MEECH WAY

STRODES LANE

SHERREN AV

Herrison
House

HERRISON ROAD

Walls
Coppice

Sewage
Works

Charminster
Down

River Cerne

1

Haydon
Hill

Cherry Close
Coppice

HERRISON RD

NORTH ST

94

A | B | C

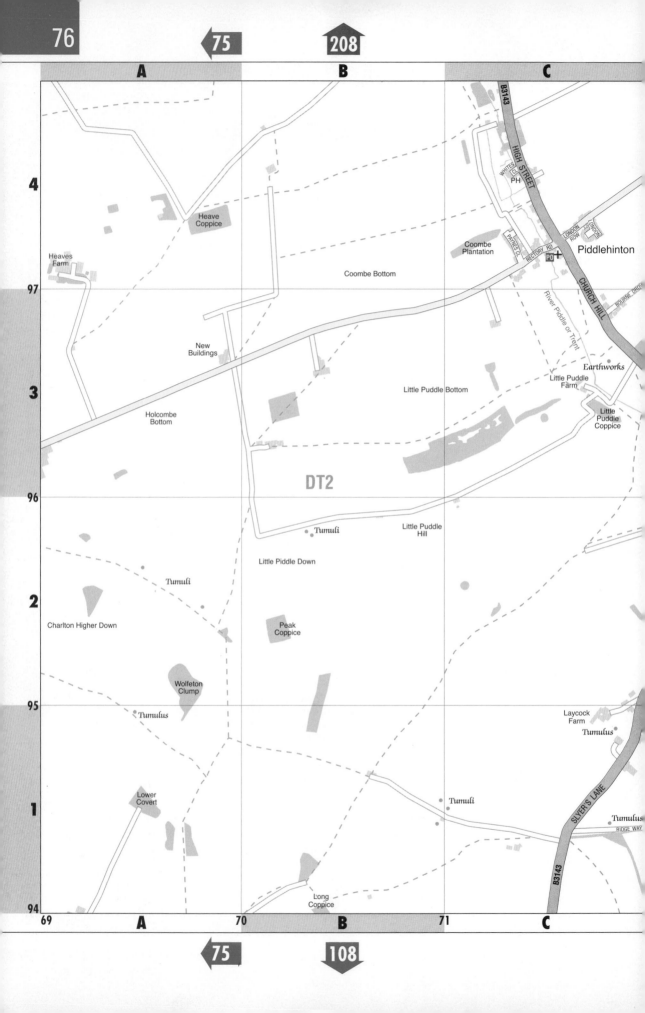

4

Heave
Coppice

Heaves
Farm

Coombe
Plantation

Coombe Bottom

WHITES CL
PH

RECTORY RD
PAYNES CL
PO

B3143
HIGH STREET
LONDON ROW
LONDON

Piddlehinton

97

New
Buildings

River Piddle or Trent

CHURCH HILL

BOURNE DROV

Earthworks

Little Puddle
Farm

Little Puddle Bottom

Little Puddle
Coppice

3

Holcombe
Bottom

DT2

96

Tumuli

Little Puddle
Hill

Little Piddle Down

Tumuli

Charlton Higher Down

Peak
Coppice

Laycock
Farm

Tumulus

2

Wolfeton
Clump

95

Tumulus

SLYER'S LANE

Lower
Covert

Tumuli

RIDGE WAY

Tumulus

1

B3143

Long
Coppice

94

69 | A | 70 | B | 71 | C

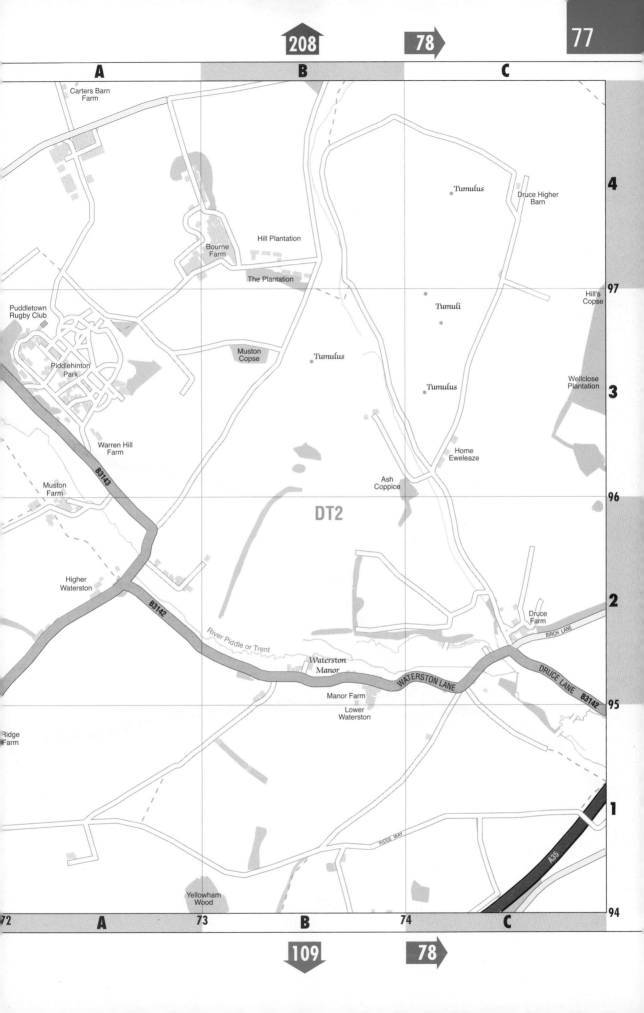

A
B
C

Carters Barn Farm

4

Tumulus

Druce Higher Barn

Hill Plantation

Bourne Farm

The Plantation

97

Hill's Copse

Puddletown Rugby Club

Tumuli

Muston Copse

Tumulus

Wellclose Plantation

Piddlehinton Park

Tumulus

3

Warren Hill Farm

Home Eweleaze

Muston Farm

Ash Coppice

B3143

96

DT2

Higher Waterston

2

Druce Farm

B3142

BIRCH LANE

River Piddle or Trent

Waterston Manor

WATERSTON LANE

DRUCE LANE B3142

Manor Farm

95

Lower Waterston

Ridge Farm

1

RIDGE WAY

A35

Yellowham Wood

94

A
B
C

Tumuli

Hazel Copse

Shailes Copse

Park Hill

Dewlish House

Puddletown Down

Hill's Copse

Warren Plantation

Lower Farm

Crawthorne Farm

Devil's Brook

WARREN HILL

WARREN ROAD

DT2

Wreden Plantation

Basan Plantation

Basan Hill

A354

Fryer's Bridge

Tumuli

Burleston Down

BIRCH LANE

LONG LANE

Bardolf Manor

Burleston Plantation

B3142

DRUCE LANE

A35

Northbrook

LONG LA

Hill Top

Home Farm

A35

BURLESTON DROVE

DRUCE LANE

THE MOOR

PH

Stafford Park Farm

Bardolfeston Village

River Piddle or Trent

THOMPSON CL

KINGSMD

PH

HIGH ST

PO

STYLES

MILL STREET

ORFORD ST

THE SQ

Ilsington House

Athelhampton House

West End

Burleston

Puddletown

Puddletown CE First Sch

Liby

St Marys CE Middle Sch

COOMBE ROAD

NEW STREET

HIGH STREET

THE

ROD HILL

BUTT CL

BEECH RD

MILOM LANE

Little Knoll Copse

Henroost Wood

ATHELHAMPTON ROAD

Athelhampton

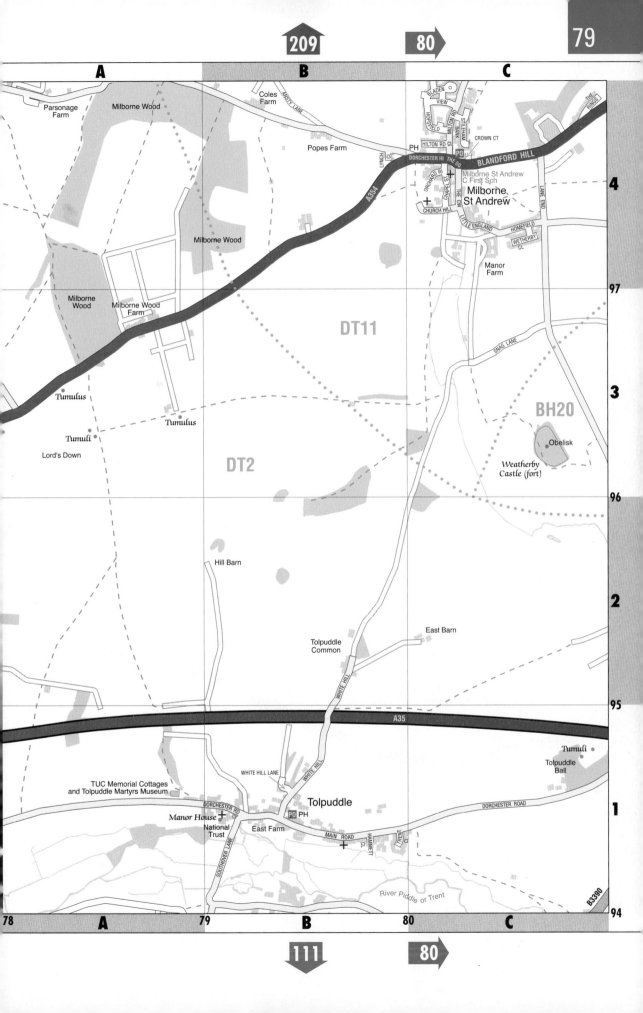

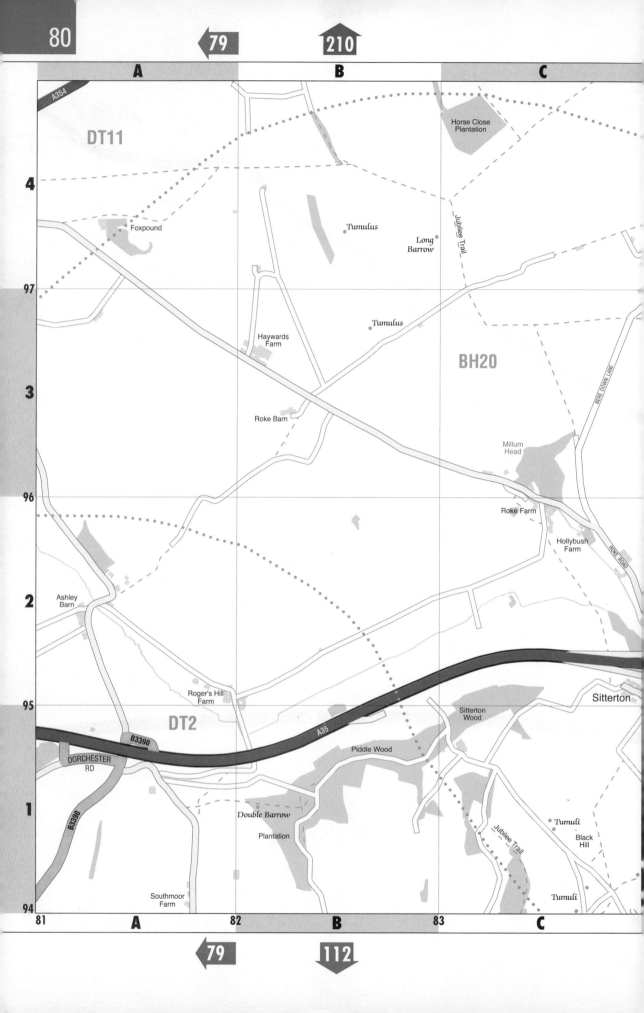

A354

DT11

4

Foxpound

Tumulus

Long Barrow

Horse Close Plantation

Jubilee Trail

97

Haywards Farm

Tumulus

BH20

3

Roke Barn

Millum Head

BERE DOWN LANE

96

Roke Farm

Hollybush Farm

Ashley Barn

ROKE ROAD

2

Roger's Hill Farm

Sitterton Wood

Sitterton

95

DT2

A35

B3390

Piddle Wood

DORCHESTER RD

Double Barrow

Jubilee Trail

1

B3390

Plantation

Tumuli

Black Hill

Southmoor Farm

Tumuli

94

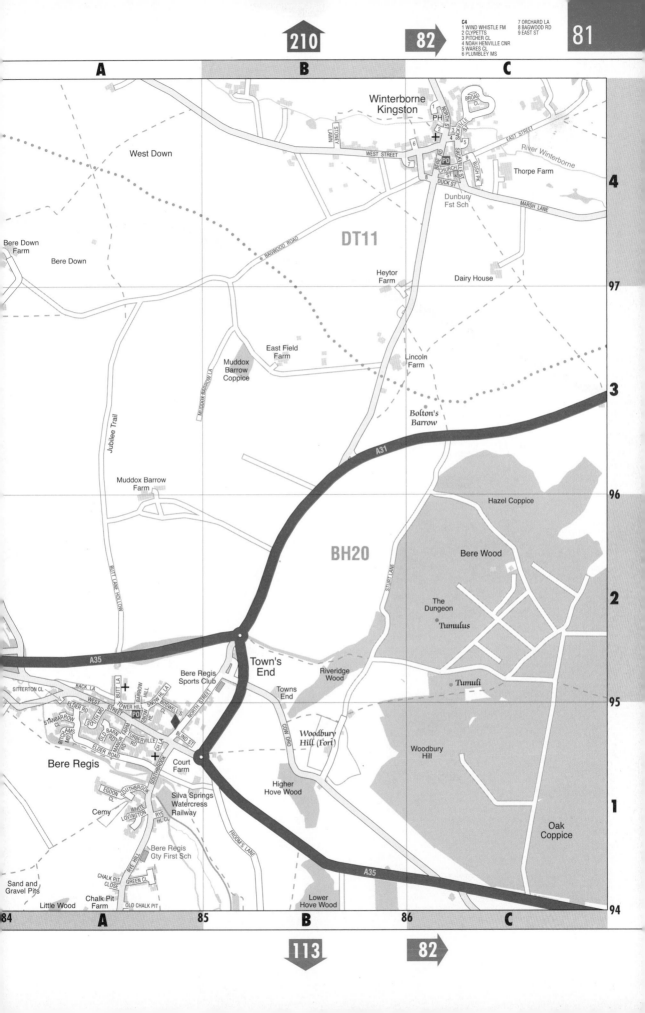

81
211

A   B   C

4

MUSTON LANE

Muston Farm

Ford

Winterborne Muston

Anderson Manor

Manor Farm

Anderson

MARSH LANE

Marsh Farm

Riverside Farm

Winterborne Tomson

River Winterborne

Hill Top

Middle Farm

Rainbow View Farm

THE STREET

Willow Farm

PH

Kiddles Farm

Rectory Farm

Winterborne Zelston

97

RED POST

A31

DT11

3

Tumulus

Tumuli

Tumuli

Botany Bay Farm

WINTERBORNE LANE

Tumulus

Bloxworth Down

96

Robinswood Farm

Waterley Wood

Pound Wood

Hazel Coppice

2

Kimberley Wood

MORDEN LANE

BH20

95

Bloxworth House

Newport

Brimland Wood

2

Bere Wood

NEWPORT LANE

Bloxworth

Manor Farm

1

Oak Coppice

East Bloxworth

Longcutters' Coppice

Humber's Coppice

East Coppice

Heron Coppice

94

87   A   88   B   89   C

A
B
C

Huish
PH
DT11

Worlds End

Miller's Farm

Hawk Wood

Eagle Plantation

Charborough House

Tower

4

VERMIN LANE
B3075

Round House Plantation

High Wood

31

97

Tumulus

EAST MORDEN DRIVE

COLEHILL ROAD

West Park Farm

3

B3075

BH20

New Plantation

Phillips's Coppice

96

West Morden Farm

PARADISE LANE

East Morden

GODWIN'S LANE

Cockett Hill

West Morden

Home Farm

HIGHER STREET

Old Park

2

Kings Corner Farm

Beacon Hill

NEW LANE

GILES'S LANE

Old Park Farm

NEW LA

GODWIN'S LANE

Dolman's Hill

Everett's Wood

95

GALLOP'S LANE

LOWER STREET

Duke's Hill

PO

Whitefield Farm

Chapel Wood

PH

Brickfield Farm

Whitefield

B3075

Brooks Farm

Sticklands Farm

1

Fry's Wood

QUARR HILL

Frogmoor Coppice

BH16

Whitmore Bottom

Bulbury

Rough Bulbury

Bulbury Coppice

90
A
91
B
92
C
94

A   B   C

High
Wood

Dullar Wood

Windmill
Barrow Farm

West Wood

West
Wood

Fox Holes
Wood

Limekiln
Coppice

Heron
Grove

Windmill
Barrow

BH21

A350

4

Combe
Almer

POOLE ROAD

Higher Coombe
Farm

Notting
Hill

BH20

97

Brock Hill

Loop
Farm

Village
Earthworks

SANDY LANE

Sandpits
Farm

Bokers
Farm

CASTLE FARM ROAD

Warmwell
Farm

FLOWERS DROVE

A350

COLEHILL ROAD

3

Winter's
Coppice

Goat House
Farm

Castle
Hill

White
Heather

POOLE ROAD

Lytchett
House

+

BH16

CRUMPETS DR

Garden
Wood

96

Phillips's
Coppice

Dyett's
Coppice

Sunnyside
Farm

Dowdens
Farm

Barrow
Hill

PEATONS LANE

WIMBORNE ROAD

Bridge End

CASTLE FARM ROAD

FLOWERS DROVE

SCUTS CL

OLD CHAPEL DR

Peatons
Farm

JENNYS LANE

HIGH STREET

CHARBOROUGH CL

LIME KILN ROAD

PURBECK ROAD

PY CT

BALLARD CL

POUND RD

Lytchett
Matravers

DOLMANS HILL

Ash Farm

HOPMANS CL

PURBECK
CL

WAREHAM RD

2

CRUMPLERS

ANNCOTT CL

+

FLIRBETTS CL

CL

ABBOTTS MD

Eddy Green
Farm

OLD POUND CLOSE

HIGH STREET

PO

Liby

Druce
Farm

VINEYARD
CL

HANNS
CL

North House
Farm

Elder
Moor

FOXHILLS
CR

ELDONS DROVE

PROSPECT RD

DCKYER'S

TREEHARD WAY

FOXHILLS RD

HUNTICK ROAD

95

Redbridge
Farm

PALMERS DR

THE SPINNEY

FOXHILLS DR

BH20

Bartom's Hill

EDDY GREEN ROAD

MIDDLE ROAD

Lytchett
Matravers
CP Sch

GIBBS
GREEN

Foxhills
Farm

1 FOSTERS SPRING
2 PRYORS WK
3 LANDERS REACH

BARTOM'S LANE

Holly
Farm

DEANS DROVE

Huntick
Farm

WAREHAM ROAD

DILLONS GD

FOXHILLS LANE

1

H Bulbury
Farm

Quarr
Hill Farm

PENROSE CL

BURBIDGE CL

Race
Farm

GLEBE ROAD

HALLS ROAD

CASTLE VW DR

94

93   A   94   B   95   C

57

C3
1 SOUTHLANDS AV
2 PHELIPPS RD
3 RUSHCOMBE WY

86

C4
1 WAREHAM RD
2 TS FARM
3 PHELIPPS RD
4 OLD RECTORY CL
5 BADBURY VW RD

85

A B C

4

97

3

96

2

95

1

94

Mountain Clump
Knoll Farm
Castle Court Sch
RED LA
BRICKYARD LA
OLD MARKET RD
KNOLL A
BROADMOOR RD
HAYWARDS LA
SHORTS LA
B3074
OLD RECTORY CL
PARDYS HILL
MEADOW FARM LA
RIDGEWAY
Cemy
NEWTOWN LA
VIOLET FARM CL
BADBURY VIEW RD
WIMBORNE RD
BLANDFORD RD
Lockyer's Mid Sch
Newtown
Mount Pleasant
HIGHER MERLEY LA
COGDEAN WAY
COGDEAN WLK
MERLEY PARK RD
ASHINGTON GDNS
Ashington
Barrow Hill
WINDGREEN EST
FIELD LA
LOCKYERS RD
ROMAN HILLS
JUPITER WAY
DIANA WAY
Rushcombe Bottom
HIGHER BLANDFORD RD
B3074
Corfe Hills
Mast
Corfe Hills Sch

Allen Hill
Home Farm
Corfe Mullen
Henbury View Fst Sch
ORCHARD LA
ORCHARD CL
TOWERS FARM
GEORGES MEWS
Liby
CENTRAL AVE
CROFT CL
BROOK LA
WAREHAM RD
RALPH RD
DIPROSE RD
WARLAND WAY
PYE
PRIMROSE WAY
SOUTHLANDS AVE
GURNEY RD
PHELPS RD
JUBILEE RD
JUBILEE CL
SOUTH
BLYTHE RD
HENBURY RISE
HENBURY VIEW RD
HAVEN RD
BLANEY WAY
LAUREL CL
ERICA DR
BIRCH CL
WYATTS RD
RUSHCOMBE WAY
LINK RISE
CECIL AVE
HEATHER
MEADOW RISE
LANCASTER DR
LANCASTER WAY
HOLLAND WAY
ANVIL CRES
BARRY GDNS
SPRINGDALE AVE
ABBOTSBURY RD

Stony Down Plantation
Little Manor Farm
CHAPEL LA
CHAPEL CL
GORSE RD
VIEWSIDE CL
THORNTON CL
CORFE VIEW RD
MOORSIDE
QUEEN'S RD
DENNIS RD
HANHAM RD
EAST WAY
HIGHMOOR RD
HIGHFIELD
INGLEY CRES
SUTHERLAND AVE
WYNNE CL
SPRINGDALE RD
CHEAM RD
HILLTOP
HIGH PARK RD
RUSHALL LA
Stoney Down Farm
BH21
WATERLOO RD
HILLSIDE RD
HILLCREST RD
HECKFORD RD
COURTNEY PL
TERENCE RD
OAK
WAREHAM RD
HARTNELL CT
VICTORIA RD
COLIN CL
ALBERT RD
BLACKSMITH CL
DALKEITH RD
IVOR RD
CAESAR'S WAY
HAMILTON RD
ROMAN RD
HIGH PARK RD

Poor Common
DAIRY CL
AMBER RD
MARIAN CL
FIRSIDE RD
FROUD WAY
Hill View
SPRINGDALE GR
WILLS CL
GLADELANDS CL
GLADELANDS WAY
SILVERDALE CL
Springdale Fst Sch
LEWESDON DR
CLARENDON RD
BARTLETTS WAY
Decoy Pond
COVENTRY
KILN CL
CORVE LODGE RD
BEECH CL
DELL CL
LAVENDER WAY
THE CLOSE
UPTON WAY
HIGH WAY
WEST WAY
BH18

Holme Bush Inn (PH)
St Leonard's Farm
OLD WAREHAM RD
BEACON HILL LA
Naked Cross
HILLSIDE GDNS
HILLSIDE MEWS
Beacon Hill Clay Pits
MAXWELL RD
HADLEY WAY
NEWLANDS WAY
BEACON GDNS
BEACON RD
CORFE WAY
MALLOW CL
SANDFORD WAY
WEST WAY

Beacon Hill Farm
Works
Beacon Hill
BH16
OLD SANDPIT LA
A350
BLANDFORD RD N
Beacon Heath
Upton Heath
BRYONY CL
SPINDLE CL
PINESPRINGS DR
SORREL GDNS
KINGCUP
DOGWOOD RD
COWSLIP RD
CHAFFINCH CL
BUTTERCUP CL
BUCKTHORN CL
SPRUCE DR
SYCAMORE CL
ROWAN DR
GREENFINCH WAY
BROADSTONE WAY
PRIMROSE WAY
REDSHANK CL
HYACINTH CL
BLUEBELL LA
HONEYSUCKLE
CREEKMOOR LA
CLOVER DR
TARN DR

Castleman Trailway
BH17

97 A 98 B 99 C

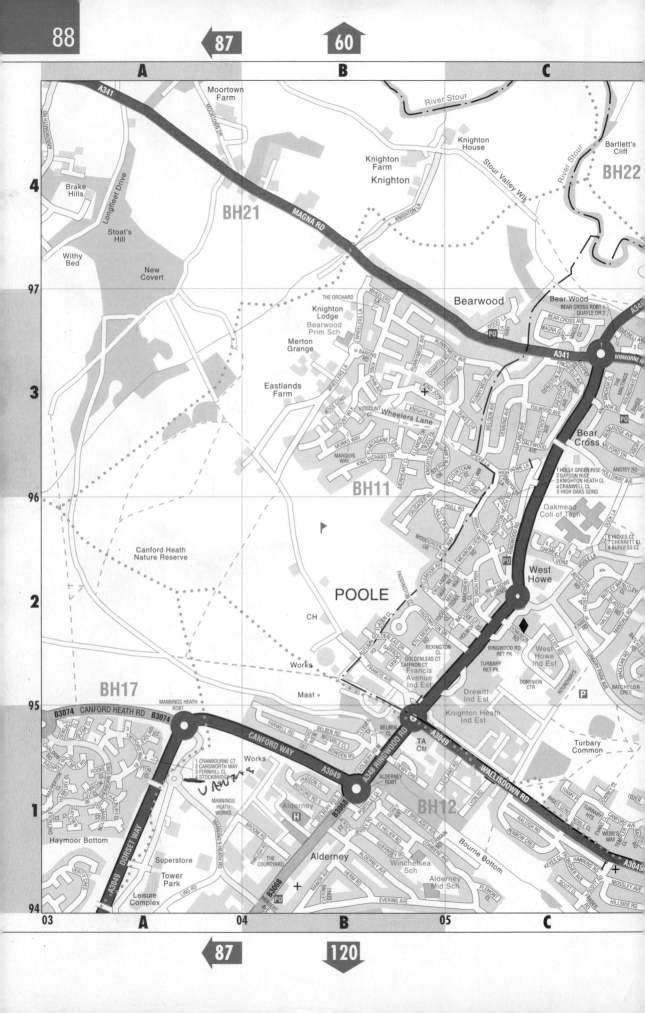

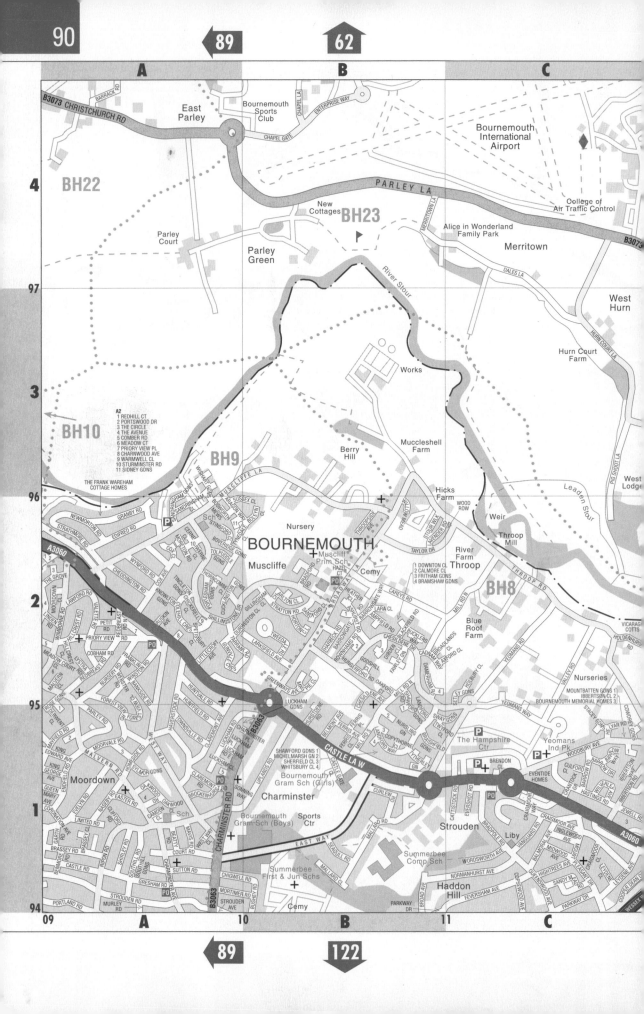

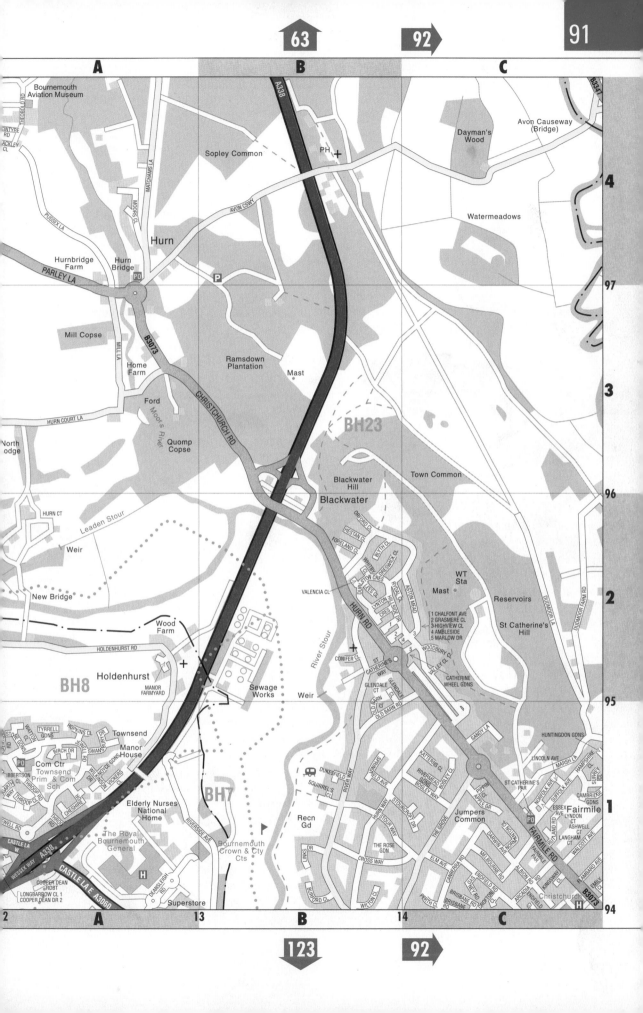

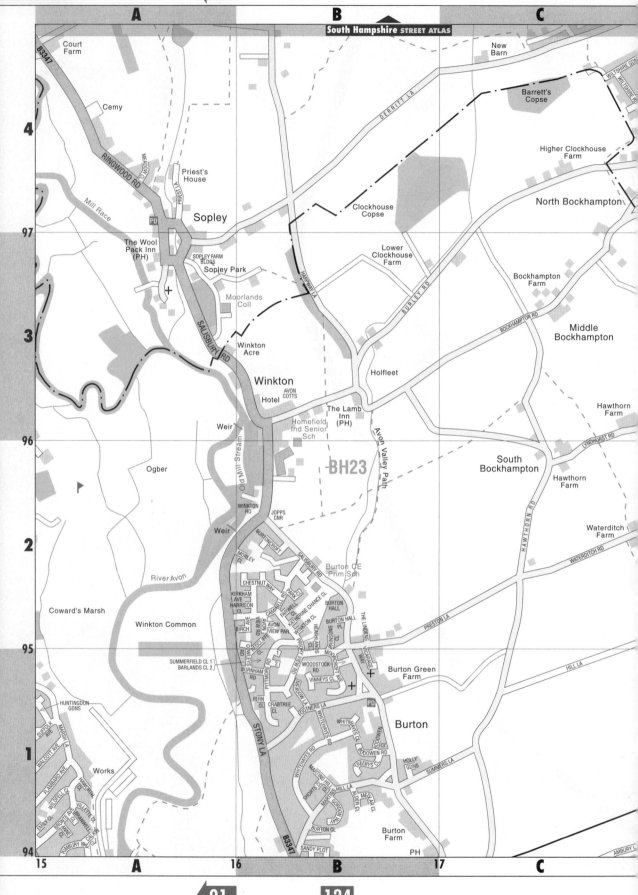

South Hampshire STREET ATLAS

A | B | C

Court Farm

B3347

Cemy

4

Ringwood Rd

Meadow Ct

Priest's House

Prest La

PO

Sopley

The Wool Pack Inn (PH)

Sopley Farm Bldgs

Sopley Park

Salisbury Rd

Mill Race

97

Derritt La

New Barn

Barrett's Copse

Wiltshire Gdns

Wiltshire Rd

Higher Clockhouse Farm

North Bockhampton

Clockhouse Copse

Lower Clockhouse Farm

Harmony La

Burley Rd

Bockhampton Farm

Bockhampton Rd

Middle Bockhampton

Moorlands Coll

3

Winkton Acre

Winkton

Hotel

Avon Cotts

Holfleet

The Lamb Inn (PH)

Homefield Ind Senior Sch

Avon Valley Path

Hawthorn Farm

96

Weir

Old Mill Stream

BH23

South Bockhampton

Hawthorn Farm

Hawthorn Rd

Lyndhurst Rd

Ogber

Winkton Ho

Jopps Cnr

Waterditch Farm

Waterditch Rd

2

Weir

Burton Croft

Morley Cl

Salisbury Rd

Chestnut Way

Burton CE Prim Sch

Preston La

The Lindens

Vicarage Way

River Avon

Winkton Common

Kirkham Ave

Harrison Cl

Birch Ave

Campbell Rd

Park Cl

Farwell Cl

Katherine Chance Cl

Burton Hall

Avon View Par

Winton Cl

Henry Rd

Priory Rd

Burton Hall Pl

Cowards Marsh

Burton Green Farm

95

Summerfield Cl 1
Barlands Cl 2

Cowleys Rd

Avon View Rd

Radcliffe

Pittmore Rd

Old Mead La

Meadow La

Woodstock Rd

Vinneys Cl

Mill Stream Dr

Moorcroft Ave

Footners La

Hill La

PO

Burnham Rd

Fern Cl

Crabtree Cl

Whitehayes Rd

White Cl

Hayes Cl

Bodowen Rd

Burton

Huntingdon Gdns

Suffolk Ave

Marsh La

Walcott Ave

Stony La

1

Freebys Cl

Holly Gdns

Summers La

Flambard Ave

Wildfell Cl

Emily Cl

Bronte Ave

Wren Cl

Branwell Cl

Villette Cl

Howarth Cl

Rimbury Way

Meyrick Cl

Alder Cl

Gordon

Martins Hill La

Shorts Cl

Martins Hill Cl

Burton Cl

Burton Farm

PH

Works

B3347

Sandy Plot

Ambury La

94

15 | 16 | 17

A | B | C

A   B   C

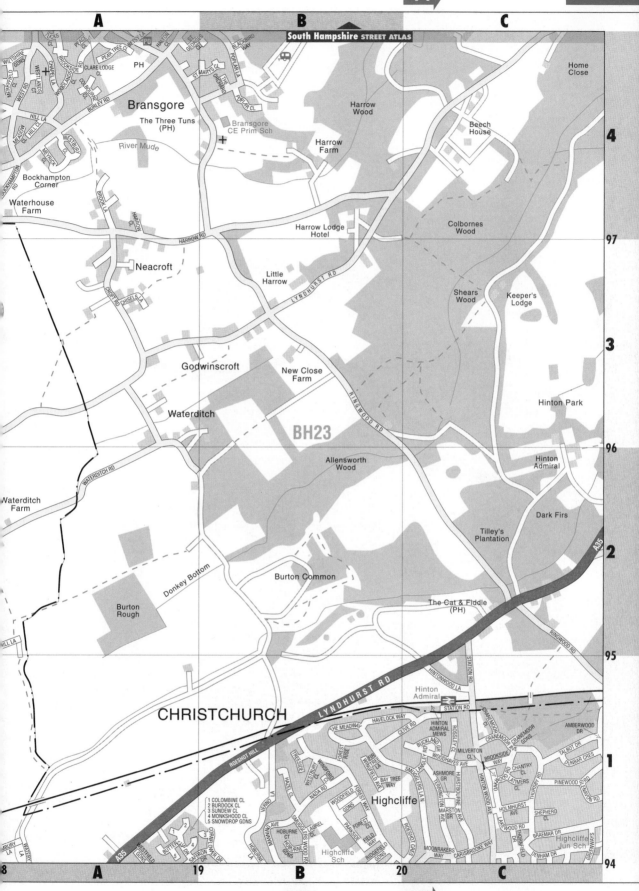

South Hampshire STREET ATLAS

Bransgore

The Three Tuns (PH)

Bransgore CE Prim Sch

River Mude

Bockhampton Corner

Waterhouse Farm

Neacroft

Godwinscroft

Waterditch

Waterditch Farm

Harrow Wood

Harrow Farm

Harrow Lodge Hotel

Little Harrow

New Close Farm

Allensworth Wood

Donkey Bottom

Burton Rough

Burton Common

Home Close

Beech House

Colbornes Wood

Shears Wood

Keeper's Lodge

Hinton Park

Hinton Admiral

Dark Firs

Tilley's Plantation

The Cat & Fiddle (PH)

BH23

HARROW RD

LYNDHURST RD

RINGWOOD RD

RINGWOOD RD

A35

CHRISTCHURCH

Highcliffe

Hinton Admiral

Hinton Admiral Mews

LYNDHURST RD

ROESHOT HILL

HINTONWOOD LA

STATION RD

1 COLOMBINE CL
2 BURDOCK CL
3 SUNDEW CL
4 MONKSHOOD CL
5 SNOWDROP GDNS

Highcliffe Sch

Highcliffe Jun Sch

4

97

3

96

2

95

1

94

A   B   C

8   19   20

A35 Southampton

South Hampshire STREET ATLAS

A   **B**   **C**

Beech Close

Bramble Copse

Ossemsley Brake

Ossemsley

The Leg

North Hinton Farm

HOLM HILL LA

Locksbridge Copse

B305A

BASHLEY RD

4

The Shrubbery

Pennyfarthing Estates Farm House

Hotel

Beckley Common

Bashley Copse

97

East Close Farm

OSSEMSLEY MANOR HO

Ossemsley Copse

WESTWOODS & GLENDENE PK

SMITHY LA

NEW LA

B305

ROBIN CRES 1
LAWN VIEW 2
CHERRY TREE DR 3

Beckley Bridge

BASHLEY CROSS RD

Ferndene Farm

3

Beckley

Bashley Manor Farm House

Mill

BH23

Beckley Farm

Sammy Miller's Motorcycle Mus

Great Woar Copse

96

Walkford Brook

BH25

New Milton

ANTLER DR

VELVET LAWN RD

ROSECR CT

Dark La

CRANBORNE PL 1
BEAULIEU CL 2
BREAMORE CL 3
FOXCOTE GDNS 4
BALMORAL WLK 5
STRATFIELD PL 6
MARRYAT CT 7
MOUNTBATTEN CT 8
RAMSEY CT 9
CUNNINGHAM CT 10
FRASER CT 11
SOMERVILLE CT 12
HARWOOD CT 13
VIAN CT 14
BROOKLYN CL 15
WALNUT CL 16.

HAZELWOOD AVE

STEM LA

2

Hinton

DARK LA

Hinton House

Walkford Moor Copse

WALKFORD LA

Walkford Farm

MARRYAT RD

Cranemoor Wood

AMBERWOOD HO

Meeting House Plantation

TURF CROFT CT

Wick 1 Ind Est

Williams Ind Pk

Wick 2 Ind Est

WICK

Gore Road Ind Est

GORE RD

Recn Ctr

95

AMBERWOOD DR

PINEWOOD RD

PINEWOOD

SOUTHWOOD CT

WILLIAM CL

GLENVILLE

GLENVILLE RD

WYNDHAM RD

BROADLANDS

WALKFORD RD

AVENUE RD

Chewton Glen Farm

Gore Farm

WAGTAIL DR 1
GOLDFINCH CL 2
WREN CL 3
MAGPIE GR 4
ROBIN GR 5
CHURCHILL CT 6

The Arnewood Sch

Cemy

1

SOUTHWOOD AVE

HEATH RD

WALKFORD RD

WYNDHAM CL

BORDER LO

Walkford

Old Milton

KING GEORGE MOBILE HOME PK

Chewton Common

HIGHLAND AVE

Highcliffe Jun Sch

Chewton Glen Hotel

CONNAUGHT CL 7
CEDAR GDNS 8
INGLEGREEN CL 9
SOUTHLAWNS WLK 10
PRESTWOOD CL 11
CHILTERN CL 12
CHAUCOMBE PL 13
THE DORMERS 14

DUNFORD CL

CHRISTCHURH RD

A35

A337

CHILTERN DR

94

21   **A**   **22**   **B**   **23**   **C**

A1
1 VINCENT RD
2 VINCENT CL
3 CHARLOTTE CL
4 ELM CT
5 SPENCER CT
6 ORCHARD LEIGH
7 CORNERWAYS CT
8 JACMAR CT
9 ASHLEY ARNEWOOD CT

10 WESTCROFT PAR
11 ELIZABETH CT
12 WAVERLEY HO
13 HOMEFIELD HO
14 ELIOT HO
15 SHELLEY HO
16 BYRON HO
17 KEATS HO
18 SHENSTONE CT
19 CLIFTON CT

20 WINSTON CT
21 SOLENT LO
22 WINSTON PAR
23 BOUVERIE CL
24 EDMUNDS CL
25 BARTON COURT AVE
26 SPINDLEWOOD CL
27 HAZEL CT
28 ST DENYS
29 DUDLEY PL

30 YEW TREE CT
31 CHERRY TREE CT
32 GREENWOODS
33 CASSELLES CT
A2
1 WHITEFIELD LO
2 HEATHER LO
3 RUSSELL CT
4 OSBOURNE HO
5 HOMEMILL HO

A2
6 MALLARD BLDGS
7 RICHMOND CT
8 PEGASUS CT
9 BEAU CT
10 ORCHARD CT
11 TANGLEWOOD CT
12 ALVANDI GDNS
13 ASHTON CT
14 MORANT CT

A2
15 TREVONE
16 FREMINGTON CT
17 YORK PL
18 FAIRCOURT
19 MERLEWOOD CT
20 CONWAY CT
21 STIRLING CT

127

B3
1 ELIZABETH CL
1 DOLPHIN CL
3 SHERBOURNE LA
4 POOLE'S CT
5 MONMOUTH ST
6 BRIDGE ST

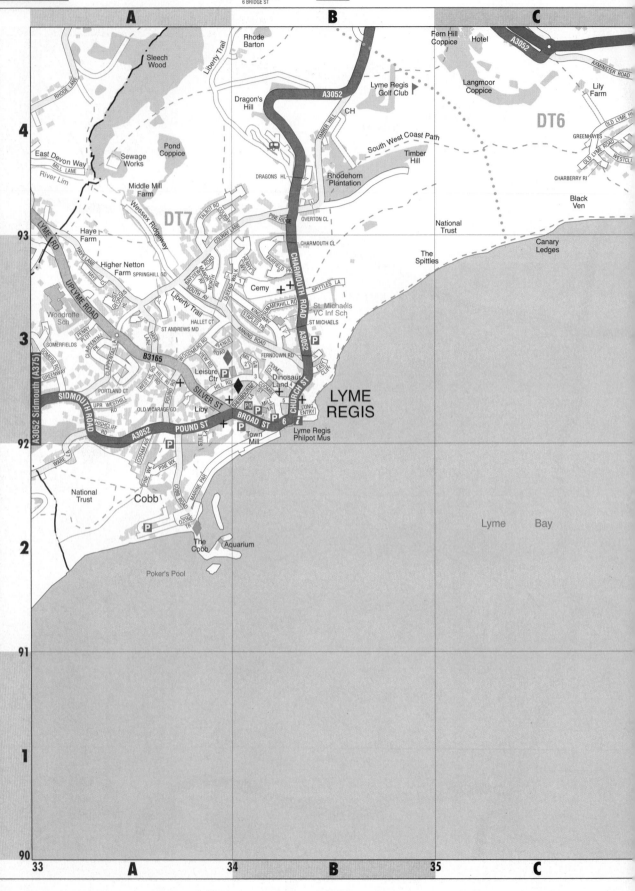

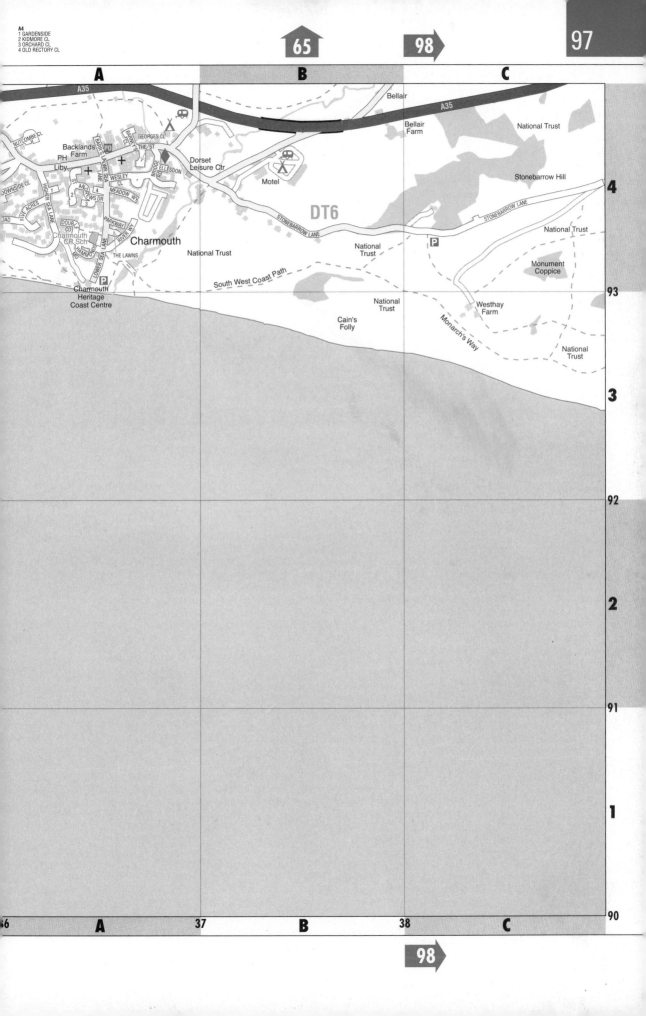

A4
1 GARDENSIDE
2 KIDMORE CL
3 ORCHARD CL
4 OLD RECTORY CL

65
98

A   B   C

A35

Bellair

A35

Bellair
Farm

National Trust

Nutcombe Cl

Backlands
Farm

PH

Liby

Georges Cl

THE ST

PO

Barrs La

Barrs Cl

Bridge Rd

Ellesdon

Dorset
Leisure Ctr

Motel

Stonebarrow Hill

St Andrews Dr

Wesley
Cl

Meadow Wy

Parkway

River Wy

Lower Sea Lane

Higher Sea Lane

Five Acres

Jowns De Cl

Doub. Co

Charmouth
C.P. Sch

Charmouth

THE LAWNS

DT6

Stonebarrow Lane

Stonebarrow Lane

National Trust

Monument
Coppice

P

National Trust

National
Trust

Charmouth
Heritage
Coast Centre

South West Coast Path

National
Trust

Cain's
Folly

Westhay
Farm

Monarch's Way

National
Trust

4

93

3

92

2

91

1

90

98

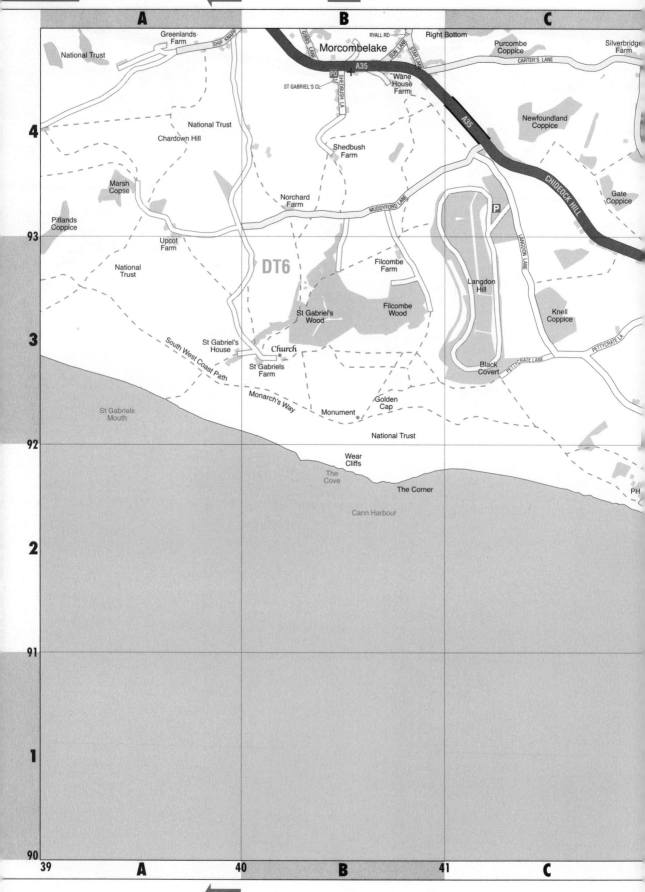

A B C

National Trust

Greenlands Farm

SHIP KNAPP

GIBBS LANE

RYALL RD

Right Bottom

Morcombelake

A35

SUN LANE

START LANE

Purcombe Coppice

CARTER'S LANE

Silverbridge Farm

National Trust

Chardown Hill

PO

ST GABRIEL'S CL

SHEDBUSH LA

Wane House Farm

A35

Newfoundland Coppice

4

Shedbush Farm

CHIDEOCK HILL

Marsh Copse

Norchard Farm

Gate Coppice

Pitlands Coppice

MUDDYFORD LANE

P

93

Upcot Farm

DT6

Filcombe Farm

LANGDON LANE

National Trust

St Gabriel's Wood

Filcombe Wood

Langdon Hill

Knell Coppice

3

South West Coast Path

St Gabriel's House

Church

St Gabriels Farm

Black Covert

PETTYCRATE LA

PETTYCRATE LANE

Monarch's Way

Monument

Golden Cap

St Gabriels Mouth

National Trust

92

Wear Cliffs

The Cove

The Corner

PH

Cann Harbour

2

91

1

90

39 A 40 B 41 C

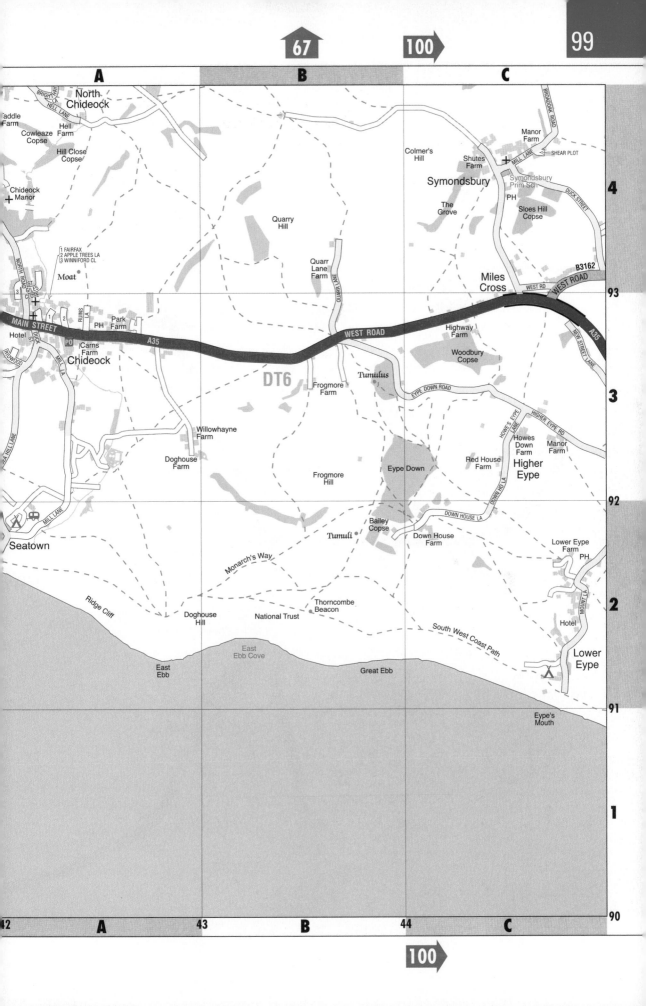

A **B** **C**

North Chideock

Taddle Farm

Cowleaze Copse

Hell Farm

Hill Close Copse

Chideock Manor

1 FAIRFAX
2 APPLE TREES LA
3 WINNIFORD CL

Moat

NORTH ROAD

ST GILES CLOSE

RUINS LA

MAIN STREET

Hotel

PO

RIDGWOOD

DUCK ST

Carns Farm

Chideock

PH

Park Farm

A35

Quarry Hill

Quarr Lane Farm

QUARR LANE

Colmer's Hill

Shutes Farm

Symondsbury

Manor Farm

BROADOAK ROAD

MILL LANE

SHEAR PLOT

Symondsbury Prim Sch

DUCK STREET

The Grove

PH

Sloes Hill Copse

Miles Cross

B3162

WEST RD

WEST ROAD

A35

NEW STREET LANE

DT6

WEST ROAD

Frogmore Farm

Tumulus

Highway Farm

Woodbury Copse

EYPE DOWN ROAD

HIGHER EYPE RD

HOWE'S EYPE LANE

Howes Down Farm

Manor Farm

Higher Eype

Red House Farm

Willowhayne Farm

Doghouse Farm

Frogmore Hill

Eype Down

DOWN HO LA

Bailey Copse

DOWN HOUSE LA

Down House Farm

Lower Eype Farm

PH

MILL LANE

Seatown

Tumuli

Monarch's Way

Ridge Cliff

Doghouse Hill

Thorncombe Beacon

National Trust

South West Coast Path

MOUNT LA

Hotel

Lower Eype

East Ebb Cove

East Ebb

Great Ebb

Eype's Mouth

SEA MILL LANE

A 43 **B** 44 **C**

42 93 92 91 90

4 3 2 1

100

A4
1 LAUREL C
2 ST LUKE'S CT
3 ALLINGTON GD

99

B4
1 HILLVIEW EST
2 DIMENTS GD
3 ALLINGTON MD
4 VICARAGE CT
5 BIDDLECOME OR
6 TRUSTIN CL

68

	A	B	C

BRIDPORT

Bridport Community

Crepe Farm

DOTTERY RD
DONKEY LA

Court Orchard

St Catherines RC Sch

St Andrew's Well

Knightstones Rd

ST ANDREWS RD

Watton Hill

St Andrews Industrial Estate

Mangerton River

Nature Reserve

Allington Hill

FULBROOKS

Coneygar

Superstore

Happy Island Wy

Allington

FOUNDRY CL

MOUNT PLEASANT

CHARDS MEAD RD

Ind Est

Bridport CP Sch

SEA ROAD NORTH

A3066

EAST ROAD

A35

FOUNDRY WEST ROAD
B3162 WEST ALLINGTON
KNAPP

WEST STREET

B3162 EAST ST

Cemy

Monarch's Way

St Michael's Trading Estate

Town Hall
Arts Ctr
Bridport Mus

Bradstock Working Horse Farm

WALDITCH ROAD

Vearse Farm

Skilling

Bridport FC
St Marys CE Prim Sch
Weir

SOUTH ST

WEST BAY RD

Weir

Superstore

SEA ROAD SOUTH

A35

Hyde

Daffodil Copse

Hyde Plantation

Bottom Wood

WATTON CROSS

BROAD LANE

Watton Farm

Watton House Farm

Watton

Bridport Leisure Centre

Recreation Gd

B3151

FLOOD LA

Mountjoy Sch

Homestead Farm

Church Farm

Church Ct

Highlands

A35

Broomhills Farm

Monarch's Way

River Brit

DT6

Bothenhampton

Nature Reserve

Middlehill Farm

Barrett's Copse

Mast

West Cliff Farm

Cowleaze Farm

ROUNDHAM GD

WYCH RIDGE

Wych

Wych Farm

BURTON ROAD

Brynvella Farm

South West Coast Path

West Cliff

West Bay

Hotel

Marshbarn Farm

Bridport & West Dorset Golf Club

East Cliff

B3157

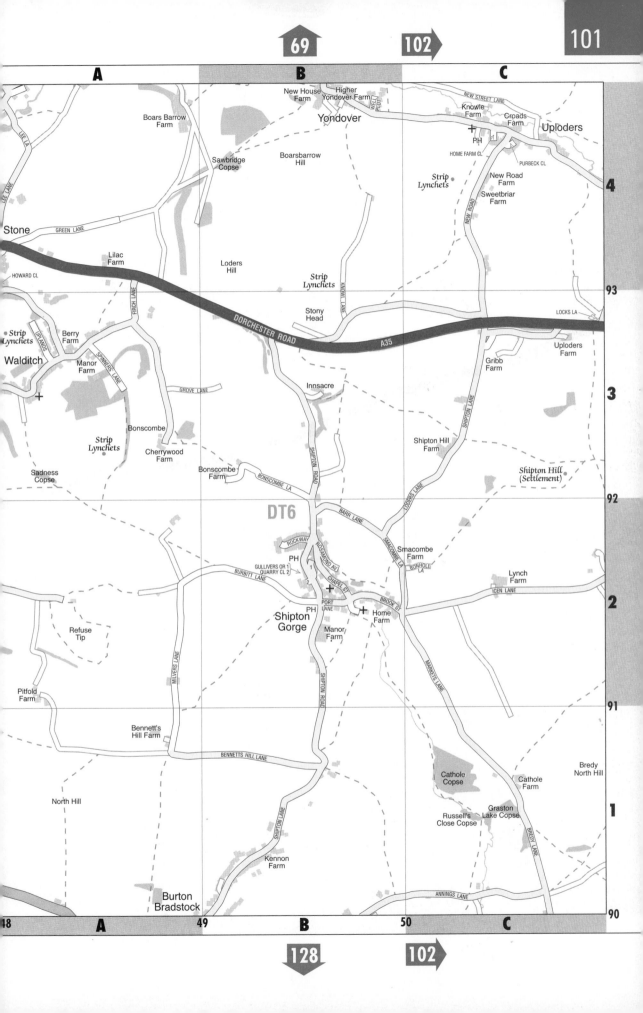

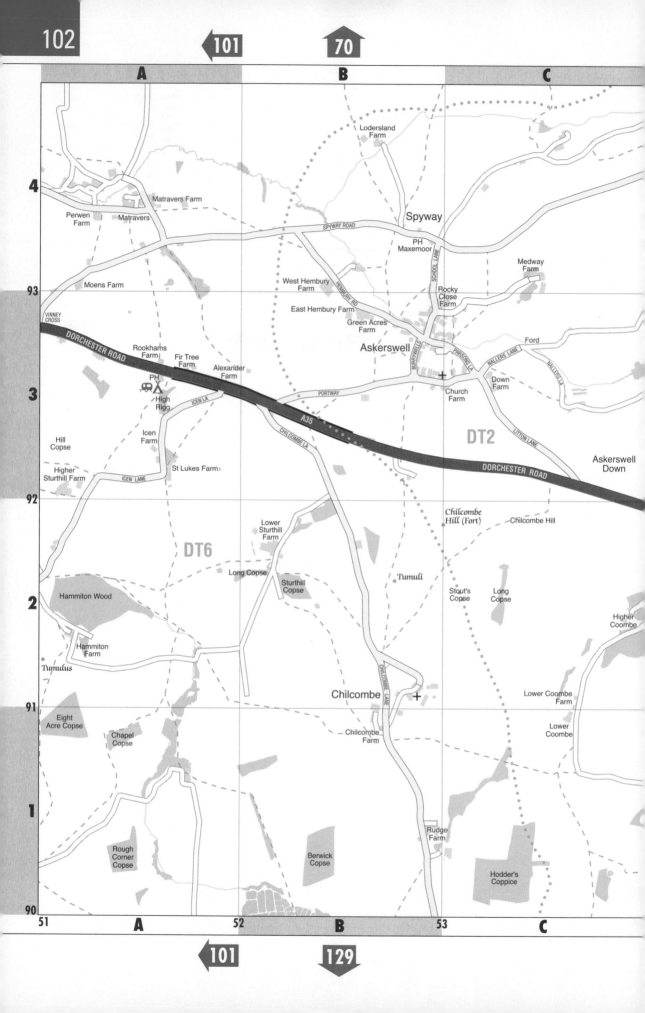

A   **B**   **C**

4

Lodersland Farm

Matravers Farm

Perwen Farm

Matravers

Spyway

SPYWAY ROAD

PH Maxemoor

SCHOOL LANE

Medway Farm

93

Moens Farm

West Hembury Farm

HEMBURY RD

East Hembury Farm

Rocky Close Farm

Green Acres Farm

Askerswell

VINNEY CROSS

DORCHESTER ROAD

Rookhams Farm

Fir Tree Farm

Alexander Farm

Ford

BURYWELLS

PARSONS LA

NALLERS LANE

NALLERS LA

PH

High Rigg

ICEN LA

PORTWAY

Church Farm

Down Farm

LITTON LANE

3

A35

Hill Copse

Icen Farm

CHILCOMBE LA

DT2

Askerswell Down

Higher Sturthill Farm

ICEN LANE

St Lukes Farm

DORCHESTER ROAD

92

Lower Sturthill Farm

Chilcombe Hill (Fort)

Chilcombe Hill

DT6

Long Copse

Sturthill Copse

Tumuli

Stout's Copse

Long Copse

Higher Coombe

2

Hammiton Wood

Hammiton Farm

CHILCOMBE LANE

Lower Coombe Farm

Tumulus

Chilcombe

Lower Coombe

91

Eight Acre Copse

Chapel Copse

Chilcombe Farm

1

Rudge Farm

Rough Corner Copse

Berwick Copse

Hodder's Coppice

90

51   **A**   52   **B**   53   **C**

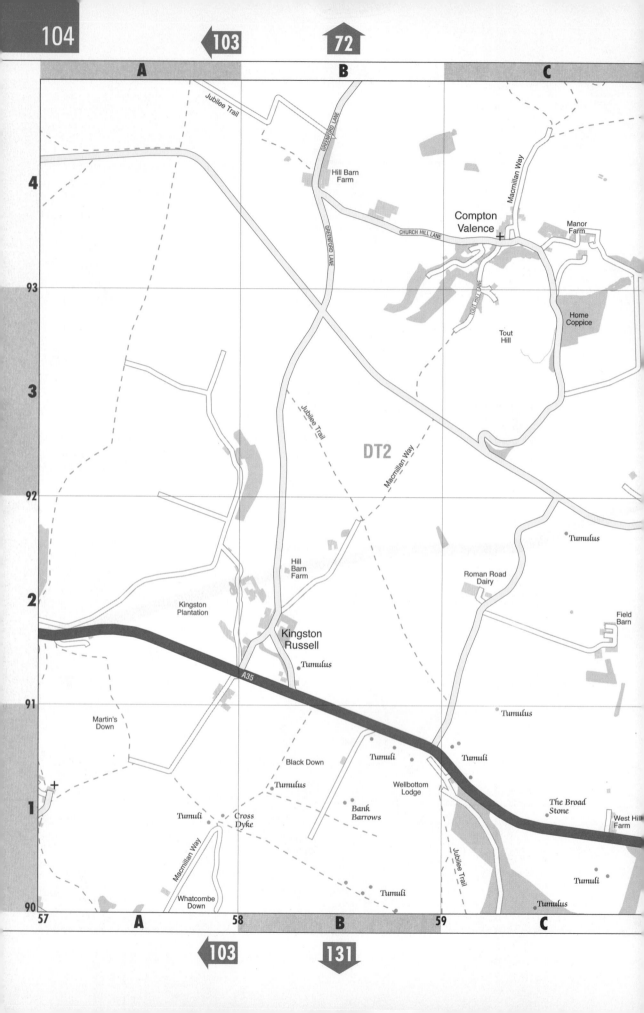

103
72

A   B   C

4

Jubilee Trail

GREENFORD LANE

Hill Barn
Farm

GREENFORD LANE

Macmillan Way

CHURCH HILL LANE

Compton
Valence

Manor
Farm

93

TOUT HILL LANE

Tout
Hill

Home
Coppice

3

Jubilee Trail

DT2

Macmillan Way

92

Tumulus

Hill
Barn
Farm

Roman Road
Dairy

Field
Barn

2

Kingston
Plantation

Kingston
Russell

Tumulus

Tumulus

91

Martin's
Down

A35

Tumulus

Tumuli

Black Down

Tumuli

The Broad
Stone

West Hill
Farm

1

Tumuli

Cross
Dyke

Tumulus

Bank
Barrows

Wellbottom
Lodge

Jubilee Trail

Tumuli

Macmillan Way

Tumuli

Whatcombe
Down

Tumulus

90

57   A   58   B   59   C

103
131

A
B
C

Compton
Bottom

Tumuli

Long
Bottom

West Hill
Bottom

Cocked Hat
Coppice

Barrow
Plantation

New
Littlewood
Farm

4

93

Tumulus

Town Hill
Coppice

Long Bottom
Plantation

Town Hill
Farm

West Hill
Bottom

Tumulus

Town Hill Slip
Plantation

Long Barrow

All Families
Plantation

Tumulus

Hogleaze
Farm

3

DT2

Field System

92

Tumulus

Tumulus

Tumulus

2

Tumuli

Tumulus

91

Midway
Down

Tumuli

Midway
Down Farm

Winterbourne
Abbas

WEST WY

Glebe
Farm

Little
Glebe

Manor
Farm

PH

BUTT FARM
CL

Little
Glebe
Farm

A35

1

Nine Stones
English Heritage

BLACKSMITH'S
PIECE

Winterbourne
Valley CE
Fst Sch

Lodge
Wood

Boxenhedge
Farm

COOMBE RD

NEWHAVEN

North Hill

Westfield
Farm

B3159

NEWHAVEN HARLANDS

Long Barrow

LONGLAND'S LANE

A
B
C

0
61
62

90

← 105
↑ 74

A B C

A37 DORCHESTER RD

LC

Long Hampton
Plantation

SAWYERS LA 1
BULL CL 2
CARPENTERS CL 3

DORCHESTER RD

Stratton

Church
Farm

WRACKLE CL

Ash
Hill

A37

4

Lower
Muckleford
Farm

Higher
Muckleford
Farm

Muckleford

Quatre
Bras

River Frome

MILL LANE

Hampton Hill
Plantation

Penns Plantation

ROMAN
AQUEDUCT

GLEBE HILLS

93

Bradford
Peverell

Home Barn
Farm

YEW TREE
LA

MANOR LA

Strap Bottom

Penn Hill

Coux Plantation

3

Long
Barrow

Tumuli

New
Barn

Seven Barrow
Plantation

New Barn
Field Centre

Tumulus

Long Walk
Plantation

MANOR LANE

Tumulus

Hampton
Plantations

Stables
Farm

Peverell

The
Coppice

92

DT2

Combe Bottom

Hampton
Farm

Lower Skippet
Farm

New
Plantation

TILLY WHIM LANE

Knowle
Hill

2

Higher
Skippet Farm

Three
Cornered
Plantation

91

Tumulus

Bradford
Down Farm

Bradford
Down

Sunnyside
Farm

Lambert's
Hill

Goldsmith's
Plantation

Mast

1

Works

Tumuli

NORTH REW LANE

Glenwood
Farm

A35

North Hill
Plantation

Tumuli

Downcroft
Farm

Purlands
Farm

Tumuli

BATS LANE

90

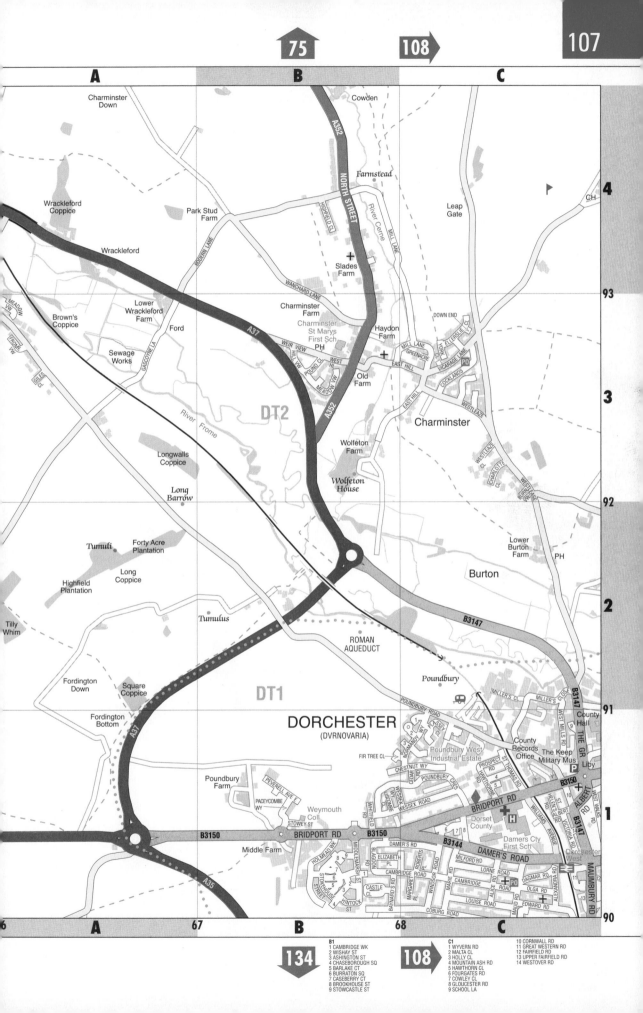

A B C

Charminster Down

Cowden

4

93

3

2

91

90

Wrackleford Coppice

Park Stud Farm

Farmstead

NORTH STREET

A352

River Cerne

Leap Gate

CH

Wrackleford

MODERN LANE

HIGHFIELD

MILL LANE

Slades Farm

DOWN END

Down End

ELERSLIE CL

PO

Brown's Coppice

Lower Wrackleford Farm

Ford

MEADOW VW

FROME VW

GILES CL

GASCOYNE LA

Sewage Works

A37

WANCHARD LANE

Charminster Farm

Charminster St Marys First Sch

WEIR VIEW

PH

HILL VW

WEST HL

POUND CL

MEADOW VW

Haydon Farm

Old Farm

MILL LANE

GREENACRE

EAST HILL

VICARAGE LANE

YORK

COCKLANDS

WESTLEAZE

Charminster

WESTLEAZE CL

CHARLOTTE CL

River Frome

Longwalls Coppice

Wolfeton Farm

Wolfeton House

Lower Burton Farm

PH

DT2

A352

EAST HILL

Long Barrow

92

Tumuli

Forty Acre Plantation

Long Coppice

Tumulus

B3147

Burton

Highfield Plantation

Tilly Whim

Fordington Down

Square Coppice

ROMAN AQUEDUCT

Poundbury

MILLER'S CL

MILLER'S CLOSE

B3147

County Hall

Fordington Bottom

A37

DT1

DORCHESTER
(DVRNOVARIA)

POUNDBURY ROAD

FIR TREE CL

Poundbury West Industrial Estate

County Records Office

The Keep Military Mus

WEST MILLS RD

THE GR

Liby

P

Poundbury Farm

PEVERELL AVE E

PACEYCOMBE WY

Weymouth Coll

CHESTNUT WY

CEDAR WY

PROSPECT

ST THOMAS RD

HAWTHORNE

County

WILLIAMS AVE

VICTORIA RD

ST ALBERT

WEST WALKS

ALBERT

B3150

Middle Farm

STOWEY ST

B3150

BRIDPORT RD

B3150

HOLMEAD WK

MIDDLEMARSH RD

POUNDBURY CRES

POUNDBURY RD

WESSEX SQUARE

WESSEX RD

Wessex Road

WHITFIELD

BRIDPORT RD

Dorset County

H

BRIDPORT RD

Damers Cty First Sch

Dorchester West

MAUMBURY RD

A35

STOUHOUSE STREET

KINTOCK ST

DAMER'S RD

BLAGDON RD

ELIZABETH PL

MARGARET ROBERTS PL

LORNE ROAD

CAMBRIDGE WK

BAYNARD'S RD

CASTLE CL

WINDSOR ROAD

MARIE RD

CAMBRIDGE

MILFORD RD

DAMER'S ROAD

ALICE RD

LOUISE ROAD

DAGMAR RD

OLGA RD

ALEXANDRA RD

MAID RD

COBURG ROAD

EDWARD RD

B3144

PO

PO

6 67 68

A
B
C

4
93
3
92
2
91
1
90

69   A   70   B   71   C

Hill Barn

Square
Coppice

Home
Farm

B3143

DT2

Higher Kingston
Farm

Limekiln Copse

SLYER'S LANE

Higher Burton
Farm

Badgers
Copse

A35

Frome
Whitfield Farm

B3143

Birkin
House

Frome
Whitfield

HOLLOW HILL

Coker's
Frome

STINSFORD HILL

Stinsford

CHURCH LA

Kingston Maurward
Agricultural Coll

County Hall

Dorchester
HM Prison

DT1

B3150

Kingston Maurward
Gardens & Animal Park

KEW COMBE LA

Kingston
Maurward

Old Crown
Ct & Cells

Dinosaur
Mus

GREENINGS CT

Greys Bridge

Colliton St
Cty Mus

TH

B3150 HIGH E ST

LONDON RD

HIGH W ST

Mus

DURNGATE

Tutankhamun
Exhibition

B3144

GT WESTERN RD 10

PRINCE OF WALES ROAD

DORCHESTER
(DVRNOVARIA)

Weir

River Frome

ALINGTON ROAD

STINSFORD
VIEW

Louds Mill Sewage
Treatment Works

Dorchester
Prep Sch

B3144

Sandringham
Sports Ctr

STATION
APP

Dorchester South

A1
1 NORTHERNWAY
2 NORTH SQ
3 THE BOW
4 ALINGTON ST
5 CHURCH ST
6 CHURCH CL
7 ACLAND RD
8 WEST WALKS RD
9 NEW ST
10 WEYMOUTH AVE
11 FAIRFIELD RD
12 UPR FAIRFIELD RD
13 CROMWELL RD
14 EARL CL
15 ATHELSTAN RD
16 FORDINGTON GD
17 SYDENHAM WAY
18 BARNES WAY
19 CULLIFORD RD NTH
20 LONDON CL
21 POUND LANE
22 CHURCH ACRE

77
110

A   B   C

Little Wood

Troytown Farm

Troytown Copse

P

Beacon Plantation

Yellowham Wood

A35

Beacon Hill

YELLOWHAM HILL

Coombe Plantation

Grey's Wood

4

Green Hill

TWO DROVES

Yellowham Hill

The Kennels

93

Tumulus

Tumuli

HE PLAIN

A35

Puddletown Forest

CUCKOO LANE

Black Bottom

Bhompston Heath

Castle Hill

Higher Bockhampton

Hardy's Birthplace

3

DT2

Puddletown Heath

X P

Thorncombe Wood

Rainbarrows

Nature Trail

92

Black Heath

Duddle Heath

ILSINGTON ROAD

Tumulus

Pine Lodge Farm

Tumulus

Tumulus

2

Thorncombe Farm

Boswell's Plantation

Ilsington Heath

BOCKHAMPTON CROSS

Heedless William's Pond

Duddle Plantation

Duck Farm

BOCKHAMPTON LANE

Norris Mill Farm

Lower Norris Mill Farm

91

Lower Bockhampton

Lower Bockhampton Farm

Bhompston Farm

Duddle Farm

1

River Frome

Weir

90

A   73   B   74   C

2

109
78

A **B** **C**

St. Marys C E
Middle Sch

WHITE HILL

WHITE HILL HL

PUTT CL

CHAPEL VW

BRYMER RD

Highwood Farm

Par
Far

4

Henroost
Wood

High
Wood

Admiston
Farm

Cowpound
Wood

Little
Copse

ROD HILL LANE

MALOM LANE

93

Tumuli

Ilsington Wood

Napier's
Copse

DARK LANE

Black
Wood

3

Hollands
Farm

TINCLETON
CROSS

Ewleaze
Farm

DT2

92

ILSINGTON ROAD

Tincleton
Farm

Tincleton

Ilsington
Farm

WATERY LANE

Boswells
Farm

Eweleaze
Farm

Clyffe
Farm

Hastings
Farm

Ilsington

Snipe
Moor

2

WATERY LANE

Ilsington Heath

White Mead

91

River Frome

Frome
Bridge

Frome Mead

River Frome

Sturt's Weir

Woodsford
House
Sch

Woodsford

Woodsford
Farm

1

SCHOOL LANE

East
Woodsford

Woodsford
Lower Dairy

Woodsford
Castle

90

75 **A** 76 **B** 77 **C**

A
B
C

Southover
Farm

Southover
House

River Piddle
or Trent

East
Farm

Affpuddle

4

B3390

Great
Copse

Southover
Heath

93

Broomhill Plantation

Wilcocks'
Wood

Lee Wood

Mansel's
Plantation

Tumulus

Allotments
Plantation

Bladen
Plantations

Southover Heath

Tumuli

Clyffe Copse

Southover Heath
Plantation

Sares Wood

Affpuddle Heath

P

Forest
Walk

Tumuli

3

Clyffe House

Tumuli

Marl Pits
Wood

92

Pallington Heath

DT2

Bryants Puddle
Heath

Squibbs
Farm

Field End

Oakers Wood

2

WADDOCK DROVE

Pallington
Lakes

Golden Springs
Farm

Pallington

Waddock
Copse

Jubilee Trail

Pallington
Farm

Spring
Coppices

91

Bound Stone
Plantation

Waddock
Farm

Hurst
Copse

Moreton
Plantation

1

B3390

Hurst
Bridges

River Frome

Jubilee Trail

Hurst

Hurst Farm

HURST ROAD

8

A

79

B

80

C

90

111
80

A **B** **C**

Spring Garden Coppice

Tumulus

Sand and Gravel Pits

Damerhill Coppice

Turners Puddle

Jubilee Trail

Turnerspuddle Farm

4

River Piddle or Trent

Jubilee Trail

Throop

Throop Farm

Brockhill Coppice

Brockhill Fish Farm

Cecily Bridge

Briantspuddle

Landshare Coppice

93

Bladen Plantations

Bryants Puddle Allotments Plantation

Battle Farm

THE HOLLOW

THROOP HOLLOW

Eweleaze Coppice

DT2

Smokeham Bottom

Cull Peppers Dish

Tumuli

Tumulus

Tumulus

Longcroft Coppice

3

Bryants Puddle Heath

Jubilee Trail

Rimsmoor Pond

Oakers Wood

Throop Heath

Tumulus

Millicent's Plantation

Tumulus

92

Okers Wood House

Moreton Plantation

Tonerspuddle Heath

DANGER AREA

BH20

Chamberlayne's Heath

East Plantation

Round Barrow

2

Clouds Hill

Lawrence of Arabia's Cottage NT

91

MORETON DRIVE

Moreton Plantation

Tank Training Area

1

90

81 **A** 82 **B** 83 **C**

111
139

A
B
C

Little Wood
Sand and Gravel Pits
Rye Hill Farm
Spear's Coppice
Silva Springs Watercress Railway
Lower Hove Wood
A35

Hundred Barrow
Hollow Oak
Dodding's Farm
Mate's Coppice
Lower Woodbury Farm

Hundred Barrow Farm
Ford
Bedlam
Sugar Hill

4

DT2

Yearlings Bottom
Heath View

Yearlings Poultry Farm
End Barrow
Jenkins Farm

Lockyer's Hill

93

Little Coppice
Snatford Bridge
Don Barrow

Bere Heath
Bere Stream
Bere Heath

Donkey Lane
Lane End Farm
Lane End

3

BH20

Culeaze Farm
Bere Heath Farm
Tumulus

Chamberlayne's Farm
Culeaze House
Tanpits Coppice
Ph_lliols Heath

River Piddle or Trent
Pickard's Coppice

Culeaze Coppice

92

Warren Farm
Higher Stockley Farm
Lower Stockley Farm

WARREN ROAD
Philliols Farm

2

Warren Heath
Warren
Philliols Coppice

91

Tumulus
Tumulus

Gallows Hill

Hyde Woods
Woodlands
Hanging Covert
Hyde Farm

Bere Heath
Skinner's Coppice
Weir

1

Heliport
Dorset Gliding Club
PUDDLETOWN ROAD
Higher Hyde Heath Nature Reserve
Heather Lodge

84
A
85
B
86
C
90

A   B   C

4

93

3

92

2

91

1

90

87   A   88   B   89   C

Humber's
Coppice

Larch
Plantation

Scotch
Plantation

Snailsbreach
Farm

A35

Mast

Ford

Black
Heath

Snail's
Bridge

Oak
Hill

Bere
Heath

SUGAR HILL

Sugar
Hill

Woolsbarrow
(Fort)

Bloxworth
Heath

Morden Heath

BH20

Wareham Forest

Stroud
Bridge

Old Ram
Plantation

Lower Hyde
Heath

North Trigon
Farm

Trent
Vale Farm

Hyde House
Country Club

Weir

Pond
Plantation

Trigon Hill
Plantation

A B C

Morden
Mill

QUARR HILL

Whitmoor
Bottom

PARK CORNER

A35

Sherford

A35

Tumulus

CHITTEN HILL

Chitten
Hill

Morden
Park

B3075

Sherford
Farm

Sherford River

Sherford
Bridge

MORDEN ROAD

Bulbury
Coppice

Bulbury
Farm

CH

HALLS ROAD

Bulbury Woods
Golf Club

BH16

Slepe

Slepe
Farm

93

3

Old Decoy
Pond

BH20

Gore
Heath

National
Nature Reserve

The
Decoy

92

Decoy
Heath

MORDEN ROAD

P

2

91

Memorial

B3075

Great Ovens
Hill

1

LILLEUL RD

Northport
Heath

A 91 B 92 C 90

4

A   **B**   **C**

Hill Wood

Post Green Farm

Shot Lake Wood

Newton Farm

Bere Farm

Post Green

4

HALLS ROAD

WAREHAM ROAD

FOXHILLS LANE

NEW ROAD

A35

Pike's Farm

French's Coppice

Cuzenage Coppice

POST GREEN ROAD

Lytchett Minster

93

OLD FORGE CL

ORCHARD CL

B3067

WAREHAM ROAD

Higher Wood

Organford

Farmer Palmers Farm Park (Adventure Farm)

BH16

Charity Farm

PH

King's Bridge

3

Lower Wood

Organford Bridge

Sherford River

King's Bridge Coppice

A351

Holton Heath

92

Youngs Farm

Heatherdene

ORGANFORD ROAD

Gore Heath

Pear Tree Farm

FANCY'S ROW

WAREHAM ROAD

Holton Heath Nature Reserve

2

Heath View

CHESTNUT AV

ASH AVE

PIKE CRESCENT

PH

BLACKHILL ROAD

Holton Heath

OAK AVE

SYCAMORE AV

ELM AVE

BIRCH AV

BEECH AVE

PARK DRIVE

LAUREL AVENUE

WILLOW CRESCENT

STATION RD

St Martin's Hill

BH20

91

Rustlings Farm

Black Hill

BLACKHILL RD W

HOLTON RD

Sandford House

SANDFORD DRIVE

A351

SANDFORD ROAD

Holton Heath Trading Park

HOLTON ROAD

Holton Heath

1

Admiralty Research Establishment

STATION ROAD

Holton Heath

Sandford Middle Sch

FILLEUL RD

A351

CEDAR GROVE

WOODLANDS DR

LC
Holton Heath

90

93   **A**   **94**   **B**   **95**   **C**

A1
1 LABURNUM CL
2 HOLLY CL
3 ALDER CL

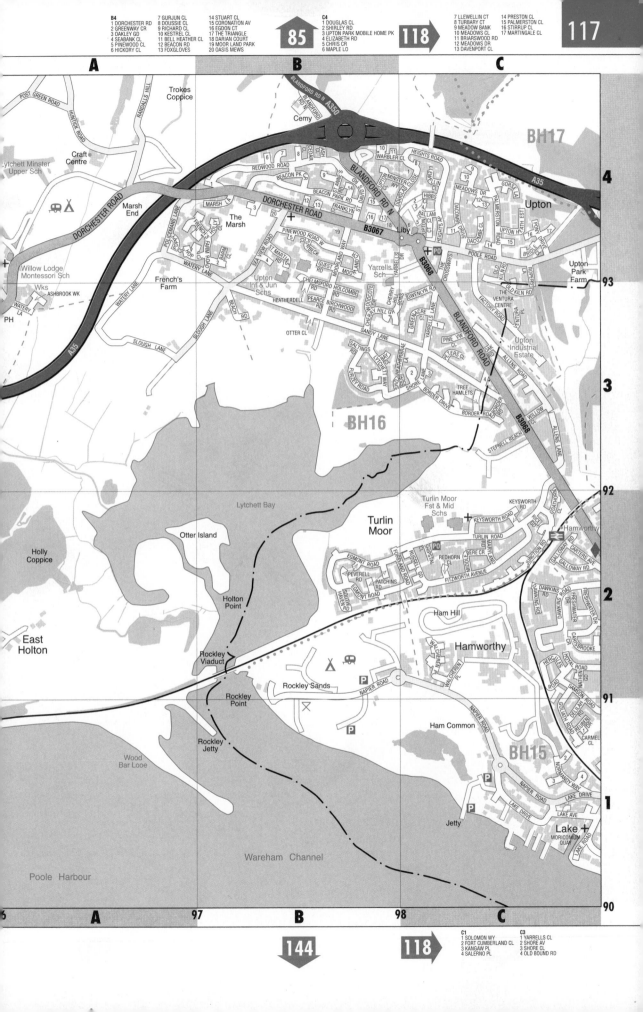

B4
1 DORCHESTER RD
2 GREENWAY CR
3 OAKLEY GD
4 SEABANK CL
5 PINEWOOD CL
6 HICKORY CL
7 GURJUN CL
8 DOUSSIE CL
9 RICHARD CL
10 KESTREL CL
11 BELL HEATHER CL
12 BEACON RD
13 FOXGLOVES
14 STUART CL
15 CORONATION AV
16 EGDON CT
17 THE TRIANGLE
18 DARIAN COURT
19 MOOR LAND PARK
20 OASIS MEWS

C4
1 DOUGLAS CL
2 SHIRLEY RD
3 UPTON PARK MOBILE HOME PK
4 ELIZABETH RD
5 CHRIS CR
6 MAPLE LO

85

118

117

7 LLEWELLIN CT
8 TURBARY CT
9 MEADOW BANK
10 MEADOWS CL
11 BRIARSWOOD RD
12 MEADOWS DR
13 DAVENPORT CL
14 PRESTON CL
15 PALMERSTON CL
16 STIRRUP CL
17 MARTINGALE CL

144

118

C1
1 SOLOMON WY
2 FORT CUMBERLAND CL
3 KANGAW PL
4 SEALERNO PL

C3
1 YARRELLS CL
2 SHORE AV
3 SHORE CL
4 OLD BOUND RD

A   **B**   **C**

BH21

Castleman Trailway

Creekmoor

BH17

A350

Cemy

1 DOUGLAS MEWS
2 LLEWELLIN CT
3 SHIRLEY RD
4 UPTON PARK MOBILE HOME PK
5 ELIZABETH RD
6 CHRIS CRES
7 MAPLE LO

A35

Upton

UPTON RD

4

B3068
BLANDFORD RD NEW
DORCHESTER RD
B3067
B3067

The Marsh

Liby
P.O.

Upton
Park
Farm

Upton House

Upton
Country Park

Yarrells
Sch

Upton Inf & Jun Schs

THE VENTURA CTR

93

Boat
House

Pergins
Island

BH16

POOLE

Holes Bay

3

Upton Ind Est

Stepnell Reach

B3068

92

Lytchett Bay

Turlin
Moor

Turlin Moor
Fst & Mid
Schs

RICE GDNS 1
RICE TERR 2

Hamworthy

BLANDFORD RD

Holton
Point

2

Dawkins
Bsns
Ctr

Cobb
Quay

Marina

Rockley
Viaduct

Ham Hill

Hamworthy

Dawkins Rd

Rockley Sands

P

Rockley
Point

91

Ham Common

BH15

Carter
Com Sch

Liby
B3068

Rockley
Jetty

1

Jetty

Lake
MORTOMLEY QUAY

LC

Wareham Channel

Hamworthy
Mid Sch

Hamworthy Park

Promenade

90

97   **A**   98   **B**   99   **C**

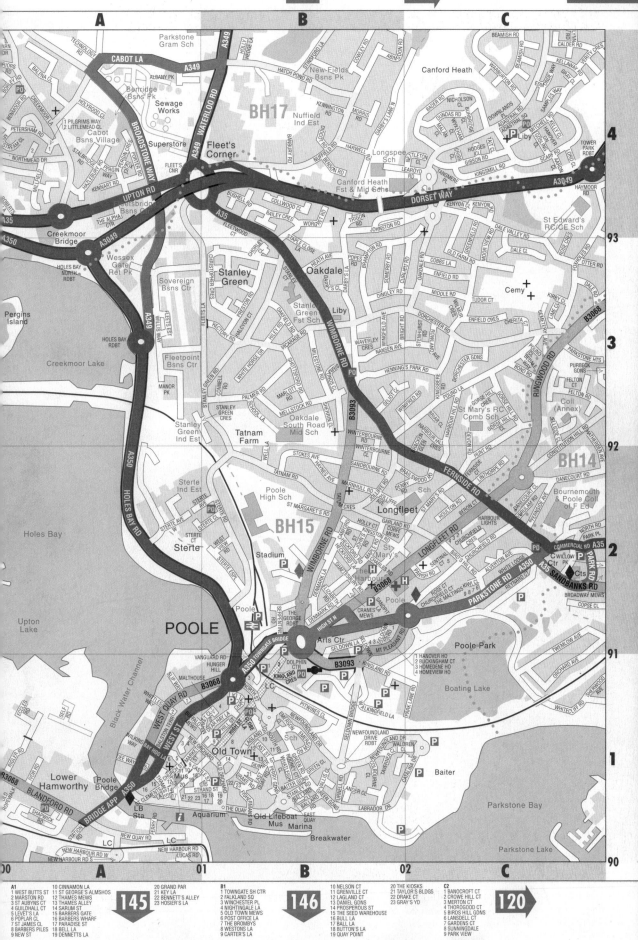

A2
1 TENNYSON RD
2 MENTONE RD
3 CLARENCE RD
4 BRANDWOOD CT
5 PARR HO
6 FRINTON CT
7 ST PETER'S CT
8 SINCLAIR CT
9 ELDON CT
10 WESTBURY CT
11 CHALBURY CT
12 HIGHFIELD HO
13 FAR ENDS

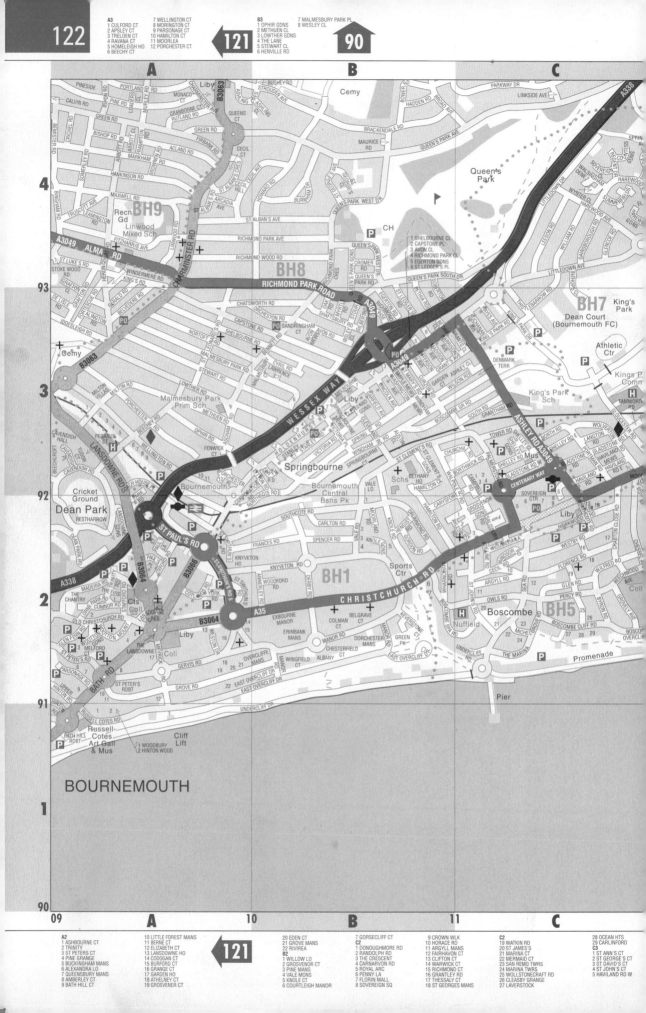

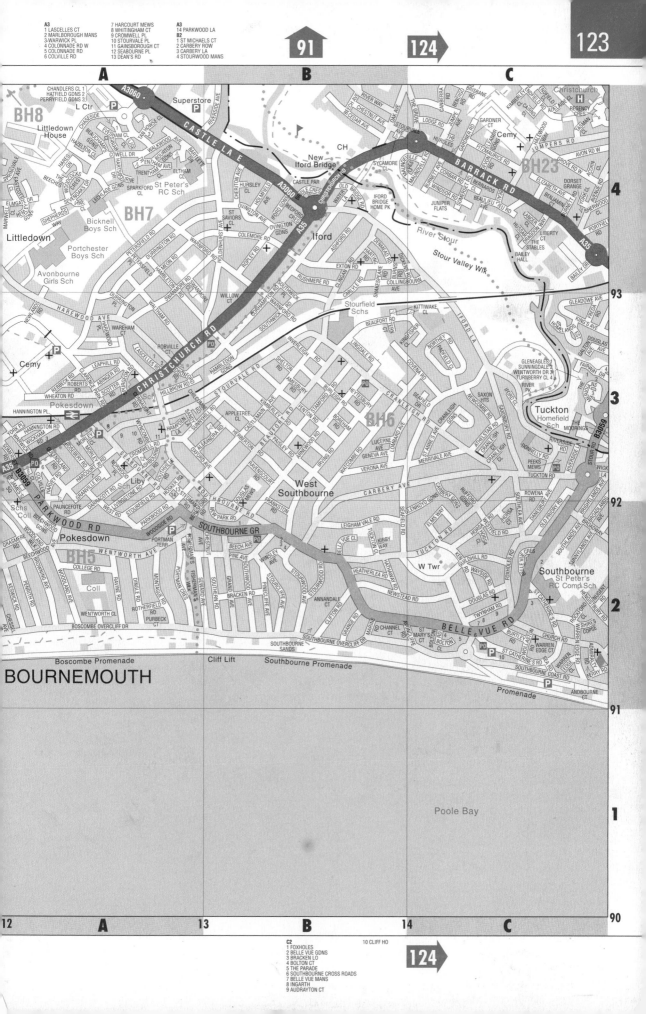

91
124
124

A3
1 LASCELLES CT
2 MARLBOROUGH MANS
3 WARWICK PL
4 COLONNADE RD W
5 COLONNADE RD
6 COLVILLE RD

7 HARCOURT MEWS
8 WHITINGHAM CT
9 CROMWELL PL
10 STOURVALE PL
11 GAINSBOROUGH CT
12 SEABOURNE PL
13 DEAN'S RD

A3
14 PARKWOOD LA

B2
1 ST MICHAELS CT
2 CARBERY ROW
3 CARBERY LA
4 STOURWOOD MANS

BH8

BH23

BH7

BH6

BH5

Littledown House

Superstore

L Ctr

CASTLE LA

New Iford Bridge

CH

BARRACK RD

Christchurch

Cemy

Littledown

Bicknell Boys Sch

Portchester Boys Sch

Avonbourne Girls Sch

St Peter's RC Sch

Iford

River Stour

Stour Valley Wlk

Stourfield Schs

Cemy

HAREWOOD AVE

CHRISTCHURCH RD

Pokesdown

West Southbourne

Tuckton

Homefield Sch

The Moorings

Pokesdown

WENTWORTH AVE

SOUTHBOURNE GR

PARKWOOD RD

Coll

Southbourne

St Peter's RC Comp Sch

W Twr

BELLE VUE RD

Boscombe Promenade

Cliff Lift

Southbourne Promenade

Southbourne Sands

Promenade

BOURNEMOUTH

Poole Bay

C2
1 FOXHOLES
2 BELLE VUE GDNS
3 BRACKEN LO
4 BOLTON CT
5 THE PARADE
6 SOUTHBOURNE CROSS ROADS
7 BELLE VUE MANS
8 INGARTH
9 AUDRAYTON CT

10 CLIFF HO

123
92
123

A   B   C

Latch Farm
1 DEVEREL CL
2 BLENHEIM CT

The Manor Arms (PH)
STAPLECROSS

Works

CHRISTCHURCH BY-PASS

B3059
Purewell

STAPLE CROSS

The Grange Comp Sch
Somerford

Schs
MARMION GN

Silver Bsns Pk

Airfield Ind Est

BH23

MASTERSON CL 1
WOLFE CL 2
MEREDITH CL 3

PUREWELL CROSS RD

Mus of Electricity

Christchurch

BARRACK RD
A35

THE CLOISTERS

Civic Ctr

2 Riversmeet Leisure Ctr
RIVERSMEET CT 1
STANIFORTH CT 2
SPRINGWATER CT 3

Ship in Distress (PH)

Mudeford Infant Sch

Mudeford Jun Sch

Castle
Red House Mus
Priory
Place Mill
Quomps
Harbour View
Priory Quay

Stanpit

CHRISTCHURCH

Ferry (F)

River Stour

Recn Gd
1 WEST CLOSE HO
2 WEST CLOSE CT

Liby

Wick Farm

Wick

Caravan Park

St Katharine's CE Prim Sch
CH

Stour Valley Wlk

Ferry (F)

Stanpit Marsh
Nature Reserve

Crouch Hill

Grimbury Marsh

Christchurch Harbour

BH6

Wick Hams

Nature Trail

Promenade

Coastguard Lookout Sta

Nature Reserve
Warren Hill

Hengistbury Head

15   16   17

90

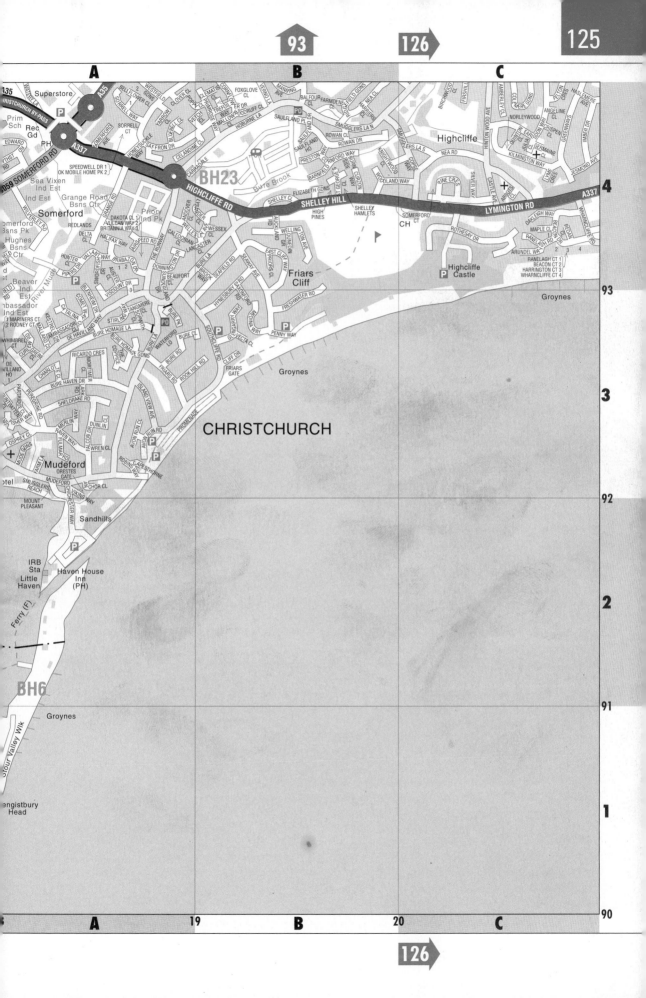

A   B   C

Superstore
435
CHRISTCHURCH BY-PASS
Prim Sch
Rec Gd
PH
A337
SOMERFORD RD
B059

Sea Vixen Ind Est
Somerford
Bsns Pk
Hughes Bsns Ctr

BH23

HIGHCLIFFE RD

Bure Brook

Highcliffe

SHELLEY HILL

LYMINGTON RD   A337

Shelley Hamlets

CH

Highcliffe Castle

Groynes

4

Beaver Ind Est

Ambassador Ind Est

River Mude

Friars Cliff

93

CHRISTCHURCH

Groynes

Friars Gate

Groynes

3

Mudeford

Sandhills

92

IRB Sta
Little Haven

Haven House Inn (PH)

Ferry (F)

2

BH6

Groynes

91

Stour Valley Wlk

engistbury Head

1

125
94

A4
1 LAVENDER VILLAS
2 BUCKINGHAM CT
3 CASTLE CT
4 CARISBROOKE CT
5 WINDSOR CT
6 HURST CT
7 BALMORAL CT
8 MERTON CT
9 BERMUDA CT
10 EXETER CT
11 PEMBROKE CT
12 HERTFORD CT
13 FRANCES CT
14 ROSEMARY CT
15 KENNETH CT
16 ALAN CT
17 WILLIAM CT
18 PENELOPE CT
19 STELLA CT

1 TRACEY CT
2 DIANA CT
3 CLAIRE CT

Barton on Sea

125

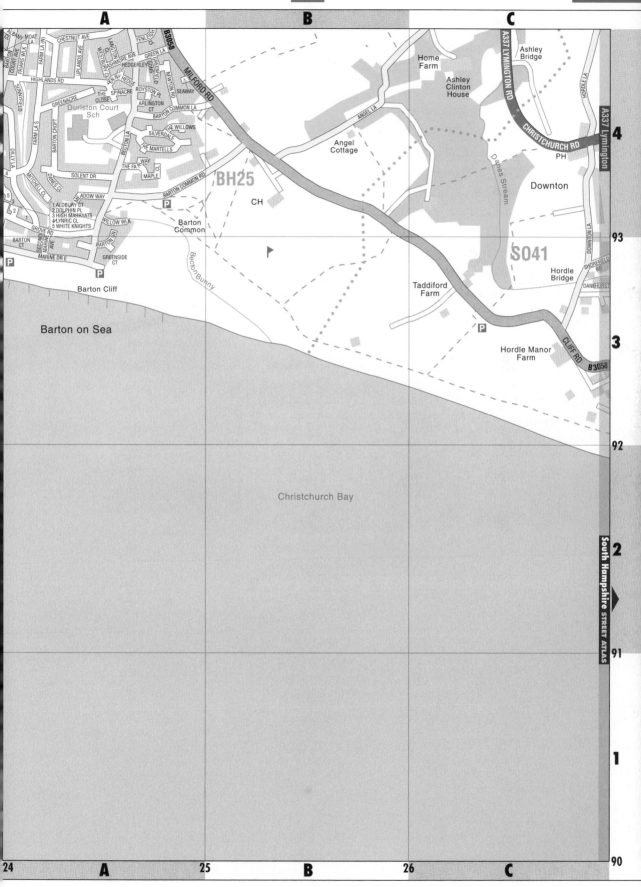

A   B   C

B3058

CHESTNUT AVE

ALBANY
MOAT LA
COURT AVE
FRIARS WLK
FARM LA (N)

UPLANDS AVE
LANGTON RD
WESTBURY CT

FENLEIGH
GREEN LA
GREENFIELD
GDNS

Milford RD

HIGHLANDS RD
ASHMORE AVE
HEDGERLEY
NEWTON RD

SEAWAY

SUNNYFIELD
GREENACRE
THE
CLOSE
SPINACRE
ROYSTON PL
BARTON COMMON LA

Home
Farm

Ashley
Bridge

Durlston Court
Sch

BARTON CROFT
BECTON LA
SILVERDALE
THE WILLOWS
ARLINGTON
CT

Ashley
Clinton
House

A337 LYMINGTON RD

CHRISTCHURCH RD

FARM LA S
THE MARTELLS

Angel
Cottage

PH

A337 Lymington

4

DILLA LA
MITCHELL CL
DONES CL
SOLENT DR
THE FA
WAY
MAPLE
CL
MAPLE

BARTON COMMON RD

ANGEL LA

Downton

BH25

Danes Stream

1 ALDBURY CT
2 DOLPHIN PL
3 HIGH MAHRYATS
4 LYNRIC CL
5 WHITE KNIGHTS

P

CH

SO41

93

GROVE RD
WILLOW WLK

Barton
Common

BARTON GN

Hordle
Bridge

BARTON
CT
SECOND
MARINE
AVE
GREENSIDE
CT

Taddiford
Farm

SHOREFIELD
RD

DANEHURST

P

MARINE DR E

Becton Bunny

P

Barton Cliff

Barton on Sea

CLIFF RD

Hordle Manor
Farm

3

B3058

92

Christchurch Bay

2

91

1

90

24   A   25   B   26   C   90

101

A   B   C

A4
1 HOWARTH CL
2 S ANNINGS
3 GROVE DR
4 ST LAWRENCE
5 DONKEY LA
6 DARBY LA

Peacehaven Farm

Burton Bradstock

Graston Copse

Graston Farm

Bredy Farm

BURTON ROAD

Shadrach

NORTH HL CL

CHARLES RD

BARROWFIELD CL

B3157

BARR LANE

Works

River Bride

SHIPTON LANE

LOWER TOWNSEND

NORTHOVER

NORTHOVER CLOSE

ANNINGS LANE

GROVE ROAD

Liby

Magnolia Farm

MIDDLE ST

CHURCH ST

PO

MILL ST

Burton Bradstock VC Prim Sch

Bredy Road

BREDY LANE

National Trust

Manor Farm

HIGH ST

PH

Burton Cliff

SOUTHOVER

Southover

CLIFF ROAD

Cliff Farm

Tumulus

DT6

4

89

3

88

2

87

1

86

COMMON LANE

HIVE CL

CROW ROAD

BEACH ROAD

BIND BR

B3157

Bind Barrow

Burton Beach

South West Coast Path

P

National Trust

Cogden Farm

Old Coastguard House

Cliff End

P

B3157

Cogden Beach

Burton Mere

100

47   48

East Cliff

DT6

89   89

47   48

48   A   49   B   50   C

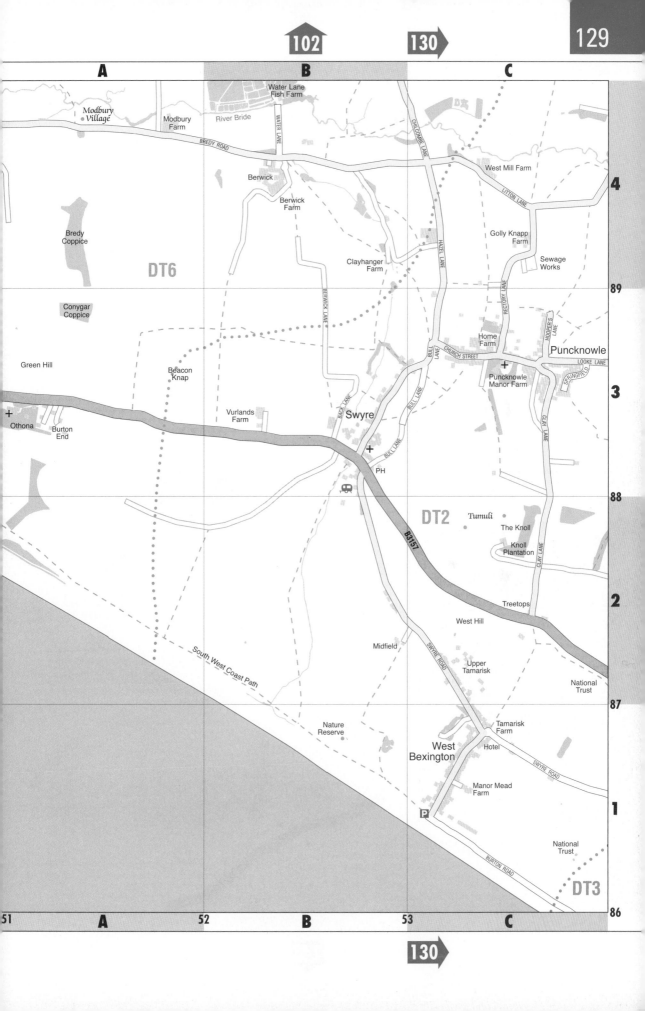

A
B
C

Modbury Village
Modbury Farm

Water Lane Fish Farm

River Bride

BREDY ROAD

West Mill Farm

4

Berwick

Berwick Farm

LITTON LANE

Golly Knapp Farm

Bredy Coppice

DT6

Clayhanger Farm

Sewage Works

89

Conygar Coppice

BERWICK LANE

HAZEL LANE

Home Farm

Puncknowle

HOOPER'S LANE

Green Hill

Beacon Knap

CHURCH STREET

BULL LANE

LOOKE LANE

SPRINGFIELD

Puncknowle Manor Farm

3

Vurlands Farm

BACK LANE

Swyre

CLAY LANE

Othona

Burton End

BULL LANE

PH

National Trust

Tumuli

The Knoll

88

DT2

Knoll Plantation

CLAY LANE

B3157

Treetops

2

West Hill

SWYRE ROAD

Midfield

Upper Tamarisk

National Trust

South West Coast Path

87

Nature Reserve

Tamarisk Farm

West Bexington

Hotel

SWYRE ROAD

Manor Mead Farm

P

1

National Trust

BURTON ROAD

DT3

86

51
A
52
B
53
C

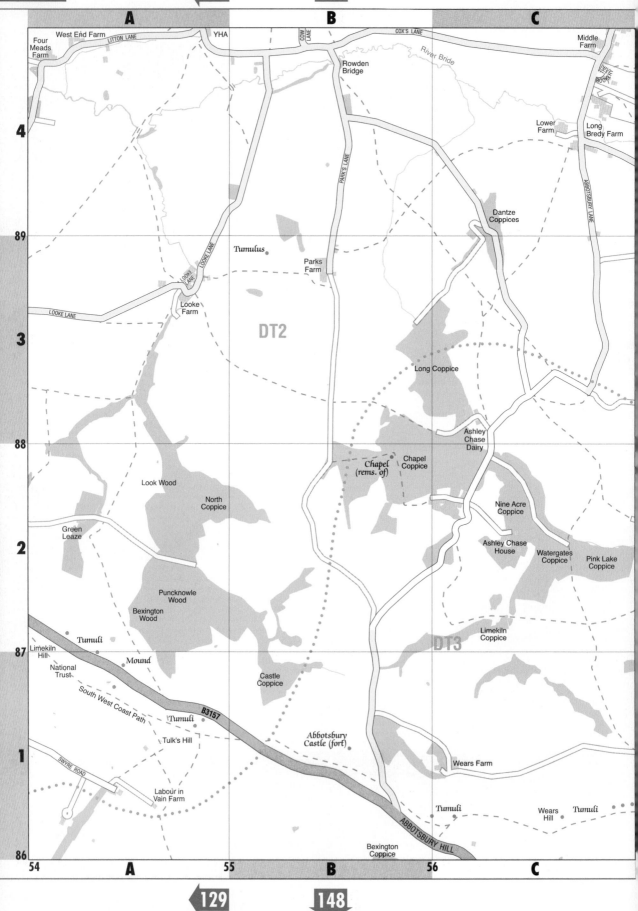

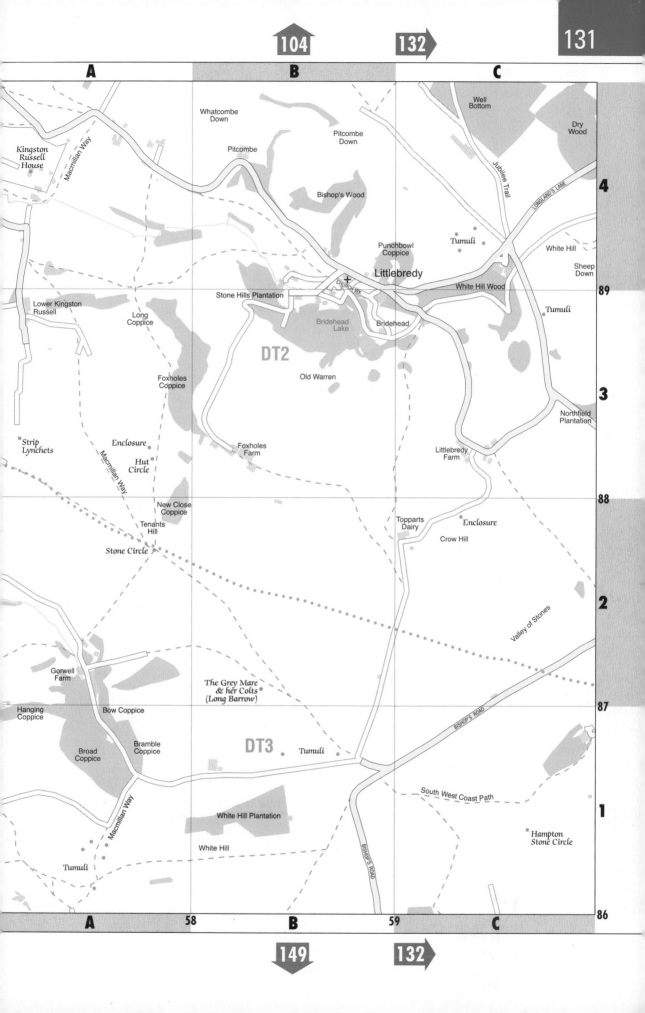

A
B
C

Kingston Russell House

Macmillan Way

Whatcombe Down

Pitcombe

Pitcombe Down

Bishop's Wood

Well Bottom

Dry Wood

Jubilee Trail

Longland's Lane

4

Tumuli

Punchbowl Coppice

White Hill

Sheep Down

CHURCH WK

Littlebredy

4

Stone Hills Plantation

White Hill Wood

89

Lower Kingston Russell

Long Coppice

Bridehead Lake

Bridehead

Tumuli

DT2

Old Warren

Foxholes Coppice

Northfield Plantation

3

Strip Lynchets

Enclosure

Macmillan Way

Hut Circle

Foxholes Farm

Littlebredy Farm

New Close Coppice

Topparts Dairy

Enclosure

88

Tenants Hill

Crow Hill

Stone Circle

Valley of Stones

2

Gorwell Farm

The Grey Mare & her Colts (Long Barrow)

Bishop's Road

Hanging Coppice

Bow Coppice

87

Broad Coppice

Bramble Coppice

DT3

Tumuli

South West Coast Path

Macmillan Way

White Hill Plantation

Bishop's Road

1

Hampton Stone Circle

White Hill

Tumuli

86

A
58
B
59
C

A **B** **C**

Longlands

Tumuli

Dry
Wood

LONGLAND'S LANE

Big
Wood

Tumulus

4

Coombe
Farm

COOMBE ROAD

Strip
Lynchets

Steepleton
Farm

B3159

Greater
Whitway Fa

MILL

Manor
Farm

Winterbourne
Steepleton

Jubilee Trail

Loscombe
Plantation

Loscombe
Farm

Loscombe
Down

Dairy

89

Sheep
Down

Tumuli

COOMBE ROAD

Loscombe
Wood

Tumulus

Tumulus

DT2

Tumulus

Ballarat
Farm

3

Long
Barrow

Conygar
Meadow
Coppice

Jubilee Trail

Tumulus

East Rew
Farm

Enclosure

Tumulus

88

Tumuli

Tumuli

South West Coast Path

Goldcombe
Farm

Black
Down

P

Hardy
Monument

National
Trust

Tumuli

Black Down
Plantation

2

Tumulus

BISHOP'S ROAD

Hardy
Coppice

Tumuli

Bronkham
Hill

Benecke
Wood

Portesham
Hill

87

South West Coast Path

Hell Stone
(Long Barrow)

Wig
Plantation

Jubilee Trail

Tumuli

Tumuli

1

Hell Bottom
Quarry
(disused)

Bench

DT3

Hell
Bottom

HAMPTON HILL
HELSTON
CL
PORTESHAM HILL
FRONT ST
BACK
ST
PO

Portesham

Portesham
Farm

86

60   A   61   B   62   C

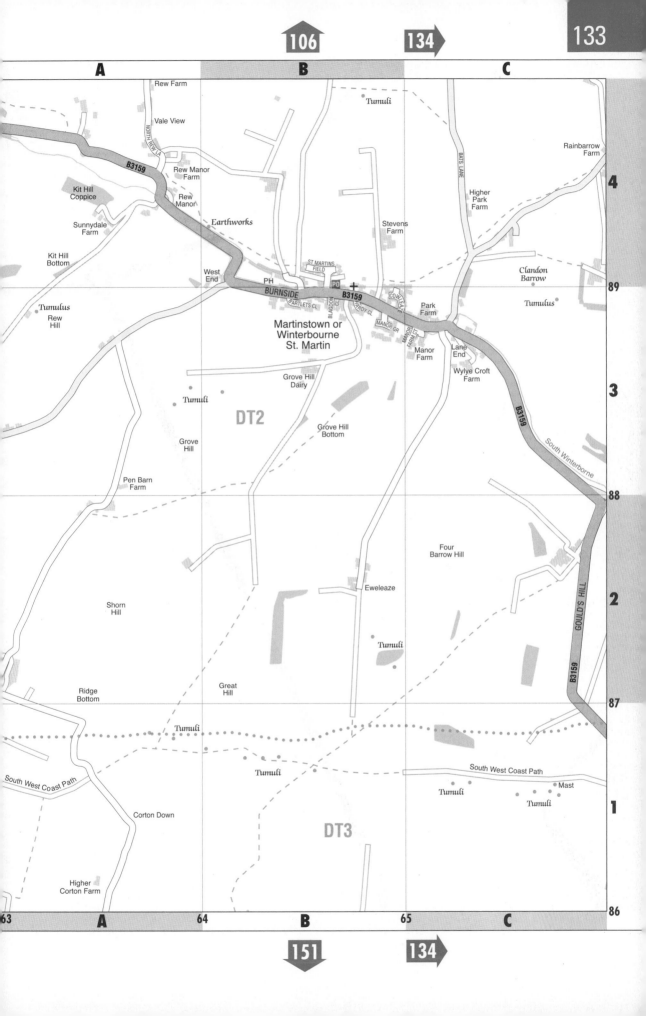

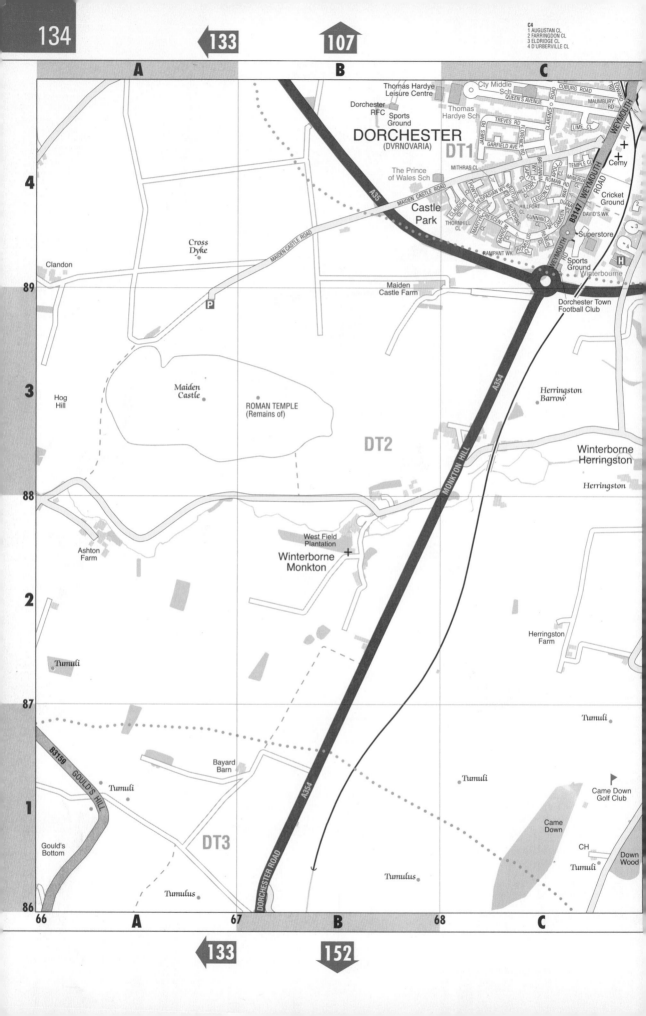

A4
1 GABRIEL GN
2 EVERDENE RD
3 NONESUCH CL
4 ST ANDREWS CL
5 HIGHGROVE CL

B4
1 SANDRINGHAM CT
2 FRIARS CL
3 SMOKEY HOLE LA

A   **B**   **C**

St Marys
Cath First
Sch

Max Gate
(NT)

Conquer
Barrow

Maumbury
Rings

DT1

St Osmunds
C E Mid Sch

Manor
Park CE
First Sch

TALBOTHAYS
RD

RENFREW CL

CARRICK CL

ALINGTON AVE

A352

A352

Henge

Tumulus

4

Frome
Hill

A35

North
Plantation

89

Tumuli

North
Plantation

Well
Plantation

Bunker's Hill
Plantation

Conygar
Hill

Came
Park

Tumulus

A352

3

South Winterborne

Cole
Hill Wood

Jubilee Trail

Winterborne
Came

Whitcombe

Winterbourne
Faringdon Village

Came
House

Home
Wood

DT2

Cole Hill
Wood

88

Jubilee Trail

Whitcombe
Manor

Tumuli

Brick Hill
Plantation

Tumulus

2

South
Plantation

Higher Came
Farm

87

Tumuli

Gallop

Down
Wood

Cripton
Cottage

Whitcombe
Down

Tumulus

1

Tumuli

Whitcombe Barn
Plantation

South Drove
Farm

Cripton
Wood

Tumuli

Whitcombe
Barn

Tumulus

Cripton
Spinney

Tumuli

SOUTH DROVE

Warren
Barn

CHALKY RD

86

A   70   **B**   71   **C**

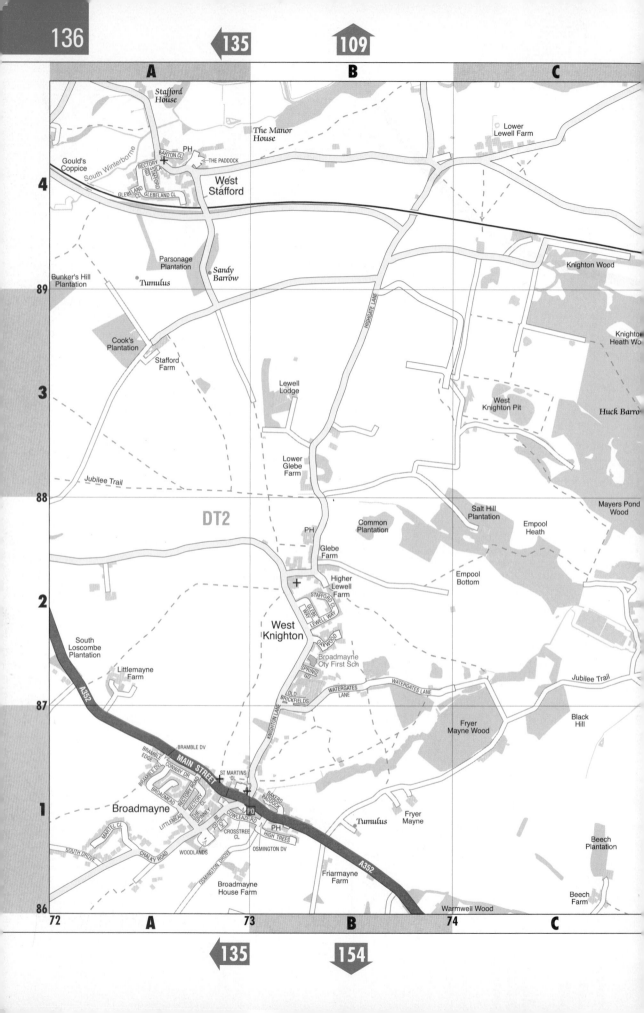

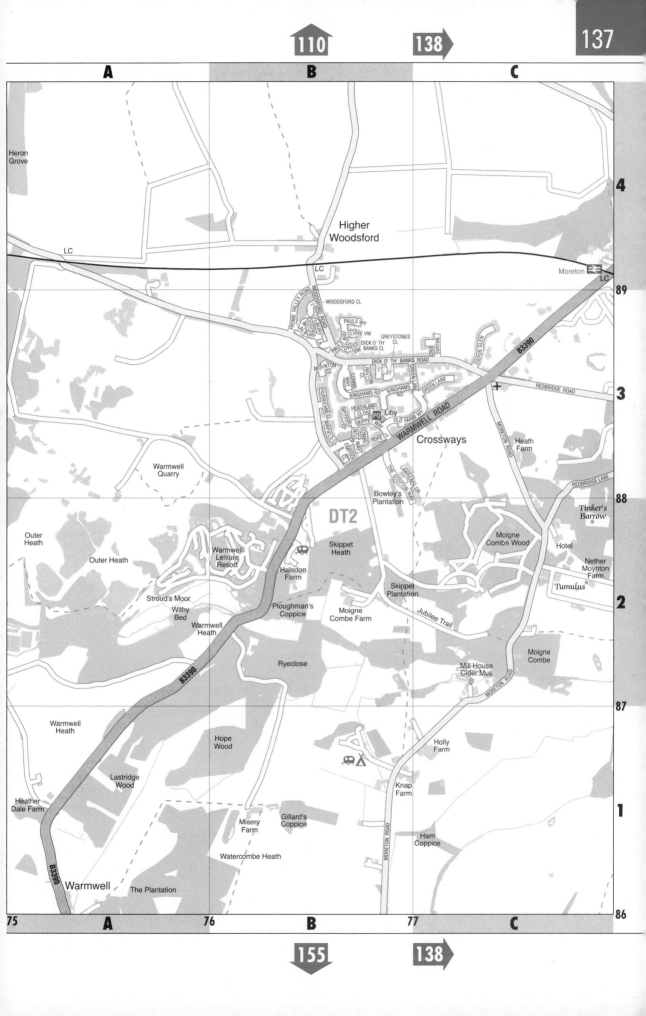

A B C

4

89

3

88

2

87

1

86

Heron Grove

Higher Woodsford

LC

LC

Moreton

LC

Woodsford CL

FROME VALLEY ROAD

WOODSFORD ROAD

WOODBURY

YALBURY LA

PAULS WY

PAULS AVE

CREST

CLYFFE VW

DICK O' TH' BANKS CL

GREYSTONES CL

BRIARS END

WARMWELL ROAD

B3390

PAULS WY

MOYNTON CL

LINGTON CL

COMBE WAY

DICK O' TH' BANKS ROAD

GREEN LANE

GREEN LANE

GOOM GLEN

REDBRIDGE ROAD

HURRICANE CL

BINGHAMS RD

BINGHAMS RD

HEATHLAND CLOSE

PO

Liby

Crossways

Heath Farm

SPITFIRE CL

AIRFIELD CL

SKIPPET WAY

LANCIA WAY

COMBE CL

HOPE CL

OLD FARM WY

LANTHORNE DR

THE SCOTTON WAY

REDBRIDGE LANE

Warmwell Quarry

DT2

Bowley's Plantation

MORETON ROAD

Tinker's Barrow

Hotel

Nether Moynton Farm

Tumulus

Outer Heath

Outer Heath

Warmwell Leisure Resort

Skippet Heath

Skippet Plantation

Moigne Combe Wood

Stroud's Moor

Withy Bed

Warmwell Heath

Halsdon Farm

Ploughman's Coppice

Moigne Combe Farm

Jubilee Trail

Moigne Combe

B3390

Ryeclose

Mill House Cider Mus

MORETON ROAD

87

Warmwell Heath

Hope Wood

Holly Farm

Lastridge Wood

Knap Farm

Heather Dale Farm

Misery Farm

Gillard's Coppice

Ham Coppice

Watercombe Heath

B3390

Warmwell

The Plantation

137
111

A **B** **C**

Hurst Heath

B3390

STATION ROAD

Nursery
Farm

THE COMMON

4

STATION ROAD

HURST ROAD

Moreton

MORETON DRIVE

Jubilee Trail

THE STREET

Lawrence of
Arabia's Grave

Cemy

Moreton
House

WOODSFORD LANE

PH

89

Moreton Park

REDBRIDGE ROAD

West
Lodge

Fir Hill

3

Redbridge

Jubilee Trail

REDBRIDGE LANE

Coombe Valley
Farm

DT2

West Wood

88

Broomhill
Farm

REDBRIDGE ROAD

Tumuli

Old
Knowle

Jubilee Trail

Tumuli

Whitcombe Hill

2

Tadnoll
Barrow

Nature
Reserve

Whitcombe
Vale

GATEMORE ROAD

87

Galton Heath

Tadnoll

Nutley
Farm

1

Blacknoll
Hill

GATEMORE ROAD

Tumuli

Tumulus

86

BLACKNOLL LANE

78 **A** 79 **B** 80 **C**

A   B   C

Moreton Plantation

Wool Heath

Bovington Heath

4

Snelling
Farm

Higher Long
Bottom

ST JULIEN RD 1
GOUZEAUCOURT RD 2
GAZA RD 3
SWINTON AV 4

HEATH
CL

CHURCHILL ROAD

ROBERTSON
RD

SEWELL
RD

MENIN RD

ARRAS RD

NEW
RD

KING GEORGE V ROAD

CACHY RD
ERIN RD

FRAMERVILLE RD

BONEY
RD

Tumulus

ELLES ROAD

SWINTON AVENUE

1 2

90

AMIENS
RD

8TH AUGUST ROAD

FOXBURY

1 2
3 4

BALACLAVA ROAD

89

SIR RICHARD HULL ROAD

WINDSOR
CLOSE

RHINE ROAD

SELLE
RD

CUNNINGHAM
CLOSE

River Frome

MENIN ROAD

HOLT
ROAD

CAPER RD E

CAPER RD WEST

COLOGNE
RD

Cranes Moor

CRANESMOOR
CL

Bovington
Camp

VICTORIA
CLOSE

CAPER
RD
EAST

ROSS
CLOSE

DUNCAN CL

MORRIS ROAD

Lower
Cranesmoor

ANDOVER
GREEN

Bovington
First Sch

Higher
Wood

Lower
Wood

Sports
Ground

Playing
Field

3

Furzy Coppice

LINSAY ROAD

RAC Tank
Museum

Playing
Field

Lays
Coppice

Bovington
Farm

BOVINGTON LANE

Bovington
Middle Sch

Broomhill
Bridge

BH20

88

Long
Coppice

Great Perry
Coppice

Tumulus

DT2

Little Perry
Coppice

Tumulus

River Frome

2

Tumulus

Burton
Heath

87

PH

Meadow
Farm

WATER MEADOW LANE

Winfrith
Heath

Winfrith
Technology Centre

PH

LC

SANDHILLS CR

The
Moors

EAST BURTON ROAD

BURTON CL

SYDENHAM
CL

THE
ALISONS

East
Burton

FROME AVE

BAILEY'S DRIVE

LAMPLATON CL

Dorset Police
Authority

GIDDY
GN LANE

LINCLIETH
ROAD

GIDDY GN
RD

1

Tumulus

BURTON ROAD

Giddy
Green

DORCHESTER ROAD

A352

COLLIER'S
LANE

CHALK PIT LANE

DARKSENE RD

HILLSIDE RD

NEW RD

Knighton
Heath

Medieval Village of
West Burton
(site of)

Gatehouse
Farm

A352

BURTON CROSS

Braytown

Balfours
Farm

86

A   82   B   83   C

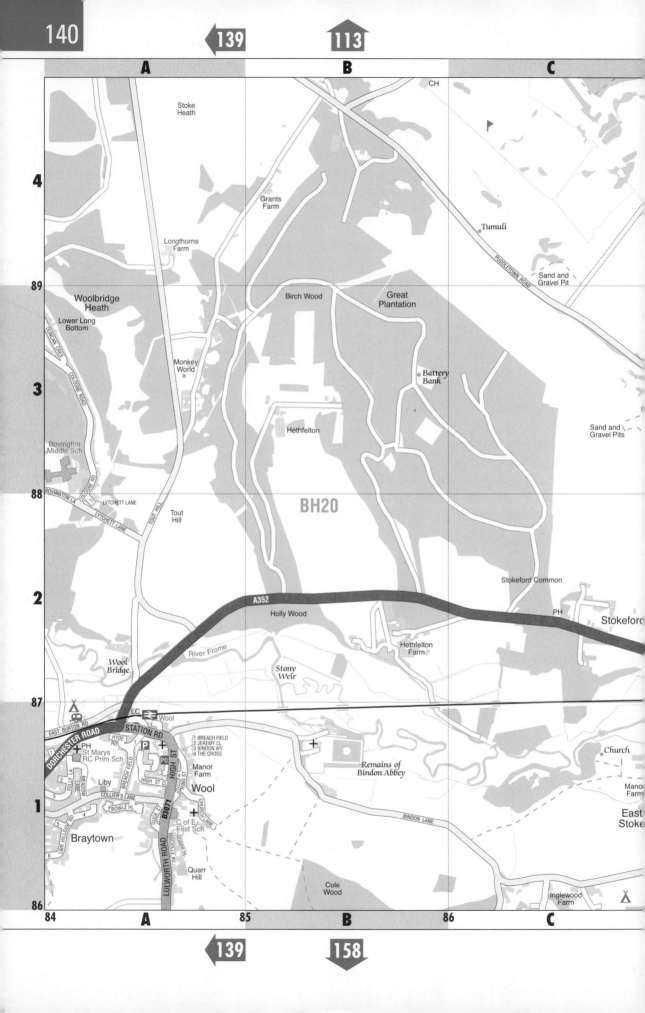

A   B   C

4

CH

Stoke
Heath

Grants
Farm

Tumuli

PUDDLETOWN ROAD

Sand and
Gravel Pit

89

Woolbridge
Heath

Birch Wood

Great
Plantation

Lower Long
Bottom

DUNCAN CRES

COLOGNE ROAD

Monkey
World

Battery
Bank

3

Bovington
Middle Sch

Hethfelton

Sand and
Gravel Pits

COLOGNE RD

88

BOVINGTON LA

LYTCHETT LANE

LYTCHETT LANE

TOUT HILL

Tout
Hill

BH20

2

Stokeford Common

A352

PH

Stokeford

Holly Wood

River Frome

Hethfelton
Farm

Wool
Bridge

Stony
Weir

87

LC   Wool

EAST BURTON RD

DORCHESTER ROAD

STATION RD

HYDE
RD

1 BREACH FIELD
2 JEREMY CL
3 BINDON WY
4 THE CROSS

Church

PH
St Marys
RC Prim Sch

P

PO

HIGH ST

Manor
Farm

Remains of
Bindon Abbey

Manor
Farm

BREACH FIELD

HIGH ST CL

SPRING ST

Liby

FOLLA LA

MEADOW LANE

COLLIER'S LANE

Wool

East
Stoke

1

2

3

KNOWLE HL

4

DUCK ST

B3071

CHURCH LANE

C of E
First Sch

BINDON LANE

Braytown

LWR HILLSIDE RD

6

LULWORTH ROAD

QUARR HL

MAIDVILLE AV

Quarr
Hill

Cole
Wood

Inglewood
Farm

86

84   A   85   B   86   C

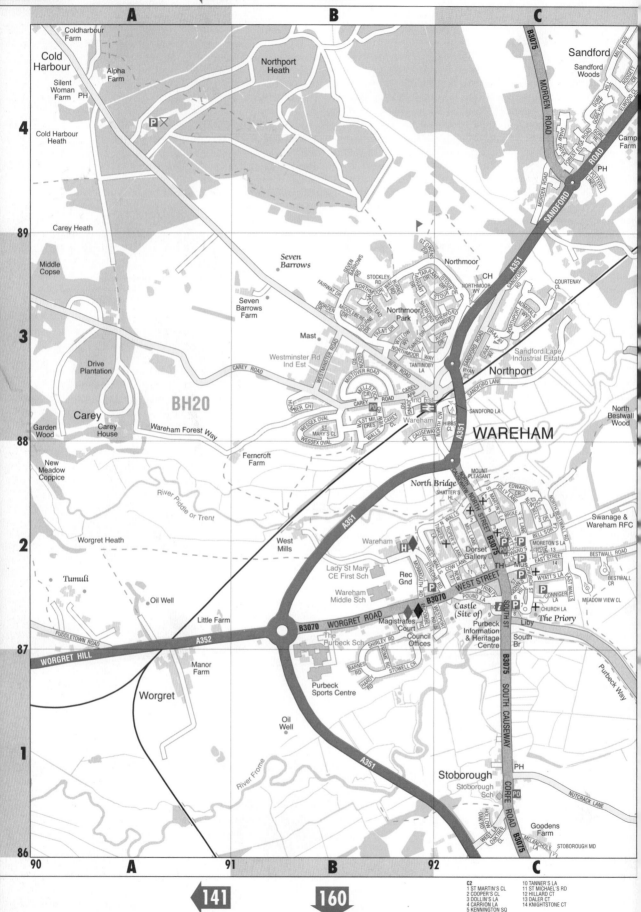

A   B   C

4

89

3

BH20

88

2

87

1

86

90   A   91   B   92   C

C2
1 ST MARTIN'S CL
2 COOPER'S CL
3 DOLLIN'S LA
4 CARRION LA
5 KENNINGTON SQ
6 HEMSBACH CT
7 CHURCH GN
8 THE QUAY
9 ABBOTS QUAY
10 TANNER'S LA
11 ST MICHAEL'S RD
12 HILLARD CT
13 DALER CT
14 KNIGHTSTONE CT

Cold Harbour
Coldharbour Farm
Alpha Farm
Silent Woman Farm PH
Cold Harbour Heath

Northport Heath

Sandford
Sandford Woods
MILES AVE
B3075
MORDEN ROAD
SHAW DRIVE
FOREST EDGE ROAD
GORE HILL
PODE HILL
ROBGETT CT
ELWOOD CT
Camp End
PH
POTTERY LANE
SANDFORD ROAD
A351

Carey Heath

Middle Copse

Seven Barrows
Seven Barrows Farm
FAIRWAY DR
SEVEN BARROWS RD
STOCKLEY RD
TAR-RANT
NORDEN DR
MIDDLEBERE
BOURNE
NORTHMOOR DR
WALSTEAD
Mast
RENT DR
WILLOW
LANE
NORTHMOOR WAY
Northmoor Park
TANTINOBY LA
AVON DR
GLOWERS
Northmoor
SHERFORD
STOUR DR
SHERFORD DRIVE
CH
NORTHMOOR WY
ADMIRAL'S WY
DRAX LA
RYAN PL
COURTENAY CL
Sandford Lane Industrial Estate
SANDFORD ROAD
SANDFORD LANE
Northport
North Bestwall Wood

Drive Plantation

Carey
Garden Wood
Carey House
Westminster Rd Ind Est
Carey Road
WESTMINSTER ROAD
MISTOVER ROAD
ESDOVE
HUMBER CR
MELLSTOCK CR
CAREY
ST MILL
W ST MILL CRES
WESSEX OVAL
ST MARY'S CL
WALLS
CAREY VIEW
CAREY JOHNS RD
CAREY APP
CR
PO
Ind Est
Wareham
HIBBS CL
CAUSEWAY CL
SANDFORD LA
WAREHAM
A351
North Bestwall Wood

Wareham Forest Way

New Meadow Coppice

River Piddle or Trent

Ferncroft Farm

North Bridge
MOUNT PLEASANT
SHATTER'S HL
N WALLS
CAUSEWAY NORTH STREET
ST MARTIN'S LA
FOLLY LANE
EDWARD
BRIXE
NORTH BESTWALL ROAD
Swanage & Wareham RFC
MORETON'S LA
EAST STREET
BESTWALL ROAD
BESTWALL CR
MEADOW VIEW CL

Worgret Heath

West Mills

A351

Wareham
ROPERS LANE
WEST STREET
TINKER LA
NEW ST
MILL LANE
COW LANE
Dorset Gallery
HOWARD'S LA
BELL ST
P
P
P
P
TH
Mus
WYATT'S LA
CONNIGER LA
CHURCH LA

Tumuli
Oil Well

Lady St Mary CE First Sch
Wareham Middle Sch
Rec Gnd
P
MONMOUTH RD
STROKE
WEST STREET
POUND LA
TRINITY
SOUTH ST
P
Liby
The Priory

Little Farm
PUDDLETOWN ROAD
A352
B3070
WORGRET ROAD
Magistrates Court
Council Offices
Castle (Site of)
WESTPORT
SHIRLEY RD
Purbeck Information & Heritage Centre
South Br
SOUTH ST
Purbeck Way

Worgret Hill
WORGRET HILL
Manor Farm
The Purbeck Sch
BARNES RD
HARDY RD
STOWELL CR
FROME RD

Worgret
Purbeck Sports Centre
Oil Well
River Frome
A351

Stoborough
Stoborough Sch
PH
B3075
SOUTH CAUSEWAY
CORFE ROAD
NUTCRACK LANE

Goodens Farm
HOLLOW OAK RD
WEST LANE
OAKTREE
MELANCHOLY LA
Stoborough MD

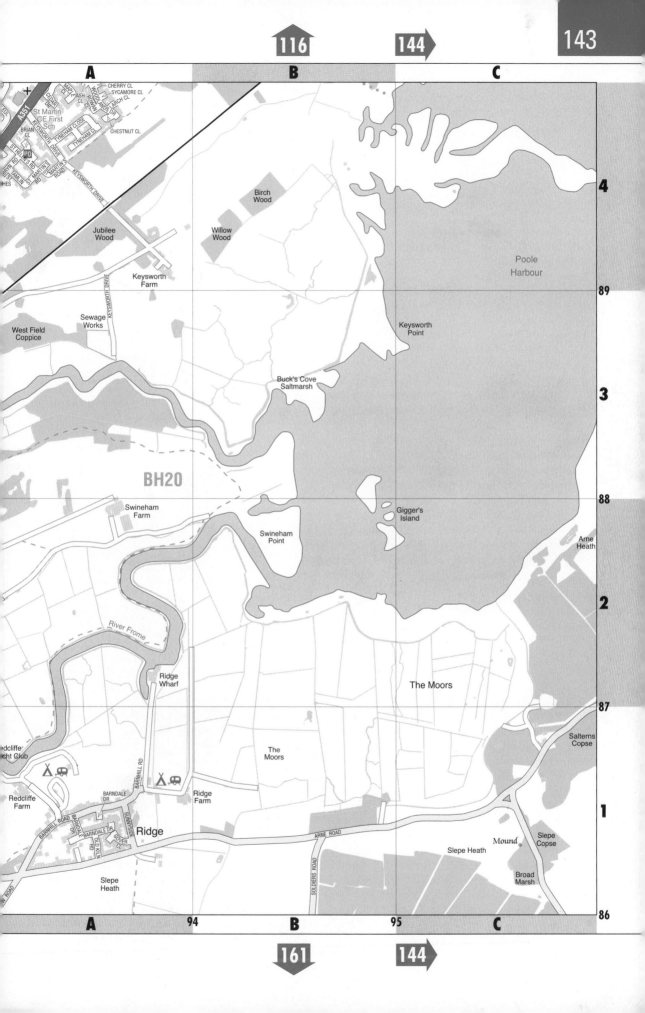

A
B
C

4

89

3

88

2

87

1

86

A
B
C

St Martin
CE First
Sch

CHERRY CL
SYCAMORE CL

CEDAR
DR
ASH CL
ROWAN
WOODLANDS DR
WINDSOR CL
BIRCH CL

MAPLE
CL
TYNEHAM CLOSE
CHESTNUT CL
BRIAN
CL
TYNEHAM CL

A351

KEYSWORTH DRIVE

MARTIN
ROAD

Jubilee
Wood

Birch
Wood

Willow
Wood

Keysworth
Farm

Poole
Harbour

Sewage
Works

West Field
Coppice

Keysworth
Point

Buck's Cove
Saltmarsh

BH20

Swineham
Farm

Gigger's
Island

Arne
Heath

Swineham
Point

River Frome

The Moors

Ridge
Wharf

Salterns
Copse

Redcliffe
Yacht Club

The
Moors

Redcliffe
Farm

BARNHILL RD

Ridge
Farm

BARNDALE
DR

SUNNYSIDE

GOVER CL

OLD KILN RD

BARNHILL ROAD

BARNDAL
DR

BARNDALE DR

Ridge

ARNE ROAD

SOLDIERS ROAD

Mound

Slepe
Copse

Slepe Heath

Slepe
Heath

Broad
Marsh

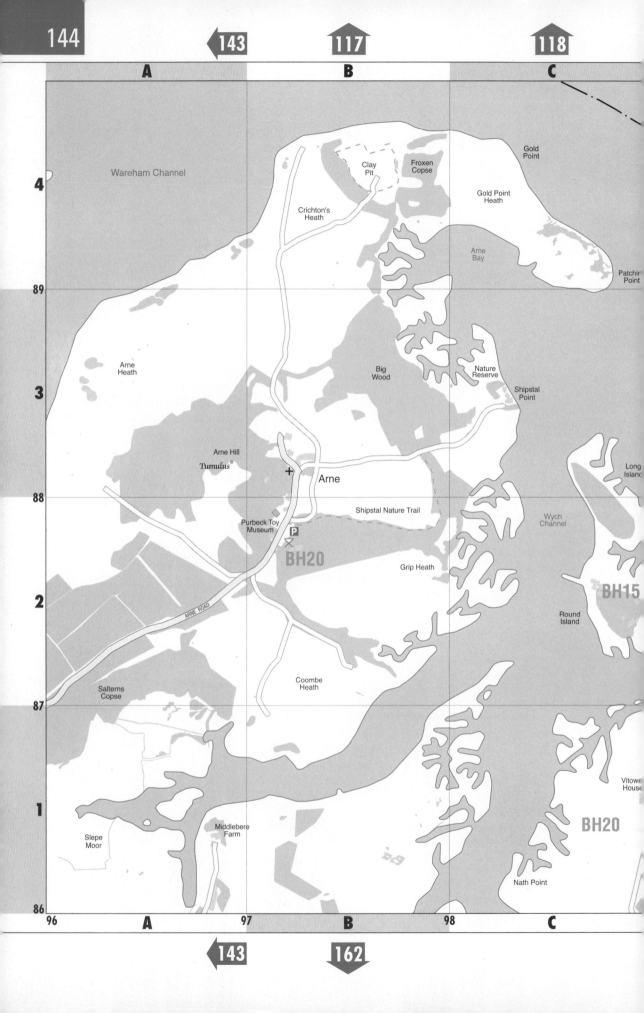

Marina

BH15

NEW HARBOUR RD

New Quay

NEW HARBOUR RD S

Ferry (F) (April to September)

Lower Hamworthy

Main Channel

4

Poole Harbour

89

3

Nature Reserve

Cambridge Wood

Maryland

Oxford Wood

Pottery Pier

Elizabeth Hill

MIDDLE STREET

Rough Brake

88

Brownsea Island

National Trust

St Michael's Mount

Fire Tower

BH13

Lincoln Cliff

Monument

William Pit

2

Slipway

Landing Stage

Oil Well

BH15

Oil Well

Furzey Island

87

Fitzworth Point

Landing Stage

BH15

Green Island

1

BH20

Fitzworth Heath

Ower Bay

South Deep

Goathorn Point

Goathorn Pier

Ower Heath

BH20

BH19

Goathorn Plantation

Brands Bay

86

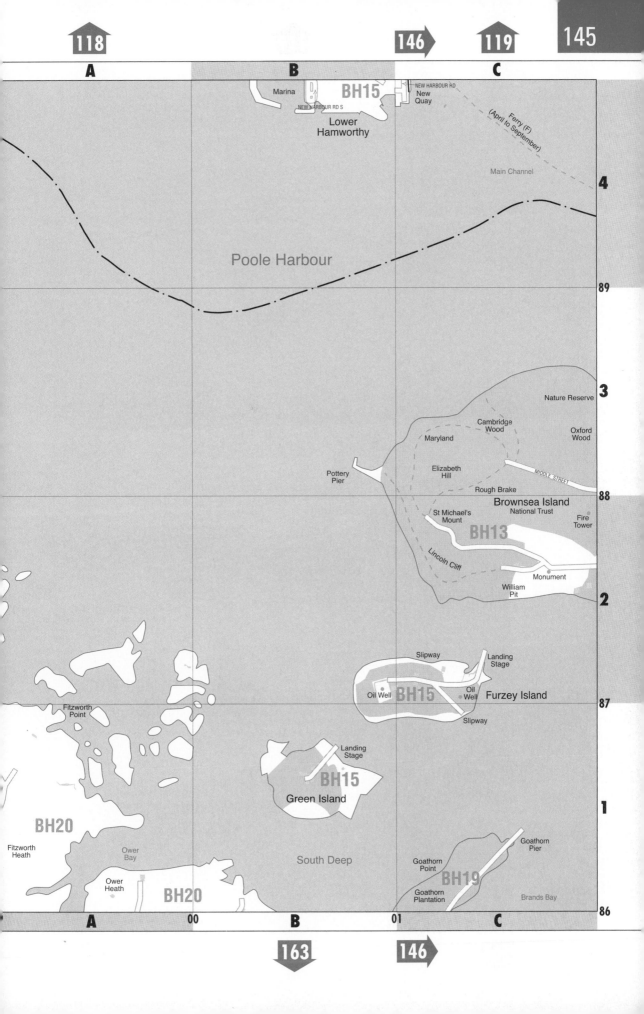

A

B

C

Marina

New Harbour Rd S

BH15

New Harbour Rd

New Quay

Main Channel

4

Ferry (F)
(April to September)

89

Poole Harbour

3

Cambridge Wood

Nature Reserve

Oxford Wood

Maryland

The Villa

West Lake

East Lake

Elizabeth Hill

MIDDLE STREET

Pottery Pier

88

Rough Brake

Brownsea Island
National Trust

BH13

St Michael's Mount

Fire Twr

Harley Wood

Church Hill

Lincoln Cliff

Monument

William Pit

Farm Buildings

2

Harry Point

Landing Stage

Oil Well

BH15

Oil Well

Furzey Island

87

Slipway

Landing Stage

BH15

Green Island

1

Goathorn Pier

South Deep

Goathorn Point

BH19

Jerry's Point

BH20

Goathorn Plantation

Brand's Bay

BH19

86

00

A

01

B

02

C

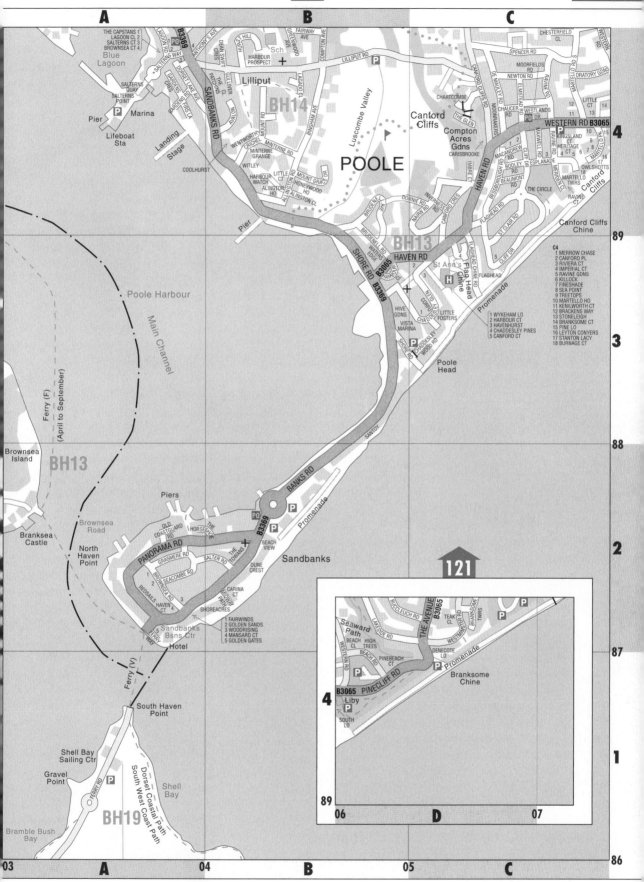

A
B
C

THE CAPSTANS 1
LAGOON CL 2
SALTERNS CT 3
BROWNSEA CT 4

B3369

Blue
Lagoon

Salterns Quay

Salterns Point

Pier   Marina

Lifeboat Sta

Landing Stage

Coolhurst

Lilliput

BH14

HARBOUR PROSPECT

Sch

LILLIPUT RD

P

Luscombe Valley

Canford Cliffs

Compton Acres Gdns

CARISBROOKE

POOLE

CHARTCOMBE

THE GLEN

WESTERN RD B3065

Kingsland Heritage

Canford Cliffs

CHESTERFIELD CL

ORATORY GDNS

12 13 14
LITTLE CT

10 15
9
8
MARTELLO PL

16
13

OWLSHOTTS
MARTELLO TWRS

Canford Cliffs

89

Pier

WATERS EDGE

B3065
B3369

HAVEN RD

BH13

St Ann's

Flag Head Chine

H

FLAGHEAD

Promenade

C4
1 MERROW CHASE
2 CANFORD PL
3 RIVIERA CT
4 IMPERIAL CT
5 RAVINE GDNS
6 KILLOCK
7 FINESHADE
8 SEA POINT
9 TREETOPS
10 MARTELLO HO
11 KENILWORTH CT
12 BRACKENS WAY
13 STONELEIGH
14 BRANKSOME CT
15 PINE LO
16 LEYTON CONYERS
17 STANTON LACY
18 BURNAGE CT

Poole Harbour

Main Channel

Poole Head

88

HIVE GDNS

VISTA MARINA

P

LITTLE FOSTERS

SHORE RD

1 WYKEHAM LO
2 HARBOUR CT
3 HAVENHURST
4 CHADDESLEY PINES
5 CANFORD CT

Ferry (F)
(April to September)

Brownsea Island

BH13

SANTOY

Brownsea Castle

Brownsea Road

North Haven Point

Piers

OLD COASTGUARD RD

PANORAMA RD

GRASMERE RD

SEACOMBE RD

REDSALLS RD

BROWNSEA RD

HAVEN CT

SALTER RD

THE HORSESHOE

THE TOWANS

BEACH VIEW

DUNE CREST

CARINA CT

DOWNS PATH

SHOREACRES

BANKS RD

P

P

B3369

PO

Promenade

Sandbanks

1 FAIRWINDS
2 GOLDEN SANDS
3 WOODRISING
4 MANSARD CT
5 GOLDEN GATES

2

121

Sandbanks Bsns Ctr

Hotel

FERRY WAY

Ferry (V)

South Haven Point

Seaward Path

BEACH CL

HIGH TREES

WESTERN RD

BUCCLEUCH RD

LAKESIDE RD

THE AVENUE

B3065

TEAK CL

BRANKSOME TWRS

P

P

P

Promenade

Branksome Chine

DENECOTE LO

PINEBEACH CT

PINECLIFF RD

B3065
Liby

SOUTH LO

87

Shell Bay Sailing Ctr

Gravel Point

Bramble Bush Bay

FERRY RD

P

BH19

Shell Bay

Dorset Coastal Path
South West Coastal Path

4

1

06
D
07

89

86

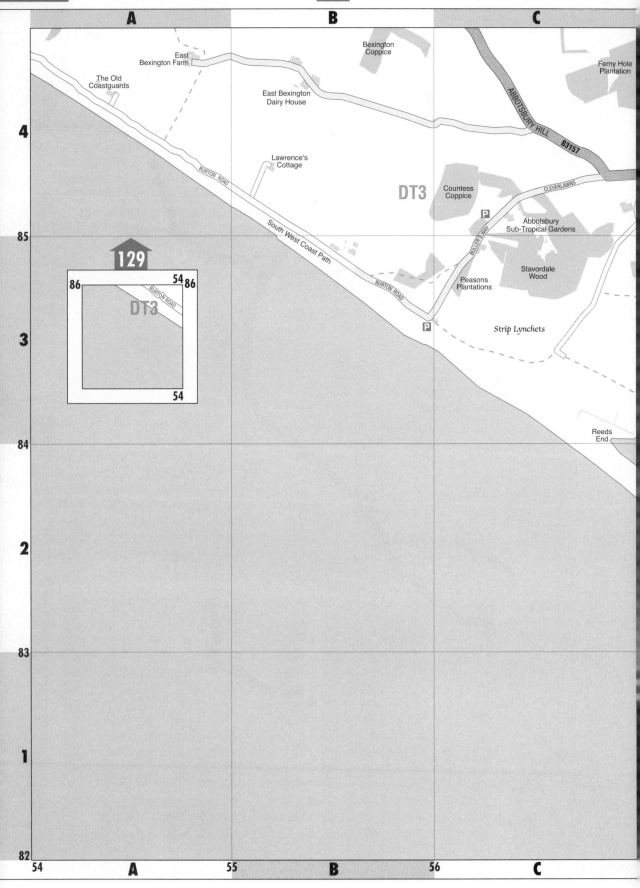

A B C

The Old
Coastguards

East
Bexington Farm

Bexington
Coppice

Ferny Hole
Plantation

East Bexington
Dairy House

ABBOTSBURY HILL

B3157

Lawrence's
Cottage

4

DT3

Countess
Coppice

CLEVERLAWNS

South West Coast Path

85

P

Abbotsbury
Sub-Tropical Gardens

129

BILLER'S WAY

86 54 86

Burton Road

BURTON ROAD

Peasons
Plantations

Stavordale
Wood

DT3

3

Strip Lynchets

P

54

54

84

Reeds
End

2

83

1

82

54 55 56

A B C

A B C

Abbotsbury Plains

Oxlip Coppice

BISHOP'S ROAD

Jubilee Coppice

Abbotsbury

ROSEMARY LA

MALTHOUSE MD

HANDS LANE

BACK STREET

WEST STREET B3157 MARKET ST

GLEBE CL

GOOSE HILL

PH

ST

PO

BISHOP'S CLOSE

RODDEN ROW

B3157

4

P

P

St Peter's Abbey

Tithe Barn Children's Farm

Goose Hill

Abbey Barn

MARKET STREET

NEW BARN RD

Oddens Wood

Sewage Works

85

St Catherines Chapel

Nunnery Grove

GROVE LANE

West Elworth Farm

Chapel Hill

Chapel Coppice

GROVE LA

Horsepool Farm

Linton Hill

Linton Barn

West Elworth

P

3

South West Coast Path

DT3

Clayhanger Farm

Merry Hill

Abbotsbury Swannery

South West Coast Path

84

Hodder's Coppice

Tiny Coppice

NEW BARN ROAD

Shipmoor Point

Cuckoo Coppice

Warre Wood

Chesters Coppice

Walls Down

2

Chesters Hill

New Barn Farm

Wyke Wood

Berry Coppice

83

Higher Barn

Chesil Beach

West Fleet

South Sleight Coppice

Holywell Spring

1

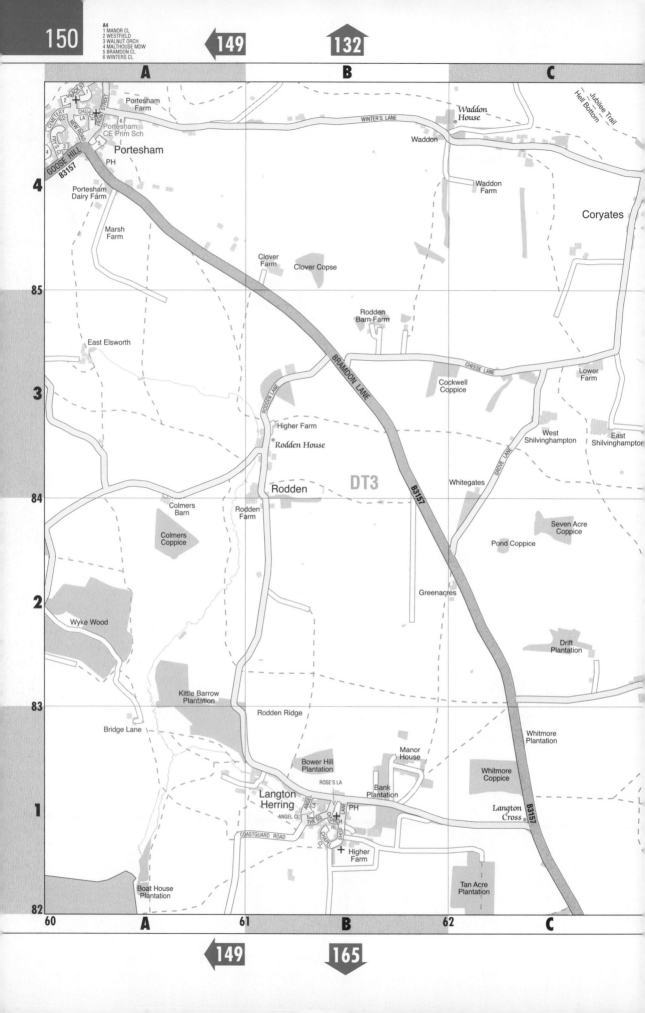

150

A4
1 MANOR CL
2 WESTFIELD
3 WALNUT ORCH
4 MALTHOUSE MDW
5 BRAMDON CL
6 WINTERS CL

149

132

A   B   C

BACK ST
CEMETERY RD
CHURCH LA
PRIM STREET
NEW ROAD
FRY'S CL
GOOSE HILL
B3157

Portesham Farm

Winter's Lane

Waddon House

Jubilee Trail
Hell Bottom

Portesham CE Prim Sch

Portesham
PH

Waddon

Waddon Farm

4

Portesham Dairy Farm

Coryates

Marsh Farm

Clover Farm
Clover Copse

85

East Elsworth

Rodden Barn Farm

Cheese Lane

Lower Farm

3

RODDEN LANE
BRAMDON LANE
GROVE LANE

Higher Farm

Rodden House

Cockwell Coppice

West Shilvinghampton

East Shilvinghampton

Rodden

Whitegates

DT3

84

Colmers Barn

Rodden Farm

B3157

Seven Acre Coppice

Colmers Coppice

Pond Coppice

Drift Plantation

2

Wyke Wood

Greenacres

83

Kittle Barrow Plantation

Rodden Ridge

Whitmore Plantation

Bridge Lane

Bower Hill Plantation

Manor House

Whitmore Coppice

ROSE'S LA

Bank Plantation

1

Langton Herring

PH

ANGEL CL
ANGEL LA
THE SQ
CHURCH HL
SHOP LANE

Langton Cross

B3157

COASTGUARD ROAD

CHAPEL LANE

Higher Farm

Boat House Plantation

Tan Acre Plantation

82

60   A   61   B   62   C

A B C

Friar Waddon

Hewish Farm

Corton Hill

Windsbatch
Farm

Yules
Farm

FRIAR WADDON
ROAD

+

Corton
Farm

Tumuli

Friar Waddon Hill

Tumuli

Jubilee Trail

4

85

Westbrook
Dairy

Pucksey Brook

3

DT3

Hewish
Farm

84

Dairy House
Coppice

Hewish
Hill

Square Coppice

Moor Coppice

Loscombe
Wood

2

Holwell Farm

Hyde Coppice

Tatton
House

Higher Moor

83

NOTTINGTON LANE

East
Farm

North Farm

Buckland
House

Tatton Farm

Broad Coppice

CHURCH LANE

Tatton
Coppice

Middle Farm

+The End

1

Buckland
Ripers

Coverwell
Coppice

Higher
Barn

63 A 64 B 65 C 82

A   **B**   **C**

4

Tumuli
Ridgeway Hill
Tumuli
Mast
Heath Dairy
Came Down
Tumuli
Came Wood

FRIAR WADDON RD
South West Coast Path
Jubilee Trail

Bincombe Down

Bayard Dairy
Tumuli

GOULD'S HILL
CHURCH ST
GOULDS HIL CL
B3159

Upwey Trout Farm

Bayard Hill
CHURCH STREET
Jubilee Trail

West Farm
Lower Bincombe

Field System

Tumuli

85

ELWELL STREET

Upwey

Elwell

DORCHESTER ROAD

The Knoll

Mast
Bincombe Hill

Middle Farm

Bincombe

South West Coast Path

East Farm

3

B3159

PH

MILES GDNS
CHAPEL LA

Coombe Farm

Combe Bottom

DT3

+ +

Westbrook House
STOTTINGWAY STREET

Cackleberry Farm

Upwey Manor Farm

North Manor Farm

WATERY LANE

SHORTLANDS RD
ST LAWRENCE RD
VICTORIA AV
OLD STATION ROAD
PO

Weyside Farm

Icen Farm

Icen Lane

Strip Lynchets

84

River Way

WATERY LANE

JESTY'S AVE
BEECH RD
WESTLAKE CL
WEYVIEW CR

ICEN LANE

NIGHTINGALE DR
MEADOW VW RD
FIR CREST
BRAMBLING CL
GOLDCREST
THE WOODPECKERS
LINNET CL
PIPIT CL

Bincombe Marsh Dairy

2

Broadwey

Higher Manor Farm

A354

MILL STREET
LITTLEMEAD
WATERY LA
ST JULIEN AV N
MERLIN AV N
SPRINGFIELD ROAD
MERLIN AV S
SPRINGFIELD CR
CAME DOWN CL
BRIDPORT WY
JUNIPER WY

WINDSOR RD
REDWOOD RD
BROADWEY CL
REEDLING CL
THE FINCHES
KESTREL VIEW
FIELDFARE
LITTLEMOOR RD
GOLDCREST
TURNSTONE CL
THE DOVES
BEVERLEY ROAD
PEMBERTON CL
SELWYN CL
CRANMER CL
WREN CL
REDIN CL
CHAFFINCH CL
Liby
ROCKHAMPTON CL
PO
CANBERRA CR
MACWEY CL
CULLIFORD CL
LITTLEMOOR WAY
HAMPTON KNOLL RD

Littlemoor

Lorton Farm

LORTON LANE

≋ Upwey

Lorton House

83

Gales End
Exmoor Lodge

Nottington

Higher Moor

NOTTINGTON LANE

COURT Y RD
THE SPINNEY
BROADLANDS RD

St Nicholas & St Laurence CE Prim Sch

BLACKBERRY LA
LORTON LANE

Coffin Plantation

CANBERRA ROAD
BRISBANE RD
GEELONG RD
LOUVIERS ROAD
CASTLEMAIN RD
HAMPTON RD
BAYARD ROAD
ALLAMANDA CL

Littlemoor CP Sch

BUDDLEIA CL
FOXGLOVE WY
HONEYSUCKLE CL
DAHLIA CL
PRIMULA CL

Nottington Farm

The Wey Valley Sch

WENTWORTH CL
CLIVIA CL

1

DORCHESTER ROAD
A354

Redlands

Weymouth Sports Club

BLENHEIM ROAD
GREENWAY ROAD
CLARENDON AVE

Two Mile Coppice

Horse Lynch Plantation

LANCASTER RD

82

66   A   67   B   68   C

B2
1 REDPOLL CL
2 ROBIN CL
3 STONECHAT CL
4 WHEATEAR CL
5 JORDAN WY
6 SANDERLING CL
7 REGENCY DR

C1
1 KIMBERLEY CL
2 GLADSTONE CL
3 MAGNOLIA CL

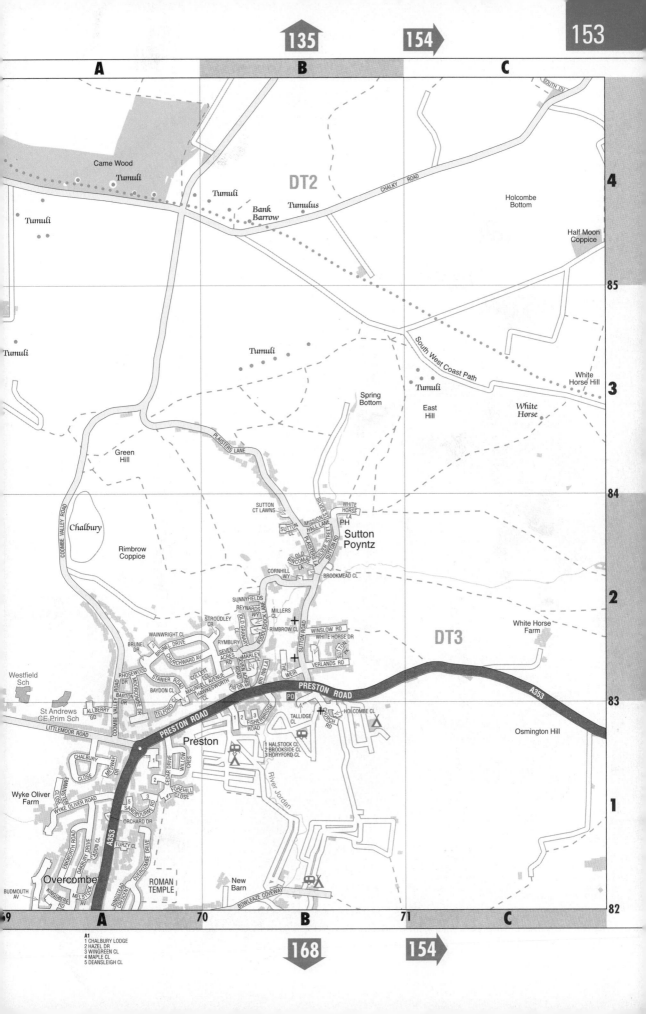

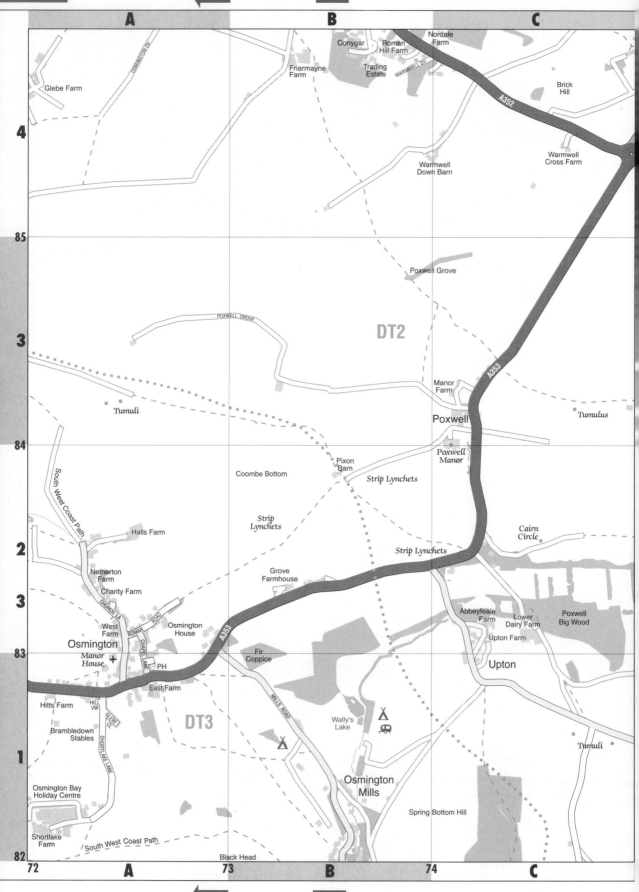

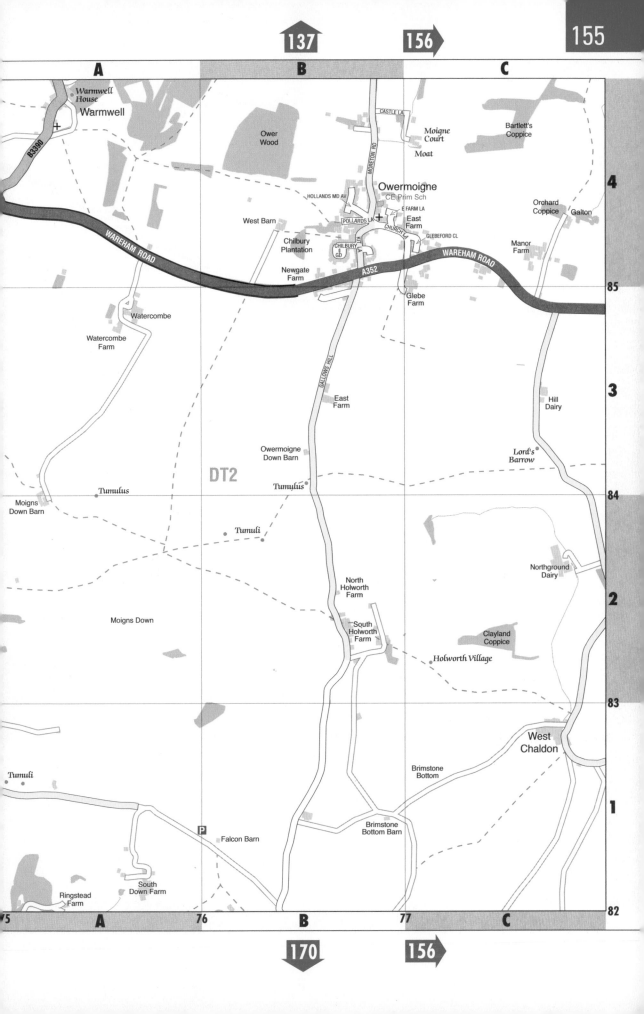

A   B   C

Warmwell House
Warmwell
B3390

Ower Wood

CASTLE LA
Moigne Court
Moat

Bartlett's Coppice

MORETON RD

Owermoigne
CE Prim Sch

HOLLANDS MD AV

West Barn

Orchard Coppice
Galton

POLLARDS LA
East Farm

E FARM LA

CHURCH LA
GLEBEFORD CL

4

Chilbury Plantation
CHILBURY GD

Manor Farm

WAREHAM ROAD

Newgate Farm
A352

WAREHAM ROAD

85

Watercombe

Glebe Farm

Watercombe Farm

GALLOWS HILL

East Farm

Hill Dairy

3

DT2

Owermoigne Down Barn

Lord's Barrow

Tumulus
Tumulus

84

Moigns Down Barn

Tumuli

Northground Dairy

North Holworth Farm

2

Moigns Down

South Holworth Farm

Clayland Coppice

Holworth Village

83

West Chaldon

Tumuli

Brimstone Bottom

1

P
Falcon Barn

Brimstone Bottom Barn

Ringstead Farm
South Down Farm

82

75   A   76   B   77   C

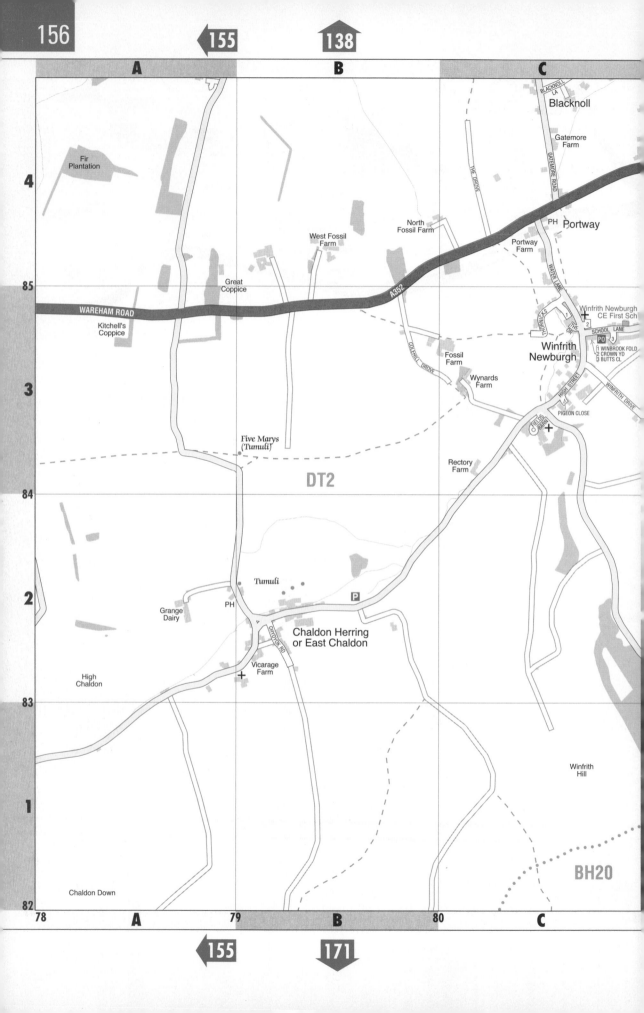

BLACKNOLL LANE

West Burton Farm

Home Farm

Longcutts Farm

PH

A352

East Knighton

North Wood

EAST KNIGHTON LANE

East Knighton Farm

Newburgh Farm

4

Claypits Farm

CLAYPITS LANE

Newburgh Dairy

85

DT2

Coombe Wood

3

Fields Farm

B3071

Drove Dairy

NEWTOWN HILL

84

2

Tumulus

BH20

Marley Bottom

Vine's Down Buildings

Lulworth Common

Belhuish House

B3071

83

Tumulus

Marley Wood

Burngate Wood

Marley Wood House

Belhuish Coppice

1

82

A B C

New
Buildings

Tumuli

Cole
Wood

Woodstreet
Farm

Long
Coppice

Woodman's
Cross

Barn
Coppice

Highwood
Wood

Highwood *Tumulus*

Dorset
Wood

Baylea
Farm

DANGER
AREA

4

Knap Coppice

B3071

Vicarage
Coppice

Haremere
Wood

Oak
Tree Farm

Coombe Heath

85

NEWTOWN HILL

Kick Hill
Coppice

Kick Hill
Farm

Coombe
Beacon

Tumuli

3

Coombe
Keynes

West
Farm

Kimbert's
End

Church
Coppice

CHURCH LA

Vary
Coppice

Lake Hill
Plantation

BH20

84

Lime Kiln
Dairy

Kennel
Wood

The
Lake

Kennel
Farm

Bellevue
Plantation

Lake
Plantation

2

Lime Kiln
Cottage

Lodge
Wood

Home
Farm

Black
Barrow

Shaggs

Park
Lodge

New Barn
Plantation

83

Burngate
Wood

Botany
Plantations

B3070

Botany
Farm

Bowling
Green Wood

Cemy

MOUNT PLEASANT

Botany
Wood

1

Park
Wood

DANGER AREA

Botany
Farm

Whiteway

Lulworth Castle

Ball
Coppice

82

84 A 85 B 86 C

Chicks
Hill Farm

Luckford
Lake Farm

West Holme
Farm

French Grass
Coppice

East
Holme

West Holme

4

HOLME LANE

Highwood
Heath

Heath
Range

DANGER AREA

West Holme
Heath

New Barn
Farm

Woodbury
Coppice

85

B3070

Luckford Lake

Tumuli

DANGER
AREA

3

Five
Barrow Hill

Tumulus

Hurst
Mill

84

BH20

Lulworth
Heath

Tumuli

Pool
Pond

Mare
Pond

2

Povington
Heath

King's Standing

Tumuli

83

Earl's
Kitchen

North Hills
Plantation

DANGER AREA
(Tank Ranges)

West
Creech

1

West Creech
Farm

Povington
Barrow

Povington
Wood

Grey's
Coppice

82

7   A   88   B   89   C

159
142

A **B** **C**

CORFE ROAD

NEW ROAD

OVAL GD

TUCKERS MILL CL

SCOTT CL

THE DROVE

HOLME TMD

STUDLD

A351

B3075

OLD FURZEBROOK RD

4

Holme Lane Plantation

Tumulus

King's Barrow

WEST LANE

HOLME LANE

Hotel

Stocks Wood

Doreys Farm

85

Battle Plain

Rifle Range

Three Lords' Barrow

Stoborough Heath

Tumulus

LC

3

Holme Heath

Tumuli

New Hall Farm

Creech Bottom

Grange Barn

DANGER AREA

84

BH20

Snug Farm

Icen Barrow

Creech Heath

GRANGE ROAD

Tumulus

Grange Heath

Haskells Farm

Clay Pits

2

Tumulus

Creech

Smithys Farm

Tumuli

DANGER AREA

Drinking Barrow

Breach Plantation

83

Great Plantation

John's Plantation

Cotness

Mine

Whitehall

Mine (dis)

East Creech

1

Alder Moor

Creech Barrow Hill

Little Wood

Grange Farm

Tumulus

Creech Grange

GRANGE HILL

Great Wood

Tumulus

Stonehill Down

Tumulus

82

90 **A** 91 **B** 92 **C**

A
B
C

4

85

3

Stoborough
Green

Nature Reserve

Slepe
Heath

Slepe
Farm

Hartland
Moor

SOLDIERS ROAD

A351

Hartland
Stud

Middlebere
Heath

National
Nature Reserve

Three
Barrows

Langton
Wallis

PH

New Mills
Heath

BH20

84

Works

Gallows
Plantation

Newline
Farm

Furzebrook

Furzebrook
House

FURZEBROOK RD

GALLOWS HILL

LC

NEW LINE

2

Blue Pool

Norden
Heath

Norden

Norden Plantation

LC

P

Norden

Norden
Farm

83

Swanage Railway

A351

Purbeck Way

P

1

Quarry

Tumuli

Corfe
Castle
NT

Knowle Hill

West
Hill

Cocknowle

The Rings

82

3
A
94
B
95
C

A

B

C

Slepe

Fitzworth Heath

Copse

Wytch Farm

Oil Wells

4

Middlebere Heath

Corfe River

Wytch Rd

Oil Wells

Wytch Farm

Oil Well

Depot

85

Sharford Bridge

Wytch Moor

Wytch Heath

Rempstone Heath

3

Flashet Plantation

Scotland Farm

84

Thrasher's Heath

BH20

Batrick's Plantation

Meadus's Plantation

Tumulus

THRASHER'S LANE

MEADUS'S LANE

Bushey

Tinker's Copse

2

Lower Bushey Farm

Brenscombe Heath

Sewage Works

BUSHEY LANE

THRASHER'S LANE

Higher Bushey Farm

83

Jack Green's Copse

Keeper's Copse

Rempstone Farm

B3351

Ashey Copse

NEW ROAD

Rollington Farm

1

East Hill

Brenscombe Farm

Bushey Wood

Corfe Castle

1 THE SQ
2 WEST ST

EAST ST

A351

SANDY HILL LANE

Rollington Hill

Brenscombe Wood

FOREST LANE

Little Wood

PO

Mus

Dairy House
Challow Farm

Rempstone Wood

82

Hotel

96

A

97

B

98

C

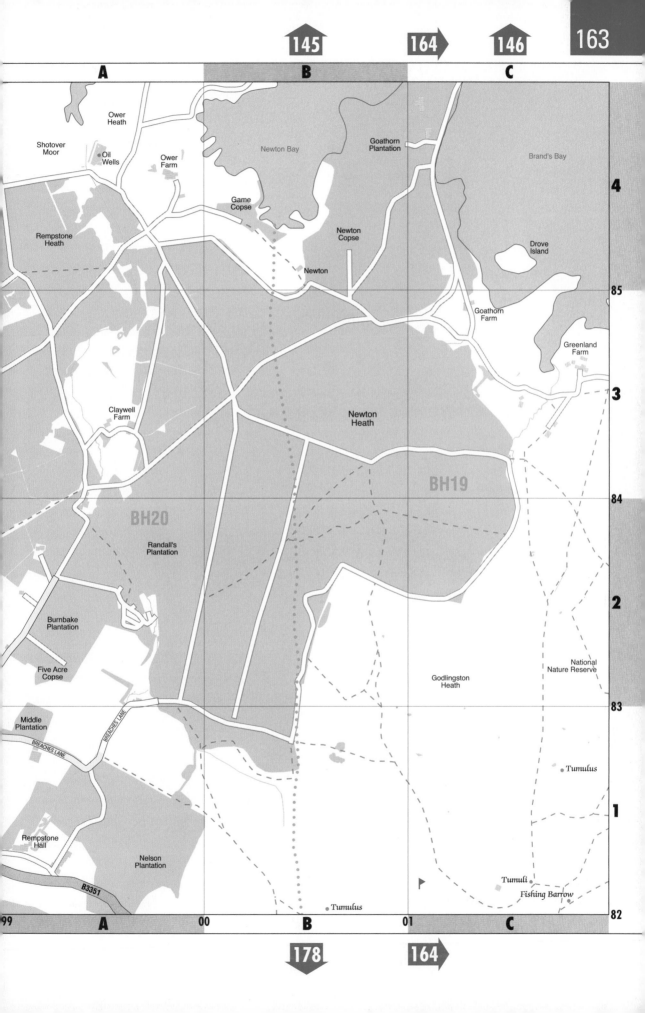

A
B
C

Ower
Heath

Shotover
Moor

• Oil
Wells

Ower
Farm

Newton Bay

Goathorn
Plantation

Brand's Bay

4

Game
Copse

Rempstone
Heath

Newton
Copse

Drove
Island

Newton

85

Goathorn
Farm

Greenland
Farm

Claywell
Farm

Newton
Heath

3

BH19

BH20

84

Randall's
Plantation

Burnbake
Plantation

2

National
Nature Reserve

Five Acre
Copse

Godlingston
Heath

83

Middle
Plantation

BREACHES LANE

BREACHES LANE

• Tumulus

Rempstone
Hall

1

Nelson
Plantation

• Tumuli

B3351

Fishing Barrow

• Tumulus

82

99
A
00
B
01
C

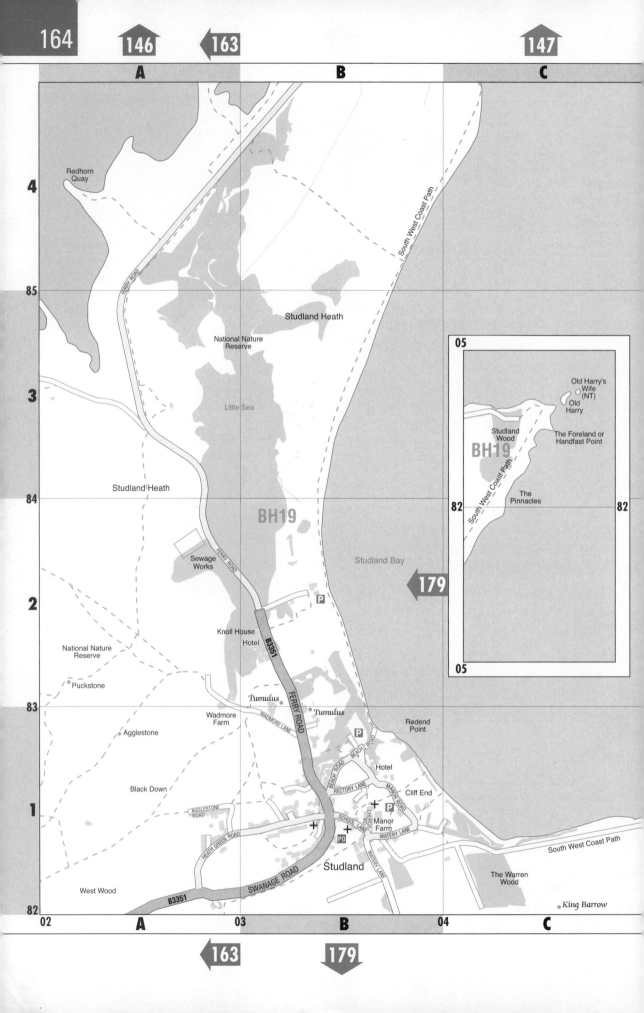

A B C

4

Redhorn
Quay

South West Coast Path

85

Studland Heath

National Nature
Reserve

3

Little Sea

05

Old Harry's
Wife
(NT)
Old
Harry

Studland
Wood

The Foreland or
Handfast Point

BH19

84

Studland Heath

82 The Pinnacles 82

BH19

South West Coast Path

Sewage
Works

FERRY ROAD

Studland Bay

179

2

Knoll House
Hotel

B3351

P

05

National Nature
Reserve

Puckstone

Tumulus

FERRY ROAD

Tumulus

Redend
Point

83

Wadmore
Farm

WADMORE LANE

Agglestone

P

BEACH ROAD

Hotel

BEACH ROAD

MANOR ROAD

Cliff End

Black Down

RECTORY LANE

1

AGGLESTONE
ROAD

SCHOOL LANE

+

P

Manor
Farm

CHURCH ROAD

+

WATERY LANE

HEATH GREEN ROAD

+

PO

WATERY LANE

South West Coast Path

West Wood

B3351

SWANAGE ROAD

Studland

The Warren
Wood

82

King Barrow

02 A 03 B 04 C

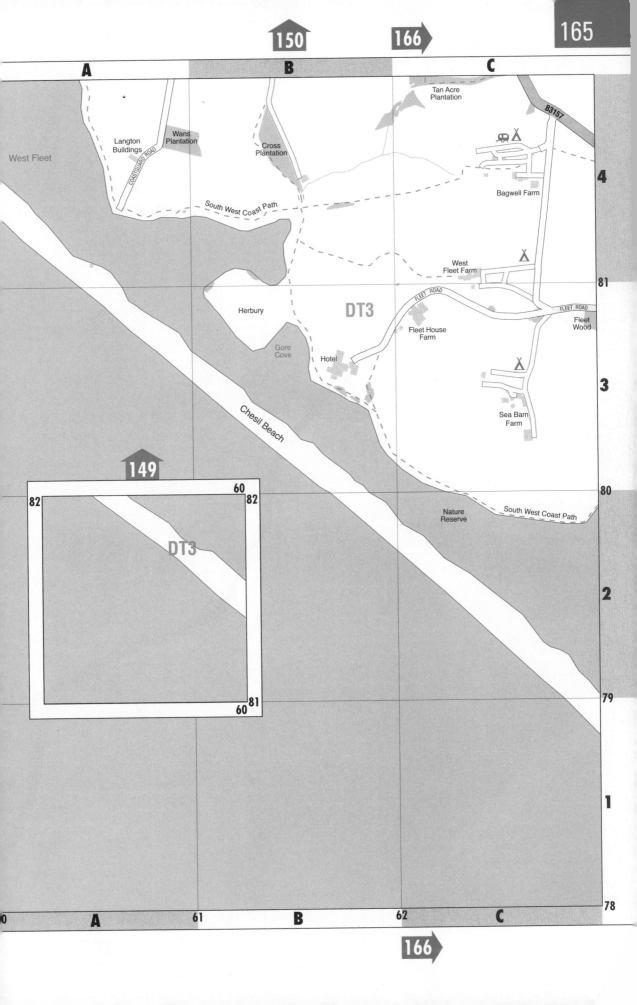

A **B** **C**

West Fleet

Langton
Buildings

Wans
Plantation

Cross
Plantation

Tan Acre
Plantation

COASTGUARD ROAD

B3157

Bagwell Farm

South West Coast Path

4

West
Fleet Farm

81

Herbury

DT3

FLEET ROAD

Fleet House
Farm

FLEET ROAD

Fleet
Wood

Gore
Cove

Hotel

3

Chesil Beach

Sea Barn
Farm

149

60   60
82   82

DT3

Nature
Reserve

South West Coast Path

80

2

81
60   81

79

1

78

0   **A**   61   **B**   62   **C**

A   **B**   **C**

4

Moor Farm

Knights in the Bottom

PH

B3157

Lower Manor Farm House

Lower Manor Farm

Heatherick

South Buckland Farm

Coldharbour

HARBOUR HILL

Eweleaze Spinneys

81

Fleet Wood

Lanehouse Equestrian Centre

Ridge Farm

WEST CL

PH

MARSHALLSAY RD

WHEAT FARLAND

WILMSLOW

MAY TR

SCHOOL CL

MARINERS WY

LERRETT CL

FISHERMANS CL

Lower Putton Lane

THE COPPICE

3

Fleet

CHICKERELL HILL

Morn Lodge

THE KNAPP

WEST STREET

WEST END

NORTH SQ

EAST ST

Liby

PH

HIGHER END

MEADOW CL

RANDALL CL

REX LA

S.MILLER RD

ROLFE

SHIRLEY RD

RASHLEY RD

THE TEA...

THE HYDE

AV

BINDO...

DRAKE

Chickerell CP Sch

PODINGTON MS

BROWN'S CR

PUTTON LANE

POGHILL...

Putton

Police

Weymouth Town Football Club

Fleet Common

GARSTON HILL

B3157

Chickerell

DT3

MASKEW CL

ELVER

WHYNOT WY

GLENNIE WY

ALDABRAND CL

PUTTON LANE

TRENC...

WY

GREEN LANE

80

Butterstreet Cove

Fleet Lane

East Fleet Farm

FLEET LANE

Bennetts Water Lily Farm

AVON CLOSE

Granby Industrial Estate

HAMPSHIRE ROAD

SURREY CL

CUMBERLAND DRIVE

COBHAM DR

COBHAM DRIVE

COB...

DT4

East Fleet

2

East Fleet

Chickerell Hive Point

South West Coast Path

CHICKERELL ROAD

AUSTRALIA RD

ELIZABETH WY

FLEET...

POTANDRA

CRETWOOD

GLOUCESTER CL

KENT CL

CAMBRIDGE ROAD

ALBANY ROAD

STAINFORTH CL

TECAN WY

WINCHESTER CL

CANTERB...

GRANBY CLOSE

B3157

Budmouth Sch

Sports & Leisure Centre

GERONG DR

MARQUIS

CLARE AV

79

DANGER AREA

Rifle Range

Charlestown

WARREN RD

CLARENCE RD

OVERBURY

ST HELENS RD

LYNCH ROAD

LUDLOW...

1

Chesil Beach

Tidmoor Point

Furzedown

Littlesea Holiday Park

Lanehouse

LANEHOUSE ROCKS ROAD

LYNCH LANE

LYNCH LANE

RAYMOND RD

ROSECROFT...

LITTLEVIEW RD

NUTGROVE...

FRASER AVENUE

CLARENCE RD

FREEMANTLE RD

SOUTHCROFT RD

VISCOUNT RD

COMET RD

RD

B3157

VULCAN CL

VANGUARD AV

ST PATRICKS AV

CONCORDE...

COCK...

78

DANGER AREA

Lynch Cove

A   **B**   **C**

63   64   65

← **165**

↓ **180**

C1
1 GORDON CR
2 LINCOLN RD
3 LIVERPOOL RD
4 TOLLERDOWN RD

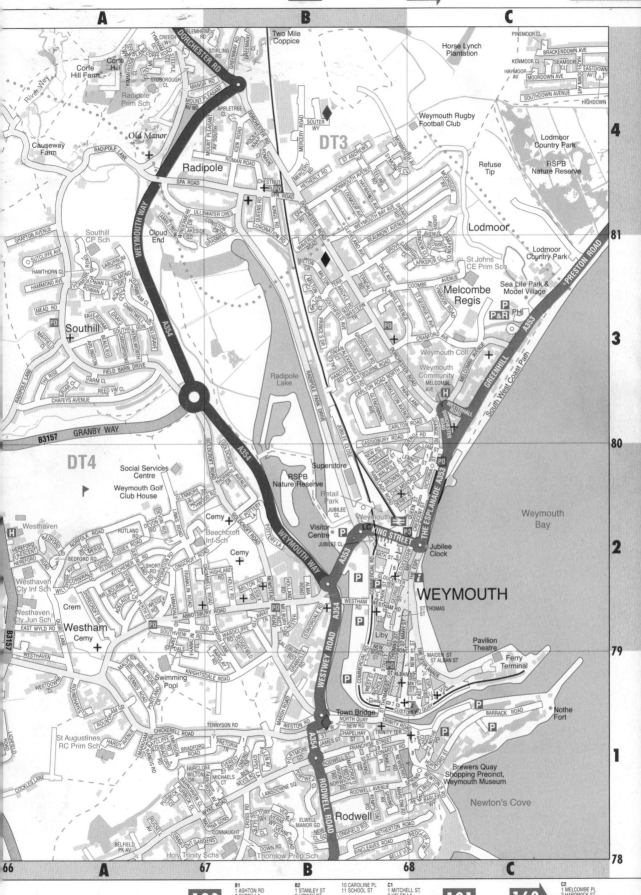

A   B   C

180   181   168

B1
1 ASHTON RD
2 GYPSY LA
3 PRINCE OF WALES RD
4 LWR ST ALBAN ST
5 LWR ST EDMUND ST
6 ST EDMUND ST
7 ST MARY ST
8 DORSET TR
9 PROSPECT PL

B2
1 STANLEY ST
2 UPWAY ST
3 TERMINUS ST
4 EDWARD ST
5 ALBERT ST
6 CLIFTON ST
7 QUEBEC PL
8 TURTON ST
9 WOOPERTON ST

10 CAROLINE PL
11 SCHOOL ST

C1
1 MITCHELL ST
2 HELEN LA
3 SOUTH PD
4 PILGRIMS WY
5 COVE ROW
6 SPRING RD
7 TRINITY ST
8 NEWBERRY GD

C2
1 MELCOMBE PL
2 HARDWICK ST
3 ASTRID WY
4 MUSGRAVE PL

A4
1 MOORCOMBE DR
2 CHALBURY LODGE
3 HAZEL DR
4 WINGREEN CL
5 MAPLE CL
6 DEANSLEIGH CL

167

153

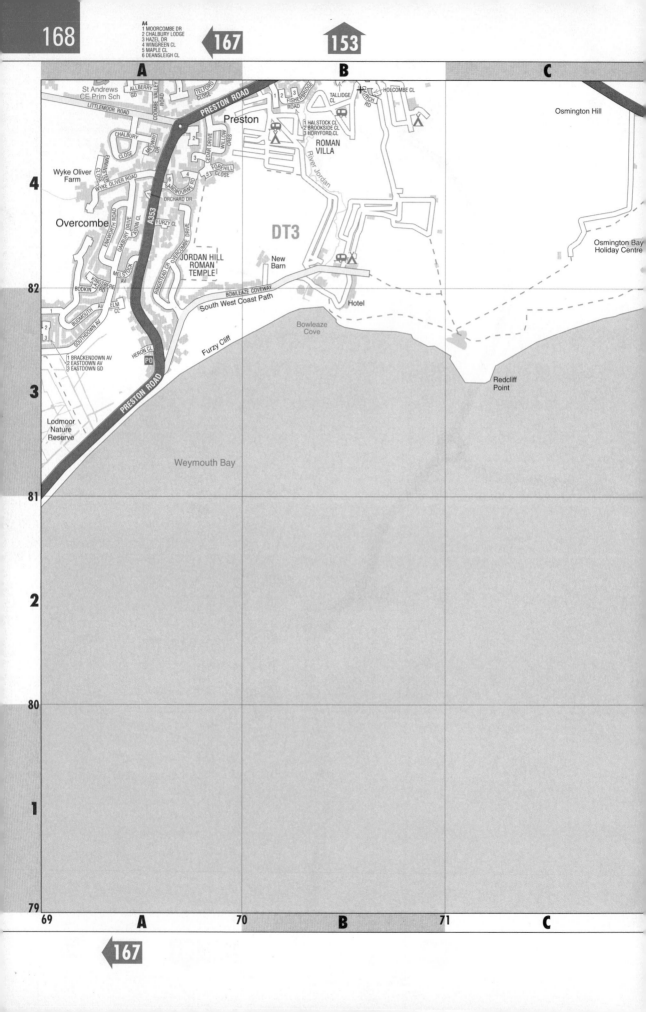

St Andrews
CE Prim Sch

ALLBERRY
GD

COMBE VALLEY

TELFORD
CLOSE

LITTLEMOOR ROAD

PRESTON ROAD

Preston

FISHERBRIDGE
ROAD

TALLIDGE
CL

HOLCOMBE CL

CHURCH
RD

Osmington Hill

CHALBURY
CLOSE

MEDWAY

CEDAR DRIVE

WILLOW
CRES

1 HALSTOCK CL
2 BROOKSIDE CL
3 HORYFORD CL

ROMAN
VILLA

Wyke Oliver
Farm

EMSWORTH
CLOSE

WYKE OLIVER ROAD

FOREHILL
CLOSE

River Jordan

DT3

4

Overcombe

OAKBURY DRIVE

ELWORTH ROAD

DENTON CL

SANDBOURNE RD

FURZY CL

ORCHARD DR

A353

OVERCOMBE DRIVE

JORDAN HILL
ROMAN
TEMPLE

New
Barn

Osmington Bay
Holiday Centre

RINGSTEAD GR

MELSTOCK
AV

KINGSBERE
RD

BODKIN

82

BOWLEAZE COVEWAY

Hotel

BUDMOUTH
AV

ELM
CL

South West Coast Path

Bowleaze
Cove

SOUTHDOWN AV

1
2
3

HERON CL

PO

Furzy Cliff

Redcliff
Point

1 BRACKENDOWN AV
2 EASTDOWN AV
3 EASTDOWN GD

3

PRESTON ROAD

Lodmoor
Nature
Reserve

Weymouth Bay

81

2

80

1

79

69

A

70

B

71

C

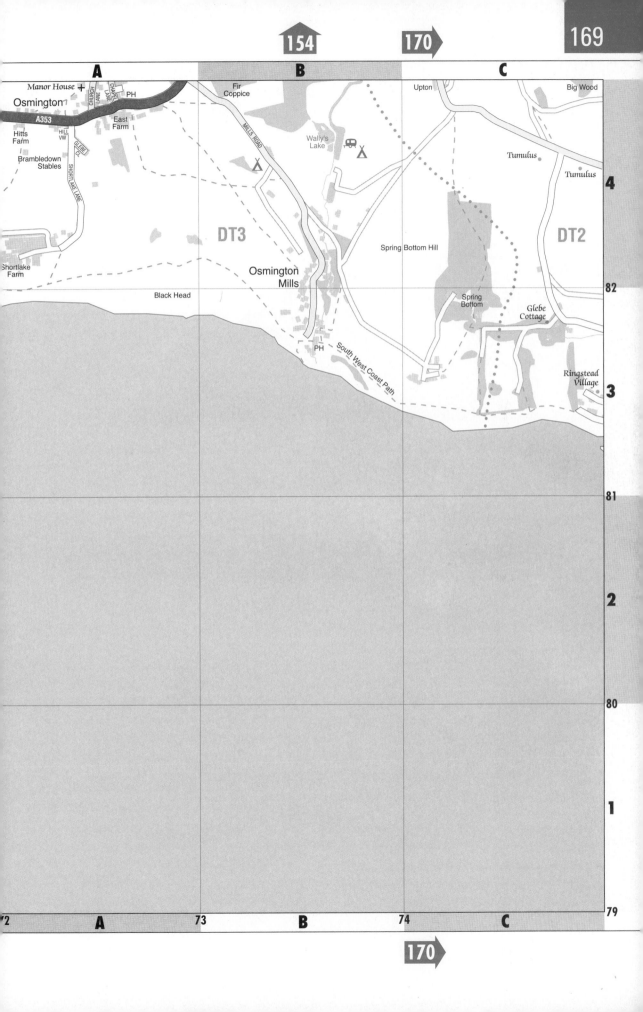

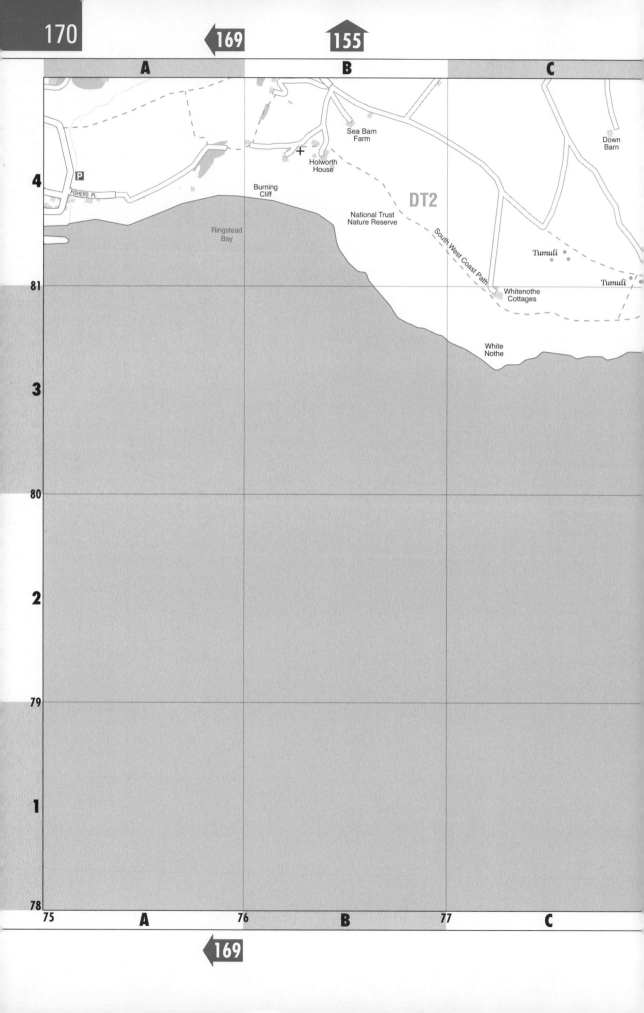

A

B

C

P

FISHERS PL

4

Burning
Cliff

Sea Barn
Farm

Holworth
House

Down
Barn

DT2

Ringstead
Bay

National Trust
Nature Reserve

81

South West Coast Path

Tumuli

Tumuli

Whitenothe
Cottages

White
Nothe

3

80

2

79

1

78

75

A

76

B

77

C

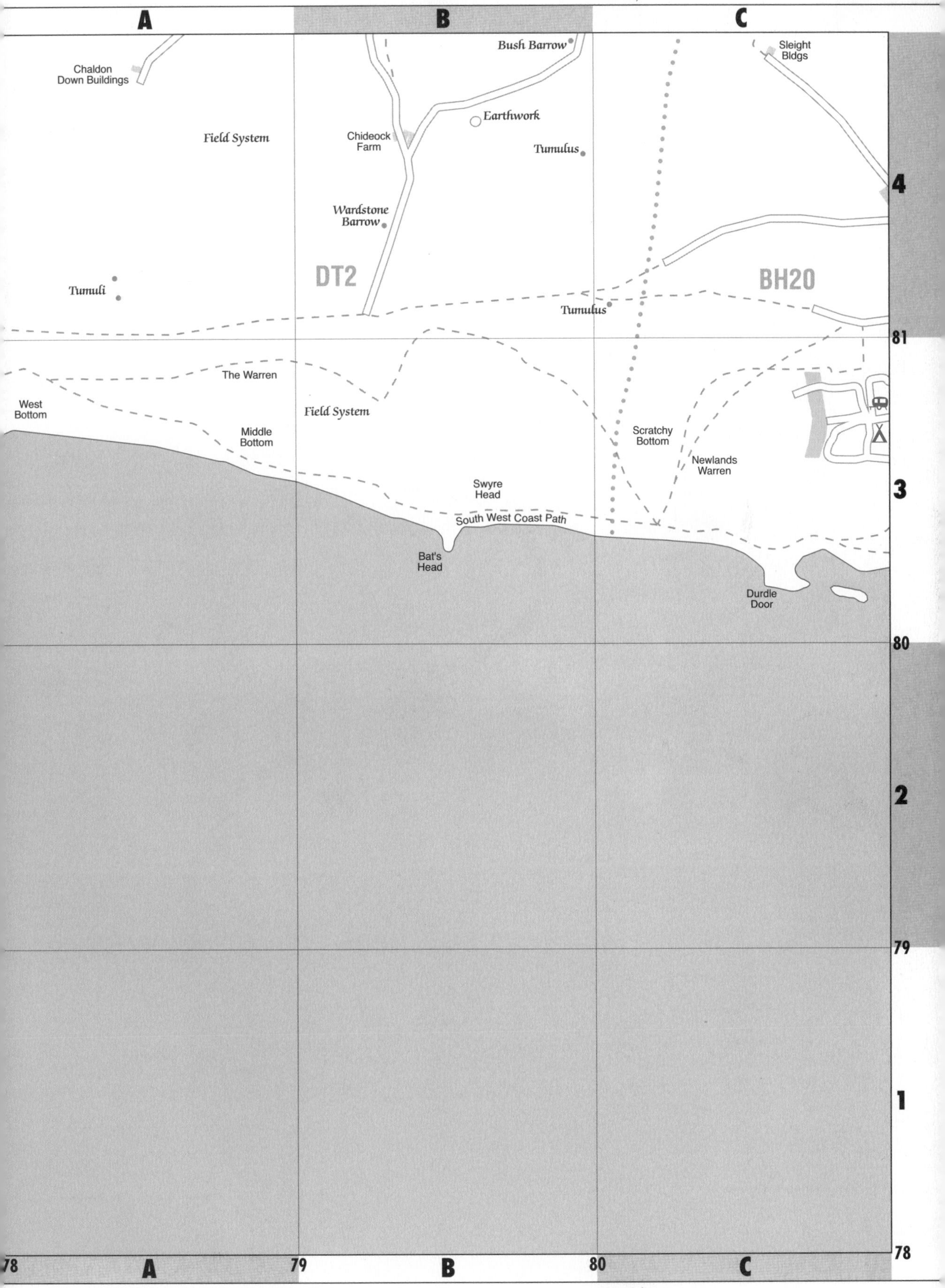

A   B   C

Chaldon Down Buildings

Field System

Bush Barrow

Earthwork

Chideock Farm

Tumulus

Wardstone Barrow

Sleight Bldgs

DT2

BH20

4

Tumuli

Tumulus

Tumulus

81

The Warren

Field System

West Bottom

Middle Bottom

Scratchy Bottom

Newlands Warren

3

Swyre Head

South West Coast Path

Bat's Head

Durdle Door

80

2

79

1

78

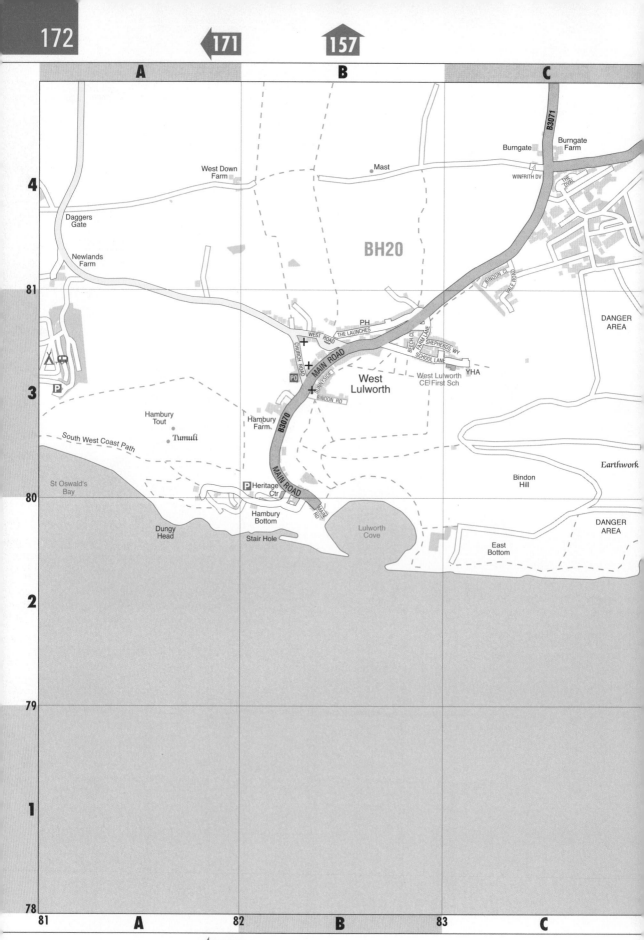

A B C

4

BH20

West Down Farm

Mast

Burngate

Burngate Farm

B3071

WINFRITH DV

THE OVAL

Daggers Gate

Newlands Farm

81

BINDON CL

VALE ROAD

DANGER AREA

PH

THE LAUNCHES

WEST ROAD

BEECH CL

FARM LANE

SHEPHERDS WY

SCHOOL LANE

YHA

CHURCH ROAD

MAIN ROAD

PO

SUNNYSIDE

West Lulworth CE First Sch

3

Hambury Tout

Tumuli

Hambury Farm

BINDON RD

West Lulworth

South West Coast Path

B3070

MAIN ROAD

Earthwork

St Oswald's Bay

P

Heritage Ctr

Bindon Hill

80

Dungy Head

Hambury Bottom

Stair Hole

MAIN RD

Lulworth Cove

East Bottom

DANGER AREA

2

79

1

78

A
B
C

Observation
Tower
P
B3070

East
Lulworth
PH

Milldown

Water
Barrows

DANGER AREA

Ferny
Barrows

Broom's
Plantation

Old Marl
Plantation

DANGER
AREA

Tumuli

4

Lulworth
Camp

BH20

Bower's
Coppice

Tumulus

Monastery
Farm

81

Bindon
Range

Maiden
Plantation

Rings
Hill

Flower's
Barrow
(Hill Fort)

Tumuli

3

Tumuli

Halcombe
Vale

DANGER
AREA

Bindon
Plantation

South West Coast Path

Arish
Mell

Cockpit
Head

Worbarrow
Bay

80

Mupe Bay

Mupe
Rocks

Worbarrow
Tout

2

79

1

78

A   B   C

Tumuli

Whiteway
Plantation

4

DANGER
AREA

Povington
Wood

West
Creech Hill

Povington
Hill

DANGER AREA

Alms
Grove

81

Whiteway
Hill

BH20

Rook
Grove

North
Egliston

3

Baltington

Long
Copse

Tyneham
+

Tyneham
Museum

Tyneham House
(remains of)

Tyneham
Great Wood

P

Tyneham
Farm

80

Worbarrow

South
Egliston

Gold
Down

South West Coast Path

Tyneham
Cap

2

Gad Cliff

DANGER
AREA

Brandy
Bay

79

Housebarrow
Bay

Broad
Bench

1

78

Great Wood

GRANGE HILL

Grange Arch

Woolland Grove

Ridgeway Hill

P ✕

Purbeck Hills

Bottom Coppice

4

Lutton Gwyle

DANGER AREA

Steeple

Horse Coppice

Whiteway Farm

Ash Coppice

Manor Farm

The Manor House

81

Lutton

+

Blackmanston Farm

Corfe River

Thornhill's Coppice

Steeple Leaze Farm

Steeple Leaze Wood

Harp Stone

3

Pole Coppice

Beach Coppice

Hyde Wood

Kimmeridge Farm

P

80

BH20

Kimmeridge Coppice

+

PO

Kimmeridge

Smedmore Hill

Higher Stonehips

2

DANGER AREA

Lower Stonehips

Oil Well

Newmead Plantation

Gaulter Gap

Metherhills

P

79

Kimmeridge Bay

Grange Plantation

Smedmore House

Barn Dairy

1

Harry's Wood

South West Coast Path

Swalland Farm

78

A B C

Heath View

+

Church
Farm

Church
Knowle

PH

Barneston
Manor

Glebe
Farm

Animal
Sanctuary

Bucknowle
House

Isle of Purbeck

4

Cemy

P

HOLLANDS
CLOSE

WEST STREET

WEBBER
CL.

West Bucknowle
House

81

Puddlemill
Farm

Tumuli

East
Orchard

Corfe Common

Bridle
Farm

West Orchard
Farm

3

Chettle Wood

Blashenwell
Farm

West
Lynch

Lynch
Farm

BH20

Willwood Plantation

80

Bradle
Barn

Orchard Hill
Farm

KINGSTON HILL

WEST ST

THE LANE

WEST STREET

P

+

2

Newfoundland

+

PH

Kingston

Quarry Wood

P

The Plantation

SOUTH STREET

79

Polar Wood

John Strange
Wood

1

Long Wood

Encombe
House

Westhill
Farm

Swyre Wood

Tumulus

Broadley
Wood

Swyre Head

Westhill
Wood

78

Big Wood

Field Systems

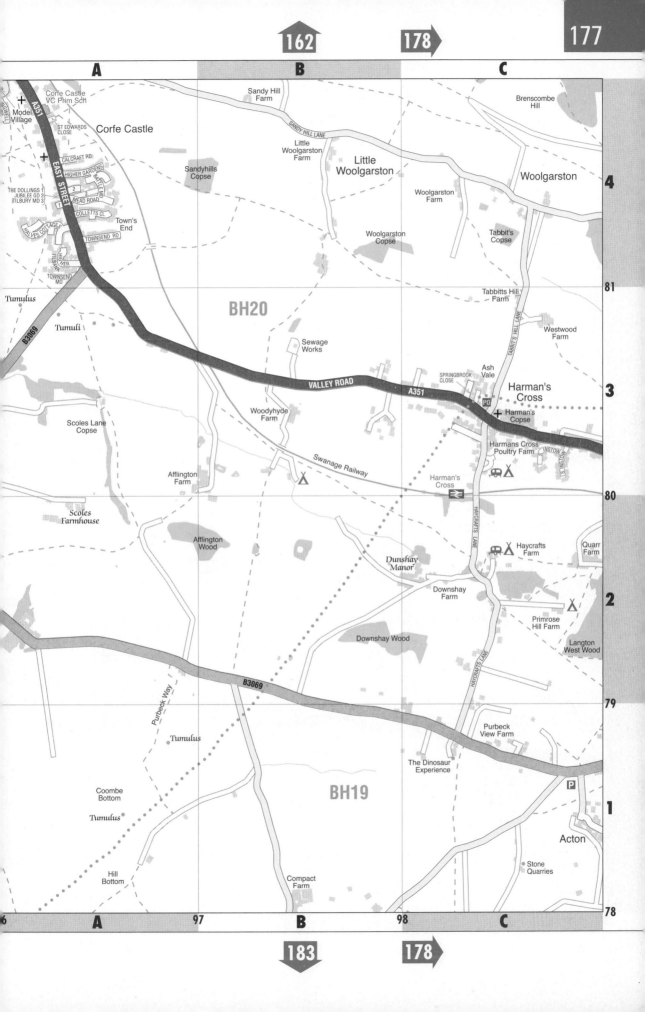

A   **B**   **C**

Corfe Castle
VC Prim Sch

Model
Village

ST EDWARDS
CLOSE

Corfe Castle

CALCRAFT RD

HIGHER GARDENS

THE DOLLINGS 1
JUBILEE GD 2
TILBURY MD 3

MEAD ROAD

COLLETTS CL

Town's
End

TOWNSEND RD

HALVES COTTAGES

HIGHCLIFFE

TOWNSEND
MD

EAST STREET

A351

B3069

Tumulus

Tumuli

BH20

Sandy Hill
Farm

SANDY HILL LANE

Little
Woolgarston
Farm

Little
Woolgarston

Woolgarston
Farm

Sandyhills
Copse

Woolgarston
Copse

Brenscombe
Hill

Woolgarston

Tabbit's
Copse

4

81

Tabbitts Hill
Farm

TABBIT'S HILL LANE

Westwood
Farm

Sewage
Works

Ash
Vale

SPRINGBROOK
CLOSE

Harman's
Cross

3

VALLEY ROAD

A351

PO

Harman's
Copse

Scoles Lane
Copse

Woodyhyde
Farm

Harmans Cross
Poultry Farm

INSTOW BRIDGE ST

Swanage Railway

Afflington
Farm

Harman's
Cross

*Scoles
Farmhouse*

Afflington
Wood

Dunshay
Manor

Downshay
Farm

Haycrafts
Farm

Quarr
Farm

HAYCRAFTS LANE

Primrose
Hill Farm

Langton
West Wood

2

80

Downshay Wood

Purbeck Way

B3069

Tumulus

BH19

Purbeck
View Farm

79

Coombe
Bottom

The Dinosaur
Experience

P

Tumulus

Acton

1

Hill
Bottom

Compact
Farm

Stone
Quarries

78

6   **A**   97   **B**   98   **C**

A **B** **C**

4

Rempstone
Wood

King's
Wood

Kingswood
Farm

B3351

Tumuli

Isle of Purbeck
Golf Club
CH

B3351

Dean
Hill

Currendon
Farm

Purbeck Way

Godlingston
Hill

Ailwood
Farm

BH20

Oakwood
Farm

Nine
Barrow Down

Giant's
Grave Bottom

Tumuli

81

Lower
Grove

Knaveswell
Farm

Knitson
Farm

Strip
Lynchets

Round
Down

Cow Leaze
Copse

Godlingston
Wood

3

Rickett's
Copse

North Lease
Farm

BURNHAM'S LANE

Godlingston
Manor

WASHPOND LANE

Seekings
Farm

New
Buildings

Marsh
Copse

Cemy

Greyseed
Farm

VALLEY ROAD

80

LC

Herston
Yards Farm

BH19

New
Barn

Square
Copse

Alderbury
Copse

Quince
Hill Wood

Great Linnings
Copse

2

Langton
West Wood

Wilkswood
Farm

Talbot's Wood

A351

VALLEY ROAD

Serrell's
Copse

Litchfield
Copse

Swanage Railway

Victoria Avenue
Industrial Estate

AIGBURTH
RD

CRACK LANE

Farm
Wood

Herston
Halt

ANCASTER
RD

Herston

Swanage Cty
Middle Sch

79

Castle
View

Langton
Matravers

Langton Matravers
Prim Sch

NORTH ST

ST GEORGE'S
CL

LWR
STEPPES

STEPPES

SERRELLS MD

THREE ACRE LA

COOMBE HILL

Coombe
Farm

HIGH STREET

A351

Superstore

PO

FINDLAY PL

Herston
CE Sch

BEALE'S WAY

JUBILE RD

STEER RD

PRIDEAUX RD

HIGH STREET

B3069

EAST DROVE

BH19

GYPSHAYES

Putlake
Adventure Farm

STEPPES
HILL

Field Studies
Centre

HIGH ST

HOLMES RD

SYDENHAM RD

DAY'S RD

MARSH WY

BELL ST

SHIRLEY CL

ASH CL

WILL'S RD

CAPSTAN FIELD

COOMS FIELD RD

BURNFORD DROVE

BH18

PRIEST'S WAY

1

Lighthouse

Langton
House

Belle Vue
Farm

78

Blacklands

Verney
Farm

99 **A** **00** **B** **01** **C**

C1
1 VICTORIA AV
2 LEESON CL
3 GLOBE CL
4 ANVIL CL
5 ALDERBURY CL
6 KINGSWOOD CL
7 SHOTTSFORD CL
8 BAY VIEW
9 CASTERBRIDGE CL
10 SHASTON CL
11 SANDBOURNE CL
12 QUARRY CL
13 PURBECK VW

A1
1 STATION PL
2 NEWTON MANOR CL
3 WEST DR
4 NEWTON RI
5 HOWARD RD
6 GORDON RD
7 HANBURY RD
8 CHURCH HL
9 CHURCH CL
10 SPRINGFIELD RD
11 ELDON TR
12 FOXHILL CL
13 COWLEASE
14 MANWELL'S LA
15 DUNFORD PL
16 QUEENS MD

B1
1 COMMERCIAL RD
2 CORNWALL RD
3 MOUNT PLEASANT LA
4 EXETER RD
5 MARSHALL ROW
6 BURT'S PL
7 BELVEDERE RD
8 KNOLLSEA CL
9 SALISBURY RD

A4
1 BEACHVIEW CL
2 JASMINE WY
3 CUNNINGHAM CL
4 FOSSETT WY
5 WESTHILL CL

B4
1 LANEHOUSE ROCKS RD
2 WYKE RD
3 LYMES CL
4 CHURCHILL CL
5 SWAFFIELD GD
6 MARTLEAVES CL

7 BELFIELD PK DR
8 BUXTON CL
9 BELFIELD CL
10 CARRINGTON CL
11 HILLBOURNE RD
12 DOWNCLOSE

C4
1 CROSS RD
2 CONNAUGHT RD

A · B · C

4

Little Bridge Farm

Camp Road

Mandeville Road
Mandeville Cl
Barrow Rise
Lea Rd
North Rd
Overland
Brants La
Tebor Rd

B3157

Wyke Road
Church Knap
Mast
Boulton Cl
Rodden Cl
Courtauld Dr
Belfield Park Ave
Lodge Wy

All Saints CE Sch

Buxton Road
A354
Whitecross Dr
Lynch La
Green La
St Martin's Rd
Whitecliffe Copse

Southlands

Khartoum Road
Southdown Rd
Southill Rd
PO
Sudan Road
Clearmount Rd
Old Castle Road
Belle Vue Road

Western Ledges

PORTLAND ROAD
All Saints Rd
Woolaway
Chamberlaine Rd
PO
Shrubbery La
Castle Hl Rd

Liby

Wyke Regis Inf Sch
Sunnyside Road
Rylands Lane
St David's Rd
St Anne's Rd
Aragon Cl
Clever Cl
Penry Cl
Boleyn Cr
Sandsfoot Castle

Collins La
High Street
West Bay Cr
Victoria Rd
Pirates La
Westhill Road
Chalbury Cr
Williams Avenue
Broadmeadow
Hillcrest Road
Howard Cl

Wyke Regis

Wyke Regis CE Jun Sch
Boney's Dr
Fleet Vw
South Rd
Gallwey Rd
Park Md
Marlborough Ave
Broughton Cl
Hillbourne Road
Stone Road
Doncaster Road
Douglas Road

77

Chesil Beach

Nature Reserve

DT4

Wyke Regis Community & Sports Centre
LESSINGHAM AV
Ryemead
Wacker Cres
Langton Ave
A354
Merley Rd
Denwent Rd
Dover Road
Dundee Road
Lyndale Rd
Dumbarton Rd
Sandpiper Rd
Osprey Rd
Bowman Cl

South West Coast Path

1 KINGFISHER CL
2 AVOCET CL
3 WHITEHEAD DR
4 SMALLMOUTH CL
5 FERRYMANS WY

3

Chesil Beach Holiday Village

PH
PORTLAND RD
Ferry Bridge
Small Mouth
Boat Yard

76

West Bay

Chesil Beach

Chesil Beach Visitor Centre

P

64 · 65
78 · 78
DT3
DT4
75
77 · 77
74
64 · 65

2

Portland Beach Road

Parasite Academy

75

1

A354

Works

DT5

74

65 · 66 · 67

A · B · C

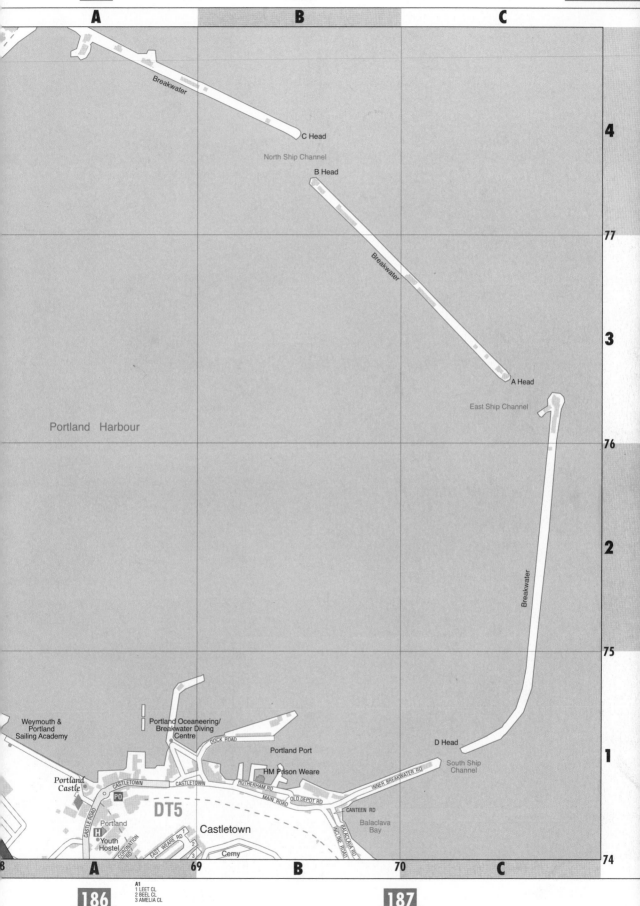

A **B** **C**

Breakwater

C Head

North Ship Channel

B Head

Breakwater

A Head

East Ship Channel

Portland   Harbour

Breakwater

Weymouth &
Portland
Sailing Academy

Portland Oceaneering/
Breakwater Diving
Centre

DOCK ROAD

Portland Port

D Head

South Ship
Channel

HM Prison Weare

Portland
Castle

CASTLETOWN

CASTLETOWN

ROTHERHAM RD

INNER BREAKWATER RD

PO

MAIN ROAD

OLD DEPOT RD

CANTEEN RD

DT5

Castletown

Portland
Youth
Hostel

EAST WEARE RD

CORONATION RD

Cemy

Balaclava
Bay

BALACLAVA RD

INCLINE ROAD

4

77

3

76

2

75

1

74

A 69 **B** 70 **C**

A1
1 LEET CL
2 BEEL CL
3 AMELIA CL

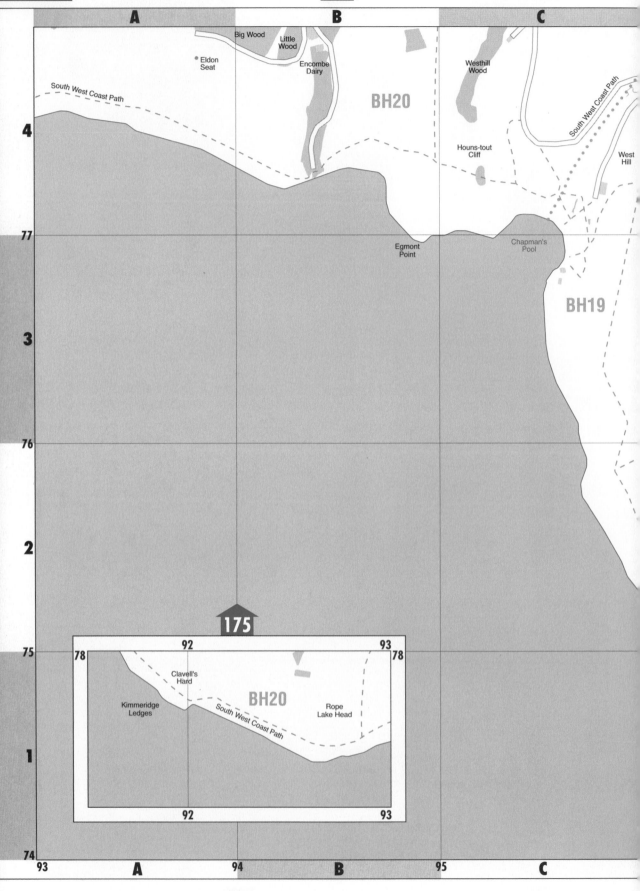

A

B

C

Big Wood

Little
Wood

Eldon
Seat

Encombe
Dairy

South West Coast Path

Westhill
Wood

South West Coast Path

BH20

Houns-tout
Cliff

West
Hill

4

77

Egmont
Point

Chapman's
Pool

BH19

3

76

2

92

93

75

78

78

Clavell's
Hard

Kimmeridge
Ledges

BH20

South West Coast Path

Rope
Lake Head

1

92

93

74

93

94

95

A

B

C

Hill Bottom

Stone Quarry

NEWFOUNDLAND CLOSE

Eastington Farm

P

Renscombe Farm

P   RENSCOMBE ROAD

PH

4

P   PO   PIKES LANE

National Trust Nature Reserve

WESTON ROAD

Worth Matravers

Weston Farm

WINSPIT RD

WINSPIT ROAD

WINSPIT ROAD

BONVILS ROAD

77

Bonvils

BH19

Seacombe Bottom

South West Coast Path

Strip Lynchets

Seacombe Cliff

3

Emmetts Hill

Winspit Bottom

East Man

Strip Lynchets

West Man

Winspit

76

Tumulus

St Aldhelm's Chapel

South West Coast Path

2

St Aldhelm's or St Alban's Head

75

1

183
178

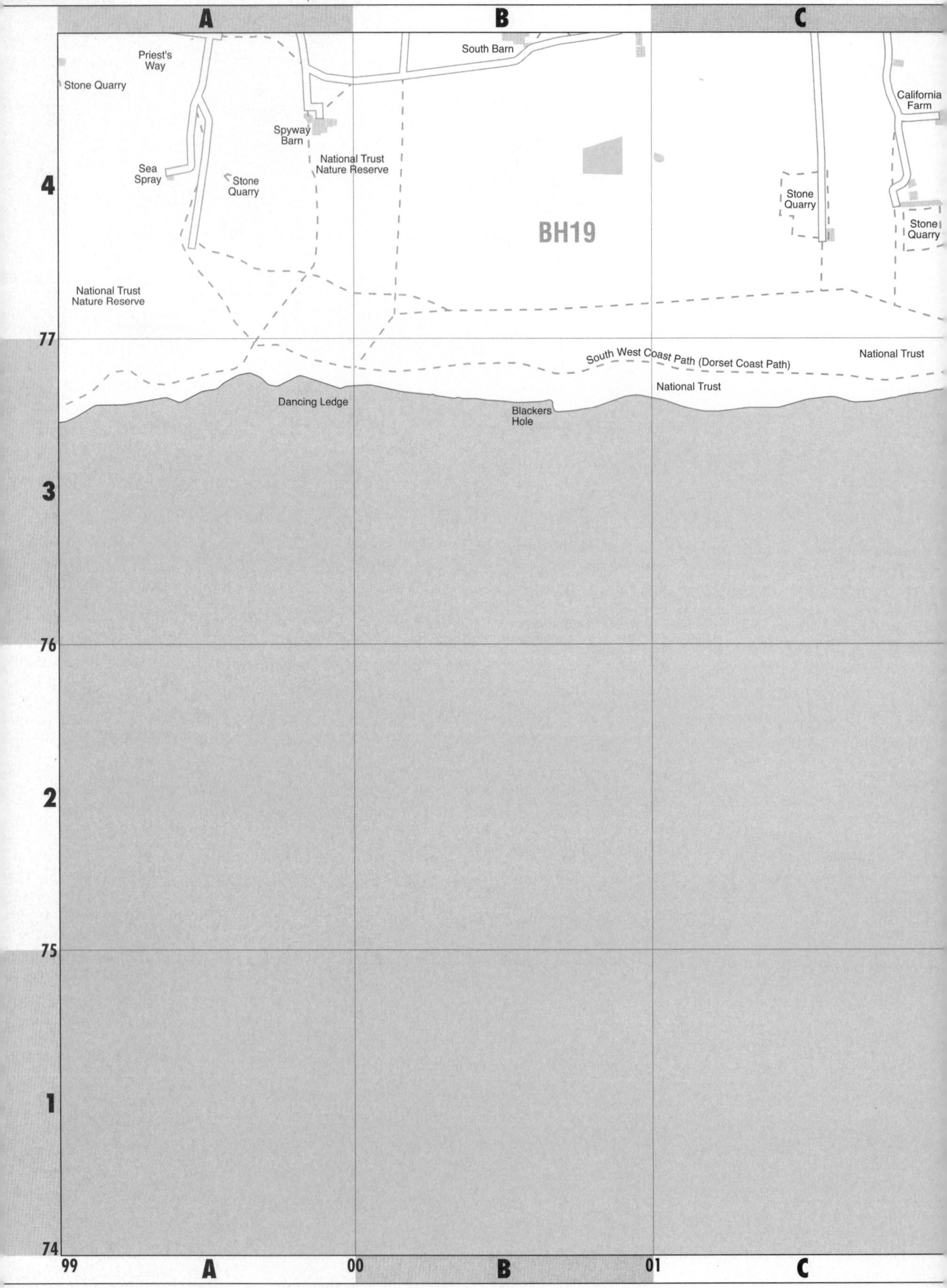

A **B** **C**

Stone Quarry

Priest's
Way

South Barn

California
Farm

Spyway
Barn

Sea
Spray

Stone
Quarry

National Trust
Nature Reserve

4

Stone
Quarry

Stone
Quarry

BH19

National Trust
Nature Reserve

77

South West Coast Path (Dorset Coast Path)

National Trust

National Trust

Dancing Ledge

Blackers
Hole

3

76

2

75

1

74

99 **A** 00 **B** 01 **C**

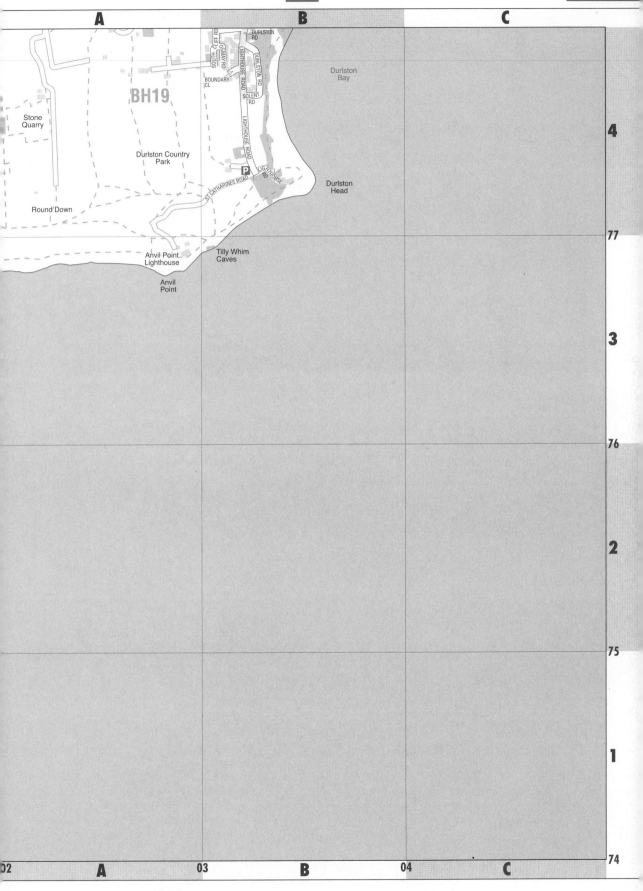

BH19

Stone Quarry

Durlston Country Park

Round Down

DURLSTON RD

CLIFF RD

OSMAY RD

SOUTH

BOUNDARY CL

DURLSTON ROAD

DURLSTON RD

SOLENT RD

LIGHTHOUSE ROAD

ST CATHARINES ROAD

LIGHTHOUSE RD

P

Durlston Bay

Durlston Head

Anvil Point Lighthouse

Tilly Whim Caves

Anvil Point

4

77

3

76

2

75

1

74

180 | 181

FORTUNESWELL

Chesil

Parrys Dive Centre & Sch

Brackenbury Cty Inf Sch
Chesil Cove
Underhill Junior Sch

Wallsend Cove

Field System

DT5

Old Higher Lighthouse

Cave Hole

Old Lower Light

Portland Bird Observatory

PH

West Weare

West Cliff

Tout Quarry Nature Reserve

Quarry

Sculpture Park

TRADECROFT

Clay Ope

Pulpit Rock

Trinity House Lighthouse

Visitor Centre

Bill of Portland

Cemy

Royal Manor Sch

DT5

BLINDMERE RD

WOOLCOMBE RD

BLACKNOR RD

WESTCLIFF RD

Blacknor

Mutton Cove

GROSVENOR ROAD

St. Georges Cty Inf Sch

Weston

COURTLANDS RD

Southwell Prim Sch

Southwell

REAP LANE

AVALANCHE ROAD

BOWN HILL

CHURCH

WEST WAY

SOUTH WAY

SWEET HILL LANE

UNDERMEDGE RD

SWEET HILL RD

A   B   C

Cemy

H.M. Prison

The Verne

Masts

LLYCOMBE ROAD VERNE HILL RD

GLACIS

NEW GROUND

P

INCLINE ROAD

INCLINE ROAD

King's Pier

4

East Weare

ISLE OF PORTLAND

73

Verne Yeates

Admiralty Quarries

Incline Rd

Grove Cty Inf Sch

Grove

HM Young Offender Institution

Portland United Football Club

GROVE ROAD

AUGUSTA CL

AUGUSTA WAY

RUFUS RD

VICTORIA RD

WITHIES CFT

SHEPHERDS CFT

GROVE RD

Mast

3

INMOSTHAY

EASTON LANE

A354

DT5

VICTORIA PL

EASTON ST

CROWN FARM TR

SHEPHERDS CROFT

LONG ACRE

NEW STREET

BROADCROFT GARDENS

Easton

STRAITS

DELHI LA

MOORFIELD RD

PARK RD

PARK RD

PARK RD

Liby

PO

1

3

4

Quarry

Grove Cliff

Durdle Pier

72

Portland Tophill Jun Sch

WANGHAM

BUMPERS LA

Bottom Coombe Quarries

Portland Mus.

CHURCH OPE

PENNSYLVANIA ROAD

Church (rems. of)

Rufus Castle

Hotel

2

WESTON STREET

Church Ope Cove

71

P

SOUTHWELL ROAD

1

Freshwater Bay

A2
1 REFORNE CL
2 STATION RD
3 LADYMDCL
4 EASTON SQ

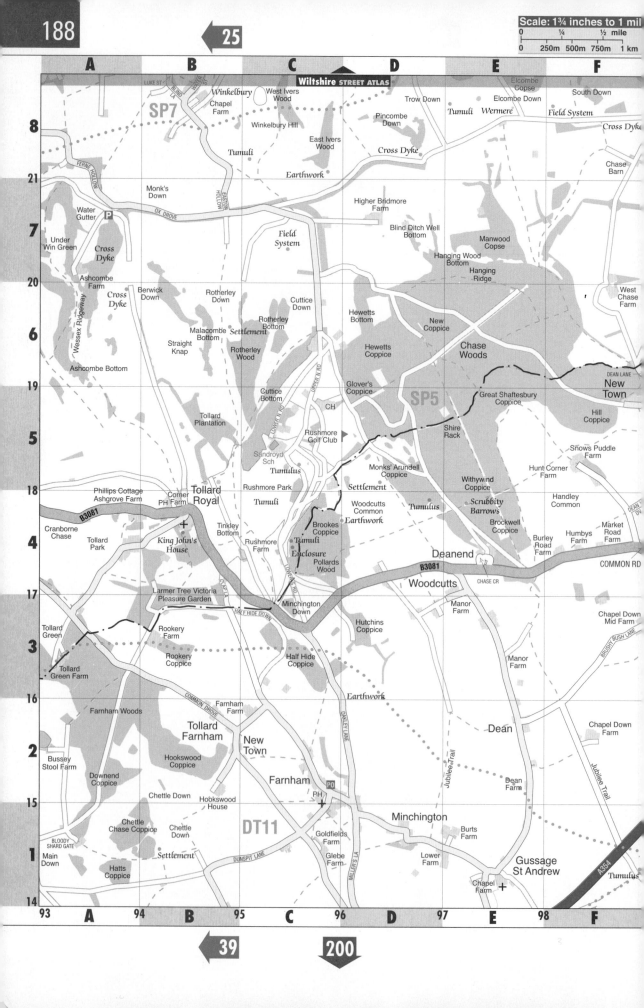

Wiltshire STREET ATLAS

8
SP7
Winkelbury
West Ivers Wood
Chapel Farm
Winkelbury Hill
Trow Down
Elcombe Copse
Elcombe Down
South Down
Tumuli
Wernere
Field System
Cross Dyke
Tumuli
East Ivers Wood
Pincombe Down
Cross Dyke

21
Earthwork
Chase Barn
Monk's Down

7
Water Gutter
Under Win Green
Cross Dyke
Field System
Higher Bridmore Farm
Blind Ditch Well Bottom
Manwood Copse
Hanging Wood Bottom
Hanging Ridge

20
Ashcombe Farm
Berwick Down
Rotherley Down
Cuttice Down
Hewetts Bottom
New Coppice
Chase Woods
West Chase Farm
Cross Dyke

6
Wessex Ridgeway
Malacombe Bottom
Straight Knap
Settlement
Rotherley Bottom
Rotherley Wood
Hewetts Coppice
Ashcombe Bottom

19
Cuttice Bottom
Glover's Coppice
SP5
Great Shaftesbury Coppice
DEAN LANE
New Town
Hill Coppice

5
Tollard Plantation
CH
Rushmore Golf Club
Shire Rack
Snows Puddle Farm
Hunt Corner Farm
Sandroyd Sch
Tumulus
Monks' Arundell Coppice
Withywind Coppice

18
Phillips Cottage
Ashgrove Farm
Corner PH Farm
Tollard Royal
Rushmore Park
Settlement
Tumulus
Scrubbity Barrows
Handley Common
Tumuli
Tinkley Bottom
Woodcutts Common Earthwork
Brockwell Coppice

4
Cranborne Chase
Tollard Park
King John's House
Rushmore Farm
Brookes Coppice
Tumuli
Enclosure
Pollards Wood
Deanend
Burley Road Farm
Humbys Farm
Market Road Farm
B3081
B3081
COMMON RD

17
Larmer Tree Victoria Pleasure Garden
Half Hide Down
Minchington Down
Woodcutts
Chase Cr
Manor Farm
Chapel Down Mid Farm

3
Tollard Green
Rookery Farm
Rookery Coppice
Half Hide Coppice
Hutchins Coppice
Manor Farm
Tollard Green Farm
Earthwork

16
Farnham Woods
Common Drive
Farnham Farm
Earthwork
Dean
Chapel Down Farm

2
Bussey Stool Farm
Tollard Farnham
Hookswood Coppice
New Town
Farnham
Jubilee Trail
Dean Farm
Jubilee Trail
Downend Coppice

15
Chettle Down
Hookswood House
PO
PH
Minchington
Burts Farm
Gussage St Andrew

1
Bloody Shard Gate
Main Down
Chettle Chase Coppice
Chettle Down
Settlement
DT11
Goldfields Farm
Glebe Farm
Dunspit Lane
Miller's La
Darkley Lane
Lower Farm
Chapel Farm
A354
Tumulus
Hatts Coppice

14

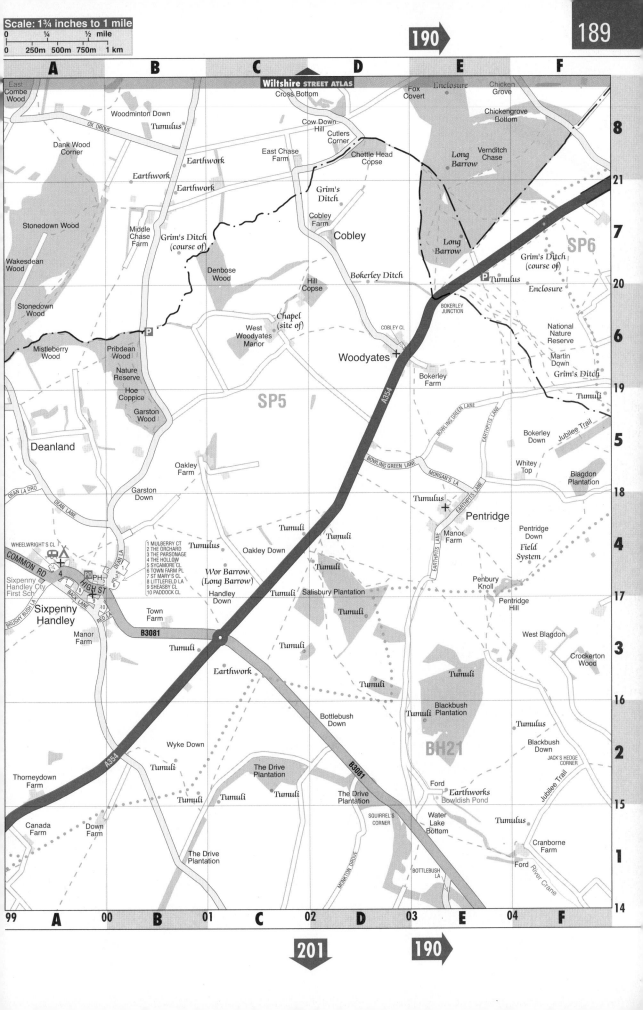

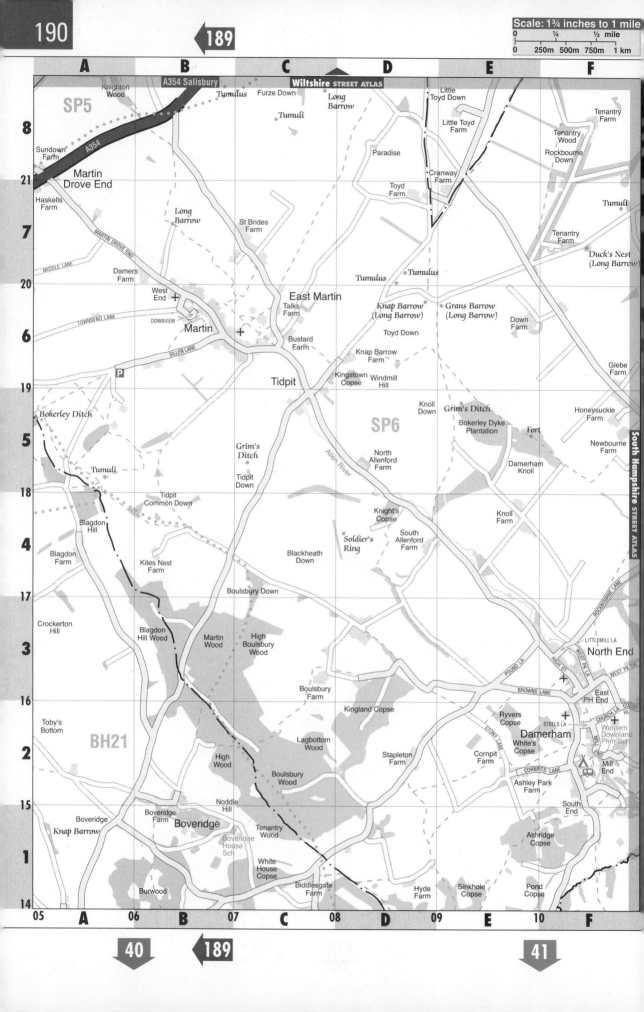

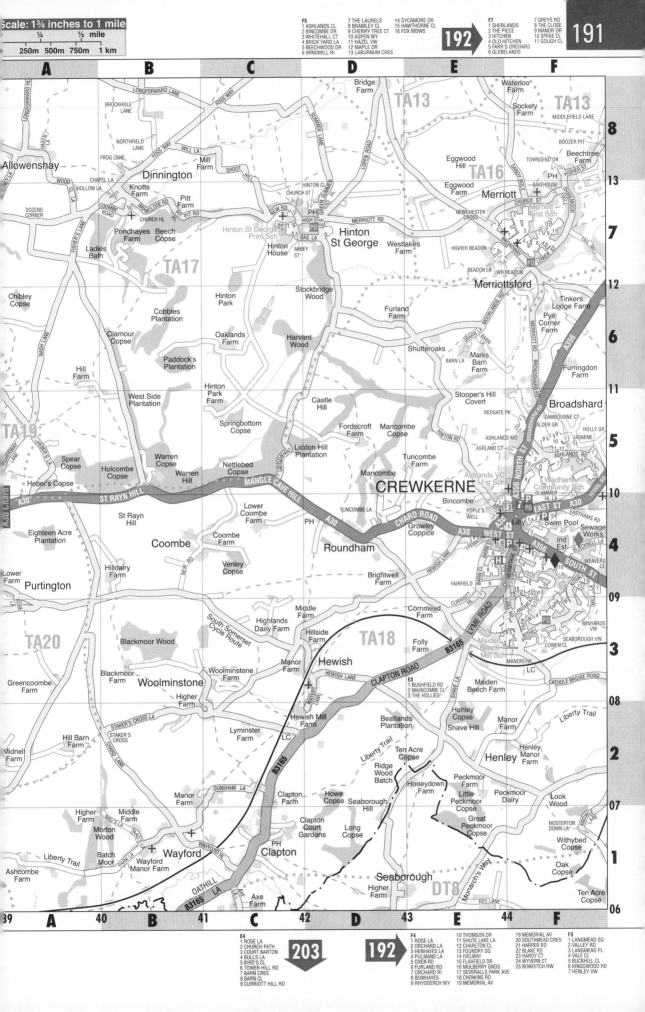

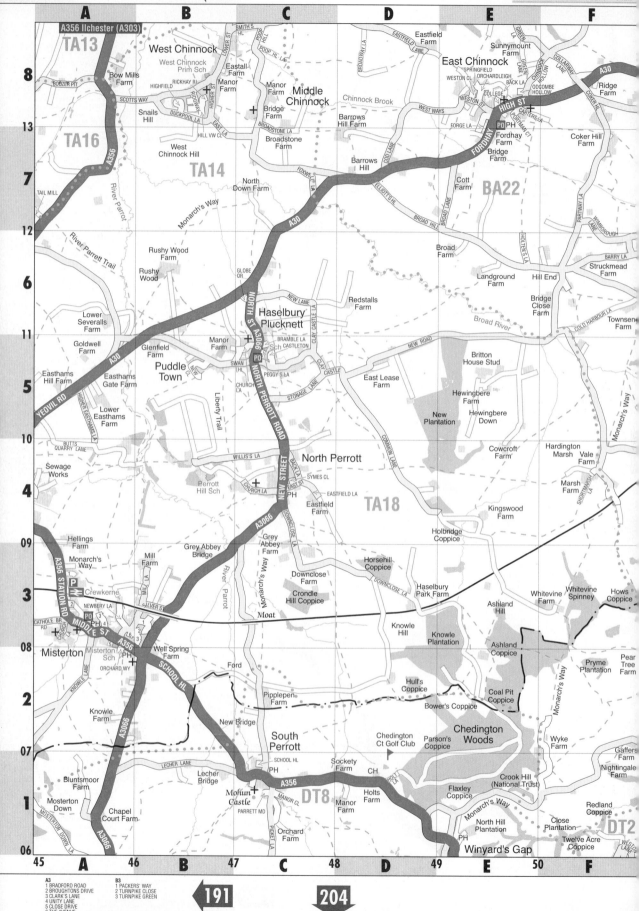

Scale: 1¾ inches to 1 mil

0   ¼   ½ mile
0 250m 500m 750m 1 km

A **B** **C** **D** **E** **F**

A356 Ilchester (A303)

TA13

West Chinnock
West Chinnock Prim Sch

SMITH'S HL
POOL HILL
POOP HL LA

East Chinnock
Sunnymount Farm
Springfield
WESTON CL ORCHARDLEIGH
BACK LA
COLLARWAY LANE
A30

8

Bow Mills Farm
BOOZER PIT
SCOTTS WAY
Eastall Farm
Manor Farm
HIGHFIELD
RICKHAY RI
HIGHER ST
Manor Farm
Middle Chinnock
Chinnock Brook
COLLEGE
WESTON ST
HIGH ST
FORDHAY
PO PH
Ridge Farm
Coker Hill Farm

TA16

13

Snails Hill
DUCKPOOL LA
EAST LA
Bridge Farm
Broadstone LA
Barrows Hill Farm
WEST WAYS
FORGE LA
Fordhay Bridge Farm
COKER HL

West Chinnock Hill
HILL VW CL
Broadstone Farm
FOXWELL LA
Barrows Hill
COLD LANE
Cott Farm
BA22

7

TA14
North Down Farm
ELLIOTT'S HL
BROAD HILL
BROAD LANE
HOLTEN'S LA
PARTWAY LA
WIMBOROUGH LANE

Tail Mill
River Parrot
A356
Monarch's Way
A30
Broad Farm
Landground Farm
Hill End
BARRY LA
Struckmead Farm
Townsen Farm

12

River Parrett Trail
Rushy Wood Farm
GLOBE OR
New Lane
Redstalls Farm
Broad River
Bridge Close Farm
COLD HARBOUR LA

6

Rushy Wood
Haselbury Plucknett
NORTH ST A3066
CLAY CASTLE LA
NEW ROAD
Britton House Stud

Lower Severalls Farm
Manor Farm
BRAMBLE LA CASTLETON
Sch
Hewingbere Farm

11

Goldwell Farm
Glenfield Farm
Puddle Town
SWAN HL
PO
PEGGY'S LA
CASTLE
East Lease Farm
Hewingbere Down

Easthams Hill Farm
YEOVIL RD
A30
Easthams Gate Farm
NEW
CHURCH LA
STONAGE LANE
New Plantation

5

Lower Easthams Farm
HIGHER EASTHAMS LA
Liberty Trail
NORTH PERROTT ROAD
COMMON LANE
Cowcroft Farm
Hardington Marsh Vale Farm

BUTTS QUARRY LANE
WILLIS'S LA
North Perrott
TA18
Kingswood Farm
Marsh Farm
SHORTMARSH LA

10

Sewage Works
Perrott Hill Sch
BACK LA
SYMES CL
Eastfield LA
Holbridge Coppice

4

Hellings Farm
Grey Abbey Bridge
CHURCH LA
NEW STREET
PH
EASTFIELD LA
Eastfield Farm

Monarch's Way
Mill Farm
A3066
DOWNCLOSE LA
Grey Abbey Farm
Horsehill Coppice
Whitevine Farm
Whitevine Spinney
Hows Coppice

09

A356 STATION RD
P
Crewkerne
River Parrot
Downclose Farm
DOWNCLOSE LA
Haselbury Park Farm
Ashland Hill
Pryme Plantation
Pear Tree Farm

3

NEWBERY LA
PO
PH
MILL LA
SILVER ST
Crondle Hill Coppice
Moat
Knowle Hill
Knowle Plantation
Ashland Coppice

CATHOLE BR RD
MIDDLE ST
A356
Well Spring Farm
Ford
Pipplepen Farm
Hull's Coppice
Coal Pit Coppice
Monarch's Way

08

Misterton
Misterton Sch
PH
ORCHARD WY
Bower's Coppice
Chedington Woods
Wyke Farm
Gaffers

2

Knowle Farm
SCHOOL HL
New Bridge
South Perrott
Chedington Ct Golf Club
Parson's Coppice
Crook Hill (National Trust)
Nightingale Farm

Bluntsmoor Farm
LECHER LANE
Lecher Bridge
SCHOOL HL
PH
Sockety Farm
CH
HOLT LA
Flaxley Coppice
Redland Coppice

07

Mosterton Down
A3066
Mohun Castle
PARRETT MD
A356
MANOR CL
DT8
Holts Farm
Monarch's Way
North Hill Plantation
Close Plantation
Twelve Acre Coppice
DT2

1

MOSTERTON DOWN LA
Chapel Court Farm
Orchard Farm
PICKET LA
Manor Farm
PH
Winyard's Gap

06

45 **A** 46 **B** 47 **C** 48 **D** 49 **E** 50 **F**

A3
1 BRADFORD ROAD
2 BROUGHTONS DRIVE
3 CLARK'S LANE
4 UNITY LANE
5 CLOSE DRIVE
6 THE AVENUE

B3
1 PACKERS' WAY
2 TURNPIKE CLOSE
3 TURNPIKE GREEN

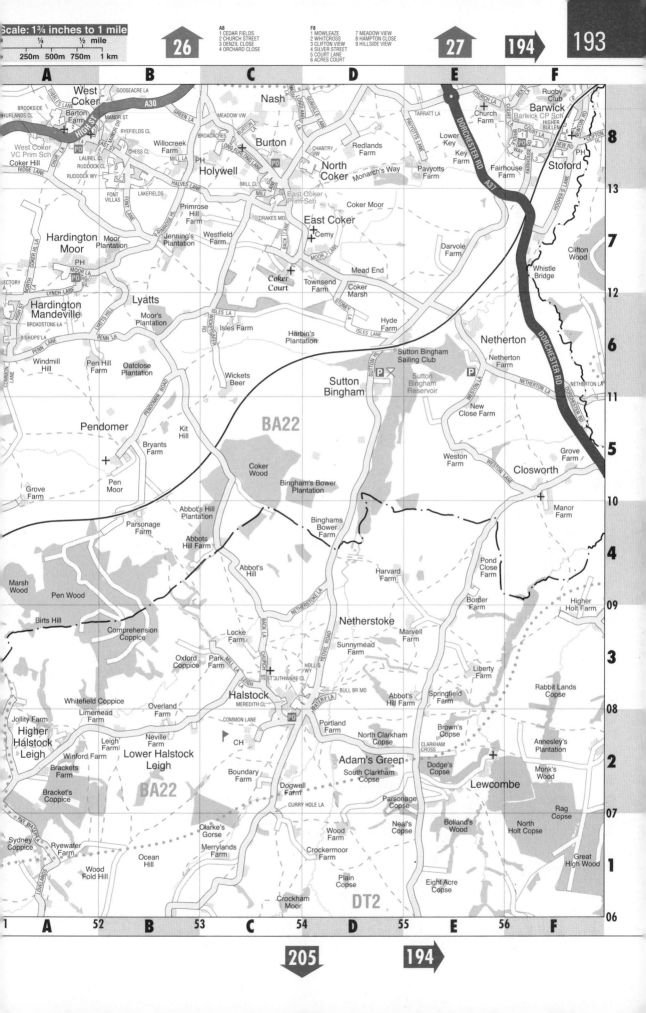

A8
1 CEDAR FIELDS
2 CHURCH STREET
3 DENZIL CLOSE
4 ORCHARD CLOSE

F8
1 MOWLEAZE
2 WHITCROSS
3 CLIFTON VIEW
4 SILVER STREET
5 COURT LANE
6 ACRES COURT
7 MEADOW VIEW
8 HAMPTON CLOSE
9 HILLSIDE VIEW

A B C D E F

Row 8
West Coker
Gooseacre La
Nash
Barwick
Rugby Club
Barwick CP Sch
Higher Bullen
Brookside
Hurlands Cl
Barton Farm
Manor St
Ryefields Cl
Meadow Vw
Burton
Tarratt La
Church Farm
Stoford
West Coker VC Prim Sch
Coker Hill
Ridge Lane
Ruddock Cl
Ruddock Wy
Willocreek Farm
Chess Cl
Broadacres
Long Furlong Lane
Holywell
North Coker
Redlands Farm
Chantry Vw
Monarch's Way
Lower Key
Key Farm
Pavyotts Farm
Fairhouse Farm
Dorchester Rd

Row 13
Lakefields
Font Villas
Halves Lane
Mill La
Mill Cl
East Coker Prim Sch
Coker Moor
Pavyotts La

Row 7
Hardington Moor
Moor Plantation
Primrose Hill Farm
Jenning's Plantation
Westfield Farm
Drakes Md
East Coker
Cemy
Mead End
Darvole Farm
Clifton Wood
Whistle Bridge

Row 12
Rectory La
North Coker Hl La
Moor La
PH
PO
Pig Hl
Lynch Lane
Lyatts
Coker Court
Townsend Farm
Coker Marsh
Netherton
Netherton Farm

Row 6
Hardington Mandeville
Broadstone La
Bishops's La
Penn Lane
Moor's Plantation
Lyatts Hill
Penn La
Isles La
Wickets-Beer Rd
Isles Farm
Harbin's Plantation
Stoney La
Isles Lane
Hyde Farm
Sutton Bingham Sailing Club
Netherton Lane
Dorchester Rd

Row 11
Windmill Hill
Common Lane
Pen Hill Farm
Oatclose Plantation
Wickets Beer
Pendomer Road
Sutton Bingham
Sutton Bingham Reservoir
New Close Farm

Row 5
Pendomer
Bryants Farm
Kit Hill
BA22
Weston Farm
Weston Lane
Closworth
Grove Farm
Grove Farm
Pen Moor
Coker Wood
Bingham's Bower Plantation

Row 10
Abbot's Hill Plantation
Parsonage Farm
Abbots Hill Farm
Binghams Bower Farm
Manor Farm

Row 4
Marsh Wood
Pen Wood
Abbot's Hill
Harvard Farm
Pond Close Farm

Row 09
Birts Hill
Comprehension Coppice
Netherstoke La
Border Farm
Higher Holt Farm

Row 3
Locke Farm
Back La
Netherstoke
Marvell Farm
Oxford Coppice
Church St
Park Farm
Mill La
Peovil Road
Sunnymead Farm
Liberty Farm
Rabbit Lands Copse

Row 08
Whitefield Coppice
Overland Farm
St Juthware Cl
Hollis Wy
Halstock
Meredith Cl
Bull Br Md
Abbot's Hill Farm
Springfield Farm
Brown's Copse
Annesley's Plantation

Row 2
Jollity Farm
Higher Halstock Leigh
Limemead Farm
Neville Farm
Lower Halstock Leigh
Winford Farm
Common Lane
CH
Portland Farm
North Clarkham Copse
Clarkham Cross
Dodge's Copse
Lewcombe
Monk's Wood
Brackets Farm
BA22
Boundary Farm
Adam's Green
South Clarkham Copse
Parsonage Copse

Row 07
Bracket's Coppice
Dogwell Farm
Curry Hole La
Neal's Copse
Bolland's Wood
North Holt Copse
Rag Copse

Row 1
Sydney Coppice
Rye Water La
Ryewater Farm
Love Lane
Clarke's Gorse
Merrylands Farm
Ocean Hill
Wood Farm
Crockermoor Farm
Eight Acre Copse
Great High Wood

Row 06
Wood Fold Hill
Crockham Moor
Plain Copse
DT2

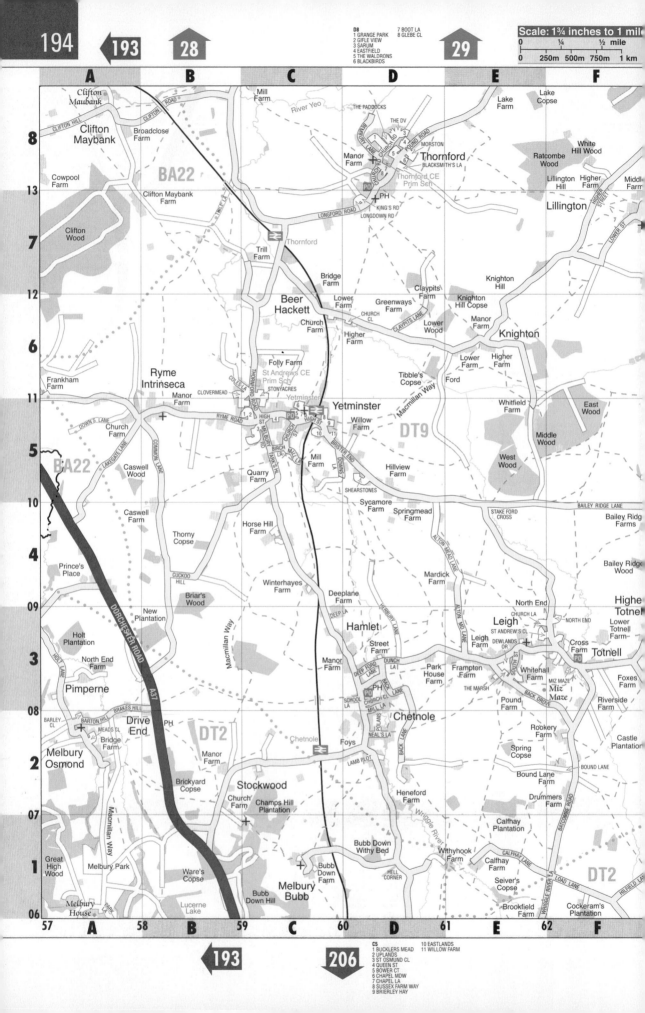

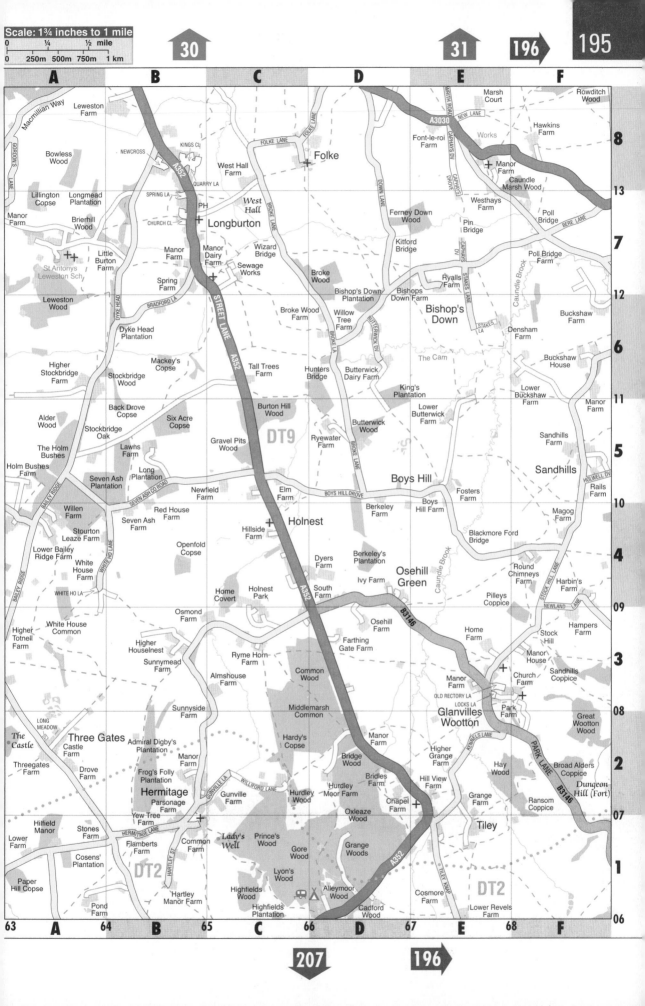

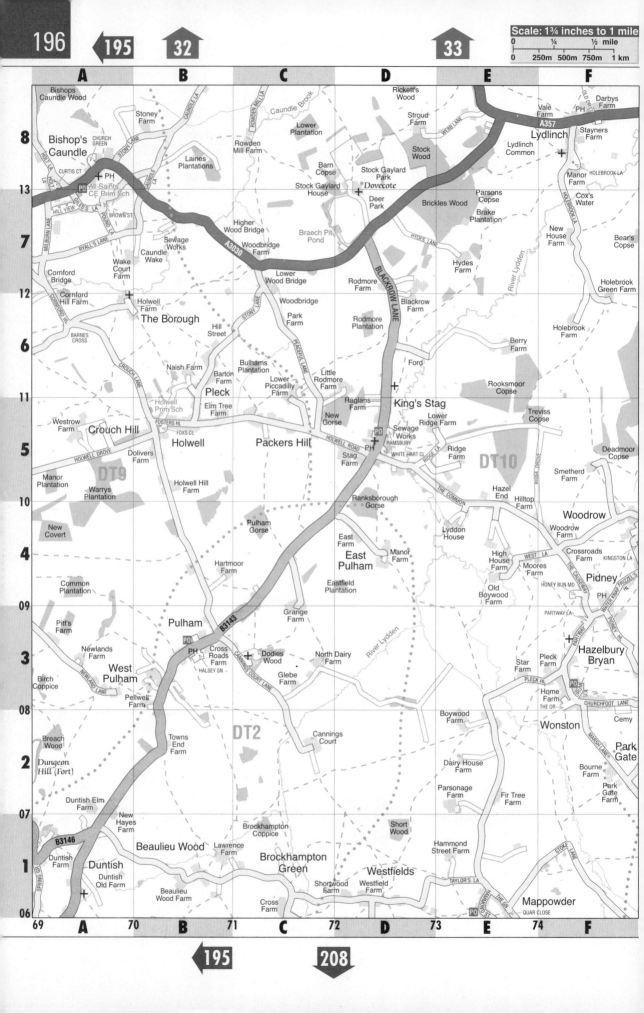

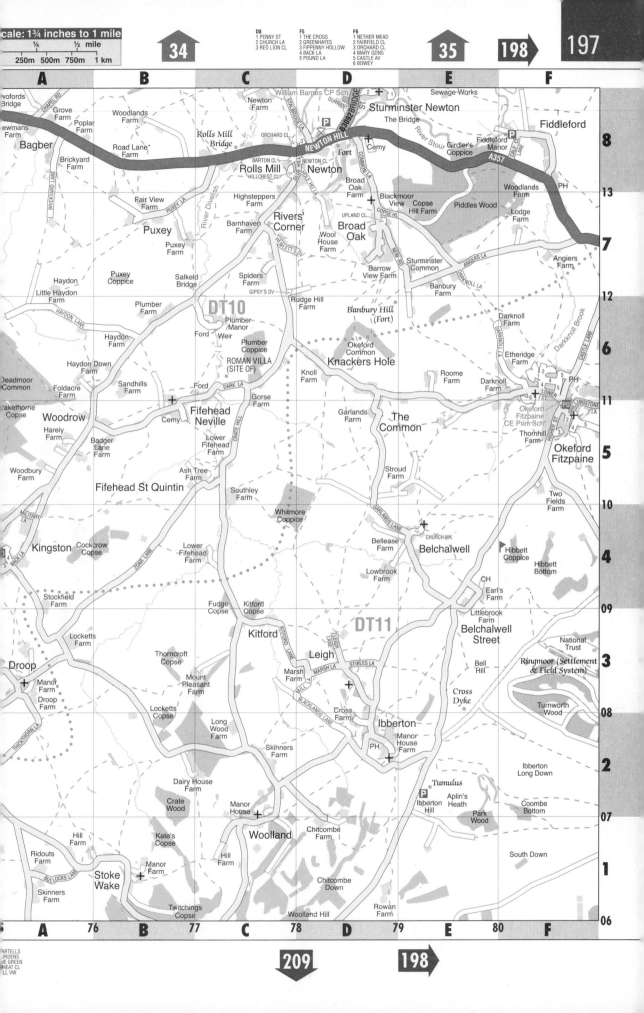

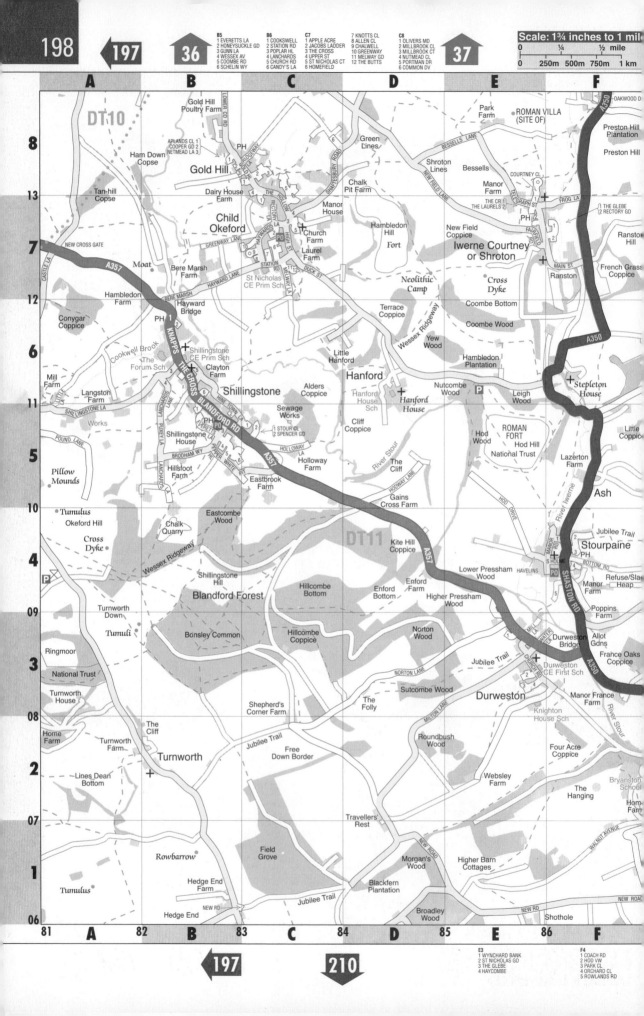

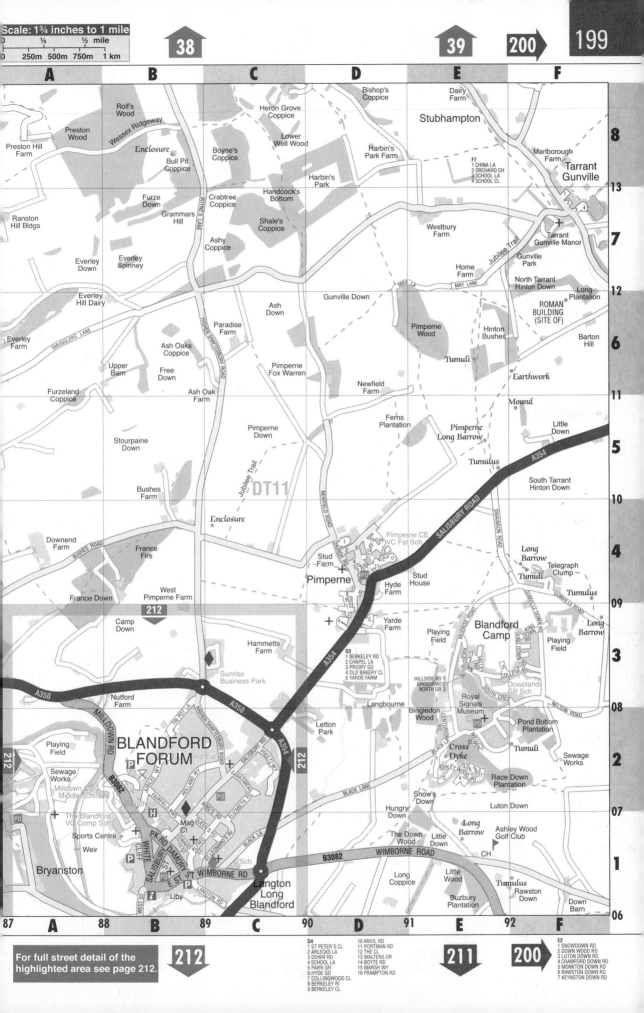

A   B   C   D   E   F

Preston Wood
Rolf's Wood
Preston Hill Farm
Wessex Ridgeway
Enclosure
Bull Pit Coppice
Boyne's Coppice
Heron Grove Coppice
Lower Well Wood
Bishop's Coppice
Harbin's Park Farm
Dairy Farm
Stubhampton
Marlborough
Tarrant Gunville

F7
1 CHINA LA
2 ORCHARD CH
3 SCHOOL LA
4 SCHOOL CL

Furze Down
Crabtree Coppice
Grammars Hill
Handcock's Bottom
Harbin's Park
Ashy Coppice
Shale's Coppice
Ranston Hill Bldgs
Westbury Farm
Tarrant Gunville Manor

Everley Down
Everley Spinney
Ash Coppice
Tarrant Gunville Manor
Gunville Park
North Tarrant Hinton Down
Long Plantation

Everley Hill Dairy
Ash Down
Gunville Down
Home Farm
May Lane
May La
ROMAN BUILDING (SITE OF)
Barton Hill

Smugglers Lane
Ash Oaks Coppice
Paradise Farm
Pimperne Wood
Hinton Bushes
Earthwork

Everley Farm
Upper Barn
Free Down
Pimperne Fox Warren
Tumuli
Mound

Furzeland Coppice
Ash Oak Farm
Newfield Farm
Little Down

Stourpaine Down
Pimperne Down
Ferns Plantation
Pimperne Long Barrow
A354
Tumulus
South Tarrant Hinton Down

Bushes Farm
Jubilee Trail
DT11
Enclosure
Pimperne CE VC Fst Sch
SALISBURY ROAD
SWANSON ROAD
Long Barrow
Telegraph Clump
Tumuli
Tumulus

Downend Farm
France Firs
Bushes Road
Hammetts Farm
Stud Farm
Pimperne
Hyde Farm
Stud House
Playing Field
Blandford Camp
Long Barrow

D3
1 BERKELEY RD
2 CHAPEL LA
3 PRIORY GD
4 OLD BAKERY CL
5 YARDE FARM

France Down
West Pimperne Farm
212
Camp Down
Yarde Farm
Langbourne
MILGERS ROAD
KING DOWN RD
GUNVILLE DOWN RD
GUNVILLE ROAD
Playing Field
Long Barrow

A350
Sunrise Business Park
A354
Letton Park
HILLSIDE RD 1
CROSSWAY 2
NORTH GR 3
Royal Signals Museum
Downlands CP Sch
COLLEGE RD
SOUTH CRES
NELSON ROAD
Pond Bottom Plantation

Nutford Farm
MILLDOWN RD
HIGHER SHAFTESBURY RD
212
Bingledon Wood
CENTURION CL
Tumuli
Sewage Works

Playing Field
BLANDFORD FORUM
Ind Est
Black Lane
Snow's Down
Cross Dyke
ASHLEY WOOD CL
Race Down Plantation

212
Sewage Works
B3082
Milldown CE Middle Sch
Hungry Down
The Down Wood
Little Down
Long Barrow
Ashley Wood Golf Club

PO
The Blandford VC Comp Sch
Sports Centre
Weir
Bryanston
Mag Ct
WIMBORNE RD
Langton Long Blandford
B3082
WIMBORNE ROAD
Little Wood
Long Coppice
Little Wood
Buzbury Plantation
Tumulus
Rawston Down
Down Barn

87   88   89   90   91   92

A   B   C   D   E   F

For full street detail of the highlighted area see page 212.

212   211   200

D4
1 ST PETER'S CL
2 ARLECKS LA
3 DOWN RD
4 SCHOOL LA
5 PARR GR
6 HYDE GD
7 COLLINGWOOD CL
8 BERKELEY RI
9 BERKELEY CL
10 ANVIL RD
11 PORTMAN RD
12 THE CL
13 WALTERS DR
14 BOYTE RD
15 MARSH WY
16 FRAMPTON RD

E2
1 SNOWDOWN RD
2 DOWN WOOD RD
3 LUTON DOWN RD
4 CRAWFORD DOWN RD
5 MONKTON DOWN RD
6 RAWSTON DOWN RD
7 KEYNSTON DOWN RD

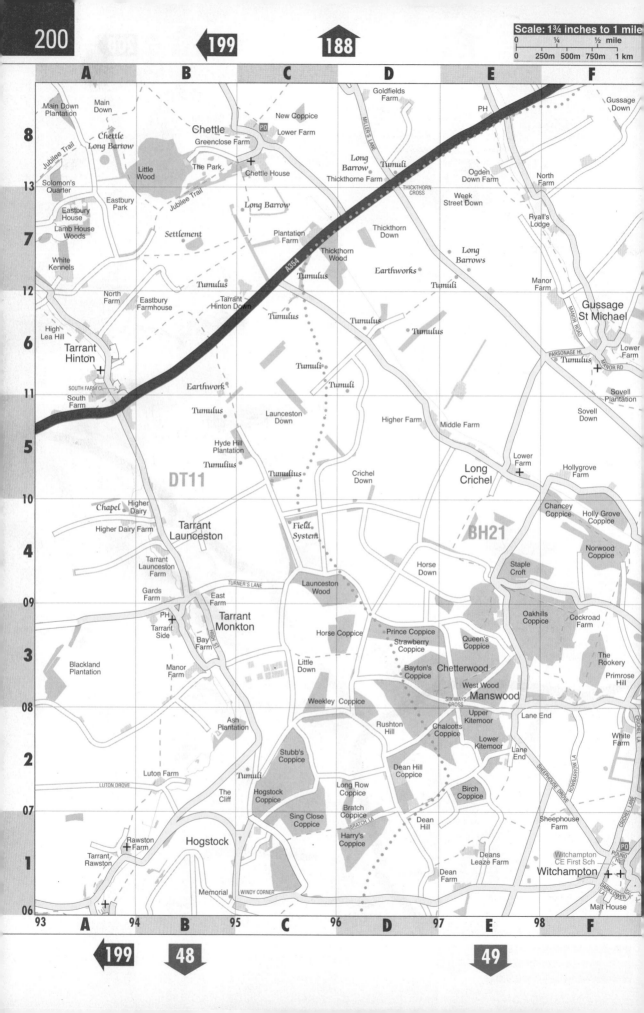

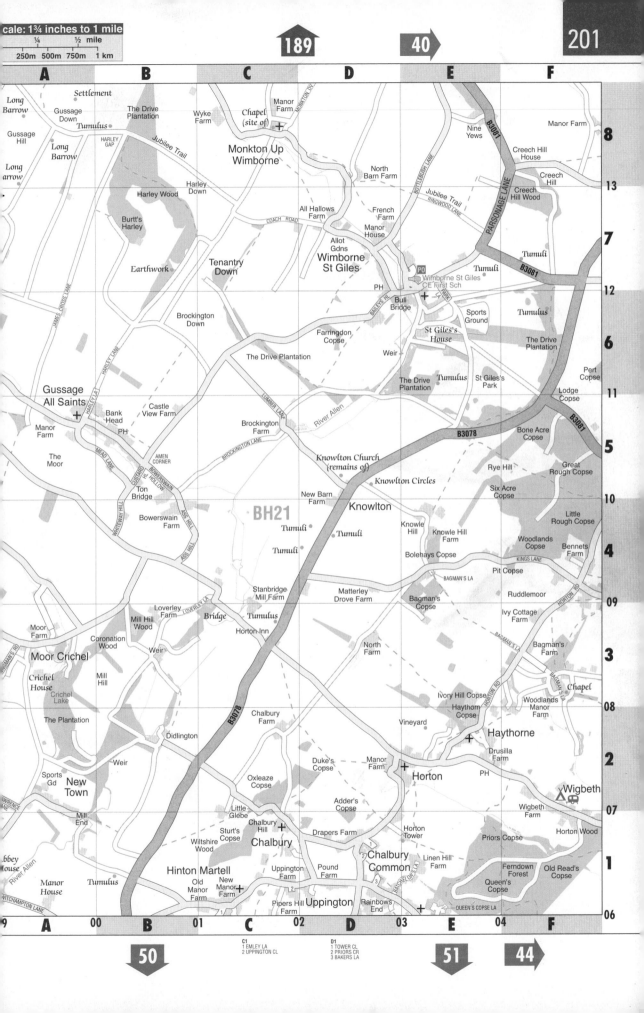

Long Barrow
Settlement
Gussage Down
Tumulus
The Drive Plantation
Wyke Farm
Chapel (site of)
Manor Farm
Nine Yews
Manor Farm

Gussage Hill
HARLEY GAP
Jubilee Trail
Monkton Up Wimborne
Creech Hill House
B3081
Creech Hill

Long Barrow
Harley Wood
Harley Down
North Barn Farm
Jubilee Trail
RINGWOOD LANE
Creech Hill Wood

Long arrow
COACH ROAD
All Hallows Farm
French Farm
BOTTLEBUSH LANE

Burtt's Harley
Manor House
Tumuli
B3081

Earthwork
Tenantry Down
Wimborne St Giles
Allot Gdns
Tumuli

PH
Wimborne St Giles CE First Sch
PO
PARSONAGE LANE

Brockington Down
Farringdon Copse
Bull Bridge
BAILEY'S HL
St Giles's House
Sports Ground
Tumulus
The Drive Plantation

JAMES CROSS LANE
The Drive Plantation
Weir
The Drive Plantation
Tumulus
St Giles's Park
Pert Copse

Gussage All Saints
Castle View Farm
LUMBER LANE
River Allen
Lodge Copse

Bank Head
PH
Brockington Farm
B3078
Bone Acre Copse
B3081

Manor Farm
HARLEY LANE
AMEN CORNER
BROCKINGTON LANE
Knowlton Church (remains of)
Rye Hill
Great Rough Copse

The Moor
MEAD LANE
BOWERSWAIN N. HOLLOW
Knowlton Circles
Six Acre Copse

Ton Bridge
Bowerswain Farm
New Barn Farm
Knowlton
Knowle Hill
Knowle Hill Farm
Woodlands Copse
Little Rough Copse

WHITEWAY HILL
ASS HILL
DUSTARD
BH21
Tumuli
Tumuli
Bolehays Copse
KINGS LANE
Bennets Farm

Moor Farm
Stanbridge Mill Farm
Matterley Drove Farm
Bagman's Copse
BAGMAN'S LA
Pit Copse
Ruddlemoor
HORTON RD

Loverley Farm
LOVERLEY LA
Bridge
Tumulus
Ivy Cottage Farm

Coronation Wood
Mill Hill Wood
Horton Inn
North Farm
BAGMAN'S LA
Bagman's Farm
BAGMAN'S LA

Moor Crichel
Weir
Mill Hill
Chapel

Crichel House
Crichel Lake
Ivory Hill Copse
Haythorn Copse
Woodlands Manor Farm

The Plantation
B3078
Didlington
Chalbury Farm
Vineyard
Haythorne
Drusilla Farm

Weir
Duke's Copse
Manor Farm
PH

Sports Gd
New Town
Oxleaze Copse
Horton
Wigbeth

Mill End
Little Glebe
Adder's Copse
Horton Tower
Wigbeth Farm

Chalbury Hill
Sturt's Copse
Chalbury
Drapers Farm
Priors Copse
Horton Wood

bbey House
River Allen
Hinton Martell
Wiltshire Wood
Chalbury Common
Horton Tower
Linen Hill Farm
Ferndown Forest
Old Read's Copse

Manor House
Tumulus
Old Manor Farm
New Manor Farm
Uppington Farm
Pound Farm
BATCHELOR'S LA
Queen's Copse

WITCHAMPTON LANE
Pipers Hill Farm
Uppington
Rainbows End
Queen's Copse LA

9   A   00   B   01   C   02   D   03   E   04   F

50

51

44

C1
1 EMLEY LA
2 UPPINGTON CL

D1
1 TOWER CL
2 PRIORS CR
3 BAKERS LA

A8
1 LANGDONS WY
2 ABBEY MS
3 WATERMEAD
4 STAPLES MD
5 DEANE WY
6 DRAKES CR
7 GULWAY MD
8 KENTS LA
9 ABBEY CL
10 KENT RD
11 LINKHAY CL
12 LINKHAY
13 CROSSWAYS
14 HOLLEYS CL
15 STOWELL LA
16 LOVERIDGE LA

Coombses
Ball's Coppice
COW DOWN RD
NEW ROAD
LEIGH LA
WHALLEY LA
Ammerham
River Axe
Wes
Woo
THE DRIFT
Leigh Farm
Bridge Farm
Trout Hall Farm
Grove Coppice
Bere Farm
Magdalen Farm
Perry Street
Marshwood Farm
Willowbed Coppice
Bridge
Forde Bridge
Baymore Coppice
MAUDLIN CROSS
SHEDICK HILL
Axeford
Forde Abbey
Copse House
Bonny Green Farm
South Chard
Ford
Hodgeditch Farm
Westmills Plantation
Goodsmore Coppice
WHEEL HO LANE
Shedrick Hill
Laymore
PH
Greenend Farm
Broadbridge Farm
Forde Grange
Chilson Common
Chard Junction
Home Farm
Compton's Coppice
Oxenleaze Coppice
Chaffeigh Farm
Weir
Westlears Farm
Forde Abbey Farm
Gribb Farm
Wessex Ridgeway
Mill
Middle Coppice
Pitmore Coppice
PARTWAY LA
Whistling Copse
TA20
Holway
Herridge Farm
Ford
Synderford
Westford Park Farm
Marlpits Plantation
Hewood Bottom
St Marys Sch
Thorncombe
Yewtree Farm
River Axe
Hewood
Hewood Bottom Coppice
ORCHARD LA
HIGH ST
Higher Holditch Farm
Lower Hewood Farm
Manor Farm
Holmbush
Monarch's Way
DT
Holditch
Gardners Farm
HOLDITCH LANE
School House
Wessex Ridgeway
River Synderford
Coggans Farm
Holditch Court
Yawlings Farm
Liberty Trail
Lower Holditch Farm
Sadborow
Buddlewall
Home Farm
Grighay Plantation
New House Farm
Tuckmill Coppice
Elmore Farm
Angels Farm
Tuckmill Farm
Beerhall Farm
Easthay Farm
Cakehorn Coppice
Grighay Coppice
Grighay Farm
Castle
Furzehill Farm
Breeches Coppice
Spearhay Coppice
Yonder Farm
Vembury Farm
Payne's Down
Doleham Coppice
Winyards Hill Coppice
Tilworth Farm
Wyld Court
Monarch's Way
Blackwater River
Ford
GASHAY LA
Hillview Farm
Coates Farm
Hawkchurch
Northay
Northay Farm
Gashay Farm
Tillworth
Piercehay Farm
PH
Hollymarsh Farm
MILL LA
NORTHAY LA
Tanyard Farm
Little Farm
BRIMLEY ROAD
Brimley
Hawkchurch Prim Sch
Westhay Farm
CULVERLAKE LA
Colmer Farm
Marshalsea
Fairwater Farm
BERRY LANE
Gladhayes Farm
EX13
PARRICKS LA
Beech Grove Farm
Pound Covert
Barcombe Farm
Hawkmoor Farm
Wellfield Farm
Foxdown Farm
Lower Checkridge Farm
Pound Farm
Pound House Farm
Bridewell Bottom
PH
Marshwoo
Higher Checkridge Farm
New House Farm
Stonebarrow Fruit Farm
Bridewell Bottom
Lambert's Castle (Fort)
DT6
Harmshay Farm
Woodhouse Farm
Scouse Lane
Roughmoor Farm
Tumulus
Nash Farm
Sminhay Farms
Woodhouse Plantations
Lambert's Castle National Trust
Nash Coppice
Babers Farm
Southmoor Farm
B3165
Woodcote Farm
Reeds Barn Farm
Fishpond Bottom
Close Coppice
Holdcroft Farm
Spearpit Coppice
Blackpool Corner
DT6
Dodpen Hill
Bridles Place Farm
ABBOTT'S WOOTTON LA

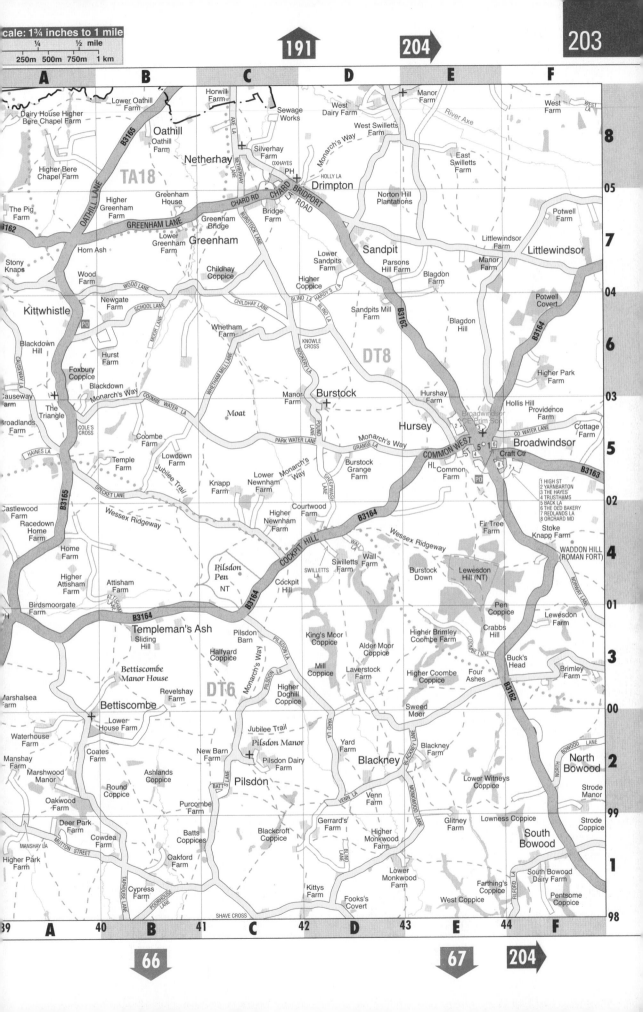

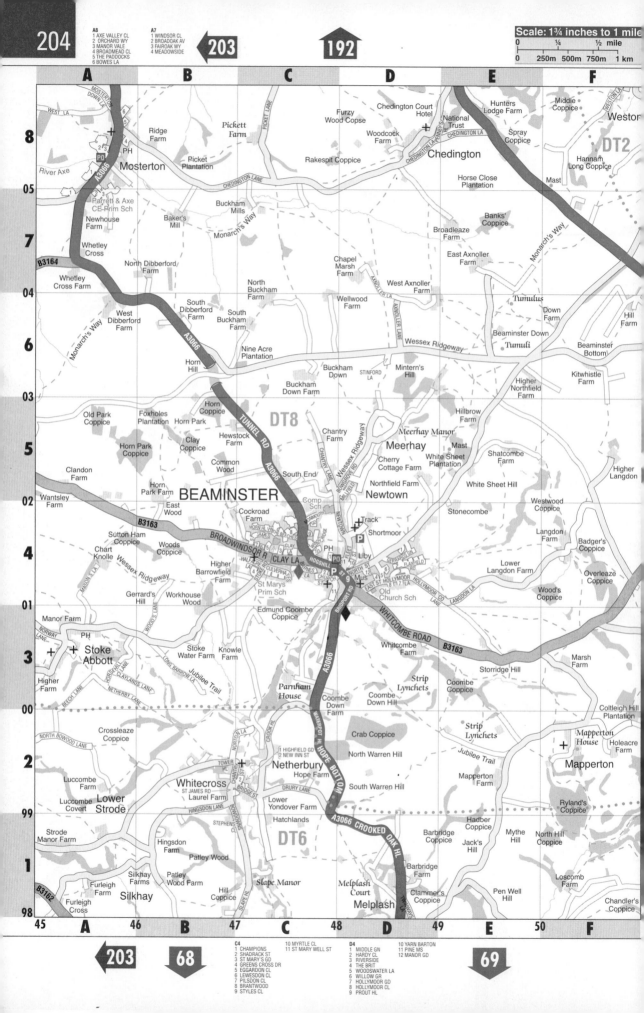

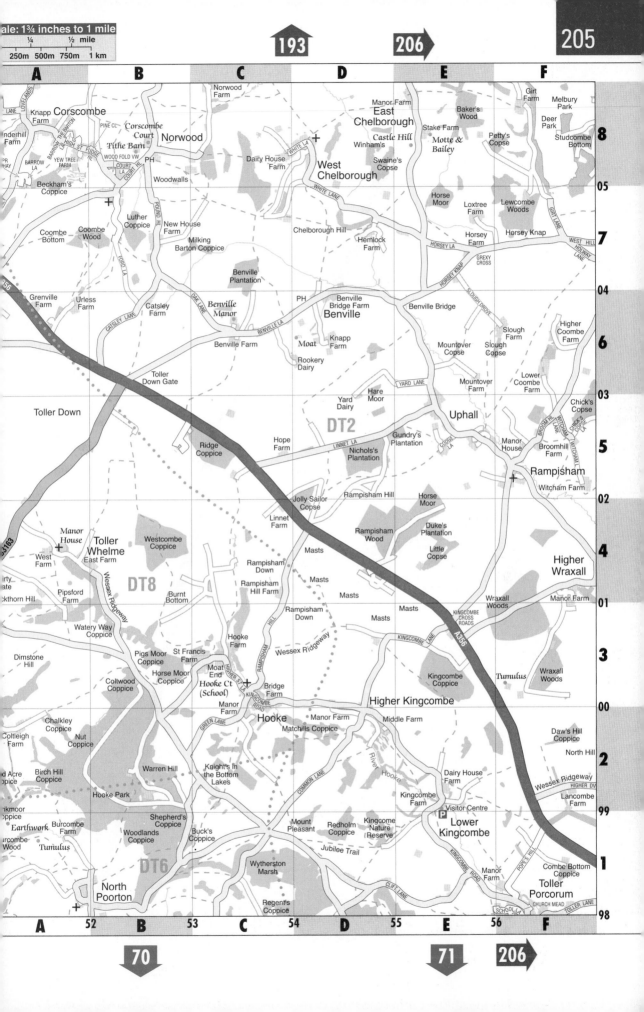

205
194

Scale: 1¾ inches to 1 mile

0 ¼ ½ mile
0 250m 500m 750m 1 km

A B C D E F

Melbury Sampford
Melbury Lake
Sares Wood
Bubb Down Plantation
Redford
Cockeram's Plantation
Lodge Farm
Melbury Park
Banger's Moor
Hazel Wood
Lower Woolcombe Farm
Redford Farm
Deansbrook Farm
Newlands Farm
Paradise Wood
Ash Copse
Hazel Farm
Higher Redford Farm
Highlands Farm
Great Head
Woolcombe Farm
Higher Woolcombe Farm
Dyers Farm
Court Farm
Flow M
TANYARD
Evershot Plantation
Parlour Moor
Spring Plantation
Baker's Moor
Harris Farm
Batcombe
West Hill Farm
BACK LA
FORE ST
EAST HL
BLIND LA
BLIND LA
Holywell Farm
Alder Moor
HAYDON LANE
PH
Stickland Sch
Evershot
SUMMER LANE
THE PARK
EAST HL
ROCKS LA
PARK LA
Burl Farm
Larkham Farm
Holywell
Horchester
Haydon Wood
Hendove Coppice
Macmillan Way
Burl Farm
Horchester Farm
Horchester
Horchester Copse
Batcombe Down
Cross & Har
West Woods Farm
Dry Hill Moor
Burl Moor
LONG ASH LANE
CHANTMARLE LANE
Batcombe Hill
East Hill
Row Hill Coppice
West Woods Plantations
Wardon Hill Farm
White's Wood
HOLWAY LANE
Fortunes Wood Farm
Chantmarle Moor
SHORT CROSS
Brookway Farm
Sydling Woods
East Coppice
CHICK'S COPSE LA
Hillcrest Farm
Park Farm
Frome Park Coppice
LONG ASH LANE
LONG ASH LANE
Sydling Woods
East Hill
Little Coppice
Voss's Moor
Dawes Barton Farm
Manor Farm
Fisher's Bottom Coppice
Tumuli
East Hill
Dudley Moor
Sewage Works
CHANTMARLE LA
CHANTMARLE LA
Frome St Quintin
Fisher's Bottom
Inpark Farm
Barnhayes Farm
DT2
Chantmarle (Police Training Centre)
Chantmarle Farm
Wardon Hill
Cross Hill
North Holway Farm
River Frome
Higher Chalmington
Ayles's Hill Bottom
West Holway
Macmillan Way
Higher Chalmington Farm
Old Wood
Brookway Farm
Holway Farm
Ayles's Hill
Lower Wraxall Farm
Chalmington Farm
Eweleaze Coppice
Stagg's Folly
North Field Hill
Lanes End
Manor
Chalmington
Norton Plantation
Loscombe Bottom
Lower Wraxall
WRAXALL LANE
Prospect Farm
Charity Bottom
Tumulus
Chalkcombe Plantation
Daw's Hill
South Wraxall Farm
Sandhills
CROSS LA
Castle Hill
Tumulus
Castle Hill (Fort)
Lankham Bottom
WEST END LA
WRAXALL LA
Castle Plantation
Folly Hill
Peak End Hill
WEST END
PO
PH
Manor Farm
MEADOW VW
DUCK ST
KENNEL ST
Lankham Bottom
The Coombe
Grove Stall Farm
Cattistock
1 MEADOW CL
2 CAMPION WLK
3 BEECH TREE CL
MILL LA
ST HELEN'S
Wessex Ridgeway
HIGHER DROVE
Wallis Farm
Norden Hill
NORDEN LANE
Court Ho
Home Farm
New Barn
Break Heart Hill
Half Moon Coppice
Chilfrome
Macmillan Way
Norden Farm
Combe Bottom
Wessex Ridgeway
DRIFT ROAD
Plain Bottom
Combe Hill
Fisher's Bottom
A356
TOLLER LA
Tumulus
Whitesheet Hill
CHILFROME LA
CATTISTOCK RD
WEBBERS PIECE
A37

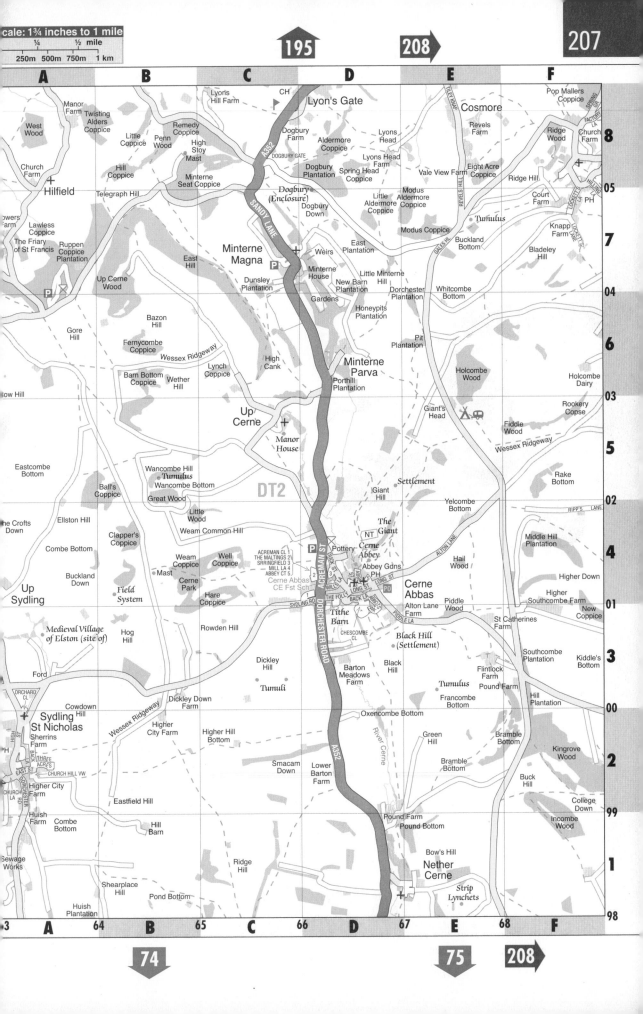

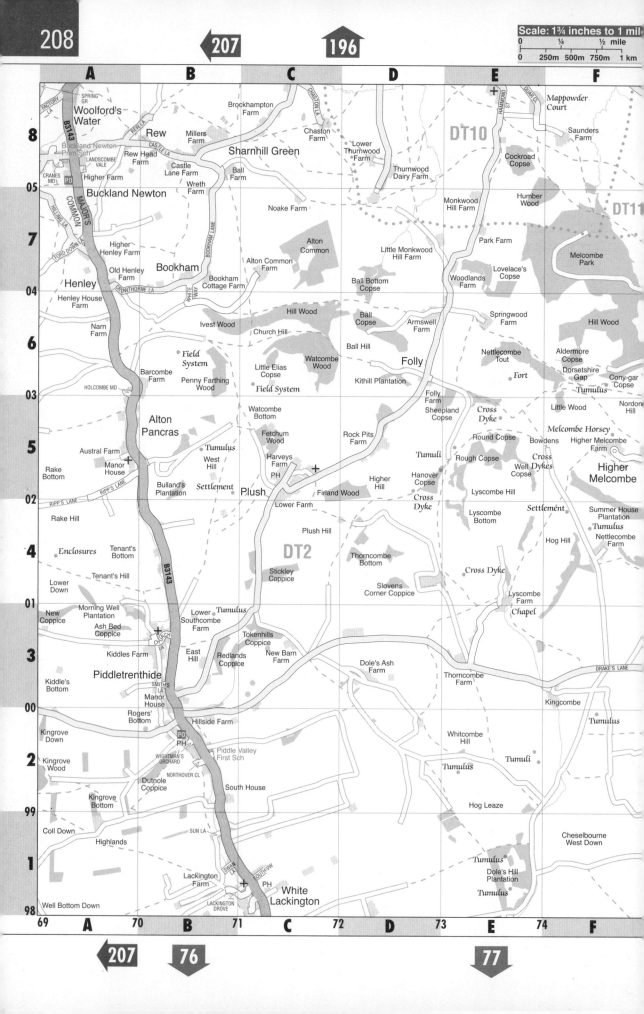

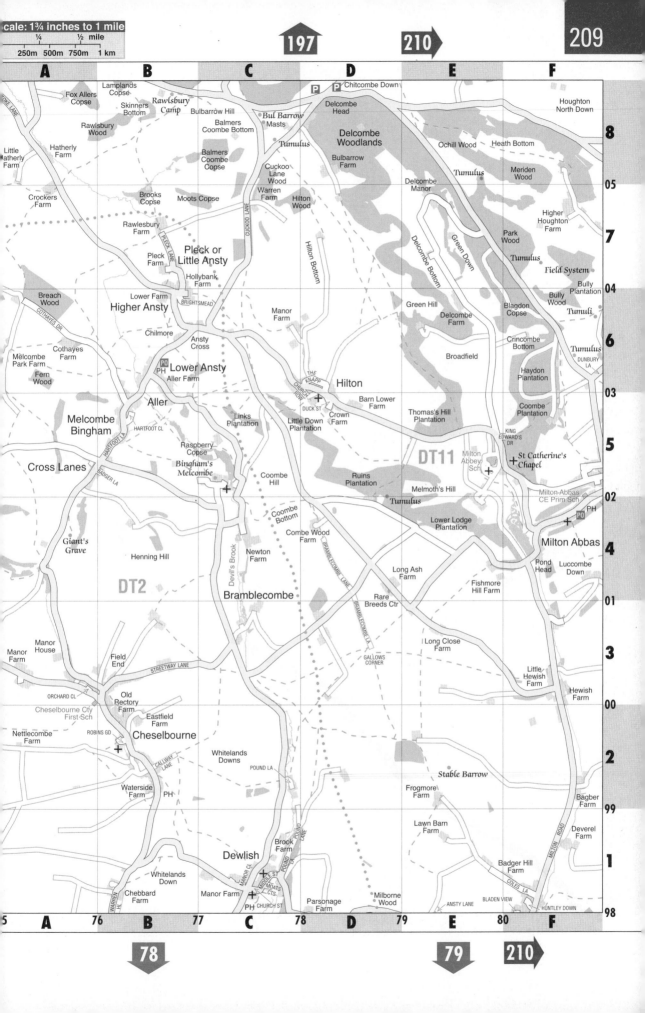

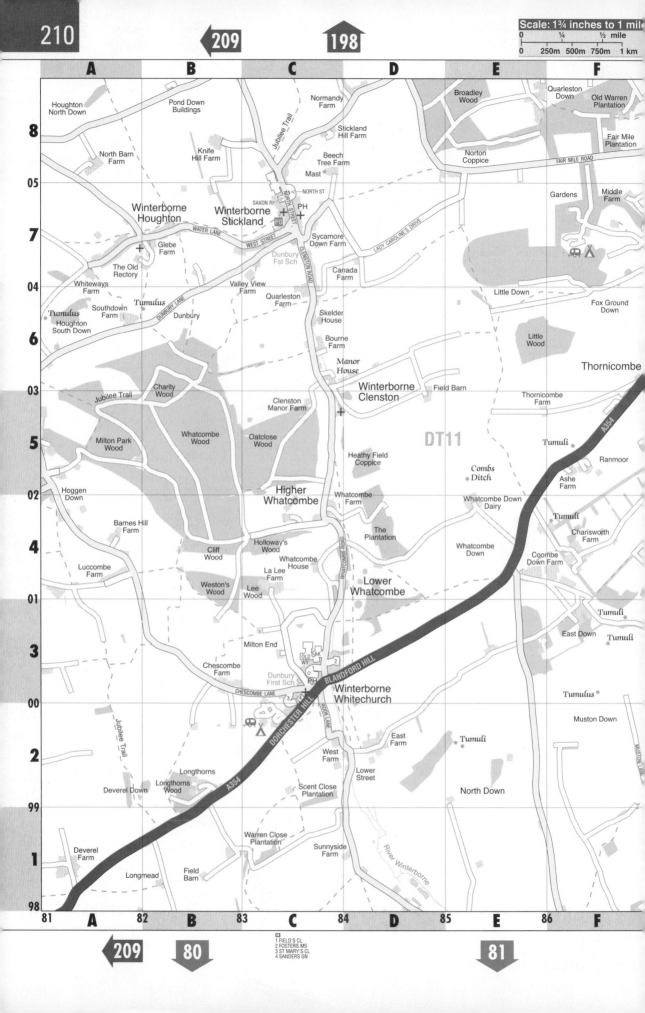

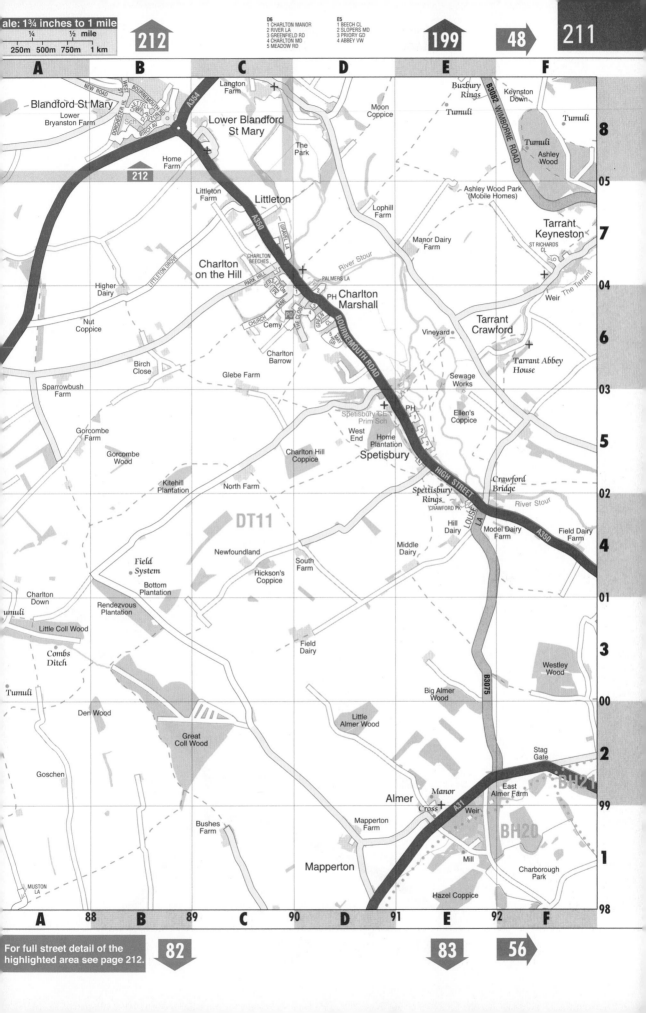

ale: 1¾ inches to 1 mile

¼ ½ mile
250m 500m 750m 1 km

212

199

48

211

D6
1 CHARLTON MANOR
2 RIVER LA
3 GREENFIELD RD
4 CHARLTON MD
5 MEADOW RD

E5
1 BEECH CL
2 SLOPERS MD
3 PRIORY GD
4 ABBEY VW

A B C D E F

NEW ROAD
Blandford St Mary
Lower
Bryanston Farm
Langton
Farm
Moon
Coppice
Buzbury
Rings
Keynston
Down
Tumuli
Tumuli
8
Lower Blandford
St Mary
Sch
Home
Farm
212
The
Park
Ashley
Wood
05
Littleton
Farm
Littleton
Lophill
Farm
Ashley Wood Park
(Mobile Homes)
Tarrant
Keyneston
ST RICHARDS
CL
7
Higher
Dairy
Charlton
Beeches
Park Hill
Charlton
on the Hill
River Stour
PALMERS LA
Manor Dairy
Farm
Weir
The Tarrant
04
Nut
Coppice
PH
Charlton
Marshall
Tarrant
Crawford
6
Birch
Close
PO
Cemy
Vineyard
Tarrant Abbey
House
Sparrowbush
Farm
Glebe Farm
Charlton
Barrow
Sewage
Works
03
Gorcombe
Farm
Spetisbury CE
Prim Sch
PH
Ellen's
Coppice
5
Gorcombe
Wood
Charlton Hill
Coppice
West
End
Home
Plantation
Spetisbury
Kitehill
Plantation
North Farm
Crawford
Bridge
River Stour
02
DT11
Spettisbury
Rings
'CRAWFORD PK
Hill
Dairy
Model Dairy
Farm
A350
Field Dairy
Farm
4
Newfoundland
South
Farm
Middle
Dairy
01
Charlton
Down
Hickson's
Coppice
Bottom
Plantation
umuli
Little Coll Wood
Rendezvous
Plantation
Field
Dairy
3
Combs
Ditch
Tumuli
Den Wood
B3075
Westley
Wood
00
Big Almer
Wood
Great
Coll Wood
Little
Almer Wood
Stag
Gate
2
Goschen
BH21
Bushes
Farm
Almer
Manor
Cross
East
Almer Farm
99
A31
Weir
BH20
Mapperton
Farm
Mill
1
Mapperton
Charborough
Park
MUSTON
LA
Hazel Coppice
98

A 88 B 89 C 90 D 91 E 92 F

For full street detail of the
highlighted area see page 212.

82

83

56

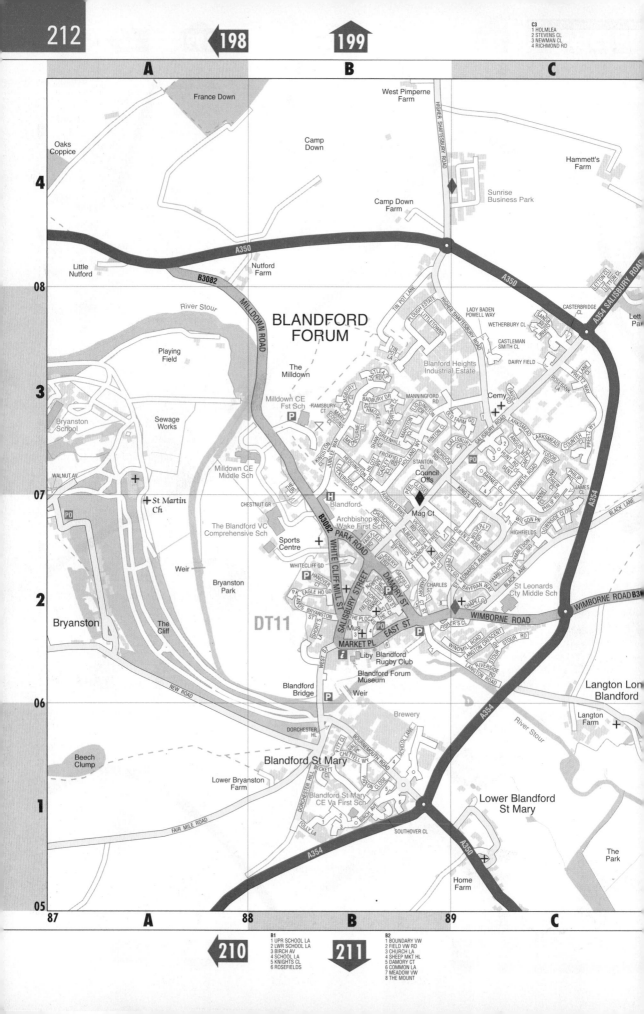

198

199

C3
1 HOLMLEA
2 STEVENS CL
3 NEWMAN CL
4 RICHMOND RD

A   B   C

France Down

West Pimperne Farm

Oaks Coppice

Camp Down

Hammett's Farm

4

Camp Down Farm

Sunrise Business Park

A350

Little Nutford

B3082

Nutford Farm

CASTERBRIDGE CL

LETTON CL
LETTON CL

A354 SALISBURY ROAD

Lett Par

08

River Stour

BLANDFORD FORUM

PLOUGH ESTATE

LITTLETOWNS

LADY BADEN POWELL WAY

WETHERBURY CL

CASTLEMAN SMITH CL

DAIRY FIELD

Playing Field

The Milldown

Blanford Heights Industrial Estate

Cemy

MILLDOWN ROAD

ROSEBANK

3

Milldown CE Fst Sch

RAMSBURY CT

Manningford RD

SALISBURY ROAD

LARKSMEAD

PREETZ WAY

Bryanston School

Sewage Works

Milldown CE Middle Sch

CHESTNUT GR

TUDOR

PHILIP RD

JAMES CL

A354

WALNUT AV

St Martin Ch

Blandford

Council Offs

07

PO

The Blandford VC Comprehensive Sch

Archbishop Wake First Sch

Mág Ct

HIGHFIELDS

DOWNSIDE CLOSE

BLACK LANE

Sports Centre

WHITECLIFF GD

PARK ROAD

WHITE CLIFF MILL ST

SALISBURY STREET

DAMORY ST

Weir

HANOVER

St Leonards Cty Middle Sch

WIMBORNE ROAD B3

Bryanston Park

EAGLE HO GD

BRYANSTON

THE PLOCKS

CHARLES ST

CHAPELGD

BAYFRAN WAY

2

Bryanston

DT11

EAST ST

WINDMILL ROAD

LANGTON CRESCENT

WIMBORNE ROAD

Langton Lor Blandford

The Cliff

WEST ST

MARKET PL

Mus

Liby

Blandford Rugby Club

FISHER'S CL

STOUR RD

Langton Farm

NEW ROAD

Blandford Bridge

Blandford Forum Museum

Weir

Brewery

River Stour

06

DORCHESTER HL

Lower Blandford St Mary

Beech Clump

Blandford St Mary

BOURNEMOUTH ROAD

SCHOOL LANE

CHETTELL WY

BECKETT CL

PIXTON CLOSE

1

Lower Bryanston Farm

Blandford St Mary CE Va First Sch

BIRCH AVE

DORCHESTER HILL

FOLLY LA

FAIR MILE ROAD

A354

SOUTHOVER CL

A350

The Park

Home Farm

05

87   A   88   B   89   C

210

211

B1
1 UPR SCHOOL LA
2 LWR SCHOOL LA
3 BIRCH AV
4 SCHOOL LA
5 KNIGHTS CL
6 ROSEFIELDS

B2
1 BOUNDARY VW
2 FIELD VW RD
3 CHURCH LA
4 SHEEP MKT HL
5 DAMORY CT
6 COMMON LA
7 MEADOW VW
8 THE MOUNT

A3
1 CHANCERY CL
2 HIGHBURY CL
3 KENSINGTON RD
4 RICHMOND RD
5 JUBILEE CT
6 HAWTHORN CL
7 CHARLES ST
8 MEADOW RD
9 GEORGE ST (STH)
10 MEADOW RD (STH)
11 WINDSOR ST
12 WINDSOR RD
13 STATION TERR
14 SANDOWN PL
15 SOUTH ST

B3
1 THE VENTRY
2 VENTRY CLOSE
3 SWAYNES CL
4 BELLE VUE RD
5 CHAPEL PL
6 SUMMERLOCK APP
7 GRIFFINS CT
8 MALTHOUSE LA
9 PRIORY SQ
10 CHEESE MARKET
11 MINSTER ST
12 ROLLESTONE ST
13 ST EDMUNDS CHURCH ST
14 BROWN ST

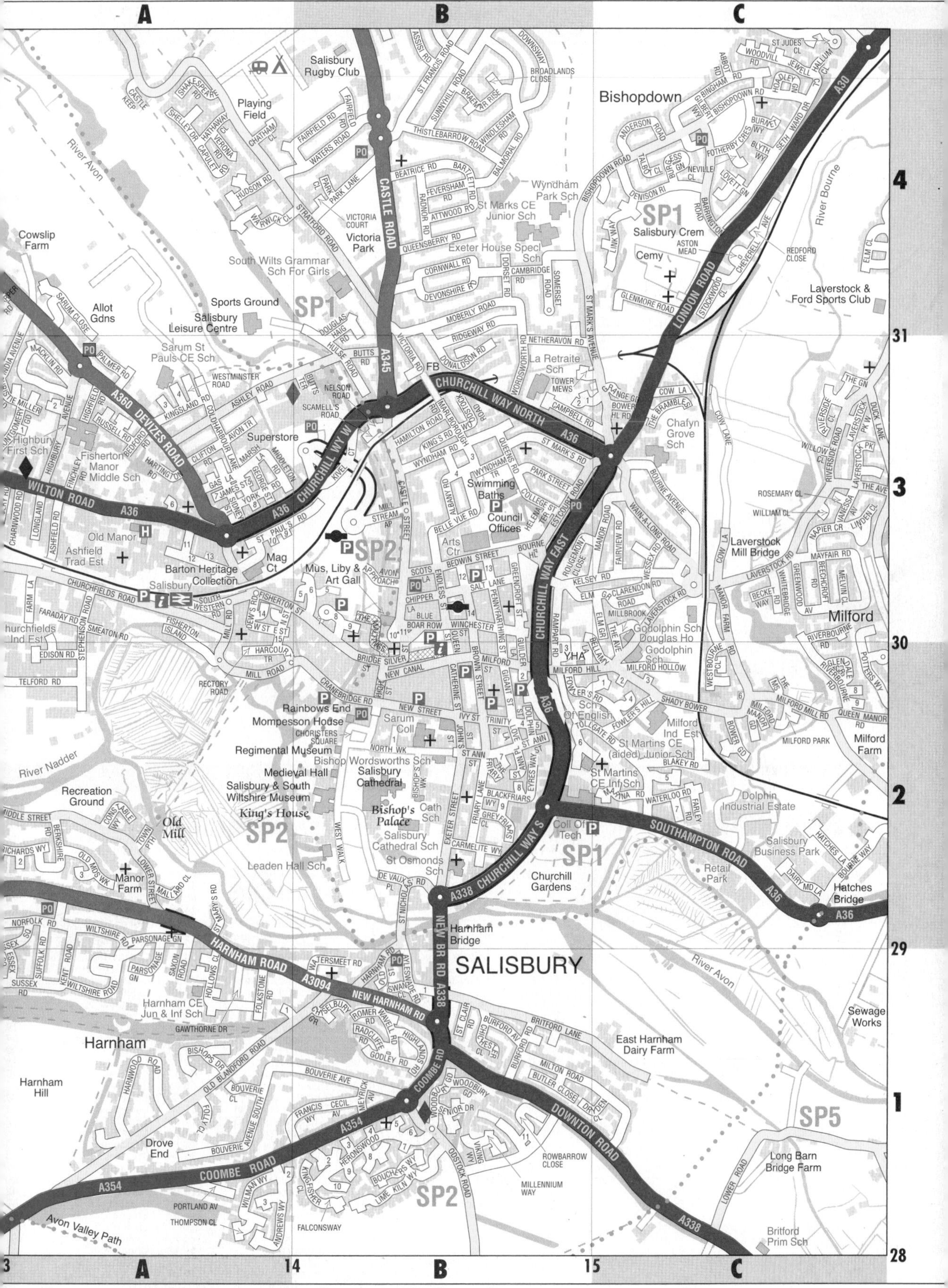

Map area labels (selection):

SP1, SP2, SP5, SALISBURY, Harnham, Harnham Hill, Bishopdown, Milford, Milford Farm, Milford Park

Streets and landmarks as shown on map:
River Avon, Castle Road, Wilton Road, A36, Devizes Road, A360, Churchill Way West, Churchill Way North, Churchill Way East, Churchill Way South, A345, A36, London Road, A30, Southampton Road, A338, New Harnham Road, A3094, Harnham Road, Coombe Road, A354, Downton Road, A338, River Nadder, River Bourne, River Avon

Salisbury Cathedral, Bishop's Palace, King's House, Salisbury & South Wiltshire Museum, Medieval Hall, Mompesson House, Rainbows End, Regimental Museum, Salisbury Leisure Centre, Sports Ground, Victoria Park, Playing Field, Salisbury Rugby Club, South Wilts Grammar Sch For Girls, Exeter House Spec Sch, St Marks CE Junior Sch, Wyndham Park Sch, Chafyn Grove Sch, Laverstock & Ford Sports Club, Salisbury Crem Cemy, Bishop Wordsworths Sch, Salisbury Cathedral Sch, St Osmonds Sch, Leaden Hall Sch, Chorister's Square, Council Offices, Swimming Baths, Arts Ctr, Mus, Liby & Art Gall, Superstore, Old Manor, Ashfield Trad Est, Churchfields Ind Est, Dolphin Industrial Estate, Salisbury Business Park, Retail Park, Sewage Works, East Harnham Dairy Farm, Long Barn Bridge Farm, Britford Prim Sch, Hatches Bridge, Harnham Bridge, Millennium Way, Churchill Gardens, Coll Of Tech, YHA, Godolphin Sch

Index

Church Rd **6** Beckenham BR2..........**53** C6

Place name	Location number	Locality, town or village	Postcode district	Page and grid square
May be abbreviated on the map	Present when a number indicates the place's position in a crowded area of mapping	Shown when more than one place has the same name	District for the indexed place	Page number and grid reference for the standard mapping

Public and commercial buildings are highlighted in magenta   **Places of interest** are highlighted in blue with a star★

Abbreviations used in the index

Acad	**Academy**	Comm	**Common**	Gd	**Ground**	L	**Leisure**	Prom	**Promenade**
App	**Approach**	Cott	**Cottage**	Gdn	**Garden**	La	**Lane**	Rd	**Road**
Arc	**Arcade**	Cres	**Crescent**	Gn	**Green**	Liby	**Library**	Recn	**Recreation**
Ave	**Avenue**	Cswy	**Causeway**	Gr	**Grove**	Mdw	**Meadow**	Ret	**Retail**
Bglw	**Bungalow**	Ct	**Court**	H	**Hall**	Meml	**Memorial**	Sh	**Shopping**
Bldg	**Building**	Ctr	**Centre**	Ho	**House**	Mkt	**Market**	Sq	**Square**
Bsns, Bus	**Business**	Ctry	**Country**	Hospl	**Hospital**	Mus	**Museum**	St	**Street**
Bvd	**Boulevard**	Cty	**County**	HQ	**Headquarters**	Orch	**Orchard**	Sta	**Station**
Cath	**Cathedral**	Dr	**Drive**	Hts	**Heights**	Pal	**Palace**	Terr	**Terrace**
Cir	**Circus**	Dro	**Drove**	Ind	**Industrial**	Par	**Parade**	TH	**Town Hall**
Cl	**Close**	Ed	**Education**	Inst	**Institute**	Pas	**Passage**	Univ	**University**
Cnr	**Corner**	Emb	**Embankment**	Int	**International**	Pk	**Park**	Wk, Wlk	**Walk**
Coll	**College**	Est	**Estate**	Intc	**Interchange**	Pl	**Place**	Wr	**Water**
Com	**Community**	Ex	**Exhibition**	Junc	**Junction**	Prec	**Precinct**	Yd	**Yard**

Index of localities, towns and villages

A

Abbotsbury 149 A4
Acton 177 C1
Adam's Green 193 D2
Adber 14 C3
Affpuddle 111 C4
Alcester 12 B1
Alderholt 42 A3
Alderney 88 B1
Aller 209 B5
Allington 100 A4
Allowenshay 191 A8
Almer 211 E2
Alton Pancras 208 B5
Alvington 26 B2
Alweston 31 A1
Ameysford 52 C1
Ammerham 202 D8
Anderson 82 A4
Arne 144 B3
Ash 68 B3
Ash 198 F5
Ashington 59 A1
Ashley 54 C3
Ashley 95 B2
Ashley Heath 53 C3
Ashmore 39 B4
Askerswell 102 B3
Athelhampton 78 C1
Atrim 68 A2
Avon 63 C1

B

Bagber 197 A8
Barrow Hill 84 C2

Barrow Street 3 C1
Barton on Sea 126 A4
Barwick 193 F8
Bashley 95 A4
Batcombe 206 E7
Bay 6 A1
Beaminster 204 B5
Bear Cross 88 C3
Bearwood 88 C3
Beaulieu Wood 196 B1
Beckley 94 B3
Bedchester 37 B4
Beer Hackett 194 C6
Belchalwell 197 E4
Belchalwell Street ..197 E3
Benville 205 D6
Bere Regis 81 A1
Bettiscombe 203 B3
Bickton 43 A3
Bincombe 152 C3
Binnegar 141 A2
Bishop's Caundle ...196 A8
Bishop's Down 195 E6
Bishopdown 213 C4
Bisterne 63 C3
Bittles Green 12 B4
Blackney 203 D2
Blacknoll 156 C4
Blackwater 91 B2
Blandford Camp 199 E3
Blandford Forum 212 B3
Blandford St Mary ..212 B1
Blashford 47 B1
Bleak Hill 42 C2
Bloxworth 82 A1
Bluntshay 66 C4
Bookham 208 B7
Boscombe 122 C2
Bothenhampton 100 C2
Bournemouth 123 A2

Bourton 1 C1
Boveridge 209 B1
Bovington Camp 139 B3
Bowden 9 C2
Bowridge Hill 6 A2
Boys Hill 195 E5
Bradford Abbas 28 B1
Bradford Peverell ...106 C3
Bradpole 69 A1
Bramblecombe 209 C4
Branksome 120 C3
Branksome Park 120 C1
Bransgore 93 A2
Braytown 139 C1
Briantspuddle 112 A4
Bridge 202 D8
Bridport 100 A3
Broad Oak 197 D7
Broadmayne 136 A1
Broadoak 67 B3
Broadshard 191 F5
Broadstone 87 A1
Broadwey 152 A2
Broadwindsor 203 F5
Brockhampton Green ..196 C1
Broom Hill 51 B1
Bryanston 212 B2
Brympton D'Evercy ...26 A2
Buckhorn Weston 9 A3
Buckland Newton 208 A7
Buckland Ripers 151 B1
Bugley 10 A3
Burleston 78 C1
Burstock 203 D6
Burton 3 B3
Burton 92 B1
Burton 107 C2
Burton 193 C8
Burton Bradstock ...101 A1
Bushey 162 B2

C

Camel Green 42 B3
Camesworth 68 C4
Canford Cliffs 147 C4
Canford Heath 87 C1
Canford Magna 60 A1
Cann 24 A4
Cann Common 24 B4
Carey 142 A3
Castle 202 A4
Castle Park 134 B4
Castletown 181 B1
Catherston Leweston ..65 B1
Cattistock 206 C2
Cerne Abbas 207 E4
Chalbury 201 C1
Chalbury Common 201 D1
Chaldon Herring 156 B2
Chalmington 206 C3
Chard Junction 202 B7
Charing Cross 42 A3
Charlestown 166 C1
Charlton Down 75 B2
Charlton Marshall ..211 D6
Charlton on the Hill .211 C7
Charminster 107 C3
Charminster 90 B1
Charmouth 97 A4
Charnage 3 C2
Chedington 204 E8
Cheselbourne 209 B2
Chesil 186 C4
Chetnole 194 D2
Chettle 200 B8
Chickerell 166 B3
Chideock 99 A3
Chilbridge 58 C4
Chilcombe 102 B2

Child Okeford 198
Chilfrome 206
Chilson Common 202
Chilton Cantelo 14
Christchurch 124
Church Knowle 176
Clapgate 50
Clapton 191
Clifton Maybank ...194
Closworth 193
Cobb 96
Cobley 189
Cocknowle 161
Cold Harbour 142
Coldharbour 166
Colehill 60
Colesbook 5
Combe Almer 84
Compton Abbas 24
Compton Valence ...104
Coneygar 100
Coombe 13
Coombe 65
Coombe 191
Coombe Keynes 158
Coombses 202
Corfe Castle 162
Corfe Mullen 86
Corscombe 205
Coryates 150
Cosmore 207
Court Orchard 100
Crab Orchard 45
Cranborne 40
Creech 160
Crendell 41
Crewkerne 191
Cripplestyle 41
Crooked Withies 52
Cross Lanes 209

rossways 137 C3
rouch Hill 196 A5
row 55 C2
ruxton 73 A3
ucklington 4 A2

D

aggons 41 C3
amerham 209 F2
ean 188 E2
eanend 188 E4
eanland 189 A5
ewlands Common ...44 C3
ewlish 209 C1
innington 191 B8
orchester 107 B1
ottery 68 A2
ownton 127 C4
rimpton 203 D8
rive End Farm 194 A2
roop 197 A3
udsbury 61 B1
untish 196 A1
urweston 198 E3

E

ast Bloxworth 82 C1
ast Brook 59 B3
ast Burton 139 C4
ast Chaldon 156 B2
ast Chelborough ..205 D8
ast Chinnock 192 E8
ast Coker 193 D7
ast Compton 24 A1
ast Creech 160 C1
ast End 58 C1
ast Fleet 166 A3
ast Holme 159 C4
ast Holton 117 A2
ast Howe 89 B2
ast Knighton 157 A4
ast Lulworth 173 B4
ast Martin 209 C6
ast Melbury 24 B3
ast Morden 83 B2
ast Orchard 36 C4
ast Parley 90 A4
ast Pulham 196 D4
ast Stoke 140 C1
ast Stour 10 C2
ast Stour Common .11 A2
aston 187 A2
bblake 45 C2
ccliffe 10 B4
dmondsham 40 B2
llingham 47 A3
lm Hill 7 A1
lwell 152 A3
nbury 89 C3
nmore Green 12 B2
nsbury Park 89 B1
vershot 206 A7

F

airmile 91 C1
arnham 188 C2
arrington 37 A2
erndown 61 B3
iddleford 197 F8
ifehead Magdalen ..20 C4
ifehead Neville ..197 C5
ifehead St Quintin 197 B5
ilford 67 C4
leet 166 A3
olke 195 D8
olly 208 D6
ontmell Magna 37 C4
ontmell Parva 36 B1
ordingbridge 43 A4
orston 75 A2
ortuneswell 186 C4
oxholes 120 A3
rampton 73 C2
riars Cliff 125 B4
rogham 43 C4
rome St Quintin ..206 D5
urzebrook 161 A2
urzehill 50 C1

G

annetts 21 B2
asper 1 B4
aunt's Common 51 A4
iddy Green 139 C1
illingham 5 C1
lanvilles Wootton 195 E2

Goathill 31 B4
God's Blessing Green ...51 B2
Godmanstone 75 A4
Godwinscroft 93 A3
Gold Hill 198 B8
Gore 14 C2
Gotham 41 A2
Grange 50 C1
Grange Estate 62 C4
Greenham 203 C7
Grimstone 74 A1
Grove 187 A3
Gussage All Saints 201 A5
Gussage St Andrew 188 E1
Gussage St Michael 200 F6
Guy's Marsh 23 A3

H

Hains 20 C2
Hale 4 A2
Halstock 193 C3
Ham Common 6 A1
Hamlet 194 D3
Hammoon 36 A1
Hampreston 60 C1
Hamworthy 118 B2
Hanford 198 D6
Harbridge 43 A1
Harbridge Green ...43 A1
Harcombe Bottom ...64 A2
Hardington Mandeville 193 A6
Hardington Moor ..193 A7
Harman's Cross ...177 C3
Harnham 213 A1
Hartgrove 22 C1
Haselbury Plucknett 192 C6
Hawkchurch 202 B3
Haydon 31 B2
Haythorne 201 F2
Hazelbury Bryan ..196 F3
Hemsworth 49 A4
Henbury 56 C1
Henley 191 E2
Henley 208 A7
Henstridge 19 A2
Henstridge Ash 19 A3
Henstridge Bowden .18 A3
Henstridge Marsh ..19 C3
Hermitage 195 B2
Herston 178 C2
Hewish 191 D3
Hewood 202 C6
Highcliffe 125 B4
Higher Ansty 209 B6
Higher Bockhampton 109 A4
Higher Chalmington 206 C4
Higher Eype 99 C3
Higher Halstock Leigh 193 A2
Higher Kingcombe .205 E3
Higher Melcombe ..208 F5
Higher Nyland 8 C1
Higher Row 51 B3
Higher Sandford ...15 C3
Higher Totnell ...194 F4
Higher Whatcombe .210 C5
Higher Woodsford .137 B4
Higher Wraxall ...205 F4
Highlands 100 A3
Hightown 55 C1
Highwood 158 C4
Hilfield 207 A7
Hillbourne 87 A1
Hillbutts 58 C3
Hilton 209 D6
Hincknowle 69 A4
Hinton 14 A1
Hinton 94 A1
Hinton Martell ...201 B1
Hinton Parva 50 A2
Hinton St George .191 D7
Hinton St Mary 35 A2
Hogstock 200 B1
Holdenhurst 91 A2
Holditch 202 B5
Hollands 27 B4
Hollow Oak 113 A4
Holmebridge 141 C1
Holnest 195 C4
Holt 51 A2
Holt Heath 52 B3
Holt Wood 51 B4
Holton Heath 116 A4
Holway 16 A3
Holway 202 E6
Holwell 3 A3
Holwell 196 B5
Holywell 193 C8
Holywell 206 C7
Hooke 205 C2
Hordle 95 C2
Horton 201 E2
Horton Common 44 C1
Horton Heath 44 B1
Hound Hill 58 C4
Houndstone 26 B3

Hummer 14 B2
Hungerford 43 C3
Huntingford 5 C4
Hurn 91 A3
Hursey 203 E5
Hurst 111 B1
Hyde 43 C3
Hyde 100 C3

I

Ibberton 197 D2
Ibsley 47 B4
Iford 123 B4
Ivy Cross 13 A2
Iwerne Courtney ..198 E7
Iwerne Minster 37 C1

K

Kimmeridge 175 B2
King's Stag 196 D5
Kingsbury Regis ...17 B2
Kingsland 68 A4
Kingston 55 A1
Kingston 63 C4
Kingston 176 C2
Kingston 197 A4
Kingston Maurward 108 C1
Kingston Russell .104 B2
Kington Magna 9 B2
Kinson 89 A3
Kit Hill 23 A2
Kitford 197 C3
Kittwhistle 203 A6
Knackers Hole 197 D6
Knapp Hill 7 B1
Knighton 194 E6
Knob's Crook 44 A2
Knowlton 201 D4

L

Lake 117 C1
Lambrook 68 C3
Lambs' Green 58 C1
Lane End 113 B3
Lanehouse 166 C1
Langham 9 C4
Langton Herring ..150 B1
Langton Long
  Blandford 212 C2
Langton Matravers 178 A2
Laymore 202 F7
Leigh 194 E3
Leigh 197 D3
Leigh 59 C2
Leigh Park 59 C2
Lewcombe 193 E2
Lillington 194 F7
Lilliput 147 B4
Limpers Hill 3 B2
Little Canford 60 B2
Little Pamphill ...58 C3
Little Woolgarston 177 B4
Littlebredy 131 B4
Littledown 123 A4
Littlemoor 152 C2
Littleton 211 B4
Littlewindsor 203 F7
Litton Cheney 103 B1
Loders 69 B1
Lodmoor 167 C4
Long Bredy 103 C1
Long Crichel 200 F3
Long Cross 2 B3
Longburton 195 C7
Longfleet 119 B2
Longham 61 A1
Loscombe 69 C2
Lower Ansty 209 B6
Lower Blandford
  St Mary 212 C1
Lower Bockhampton 109 A1
Lower Daggons 41 B4
Lower Eype 99 C2
Lower Halstock Leigh 193 B2
Lower Hamworthy ..119 A1
Lower Holwell 40 C3
Lower Kingcombe .205 E1
Lower Mannington .52 B4
Lower Nyland 19 C3
Lower Odcombe 26 A2
Lower Parkstone ..120 A2
Lower Row 51 C4
Lower Strode 204 A2
Lower Turmer 46 A2
Lower Whatcombe .210 D4
Lower Wraxall 206 A3
Lower Zeals 2 B3
Lufton 26 A3
Lulworth Camp 173 A4

Lyatts 193 B6
Lydlinch 196 F8
Lyme Regis 96 B3
Lyon's Gate 207 D8
Lytchett Matravers 84 B2
Lytchett Minster .116 C4

M

Madjeston 10 C4
Maiden Newton 73 A4
Mangerton 69 A2
Mannington 52 B4
Manston 36 A2
Manswood 200 E3
Mapperton 204 F2
Mapperton 211 D1
Mappowder 196 F1
Margaret Marsh 22 B1
Marnhull 20 C1
Marshalsea 202 F3
Marshwood 202 F2
Martin 209 B6
Martin Drove End .209 A8
Martinstown or Winterbourne
  St Martin 133 B3
Meerhay 204 D5
Melbury Abbas 24 B3
Melbury Bubb 194 C1
Melbury Osmond ...194 A2
Melbury Sampford 206 A8
Melcombe Bingham 209 A5
Melcombe Regis ...: 167 C3
Melplash 204 D1
Mere 3 A3
Merley 59 B1
Merriott 70 A2
Merriott 191 E7
Merriottsford 191 E7
Merritown 90 C4
Middle Bockhampton 92 C3
Middle Chinnock .192 C8
Milborne Port 17 B1
Milborne St Andrew 79 C4
Milborne Wick 17 A3
Miles Cross 99 C4
Milford 213 C3
Milton Abbas 209 F4
Milton on Stour ...5 B3
Minchington 188 D1
Minterne Magna ..207 C7
Minterne Parva ..207 D6
Misterton 192 A2
Mockbeggar 47 C4
Monkton Up Wimborne 201 C8
Monkton Wyld 64 A3
Moor Crichel 201 A3
Moorbath 67 B2
Moordown 90 A1
Moorside 21 B2
Moortown 55 B3
Morcombelake 98 B4
Moreton 138 C4
Mosterton 204 A8
Motcombe 12 A4
Mount Pleasant ...86 C4
Mounters 20 C1
Muckleford 106 A4
Mudeford 125 A3
Mudford 14 A2
Muscliffe 90 B2

N

Nash 193 C8
Neacroft 93 A3
Nether Cerne 207 E1
Nether Compton ...28 C4
Netherbury 204 C2
Netherhay 203 C8
Netherstoke 193 D3
Netherton 193 E6
Nettlecombe 70 A2
New Milton 94 C1
New Swanage 179 A3
New Town 9 B1
New Town 17 A1
New Town 27 C3
New Town 188 C2
New Town 188 F6
New Town 201 A2
New Town 120 A4
Newport 82 B1
Newton 197 D8
Newton Peveril 56 A2
Newtown 204 D5
Norden 161 B2
North Bockhampton 92 C4
North Bowood 203 F2
North Chideock ...99 A4
North Coker 193 D8
North End 7 A2
North Gorley : 43 B2
North Kingston 55 C1

North Perrott 192 C4
North Poorton 205 B1
North Poulner 47 C1
North Wootton 30 C1
Northay 202 D3
Northbourne 89 C2
Northbrook 78 A1
Northport 142 C3
Norwood 205 B8
Nottington 152 A1
Notton 73 A2

O

Oakdale 119 B3
Oakley 59 C1
Oathill 203 B8
Oborne 16 C1
Okeford Fitzpaine 197 F5
Old Milton 94 C1
Organford 116 A3
Osehill Green 195 E4
Osmington 169 A4
Osmington Mills ..169 B4
Over Compton 28 C4
Overcombe 168 A4
Owermoigne 155 B4
Oxbridge 68 C4

P

Packers Hill 196 C5
Pallington 111 B2
Pamphill 58 A3
Park Gate 196 F2
Parkstone 120 A2
Parkway 14 C4
Parley Green 90 B4
Peacemarsh 5 C2
Pear Ash 1 B2
Pen Mill 28 A3
Pendomer 193 B5
Penn 64 B2
Penselwood 1 A2
Pentridge 189 E4
Perry Street 202 B8
Piddlehinton 76 C4
Piddletrenthide ..208 A3
Pidney 196 F4
Pig Oak 51 B3
Pilford 60 A4
Pillwell 21 C2
Pilsdon 203 C2
Pimperne 194 A3
Pimperne 199 D4
Pleck 34 C4
Pleck 196 B6
Pleck or Little Ansty 209 C2
Plush 208 C5
Pokesdown 123 A2
Poole 119 A1
Poolestown 33 C3
Portesham 132 A1
Portway 156 C4
Post Green 116 C4
Poulner 47 C1
Powerstock 70 A3
Poxwell 154 C3
Poyntington 16 C2
Preston 168 A4
Preston Plucknett .26 C2
Puddle Town 192 B5
Puddletown 78 A1
Pulham 196 B3
Puncknowle 129 C3
Purewell 124 B4
Purse Caundle 32 A4
Purtington 191 A4
Putton 166 C3
Puxey 197 B7
Pymore 68 B1

Q

Queen Oak 2 A2

R

Radipole 167 A4
Rampisham 205 F5
Red Hill 89 C3
Redbridge 138 A3
Redford 206 D8
Redlands 152 A1
Rew 208 B8
Ridge 143 A1
Rimpton 15 A4
Ringwood 47 B1
Rivers' Corner ...197 C7
Rixon 35 B1

Rockford 47 C2
Rodden 150 B3
Rodgrove 8 C3
Rodwell 167 B1
Rolls Mill 197 C8
Romford 44 C4
Rook Street 3 A4
Rossmore 120 C4
Roundham 191 D4
Rowlands 59 B3
Rushton 141 A1
Ryall 66 B1
Ryme Intrinseca 194 B6

S

St Andrew's Well 100 C4
St Ives 54 B3
St James 12 C1
St Johns 59 B2
St Leonards 54 A1
Salisbury 213 B1
Salwayash 68 A3
Sandbanks 147 B2
Sandford 142 C4
Sandford Orcas 15 C3
Sandhills 195 F5
Sandhills 206 B3
Sandpit 203 D7
School House 202 D5
Seaborough 191 D1
Seatown 99 A2
Sedgehill 7 C3
Shaftesbury 12 C2
Shaggs 158 B2
Shapwick 56 B4
Sharnhill Green 208 C8
Sherborne 30 A4
Sherford 115 B4
Shillingstone 198 C6
Shipton Gorge 101 B2
Shroton 198 E7
Silkhay 204 A1
Silton 5 A4
Sitterton 80 C2
Sixpenny Handley 189 A3
Skilling 100 A3
Slepe 115 C4
Somerford 124 C3
Sopley 92 A3
South Bockhampton ..92 C2
South Bowood 203 F1
South Chard 202 A7
South Gorley 43 C1
South Perrott 192 C2
South Poorton 70 B4
Southbourne 123 C2
Southbrook 3 A5
Southill 167 A3
Southlands 180 C4
Southover 73 B1

Southover 128 A4
Southwell 186 C1
Spetisbury 211 D5
Springbourne 122 B3
Spyway 102 B4
Stafford's Green 16 A4
Stalbridge 33 C4
Stalbridge Weston 33 A3
Stallen 29 A3
Stanbridge 50 B2
Stanley Green 119 B3
Stanpit 124 C3
Stapehill 60 C3
Steeple 175 B4
Sterte 119 A2
Stinsford 108 C2
Stoborough 142 C1
Stoborough Green ...161 A4
Stockwood 194 C2
Stoford 193 F8
Stoke Abbott 204 A3
Stoke Wake 197 B1
Stokeford 140 C2
Stone 101 A4
Stone 59 A3
Stour Provost 21 B4
Stour Row 22 B4
Stourpaine 198 F4
Stourton Caundle 32 C2
Stratton 106 C4
Strouden 90 C1
Stubhampton 199 E8
Stuckton 43 C4
Studland 164 B1
Sturminster Marshall .56 C2
Sturminster Newton ..35 A1
Summerlands 27 A3
Sutton Bingham 193 D6
Sutton Holms 44 A4
Sutton Poyntz 153 B2
Sutton Waldron 37 C3
Swanage 179 B2
Swyre 129 B3
Sydling St Nicholas ..207 A2
Symondsbury 99 C4
Synderford 202 F6

T

Tadnoll 138 B1
Talbot Village 89 B1
Tarrant Crawford ...211 E6
Tarrant Gunville ...199 F8
Tarrant Hinton 200 A6
Tarrant Keyneston ...48 A3
Tarrant Launceston .200 B4
Tarrant Monkton ...200 B3
Tarrant Rushton 48 A4
Templeman's Ash ...203 B3
The Borough 196 B6
The Causeway 3 B2

The Common 197 D5
The Mount 69 A3
Thorncombe 202 E6
Thorne Coffin 26 B4
Thornford 194 D8
Thornicombe 210 F6
Three Gates 195 A2
Three Legged Cross ..45 A1
Throop 112 B4
Throop 90 C2
Tidpit 209 C6
Tiley 195 E1
Tillworth 202 A3
Tincleton 110 B2
Tiptoe 95 B4
Todber 21 B2
Tollard Farnham 188 B2
Tollard Royal 188 B4
Toller Fratrum 72 B4
Toller Porcorum 71 C4
Toller Whelme 205 B4
Tollerford 72 C4
Tolpuddle 79 B1
Totnell 194 F3
Town's End 81 B2
Trent 14 C1
Trickett's Cross 61 C4
Tuckton 123 C3
Turlin Moor 117 B2
Turmer 46 C4
Turners Puddle 112 B4
Turnworth 198 B2
Twyford 23 B1
Tyneham 174 B3

U

Ulwell 179 A3
Up Cerne 207 C5
Up Mudford 14 A1
Up Sydling 207 A4
Uphall 205 E5
Uploders 101 C4
Upper Parkstone ...120 A3
Uppington 201 D1
Upton 118 B4
Upwey 152 A3

V

Verwood 45 A3

W

Walditch 101 A3
Walkford 94 B1
Wallisdown 89 A1

Walton Elm 34 C4
Wareham 142 C3
Warmwell 137 A1
Warren 113 B2
Waterditch 93 A3
Waterloo 87 A1
Watton 100 A2
Wayford 191 B1
Waytown 68 C4
Well Bottom 39 B3
West Bay 100 B1
West Bexington 129 C1
West Bourton 4 B4
West Chaldon 155 C1
West Chelborough ..205 D8
West Chinnock 192 B8
West Cliff 121 B1
West Coker 193 A8
West Compton 71 C1
West End 29 C3
West Holme 159 B4
West Howe 88 C2
West Hurn 90 C3
West Knighton 136 B2
West Lulworth 172 B3
West Melbury 24 A3
West Milton 69 C3
West Moors 53 A1
West Morden 83 A2
West Orchard 36 B3
West Parley 89 F4
West Pulham 196 A3
West Southbourne ..123 B3
West Stafford 136 A4
West Stour 10 A1
Westbourne 121 B2
Westfields 196 D1
Westham 167 A2
Weston 186 C2
Weston 204 F8
Weymouth 167 C2
Whitchurch 19 A3
Whitchurch
  Canonicorum 66 A2
Whitcombe 135 C3
White Cross 1 C3
White Hill 3 B1
White Lackington ..208 C1
Whitecross 204 B2
Whitefield 83 A1
Whitmore 44 A3
Wick 124 A2
Wigbeth 201 F2
Wimborne Minster ...59 A3
Wimborne St Giles .201 D7
Winfrith Newburgh ..156 C3
Winkton 92 B1
Winterborne Came ..135 B3
Winterborne Clenston .210 D6
Winterborne
  Herringston 134 C3
Winterborne Houghton .210 B7
Winterborne Kingston ..81 B4

Winterborne Monkton .134
Winterborne Muston 82
Winterborne Stickland .210
Winterborne Tomson ...82
Winterborne
  Whitechurch 210
Winterborne Zelston ...82
Winterbourne Abbas ..105
Winterbourne
  Steepleton 132
Winton 121
Winyard's Gap 192
Witchampton 200
Wolverton 2
Wonston 196
Woodbridge 23
Woodcutts 188
Woodlands 44
Woodlands Common ..44
Woodrow 196
Woodsford 110
Woodville 21
Woodyates 189
Wool 140
Woolbridge Heath ..140
Woolford's Water ..208
Woolgarston 177
Woolland 197
Woolminstone 191
Woolsbridge 53
Wooth 68
Wooton 95
Wootton Fitzpaine ..65
Worgret 142
Worth Matravers ...183
Wych 100
Wyke 5
Wyke Regis 180
Wynford Eagle 72

Y

Yenston 18
Yeovil 27
Yetminster 194
Yondover 101

Z

Zeals 1

8

8th August Rd BH20 ...139 C4

A

Aaron Cl BH17 ...119 C4
Abbey Barn★ DT3 ...149 A4
Abbey CE VC Prim Sch The DT9 ...29 C2
Abbey CE Voluntary Aided Fst Sch The SP7 ...12 B1
Abbey Cl 9 TA20 ...202 A8
Abbey Ct DT2 ...207 D4
Abbey Gdns★
Cerne Abbas DT2 ...207 D4
Ferndown BH21 ...60 B3
Abbey House★ BH21 ...201 A1
Abbey Mews 2 TA20 ...202 A8
Abbey Mus★ SP7 ...12 C1
Abbey Rd Sherborne DT9 ...30 A3
West Moors BH22 ...62 A4
Yeovil BA21 ...26 C3
Abbey St
Cerne Abbas DT2 ...207 D4
Crewkerne TA18 ...191 E4
Hinton St George TA17 ...191 C7
Abbey View 4 DT11 ...211 E5
Abbey Wlk SP7 ...12 C1
Abbot Rd SP1 ...213 C4
Abbots Cl BH23 ...125 C4
Abbots Meade BA21 ...26 C3
Abbots Quay 9 BH20 ...142 C2
Abbots Way
Sherborne DT9 ...29 C3
Yeovil BA21 ...26 C4
Abbots Wlk DT2 ...207 D4
Abbotsbury Castle (Fort)★ DT3 ...130 B1
Abbotsbury Hill DT3 ...130 B1
Abbotsbury La DT2 ...130 C4
Abbotsbury Rd
Broadstone BH18 ...86 C3
Weymouth DT4 ...167 A2
Abbotsbury Swannery★ DT3 ...149 A3
Abbott Cl BH9 ...122 A4
Abbott Rd BH9 ...122 A4
Abbott St BH21 ...58 B3
Abbott's Way SP8 ...5 C2
Abbott's Wootton La
Marshwood DT6 ...202 E1
Whitechurch Canonicorum DT6 ...65 B4
Abbotts Mdw BH16 ...84 B2
Abbotts Way BH22 ...62 A4
Abder Cross DT9 ...14 C2
Abels La DT9 ...14 C1
Aberdare Rd BH10 ...89 C4
Abingdon Dr BH23 ...126 B4
Abingdon Rd BH17 ...119 B4
Abinger Rd BH7 ...123 A3
Abney Rd BH10 ...89 B2
Acacia Ave BH31 ...45 C2
Acacia Cl DT4 ...167 A3
Acacia Rd SO41 ...95 C2
Acer Ave 2 Bridport DT6 ...68 C1
Bridport DT6 ...100 C4
Acer Dr BA21 ...26 C4
Ackerman Rd DT1 ...108 B1
Acland Rd
Bournemouth BH9 ...122 A4
7 Dorchester DT1 ...108 A1
Acorn Bsns Pk BH12 ...120 A4
Acorn Cl
Christchurch BH23 ...123 C4
New Milton BH25 ...95 B2
St.Leonards BH24 ...54 A2
Acorn Way BH31 ...45 B3
Acorns The BH21 ...60 A2
Acreman Cl DT2 ...207 D4
Acreman Pl DT9 ...30 A3
Acreman St
Cerne Abbas DT2 ...207 D4
Sherborne DT9 ...30 A3
Acres Ct 6 BA22 ...193 F8
Acres Rd BH11 ...89 A1
Acton Rd BH10 ...89 A1
Ad Astro Fst Sch BH17 ...87 C1
Adamsfield Gdns BH10 ...89 B1
Adastral Rd BH17 ...119 C4
Adastral Sq BH17 ...119 C4
Adber Cl BA21 ...28 A4
Addington Pl BH23 ...124 B3
Addiscombe Rd BH23 ...124 A4
Addison Cl SP8 ...6 A1
Addison Sq BH24 ...55 B4
Addlewell La BA20 ...27 B2
Adelaide Cl BH23 ...123 C4
Adelaide Cres DT4 ...167 A2
Adelaide La 40 BH1 ...121 C2
Adeline Rd BH5 ...122 C2
Admirals Cl DT9 ...30 B4
Admirals Way BH20 ...142 C3
Admirals Wlk BH2 ...121 B1
Admiralty Rd BH6 ...123 C2
Aggis Farm Rd BH31 ...45 A3
Agglestone Rd BH19 ...164 A1
Aigburth Rd BH19 ...178 C2
Airetons Cl BH18 ...87 B2
Airfield Cl DT2 ...137 B3
Airfield Ind Est BH23 ...124 C3
Airfield Rd BH23 ...124 C3
Airfield Way BH23 ...124 C4
Airspeed Rd BH23 ...125 A4
Akeshill Cl BH25 ...95 A3
Alamein Rd BH20 ...139 C3
Alan Ct 16 BH23 ...126 A4
Alastair Cl BA21 ...27 A4
Alastair Dr BA21 ...27 A4
Albany BH1 ...122 B2
Albany Cl
Barton on Sea BH25 ...94 C1
Sherborne DT9 ...30 B4
Albany Dr Horton BH21 ...52 C4
Three Legged Cross BH21 ...45 A1
Albany Gdns BH15 ...118 C1
Albany Pk BH17 ...119 A4
Albany Rd
Salisbury SP1 ...213 B3
Weymouth DT4 ...166 C2
Albemarle Rd BH3 ...121 C4
Albert Cl BA21 ...27 A4
Albert Rd
Bournemouth BH1 ...121 C2
Corfe Mullen BH21 ...86 B3
Dorchester DT1 ...107 C1
Ferndown BH22 ...61 B3
New Milton BH25 ...94 C1
Poole BH12 ...120 B3
Albert St
Blandford Forum DT11 ...212 B2
5 Radipole DT4 ...167 B2
Albert Terr 5 DT5 ...186 C4
Albion Cl BH12 ...120 A4
Albion Rd BH23 ...91 C1
Albion Way BH31 ...44 C3
Alby Rd BH12 ...120 C3
Alcester Rd BH12 ...120 B3
Aldabrand Cl DT3 ...166 B2
Aldbury Ct BH25 ...127 A4
Alder Cl Burton BH23 ...92 B1
3 Sandford BH20 ...116 A1
Sturminster Newton DT10 ...35 B1
Alder Cres BH12 ...120 C4
Alder Dr SP6 ...42 A3
Alder Gr
Crewkerne TA18 ...191 F5
Yeovil BA20 ...27 A1
Alder Hills BH12 ...121 A4
Alder Hills Ind Est BH12 ...121 A4
Alder Rd Poole BH12 ...120 C3
Sturminster Newton DT10 ...35 B1
Alderbury Cl 5 BH19 ...178 C1
Alderbury Ct 6 BH23 ...124 C3
Alderholt Pk★ SP6 ...42 A4
Alderley Rd BH10 ...89 C2
Alderney Mid Sch BH12 ...88 B1
Alderney Ave BH12 ...88 B1
Alderney Hospl BH12 ...88 B1
Aldis Gdns BH15 ...118 C1
Aldondale Gdns BA20 ...27 B2
Aldridge Rd
Bournemouth BH10 ...89 B3
Ferndown BH22 ...61 C2
Aldridge Way BH22 ...61 C2
Alexander Cl BH23 ...124 C3
Alexandra Ct DT6 ...100 B3
Alexandra Lodge 6 BH1 ...122 A2
Alexandra Rd
Bournemouth BH6 ...123 B3
Bridport DT6 ...100 B3
Dorchester DT1 ...107 C1
Poole BH14 ...120 C2
Radipole DT4 ...167 B3
Weymouth DT4 ...166 C2
Yeovil BA21 ...27 C3
Alexandra St DT11 ...212 B2
Alexandria Ct BH22 ...61 C2
Alford Rd BH3 ...121 B4
Alfred Pl DT1 ...108 A1
Alfred Rd DT1 ...108 A1
Alfred St DT11 ...212 B2
Alice in Wonderland Family Pk★ BH23 ...90 C4
Alice Rd DT1 ...107 C1
Alington 18 BH4 ...121 B2
Alington Ave DT1 ...135 B4
Alington Cl BH14 ...147 B4
Alington House BH14 ...147 B4
Alington Rd
Bournemouth BH3 ...122 A3
Dorchester DT1 ...108 A1
Alington St 4 DT1 ...108 A1
Alipore Cl BH14 ...120 B2
Alipore Hts BH14 ...120 B2
Alisons The BH20 ...139 C1
All Saints CE Prim Sch DT9 ...196 A8
All Saints CE Sch DT4 ...180 B4
All Saints' Rd
Dorchester DT1 ...108 A1
Weymouth DT4 ...180 B4
Allamanda Rd DT3 ...152 C1
Allberry Gdns DT3 ...168 A4
Allen Cl 8 DT11 ...198 C7
Allen Ct BH21 ...59 B3
Allen Rd BH21 ...59 B2
Allenbourn Mid Sch BH21 ...59 B3
Allenby Cl BH17 ...87 A1
Allenby Rd BH17 ...87 A1
Allens La BH16 ...118 B3
Allens Rd BH16 ...118 B3
Allenview Rd BH21 ...59 B3
Allingham Rd BA21 ...27 C4
Allington Gdns 3 DT6 ...100 A4
Allington Mead 3 DT6 ...100 B4
Allington Pk DT6 ...100 A4
Allington Rd BH14 ...147 B4
Alma Rd
Bournemouth BH9 ...122 A4
Weymouth DT4 ...167 B2
Almer Rd BH15 ...118 C2
Almond Gr Poole BH12 ...120 B4
Radipole DT4 ...167 A3
Almshouses BH10 ...89 B1
Alpha Ctr The BH17 ...119 A4
Alpine Rd BH24 ...54 C1
Alton La DT2 ...207 E4
Alton Mead La DT9 ...194 E4
Alton Rd
Bournemouth BH10 ...89 A1
Poole BH14 ...120 B2
Alton Rd E BH14 ...120 B1
Alum Chine Rd BH4 ...121 A2
Alumdale Rd BH4 ...121 A1
Alumhurst Rd BH4 ...121 A1
Alvandi Gdns 12 BH25 ...95 A2
Alverton Ave BH15 ...119 C2
Alverton Hall BH4 ...121 B1
Alvington La BA22 ...26 B2
Alyth Rd BH3 ...121 B3
Ambassador Cl BH23 ...125 A3
Ambassador Ind Est BH23 ...125 A3
Amber Rd BH21 ...86 B2
Amberley Cl BH23 ...125 C4
Amberley Ct 8 BH1 ...122 A2
Amberwood BH22 ...61 C3
Amberwood Dr BH23 ...93 C1
Amberwood Gdns BH23 ...94 A1
Amberwood House BH23 ...94 A1
Ambleside
Christchurch BH23 ...91 C2
Radipole DT4 ...167 A4
Ambrose Cl DT9 ...28 B1
Ambury La BH23 ...124 C4
Amelia Cl 3 DT5 ...181 A1
Amen Cnr BH21 ...201 B5
Amesbury Rd BH6 ...123 B3
Amethyst Rd BH23 ...124 C4
Ameys La BH22 ...61 C4
Ameysford Rd BH22 ...52 B1
Amiens Rd BH20 ...139 C4
Amira Ct 9 BH2 ...121 C2
Ammerham La TA20 ...202 D8
Ampfield Rd BH8 ...90 B2
Amsterdam Sq BH23 ...124 B3
Ancaster Rd BH19 ...178 C2
Anchor Cl
Bournemouth BH11 ...88 C3
Christchurch BH23 ...125 A3
Anchor Rd BH11 ...88 C3
Ancrum Lodge BH4 ...121 A2
Andbourne Ct BH6 ...123 C2
Anderson Manor★ DT11 ...82 B4
Anderson Rd SP1 ...213 C4
Andover Cl BH23 ...125 A4
Andover Gn BH20 ...139 B3
Andree Ct BH23 ...126 A4
Andrew Cl DT11 ...212 C3
Andrew La BH25 ...95 B1
Andrews Cl BH11 ...89 A2
Andrews Way SP2 ...213 A1
Angel Cl DT3 ...150 B1
Angel La
Barton on Sea BH25 ...127 B4
Ferndown BH22 ...61 A2
Langton Herring DT3 ...150 B1
Mere BA12 ...3 A3
Shaftesbury SP7 ...12 C2
Stour Provost SP8 ...10 C1
Angeline Cl BH23 ...125 C4
Angers La DT10 ...197 E7
Anglebury Ave BH19 ...179 A2
Anglewood Mans 9 BH4 ...121 B2
Anglo-European Coll of Chiropractic BH5 ...123 A2
Angus Cl DT11 ...212 C3
Anjou Cl BH11 ...88 B3
Annandale Ct BH6 ...123 B2
Anncott Cl BH16 ...84 B2
Anne Cl
Blandford Forum DT11 ...212 C2
Christchurch BH23 ...92 A1
Annerley Rd BH1 ...122 B2
Annet Cl BH15 ...118 C1
Anning Rd DT7 ...96 B3
Annings La DT6 ...101 C1
Anson Cl
Christchurch BH23 ...124 C3
Ringwood BH24 ...55 C4
Anstey Cl BH11 ...89 A3
Anstey Rd BH11 ...89 A3
Ansty La DT11 ...79 B4
Antell's Way SP6 ...42 B3
Antelope Wlk DT1 ...108 A1
Anthony's Ave BH14 ...120 B1
Antler Dr BH25 ...94 C2
Anvil Cl 4 BH19 ...178 C1
Anvil Cres BH18 ...86 C3
Anvil Rd 10 DT11 ...199 D4
Aplands Cl DT11 ...198 B8
Apollo Cl
Dorchester DT1 ...134 C4
Poole BH12 ...120 B4
Apple Acre 1 DT11 ...198 C7
Apple Cl BH12 ...121 A2
Apple Gr BH23 ...91 C1
Apple Tree Gr BH22 ...61 C3
Apple Tree Rd SP6 ...42 A3
Apple Trees La DT6 ...99 A3
Appleslade Way BH25 ...95 A3
Appletree Cl
Bournemouth BH6 ...123 B3
New Milton BH25 ...95 A1
Radipole DT3 ...167 B4
Approach Rd BH14 ...120 A2
April Cl BH11 ...89 A2
Apsley Cres BH17 ...87 B1
Apsley Ct 2 BH8 ...122 A3
Aragon Cl DT4 ...180 C4
Aragon Way BH9 ...90 A2
Arbutus Cl DT1 ...108 A1
Arcade BH4 ...121 A2
Arcade The 37 BH1 ...121 C2
Arcadia Ave BH8 ...122 A4
Arcadia Rd BH23 ...91 C1
Archbishop Wake Fst Sch DT11 ...212 B2
Archdale Cl BH10 ...89 B1
Archway Rd BH14 ...120 C2
Arden Rd BH9 ...89 C2
Arden Wlk BH25 ...95 A1
Ardmore Rd BH14 ...120 A2
Argyle Rd
Christchurch BH23 ...124 C3
Radipole DT4 ...167 B3
Swanage BH19 ...179 A1
Argyll Mans 11 BH5 ...122 C2
Argyll Rd
Bournemouth BH5 ...122 C2
Poole BH12 ...120 B3
Ariel Cl BH6 ...124 A2
Ariel Dr BH6 ...124 A2
Ark Dr BH22 ...61 C2
Arlecks La 2 DT11 ...199 D4
Arley Rd BH14 ...120 A1
Arlington DT4 ...167 A3
Arlington Cl BA21 ...26 C4
Arlington Ct BH25 ...127 A4
Armada Way DT1 ...135 B4
Armoury Rd BA22 ...26 B3
Armoury Yd SP7 ...12 C2
Armstrong Rd DT6 ...100 B4
Arne Ave BH12 ...120 C4
Arne Cres BH12 ...120 C4
Arne Rd BH20 ...143 B1
Arnewood Ct BH2 ...121 C1
Arnewood Gdns BA20 ...27 A1
Arnewood Rd BH6 ...123 B3
Arnewood Sch The BH25 ...94 C1
Arnold Cl BH22 ...53 A2
Arnold Rd BH22 ...53 A2
Arnolds Cl BH25 ...126 C4
Arran Way BH23 ...94 A1
Arras Cres BH20 ...139 B4
Arras Rd BH20 ...139 B4
Arrow Field DT6 ...100 B3
Arrowfield DT6 ...100 B3
Arrowsmith Ct BH18 ...87 A2
Arrowsmith La BH21 ...87 C4
Arrowsmith Rd BH21 ...87 C4
Arthur Cl BH2 ...121 C3
Arthur La 3 BH23 ...124 A4
Arthur Rd BH23 ...124 A4
Artillery Rd BA22 ...26 B3
Artist Row DT5 ...186 C4
Arts Inst of Bournemouth The BH12 ...121 B4
Arun Cl 2 SP8 ...5 C2
Arundel Cl BH25 ...94 C2
Arundel Rd BA21 ...28 A3
Arundel Way BH23 ...125 C4
Ascham Rd BH8 ...122 A3
Ascot Rd BH18 ...87 A2
Ash Ave BH20 ...116 A2
Ash Cl Alderholt SP6 ...42 B3
Sandford BH20 ...143 A4
Shaftesbury SP7 ...13 A2
Swanage BH19 ...178 C1
Upton BH16 ...118 A4
Ash End BA8 ...19 A3
Ash Gr BH24 ...55 C4
Ash Hill DT2 ...106 C4
Ash La DT6 ...68 B3
Ash Tree Cl 2 DT2 ...78 A1
Ash Tree La SP7 ...24 B3
Ash Wlk BA8 ...19 A3
Ashbourne Ct 1 BH1 ...122 A2
Ashbourne Rd BH5 ...123 A3
Ashbrook Wlk BH16 ...117 A3
Ashburn Garth 5 BH24 ...55 C3
Ashburton Gdns BH10 ...89 B1
Ashcombe La DT9 ...31 B2
Ashdene Cl BH21 ...59 B3
Ashdown BH2 ...121 B1
Ashdown Cl BH17 ...87 C1
Ashdown Sch BH17 ...87 C1
Ashdown Wlk BH25 ...95 B1
Ashfield Rd SP2 ...213 A3
Ashfield Trad Est SP2 ...213 A3
Ashford Gr BA21 ...27 B4
Ashford Rd
Bournemouth BH6 ...123 B4
Fordingbridge SP6 ...42 C4
Ashgrove BA12 ...3 A2
Ashington Gdns BH21 ...86 C4
Ashington La BH21 ...59 A1
Ashington Pk BH25 ...95 A1
Ashington St 3 DT1 ...107 B1
Ashland Ct TA18 ...191 E5
Ashlands Cl 1 TA18 ...191 F5
Ashlands Mdw TA18 ...191 F5
Ashlands Rd TA18 ...191 F5
Ashlands VC Fst Sch TA18 ...191 E5
Ashleigh Ave DT2 ...72 C4
Ashleigh Rise BH10 ...89 B1
Ashlett Gdns BH25 ...95 B2
Ashley Arnewood Ct 9 BH25 ...95 A1
Ashley Cl
Bournemouth BH1 ...122 C3
Ringwood BH24 ...55 C3
Ashley Comm Rd BH25 ...95 B2
Ashley Ct BH22 ...62 A4
Ashley Dr BH24 ...46 C1
Ashley Dr N BH24 ...54 A3
Ashley Dr S BH24 ...54 A3
Ashley Dr W BH24 ...54 A3
Ashley Inf Sch BH25 ...95 B2
Ashley Jun Sch BH25 ...95 B2
Ashley La SO41 ...95 C2
Ashley Meads BH25 ...95 B2
Ashley Pk BH24 ...54 B3
Ashley Rd
Bournemouth BH1 ...122 C3
Dorchester DT1 ...135 A4
Marnhull DT10 ...21 A1
New Milton BH25 ...95 B2
Poole BH14 ...120 B3
Salisbury SP2 ...213 A3
Ashley Wood Golf Club DT11 ...199 E1
Ashley Wood Pk DT11 ...211 E7
Ashley Wood Rd DT11 ...199 E2
Ashling Cl BH8 ...122 B4
Ashling Cres BH8 ...122 A4
Ashmead BA20 ...26 C1
Ashmeads Cl BH21 ...60 A3
Ashmeads Way BH21 ...60 A3
Ashmede BH4 ...121 B1
Ashmore BH21 ...59 B2
Ashmore Ave
Barton on Sea BH25 ...127 A4
Hamworthy BH15 ...118 C1
Ashmore Bottom DT11 ...39 B1
Ashmore Cl DT11 ...212 B3
Ashmore Cres BH15 ...118 C1
Ashmore Gr BH23 ...93 C1
Ashridge Ave 1 BH10 ...89 B3
Ashridge Gdns BH10 ...89 B3
Ashridge Par 2 BH10 ...89 B3
Ashton Ct
13 New Milton BH25 ...95 A2
Poole BH13 ...121 A1
Ashton Rd
Bournemouth BH9 ...89 C1
1 Weymouth DT4 ...167 B1
Ashtree Cl BH25 ...95 B1
Ashurst Rd
Bournemouth BH8 ...90 B2
Ferndown BH22 ...53 A2
Ashwell Ct BH23 ...91 C1
Ashwood Dr
Broadstone BH18 ...87 B2
Yeovil Without BA21 ...28 A4
Asker Gdns DT6 ...100 B3
Askwith Cl DT9 ...29 C3
Aspen Dr BH31 ...45 B3
Aspen Gdns BH12 ...120 C4
Aspen Pl BH25 ...95 A1
Aspen Rd BH12 ...120 C4
Aspen Way
10 Crewkerne TA18 ...191 F5
Poole BH12 ...120 C4
Asquith Cl BH23 ...124 B3
Ass Hill BH21 ...201 B4
Assisi Rd SP1 ...213 B4
Astbury Ave BH12 ...89 A1
Aston Mead
Christchurch BH23 ...91 C2
Salisbury SP1 ...213 C4
Astrid Way 3 DT4 ...167 C2
Athelhampton House★ DT2 ...78 C1
Athelhampton Rd DT2 ...78 C1
Athelney Ct 18 BH1 ...122 A2
Athelney Way BA21 ...26 C3
Athelstan Rd
Bournemouth BH6 ...123 C3
15 Dorchester DT1 ...108 A1
Atlantic Rd BH19 ...179 A1
Attisham La DT6 ...203 B4
Attwood Cl SP6 ...42 A3
Attwood Rd SP1 ...213 B4
Auckland Rd BH23 ...125 B4
Audemer Ct BH24 ...55 C4
Audrayton Ct 9 BH6 ...123 C2
Augusta Cl DT5 ...187 A3
Augusta Rd DT5 ...187 A3
Augustan Cl 1 DT1 ...134 C4
Austen Ave BH10 ...89 C3
Auster Cl BH23 ...125 A4
Austin Ave BH14 ...120 A1
Austin Cl BH1 ...122 B3
Australia Rd DT3 ...166 B2
Autumn Cl BH22 ...61 A4
Autumn Copse BH25 ...95 B1
Autumn Rd BH11 ...88 B2
Avalanche Rd DT5 ...186 C1
Avalon BH14 ...147 B4
Avebury Ave BH10 ...89 C3
Avenue Ct BH13 ...121 A2
Avenue La 20 BH2 ...121 C2
Avenue Rd
Bournemouth BH2 ...121 C2
Christchurch BH23 ...94 B1
Lyme Regis DT7 ...96 A3
New Milton BH25 ...95 A2
Radipole DT4 ...167 B2
Wimborne Minster BH21 ...59 B2
Avenue Shopping Ctr The 21 BH2 ...121 C2

Avenue The
Bournemouth BH9 ....89 C2
[6] Crewkerne TA18 ...192 A3
Ferndown BH22 ....53 A2
Poole BH13 ....121 A1
Salisbury SP1 ....213 C3
Sherborne DT9 ....30 B4
Yeovil BA21 ....27 B3
Avocet Cl DT4 ....180 B3
Avon Approch SP2 ....213 B3
Avon Ave BH24 ....54 C2
Avon Bldgs BH23 ....124 A4
Avon Castle★ BH24 ....54 C2
Avon Castle Dr BH24 ....54 C2
Avon Cl
Bournemouth BH8 ....122 B3
Weymouth DT4 ....166 C2
Yeovil BA21 ....27 C3
Avon Cotts BH23 ....92 B3
Avon Cswy BH23 ....91 B4
Avon Ct BH23 ....124 B3
Avon Dr BH20 ....142 C3
Avon Farm Cotts 63 C2
Avon Heath Ctry Pk★
BH24 ....54 B2
Avon Heath Ctry Pk (South Pk)★ BH24 ....63 A4
Avon House BH2 ....121 C1
Avon Mews BH8 ....122 B3
Avon Pk BH24 ....54 C3
Avon Rd
Bournemouth BH8 ....122 B3
Ferndown BH22 ....53 A1
Avon Rd E BH23 ....124 A4
Avon Rd W BH23 ....123 C4
Avon Run Cl BH23 ....125 A3
Avon Run Rd BH23 ....125 A3
Avon Terr SP2 ....213 A3
Avon View Par BH23 ....92 B2
Avon View Rd BH23 ....92 B2
Avon Wharf BH23 ....124 B3
Avonbourne Girls Sch BH7 ....123 A4
Avoncliffe Rd BH6 ....123 C2
Avondale Gdns SP8 ....5 C1
Avonlea Prep Sch BH24 ....55 B4
Award Rd BH24 ....60 C3
Axe La
Broadwindsor DT8 ....203 C8
West Crewkerne TA18 ....191 C1
Axe Valley [1] DT8 ....204 A8
Axeford TA20 ....202 B8
Axford Cl BH8 ....90 B2
Axminster Rd DT6 ....96 C4
Axnoller La DT8 ....204 D6
Aylesbury Rd BH1 ....122 C2
Ayleswade Rd SP2 ....213 B1
Aysha Cl BH25 ....95 A1
Azalea Cl BH24 ....54 B3
Azura Cl BH21 ....53 B3

B

Babwell Rd BA9 ....4 A2
Babylon Hill DT9 ....28 B3
Babylon View BA21 ....28 A4
Back Dro DT9 ....194 E3
Back La Bere Regis BH20 ....81 A2
Bradford Abbas DT9 ....28 B1
Broadwindsor DT8 ....203 E5
Cerne Abbas DT2 ....207 D4
Chetnole DT9 ....194 D3
East Chinnock BA22 ....192 E8
East Coker BA22 ....193 C4
Evershot DT2 ....206 A7
Frome Vauchurch DT2 ....72 C4
Gillingham SP8 ....5 B3
Halstock BA22 ....193 C3
Hazelbury Bryan DT10 ....197 A4
Kington Magna SP8 ....9 B2
North Perrott TA18 ....192 C4
[4] Okeford Fitzpaine DT11 197 F5
Rimpton BA22 ....15 A4
Sherborne DT9 ....30 A3
Sixpenny Handley SP5 ....189 A4
Sturminster Marshall BH21 ....56 B3
Swyre DT2 ....129 B3
Sydling St Nicholas DT2 ....207 A2
Back St Abbotsbury DT3 ....149 A4
East Stour SP8 ....10 C2
Portesham DT3 ....132 A1
Badbury Cl BH18 ....87 B2
Badbury Ct [8] BH23 ....124 C3
Badbury Dr DT11 ....212 B3
Badbury Rings (Hill Fort)★ DT11 ....49 A2
Badbury View BH21 ....59 B3
Badbury View Rd BH21 ....86 B4
Baden Cl BH25 ....95 A1
Baden Powell & St Peter's Mid Sch BH14 ....120 A2
Bader Rd BH17 ....119 C4
Badger Hts BA22 ....26 B3
Badger La DT2 ....209 A5
Badger Way BH31 ....45 A3
Badgers BH24 ....54 A3
Badgers Copse BH25 ....95 B3
Badgers Way DT10 ....35 A1
Badgers Wlk BH24 ....61 C4
Baglake DT2 ....103 B1
Bagman's La BH21 ....201 E3
Bagwood Rd [5] DT11 ....81 C4
Bailey Cl BH25 ....95 B2

Bailey Cres BH15 ....119 B4
Bailey Dr BH23 ....123 C4
Bailey Gate Ind Est BH21 ....56 C2
Bailey Hall BH23 ....123 C4
Bailey Ridge DT9 ....195 A4
Bailey Ridge La DT9 ....194 F4
Bailey's Dro BH20 ....139 C1
Baileys Hill BH21 ....201 D6
Baiter Gdns BH15 ....119 B1
Bakehouse TA16 ....191 F7
Bakehouse La [1] DT9 ....28 B1
Baker Rd BH11 ....89 A3
Baker's Cross DT6 ....65 B2
Bakers Farm Rd BH31 ....45 A4
Bakers La [3] BH21 ....201 D1
Bakers Paddock DT2 ....136 B1
Balaclava Rd
Bovington Camp BH20 ....139 C4
Fortuneswell DT5 ....181 B1
Balcombe Rd BH13 ....121 A2
Baldwin Cl BH21 ....124 B3
Balena Cl BH17 ....119 A4
Balfour Cl BH23 ....125 B4
Balfour Rd BH9 ....89 C1
Ball La [17] BH15 ....119 B1
Ballam Cl BH16 ....118 B4
Ballard Cl
Lytchett Matravers BH16 ....84 B2
New Milton BH25 ....95 A2
Poole BH15 ....119 B1
Ballard Coll BH25 ....95 A2
Ballard Lee BH19 ....179 B3
Ballard Rd Poole BH15 ....119 B1
Swanage BH19 ....179 B3
Ballard Sch BH25 ....95 A2
Ballard Way BH19 ....179 B3
Balls Hill BA22 ....26 A4
Ball's La BH21 ....56 B3
Balmoor Cl BA12 ....3 A2
Balmoral Ave BH8 ....90 C1
Balmoral Cres DT1 ....135 B4
Balmoral Ct [7] BH23 ....126 A4
Balmoral House BH2 ....121 B2
Balmoral Rd
Poole BH14 ....120 B2
Salisbury SP1 ....213 B4
Yeovil BA21 ....28 A3
Balmoral Wlk BH25 ....94 C2
Balston Rd BH14 ....120 A3
Balston Terr BH15 ....119 A1
Banbury Hill (Fort)★ DT10 ....197 D6
Banbury Rd BH17 ....119 B4
Bank Chambers BH14 ....120 C2
Bank Cl BH23 ....124 A3
Banks Rd BH13 ....147 B2
Bankside Rd BH9 ....90 A2
Banocroft Ct [1] BH15 ....119 C2
Banstead Rd BH18 ....87 A3
Banton Shard DT6 ....68 C1
Barberry Way BH31 ....45 C3
Barbers Gate [15] BH15 ....119 A1
Barbers Piles [8] BH15 ....119 A1
Barbers Wharf [16] BH15 ....119 A1
Barclay Mans BH2 ....121 C3
Barclay Rd DT4 ....167 B2
Bardolfeston Village★ DT2 ....78 B1
Bargates BH23 ....124 A4
Barges Cl DT2 ....103 B1
Baring Rd BH6 ....124 C2
Barlake Ct [5] DT1 ....107 B1
Barlands Cl BH23 ....92 B1
Barley Cl DT2 ....194 A2
Barley Way DT4 ....167 C1
Barleycroft Rd [3] DT5 ....186 C2
Barleyfields [10] SP8 ....5 C2
Barlynch Ct [6] BA21 ....26 C3
Barn Cl
[8] Crewkerne TA18 ....191 E4
Upton BH16 ....118 A4
Barn Cres [7] TA18 ....191 E4
Barn La TA18 ....191 E6
Barn Rd BH18 ....87 A2
Barn St TA18 ....191 E4
Barnaby Mead SP8 ....5 C1
Barnard St [4] SP1 ....213 B2
Barndale Dr BH20 ....143 A1
Barnes Cl
Blandford Forum DT11 ....212 C3
Bournemouth BH10 ....89 B2
Marnhull DT10 ....21 A1
Sturminster Newton DT10 ....35 A1
Barnes Cres
Bournemouth BH10 ....89 B2
Wimborne Minster BH21 ....59 C2
Barnes Cross DT9 ....196 A6
Barnes La DT8 ....204 C4
Barnes Pl BA12 ....3 A3
Barnes Rd
Bournemouth BH10 ....89 B2
Wareham Town BH20 ....142 B1
Barnes Way [18] DT1 ....108 A1
Barneston Manor★ BH20 ....176 A4
Barnet Cl BA21 ....27 A4
Barney's Cl DT6 ....97 A4
Barnfield BH23 ....125 B4
Barnhaven Cl DT4 ....167 A1
Barnhill Rd BH20 ....143 A1
Barns Rd BH22 ....62 A3
Barnsfield Rd BH24 ....54 B1
Barnsley Dro BH21 ....50 A2
Barons Ct [8] BH12 ....121 A2
Barons Rd BH11 ....88 B3
Barr La DT6 ....101 B2

Barrack La BH24 ....55 C2
Barrack Rd
Christchurch BH23 ....123 C4
Ferndown BH22 ....62 A1
Weymouth DT4 ....167 C1
Barrack St DT6 ....100 B4
Barr's La DT6 ....97 A4
Barrie Rd BH9 ....89 C2
Barrington Rd SP1 ....213 C4
Barrow Cl DT1 ....134 C4
Barrow Dr BH8 ....90 C1
Barrow Hill
Bere Regis BH20 ....81 A2
Stalbridge DT10 ....33 B4
Stourton Caundle DT10 ....32 C1
Barrow La DT2 ....205 A8
Barrow Rd BH8 ....90 C1
Barrow Rise DT4 ....180 A4
Barrow St La BA12 ....3 C2
Barrow View BH22 ....61 A3
Barrow Way BH8 ....90 C1
Barrowfield Cl DT6 ....128 A4
Barrowgate Rd BH8 ....90 B2
Barrowgate Way BH8 ....90 B2
Barrowland La DT2 ....71 A3
Barrs Ave BH25 ....95 A4
Barrs Wood Dr BH25 ....95 A4
Barrs Wood Rd BH25 ....95 A4
Barry Gdns BH18 ....86 C3
Barry La BA22 ....192 F6
Barters La
Broadstone BH18 ....86 C2
Donhead St Mary SP7 ....25 A4
Bartlets Cl DT2 ....133 B3
Bartlett Dr BH7 ....123 A4
Bartlett Rd SP1 ....213 B4
Bartletts The BA12 ....3 A2
Bartley Ct [6] BH21 ....59 A3
Bartom's La BH16 ....84 A1
Barton Cl
Sturminster Newton DT10 ....197 C8
Toller Porcorum DT2 ....71 B4
West Stafford DT2 ....136 A4
Barton Comm La BH25 ....127 A4
Barton Comm Rd BH25 ....127 A4
Barton Croft BH25 ....127 A4
Barton Ct BH25 ....127 A3
Barton Ct Ave BH25 ....127 A4
Barton Ct Rd BH25 ....95 A1
Barton Dr
Barton on Sea BH25 ....126 C4
Overcombe/Preston DT3 ....153 A2
Barton Gdns DT9 ....29 C3
Barton Gn BH25 ....127 A4
Barton Heritage Collection★ SP2 ....213 A3
Barton Hill
Kington Magna SP8 ....9 B2
Melbury Osmond DT2 ....194 A2
Shaftesbury SP7 ....12 C2
Barton Hill House Sch SP7 ....12 C2
Barton House BH25 ....126 C4
Barton La
Barton on Sea BH25 ....126 C4
Mere BA12 ....3 A3
Barton Lodge BH12 ....120 A3
Barton The DT2 ....205 A8
Barton Way BH25 ....126 C4
Barton Wood Rd BH25 ....126 C4
Bartonside Rd BH25 ....126 C4
Barwick CP Sch BA22 ....193 F8
Bascott Cl BH11 ....89 A1
Bascott Rd BH11 ....89 A1
Bashley Comm Rd BH25 ....95 A4
Bashley Cross Rd BH25 ....94 C3
Bashley Dr BH25 ....95 A3
Bashley Rd BH25 ....95 A3
Bassett Rd BH12 ....120 A3
Bastone Way BH22 ....61 A3
Bat Alley DT4 ....20 C1
Batchelor Cres BH11 ....88 C2
Batchelor Rd BH11 ....88 C2
Batchelor's La BH21 ....201 D1
Batchpool La BA8 ....8 A4
Batcombe Cl BH11 ....88 C2
Batcombe Rd DT9 ....194 F1
Bath Hill Ct [9] BH1 ....122 A2
Bath Orch [6] DT6 ....68 C1
Bath Rd
Bournemouth BH1 ....122 A2
Sturminster Newton DT10 ....35 A1
Bath St DT4 ....167 B2
Bathwell La DT9 ....17 B1
Bats La DT2 ....106 C1
Batten Cl BH23 ....124 B4
Batterley Dro BH21 ....41 A2
Battle Mead
Corfe Castle BH20 ....177 A4
Swanage BH19 ....179 A2
Batts La DT2 ....203 C2
Baunton's Orch DT9 ....17 B1
Bauntons Cl [10] DT9 ....17 B1
Baverstock Rd BH21 ....121 A4
Bay Cl Swanage BH19 ....179 B3
Three Legged Cross BH21 ....53 A4
Upton BH16 ....118 A3
Bay Cres BH19 ....179 A3
Bay Hog La BH15 ....119 A1
Bay La SP8 ....6 A1
Bay Rd SP8 ....5 C1
Bay Tree Way BH23 ....93 B1

Bay View [8] BH19 ....178 C1
Bayard Rd DT3 ....152 C1
Baycliffe Rd DT4 ....167 A1
Baydon Cl DT3 ....153 A2
Bayfran Way DT11 ....212 C2
Bayview Rd DT7 ....96 A3
Beach Ave BH25 ....126 C4
Beach Cl BH13 ....147 D4
Beach Gdns BH19 ....179 A2
Beach Rd
Burton Bradstock DT6 ....128 B4
Poole BH13 ....147 D4
Studland BH19 ....164 B1
Upton BH16 ....118 A3
Beach View BH13 ....147 B2
Beachcroft BH13 ....147 B2
Beachview Cl [1] DT4 ....180 A4
Beacon Cl BH23 ....125 C4
Beacon Dr BH23 ....125 C4
Beacon Gdns BH18 ....86 C2
Beacon Hill La BH21 ....86 A2
Beacon Pk Cres BH16 ....118 A4
Beacon Pk Rd BH16 ....118 A4
Beacon Rd
Bournemouth BH2 ....121 C1
Broadstone BH18 ....86 C2
Upton BH16 ....118 A4
Beacon Way BH18 ....86 C2
Beaconfield Rd BA20 ....27 A1
Beaconsfield Rd
Christchurch BH23 ....124 A4
Poole BH12 ....120 B3
Beadon La TA16 ....191 E7
Beaminster Mus★ DT8 ....204 D4
Beaminster Rd DT6 ....68 C1
Beaminster VC Comp Sch DT8 ....204 C4
Beamish Rd BH17 ....119 C4
Bear Cross Ave BH11 ....88 C3
Bearwood Prim Sch BH11 ....88 B3
Beatrice Rd SP1 ....213 B4
Beatty Cl BH24 ....55 C4
Beatty Rd BH9 ....90 A1
Beau Ct
[31] Bournemouth BH4 ....121 B2
[9] New Milton BH25 ....95 A2
Beauchamps Gdns BH7 ....123 A4
Beaucroft La BH21 ....59 C3
Beaucroft Rd BH21 ....59 C3
Beaucroft Sch BH21 ....59 C3
Beaufort Cl BH23 ....125 A4
Beaufort Dr BH21 ....59 B3
Beaufort Mews BH21 ....59 A2
Beaufort Rd BH6 ....123 B3
Beaufoy Cl SP7 ....13 A2
Beaufoys Ave BH22 ....61 B4
Beaufoys Cl BH22 ....61 B4
Beaufoys Ct BH22 ....61 B3
Beaulieu Cl DT4 ....167 A3
Beaulieu Ave BH23 ....123 C4
Beaulieu Cl BH25 ....94 C2
Beaulieu Dr BA21 ....26 C3
Beaulieu Rd
Bournemouth BH4 ....121 A1
Christchurch BH23 ....123 C4
Beaumont Ave
Bridport DT6 ....100 B4
Radipole DT4 ....167 B3
Beaumont Rd BH13 ....147 C4
Beaver Ind Est BH23 ....125 A3
Beccles Cl BH15 ....118 C1
Becher Rd BH14 ....120 C2
Becket Way SP1 ....213 C3
Beckett Cl DT11 ....212 B1
Beckhampton Rd BH15 ....118 C2
Becklands La DT6 ....65 C2
Beckley Copse BH23 ....94 A1
Becton La BH25 ....127 A4
Becton Mead BH25 ....95 A1
Bedale Way BH15 ....119 C3
Bedford Cres BH7 ....123 B4
Bedford Pl DT6 ....100 B4
Bedford Rd
Salisbury SP2 ....213 A3
Weymouth DT4 ....167 A2
Yeovil BA21 ....27 C4
Bedford Rd N BH12 ....88 B1
Bedford Rd S BH12 ....88 B1
Bedford Terr DT6 ....100 B4
Bedwin St SP1 ....213 B3
Beech Ave
Bournemouth BH6 ....123 B2
Holton Heath BH20 ....116 A2
Beech Cl Alderholt SP6 ....42 B3
Broadmayne DT2 ....136 A1
Broadstone BH18 ....86 C2
[1] Spetisbury DT11 ....211 E5
Verwood BH31 ....45 A3
West Lulworth BH20 ....172 B3
Beech Ct BH21 ....59 C2
Beech La
Hawkchurch EX13 ....202 B1
Netherbury DT8 ....204 A3
St.Leonards BH24 ....54 A1
Beech Rd
Puddletown DT2 ....78 A1
Radipole DT4 ....152 A2
Beech Tree Cl DT2 ....206 C2
Beech Wood Cl BH8 ....87 A2
Beechbank Ave BH17 ....86 C1
Beechcroft BH1 ....122 A3
Beechcroft Inf Sch DT4 ....167 B2

Beechcroft La [1] BH24 ....55 B4
Beechcroft Mews [2] BH24 ....55 B4
Beechcroft Rd SP1 ....213 C4
Beeches The
Beaminster DT8 ....204 C4
Bournemouth BH7 ....123 A4
[5] Salisbury SP1 ....213 C2
[1] Shaftesbury SP7 ....12 C2
Wareham St Martin BH20 ....143 A4
Beechey Ct [6] BH8 ....122 A3
Beechey Rd BH8 ....122 A3
Beechfield [30] BH4 ....121 B2
Beechwood BA20 ....27 A1
Beechwood Ave
Bournemouth BH5 ....122 C2
New Milton BH25 ....94 C2
Beechwood Ct BH2 ....121 C1
Beechwood Dr [5] TA18 ....191 F5
Beechwood Gdns BH5 ....123 A2
Beechwood Rd BH22 ....53 C1
Beel Cl [2] DT5 ....181 A1
Beer St BA20 ....27 A2
Belben Cl BH12 ....88 B1
Belben Rd BH12 ....88 B1
Belfield Pk Ave DT4 ....167 A1
Belfield Rd BH6 ....124 A2
Belgrave DT4 ....167 A3
Belgrave Ct BH1 ....122 B4
Belgrave Pl [3] DT5 ....186 C4
Belgrave Rd BH3 ....121 A1
Bell Heather Cl BH16 ....118 A4
Bell La [18] BH15 ....119 A1
Bell St Shaftesbury SP7 ....12 C2
Swanage BH19 ....178 C1
Bellamy La SP1 ....213 B4
Bell's Orch La BH20 ....142 C2
Bellbury Cl [1] DT2 ....78 A1
Belle Vue BH19 ....167 C1
Belle Vue Cl BH6 ....123 B2
Belle Vue Cres BH6 ....123 C2
Belle Vue Gdns [2] BH6 ....123 C2
Belle Vue Gr BH22 ....53 A1
Belle Vue Mans [7] BH6 ....123 C2
Belle Vue Rd
Bournemouth BH6 ....123 C2
Poole BH14 ....120 B3
[4] Salisbury SP1 ....213 B3
Swanage BH19 ....179 B1
Weymouth DT4 ....167 A1
Belle Vue Terr [15] DT5 ....186 C4
Belle Vue Wlk BH22 ....61 C1
Bellflower Cl BH23 ....125 A4
Bellman's Cross BA8 ....19 B3
Bellows Cross BH21 ....40 B4
Bells House BH21 ....59 B3
Bells La BA12 ....1 C4
Belmont Ave BH8 ....90 B1
Belmont Cl
Shaftesbury SP7 ....12 C1
Verwood BH31 ....45 B3
Belmont Rd
New Milton BH25 ....95 A1
Poole BH14 ....120 B3
Belmour Lodge [26] BH4 ....121 B2
Belvedere Rd
Bournemouth BH3 ....122 A3
Christchurch BH23 ....124 A4
[7] Swanage BH19 ....179 B1
Bembury La DT9 ....194 D8
Bemister Rd BH9 ....122 A4
Ben Nevis Rd DT4 ....167 B2
Benbow Cres BH12 ....88 C1
Benbridge Ave BH11 ....88 C3
Bendigo Rd BH23 ....123 C4
Benellen Ave BH4 ....121 B2
Benellen Gdns BH4 ....121 B2
Benellen Rd BH4 ....121 B3
Benellen Twrs BH4 ....121 B2
Bengal Rd BH9 ....121 C4
Benjamin Ct BH23 ....123 C4
Benjamin Rd BH15 ....118 C1
Benlease Way BH19 ....178 C1
Benmoor Rd BH17 ....119 A4
Benmore Cl BH25 ....95 B1
Benmore Rd BH9 ....90 A2
Bennett House [11] BH4 ....121 B2
Bennett Rd BH8 ....122 B3
Bennett's Alley [22] BH15 ....119 A1
Bennetts Hill La DT6 ....101 B1
Bennion Rd BH10 ....89 B2
Benridge Cl BH18 ....87 A2
Benson Rd BH17 ....119 B4
Bentley Rd BH9 ....89 C2
Benville La DT2 ....205 C6
Benville Manor★ DT2 ....205 C6
Benville Rd DT4 ....166 C1
Bere Cl BH17 ....87 B1
Bere Down La BH20 ....80 C3
Bere La DT9 ....195 B7
Bere Marsh DT11 ....198 B7
Bere Rd
Northport BH20 ....142 B3
Winterborne Kingston DT11 ....81 C4
Bere Regis Cty Fst Sch BH20 ....81 A1
Bere Regis Sports Club BH20 ....81 B2
Beresford Cl BH12 ....120 B3
Beresford Gdns BH23 ....124 C3
Beresford Rd
Bournemouth BH6 ....123 C4
Poole BH12 ....120 B4
Berkeley Ave BH12 ....120 B4

Berkeley Cl
9 Pimperne DT11 ......199 D4
Verwood BH31 ....45 A4
Berkeley Ct DT6 ....100 B3
Berkeley Rd
Bournemouth BH3 .....121 C4
1 Pimperne DT11 ......199 D3
16 Yeovil BA20 ....27 B2
Berkeley Rise 8 DT11 ..199 D4
Berkley Ave BH22 .....61 B1
Bermuda Ct 9 BH23 ...126 A4
Bernards Ct BH23 .....123 C4
Berne Ct 11 BH1 ......122 A2
Beron Ct BH15 ....119 C2
Berrans Ave BH11 .....89 A3
Berrans Ct BH11 ......89 A3
Berry La EX13 ....202 D3
Bertram Rd BH25 .....95 B2
Berwick Cl DT6 ....129 B3
Berwick Rd BH3 ......121 C3
Berwyn Ct BH18 ......87 A2
Bessborough Rd
BH13 ....147 C4
Bessells La DT11 .....198 D8
Bessemer Cl BH31 ....45 C2
Bestwall Cres BH20 ...142 C2
Bestwall Rd BH20 ....142 C2
Beswick Ave BH10 ....89 B1
Bethany Ct BH12 .....121 A4
Bethany House BH1 ...122 B3
Bethany Jun CE Sch
BH1 ....122 B3
Bethia Cl BH8 ....122 B3
Bethia Rd BH8 ....122 B3
Bettiscombe Cl BH17 ..87 C1
Bettiscombe Manor House*
DT6 ....203 B3
Beverley Gdns BH10 ..89 B2
Beverley Grange 29
BH4 ....121 B2
Beverley Rd DT3 ......152 B2
Bexington Cl BH11 ....88 C2
Bicknell Boys Sch
BH7 ....123 A4
Bicknell Ct 10 BH4 ...121 B2
Bicknell La BA21 .....27 B4
Bicton Rd BH10 ......89 A2
Biddlecome Orch 5
.....................100 B4
Big Ope DT5 ....186 C4
Bilshay La DT6 ....68 A1
Bimport SP7 ....12 B1
Bincleaves Rd DT4 ...167 B1
Bincombe Dr 2 TA18 .191 F5
Bincombe Rise DT3 ...152 C2
Bindbarrow Rd DT6 ...128 B3
Bindells The DT3 .....166 B3
Bindon Abbey (rems of)*
BH20 ....140 B1
Bindon Cl Poole BH12 .120 C4
West Lulworth BH20 ..172 C4
Bindon La BH20 ......140 B1
Bindon Rd BH20 .....172 B3
Bindon Way BH20 ....140 A1
Bingham Ave BH14 ...147 B4
Bingham Cl
Christchurch BH23 ...124 C4
Verwood BH31 ....45 B2
Bingham Dr BH31 ....45 B2
Bingham Rd
Bournemouth BH9 ....122 A4
Christchurch BH23 ...124 C4
Salisbury SP1 ....213 C4
Verwood BH31 ....45 B2
Binghams Rd DT2 ....137 B3
Binnegar La BH20 ....141 B2
Binnie Rd BH12 ......120 C3
Birch Ave
3 Blandford St Mary
DT11 ....212 B1
Burton BH23 ....92 B2
Ferndown BH22 ......61 C1
Holton Heath BH20 ..116 A2
New Milton BH25 ....94 B3
Birch Cl
Corfe Mullen BH21 ...86 B3
Poole BH14 ....120 C2
St.Leonards BH24 ....53 C2
Birch Dr BH8 ....91 A1
Birch Gr Ferndown BH22 .52 C1
New Milton BH25 ....95 A1
Birch La Puddletown DT2 .77 C2
Yetminster DT9 ......194 C5
Birch Rd BH24 ....54 B2
Birch Wlk BH22 ......61 C2
Birchdale 6 BA20 ....26 C1
Birchdale Rd BH21 ...59 B3
Birchfield Prim Sch
BA21 ....27 C4
Birchfield Rd BA21 ...27 C4
Birchwood Cl BH23 ..125 C4
Birchwood Dr SP6 ....42 B3
Birchwood Mews
BH14 ....120 B2
Birchwood Rd
Poole BH14 ....120 B2
Upton BH16 ....118 A3
Bird's Cl 5 TA18 ....191 E4
Bird's Hill Rd BH15 ..119 C2
Birds Hill Gdns 5 BH15 .119 C2
Birkdale Ct BH18 ....87 A3
Birkdale Rd BH18 ....87 A3
Bishop Cl BH12 ......121 B4
Bishop Ct BH24 ......55 B4
Bishop Rd BH9 ......122 A4

Bishop Wordsworths Sch
SP1 ....213 B2
Bishop's Cl SP1 ......213 B2
Bishop's Palace* SP1 213 B2
Bishop's Rd
Abbotsbury DT3 .....149 B4
Portesham DT3 ......131 B1
Bishop's Wlk SP1 ....213 B2
Bishopdown Rd SP1 ..213 B4
Bishops Cl
Abbotsbury DT3 .....149 A4
Bournemouth BH7 ...122 C4
Mere BA12 ....3 A3
Bishops Dr SP2 ......213 A1
Bishops La BA22 .....193 A6
Bitchams Mead BH20 .81 A1
Bitterne Way BH31 ...45 B3
Black Hill BH31 .....45 B3
Black La DT11 ....212 C2
Black Lawn SP8 .....5 C2
Black Mere BA12 ....26 B3
Black Moor Rd BH31 .45 C2
Blackberry La
Christchurch BH23 ...124 C3
Radipole DT3 ....152 B1
Sherborne DT9 ......30 A4
Blackbird Cl BH17 ...118 C4
Blackbird Way BH21 .93 B4
Blackbirds 6 DT9 ....194 D8
Blackburn Rd BH12 ..120 A3
Blackers Hole (Cave)*
BH19 ....184 B3
Blackfield La BH22 ..53 A2
Blackfield Rd BH8 ...90 B2
Blackfriars Way SP1 .213 B2
Blackhill Rd BH16 ...116 B2
Blackhill Rd W BH16 .116 B1
Blacklands La DT11 ..197 D3
Blackmoor BA8 ......19 A3
Blackmoor La BA8 ...19 A2
Blackmore Rd
Shaftesbury SP7 .....13 A2
Stalbridge DT10 .....33 B4
Blacknell La TA18 ...191 F4
Blackney La DT6 .....203 E2
Blacknoll La DT2 ....138 C2
Blacknor Rd DT5 ....186 C2
Blackpool Cnr DT6 ..202 B1
Blackrow La DT10 ...196 D7
Blacksmith Cl BH21 .86 B3
Blacksmith's La DT9 .194 D8
Blacksmith's Piece
DT2 ....105 B1
Blackthorn Way
New Milton BH25 ....95 B2
Verwood BH31 ......45 B3
Blackwater Dr BH21 .87 B4
Blackwater Gr SP6 ..42 A3
Blackwater La EX13 .202 C3
Bladen View DT11 ...79 C4
Blagdon Cl DT2 .....133 B3
Blagdon Rd DT1 ....107 B3
Blair Ave BH14 .....120 B2
Blair Cl BH25 ....94 C2
Blake Dene Rd BH14 .120 A1
Blake Hill Ave BH14 .120 B1
Blake Hill Cres BH14 .120 B1
Blake Rd 22 TA18 ...191 F4
Blakey Rd SP1 ......213 C2
Blandford Cl BH15 ..118 C1
Blandford Hill
Milborne St Andrew DT11 .79 C4
Winterborne Whitechurch
DT11 ....210 C3
Blandford Hospl DT11 212 B1
Blandford Rd
Corfe Mullen BH21 ..86 B4
Hamworthy BH15 ...118 B2
Iwerne Minster DT11 .37 C1
Pamphill BH21 ......58 B4
Shapwick DT11 .....48 C1
Shillingstone DT11 ..198 B6
Sturminster Marshall
BH21 ....56 B2
Blandford Rd N
Lytchett Minster & Upton
BH16 ....85 A1
Upton BH16 ....118 A4
Blandford Sports Ctr
DT11 ....212 B2
Blandford St Mary CE VA Fst
Sch DT11 ....212 B1
Blandford VC Comp Sch The
DT11 ....212 B2
Blaney Way BH21 ...86 B3
Blanford Hts Ind Est
DT11 ....212 B1
Blashford Lakes Study Ctr*
BH24 ....47 B3
Bleak St BA9 ....1 B2
Bleax Cl SP7 ....22 C1
Bleet La SP8 ....10 B3
Bleke St SP7 ....12 C2
Blemheim Rd DT3 ...152 A1
Blenheim Cres SO41 .95 C3
Blenheim Dr
25 Bournemouth BH4 .121 B2
Christchurch BH23 ..124 A4
Blenheim Dr BH23 ..125 A3
Blenheim Rd BA21 ..27 C4
Blind La
Berwick St John SP7 .188 B3
Burstock DT8 ....203 C6
Ellingham Harbridge & Ibsley
SP6 ....43 C1
Evershot DT2 ....206 B7
Marshwood DT6 ....203 D1
Thorncombe TA20 ..202 E6

Blind La continued
Wimborne Minster BH21 .59 A3
Blind La Cl DT6 .....68 C1
Blind St BH20 ....81 A1
Blindmere Rd DT5 ..186 C2
Blissford Hill SP6 ...43 C3
Bloody Shard Gate
DT11 ....188 A1
Bloomfield Ave BH9 .89 C1
Bloomfield Pl BH9 ..89 C1
Bloxworth Rd BH12 .120 C4
Blue Boar Row SP1 .213 B3
Bluebell Cl BH23 ...125 A4
Bluebell Cl BH17 ...86 C1
Bluebell Rd BA22 ..26 B3
Bluntshay La DT6 ...66 C2
Blyth Cl DT3 ....91 B2
Blyth Way SP1 .....213 C4
Blythe Rd BH21 ....86 B3
Blythswood Ct BH25 .126 C4
Boar St BA12 ......3 A3
Bob Hann Cl BH12 ..120 B3
Bockhampton Cross
DT2 ....109 A2
Bockhampton La DT2 .109 A2
Bockhampton Rd BH23 .92 C3
Bodkin La DT3 .....168 A3
Bodley Rd BH13 ....147 C4
Bodorgan Rd BH2 ..121 C2
Bodowen Cl BH23 ..92 B1
Bodowen Rd BH23 ..92 B1
Bodsmarsh La DT10 .21 C1
Bognor Rd BH18 ...86 C2
Bohay's Dr DT4 ....180 B4
Bokerley Ditch* SP6 .190 A5
Boldre Cl
Barton on Sea BH25 .126 B4
Poole BH20 ....120 B4
Boleyn Cl BH9 .....90 A2
Boleyn Cres DT4 ...180 C4
Bolton Cl BH6 .....123 C2
Bolton Cres BH22 ..62 A3
Bolton Ct 4 BH6 ...123 C2
Bolton Rd BH6 .....123 C2
Bon Accord Rd BH19 .179 A1
Bond Ave BH22 ....52 C2
Bond Rd BH15 .....119 C3
Bond St Radipole DT4 .167 B2
4 Yeovil BA20 ......27 B2
Boney Rd DT4 .....139 C4
Bonfields Ave BH19 .179 A2
Bonham La BA12 ...1 C4
Bonham Rd BH3 ...121 C4
Bonhole La DT6 ...101 C2
Bonington Cl BH23 .124 C4
Bonnett's La BH20 .142 C2
Bonscombe La DT6 .101 B3
Bonvils Rd BH19 ...183 A4
Bookham La DT2 ...208 B7
Boot La 7 DT9 ....194 D8
Boozer Pit TA16 ...191 F8
Border Dr BH16 ...118 B3
Border Lodge BH23 .94 B1
Border Rd BH16 ...118 B3
Boreham Rd BH23 .123 B3
Borley Rd BH17 ...119 A4
Borthwick Rd BH1 ..122 C3
Boscombe Cliff Rd
BH5 ....122 C2
Boscombe Gr Rd BH1 .122 B3
Boscombe Overcliff Dr
BH5 ....123 A2
Boscombe Spa Rd
BH5 ....122 B2
Bosley Cl BH23 ....91 C1
Bosley Way BH23 ..91 C1
Boston Lodge 22 BH4 .121 B2
Boswell's Cl BH21 ..81 A2
Bosworth Mews BH9 .90 A2
Bothen Dr DT6 .....100 C3
Bothenwood La BH21 .189 E1
Bottom Rd DT11 ...198 F4
Bottlebush La BH21 .189 E1
Bouchers Way SP2 .213 B1
Boulnois Ave BH14 .120 C2
Boulton Cl DT4 ....180 B4
Bound La DT9 .....194 F2
Boundary Ave BH25 .26 B4
Boundary Cl
Swanage BH19 .....185 B4
Yeovil BA21 ....27 A4
Boundary Dr BH23 .59 B3
Boundary La BH24 .53 C2
Boundary Rd
Bournemouth BH10 .89 C2
Yeovil BA22 ....26 A4
Boundary View 1 DT11 212 B2
Bountys La BH12 ...120 C3
Bourne Ave
Bournemouth BH2 ..121 C2
Salisbury SP1 ......213 C3
Bourne Cl
Bournemouth BH4 ..121 B2
8 Salisbury SP1 ....213 C2
Bourne Ct
24 Bournemouth BH2 .121 C2
Wimborne Minster BH21 .59 B2
Bourne Dr BH20 ...142 B3
Bourne Dro DT2 ...76 C3
Bourne Hill SP1 ....213 B3
Bourne Pines BH1 .121 C2
Bourne Valley Rd
BH12 ....121 A3
Bourne Way
Gillingham SP8 .....5 C2
Salisbury SP1 ......213 C3
Bournemouth & Poole Coll of
F Ed BH14 ....119 C2

Bournemouth & Poole Coll
The BH1 ....122 A2
Bournemouth Aquarium*
BH2 ....121 C1
Bournemouth Aviation Mus*
BH23 ....91 A4
Bournemouth Central Bsns
Pk BH1 ....122 B3
Bournemouth Crown & Cty
Cts* BH7 ....91 B1
Bournemouth Gram Sch
(Boys) BH8 ....90 B1
Bournemouth Gram Sch
(Girls) BH8 ....90 A1
Bournemouth Int Airport
BH23 ....90 C4
Bournemouth Int Ctr*
BH2 ....121 C1
Bournemouth Meml Homes
BH8 ....90 C1
Bournemouth Nuffield Hospl
BH8 ....122 A3
Bournemouth Rd
Blandford St Mary DT11 .212 B1
Charlton Marshall DT11 .211 D6
Poole BH14 ....120 B2
Bournemouth Sta
BH1 ....122 A2
Bournemouth Univ
BH12 ....121 B4
Bournewood Dr BH4 .121 B2
Bourton Gdns BH7 .123 A4
Bourton Prim Sch SP8 .1 C1
Bouverie Ave SP2 ..213 A1
Bouverie Ave S SP2 .213 A1
Bouverie Cl
28 Barton on Sea BH25 .95 A1
Salisbury SP2 ......213 A1
Boveridge Gdns BH9 .90 A2
Boveridge House Sch
BH21 ....190 B1
Bovington Cl BH17 .87 C1
Bovington Fst Sch
BH20 ....139 B3
Bovington La BH20 .139 C3
Bovington Mid Sch
BH20 ....139 C3
Bow The 3 DT1 ...108 A1
Bowden La BA8 ....18 B3
Bowden Rd
Abbas & Templecombe
BA8 ....18 A4
Poole BH12 ....88 B1
Bowditch Row 25 TA18 191 F4
Bowdowns DT6 ....204 B3
Bower Ct 5 DT9 ...194 C5
Bower Gdns SP1 ...213 C3
Bower Rd BH8 .....122 B4
Bowers Rd 6 DT5 ..186 C2
Bowerswain Hollow
BH21 ....201 B5
Bowerwood Rd SP6 .42 C4
Bowes La 6 DT8 ...204 A8
Bowey DT11 ....197 F6
Bowgrove Rd DT8 ..204 D5
Bowhayes Bridport DT6 .100 C3
8 Crewkerne TA18 ..191 F4
Bowland Rise BH25 .95 B1
Bowleaze BA21 ....26 C3
Bowleaze Coveway
DT3 ....168 A3
Bowling Gn La SP5 .189 D5
Bown Hill DT5 .....186 C1
Box Cl BH17 ......119 A4
Boyd Rd BH12 .....120 C3
Boyle Cl DT10 .....33 B4
Boyne's La
Iwerne Minster DT11 .38 B1
Iwerne Stepleton DT11 .199 B7
Boys Hill Dro DT9 .195 D5
Boyte Rd 14 DT11 .199 D4
Bozley Hill SP7 ....24 C3
Brabazon Dr BH23 .125 A4
Brabazon Rd BH21 .59 C1
Brabourne Ave BH22 .61 B2
Bracken Cl BH24 ..53 C2
Bracken Glen BH15 .119 C3
Bracken Lodge 3 BH6 .123 C2
Bracken Rd
Bournemouth BH6 ..123 B2
Ferndown BH22 ....61 A4
Bracken Way BH23 .94 A1
Brackenbury Cty Infs Sch
DT5 ....186 C4
Brackendale Ct BH1 .52 C4
Brackendale Rd BH8 .122 B4
Brackendown Ave
DT3 ....167 C4
Brackenhill BH13 ..121 A1
Brackenhill Rd BH6 .60 A4
Brackens Way 12 BH13 .147 C4
Brackley Cl BH23 ..91 A4
Bradbourne Rd BH2 .121 C2
Bradford Abbas Prim Sch
DT9 ....28 B1
Bradford La DT9 ...195 B6
Bradford Rd
Bournemouth BH9 ..90 B2
1 Crewkerne TA18 ..192 A3
Sherborne DT9 .....29 C3
Weymouth DT4 .....167 A1
Bradpole Rd BH8 ..90 C1
Bradstock Cl BH17 .119 A4
Braemar Ave BH6 ..124 C4
Braemar Cl BH6 ...124 A2
Braemar Dr BH23 ..93 C1
Braemar Rd DT1 ...135 B4

Ber - Bri 219

Braeside Rd
Ferndown BH22 ....53 A2
St.Leonards BH24 ..54 A2
Braidley Rd BH2 ...121 C2
Brailswood Rd BH15 .119 C2
Braishfield Gdns BH8 .90 B1
Brakes Hill DT2 ....194 A2
Bramar Ct BH4 ....121 B1
Bramble Cl SP6 ...42 B3
Bramble Ct BH22 ..53 A1
Bramble Dr DT6 ...100 B3
Bramble Dro DT2 ..136 A1
Bramble Edge DT2 .136 A1
Bramble La
Christchurch BH23 ..94 A1
Haselbury Plucknett
TA18 ....192 C5
Bramblecombe La
DT11 ....209 D4
Brambles The SP1 ..213 C3
Brambling Cl DT3 ..152 B2
Bramdon Cl 5 DT3 .150 A4
Bramdon La DT3 ...150 B3
Bramley Cl 8 TA18 .191 F5
Bramley Ct BH22 ..61 B3
Bramley Hill
Bridport DT6 ....100 C4
Mere BA12 ....2 C3
Bramley Rd
Bournemouth BH10 .89 B3
Ferndown BH22 ....61 B3
Brampton Rd BH15 .119 B3
Bramshaw Gdns BH8 .90 B1
Bramshaw Way BH25 .126 B4
Branders Cl BH6 ...124 C3
Branders La BH6 ..124 A3
Brandwood Ct 4 BH14 .120 C2
Brandy La 9 DT5 ..186 C4
Brandy Row 8 DT5 .186 C4
Branksea Ave BH15 .118 C1
Branksea Cl BH15 .118 C1
Branksome Cl BH25 .95 A1
Branksome Ct 14 BH13 .147 C4
Branksome Dene Rd
BH4 ....121 A1
Branksome Heath Mid Sch
BH12 ....120 B3
Branksome Hill Rd
BH4 ....121 A3
Branksome Sta BH12 .120 C2
Branksome Twrs
BH13 ....147 D4
Branksome Wood Gdns
BH2 ....121 B4
Branksome Wood Rd
BH2 ....121 C1
Branscombe Cl 1 DT5 .186 C1
Bransgore CE Prim Sch
BH23 ....93 B4
Brantwood 8 DT8 ..204 C4
Branwell Cl BH23 ..92 A1
Brassey Cl BH9 ....90 A1
Brassey Rd BH9 ...90 A1
Brassey Terr BH9 ..89 C1
Bratch La DT11 ....200 D1
Breach Cl SP8 .....1 C1
Breach Field BH20 .140 A1
Breach La
Kington Magna SP8 .9 B2
Shaftesbury SP7 ...12 B1
Breaches La BH25 .163 A1
Breamore Cl BH25 .94 C2
Brearley Cl BH23 ..126 A4
Brecon Cl
Bournemouth BH10 .89 C3
New Milton BH25 ..95 B1
Bredy Cl BH17 ....87 B1
Bredy End DT6 ....101 C1
Bredy Rd DT6 .....128 B4
Bremble Cl BH12 ..88 B1
Brendon Cl BH8 ...90 C1
Breston Cl 5 DT5 ..186 C1
Brian Cl BH23 .....143 A4
Briar Cl
Christchurch BH23 ..124 C1
Gillingham SP8 ....5 C1
Mudford BA21 .....28 A4
Poole BH15 ....119 C3
Radipole DT4 ......167 A3
Briar Way BH21 ...60 A3
Briarfield 28 BH4 ..121 B2
Briars End DT2 ....137 C3
Briars The 3 BA20 .26 C1
Briarswood Rd BH16 .118 B4
Brick Yd La 4 TA18 .191 F5
Brickyard La Bourton SP8 .1 C1
Broadstone BH21 ..58 A1
Ferndown BH21 ....61 A3
1 Gillingham SP8 ...6 A1
Gillingham SP8 ....10 C1
Silton SP8 ....4 C1
Sturminster Newton
DT10 ....197 A7
Swanage BH19 .....179 A3
Bridewell La SP7 ..7 A1
Bridge App BH15 ..119 A1
Bridge Cl SP8 .....6 A1
Bridge Inn La DT3 .153 B2
Bridge Pl BH10 ...89 B4
Bridge Rd DT6 ....97 A4
Bridge St Bourton SP8 .1 C1
Christchurch BH23 ..124 B3
6 Lyme Regis DT7 ..96 B3
Netherbury DT6 ...204 C2

Bridge St continued
Salisbury SP2 ....213 B2
Sturminster Marshall
BH21 ....56 B2
Sturminster Newton
DT10 ....197 D8
Bridges Cl BH22 ....53 A2
Bridges The BH24 ....55 A4
Bridgewater Rd BH12 .120 B3
Bridle Cl BH16 ....118 B4
Bridle Cres BH7 ....123 B4
Bridle Way
Stofold BA22 ....193 F8
Wimborne Minster BH21 ...60 B3
Bridlebank Way DT3 ..152 A4
Bridleways BH31 ....45 A3
Bridport & W Dorset Golf
Club DT6 ....100 B1
Bridport Com Hospl
DT6 ....100 A4
Bridport CP Sch DT6 ..100 C4
Bridport Leisure Ctr
DT6 ....100 B3
Bridport Rd
Beaminster DT8 ....204 D3
Broadwindsor DT8 ....203 C8
Dorchester DT1 ....107 B1
Poole BH12 ....120 C4
Verwood BH31 ....45 A3
Brierley Ave BH22 ....61 C1
Brierley Cl BH10 ....89 C3
Brierley Hay [9] DT9 ..194 C5
Brierley Rd BH10 ....89 C2
Brigadier Cl [1] BA22 ...26 B3
Bright Rd BH15 ....119 B3
Brighthay La DT6 ....67 A1
Brightlands Ave BH6 ..123 C3
Brightsmead DT2 ....209 B6
Brimclose Rd TA17 .....191 B7
Brimley Hill EX13 ....202 A2
Brimley Rd EX13 ....202 A3
Brinscombe La [3] SP7 ...13 A1
Brinsley Cl DT10 ....35 A1
Brinsons Cl BH23 ....92 B2
Brionne Way SP7 ....13 C1
Brisbane Rd
Christchurch BH23 ....91 C1
Radipole DT3 ....152 C1
Brister End DT9 ....194 C5
Bristol Rd DT9 ....30 A4
Brit The [4] DT8 ....204 D4
Brit View Rd DT6 ....100 A1
Britannia Ct BH12 ....120 A4
Britannia Rd BH14 .....120 A2
Britannia Way
Christchurch BH23 ....125 A4
Dorchester DT1 ....134 C4
Britford La SP2 ....213 B1
Britford La W [1] SP2 ..213 B1
Britford Prim Sch
SP5 ....213 C1
Britmore La SP7 ....13 C1
Brixey Cl BH12 ....120 B4
Brixey Rd BH12 ....120 B4
Brixey's La BH20 ....142 C2
Broad Ave BH8 ....122 B4
Broad Cl DT11 ....81 C4
Broad Hill BA22 ....192 D7
Broad La Bridport DT6 ..100 A3
East Chinnock BA22 .....192 E7
Broad Mead Rd BA21 ...45 A1
Broad Rd BH19 ....179 B1
Broad Robin SP8 ....5 C1
Broad St DT7 ....96 B3
Broad Stone The★
DT2 ....104 C1
Broadacres
East Coker BA22 ....193 C8
Gillingham SP8 ....5 C2
Broadcroft Gdns DT5 ..187 A2
Broadhill La SP6 ....43 C4
Broadhurst Ave BH10 ...89 C2
Broadlands Ave BH6 ..123 C3
Broadlands Cl
Bournemouth BH8 ....90 B2
Christchurch BH23 ....94 A1
Salisbury SP1 ....213 B4
Broadlands Rd DT3 ....152 A1
Broadleaze BA21 ....206 C4
Broadmayne Cty Fst Sch
DT2 ....136 B2
Broadmayne Rd BH12 ..121 A4
Broadmead DT2 ....136 A1
Broadmead Ave DT6 ..100 B4
Broadmead Cl [4] DT8 ..204 A8
Broadmeadow Rd
DT4 ....180 B4
Broadmoor Rd BH11 .....86 B4
Broadoak Ave [2] DT8 ..204 A4
Broadoak Rd DT6 ....67 C1
Broads The BH21 ....58 C3
Broadshard La BH24 .....47 B1
Broadshard Rd TA18 ..191 F5
Broadstone Fst Sch
BH18 ....87 A2
Broadstone La
Hardington Mandeville
BA22 ....193 A6
West Chinnock TA18 .....192 C8
Broadstone Mid Sch
BH18 ....87 B3
Broadstone Way BH18 ..86 C1
Broadwater Ave BH14 ..120 B1
Broadway
Bournemouth BH6 ....124 A2

Broadway continued
Merriott TA16 ....191 E7
Broadway Ct BH12 ....121 A3
Broadway Gables
BH14 ....120 C2
Broadway Gdns [6] BH21 .59 B2
Broadway La
Bournemouth BH8 ....90 B2
West Chinnock BA22 ...192 D8
Broadway Mews BH14 ..119 C2
Broadway Pk [4] BH21 ...59 B2
Broadway The BH10 .....89 B3
Broadwey Cl DT3 ....152 B2
DT8 ....203 E5
Broadwindsor CE Prim Sch
DT8 ....203 E5
Broadwindsor Craft & Design
Ctr★ DT8 ....203 E5
Broadwindsor Rd DT8 ..204 B4
Brockenhurst Rd BH9 ...90 A1
Brockhills La BH25 ....95 B3
Brockhole La TA17 .....191 B8
Brockington La BH21 ..201 C5
Brockley Rd BH10 ....89 C2
Brocks Pine BH24 ....54 A2
Brodham Way DT11 ....198 B5
Brog St BH21 ....58 B1
Broke La DT9 ....195 D6
Brombys The [7] BH15 ..119 B1
Bromley House BH14 ..121 A3
Bromley Rd BH23 ....92 A1
Bronte Ave BH23 ....92 A1
Brook Ave BH25 ....95 A2
Brook Ave N BH25 ....95 A2
Brook Cl BH10 ....89 B2
Brook Dr BH31 ....45 B2
Brook La
Bransgore BH23 ....93 A4
Corfe Mullen BH21 ....86 B3
Henstridge BA8 ....19 A2
Woodlands BH21 ....44 A4
Brook Rd
Bournemouth BH10 ....89 B2
Poole BH12 ....120 B3
Wimborne Minster BH21 ...59 C2
Brook St
Milborne Port DT9 ....17 B1
Shipton Gorge DT6 ....101 B2
Brook Terr SP6 ....43 A4
Brook Way BH23 ....125 B4
Brookdale Cl BH18 ....87 A2
Brookdale Farm BH18 ...87 A2
Brookhouse St [8] DT1 ..107 B1
Brookland Way [4] BA8 ..19 A2
Brooklands BH4 ....121 A2
Brooklyn Ct BH25 ....94 C2
Brookmead Cl DT3 .....153 B2
Brooks Cl BH24 ....55 B3
Brookside
Ellingham Harbridge & Ibsley
SP6 ....43 C1
[8] Gillingham SP8 ....5 C2
Milborne Port DT9 ....17 B1
West Coker BA22 ....193 A8
Brookside Cl DT3 ....168 B4
Brookside Pk Homes
BH21 ....86 A2
Brookside Rd
Bransgore BH23 ....93 A4
Wimborne Minster BH21 ...59 C2
Brookside Way BH23 .....93 C1
Broom Hill DT2 ....205 F5
Broom Rd BH12 ....88 B1
Broomfield Ct BH22 ....61 C3
Broomfield Dr SP6 ....42 B3
Broughton Ave BH10 ....89 C2
Broughton Cl BH10 ....89 C2
Broughton Cres DT4 ..180 B4
Broughtons Dr [2] TA18 .192 A3
Brown St
Bishop's Caundle DT9 ..196 A7
[14] Salisbury SP1 ....213 B3
Brown's Cres DT3 ....166 C3
Brown's La SP8 ....10 C2
Browen Rd BH9 ....122 A4
Brownes Pl DT2 ....73 C2
Browning Ave BH5 .....123 A2
Browning Rd BH12 .....120 B3
Brownlow Ct [23] BH4 ..121 B2
Brownlow St DT4 ....167 B2
Browns La SP6 ....190 E3
Brownsea Ave BH21 .....86 B3
Brownsea Cl BH25 ....94 C2
Brownsea Ct BH14 .....147 A4
Brownsea Island (NT)★
BH15 ....146 B2
Brownsea Rd BH13 .....147 A4
Brownsea View Ave
BH14 ....120 B1
Brownsea View Cl
BH14 ....120 B1
Brudenell Ave BH13 ....147 B4
Brudenell Rd BH13 .....147 B3
Brune Way BH22 ....61 B2
Brunel Cl BH31 ....45 C2
Brunel Dr DT3 ....153 C2
Brunsell's Knap DT10 ...33 A1
Brunstead Pl BH12 .....121 A2
Brunstead Rd BH12 ....121 A2
Brunswick St BA20 .....27 B2
Brushy Bush La SP5 ..188 F3
Brutus Cl DT1 ....134 C4
Bryanston Pk★ DT11 ..212 A2
Bryanston Sch DT11 ...212 A3
Bryanston St DT11 .....212 A2
Bryanstone Rd BH3 ....121 C4
Bryant Rd BH12 ....121 A4
Bryants La DT4 ....180 A4
Brymer Rd
[4] Puddletown DT2 ....78 A1

Brymer Rd continued
Puddletown DT2 ....110 A4
Brymers Rd [14] DT5 ....186 C4
Brympton Ave BA22 .....26 C4
Brympton Way BA20 ....26 C2
Bryn Rd Sandford BH20 .143 A4
Weymouth DT4 ....167 A1
Bryony Cl BH18 ....86 C2
Bryony Gdns SP8 ....5 B1
Bub La BH23 ....124 C3
Buccaneers Cl BH23 ..124 C3
Buccleuch Rd BH13 ....121 A1
Bucehayes Cl BH23 ....126 A4
Buchanan Ave BH7 ....122 C3
Buckhill Cl [5] TA18 ....191 F3
Buckhorn Cl DT6 ....69 A4
Buckingham Ct
[2] Christchurch BH23 ..126 A4
Poole BH15 ....119 B2
Buckingham Mans [5]
BH1 ....122 A2
Buckingham Rd
Gillingham SP8 ....5 C1
Poole BH12 ....120 B4
Buckingham Way DT1 ..135 B4
Buckingham Wlk BH25 .94 C2
Buckland Gr BH23 ....93 C1
Buckland Newton Prim Sch
DT2 ....208 A8
Buckland Rd
Poole BH12 ....120 B3
Yeovil BA21 ....28 A3
Buckland Terr BH12 ....120 B3
Buckle Pl BA22 ....26 B3
Bucklers Mead [1] DT9 .194 C5
Bucklers Mead Rd
BA21 ....27 C4
Bucklers Mead Sch
BA21 ....27 C4
Bucklers Way BH8 ....90 B2
Buckthorn Cl BH17 ....86 C1
Buddens La SP7 ....23 C2
Buddle Hill SP6 ....43 C2
Buddleia Cl DT3 ....152 C1
Budmouth Ave DT3 ....168 A3
Budmouth Sch DT4 ....166 C2
Buffalo Mews BH15 ....119 A1
Buffetts Rd DT10 ....35 A1
Bugdens La BH31 ....45 B3
Bugway La DT10 ..202 B8
Bulbury Woods Golf Club
BH16 ....115 C4
Bull Bridge Mead
BA22 ....193 D3
Bull Cl DT2 ....106 C2
Bull Gd La DT10 ....35 B1
Bull La
Maiden Newton DT2 ....72 C4
[16] Poole BH15 ....119 B1
Punknowle DT2 ....129 B3
Buller Ave BA22 ....26 B3
Buller's Way DT3 ....148 C3
Bullfinch Cl BH17 ....86 C1
Bullocks La DT11 ....197 A1
Bulls La [4] TA18 ....191 E4
Bumpers La DT5 ....187 A2
Bunford La BA20 ....26 C2
Bunting Rd BH22 ....61 A4
Burbidge Cl BH16 ....84 B1
Burbitt La DT6 ....101 B2
Burbridge Cl BH17 .....119 C4
Burcombe Rd BH10 .....89 B3
Burdens [2] DT10 ....197 A4
Burdock Rd BH23 ....93 A1
Bure Cl BH23 ....125 A3
Bure Haven Dr BH23 ..125 A3
Bure Homage Gdns
BH23 ....125 A3
Bure Homage La
BH23 ....125 A3
Bure La BH23 ....125 A3
Bure Pk BH23 ....125 A3
Bure Rd BH23 ....125 A3
Burford Ave SP2 ....213 A3
Burford Cl BH23 ....91 B1
Burford Ct [15] BH1 ....122 A4
Burford Rd SP2 ....213 B1
Burges Cl DT10 ....20 C2
Burgess Cl BH11 ....88 C2
Burgess Field BH21 .....44 B3
Burgess Gn SP1 ....213 C4
Burleigh Rd BH6 ....123 B3
Burleston Dro DT2 ....78 C1
Burley Cl
Barton on Sea BH25 ....126 B4
Verwood BH31 ....45 A3
Burley Rd
Bransgore BH23 ....93 A4
Burton BH23 ....92 B3
Poole BH12 ....120 B3
Burling Terr [1] BH12 ..121 A2
Burlington Arc [34] BH1 .121 C2
Burlington Rd BH19 ....179 B2
Burn Cl BH31 ....45 C2
Burn View DT2 ....107 C3
Burnaby Cl BH4 ....121 B1
Burnaby Rd BH4 ....121 B1
Burnage Ct [18] BH13 ..147 C4
Burnbake Rd BH31 ....45 A3
Burnbrae Rd BH22 ....61 B1
Burnet Way SP1 ....213 C4
Burnett Ave BH23 .....123 C4
Burnett Rd BH23 ....123 C4
Burngate Rd BH15 .....118 C1
Burnham Dr BH8 ....122 B4
Burnham's La BH19 ....178 B3
Burnleigh Gdns BH25 ...95 B2

Burns Rd
Bournemouth BH6 ....123 B4
Northport BH20 ....142 B3
Burnside
Christchurch BH23 ....125 B4
Winterborne St Martin
DT2 ....133 B3
Burraton Sq [6] DT1 ....107 B1
Burroughes Ave BA21 ...27 A3
Burrows La BH31 ....41 A1
Burrywells BH21 ....102 B3
Burstock La DT8 ....203 C7
Burt's La Holt BH21 .....52 B4
Horton BH21 ....44 B1
Burt's Pl [6] BH19 ....179 B1
Burtley Rd BH6 ....123 C2
Burton Bradstock VC Prim
Sch DT6 ....128 A4
Burton CE Prim Sch
BH23 ....92 B2
Burton Cl Burton BH23 ..92 B1
Shaftesbury SP7 ....13 A2
St.Leonards BH24 ....53 C3
Wool BH20 ....139 C1
Burton Cross BH20 ....139 C1
Burton Hall BH23 ....92 B2
Burton Hall Pl BH23 .....92 B2
Burton La BA22 ....193 C8
Burton Rd
Abbotsbury DT3 ....148 A4
Bothenhampton DT6 .....100 C1
Burton Bradstock DT6 ..128 A4
Christchurch BH23 ....124 C4
Poole BH13 ....121 A2
Puncknowle DT2 ....129 C1
Wool BH20 ....139 C1
Burton St DT10 ....20 C2
Burton Wood BH20 ....139 C1
Burtoncroft BH23 ....92 B2
Burts Hill BH21 ....59 B3
Bury Rd BH13 ....120 C1
Bush Pk DT11 ....81 C4
Bushell Rd BH15 ....119 B4
Bushes Hill SP6 ....5 A4
Bushes Rd DT11 ....199 A4
Bushey La BH20 ....162 B2
Bushey Rd BH8 ....90 B1
Bushfield Rd [1] TA18 ..191 E3
Bushmead Dr BH24 .....54 A3
Bute Dr BH23 ....126 A4
Butler Cl SP2 ....213 B1
Butlers La BH23 ....47 C1
Butt Cl DT2 ....78 A1
Butt Farm Cl DT2 .....105 B1
Butt La Bere Regis BH20 .81 A2
Chideock DT6 ....66 C1
Butt La Hollow BH20 .....81 A2
Buttercup Cl [2] SP8 .....5 B1
Buttercup Dr BH23 ....93 A1
Buttercup Way DT4 ....100 B1
Butterwick Dro DT9 ....195 D6
Buttery The BH23 ....124 B4
Button's La [18] BH15 ..119 B1
Butts Cl Marnhull DT10 ..20 C1
Winfrith Newburgh DT2 ..156 C3
Butts La SP8 ....21 B4
Butts Mead [1] SP7 ....13 A1
Butts Quarry La TA18 ..192 A4
Butts Rd SP1 ....213 B3
Butts Terr SP2 ....213 B3
Butts The
[12] Child Okeford DT11 .198 C7
Shaftesbury SP7 ....12 B2
Buxton Cl [8] DT4 ....180 B4
Buxton Rd DT4 ....180 B4
Buzbury Rings★ DT11 .211 E8
Byron Cl BH23 ....61 B3
Byron House [16] BH25 ..95 A1
Byron Rd
Barton on Sea BH25 ....126 C4
Bournemouth BH5 ....122 C2
Wimborne Minster BH21 ..59 B3
Byways Cl [4] SP1 ....213 C2

C

Cabot Bsns Village
BH17 ....119 A4
Cabot La BH17 ....119 A4
Cabot Way BH25 ....94 C2
Cachy Rd BH20 ....139 C4
Caddy La BA12 ....2 C3
Cadhay Cl BH25 ....94 C2
Cadley Cl DT11 ....212 B3
Cadnam Way BH8 ....90 B2
Cadogan Rd BH24 ....55 B4
Caesar's Way BH18 .....86 C2
Caird Ave BH25 ....95 B1
Cairns Cl BH23 ....123 C4
Caister Cl BA22 ....61 B3
Calcraft Rd BH20 ....177 A4
Calder Rd BH17 ....119 C4
Caledon Rd BH14 .....120 C2
Caledonian Cl
Christchurch BH23 ....125 A4
Radipole DT4 ....167 B3
Caley Way DT6 ....69 A1
Calf Cl La DT10 ....197 F8
Calfhay La DT9 ....19 C4
Calkin Cl BH23 ....92 A1
Calluna Rd BH12 ....120 B3
Callway La DT12 ....209 B2
Calmore Cl BH8 ....90 B2
Calves La SP7 ....12 A2
Calvin Rd BH9 ....121 C4
Camborne Pl BA22 .....28 A3

Camborne St BA21 ....28 A3
Cambridge Cl BA20 .....26 C3
Cambridge Gdns BH23 ..91 C3
Cambridge Rd
Bournemouth BH2 ....121 C3
Dorchester DT1 ....107 B3
Salisbury SP1 ....213 A4
Weymouth DT4 ....166 C2
Cambridge Wlk [1] DT1 .107 B1
Camden Cl BH9 ....90 A1
Camden Way DT1 ....134 C4
Came Down Cl DT3 .....152 B2
Came Down Golf Club
DT2 ....134 C1
Came House★ DT2 .....135 B3
Came View Cl DT1 .....135 B4
Came View Rd DT1 .....135 B4
Camel Gn Rd SP6 ....42 B3
Camellia Cl BH31 ....45 A1
Camellia Gdns BH25 ....95 A1
Camelot Way SP8 ....5 B1
Cameron Rd BH23 .....124 B4
Camesworth La DT6 .....69 A4
Cammel Rd BH22 ....61 B1
Camp Rd
Chickerell DT4 ....180 A4
West Coker BA22 ....26 B1
Campbell Rd
Bournemouth BH1 ....122 C3
Burton BH23 ....92 B2
Salisbury SP1 ....213 B3
Campion Cl
[5] Gillingham SP8 ....5 B1
Radipole DT4 ....167 C4
Campion Dr BA22 ....26 B3
Campion Gr BH23 ....124 C3
Canberra Cres DT3 .....152 C2
Canberra Rd
Christchurch BH23 ....91 C3
Radipole DT3 ....152 C1
Candy's La [6] DT11 ....198 B6
Candys Cl BH21 ....58 C1
Candys La BH21 ....58 C1
Canford Ave BH11 ....89 A1
Canford Bottom BH21 ...60 B3
Canford Cliffs Ave
BH14 ....120 C1
Canford Cliffs Rd
BH13 ....120 C1
Canford Cres BH13 ....147 C4
Canford Ct BH13 ....147 C3
Canford Gdns BH11 .....89 A1
Canford Heath Fst & Mid
Schs BH17 ....119 B4
Canford Heath Nature
Reserve★ BH11 ....88 A2
Canford Heath Rd
BH17 ....87 C1
Canford Magna BH21 ...60 A1
Canford Pl [2] BH13 ....147 C4
Canford Rd
Bournemouth BH11 ....89 A1
Poole BH15 ....119 B2
Canford Sch BH21 ....60 A1
Canford View Dr BH21 ..60 A3
Canford Way BH12 ....88 B1
Cann Hill SP7 ....24 A3
Cannings Ct La DT2 ...196 C3
Cannington Coll BA22 ...26 C3
Cannon Cl BH18 ....87 A1
Cannon Ct Mews [8] DT9 .17 B1
Cannon Hill Gdns BH21 .60 A4
Cannon Hill Rd BH21 ....60 A4
Canteen Rd DT5 ....181 B1
Canterbury Cl
Ferndown BH22 ....53 A1
Weymouth DT4 ....166 C2
Capella Ct BH22 ....121 C1
Capesthorne BH23 .....125 A3
Caphays Dro DT9 ....195 E2
Capitol Cl DT1 ....134 C4
Capper Rd E BH20 .....139 C3
Capper Rd W BH20 ....139 C3
Capstan Field BH19 ...178 A3
Capstans The BH14 ....147 A4
Capstone Pl BH8 ....122 B3
Capstone Rd BH8 ....122 A4
Capulet Rd SP1 ....213 A4
Carbery Ave BH6 ....123 B3
Carbery Gdns BH6 .....123 C3
Carbery La [3] BH6 .....123 B2
Carbery Row [2] BH6 ...123 B2
Cardigan Rd
Bournemouth BH9 ....121 C4
Poole BH12 ....120 C2
Cards Mill La DT6 ....66 A4
Carent Cl DT10 ....21 A1
Carey App BH20 ....142 B3
Carey Cl BH20 ....142 B3
Carey Rd
Bournemouth BH9 ....89 C2
Northport BH20 ....142 B3
Careys Rd BH8 ....90 B2
Carina Ct BH13 ....147 B2
Carisbrook Cres BH15 .118 B2
Carisbrooke
Poole BH13 ....147 C4
Radipole DT4 ....167 A4
Carisbrooke Ct
[4] Christchurch BH23 ..126 A4
New Milton BH25 ....94 C1
Carisbrooke Gdns
BA20 ....27 A3
Carisbrooke Way BH23 ..93 C1
Carlinford [29] BH15 ....122 C2
Carlton Ave BH25 ....126 C4
Carlton Gr BH12 ....120 B3
Carlton Rd BH1 ....122 C4

Carlton Rd N DT4 .....167 B3
Carlton Rd S DT4 .....167 B3
Carlyle Rd BH6 ....123 B3
Carmel Cl BH15 ......118 B1
Carmelite Way SP1 ...213 B2
Carnarvon Rd 4 BH1 ..122 C2
Carnegie Cl BH14 .....120 B3
Caroline Ave BH23 ...124 C3
Caroline Pl 10 DT4 ...167 B2
Caroline Rd BH11 ......89 A2
Carpenters Cl DT2 ...106 C4
Carradale BH23 ....125 A4
Carraway La 20 C1
Carrbridge Cl BH3 ...121 B4
Carrbridge Gdns BH3 .121 B4
Carrbridge Rd BH3 ...121 B4
Carrick Cl DT1 ....135 B4
Carrick Way BH25 .....95 B1
Carrington Cl 10 DT4 ..180 B4
Carrion La 4 BH20 ...142 C2
Carroll Ave BH22 .....61 C3
Carroll Cl BH12 ......121 A3
Carsworth Way BH17 ..88 A1
Carter Cl DT11 ....212 C3
Carter Com Sch BH15 .118 C1
Carter's La Chideock DT6 .98 C4
9 Poole BH15 ....119 B1
Carters Ave BH15 ....118 B2
Carters La BA22 .....192 E8
Cartref Cl BH31 ......45 A3
Cartwright Cl BH10 ...89 B2
Carvers La BH24 ......55 B4
Carysfort Rd BH1 ....122 B2
Caseberry Ct 7 DT1 ..107 B2
Cashmoor Cl BH12 ...120 C4
Caslake Cl BH25 ......94 C1
Cassel Ave BH13 .....121 A1
Casselles Ct 33 BH15 ..95 A1
Cassiobury Rd DT4 ...167 B2
Casterbridge Cl
  Blandford Forum DT11 ..212 C3
  9 Swanage BH19 ...178 C1
Casterbridge Rd
  Dorchester DT1 .....135 B4
  Ferndown BH22 ......61 B2
Castle Ave
  Christchurch BH23 ...125 C4
  5 Okeford Fitzpaine DT11 197 F6
Castle Cl
  Cranborne BH21 ......40 A4
  Dorchester DT1 .....107 B1
Castle Ct 3 BH23 ....126 A4
Castle Ct Sch BH21 ...86 A4
Castle Farm Rd BH16 ..84 B2
Castle Gate Cl BH8 ...90 B1
Castle Hill BH14 .....120 A2
Castle Hill Cl SP7 ....12 B2
Castle Hill Cres BA12 ..3 A3
Castle Hill La
  Cranborne BH21 ......40 A3
  Mere BA12 ....3 A3
Castle Hill Rd DT4 ...180 A1
Castle Keep SP1 .....213 A4
Castle La
  Buckland Newton DT2 ...208 B8
  Okeford Fitzpaine DT11 ...197 F6
  Owermoigne DT2 ...155 B4
Castle La E BH7 .....123 B4
Castle La W BH8 .....90 B1
Castle Par BH7 ......123 B4
Castle Rd
  Bournemouth BH9 ....90 A1
  Fortuneswell DT5 ...181 A1
  Salisbury SP1 ......213 B4
  Sherborne DT9 ....30 B4
Castle Sq DT6 ....100 B3
Castle St
  Christchurch BH23 ...124 B3
  Cranborne BH21 ......40 A4
  Mere BA12 ....2 C3
  Poole BH15 ....119 B1
  Salisbury SP2 ......213 B3
Castle Town Way DT9 ..16 A1
Castle View Dr BH16 ..84 B1
Castledene Cres BH14 .120 A1
Castlemain Ave BH6 ..123 B4
Castlemaine Rd DT3 ..152 C1
Castleman Smith Cl
  DT11 ....212 C3
Castleman Way BH24 ..55 B3
Castlemews BH24 .....54 C3
Castleton TA18 ......192 C5
Castleton Ave BH10 ..89 B3
Castleton Rd DT9 .....30 B3
Castletown DT5 .....181 A1
Castlewood BH24 ....54 C3
Cat La DT10 ....33 A3
Catalina Cl BH23 ....125 A4
Catalina Dr BH15 ....119 C1
Caters Pl DT1 ....108 A1
Cathedral Sch SP1 ...213 B2
Catherine St SP1 ....213 B2
Catherine Wheel Gdns
  BH23 ....91 C2
Cathole Bridge Rd
  TA18 ....191 F3
Caton Cl BH12 ......121 A4
Catsley La DT2 ......205 B6
Cattistock Rd
  Bournemouth BH8 ....90 C1
  Maiden Newton DT2 ..72 C4
Cauldon Ave BH19 ...179 A2
Cauldron Barn Rd
  BH19 ....179 A2
Cauldron Cres BH19 ..179 A2
Cauldron Mdws BH19 .179 A2
Caundle La
  Stalbridge DT10 .....33 A3

Caundle La continued
  Stourton Caundle DT10 ..32 C1
Causeway La BH20 ...142 B3
Causeway La DT8 ....203 A6
Causeway The
  Hazelbury Bryan DT10 ..196 F4
  Milborne St Andrew DT11 ..79 C4
Cavalier Cl BA21 .....27 C4
Cavalier Way BA21 ...27 C4
Cavan Cres BH17 .....87 A1
Cavendish Hall BH1 ..122 A3
Cavendish Pl BH1 ...122 A3
Cavendish Rd BH1 ...122 A3
Cawdor Rd BH3 ......121 B4
Caxton Cl BH23 .....125 A4
Cecil Ave
  Bournemouth BH8 ....122 B4
  Salisbury SP2 ......213 B1
Cecil Cl BH21 ....86 C3
Cecil Ct BH21 ....86 C3
Cecil Hill BH8 ....122 A4
Cecil Rd
  Bournemouth BH5 ...122 C2
  Poole BH12 ....120 B3
  Swanage BH19 ......179 A1
Cecil St BA20 ....27 B3
Cedar Ave
  Bournemouth BH10 ...89 B3
  Christchurch BH23 ..123 B4
  3 St.Leonards BH24 ..53 C2
Cedar Cl Upton BH16 ..118 A4
  1 Wool BH20 ....140 A1
Cedar Ct BH4 ....121 A1
Cedar Dr
  11 Easton/Weston DT5 ..186 C1
  Overcombe/Preston
    DT3 ....168 A4
  Sandford BH20 .....116 A1
  Wimborne Minster BH21 ..60 A3
Cedar Fields 1 BA22 ..193 A8
Cedar Gdns BH25 .....94 C1
Cedar Gr BA21 ....27 A3
Cedar Manor BH4 ....121 B2
Cedar Rd DT1 ....107 C1
Cedar Trad Pk BH21 ..60 C3
Cedar Way BH22 .....61 B4
Cedars The BH4 .....121 B2
Celandine Cl BH23 ...125 A4
Celandine Rd 3 BA22 ..26 B3
Cellars Farm Rd BH6 .124 A2
Celtic Cres DT1 .....134 C4
Cemetery Ave BH15 ..119 C3
Cemetery Rd
  10 Gillingham SP8 ....5 C1
  Portesham DT3 .....150 A4
  Wimborne Minster BH21 ..59 A3
Centenary Gdns BA8 ..19 A2
Centenary House 6
  BH23 ....124 A4
Centenary Way BH1 ..122 C3
Central Acre 13 BA20 ..27 B2
Central Ave
  Corfe Mullen BH21 ...86 B4
  Poole BH12 ....120 A3
Central Dr BH2 ......121 C3
Central Rd 2 BA20 ...27 C2
Centre Pl BH24 ....55 A4
Centurion Rd DT11 ..199 E2
Cereleton Pk DT11 ...211 C6
Cerne Abbas BH1 ....121 A1
Cerne Abbas CE Fst Sch
  DT2 ....207 D4
Cerne Abbas Giant★
  DT2 ....207 D4
Cerne Abbey★ DT2 ..207 D4
Cerne Cl BH9 ....90 A2
Chaddesley Glen
  BH13 ....147 C3
Chaddesley Pines
  BH13 ....147 C3
Chaddesley Wood Rd
  BH13 ....147 C3
Chafeys Ave DT4 ....167 A3
Chaffey Cl BH24 ......55 C4
Chaffeymoor Hill SP8 ..1 A1
Chaffinch Cl
  Bincombe DT3 ......152 B2
  Broadstone BH17 ....86 C1
  New Milton BH25 .....94 C1
Chafyn Gr Sch SP1 ..213 C3
Chalbury (Hill Fort)★
  DT3 ....153 A2
Chalbury Cl
  Overcombe/Preston
    DT3 ....168 A4
  Poole BH17 ....88 A1
Chalbury Ct
  7 Christchurch BH23 ..124 C3
  11 Poole BH14 .....120 A2
Chalbury Lodge 1 DT3 ..168 A4
Chaldecott Gdns BH10 ..89 B2
Chaldon Rd BH17 ....87 C1
Chalfont Ave BH23 ...91 B2
Chalice Cl BH14 .....120 A2
Chalk Pit Cl BH20 ....81 A1
Chalk Pit La
  Litton Cheney DT2 ..103 A1
  Wool BH20 ....139 C1
Chalk The 2 DT11 ....37 C1
Chalky Rd DT1 ......135 C1
Chalwell 9 DT11 .....37 C1
Chalwell Gr BH14 ...120 A2
Chalwyn Ind Est BH12 ..120 A4
Chamberlaine Rd DT4 ..180 B4
Champernhayes La
  DT6 ....64 C3
Champions 1 DT8 ...204 C4
Chancery Cl 1 SP2 ..213 A3

Chancery La DT6 ....100 B3
Chander Cl BH22 .....61 C2
Chandlers BH9 ....30 B4
Chandlers Cl BH7 ...123 A4
Chandos Ave BH12 ..121 A4
Channel Ct
  Barton on Sea BH25 ..126 C4
  Bournemouth BH6 ...123 B2
Channel View Rd DT5 ..186 C2
Chant Cl BH23 ....124 B4
Chantmarle La DT2 ..206 B5
Chantry Cl BH1 ......122 A3
Chantry La DT8 .....204 C5
Chantry St DT6 .....204 C2
Chantry The BH1 ....122 A3
Chantry View BA22 ..193 D8
Chapel Cl
  Corfe Mullen BH21 ...86 B3
  Langton Herring DT3 ..150 B1
Chapel Gate BH23 ...90 B4
Chapel Gdns DT11 ...212 C2
Chapel Hill SP8 ......9 B1
Chapel La
  Bransgore BH23 ....93 A4
  Corfe Mullen BH21 ...86 B3
  Dinnington TA17 ...191 B8
  Henstridge BA8 .....18 B3
  Hurn BH23 ....90 B4
  Maiden Newton DT2 ..72 C4
  7 Milborne Port DT9 ..17 B1
  Osmington DT3 .....154 A2
  Pen Selwood BA9 ....1 B2
  2 Pimperne DT11 ...199 D3
  Poole BH15 ....119 B1
  Radipole DT3 ......152 B3
  Wimborne Minster BH21 ..59 A3
  Woodlands BH21 .....44 A4
  7 Yetminster DT9 ...194 C5
  Zennor BA12 ....1 C3
Chapel Mdw 6 DT9 ..194 C5
Chapel Pl 5 SP2 ....213 B3
Chapel Rd Poole BH14 ..120 A2
  Sturminster Newton
    DT10 ....197 A8
Chapel Rise BH24 ...54 C1
Chapel St
  Milborne St Andrew DT11 ..79 C4
  Shipton Gorge DT6 ..101 B2
Chapel View 6 DT2 ..78 A1
Chapelhay St DT4 ...167 B1
Charberry Rise DT6 ..96 C4
Charborough Cl BH16 ..84 B2
Charborough House★
  BH20 ....83 C4
Charborough Pk★
  BH20 ....211 F1
Charborough Rd BH18 ..87 A2
Charborough Way 1
  BH21 ....56 B2
Chard La
  Broadwindsor DT8 ..203 C7
  Wayford TA18 ......191 B2
Chard Rd
  Broadwindsor DT8 ..203 C7
  Crewkerne TA18 ....191 D4
Chard St TA20 ......202 E6
Chards Mead Rd DT6 ..100 B4
Charing Cl 2 BH24 ..55 B3
Charing Cross SP6 ..42 A3
Charles Cres BH25 ..95 A3
Charles Garrett Cl 7
  SP7 ....12 C2
Charles Gdns BH10 ..89 B1
Charles Keightley Ct
  BH21 ....59 B2
Charles Rd
  Burton Bradstock DT6 ..128 A4
  Christchurch BH23 ..124 C4
  Poole BH15 ....119 B2
  Yeovil BA21 ....27 C3
Charles St
  Blandford Forum DT11 ..212 B2
  Dorchester DT1 .....108 A1
  Radipole DT4 ....167 B2
  7 Salisbury SP2 ...213 A3
Charles's La BH24 ...55 C1
Charlotte Cl
  Charminster DT2 ...107 C3
  Christchurch BH23 ..125 A3
  3 New Milton BH25 ..95 A1
  Poole BH12 ....121 B4
Charlton Beeches
  DT11 ....211 C7
Charlton Cl
  Bournemouth BH9 ...90 B2
  12 Crewkerne TA18 ..191 F4
  Hordle SO41 ....95 C2
Charlton La SP7 .....13 C1
Charlton Manor 1
  DT11 ....211 D6
Charlton Mead 4 DT11 211 D6
Charltons The BH21 ..121 C3
Charminster Ave BH9 ..90 C1
Charminster Cl 5 BH8 ..90 B1
Charminster Pl BH8 ..90 B1
Charminster Rd BH8 ..122 A4
Charminster St Marys Fst Sch
  DT2 ....107 B3
Charmouth Cl DT7 ...96 B3
Charmouth CP Sch
  DT6 ....97 A4
Charmouth Gr BH14 ..120 A2
Charmouth Heritage Coast
  Ctr★ DT6 ....97 A4
Charmouth Rd DT7 ..96 B3
Charnock Cl SO41 ...95 C2
Charnwood Ave 8 BH9 ..90 A2

Charnwood Cl BH22 ..53 A1
Charnwood Rd SP2 ..213 A3
Chartcombe BH13 ...147 C4
Charter Rd BH11 .....88 B3
Chartwell DT4 ......167 A3
Chase Cres SP5 .....188 C3
Chase The
  St.Leonards BH24 ...54 C3
  Verwood BH31 ......45 C3
Chaseborough Sq 4
  DT1 ....107 B1
Chaseside BH7 .....123 A4
Chaston La DT2 .....208 C8
Chatham Cl SP1 ....213 A4
Chatsworth Rd
  Bournemouth BH8 ...122 B4
  Poole BH14 ....120 A3
  Yeovil BA21 ....27 C4
Chatsworth Way BH25 ..94 C2
Chaucer Cl BH21 .....59 B3
Chaucer Rd BH13 ...147 C4
Chaucombe Pl BH25 ..94 C1
Cheam Rd BH18 .....86 C2
Cheap St DT9 ....30 A3
Checkridge La EX13 ..202 A2
Cheddington Rd BH9 ..90 A2
Chedington Cl BH17 ..87 C1
Chedington Ct Golf Club
  DT8 ....192 D2
Chedington La DT8 ..204 D8
Cheese La DT3 .....150 C3
Cheese Mkt 10 SP1 ..213 B2
Chelmsford Rd BH16 ..118 A4
Chelmsford St DT4 ..167 B2
Chelston Ave BA21 ..27 A4
Cheltenham Rd BH12 ..120 B3
Chelwood Gate DT4 ..166 C2
Chene Rd BH21 ......59 B2
Cherford Rd BH11 ...89 A1
Cherita Ct BH15 ....119 C3
Cheriton Ave BH7 ..123 B4
Cheriton Way BH21 ..59 B3
Cherrett Cl BH11 ....88 C2
Cherries Dr BH9 .....89 C1
Cherry Cl Poole BH14 ..120 A2
  Sandford BH20 .....143 A4
Cherry Ct BH14 .....120 A3
Cherry Gr BH22 .....61 B3
Cherry Hill Gdns
  BH16 ....118 A3
Cherry Hill Gr BH16 ..118 A3
Cherry Orch La
  Cann SP7 ....11 C1
  Gillingham SP8 .....5 B1
Cherry Tree DT6 ....100 A4
Cherry Tree Cl BH24 ..53 C2
Cherry Tree Ct
  9 Crewkerne TA18 ..191 F5
  31 New Milton BH25 ..95 A1
Cherry Tree Dr BA20 ..26 C1
Cherryfields SP8 ....5 C2
Chescombe Cl DT2 ..207 D3
Chescombe La DT11 ..210 B3
Cheselbourne Cty Fst Sch
  DT2 ....209 A2
Cheshire Dr BH8 ....91 A1
Chesil Beach Visitor Ctr★
  DT4 ....180 B2
Chesil View DT4 ....180 A1
Chesildene Ave BH8 ..90 B1
Chesildene Dr BH8 ..90 B2
Chessel Ave BH5 ...122 C2
Chessels Cl BA22 ...193 B8
Chester Cl DT1 .....135 B4
Chester Rd BH13 ...121 A1
Chesterfield Cl BH13 ..147 C4
Chesterfield Ct BH1 ..122 B2
Chestnut Ave
  Barton on Sea BH25 ..127 A4
  Bournemouth BH6 ...123 B2
  Ellingham Harbridge & Ibsley
    BH24 ....46 B3
  Wareham St Martin
    BH20 ....116 A2
Chestnut Cl BH20 ...143 A4
Chestnut Dr BA20 ...27 A2
Chestnut Gr
  Blandford Forum DT11 ..212 B2
  Ferndown BH21 .....60 C3
Chestnut Pl DT3 ....167 B4
Chestnut Rd DT6 ...100 B2
Chestnut Way
  Burton BH23 ....92 B2
  Dorchester DT1 .....107 B1
  Gillingham SP8 .....5 B1
Chetcombe Rd BA12 ..3 A3
Chetnole Cl BH17 ...88 C1
Chetnole Sta DT9 ...194 C2
Chettell Way DT11 ..212 B1
Cheverell Ave SP1 ..213 C4
Cheviot Ct Flats BH23 .124 C4
Cheviot Way BH31 ...45 A3
Cheviots The BH14 ..120 B2
Chewton Comm Rd
  BH23 ....126 A4
Chewton Farm Rd
  BH23 ....126 A4
Chewton Lodge BH23 .126 A4
Chewton Way BH23 ..94 A1
Cheyne Cl 4 DT5 ....186 C1
Cheyne Gdns BH4 ...121 B1
Cheyne Ct
Chichester Cl SP2 ...213 B1
Chichester Rd 1 BH24 ..47 C1
Chichester Way BH23 .125 A3
Chichester Wlk BH21 ..59 C1
Chick's Copse La
  Cattistock DT2 .....206 A5

Car - Chu 221

Chick's Copse La continued
  Rampisham DT2 ....205 F5
Chickerell Cl BH9 ....90 A2
Chickerell CP Sch
  DT3 ....166 A3
Chickerell Hill DT3 ..166 A3
Chickerell Rd DT3 ..166 B2
Chideock Cl BH12 ...120 C3
Chideock Ct BH12 ...120 C3
Chideock Hill DT6 ...98 C4
Chigwell Rd BH8 ....90 A1
Chilbury Gdns DT2 ..155 B4
Chilcombe Hill (Fort)★
  DT2 ....102 C2
Chilcombe La
  Chilcombe DT6 .....102 B2
  Shipton Gorge DT6 ..102 B3
Chilcombe Rd BH6 ..123 A3
Childhay La DT8 ....203 C6
Chilfrome La
  Chilfrome DT2 .....206 B1
  Maiden Newton DT2 ..72 C4
Chiltern Cl
  Barton on Sea BH25 ..94 C1
  Poole BH21 ....121 A3
Chiltern Ct 5 BH23 ..124 C4
Chiltern Dr
  Barton on Sea BH25 ..126 C4
  Verwood BH31 ......45 A3
Chilton Gr BA21 .....27 B4
Chimes The BH4 ....121 A2
China La 1 DT11 ...199 F7
Chine Cres BH2 .....121 B1
Chine Cres Rd BH2 ..121 B1
Chine Wlk BH22 .....61 C1
Chinnock Hollow
  BA22 ....192 E8
Chippel La DT10 ....20 C1
Chipper La SP1 .....213 B3
Chiselbury Gr SP2 ..213 B1
Chisels La BH23 ....93 A3
Chiswell DT5 ....186 C4
Chiswell Rd BH17 ...87 B1
Chitten Hill BH20 ...115 B4
Choristers Sq SP1 ..213 B2
Chorley Cl BH15 ....119 B3
Chowins Rd 18 TA18 ..191 F4
Chris Cres BH16 ....118 B4
Christ the King RC Prim Sch
  BH11 ....89 A3
Christchurch Bay Rd
  BH25 ....126 C4
Christchurch By-pass
  BH23 ....124 B4
Christchurch Castle★
  BH23 ....124 B3
Christchurch Cty Jun Sch
  BH23 ....124 A4
Christchurch Cty Prim Sch
  BH23 ....124 A4
Christchurch Hospl
  BH23 ....123 C4
Christchurch Priory★
  BH23 ....124 B3
Christchurch Rd
  Barton on Sea BH25 ..126 B4
  Bournemouth BH1 ..122 B2
  Ferndown BH22 .....61 B1
  Hurn BH23 ....91 B3
  Ringwood BH24 .....55 A4
Christchurch Ski Ctr★
  BH23 ....63 A2
Christchurch Sta
  BH23 ....124 A4
Christie Miller Rd
  SP2 ....213 A3
Christopher Cl
  3 Salisbury SP1 ...213 A1
  Yeovil BA20 ....27 A3
Christopher Cres
  BH15 ....119 B3
Christophers BH21 ..59 B1
Christy's La SP7 ....12 C2
Chur La BA22 ......193 A8
Church Acre 22 DT1 ..108 A1
Church Cl
  Beer Hackett DT9 ...194 D6
  Bourton SP8 ....1 B1
  Bridport DT6 ....69 A1
  Chetnole DT9 ......194 D3
  6 Dorchester DT1 ..108 A1
  Fontmell Magna SP7 ..37 C4
  Longburton DT9 ...195 B7
  Stour Provost SP7 ..22 B4
  9 Swanage BH19 ..179 A1
  Todber DT10 ....21 B2
Church Farm SP6 ...43 A4
Church Gn
  Bishop's Caundle DT9 ..196 A8
  7 Wareham BH20 ..142 C2
Church Hill
  Buckhorn Weston SP8 ..9 A3
  Dinnington TA17 ...191 B7
  Iwerne Minster DT11 ..37 C1
  Kington Magna SP8 ..9 B2
  Langton Herring DT3 ..150 B1
  Marnhull DT10 .....21 A2
  Milborne St Andrew DT11 ..79 C4
  Piddlehinton DT2 ..76 C4
  Shaftesbury SP7 ...12 B1
  Stalbridge DT10 ...19 B1
  8 Swanage BH19 ..179 A1
  Verwood BH31 ......45 A3
  West Stour SP8 ....10 A2

Church Hill continued
Woodlands BH21 ....44 A4
Church Hill La DT2 ....104 B4
Church Hill View DT2 ...207 A2
Church Knap DT4 ......180 B4
Church Knowle Animal
Sanctuary & Rehoming Ctr★
BH20 ....176 A4
Church La
Barwick BA22 ....193 E8
Bere Regis BH20 ....81 A1
3 Blandford Forum DT11 .212 B2
Charlton Marshall DT11 ...211 C6
Chickerell DT3 ....151 B1
Christchurch BH23 ....124 A3
Coombe Keynes BH20 .....158 A3
Crewkerne TA18 ....192 A3
Damerham SP6 ....190 F2
East Orchard SP7 ....36 C4
Easton/Weston DT5 ....186 C1
Ferndown BH22 ....89 C4
Frampton DT2 ....73 C2
Godmanstone DT2 ....75 A4
Haselbury Plucknett
 TA18 ....192 C5
Leigh DT9 ....194 E3
Margaret Marsh SP7 ......22 B1
New Milton BH25 ....94 C1
Osmington DT3 ....154 A2
Owermoigne DT2 ....155 B4
Piddletrenthide DT2 ......208 B3
Portesham DT3 ....150 A4
Rimpton BA22 ....15 A4
Shaftesbury SP7 ....12 C1
Stinsford DT2 ....108 C2
Stour Provost SP8 ....21 B4
2 Sturminster Newton
 DT10 ....197 D8
Sutton Waldron DT11 .....37 C2
Sydling St Nicholas DT2 ..207 A2
Wareham BH20 ....142 C2
Wool BH20 ....140 A1
Church Mead DT2 .....205 F1
Church Ope DT5 ......187 A2
Church Path
2 Crewkerne TA18 ......191 E4
Litton Cheney DT2 ....103 B1
Yeovil BA20 ....27 B3
Church Rd
Bournemouth BH6 ....123 C2
Bradford Abbas DT9 ......28 B1
Durweston DT11 ....198 E3
Ferndown BH22 ....61 B3
Iwerne Minster DT11 .....37 C1
Maiden Newton DT2 ......72 C4
Overcombe/Preston
 DT3 ....168 B4
Pimperne DT11 ....199 D4
Poole BH14 ....120 A2
5 Shillingstone DT11 ...198 B6
Silton SP8 ....2 A1
Studland BH19 ....164 B1
Thornford DT9 ....194 D8
Three Legged Cross BH21 .45 A1
West Lulworth BH20 ......172 B3
Church Row DT11 .....209 C6
Church St
Beaminster DT8 ....204 C4
Bridport DT6 ....100 B3
Burton Bradstock DT6 ....128 A4
Christchurch BH23 ....124 A3
Cranborne BH21 ....40 A4
Dewlish DT2 ....209 C1
5 Dorchester DT1 ....108 A1
Fontmell Magna SP7 ......37 C1
Fordingbridge SP6 ....43 A4
Halstock BA22 ....193 C3
Henstridge BA8 ....19 A2
Hinton St George TA17 ...191 C7
Kington Magna SP8 ....9 B2
Lyme Regis DT7 ....96 B3
Mere BA12 ....3 A3
Merriott TA16 ....191 F7
Milborne Port DT9 ....17 B1
Poole BH15 ....119 A1
Puncknowle DT2 ....129 C3
Radipole DT3 ....152 A4
Shapwick DT11 ....56 A4
Sturminster Newton DT10 .35 A1
Wareham BH20 ....142 C2
2 West Coker BA22 .....193 A8
West Stour SP8 ....10 A1
10 Wimborne Minster BH21 59 A3
Winterborne Kingston
 DT11 ....81 C4
Yeovil BA20 ....27 B3
Yetminster DT9 ....194 C5
Church Track SP8 .....1 B1
Church View SP8 ......5 C1
Church Wlk
Littlebredy DT2 ....131 B4
Motcombe SP7 ....12 A4
Okeford Fitzpaine DT11 ...197 E4
Churchfield BH31 ......45 A3
Churchfield Cres
BH15 ....119 C2
Churchfield Cl BH15 ...119 C2
Churchfield La BH24 ...43 A1
Churchfield Rd BH15 ..119 C2
Churchfields Ind Est
SP2 ....213 A3
Churchfields Rd SP2 ...213 A3
Churchfoot La DT10 ...196 F3
Churchill Cl
Alderholt SP6 ....42 A3

Churchill Cl continued
Sturminster Marshall
 BH21 ....56 B2
4 Weymouth DT4 ....180 B4
Churchill Cres DT4 ...120 B3
Churchill Ct BH25 .....94 C1
Churchill Dro BH21 ....40 C4
Churchill Gdns BH12 ..120 B3
Churchill Rd
Blandford Forum DT11 ....212 B2
Bournemouth BH1 ....122 B3
Bovington Camp BH20 ....139 B4
Poole BH12 ....120 B3
Wimborne Minster BH21 ..59 C2
Churchill Way E SP1 ...213 B3
Churchill Way N SP1 ...213 B3
Churchill Way S SP1 ...213 B2
Churchill Way W SP2 ..213 B3
Churchmoor Rd BH21 ..60 A3
Churchward Ave DT3 ...153 A2
Churchwell St DT9 .....28 B1
Churlands Cl BA22 .....193 A8
Chydok Rd DT2 ....156 B2
Cinnamon La 10 BH15 ..119 A1
Circle The
3 Bournemouth BH9 .....90 A2
Poole BH13 ....147 C4
Claire Ct BH23 ....126 A4
Clammer Hill La TA18 ..191 F4
Clanfield 29 C2
Clap La SP5 ....188 B4
Clappentail La DT7 ....96 A3
Clappentail Pk DT7 ....96 A3
Clapton Ct Gdns★
 TA18 ....191 D1
Clapton Rd TA18 ......191 D3
Clare Ave DT4 ....166 C1
Claremont Ave
Bournemouth BH9 ....90 A1
Gillingham SP8 ....5 C2
Claremont Gdns DT6 ...100 B4
Claremont Rd
Bournemouth BH9 ....90 A1
Bridport DT6 ....100 B4
Clarence Cl 2 DT5 .....186 C2
Clarence Pk Rd BH7 ...123 A3
Clarence Rd
Dorchester DT1 ....134 C4
Easton/Weston DT5 ......186 C2
3 Poole BH14 ....120 A2
Weymouth DT4 ....166 C1
Clarence St BA20 ......27 B2
Clarendon Ave DT3 ....152 B1
Clarendon Cl
Broadstone BH18 ....87 A2
Gillingham SP8 ....5 B1
Clarendon Ct BH22 ....121 B1
Clarendon Rd
Bournemouth BH4 ....121 B2
Broadstone BH18 ....86 C2
Christchurch BH23 ....124 A4
Salisbury SP1 ....213 C3
Clark's Cl BH24 ....55 B4
Clark's La 3 TA18 ......192 A3
Clarkham Cross BA22 ..193 E2
Clarks Cl BA22 ....26 B3
Clatcombe La DT9 .....15 C2
Claudius Cl DT1 ....134 C4
Clay Castle TA18 ......192 C5
Clay Castle La TA18 ...192 C5
Clay La Beaminster DT8 204 C4
 Puncknowle DT2 ....129 C2
Clayesmore Prep Sch
 DT11 ....37 C1
Clayesmore Sch DT11 ...37 C1
Clayford Ave BH22 ....61 A4
Clayford Cl BH17 ......87 B1
Claylake Dr BH31 ......45 B3
Claylands La DT8 ......204 A3
Claypits La
Beer Hackett DT9 ....194 D6
Winfrith Newburgh DT2 ..157 A3
Clayton Cl
Radipole DT3 ....152 B2
Yeovil BA22 ....26 B3
Clearmount Rd DT4 ....180 C4
Cleasby Grange 26 BH5 .122 C2
Cleeves Cl BH12 ....88 B1
Clematis Cl BH23 ......125 B4
Clement Mews BH4 ....121 A2
Clement's La BA12 .....3 A2
Clements La DT5 ......186 C4
Clenston Rd DT11 .....210 C7
Cleve The BA21 ....26 C3
Cleveland Ave DT4 ....167 B4
Cleveland Cl BH25 .....126 B4
Cleveland Ct BH2 ......121 B1
Cleveland Gdns BH1 ...122 B3
Cleveland Rd BH1 .....122 B3
Cleverlawns DT3 ......148 C4
Cleves Cl DT4 ....180 C4
Cliff Ave BH19 ....179 B2
Cliff Cres BH25 ....126 C4
Cliff Dr
Christchurch BH23 ....125 B3
Poole BH13 ....147 C3
Cliff House 10 BH6 ....123 C4
Cliff Rd DT6 ....128 A4
Cliff Terr BH25 ....126 C3
Cliff Way DT5 ....186 B1
Cliffe La BH25 ....126 C4
Clifford Rd BH9 ....90 A1
Clift La DT2 ....205 D1
Clifton Cl
Swanage BH19 ....179 B2
Yeovil BA21 ....28 A3
Clifton Ct
18 Bournemouth BH5 ....122 C2

Clifton Ct continued
19 New Milton BH25 .....95 A1
Clifton Gdns BH22 ....61 B2
Clifton Hill BA22 ......193 F8
Clifton Pl 6 DT4 ......167 B2
Clifton Rd
Bournemouth BH6 ....123 B2
Clifton Maybank BA22 ....194 B8
Poole BH14 ....120 C1
Salisbury SP2 ....213 A3
Swanage BH19 ....179 A2
Clifton View 3 BA22 ...193 F8
Clingan Rd BH6 ....123 B4
Clinton Cl BH23 ....94 A1
Clive Ct 19 BH4 ....121 B2
Clive Rd
Bournemouth BH9 ....89 C1
Christchurch BH23 ....93 C1
Cliveden Cl BH22 ......61 B4
Clivia Cl DT3 ....152 C1
Cloisters The
Christchurch BH23 ....124 A3
2 Ringwood BH24 ....55 C3
Close Dr 5 TA18 ....192 A3
Close The
Barton on Sea BH25 .....127 A4
Blandford Forum DT11 ...212 B2
Broadstone BH18 ....86 C2
Charlton Marshall DT11 ..211 D6
8 Merriott TA16 ....191 F6
12 Pimperne DT11 ......199 D4
Ringwood BH24 ....55 A4
St.Leonards BH24 ....54 B2
Clough's Rd BH24 ......55 B4
Clovens Rd DT5 ....186 C4
Clover Cl BH23 ....125 A4
Clover Ct BH25 ....95 B2
Clover Dr BH17 ....86 C1
Cloverfields SP8 ....5 C2
Clovermead DT3 ......194 B6
Clovers The BH12 .....121 A4
Clovers Wlk 5 BA20 ...27 B2
Clowes Ave BH6 ......124 A2
Clump Hill BH21 ....44 B1
Cluny Cres BH19 ......179 B1
Clyde Rd BH17 ....87 A1
Clyffe View DT2 ......137 B3
Clyppetts 2 DT11 .....81 C4
Coach House Pl BH1 ...122 A3
Coach Rd
1 Stourpaine DT11 .....198 F4
Wimborne St Giles
 BH21 ....201 C7
Coach Rd The DT7 ....64 A1
Coastguard Rd
6 Fortuneswell DT5 ....186 C4
Langton Herring DT3 .....150 A1
Coastguard Way BH23 .124 A3
Cobb Rd DT7 ....96 A2
Cobb's Rd BH23 ......59 C3
Cobbs La BH15 ....119 C3
Cobham Dr DT4 ......166 C2
Cobham Rd
Bournemouth BH9 ....90 A2
Ferndown BH21 ....61 A4
Ferndown Town DT22 ....52 B1
Cobham Way BH21 ....59 C1
Cobley Cl SP5 ....189 D6
Coburg Rd DT1 ....107 C1
Cockerell Cl BH21 .....59 C1
Cocklands DT2 ....107 C2
Cockles La Fleet DT4 ..166 C1
 Weymouth DT4 ....167 A1
Cockpit Hill DT6 ......203 C4
Cod La BA22 ....192 D7
Codge La DT2 ....205 E5
Codogan Ct 14 BH1 ...122 A2
Cogdean Cl BH21 ......86 C4
Cogdean Way BH21 ...86 C4
Cogdean Wlk BH21 ....86 C4
Cogdeane Rd BH17 ....87 B1
Coker Ct★ BA22 ....193 C7
Coker Hill BA22 ....192 F8
Coker Hill La BA22 ....193 A7
Colber Medieval Village of★
 DT10 ....34 C1
Colborne Ave BH21 ...59 C3
Colbourne Cl
Bransgore BH23 ....93 A4
Poole BH15 ....119 B1
Cold Harbour
Milborne Port DT9 ......17 B1
Sherborne DT9 ....30 B4
Cold Harbour La BA22 .192 F6
Coldharbour SP8 ......5 C1
Coldharbour La SP2 ...213 A3
Cole St La SP8 ....11 A3
Cole's Cross SP8 ......203 A5
Cole's La SP7 ....12 A1
Colehill Cres BH9 .....90 A2
Colehill Dro DT2 ......156 B3
Colehill Fst Sch BH21 ..60 A4
Colehill La Holt BH21 ..51 B1
 Wimborne Minster BH21 .59 C4
Colehill Rd BH20 ......83 C3
Coleman Rd BH11 .....89 A2
Colemore Rd BH7 .....123 B4
Coleridge Gn BH23 ....124 C4
Coles Ave BH15 ....118 C1
Coles Cl DT10 ....35 B1
Coles Gdns BH15 ......118 C1
Coles La
Milborne St Andrew
 DT11 ....209 F1
Yetminster DT9 ....194 B6
Colin Cl BH21 ....86 B3
Coll of Air Traffic Control
 BH23 ....90 C4

Collarway La BA22 .....192 F8
College BA22 ....192 E8
College Arms Cl SP7 ...22 A4
College Gn BA21 ......27 B3
College Rd
Blandford Camp DT11 ....199 E3
Bournemouth BH5 ....123 A2
Ringwood BH24 ....55 B4
College St SP1 ....213 B3
Collett Cl DT3 ....153 A2
Colletts Cl BH20 ......177 A4
Collier's La BH20 .....139 C1
Collingbourne Ave
BH6 ....123 B4
Collingwood Cl 7 DT11 199 D4
Collingwood Rd 53 A3
Collins La
Ringwood BH24 ....55 B4
Weymouth DT4 ....180 B4
Colliton St DT1 ....108 A1
Collwood Cl BH15 .....119 B4
Collyer's Rise SP7 .....37 C3
Colman Cl BH1 ....122 B2
Colmer Rd BA21 ......27 B3
Cologne Rd
Bovington Camp BH20 ...140 A3
Wool BH20 ....139 C3
Colombine Cl BH23 ....93 A1
Colonnade Rd 5 BH5 ..123 A3
Colonnade Rd W 4
BH5 ....123 A3
Colt Cl BH21 ....60 A3
Columbia Rd BH10 ....89 B1
Columbia Trees La
BH10 ....89 B1
Columban Way BH10 ..89 B1
Colville Cl BH5 ....123 A3
Colville Rd 6 BH5 .....123 A3
Colway Cl DT7 ....96 A4
Colway La DT7 ....96 A4
Combe Hill
Milborne Port DT9 ......17 A2
Templecombe BA8 ....18 C4
Combe Pk BA21 ....27 A4
Combe Way DT2 ......137 B3
Comber Rd 5 BH9 .....90 A2
Comet Cl DT4 ....166 C1
Comet Way BH23 .....125 A4
Comley Rd BH9 ....89 C1
Commercial Rd
Bournemouth BH2 ....121 C2
Poole BH14 ....120 A2
Radipole DT4 ....167 B1
1 Swanage BH19 ....179 B1
Common Dro
6 Child Okeford DT11 ..198 C8
Farnham DT11 ....188 B3
Common Hill DT8 .....203 E5
Common La
6 Blandford Forum DT11 212 B2
Burton Bradstock DT6 ...128 A4
East Stour SP8 ....11 A2
Halstock BA22 ....193 C2
Haselbury Plucknett
 TA18 ....192 D5
Henstridge BA8 ....18 C4
Kington Magna SP8 .....9 B1
Marnhull DT10 ....34 B4
Ryme Intrinseca DT9 ....194 B5
Sturminster Newton
 DT10 ....197 D8
Toller Porcorum DT2 ....205 D2
Common Mead Ave SP8 .5 C1
Common Mead La SP8 ..5 B1
Common Rd SP5 ......188 F4
Common The
Evershot DT2 ....206 A7
Hazelbury Bryan DT10 ...196 E5
Moreton DT2 ....138 B4
Common Wr La DT8 ...203 F5
Compton Abbas Airfield
 SP5 ....24 C1
Compton Acres Gdns★
BH13 ....147 C4
Compton Ave BH14 ...120 B1
Compton Beeches
BH24 ....54 B3
Compton Cl
Verwood BH31 ....45 A3
Yeovil BA21 ....28 A4
Compton Cres BH22 ...53 B1
Compton Ct BH14 .....120 B2
Compton Dr BH14 .....120 B1
Compton Gdns BH14 ..120 B1
Compton Rd
New Milton BH25 ....95 A1
Over Compton DT9 ......28 B3
Concorde Cl DT4 ......166 C1
Condor Cl BH21 ......53 B3
Coney's Castle (Fort)★
 DT6 ....65 B4
Coneygar Cl DT6 ......100 A4
Coneygar La DT6 ......100 B4
Coneygar Rd DT6 .....100 B4
Conifer Ave BH14 .....120 A1
Conifer Cl
Christchurch BH23 ....91 B2
Ferndown BH22 ....61 C1
St.Leonards BH24 ....53 C2
Coniston Ave BH11 ...88 C3
Coniston Cl BH31 .....45 A3
Coniston Cres DT3 ....166 B1
Coniston Gdns BA21 ..27 A4
Coniston Rd BH24 ....55 B3
Connaught Cl BH25 ...94 C1
Connaught Cres BH12 .120 C3
Connaught Gdns DT4 ..167 A1

Connaught Rd
Bournemouth BH5 ....123 A3
2 Weymouth DT4 ....180 C4
Connell Rd BH15 ......119 B3
Conniger La BH20 .....142 C2
Consort Cl BH12 ......120 B3
Constable Cl BA21 ....28 A4
Constable Way SP2 ...213 A2
Constitution Hill Gdns
BH14 ....120 A3
Constitution Hill Rd
BH14 ....120 A3
Conway Cl BH25 ......95 A2
Conway Ct 20 BH25 ...95 A2
Conway Dr DT2 ....136 A1
Conways Dr BH14 .....120 A2
Cook Cl BH24 ....55 C4
Cook Row BH21 ....59 A2
Cook's La DT10 ....33 B2
Cooke Gdns BH12 .....120 C3
Cooke Rd BH12 ....120 C3
Cooks La DT9 ....30 A3
Cookswell 1 DT11 ....198 B8
Coolhurst BH14 ....147 B4
Coombe DT9 ....30 A4
Coombe Ave
Bournemouth BH10 ......89 C2
Radipole DT4 ....167 C3
Coombe Cl BA21 ......27 B4
Coombe Gdns BH10 ...89 C1
Coombe Hill BH19 ....178 B1
Coombe La
Castleton DT9 ....15 B1
Stoke Abbott DT8 ....203 E3
Coombe Rd
Dinnington TA17 ....191 B7
Puddletown DT2 ....78 A1
Salisbury SP2 ....213 A1
5 Shillingstone DT11 ...198 B5
Winterbourne Steepleton
 DT2 ....105 C1
Coombe St
Lyme Regis DT7 ....96 B3
Pen Selwood BA9 ......1 B3
Coombe St La BA21 ...27 B4
Coombe Valley Rd
Bincombe DT3 ....153 A2
Overcombe/Preston
 DT3 ....168 A4
Coombe Wr La DT8 ...203 B6
Coombes Cl DT2 ......103 B1
Cooper Dean Dr BH8 ..90 C1
Cooper Gdns DT11 ....198 B8
Cooper's Cl 2 BH20 ...142 C2
Coopers Dr DT6 ....100 B2
Coopers La BH31 .....45 A4
Copeland Dr BH14 ....120 A1
Copper Beech Cl
BH12 ....121 A2
Copper Beech Gdns
BH10 ....89 B1
Coppercourt Leaze 5
BH21 ....59 B2
Coppern Way DT10 ...33 B4
Coppers Cl SP6 ....42 B3
Coppice Ave BH22 ....61 A4
Coppice Cl
New Milton BH25 ....95 B2
St.Leonards BH24 ....54 A2
Coppice St SP7 ....12 C1
Coppice The
Chickerell DT3 ....166 C1
Christchurch BH23 ....125 A3
Coppice View BH10 ...89 C2
Copse Ave BH25 ......95 A1
Copse Cl BH14 ....119 C2
Copse Hill DT10 ......197 D7
Copse Rd
Brympton BA22 ....26 B4
New Milton BH25 ....95 A1
Verwood BH31 ....45 A3
Copse Way BH23 .....125 C4
Copsewood Ave BH8 ..90 C1
Copythorne Cl BH8 ...90 B1
Coral Cl 2 BH12 ......121 A2
Coram Ave DT7 ....96 A2
Corbar Rd BH23 ......123 C4
Corbiere Ave BH12 ...88 B1
Corbin Ave BH22 .....62 A3
Corbin Way DT6 ......68 C1
Cordery Gdns SP8 ....5 C2
Cordova Gdns DT6 ...100 B4
Corfe Castle★ BH20 ..161 B1
Corfe Castle Model Village★
BH20 ....177 A4
Corfe Castle Mus★
BH20 ....162 A1
Corfe Castle VC Prim Sch
BH20 ....177 A4
Corfe Halt Cl BH21 ...58 C1
Corfe Hills Sch BH21 ..86 C3
Corfe Lodge Rd BH18 .86 B2
Corfe Mews BH15 ....119 B2
Corfe Rd Arne BH20 ..160 C4
 Radipole DT3 ....167 A4
Corfe View Rd
Corfe Mullen BH21 .....86 B3
Poole BH14 ....120 B2
Corfe Way BH18 ......86 C2
Corfu BH13 ....147 C3
Corhampton Rd BH6 ..123 B3
Cornelia Cres BH12 ...121 A3
Corner Cl DT10 ....21 A2
Corner La SP7 ....7 B1
Corner The DT11 .....198 E7
Cornerways Ct 7 BH25 .95 A1
Cornflower Dr BH23 ...125 B4
Cornford Hill DT9 .....196 A6

Cornford Way BH23	125	B4
Cornhill Way DT3	153	B2
Cornish Gdns BH10	89	B1
Cornpits La SP6	190	E2
Cornwall Cl DT4	167	A2
Cornwall Rd		
10 Dorchester DT1	107	C1
Salisbury SP1	213	B4
2 Swanage BH19	179	B1
Coronation Ave		
Bournemouth BH9	89	C1
Upton BH16	118	A4
Yeovil BA21	27	A4
Coronation Cl BH31	45	A4
Coronation Rd		
Bridport DT6	100	B3
1 Fortuneswell DT5	186	C4
Gillingham SP8	5	C1
Radipole DT3	167	B4
Verwood BH31	45	A4
Corporation Rd		
Bournemouth BH1	122	B3
Weymouth DT4	167	A2
Corpus Christi RC Prim Sch		
BH5	123	A3
Corscombe Cl BH7	87	C1
Corscombe Ct* DT2	205	B8
Corton Cl BA21	28	A4
Cortry Cl BH12	87	B2
Cossins La 1 TA18	191	F4
Cotes Ave BH14	120	A3
Cotes Ct BH14	120	A3
Cothayes Dro DT2	209	A6
Cotlands Rd BH1	122	C2
Cotswold Cl BH31	45	A3
Cotswold Ct 6 BH20	140	A1
Cottage Cl 2 BH20	140	A1
Cottage Gdns BH12	120	B3
Cottage Mews BH24	55	A4
Cotton Cl BH18	86	C3
Counter Cl DT11	212	C3
Countess Cl BH21	87	C4
Countess Gdns BH7	122	C4
County Mus* DT1	108	A1
Court Ash BA20	27	B3
Court Barton		
3 Crewkerne TA18	191	E4
Easton/Weston DT5	186	C4
Court Cl Bridport DT6	68	C1
12 Christchurch BH23	124	C4
Court Gdns BA21	27	A4
Court Hill		
Corscombe DT2	205	B8
Damerham SP6	190	F2
Swanage BH19	179	A1
Court La		
Corscombe DT2	205	B8
Milborne Port DT9	17	B2
5 Stofold BA22	193	F8
Court Orch Rd DT6	100	B3
Court Rd		
Bournemouth BH9	90	A1
Radipole DT3	152	A1
Swanage BH19	179	A1
Courtauld Dr DT4	180	A4
Courtenay Cl BH20	142	C3
Courtenay Dr BH21	59	B3
Courtenay Rd BH14	120	A2
Courthill Fst Sch		
BH14	120	B2
Courthill Rd BH14	120	B2
Courtlands Rd DT5	186	C2
Courtleigh Manor 6		
BH5	122	B2
Courtney Cl DT11	198	E8
Courtney Pl BH21	86	B3
Courtwood Cl 3 SP1	213	C2
Courtyard Craft Ctr*		
BH16	117	A4
Courtyard The		
Christchurch BH23	124	B3
Poole BH12	88	B1
Cove Rd BH10	89	B1
Cove Row 5 DT4	167	C1
Cove St DT4	167	C1
Covena Rd BH6	123	C3
Coventry Cl BH21	86	B2
Coventry Cres BH17	87	A1
Cow Down Rd TA20	202	C8
Cow Dro BH20	81	B1
Cow La Laverstock SP1	213	C3
Long Bredy DT2	103	B1
Salisbury SP1	213	C3
Swanage BH19	179	A1
Wareham BH20	142	C3
Cowards La DT3	149	A4
Cowdrey Gdns BH8	90	C1
Cowdrys Field 2 BH21	59	A3
Cowell Dr BH21	123	A4
Cowgrove Rd BH21	58	C3
Cowlease 13 BH19	179	A1
Cowleaze DT2	133	B3
Cowleaze Rd DT2	136	A1
Cowley Cl 7 DT1	107	C1
Cowley Rd BH17	119	B4
Cowleys Rd BH23	92	B1
Cowper Ave BH25	95	A1
Cowper Rd BH9	89	C1
Cowpitts La BH24	47	C1
Cowslip Rd BH18	86	C1
Cox Ave BH9	90	A2
Cox Cl BH9	90	A2
Cox Hill DT10	34	B4
Cox's La BH23	130	B4
Coxstone La BH24	55	A3
Coy Pond Rd BH12	121	A3
Crab La BA12	2	A4

Crab Orch Way BH21	45	A1
Crabbswood La SO41	95	C4
Crabton Cl Rd BH5	122	C2
Crabtree Cl BH23	92	B1
Crack La BH19	178	B2
Crackmore DT9	17	B1
Craigmoor Ave BH8	90	C1
Craigmoor Cl BH8	90	C1
Craigmoor Way BH8	90	C1
Craigside Rd BH24	53	C2
Craigwood Dr BH22	61	C2
Cranborne CE Fst Sch		
BH21	40	A4
Cranborne Cres BH12	120	C4
Cranborne Ct		
14 Bournemouth BH4	121	B4
Bournemouth BH9	122	A4
Cranborne Cty Mid Sch		
BH21	40	A4
Cranborne Dr 9 SP7	12	C2
Cranborne Lodge*		
BH21	40	A4
Cranborne Pl BH25	94	C2
Cranborne Rd		
Alderholt SP6	41	B3
Bournemouth BH2	121	C1
Hinton Parva BH21	50	B3
Swanage BH19	179	A2
Wimborne Minster BH21	59	B2
Cranbourne Ct BH17	88	A1
Cranbrook Mews		
BH12	120	A3
Cranbrook Rd BH12	120	A3
Crane Cl BH31	45	A4
Crane Dr BH31	45	A4
Crane St BH21	40	A4
Crane Valley Golf Club		
BH21	44	B3
Crane Way BH21	53	B3
Cranebridge Rd SP2	213	B2
Cranemoor Ave BH23	93	C3
Cranemoor Cl BH23	93	C3
Cranemoor Gdns BH23	93	C1
Cranes Mdw DT2	208	A8
Cranes Mews BH15	119	B2
Cranesmoor Cl BH20	139	B2
Cranfield Ave BH21	59	B3
Cranford Ave DT4	167	C3
Cranleigh Cl BH6	123	C3
Cranleigh Cl BH6	123	C3
Cranleigh Gdns BH6	123	C3
Cranleigh Rd BH6	123	C3
Cranmer Rd BH9	121	C4
Cransley St SH4	121	B1
Crantock Gr BH8	90	C1
Cranwell Cl BH11	88	C2
Crate Hill DT10	197	C5
Crate La SP7	7	C3
Crawford Bridge*		
DT11	211	E5
Crawford Down Rd 4		
DT11	199	E2
Crawford Pk DT11	211	E4
Crawshaw Rd BH14	120	A1
Creasey Rd BH11	89	A3
Creech Grange*		
BH20	160	B1
Creech Rd BH12	120	B3
Creech Way DT3	167	A4
Creekmoor La BH17	119	A4
Crescent Ct BH25	126	C4
Crescent Dr BH25	126	C4
Crescent Rd		
Bournemouth BH2	121	C2
Poole BH14	120	C2
Verwood BH31	45	B3
Wimborne Minster BH21	59	B2
Crescent St DT4	167	C2
Crescent The		
Barton on Sea BH25	126	B4
3 Bournemouth BH7	122	C2
14 Yeovil BA21	27	B2
Crescent Wlk BH22	61	C3
Crest Rd BH12	120	B3
Cresta Gdns BH22	61	C2
Crewkerne Sta TA18	192	A3
Cribb Cl BH17	119	C4
Crichel House* BH21	201	A3
Crichel La BH21	200	F1
Crichel Mount Rd		
BH14	147	B4
Crichel Rd BH9	122	A4
Cricket Cl BH23	124	C3
Crimea Rd BH9	121	C4
Cringle Ave BH6	124	A2
Crispen Cl DT3	167	A4
Criterion Arc 39 BH1	121	C2
Crock La DT6	100	C3
Crockford Rd BH25	95	A3
Croft Cl BH21	86	B4
Croft Rd		
Bournemouth BH9	89	C1
Bransgore BH23	93	A3
Christchurch BH23	124	C4
Easton/Weston DT5	186	C2
Poole BH12	120	B3
Ringwood BH24	47	C1
Croft The		
Wareham BH20	142	C2
10 Yeovil BA21	26	C1
Crofton Ave BA21	27	B3
Crofton Cl BH23	91	C1
Crofton Pk BA21	27	B3
Crofton Rd BA21	27	B3
Cromer Gdns BH12	120	C3
Cromer Rd		
Bournemouth BH8	122	B4
Poole BH12	120	C4

Cromwell Pl 9 BH5	123	A3
Cromwell Rd		
Bournemouth BH5	123	A3
13 Dorchester DT1	108	A3
Poole BH12	120	B3
Weymouth DT4	167	A2
16 Wimborne Minster BH21	59	B2
Crook Hill (National Trust)*		
DT8	192	E1
Crooked La BH9	4	B2
Crooked Oak Hill DT6	204	C5
Crookhays SP7	12	C2
Cropmead Ind Est		
TA18	191	F4
Crosby Rd BH4	121	B1
Cross La SP8	5	C4
Cross Rd		
Bradford Abbas DT9	28	A3
1 Weymouth DT4	180	C3
Cross The		
2 Bradford Abbas DT9	28	B1
3 Child Okeford DT11	198	C7
5 Henstridge BA8	19	A2
1 Okeford Fitzpaine DT11	197	F5
Shillingstone DT11	198	B6
Wool BH20	140	A1
Cross Way		
Bradford Abbas DT9	28	A1
Christchurch BH23	91	B1
Crossfields DT9	28	C4
Crossmead Ave BH25	95	A1
Crosstree Cl DT2	136	A1
Crossway DT11	199	E3
Crossways 13 TA20	202	A8
Crouch La DT9	196	A6
Crow Arch La 5 BH24	55	B3
Crow La BH24	55	C3
Crowe Hill Ct 2 BH15	119	C2
Crown Cl BH12	120	B3
Crown Ct		
Milborne St Andrew DT11	79	C4
8 Wimborne Minster BH21	59	A3
Crown Farm Terr DT5	187	A3
Crown Mead BH21	59	B2
Crown Rd DT10	21	A1
Crown Wlk 9 BH7	122	C2
Crown Yd DT2	156	C3
Crowthorne La DT2	208	A8
Crumpets Dr BH16	84	C3
Crumplers Cl BH16	84	A2
Crusader Rd BH12	88	B2
Cruxton Farm Ctyd		
BH21	59	B1
Cruxton La DT2	73	A3
Cucklington Gdns BH9	90	A2
Cuckoo Cl BH20	120	A4
Cuckoo La		
Broadwindsor TA20	202	F7
Hilton DT11	209	C7
Stinsford DT2	109	A3
Cuckoo Rd DT4	120	A4
Cudnell Ave BH11	89	A4
Cuffnells Cl BH24	47	B4
Cul-de-sac BH25	126	B4
Culford Cl BH8	90	C1
Culford Ct 1 BH8	122	A3
Cull Cl BH21	121	B4
Cull La BH25	95	A3
Culliford Cres BH17	87	C1
Culliford Rd DT1	135	A4
Culliford Rd N 19 DT1	108	A1
Culliford Way DT3	152	C2
Cullwood La BH25	95	B3
Culver Rd BH25	94	C1
Culver St 2 SP1	213	B2
Culverhayes DT8	204	C4
Culverhayes Pl BH21	59	A3
Culverhayes Rd BH21	59	A3
Culverlake La EX13	202	D3
Culvers Cl DT3	30	A3
Culvers La SP8	5	B1
Cumberland Dr DT4	166	C2
Cumnor Rd BH1	122	A2
Cunnage La BA12	3	C1
Cunningham Cl		
Bournemouth BH11	89	A2
Bovington Camp BH20	139	C3
Christchurch BH23	125	A3
4 Ringwood BH24	55	C4
3 Weymouth DT4	180	A4
Cunningham Cres		
BH11	89	A2
Cunningham Ct BH25	94	C2
Cunningham Pl BH11	89	A2
Cunnington Cl DT1	134	C4
Curlew Cl		
1 Chickerell DT3	166	B3
Ferndown BH22	61	A4
Curlew Rd		
Bournemouth BH8	90	B1
Christchurch BH23	125	A3
Curlews The BH31	45	B3
Curlieu Rd DT4	167	A4
Curriott Hill TA18	191	E4
Curriott Hill Rd 9 TA18	191	E4
Curry Hole La DT2	193	D2
Curtis Ct DT9	196	A8
Curtis Rd BH12	120	B3
Curzon Ct 32 BH4	121	B4
Curzon Rd		
Bournemouth BH1	122	A2
Poole BH12	120	A2
Curzon Way BH23	125	B4

Custard Hill BH21	201	B5
Custom House Quay		
DT4	167	B1
Cuthburga Rd BH21	59	B2
Cuthbury Cl BH21	59	A3
Cuthbury Gdns BH21	59	A3
Cutler Cl		
New Milton BH25	95	B2
Poole BH12	121	B4
Cutlers Pl BH21	60	A3
Cutt Mill La DT10	34	C3
Cynthia Cl BH12	120	A4
Cynthia House BH12	120	A4
Cynthia Rd BH12	120	A4
Cypress Dr BA20	27	A1
Cypress Way 9 SP8	5	C1
Cyril Rd BH8	122	B3

D

Dacombe Cl BH16	118	B4
Dacombe Dr BH16	118	B4
Daggons Rd SP6	41	C3
Dagmar Rd DT1	107	C1
Dahlia Cl DT3	152	C1
Dairy Cl		
Christchurch BH23	124	B4
Corfe Mullen BH21	86	A2
Dairy Field DT11	212	C3
Dairy Mdw La DT1	213	C2
Dakota Cl BH23	125	A4
Dale Ave DT4	167	A3
Dale Cl BH15	119	C3
Dale Rd BH15	119	C3
Dale Valley Rd BH15	119	C4
Daler Ct 13 BH20	142	C2
Dales Cl BH21	60	A3
Dales Dr BH21	60	A3
Dales La BH23	90	C4
Dalewood Ave BH11	88	C3
Dalkeith Rd		
Corfe Mullen BH21	86	B2
Poole BH13	121	A1
Dalling Rd BH12	121	A3
Dalmeny Rd BH6	124	A2
Dalwoods DT9	30	A3
Damer's Rd DT1	107	B1
Damerham Rd BH8	90	B2
Damers Cty Fst Sch		
DT1	107	C1
Damory Ct 5 DT11	212	B2
Damory Ct St DT11	212	B2
Damory St DT11	212	B2
Dampier Pl 2 BA21	27	C3
Dampier St 3 BA21	27	C3
Dane Ct BH14	120	A3
Dane Dr BH22	61	C2
Danecourt Cl BH14	119	C2
Danecourt Rd BH14	119	C2
Danecrest Rd SO41	95	C3
Danehurst New Rd		
SO41	95	A4
Danes Cl BH25	127	A4
Danesbury Ave BH6	123	C2
Danesbury Mdws BH25	95	B3
Daneswood Rd BH25	95	B2
Daniel Dr BH20	142	B3
Daniel Gdns 13 BH15	119	B1
Danielsfield Rd BA20	27	A1
Dansie Cl BH14	120	A3
Darby La 6 DT6	128	A4
Darby's Cl BH15	119	B3
Darby's Cnr BH17	87	B1
Darby's La BH15	119	B3
Darby's La N BH17	119	B3
Dark La Bransgore BH23	94	A2
Fifehead Neville DT10	197	C6
Mere BA12	3	A3
Sandford Orcas DT9	15	B3
Tincleton DT2	110	B3
Witchampton BH21	200	F1
Darkie La BH19	179	A3
Darknoll La DT11	197	E6
Darley Rd BH22	61	B2
Darracott Rd BH5	123	A3
Darrian Ct BH16	118	A4
Darwin Ave BH23	91	C1
Darwin Cl DT3	152	B2
Darwin Ct 4 BH21	121	B4
Dashwood Cl DT10	35	B1
D'Urberville Cl 4 DT1	134	C4
D'Urberville Dr BH19	179	A2
Davenant Cl 5 SP8	5	C1
Davenport Cl BH16	118	B4
David Way BH15	118	C1
David's La BH24	54	C3
David's Wlk DT1	134	C4
Davis Cl BH12	120	C3
Davis Field BH25	94	C1
Davis Gdns DT11	212	C3
Davis Rd BH12	120	C3
Dawkins Bsns Ctr		
BH15	118	B2
Dawkins Rd BH15	118	B2
Dawkins Way BH25	95	A1
Dawn Chorus BH14	120	A2
Dawn Cl BH10	89	B1
Daws Ave BH11	89	A1
Day's La DT11	59	B2
Day's Rd BH19	178	C1
Daylesford Cl BH14	120	A1
De Courtenai Cl BH11	88	C3
De Haviland Cl DT11	59	C1
De Havilland Ho BH23	125	A3
De Havilland Way		
BH23	125	A3

Cor - Dic 223

De Lisle Rd BH3	121	C4
De Mauley Rd BH13	147	C4
De Montfort Rd BH21	59	C1
De Moulham Rd BH19	179	A2
De Redvers Rd BH14	120	B1
De Vaux Pl SP1	213	B2
Deacon Gdns BH11	89	A3
Deacon Rd BH11	89	A3
Dean Cl BH15	118	C2
Dean La SP5	188	F6
Dean La Dro SP5	188	F4
Dean Pk Cres BH1	121	C2
Dean Pk Rd BH1	121	C2
Dean Swift Cres BH14	147	B4
Dean's Rd 18 BH5	123	A3
Deane Ave SP5	5	C1
Deane Way 5 TA20	202	A8
Deanes Ct La BH21	59	B2
Deans Dro BH16	84	B1
Deans Gr BH21	59	B4
Deans The BH1	121	C2
Deanscroft Rd BH10	89	C2
Deansleigh Cl 5 DT3	168	A4
Deansleigh Rd BH7	91	A1
Dear Hay La BH15	119	B1
Decies Rd BH14	120	A3
Dee Way BH15	119	A1
Deep Ford La DT9	194	D3
Deep La DT9	194	C3
Deepdene La BH11	88	C3
Deer Pk Cl BH25	94	C2
Deerleap Way BH25	95	A3
Delamere Gdns BH10	89	C2
Delft Mews BH23	124	B3
Delhi Cl BH14	120	B2
Delhi La DT5	187	A2
Delhi Rd BH9	89	C1
Delilah Rd BH15	118	B3
Delkeith Ct BH22	61	B2
Dell Cl BH18	86	C2
Dell The BH25	126	B4
Delph Rd BH21	87	B4
Delph Woods Woodland		
Trail* BH21	87	B4
Delta Cl BH23	125	B4
Denby Rd BH15	119	C2
Dene Cl BH24	47	C1
Dene Wlk BH22	61	C1
Denecote Lodge		
BH13	147	D4
Denes Ave BA12	3	A3
Deneve Ave BH17	87	B1
Denewood Copse BH22	52	C2
Denewood Rd BH22	52	C2
Denhall Cl DT10	35	A1
Denham Cl DT11	59	C1
Denham Dr Cann SP7	23	A3
Christchurch BH23	93	C1
Denhay La DT6	67	C3
Denholm Cl BH24	47	C1
Denison Rd BH17	87	B1
Denison Rise SP1	213	C4
Denmark La BH15	119	B2
Denmark Rd		
Bournemouth BH9	89	C1
Poole BH15	119	B2
Denmark Terr BH1	122	C3
Denmead BH25	95	B2
Denmead Rd BH6	123	C3
Dennetts La 19 BH15	119	A1
Dennis Rd		
Corfe Mullen BH21	86	B3
Weymouth DT4	167	A4
Dennistoun Ave BH23	124	C4
Denwood Rd BH4	121	A2
Denzil Cl 3 BA22	193	A8
Derby Rd BH1	122	B2
Derby St DT4	167	B2
Dereham Way BH12	120	C3
Derritt La BH23	92	B4
Derrybrian Gdns BH25	95	A1
Derwent Cl		
Bournemouth BH9	90	A1
Ferndown BH22	62	A3
Derwent Gdns BA21	27	C3
Derwent Rd		
New Milton BH25	95	A3
Weymouth DT4	180	B3
Derwent Way 3 BA21	26	C3
Derwentwater Rd BH21	59	B1
Deverel Cl BH23	124	A4
Devizes Rd SP2	213	A3
Devon Rd		
Christchurch BH23	123	C4
Poole BH15	119	C3
Weymouth DT4	167	A2
Devonshire Rd SP1	213	B4
Dew's Rd SP2	213	A3
Dewey's Way SP8	5	C1
Dewlands Orch DT2	194	E3
Dewlands Rd BH31	44	C3
Dewlands Way BH31	45	A3
Dewlish Cl BH17	88	A1
Dewlish House* DT2	78	C4
Diamond Rd SP6	43	A4
Diana Cl DT1	134	C4
Diana Ct BH23	126	A4
Diana Way BH21	86	C4
Dibbles La BA22	193	A8
Dibden Cl BH8	90	B2
Dick o' Th' Banks Cl		
DT2	137	B3
Dick o' Th' Banks Rd		
DT2	137	B3
Dickens Rd BH6	123	B4

Didcot Rd BH17 .....119 B4
Digby Rd DT9 ......30 A3
Diggory Cres DT1 ...135 A4
Dillons Gdns BH16 ....84 B1
Dilly La DT5 ......127 A4
Diments Gdns **2** DT6 ..100 B4
Dinah's Hollow SP7 ....24 B3
Dingle Rd BH5 .....123 A2
Dingley Rd BH15 ....119 B3
Dinham Ct BH25 .....95 B2
Dinham Rd BH25 .....95 B2
Dinhay DT10 ......20 C2
Dinosaur Experience The★
 BH19 ......177 C1
Dinosaur Mus★ DT1 ..108 A1
Diprose Rd BH21 .....86 C4
Discover Salisbury (Medieval
 Hall)★ SP1 .....213 B2
Disraeli Dr BH23 ....124 B3
Dock Rd DT5 .....181 B1
Dodhams Farm Cl DT6 ..68 C1
Doe Copse Way BH25 ..94 C2
Dogbury Gate DT2 ...207 C8
Dogdean BH21 .....59 B4
Dogwood Rd BH18 ....86 C1
Dolbery Rd N BH12 ....88 B1
Dolbery Rd S BH12 ....88 B1
Dollin's La **3** BH20 ..142 C2
Dollings The BH20 ...177 A4
Dolmans Hill BH20 ....84 A2
Dolphin Ave BH10 ....89 C3
Dolphin Cl **2** DT7 ....96 B3
Dolphin Ctr BH15 ...119 B1
Dolphin Ind Est SP1 ..213 C2
Dolphin La SP8 ......5 C2
Dolphin Pl BH25 ....127 A4
Dolphin St SP1 ....213 B2
Dominion Ctr★ BH11 ..88 C2
Dominion Rd BH11 ...88 C2
Donaldson Rd SP1 ...213 B3
Doncaster Rd DT4 ...180 B3
Donhead Hollow SP7 ...25 B4
Donkey La
 Bere Regis BH20 ....113 A3
 Bridport DT6 .....100 B4
 5 Burton Bradstock DT6 .128 A4
Donnelly Rd BH6 ....123 C3
Donnington Dr BH23 ..125 A4
Donoughmore Rd **1**
 BH1 ......122 C2
Dorchester Cty Mid Sch
 DT1 ......134 C4
Dorchester Gdns
 BH15 ......119 C3
Dorchester Hill
 Blandford St Mary DT11 .212 B1
 Milborne St Andrew DT11 .79 C4
 Winterborne Whitechurch
 DT11 ......210 C4
Dorchester Mans BH1 .122 B2
Dorchester Mus★
 DT1 ......108 A1
Dorchester Prep Sch
 DT1 ......108 A1
Dorchester Rd
 Affpuddle DT2 ......79 C1
 Askerswell DT2 ....103 A2
 Bincombe DT3 ....134 B1
 Cerne Abbas DT2 ...207 D4
 Closworth BA22 ...193 F6
 Frampton DT2 ......74 A1
 Loders DT6 .....101 B3
 Lytchett Minster & Upton
  BH16 ......117 A4
 Maiden Newton DT2 ...73 A4
 Melbury Osmond BA22 ..194 A4
 Poole BH15 .....119 C3
 Radipole DT3 .....152 A4
 Stratton DT2 .....106 B4
 Sydling St Nicholas DT2 .207 A4
 Tolpuddle DT2 .....79 A1
 Upton BH16 .....118 A4
 Wool BH20 .....139 C1
 Yeovil BA20 ......27 B1
Dorchester S Sta DT1 .108 A1
Dorchester W Sta
 DT1 ......107 C1
Dormers The BH25 ....94 C1
Dornie Rd BH13 ....147 C4
Dorset Ave BH22 .....61 C2
Dorset Cl DT4 ....167 A2
Dorset Cty Hospl DT1 .107 C1
Dorset Gall★ BA20 ...142 C2
Dorset Grange BH23 ..123 C4
Dorset House BH13 ...121 A1
Dorset Lake Ave BH14 .147 A4
Dorset Lake Manor
 BH14 ......120 A1
Dorset Leisure Ctr DT6 .97 A4
Dorset Rare Breeds Ctr★
 SP8 ......11 B4
Dorset Rd
 Bournemouth BH4 ...121 B3
 Christchurch BH23 ...124 C4
 Salisbury SP1 .....213 B4
Dorset St DT11 ....212 B2
Dorset Terr **8** DT4 ...167 B1
Dottery Rd DT6 ......68 B1
Double Comm DT6 ....97 A4
Douglas Ave BH23 ...124 A3
Douglas Cl BH16 ....118 B4
Douglas Gdns BH12 ...120 C3
Douglas Haig Rd SP1 .213 B3
Douglas Mews
 Bournemouth BH6 ...123 B3

Douglas Mews continued
 Upton BH16 .....118 B4
Douglas Rd
 Bournemouth BH6 ...123 C2
 Poole BH12 .....120 C3
 Weymouth DT4 .....180 B3
Doulton Gdns BH14 ...120 A1
Doussie Cl BH16 ....118 A4
Dover Cl BH13 ....121 A2
Dover Rd Poole BH13 ..121 A2
 Weymouth DT4 .....180 B3
Dover St SP7 ......21 C3
Doves The DT3 ....152 B2
Doveshill Cres BH10 ...89 B2
Doveshill Gdns BH10 ...89 B2
Doveshill Mobile Home Pk
 BH10 ......89 B2
Dowlands Cl BH10 ....89 B2
Dowlands Rd BH10 ...89 B2
Dowman Pl DT4 ....180 B3
Down End DT2 ....107 C3
Down House La DT2 ....99 C2
Down La Folke DT9 ...195 D8
 Trent DT9 ......14 C1
Down Lodge Cl SP6 ....42 B3
Down Rd
 3 Pimperne DT11 ...199 D4
 Weymouth DT4 .....167 B1
Down Wood Rd **2** DT11 .199 E2
Down's La DT9 ....194 C5
Downash La EX13 ...202 B3
Downclose **12** DT4 ...180 B4
Downclose La TA18 ...192 C4
Downes St DT6 ....100 B3
Downey Cl BH11 .....88 C1
Downlands CP Sch
 DT11 ......199 E3
Downlands Pl BH17 ...119 C4
Downleaze **1** BA20 ...26 C1
Downs La DT9 ....194 C5
Downside Cl
 Blandford Forum DT11 .212 C2
 Charmouth DT6 .....97 A4
 Mere BA12 ......3 A3
Downsview Dr SP8 ....5 C2
Downsway SP1 ....213 B1
Downton Cl BH8 ......90 B2
Downton La SO41 ...127 C4
Downton Rd SP2 ...213 B1
Downview Rd SP6 ...190 B6
Doyne Rd BH14 ....120 C2
Dozens Cnr TA17 ...191 A7
Dragons Hill DT7 ....96 B3
Dragoon Way BH23 ...123 C4
Drake Ave DT3 ....166 B3
Drake Cl
 Christchurch BH23 ...124 C3
 New Milton BH25 ....94 C2
 Ringwood BH24 ......47 C1
Drake Ct **22** BH15 ...119 B1
Drake Rd BH15 ....119 B1
Drake's La DT2 ....208 F3
Drakes Cres **6** TA20 .202 A8
Drakes Mdw BA22 ...193 C7
Drakes Rd BH22 .....61 C2
Draper Rd
 Bournemouth BH11 ...89 A2
 Christchurch BH23 ...124 C4
Drax Ave BH20 ....142 C3
Draycott Rd BH10 ....89 B1
Dreswick Cl DT3 ....91 B2
Drew Cl Bridport DT6 ...68 C1
 Poole BH12 .....121 B4
Drew's La DT10 ......19 B1
Drewitt Ind Est BH11 ...88 C2
Drift Rd DT2 ......72 C4
Drive The BH12 ....120 B3
Drones La SP7 ......23 B1
Drove La SP7 ......36 C3
Drove Rd DT10 ......32 C2
Drove The Arne BH20 .160 C4
 Shapwick DT11 .....56 C4
 Thornford DT9 .....194 D8
 Winfrith Newburgh DT2 .156 C4
Droveway La BA21 ....14 A3
Droxford Rd BH6 ....123 A3
Druce La DT2 ......77 C2
Druids Cl BH22 .....61 B1
Druitt Rd BH23 ....124 C4
Drum La DT10 ....196 F3
Drummond Rd
 Bournemouth BH1 ...122 B2
 Swanage BH19 ....179 B1
Drury La DT6 ....204 C2
Drury Rd BH14 ....121 A1
Dry La SP8 ......5 B1
Dryden Cl
 Salisbury SP2 .....213 B1
 St.Leonards BH24 ....54 A3
Duart Ct BH25 ......95 B2
Duchy Cl DT1 ....135 B4
Duchy Manor Mid Sch
 BA12 ......3 A3
Duck Island La BH24 ...55 A3
Duck La
 Bournemouth BH11 ...88 C2
 Salisbury SP1 .....213 C3
 Stalbridge DT10 ......19 B1
Duck St Bridport DT6 .100 C2
 Cattistock DT2 ....206 C2
 Cerne Abbas DT2 ...207 D4
 Chideock DT6 ......99 A3
 Child Okeford DT11 ...198 C4
 Hilton DT11 .....209 D5
 Symondsbury DT6 ....99 C4
 Winterborne Kingston
 DT11 ......81 C4

Duck St continued
 Wool BH20 .....140 A1
Duck's Nest (Long Barrow)★
 SP6 ......190 F7
Ducking Stool La
 BH23 ......124 A3
Duckpool La TA18 ...192 B8
Dudley Cl SO41 ......95 C2
Dudley Gdns BH10 ...89 B3
Dudley Pl **29** BH25 ...95 A1
Dudley Rd BH10 ....89 B3
Dudmoor Farm Rd
 BH23 ......91 C2
Dudmoor La BH23 ....91 C2
Dudsbury Ave BH22 ...61 B2
Dudsbury Cres BH22 ...61 C2
Dudsbury Ct **9** BH23 .124 C3
Dudsbury Gdns BH22 ..89 C4
Dudsbury Rd BH22 ...61 B2
Dudsway DT4 ....167 B2
Dugberry Hill DT6 ....70 A3
Dugdell Cl BH22 .....61 C3
Duke's Ave DT1 ....108 A1
Dukes Dr BH11 ......88 C3
Dukesfield BH23 .....91 B1
Dullar La BH21 ......56 B1
Dulsie Rd BH3 ....121 B4
Dumbarton Rd DT4 ...180 B3
Dumpton Sch BH21 ...59 B4
Dunbar Cres BH22 ....93 C1
Dunbar Rd BH3 ....121 C3
Dunbury Fst Sch
 Winterborne Kingston
 DT11 ......81 C4
 Winterborne Stickland
 DT11 ......210 C7
 Winterborne Whitechurch
 DT11 ......210 C3
Dunbury La DT11 ...209 F6
Duncan Cres BH20 ...139 C3
Duncan Rd BH25 .....95 B2
Dunch La DT9 ....194 D3
Duncliff Rd BH6 ....124 A2
Duncliffe Cl DT10 ....33 C4
Duncombe Dr BH24 ...46 C2
Dundas Rd BH17 ...119 C4
Dundee Rd DT4 ....180 B3
Dune Crest BH13 ...147 B2
Dunedin Cl BH22 ....61 A2
Dunedin Dr BH22 ....61 A2
Dunedin Gdns BH22 ...61 A2
Dunedin Gr BH23 ...125 B4
Dunford Cl
 Barton on Sea BH25 ..126 C4
 New Milton BH25 ....94 C1
Dunford Pl **15** BH19 .179 A1
Dunford Rd BH12 ...120 B3
Dungeon Hill (Fort)★
 DT9 ......195 F2
Dunkeld Rd BH3 ....121 C3
Dunlin Cl BH23 ....125 A3
Dunn's La
 Iwerne Minster DT11 ...37 C1
 Silton SP8 ......2 A1
Dunnock Cl BH22 ....61 A4
Dunsham La TA18 ...191 C2
Dunshay Manor★
 BH19 ......177 B2
Dunspit La DT11 ...188 B1
Dunstans La BH15 ...120 A3
Dunyeats Rd BH18 ....87 A2
Durdells Ave BH11 ...89 A3
Durdells Gdns BH11 ...89 A3
Durland Cl BH25 .....95 A1
Durley Chine Ct BH2 .121 B1
Durley Chine Rd BH2 .121 B1
Durley Chine Rd S
 BH2 ......121 B1
Durley Gdns BH2 ...121 B1
Durley Rd BH2 ....121 C1
Durley Rd S BH2 ...121 B1
Durlston Cres BH23 ...91 B2
Durlston Ct Sch BH25 .127 A4
Durlston Ctry Pk★
 BH19 ......185 A4
Durlston Farm BH19 .179 A3
Durlston Rd
 Poole BH14 .....120 B1
 Swanage BH19 ....179 B1
Durnford Dro BH19 ...178 A1
Durngate St DT1 ...108 A1
Durnover Ct DT1 ...108 A1
Durrant Rd DT10 ...197 D8
Durrant Cl DT9 ......30 A3
Durrant Rd
 7 Bournemouth BH2 .121 C2
 Poole BH14 .....120 B2
Durrington Pl BH7 ...123 C4
Durrington Rd BH7 ...123 A4
Durweston CE Fst Sch
 DT11 ......198 E3
Durweston Cl BH9 ....90 A2
Dyke Head DT9 ....195 B6
Dymewood Rd BH21 ...53 A4

E

Eadon Cl DT3 ....168 A4
Eagle House Gdns
 DT11 ......212 B1
Eagle House Sch
 BH14 ......120 A1
Eagle Rd BH12 ....121 A2
Eaglehurst **5** BH12 ...121 A2
Earl Cl **14** DT1 ....108 A1
Earle Rd BH4 ....121 B1
Earls La BA20 ......27 C2

Earlham Dr BH14 ...120 B2
Earls Cl DT9 ......30 A3
Earlsdon Way BH23 ..125 C4
Earlswood Dr SP6 ....42 A3
Earlswood Pk BH25 ...95 B2
Earthpits La SP5 ...189 E4
East Ave
 Barton on Sea BH25 ..126 B4
 Bournemouth BH3 ...121 B3
East Borough BH21 ...59 A3
East Burton Rd BH20 .139 C1
East Cl BH25 ....126 B4
East Cliff DT7 ......96 B3
East Cliff Way BH23 ..125 C4
East Coker Prim Sch
 BA22 ......193 C7
East Coker Rd BA22 ...27 A1
East Dro DT2 ....178 A1
East Farm La DT2 ...155 B4
East Hill
 Charminster DT2 ...107 B3
 Evershot DT2 .....206 A7
East Howe La BH10 ...89 B2
East Knighton La DT2 .157 A4
East La TA18 ....192 B8
East Mill La DT9 ......30 A3
East Morden Dro BH20 .83 B3
East Overcliff Dr BH1 .122 B2
East Quay BH15 ....119 B1
East Quay Rd BH15 ...119 B1
East St Beaminster DT8 .204 D4
 Blandford Forum DT11 .212 B3
 Bourton SP8 ......1 C1
 Bridport DT6 .....100 B3
 Chickerell DT3 ....166 B3
 Corfe Castle BH20 ...162 A1
 Crewkerne TA18 ...191 F4
 Fortuneswell DT5 ...186 C4
 Milborne Port DT9 ....17 B1
 North Perrott TA18 ...192 C4
 Poole BH15 .....119 B1
 Radipole DT4 .....167 C1
 Salisbury SP2 .....213 A3
 Sydling St Nicholas DT2 .207 A2
 Wareham BH20 .....142 C2
 West Coker BA22 ...193 A8
 Wimborne Minster BH21 ..59 B2
 9 Winterborne Kingston
 DT11 ......81 C4
East View Rd BH24 ...55 B4
East Walls BH20 ....142 C2
East Way
 Bournemouth BH8 ....90 B1
 Corfe Mullen BH21 ...86 B3
East Weare Rd DT5 ...181 A1
East Wyld Rd DT4 ...167 A2
Eastbrook Row BH21 ...59 B2
Eastbury Ct BH23 ...124 C2
Eastcott Cl BH7 ....123 A4
Eastdown Ave DT3 ...167 C4
Eastdown Gdns DT3 ..168 A3
Easter Rd BH9 ......90 A1
Eastfield **4** DT9 ...194 D8
Eastfield Ct BH24 ....55 C4
Eastfield La
 North Perrott TA18 ...192 C4
 Ringwood BH24 ......55 C4
 West Chinnock BA22 .192 D8
Easthams Rd TA18 ...191 F4
Eastlake Ave BH12 ...120 B3
Eastland Rd BA21 ....27 C3
Eastlands
 New Milton BH25 ....95 A1
 10 Yetminster DT9 ...194 D8
Eastleaze Rd DT11 ...212 B3
Easton Hollow SP5 ...188 B7
Easton La DT5 ....187 A3
Easton Sq **4** DT5 ...187 A2
Easton St DT5 ....187 A2
Eastop La DT10 ......33 A3
Eastville BA21 ......27 C3
Eastwood Ave BH7 ...61 C3
Eastworth Rd BH31 ...45 A4
Eaton Rd BH13 ....121 A1
Ebor Cl BH22 ......61 C1
Ebor Rd Poole BH12 ..120 B3
 Weymouth DT4 .....180 B4
Eccles Rd BH15 ....119 A1
Ecclestone Ave DT1 ..108 B1
Eddy Green Rd BH16 ...84 A1
Eden Cl **20** BH1 ...122 A2
Eden Gr BH21 ......59 B2
Edgarton Rd BH17 ....87 B2
Edgehill Rd
 Bournemouth BH9 ...89 C1
 Bridport DT6 .....100 A3
Edgemoor Rd BH22 ...53 B1
Edifred Rd BH9 ......90 A2
Edison Rd SP2 ....213 A4
Edith Ct **2** SP8 ......5 C1
Edmondsham House★
 BH21 ......40 B2
Edmondsham Rd BH31 .45 A4
Edmonsham House **23**
 BH21 ......59 B2
Edmunds Cl BH25 ....95 A1
Edward Cl BA22 ......26 B3
Edward Cres BH20 ...142 C2
Edward Rd
 Bournemouth BH11 ...89 A2
 Christchurch BH23 ...124 C4
 Dorchester DT1 .....107 C1
 Poole BH14 .....120 B3
Edward St
 Blandford Forum DT11 .212 B2

Edward St continued
 4 Radipole DT4 ...167 B2
Edward Way Ct DT4 ...89 A2
Edwina Cl BH24 ......47 C1
Edwina Dr BH17 ......87 A1
Egdon Cl
 Bere Regis BH20 ....81 A1
 Ferndown BH22 ......61 A2
Egdon Ct BH16 ....118 A4
Egdon Dr BH21 ......87 C4
Egdon Glen DT2 ....137 C3
Egdon Rd
 Dorchester DT1 .....135 A4
 Northport BH20 .....142 B3
Egerton Gdns BH8 ...122 B3
Egerton Rd BH8 ....122 B3
Eggardon Cl **5** DT8 ..204 C4
Eggardon Hill (Fort)★
 DT6 ......71 A1
Egmont Cl BH24 ......54 C1
Egmont Dr BH24 ......54 C1
Egmont Gdns BH24 ...54 C1
Egmont Rd BH16 ...118 A2
Elbury View SP7 ......37 C4
Elder Rd BH20 ......81 A1
Elderberry La BH23 ..124 C3
Eldon Ave BH25 ....126 C4
Eldon Cl BH25 ....126 C4
Eldon Ct **9** BH14 ...120 A2
Eldon Pl BH4 ....121 A2
Eldon Rd BH9 ......89 C1
Eldon Terr **11** BH19 .179 A1
Eldons Dro BH16 ......84 B2
Eldridge Cl **3** DT1 ..134 C4
Eleanor Dr BH11 ......88 B3
Eleanor Gdns BH23 ..123 C4
Elfin Dr BH22 ......61 B4
Elgar Rd BH10 ......89 B2
Elgin Rd
 Bournemouth BH3 ...121 B3
 Poole BH14 .....120 B1
Elijah Cl BH15 ....118 C1
Eliot House **14** BH25 ..95 A1
Eliotts Dr BA21 ......27 A4
Elise Cl DT4 ....123 A4
Elizabeth Ave
 Bridport DT6 .....100 B3
 Christchurch BH23 ...123 C4
Elizabeth Cl **1** DT7 ...96 B3
Elizabeth Ct
 12 Bournemouth BH1 ..122 A2
 11 New Milton BH25 ...95 A1
Elizabeth Gdns BH23 .125 B4
Elizabeth Pl DT1 ...107 B1
Elizabeth Rd
 Blandford Forum DT11 .212 C4
 Poole BH15 .....119 B2
 Upton BH16 .....118 B4
 Wimborne Minster BH21 ..59 B3
Elizabeth Way DT3 ...166 C3
Ellerslie Cl DT2 ....107 C3
Elles Rd BH20 ....139 B4
Ellesdon DT6 ....97 A4
Ellesfield Dr BH22 ...61 B1
Ellingham Dr BH24 ...46 C2
Ellingham Dro BH24 ...47 C3
Ellingham Rd BH25 ..126 B4
Elliot Rd BH11 ......88 C2
Elliott's Hill BA22 ...192 D7
Elm Ave
 Christchurch BH23 ....91 C1
 Holton Heath BH20 ..116 A2
 New Milton BH25 ....95 A1
Elm Cl Motcombe SP7 ...7 A1
 Overcombe/Preston
 DT3 ......168 A3
 Salisbury SP1 .....213 C4
 Sturminster Newton DT10 .35 B2
Elm Ct **4** BH25 ......95 A1
Elm Gdns BH4 ....121 B3
Elm Gr SP1 ....213 B3
Elm Gr Rd SP1 ....213 B3
Elm Tree Wlk DT6 ....89 C4
Elmes Rd BH9 ......89 C4
Elmgate Dr BH7 ....123 A4
Elmhurst Ave BA21 ...27 B4
Elmhurst Rd
 Bournemouth BH11 ...89 A3
 Ferndown BH22 ......53 A1
Elmhurst Way BH22 ...53 A1
Elmore Dr BH24 ......54 A3
Elmrise Prim Sch BH11 .89 A2
Elms Ave BH14 ....120 A1
Elms Cl BH14 ....120 A1
Elms Way BH6 ....123 C2
Elmstead Rd BH13 ...147 C4
Elmwood Way BH23 ..126 A4
Elphinstone Rd BH23 ..94 A1
Elsdon's La DT6 ......64 A2
Elston Medieval Village of★
 DT2 ......207 A3
Eltham Cl BH7 ....123 C4
Elvin Cl SO41 ......95 C2
Elwell DT6 ....100 C3
Elwell Manor Gdns
 DT4 ......167 B1
Elwell St DT3 ....152 B2
Elwood Cl BH20 ....142 C4
Elwyn Rd BH1 ....122 B3
Elysium Ct BH21 ......61 C2
Elziver Cl DT3 ....166 B3
Embankment Way
 BH24 ......55 B3
Emberley Cl BH22 ....62 A3
Emerald Cl BH24 ......54 A3
Emerson Cl BH15 ...119 B1
Emerson Rd
 Poole BH15 .....119 B1

Emerson Rd continued
Weymouth DT4 ....167 A1
Emily Cl BH23 ....45 A3
Emily Ct BH14 ....120 C3
Emley La **1** BH21 ......201 C1
Emmadale Rd DT4 ......167 A2
Emmanuel CE Mid Sch
BH31 ....45 A3
Emmdale Cl DT4 ....167 A1
Emminster Cl DT3 .....168 A4
Empool Cl DT2 ....137 B3
Encombe Cl BH12 ......120 C4
Encombe Rd BH20 .....142 B2
Endfield Cl BH23 ....91 C1
Endfield Rd
Bournemouth BH9 ....90 A1
Christchurch BH23 ....91 C1
Endless St SP1 ....213 B3
Enfield Cres BH15 .....119 C3
Enfield Rd BH15 ....119 C3
Englands Way BH11 .....88 B2
Enkworth Rd DT3 ......168 A4
Ensbury Ave BH10 ......89 B1
Ensbury Cl BH10 ....89 B1
Ensbury Ct BH10 ....89 C1
Ensbury Pk Rd BH9 .....89 C1
Enterprise Way BH23 ...90 B4
Epiphany CE Prim Sch
BH9 ....90 A2
Erica Dr BH21 ....86 B3
Ericksen Rd BH11 ......89 B2
Erin Rd BH20 ....139 C4
Erinbank Mans BH1 ...122 B2
Erpingham Rd BH12 ...121 A3
Esmonde Way BH17 ...119 C4
Esplanade
Bridport DT6 ....100 A1
Poole BH13 ....147 C1
Portland DT5 ....186 C4
Radipole DT4 ....167 C2
Essex Ave BH23 ....91 C1
Essex Rd DT4 ....167 B2
Essex Sq SP1 ....213 A4
Estcourt Rd SP1 ....213 B3
Ethelbert Rd BH21 .....59 B2
Eton Gdns BH4 ....121 B2
Ettrick Rd BH13 ....121 A1
Eucalyptus Ave BH24 ..54 B1
Euston Gr BH24 ....55 B3
Evans Cl
Bournemouth BH11 .....88 C1
St.Leonards BH24 ......54 A3
Evelyn Mews **1** BH9 ..89 C1
Evelyn Rd BH9 ....90 A1
Evening Glade BH22 ...61 C2
Eventide Homes BH8 ..90 C1
Everdene Cl BH22 .....61 B1
Everdene Dr DT4 ......166 C2
Everdene Rd **2** DT1 ..135 A4
Everest Rd
Christchurch BH23 .....124 C4
Weymouth DT4 ....167 B1
Everglades Cl BH21 ....61 B4
Evergreen Cl BH21 ....53 C4
Evergreens BH24 ......54 A3
Evering Ave BH12 ......88 B1
Evering Gdns BH12 ....88 B1
Evershot Rd BH8 ......90 C1
Eversleigh BH2 ....121 B1
Everton Rd **15** BA20 ..27 B2
Evesham Ave BA21 ....26 C3
Evesham Cl BH7 ......123 A4
Evesham St BH1 ......121 A1
Exbourne Manor BH1 .122 B3
Exbury Dr BH11 ....88 C3
Excelsior Rd BH14 ....120 B2
Exeter Cres BH2 ......121 C2
Exeter Ct **10** BH2 ....126 A4
Exeter House Specl Sch
SP1 ....213 B4
Exeter La BH2 ....121 C1
Exeter Pk Mans BH2 ..121 C1
Exeter Pk Rd BH2 ....121 C1
Exeter Rd
Bournemouth BH2 ....121 C2
4 Swanage BH19 ....179 B1
Exeter St SP1 ....213 B2
Exton Rd BH6 ....123 C4
Eynon Mews BH24 .....55 A3
Eype Down Rd DT6 ....99 C3
Eyres Way SP1 ....213 B2

F

Factory Hill SP8 ....1 C2
Factory La
Buckland Newton DT2 ..207 F8
Tatworth & Forton
TA20 ....202 A8
Factory Rd BH16 ......118 B3
Fair Lea BH2 ....121 C1
Fair Mile Road DT11 ..212 A1
Fairclose DT2 ....167 A1
Faircourt **18** BH25 ....95 B4
Faircross Ave DT4 ....167 B1
Fairey Cl SP8 ....5 C2
Fairfax DT6 ....99 A3
Fairfield
Christchurch BH23 .....124 A4
Crewkerne TA18 ......191 E4
Sherborne DT9 ....30 A4
Fairfield Bglws DT11 ..212 B1
Fairfield Cl
Christchurch BH23 .....124 A4
2 Okeford Fitzpaine DT11 197 F6

Fairfield Cl continued
Wimborne Minster BH21 ..59 C3
Fairfield Pk DT7 ....96 B3
Fairfield Rd
Barton on Sea BH25 ...126 C4
Blandford Forum DT11 .212 B2
11 Dorchester DT1 ....108 A1
Iwerne Courtney or Shroton
DT11 ....198 E7
Salisbury SP1 ....213 B4
Wimborne Minster BH21 ..59 B3
Fairhavon Ct **12** BH5 .122 C2
Fairhouse Rd BA22 ...193 F8
Fairies Dr BH22 ....61 C2
Fairlane SP7 ....13 A1
Fairlie BH24 ....47 C1
Fairlie Pk BH24 ....47 B1
Fairlight La SO41 ....95 B4
Fairmead Rd BA21 ....27 C4
Fairmead Sch BA21 ...27 C4
Fairmile Par BH23 .....91 C1
Fairmile Rd BH23 .....91 C1
Fairoak Way **3** DT8 .204 A7
Fairthorn Ct **2** BH2 ..121 C2
Fairview Cres BH18 ...87 A3
Fairview Dr BH18 .....87 A3
Fairview Pk BH14 ....120 B2
Fairview Rd
Broadstone BH18 ......87 A3
Salisbury SP1 ....213 C3
Weymouth DT4 ....180 B4
Fairway Ave BH14 ....147 B4
Fairway Dr
Christchurch BH23 ....123 C3
Wareham Town BH20 ..142 B3
Fairway The BH25 ....127 A4
Fairway View BA21 ....27 C3
Fairways BH22 ....61 C3
Fairwinds BH13 ....147 A2
Fairwood Rd BH31 .....45 C3
Fairy Bridge Wlk **1** SP8 ..5 C2
Fairy Cres SP8 ....5 C2
Falcon Dr BH23 ......125 A3
Falconer Dr BH15 ....118 C2
Falconsway SP2 ......213 B1
Fallows The BH25 .....95 A3
Fancy Rd BH12 ......120 A4
Fancy's Row BH20 ...116 A2
Fantley La SP8 ....2 A1
Far Ends **13** BH14 ...120 A4
Faraday Rd SP2 ......213 A4
Farcroft Rd BH12 ....120 A3
Farfrae Cres DT1 .....135 A4
Farley Rd SP1 ....213 C2
Farm Cl Radipole DT4 .167 A3
Ringwood BH24 ....55 B4
Farm La
Christchurch BH23 ....125 A3
Salisbury SP2 ....213 A3
West Lulworth BH20 ..172 B3
Farm La N BH25 ......127 A4
Farm La S BH25 ......127 A4
Farm Rd
Bradford Abbas DT9 ...28 B1
Ferndown BH22 ....52 C1
Farmdene Cl BH23 ...125 B4
Farmer Palmers Farm Pk★
BH16 ....116 A2
Farmers Wlk **1** BH21 ..59 A3
Farnham Rd DT1 ......121 A4
Farr's Orch **5** TA16 ..191 F7
Farriers Cl BH24 ....60 A3
Farringdon Cl **2** DT1 .134 C4
Farrington BH4 ....121 B1
Farwell Cl BH23 ....92 B2
Farwell Rd BH12 ......88 B1
Faversham
Bournemouth BH2 ....121 B1
Radipole DT4 ....167 A3
Fawcett Rd BH25 .....94 C1
Fawley Gn BH8 ....90 B2
Fawn Gdns BH25 .....94 C2
Fellowsmead DT10 ....20 C1
Felton Cres BH23 ....125 C4
Felton Ct BH14 ......119 C3
Felton Rd BH14 ......119 C3
Fenleigh Cl BH25 .....95 A1
Fennel Rd BA12 ....3 A3
Fennel Way BA22 .....26 B3
Fenton Rd BH6 ....123 B3
Fenway Cl DT1 ....108 B1
Fenwick Ct BH8 ......122 A3
Fern Bank
28 Bournemouth BH2 .121 C2
Three Legged Cross BH21 ..53 A4
Fern Barrow BH12 ....121 A4
Fern Cl Alderholt SP6 ..42 B3
Burton DT3 ....92 B1
Fern Hill SP8 ....11 A2
Ferncroft Gdns BH10 ..89 B3
Ferncroft Rd BH10 ....89 B3
Ferndale Gdns BA21 ..27 A3
Ferndale Rd
New Milton BH25 ......95 A3
Radipole DT4 ....167 A3
Ferndown Forest Golf Club
BH22 ....52 C1
Ferndown Fst Sch
BH22 ....61 B3
Ferndown Ind Est BH21 .60 C4
Ferndown Mid Sch
BH22 ....61 B3
Ferndown Rd DT7 .....96 B3
Ferndown Upper Sch
BH22 ....61 A3
Ferne Hollow SP5 ....188 A8
Fernery Rd BA21 ......27 C3

Fernglade BH25 ....95 A2
Fernheath Cl BH11 ....89 A2
Fernheath Rd BH11 ...89 A2
Fernhill Ave DT4 .....167 B3
Fernhill Cl BH17 ......88 A1
Fernhill Flats **29** BH2 .121 C2
Fernhill Gate BH25 ...95 A2
Fernhill La BH25 ......95 A2
Fernhill Rd BH25 .....95 A2
Fernlea Ave BH22 .....61 B2
Fernlea Cl
Ferndown BH22 ....61 B2
St.Leonards BH24 .....54 A2
Fernlea Gdns BH22 ...61 B2
Fernside Ave BH14 ...119 C2
Fernside Ct BH15 ....119 C2
Fernside Rd
Bournemouth BH9 ...121 C4
Ferndown BH22 ....53 A1
Poole BH15 ....119 C2
Studland BH19 ....164 A2
Ferry Way BH13 .....147 A2
Ferrymans Way DT4 .180 B3
Feversham Ave BH8 ..90 C1
Feversham Rd SP1 ...213 B4
Fiddleford Manor★
DT10 ....197 F8
Field Barn Dr DT4 ...167 A3
Field La Gillingham SP8 ..5 A2
Kington Magna SP8 .....9 B1
Pen Selwood BA9 ......1 A1
Field Pl
Barton on Sea BH25 ..126 B4
Verwood BH31 ....45 A4
Field View Rd **2** DT11 .212 B2
Field Way
Christchurch BH23 ....93 B1
Corfe Mullen BH21 ....86 C4
Field's Cl **1** DT11 ...210 C3
Fieldfare Cl DT3 .....152 B2
Fielding Rd BA21 .....27 C3
Fieldings The SP8 ....10 B2
Fields Barn DT2 ......156 C3
Fields Mead DT6 ....100 A4
Fields Oak DT11 .....212 B2
Fields The BA12 ....3 A3
Fieldway BH24 ....55 B4
Fifehead Hill SP8 .....20 C4
Filbridge Rise DT10 ..35 B1
Filford La DT6 ....67 C4
Filleul Rd BH20 .....115 C1
Finches The DT3 ....152 B2
Finchfield Ave BH11 ..88 C3
Finchley Rd SP2 .....213 A3
Findlay Pl BH19 .....178 C2
Fineshade **7** BH13 .147 C3
Fippenny Hollow **3**
DT11 ....197 F5
Fir Ave
Holton Heath BH20 ...116 A2
New Milton BH25 .....95 A1
Fir Cl BH22 ....53 A2
Fir Dr DT3 ....153 B2
Fir Tree Cl
Dorchester DT1 ....107 B1
Netherbury DT6 ....68 A3
St.Leonards BH24 .....53 C1
Fir Tree Hill SP6 ......42 B3
Fir Tree La BH23 .....93 B1
Fir Vale Rd BH1 .....121 C2
Firbank Rd BH9 .....122 A4
Firch La DT6 ....101 A3
Firecrest Cl DT3 .....152 B2
Firmain Rd BH12 ......88 B1
Firs Glen Rd
Bournemouth BH9 ...121 C4
Ferndown BH22 ....53 A1
Verwood BH31 ....45 A3
Firs La BH14 ....147 A4
Firs The BH1 ....122 A2
Firshill BH23 ....125 C4
Firside Rd BH21 ......86 B2
First Cliff Wlk **1** DT6 .100 A1
First Marine Ave
BH25 ....126 C4
Firsway BH16 ....118 B4
Firtree Cres SO41 ....95 C2
Fisher's Cl DT11 .....212 B2
Fisher's La TA17 ....191 A7
Fisherbridge Rd DT3 .168 B4
Fisherman's Ave BH5 .123 A4
Fisherman's Wlk BH5 .123 A2
Fishermans Cl DT3 ..166 B3
Fishermans Rd BH15 .119 B1
Fishers Cl DT9 ....14 C1
Fishers Pl DT2 ......170 A4
Fisherton Island SP2 .213 A3
Fisherton Manor Mid Sch
SP2 ....213 A3
Fisherton St SP2 ....213 A3
Fisherway La TA19 ..191 A5
Fishey La SP7 ....36 C3
Fishpond Bottom Rd
DT6 ....202 D1
Fishweir Fields **1** DT6 .68 C1
Fishweir La DT6 ......68 C1
Fitzharris Ave BH9 ..122 A4
Fitzmaurice Rd BH23 .123 C4
Fitzpain Rd BH22 .....61 B1

Fitzpain Rd BH22 .....61 B1
Fitzwilliam Cl BH11 ..88 C3
Fitzworth Ave BH16 ..118 B2
Five Acres DT6 ....97 A3
Five Marys (Tumuli)★
DT2 ....156 B3
Fiveways Specl Sch
BA21 ....27 C3
Flaghead BH13 ......147 C3
Flaghead Chine Rd
BH13 ....147 C3
Flaghead Rd BH13 ..147 C3
Flambard Ave BH23 ..92 A1
Flambard Rd BH14 ..120 B2
Flanders Cl DT10 .....21 A1
Flax La DT9 ....28 C4
Flax Way BA21 ....26 C3
Flaxfield Dr **15** TA18 .191 F4
Flaxfield Rd DT8 ....204 B4
Flazen Cl BH11 ....88 B2
Fleet Ct DT3 ....166 C2
Fleet La DT3 ....166 C3
Fleet Rd DT3 ....165 C3
Fleet St DT4 ....204 D4
Fleet View DT4 .....180 B4
Fleet's Cnr BH17 ....119 A4
Fleetpoint Bsns Ctr
BH15 ....119 A3
Fleets Est BH15 ....119 A3
Fleets La BH15 ......119 B3
Fleetsbridge Bsns Ctr
BH17 ....119 A4
Fleetwood Ct BH15 .119 B4
Fletcher Cl BH10 .....89 B2
Fletcher Rd BH10 ....89 B2
Flood La DT6 ....100 B2
Floral Farm BH21 ....60 A1
Florence Rd
Bournemouth BH5 ...122 C2
Dorchester DT1 ......134 C4
Poole BH14 ....120 B2
Florin Mall **7** BH7 .122 C2
Floriston Gdns BH25 ..95 B2
Flower Ct **10** BH21 ..59 B2
Flowers Dro BH14 ....84 B2
Flushing Mdw BA21 ..28 A3
Folke La DT9 ....31 A1
Folkstone Rd SP2 ...213 A1
Folly Cl SP2 ....213 A1
Folly Farm La BH24 ..54 C3
Folly Fields BA21 .....27 B4
Folly La
Blandford St Mary DT11 .212 B1
Gillingham SP8 ....10 B3
Kington Magna SP8 ....9 C1
Nether Compton DT9 ..28 C4
Wareham BH20 ......142 C2
Wool BH20 ....140 A1
Folly Mill Gdns DT6 ..100 B3
Folly Mill La DT6 ....100 B3
Folly The DT2 ....207 D4
Font La BA22 ....193 B2
Font Villas BA22 ....193 B2
Fontmell Magna St Andrews
CE Sch SP7 ....37 C3
Fontmell Rd BH18 ....87 B2
Foot's Hill SP7 ....24 C3
Footners La BH23 ....92 B1
Ford Cl BH22 ....61 C4
Ford Down La DT2 ..208 A7
Ford La Corscombe DT2 ..205 B7
Ferndown BH22 ....62 A4
Forde Abbey★ TA20 .202 D8
Forde Pk BH23 ....26 C4
Fordhay BA21 ....192 E7
Fordingbridge Rd SP6 .42 B4
Fordington Gdns **16**
DT1 ....108 A1
Fore St Evershot DT2 .206 A7
Thorncombe TA20 ....202 E6
Forehill Cl DT3 ......168 A4
Foreland Cl BH23 ....91 B2
Foreland Rd BH16 ..118 B2
Forest Cl
Christchurch BH23 ....93 B1
Verwood BH24 ....45 A4
Forest Ct BH25 ....95 A1
Forest Ct Hills **6** BH24 .55 C3
Forest Edge Dr BH24 .53 C3
Forest Edge Rd BH20 .142 C4
Forest Hill BA20 ......27 A1
Forest La
Corfe Castle BH20 ...162 C1
Verwood BH24 ....45 A4
Forest Links Rd BH21 .52 B1
Forest Oak Dr BH25 ..95 A3
Forest Pines BH25 ...95 A2
Forest Rd
Ferndown BH22 ....53 A1
Poole BH13 ....121 A1
Forest Rise BH23 .....93 B1
Forest View
Crossways DT2 ......137 B3
New Milton BH25 .....94 B3
Forest View Cl BH9 ...90 A1
Forest View Dr BH21 .61 A3
Forest View Rd BH9 ..90 A1
Forest Way
Christchurch BH23 ....93 B1
Ferndown BH21 ....61 A3
Forestlake Ave BH24 .55 C3
Forestside Gdns BH24 .47 C1
Forestside The BH31 ..45 C3
Forge End SP8 ....10 B2
Forge La
East Chinnock BA22 ..192 E8
Zennor BA12 ....1 C2
Forsters La DT6 ......69 A1

Forsyth Gdns BH10 ..89 B1
Fort Cumberland Pl
BH15 ....118 B1
Fortescue Rd
Bournemouth BH3 ...122 A3
Poole BH12 ....120 B3
Fortuneswell DT5 ...186 C4
Forty Foot Way DT6 .100 A1
Forum Sch The DT11 .198 B6
Foss Way TA17 ......191 C8
Fosse Cl BA21 ....26 C4
Fosse Way BA21 .....26 C4
Fossett Way **4** DT4 .180 A4
Foster's Rd DT9 ......30 B3
Fosters Hill DT9 .....196 B5
Fosters Mdws **2** DT10 .210 C3
Fosters Spring BH16 ..84 B1
Fotherby Cres SP1 ..213 C4
Foundry Cl DT6 .....100 A4
Foundry Knapp DT6 ..100 A4
Foundry La DT6 ......100 B3
Foundry Sq **18** TA18 .191 F4
Fountain Mead **11** SP7 .37 C3
Fountain Way BH23 .124 A3
Four Acres DT5 .....186 C2
Four Wells Rd BH21 ..60 A4
Fouracre Cl DT6 .....100 B4
Fourgates Rd DT1 ...107 C1
Fourth Cliff Wlk DT6 .100 A1
Fowler's Hill SP1 ....213 C2
Fowler's Rd SP1 .....213 B2
Fox Cl DT6 ....69 A1
Fox La BA21 ....60 B3
Fox La Terr DT10 .....35 A1
Fox Mdws **16** TA18 .191 F5
Foxbury BH20 ....139 B4
Foxbury Rd
St Leonards BH24 .....62 C4
St.Leonards BH24 .....54 A1
Foxcote **8** BA20 .....26 C1
Foxcote Gdns BH25 ..94 C2
Foxcroft Dr BH21 ....60 A3
Foxes Cl BH31 ....45 A3
Foxglove Cl
Christchurch BH23 ...125 B4
Gillingham SP8 ....5 C1
Foxglove Pl BH25 ....95 B2
Foxglove Way
Radipole DT3 ....152 C1
Yeovil BA22 ....26 B3
Foxgloves BH16 ......118 A4
Foxhill BH31 ....45 A3
Foxhills **12** BH19 ...179 A1
Foxhills Cres BH16 ...84 B2
Foxhills Dr BH16 .....84 B2
Foxhills La BH16 .....84 B1
Foxhills Rd BH16 .....84 B2
Foxholes **1** BH6 ....123 C2
Foxholes Rd
Bournemouth BH6 ...123 C2
Poole BH15 ....119 C3
Foxs Cl DT9 ....196 B5
Foxwell La TA18 ....192 C7
Foxwood Ave BH23 .124 C3
Foyle Hill SP7 ....12 B1
Framerville Rd BH20 .139 C4
Frampton Cl BH25 ...95 B3
Frampton Pl BH24 ....55 B4
Frampton Rd
Bournemouth BH9 ...122 A4
16 Pimperne DT11 ...199 D4
Frances Ct **13** BH23 .126 A4
Frances Rd BH1 .....122 B2
Francesca Ct **14** BH23 .124 C4
Francesca Grange **13**
BH23 ....124 C4
Francesca Lodge **1**
..................124 C3
Franchise St DT4 ....167 B1
Francis Ave BH11 .....88 B2
Francis Ave Ind Est
BH11 ....88 B2
Francis Rd Poole BH12 .120 C3
Weymouth DT4 ......167 A1
Francis Way SP2 ....213 B1
Frank Wareham Cottage
Homes The BH9 ......90 A2
Frankland Cres BH14 .120 C2
Franklin Cl DT4 .....167 A1
Franklin Rd
Bournemouth BH9 ....90 A2
New Milton BH25 .....95 B2
Weymouth DT4 ......167 A2
Franklyn Cl BH16 ...118 A4
Franks Way BH12 ...120 A4
Frankston Rd BH6 ..123 B2
Fraser Ave DT4 ......166 C1
Fraser Ct BH25 ......94 C2
Fraser Rd BH12 .....120 C4
Freame Way SP8 ......5 B1
Freda Rd BH23 ......123 C3
Frederica Rd BH9 ...121 C4
Freedom Ave BA21 ..27 A3
Freemans Cl BH21 ...60 A3
Freemans La BH21 ..60 A3
Freemantle Rd DT4 .166 C1
Freesia Cl DT3 ......152 C1
Fremington Ct **16** BH25 .95 A2
French Mill La
Cann SP7 ....23 C4
Shaftesbury SP7 ......12 C1
French Mill Rise SP7 .12 C1
French Rd BH17 ......87 A1
French's Farm Rd
BH16 ....117 A4

Frensham Cl BH10 ....89 C2
Freshwater Cl **8** DT5 .186 C1
Freshwater Dr BH15 ...118 B2
Freshwater Rd BH23 ..125 B3
Friar Waddon Rd
　Chickerell DT3 ....151 C4
　Radipole DT3 ....152 A4
Friar's Orch **8** SP1 ..213 B2
Friars Ave BA21 ....26 C3
Friars Cl **2** DT1 ......135 B4
Friars Gate BH23 .....125 B3
Friars Moor DT10 ......35 B1
Friars Rd BH23 ....125 A3
Friars Wlk BH25 ......127 A4
Friary Hill DT1 ....108 A1
Friary La
　Dorchester DT1 ......108 A1
　Salisbury SP1 ....213 B2
Friary The SP1 ....213 B2
Friday's Heron BH21 ...40 A4
Frinton Ct **6** BH14 ...120 A2
Fritham Gdns BH8 ......90 B2
Frizzel's Hill DT10 ..196 F4
Frobisher Ave BH12 ....88 C1
Frobisher Cl
　Christchurch BH23 ...124 C3
　3 Ringwood BH24 ...47 C1
Frog La
　Dinnington TA17 .....191 B8
　Fordingbridge SP6 ....43 A4
　Iwerne Courtney or Shroton
　　DT11 ....198 F7
　Motcombe SP7 ....12 B4
Frogham Hill SP6 ......43 C3
Frogmore La DT2 ....71 C4
Frome Ave BA20 ......139 C1
Frome La DT2 ....72 C4
Frome Rd BH20 ....142 B2
Frome Terr DT1 ......108 A1
Frome Valley Rd DT2 .137 B3
Frome View
　Bradford Peverell DT2 ..107 A3
　Maiden Newton DT2 ....73 A4
Front La BH21 ....56 B3
Front St East Stour SP8 ..10 C2
　Portesham DT3 ....132 A1
Froom's La BH20 ....81 B1
Frost Rd BH11 ....88 C2
Froud Way BH21 ....86 B2
Froxfield Rd DT11 ....212 B3
Fry's Cl DT3 ....150 A4
Fry's La DT2 ....75 A4
Fryer Cl DT1 ....89 A3
Fryers Copse BH21 ....60 B3
Fryers Rd BH21 ....52 C4
Frys Cl BH16 ....84 B2
Fudge Hill DT2 ....205 A8
Fulbrooks Cl DT6 .....100 B4
Fulbrooks La DT6 .....100 B4
Fulmar Rd BH23 ......125 A3
Fulwood Ave BH11 .....88 C3
Furge Gr BA8 ....19 A2
Furge La BA8 ....19 A2
Furland Rd **6** TA18 ..191 F4
Furlands BH23 ....186 C2
Furlong La DT9 ....17 C2
Furlong The BH24 .....55 A4
Furlongs The DT9 .....30 A4
Furnell Rd BH15 .....119 B1
Furze Hill Dr BH14 ..120 B1
Furze The **9** BA20 ...26 C1
Furzebrook Cl BH17 ...87 C2
Furzebrook Rd BH20 ..161 A2
Furzehill BH21 ....50 C1
Furzelands Rd
　Verwood BH21 ....45 A1
　Verwood BH21 ....53 A4
Furzey Rd BH16 ......118 A3
Furzy Cl DT3 ....168 A4

G

Gabriel Gn **1** DT1 ...135 A4
Gainsborough DT9 .....17 B1
Gainsborough Ave
　BH25 ....95 A3
Gainsborough Ct **11**
　BH5 ....123 A3
Gainsborough Dr DT9 ..29 C3
Gainsborough Hill DT9 .30 B2
Gainsborough Rd
　Bournemouth BH7 ....122 C4
　St.Leonards BH24 .....54 A4
Gainsborough Way
　BA21 ....28 A4
Gale Cres DT6 ....100 B3
Gales Hill DT2 ......207 E7
Gallop Way BH12 .....121 B4
Gallop's La BH20 .....83 B1
Galloway Rd BH15 ....118 B2
Gallows Cnr
　Iwerne Courtney or Shroton
　　DT11 ....36 C1
　Milton Abbas DT11 ...209 D3
Gallows Dr BH22 ......61 C1
Gallows Hill Arne BH20 .161 B2
　Owermoigne DT2 .....155 B3
Gallwey Rd DT4 ......180 B4
Galton Ave BA23 .....123 C3
Gannetts Pk BH19 ....179 A2
Garden Cl Bridport DT6 .100 B4
　Litton Cheney DT2 ...103 A1

Garden Cl continued
　New Milton BH25 .....95 A1
Garden Ct BH1 ....122 B3
Garden House **17** BH1 .122 B3
Garden Wlk BH22 .....61 C4
Garden-Lane BA24 .....54 A2
Gardens Cres BH14 ...147 A4
Gardens Ct **7** BH15 ..119 C2
Gardens Rd BH14 ....147 A4
Gardenside **1** DT6 ...97 A4
Gardner Ct BH23 .....123 C4
Gardner Rd
　Christchurch BH23 ...123 C4
　Ringwood BH24 ......55 B3
Garfield Ave
　Bournemouth BH1 ....122 B3
　Dorchester DT1 .....134 C4
Garland Cres DT1 ....135 A4
Garland Rd BH15 .....119 B2
Garlands La DT11 ....197 D4
Garrett Rd BA20 ......26 C2
Garsdale Cl BH11 .....89 A3
Garston Hill DT3 ....166 B3
Gartells **1** DT10 ....197 A4
Garth Cl DT4 ....53 C2
Garth Rd BH9 ....90 A1
Gas La
　Hinton St George TA17 .191 C7
　Salisbury SP2 ....213 A3
Gascoigne's La SP7 ...12 C1
Gascoyne La DT2 .....107 A3
Gashay La EX13 ......202 E3
Gasper St BA12 ....1 B3
Gassons La DT6 ....66 A2
Gate Cl EX13 ....202 A3
Gatemore Rd DT2 ....138 C1
Gateway The BH13 ...120 C2
Gawthorne Dr SP2 ...213 A1
Gaydon Rise BH11 .....88 C2
Gaza Rd BA20 ....139 B4
Gazelle Rd BA20 ......26 C2
Geelong Cl DT3 ......152 C1
Geneva Ave BH6 .....123 B3
Gent Cl DT11 ....212 C3
George St (South) **9**
　SP2 ....213 A3
George St Bridport DT6 .100 B1
　Salisbury SP3 ....213 A3
　Sherborne DT9 ....30 A3
Georges Cl DT6 ....97 A4
Georges Mews BH21 ...86 B4
Georgian Cl BH24 .....55 B4
Georgian Way BH10 ...89 C2
Georgina Cl BH21 ....121 B4
Georgina Talbot House
　BH12 ....121 A4
Gerald Rd BH3 ......122 A3
Germaine St BH23 ...125 C4
Gerrards Gn DT8 ....204 D4
Gervis Cres BH14 ....120 A2
Gervis Pl BH1 ....121 C2
Gervis Rd BH1 ......122 C2
Giant's Grave★ DT2 .209 A4
Gibbs Gn BH16 ....84 B1
Gibbs La DT6 ....66 B1
Gibbs Marsh Trading Est
　DT10 ....20 A2
Gibson Rd DT11 .....119 C4
Giddy Gn La BH20 ...139 C1
Giddy Gn Rd BH20 ...139 C1
Giddylake BH21 ....59 B3
Gifle View **2** DT9 ..194 D8
Gigant St SP1 ......213 B2
Gigg La SP8 ....8 C2
Gilbert Cl SP6 ....42 B3
Gilbert Ct **5** BH23 ..124 A4
Gilbert Rd
　Bournemouth BH1 ....122 B3
　Swanage BH19 ......179 A1
Gilbert Way SP1 ....213 C4
Giles Cl DT2 ....107 A3
Giles's La
　Bishop's Caundle DT9 .196 A7
　Morden BH20 ....83 B2
Gillam Rd BH3 ....89 B3
Gillett Rd BH12 ....121 B4
Gillingham CP Sch SP8 ..5 C1
Gillingham Milton Prim Sch
　SP8 ....5 C3
Gillingham Mus★ SP8 ..5 C1
Gillingham Sch SP8 ...6 A1
Gillingham Sta SP8 ...5 C1
Gillion Ct **2** BH23 ..124 C3
Gipsy La DT6 ....68 C1
Gipsy's Dro DT10 ....197 C7
Girt La DT2 ....205 F7
Glacis DT5 ....187 A4
Gladdis Rd BH11 ......88 C2
Glade The BH24 ......54 A3
Gladelands Cl BH18 ...86 C2
Gladelands Mobile Home Pk
　BH22 ....61 C4
Gladelands Way BH18 ..86 C2
Gladstone Cl
　Bridport DT6 ....100 C4
　Christchurch BH23 ...124 B3
　2 Radipole DT3 ...152 C1
Gladstone Rd
　Bournemouth BH7 ....122 C4
　Poole BH12 ....120 B4
Gladstone Rd E BH7 ..122 C4
Gladstone Rd W BH1 .122 C3
Glamis Ave BH10 .....89 C3
Glastonbury Ct BA21 ..26 C3
Gleadowe Ave BH23 ..123 C4
Glebe Cl
　Abbotsbury DT3 .....149 B4

Glebe Cl continued
　Bridport DT6 ....100 B3
　Maiden Newton DT2 ...72 C4
　Osmington DT3 .....169 A4
　8 Thornford DT9 ...194 D8
　Weymouth DT4 ....167 B1
Glebe Cottage★ DT2 .169 C3
Glebe Ct **4** DT11 ....37 C1
Glebe Gdns SP7 ....12 A4
Glebe Rd BH16 ....84 B3
Glebe The
　3 Durweston DT11 ..198 E3
　3 Iwerne Minster DT11 ..37 C1
Glebe Way DT2 ......136 B2
Glebefields DT2 .....106 C4
Glebeford Cl DT2 ....155 C4
Glebeland Cl DT2 ....136 A4
Glebeland La DT6 .....65 C4
Glebelands **6** TA16 ..191 F7
Glen Ave DT4 ....167 B1
Glen Cl BH25 ....126 B4
Glen Fern Rd BH1 ...122 A4
Glen Rd
　Bournemouth BH5 ....122 C2
　Poole BH14 ....120 A4
　6 Swanage BH19 ...179 A1
　Wimborne Minster BH21 .59 C2
　Yeovil BA21 ....27 C3
Glen Spey BH25 ......95 B1
Glen The DT12 ......120 B3
Glenair Ave BH14 ...120 A2
Glenair Cres BH14 ...120 A2
Glenair Rd BH14 ....120 A2
Glenavon BH25 ....95 B1
Glenavon Rd BH23 ....93 C1
Glencoe Rd
　Bournemouth BH7 ....122 C4
　Poole BH12 ....120 B3
Glendale Ave BH22 ...61 C3
Glendale Cl
　Christchurch BH23 ...91 B2
　Wimborne Minster BH21 .59 B3
Glendale Cres SP1 ..213 C2
Glendale Ct BH23 ....91 B2
Glendale Rd BH6 ....124 A2
Glendinning Ave DT4 .167 B3
Glendon Ave BH10 ....89 B3
Glendrive BH25 .....126 B4
Gleneagles BH23 ....123 C3
Gleneagles Ave BH14 .120 B1
Gleneagles Cl BH22 ..61 C3
Glenferness Ave BH3 .121 B3
Glengariff Rd BH14 .120 B2
Glengarry BH25 ......95 B1
Glengarry Way BH23 .125 B3
Glenives Cl BH24 .....54 A2
Glenmeadows Dr BH10 .89 A3
Glenmoor (Girls) Sch
　BH10 ....89 B1
Glenmoor Cl BH10 ....89 B1
Glenmoor Rd
　Bournemouth BH9 ...121 C4
　Ferndown BH22 ......61 B2
Glenmore Rd
　Salisbury SP1 ......213 C4
　Weymouth DT4 ......167 A2
Glenmount Dr BH14 ..120 A2
Glennie Way DT3 ....166 B2
Glenroyd Gdns BH6 ..123 C2
Glenside BH25 ......126 A4
Glenthorne Ave BA21 ..27 B4
Glenville Cl BH23 ....94 A1
Glenville Gdns BH10 ..89 B1
Glenville Rd
　Bournemouth BH10 ...89 B1
　Christchurch BH23 ...94 A1
　Yeovil BA21 ....27 C3
Glenwood Cl BH22 ....53 A1
Glenwood La BH22 ....53 A1
Glenwood Rd
　Ferndown BH22 ......53 A1
　Verwood BH31 ....45 A3
Glenwood Way BH22 ..53 A1
Glissons BH22 ....61 A1
Globe Cl **3** BH19 ...178 C1
Globe La BH15 ......119 B1
Globe Orch TA18 ....192 C6
Gloucester Cl DT3 ..166 C2
Gloucester Mews DT4 .167 B2
Gloucester Rd
　Bournemouth BH7 ....122 C3
　8 Dorchester DT1 ..107 C1
　Poole BH12 ....120 C3
Gloucester St DT4 ..167 B2
Glovers Cl **2** DT9 ...17 B1
Glue Hill DT10 .....197 C8
Glyde Path Rd DT1 ..108 A1
Glyn Pl SP7 ....24 B3
Glynville Cl BH21 ....60 A4
Glynville Ct BH21 ....60 A4
Glynville Rd BH21 ....60 A4
Goathill Rd DT9 .....17 B1
Goathorn Cl BH16 ...118 B2
God's Blessing La BH21 .51 A4
Godley Rd SP2 ......213 B1
Godlingston Manor★
　BH19 ....178 C3
Godmanstone Cl BH17 .88 A1
Godolphin Sch SP1 ..213 C2
Godolphin Sch Douglas
　House SP1 ....213 C3
Godshill Cl BH8 ......90 B2
Gold Hill
　Child Okeford DT11 .198 B8
　Shaftesbury SP7 .....12 C1
Gold St DT10 ....33 B4
Goldcrest Cl DT3 ...152 B2
Goldcroft BA21 ......27 B3
Goldcroft Ave DT4 ..167 B2
Goldcroft Rd DT4 ...167 B2
Golden Gates BH13 ..147 A2

Golden Hill DT10 .....32 C1
Golden Sands BH13 ..147 A2
Goldenleas Ct BH11 ...88 B2
Goldenleas Dr BH11 ..88 B2
Goldenstones Pool & Leisure
　Ctr BA20 ....27 B2
Goldfinch Cl BH25 ....94 C1
Goldfinch Rd BH17 ..118 C4
Golding's La DT9 .....17 B1
Golf Links Rd
　Broadstone BH18 .....87 A3
　Ferndown BH22 ......61 C2
Goliath Rd BH15 ....118 B1
Good Rd BH12 ......120 B4
Goodwin's La BH20 ...83 B1
Goose Hill DT3 .....149 C4
Gooseacre La BA22 ...26 B1
Gordon Cres **1** DT4 .166 C1
Gordon Ct BH4 ......121 B2
Gordon Mount BH23 .126 A4
Gordon Rd
　Bournemouth BH1 ...122 B2
　Christchurch BH23 ...126 A4
　Poole BH12 ....121 A3
　6 Swanage BH19 ...179 A1
　Wimborne Minster BH21 .59 C2
　Yeovil BA21 ....27 C3
Gordon Rd S BH12 ...121 A3
Gordon Way BH23 ....92 B1
Gordon's La DT9 ....195 A8
Gore Cross DT6 ......68 C1
Gore Cross Way **5** DT6 .68 C1
Gore Grange BH25 ....94 C1
Gore Hill BH20 .....142 C4
Gore La DT6 ....68 C1
Gore Rd BH25 ....94 C1
Gore Rd Ind Est BH25 .94 C1
Gorey Ave BH12 ......88 B1
Gorleston Rd BH12 ..120 C3
Gorley Lynch SP6 ....43 C2
Gorley Rd BH24 ......47 C1
Gorse Cl
　New Milton BH25 .....95 B2
　St.Leonards BH24 ....53 C2
Gorse Hill Cl BH15 ..119 C3
Gorse Hill Cres BH15 .119 C3
Gorse Hill Rd BH15 ..119 C3
Gorse La BH16 ......118 B4
Gorse Rd BH21 ....86 B3
Gorsecliff Ct **7** BH5 .122 B2
Gorsecliff Rd BH10 ...89 B1
Gorsefield Rd BH25 ...95 A2
Gorseland Ct BH22 ...61 C2
Gort Rd
　Bournemouth BH11 ...89 A2
　Poole BH17 ....87 A1
Gosling Cl BH17 ....119 C4
Gough Cl **11** TA16 ..191 F7
Gough Cres BH17 .....87 A1
Goughs Cl DT10 ......35 A1
Gould's Hill
　Radipole DT3 ......152 A4
　Winterborne St Martin
　　DT2 ....133 C2
Goulds Hill Cl DT3 ..152 A4
Gover Cl BH20 ....143 A1
Gower Rd SP7 ....13 A1
Grafton Ave DT4 ....167 A3
Grafton Cl
　Bournemouth BH3 ...122 A4
　Christchurch BH23 ...124 B3
Grafton Rd BH3 .....122 A4
Grammar Sch La BA21 .59 A2
Granby Cl DT4 ......166 C2
Granby Rd BH9 ....90 A2
Granby Way DT4 ....167 A3
Grand Ave BH6 .....123 B2
Grand Par **20** BH15 ..119 A1
Grange BH21 ....50 C1
Grange Arch★ BH20 .175 B4
Grange Ct **16** BH1 ...122 A2
Grange Gdns
　Poole BH12 ....120 C4
　Salisbury SP1 ......213 C4
Grange Hill BH20 ...160 B1
Grange La DT8 ......203 D5
Grange Pk **1** DT9 ..194 D8
Grange Rd
　Bournemouth BH6 ...123 B2
　Broadstone BH18 .....87 A2
　Christchurch BH23 ...125 A4
　Church Knowle BH20 .160 B2
　Radipole DT4 ......167 C3
　St.Leonards BH24 ....53 C1
Grange Rd Bsns Ctr
　BH23 ....125 A4
Grange Sch The BH23 .124 C4
Grangecroft Rd **5** DT5 .186 C2
Grangewood Hall BH21 .59 B3
Grans Barrow (Long
　Barrow)★ SP6 .....190 E6
Grant's Ave BH1 .....122 B3
Grantham Rd BH1 ...122 C4
Grantley Rd **16** BH5 .122 C2
Grants Cl BH1 ......122 C3
Granville Gdns **6** SP7 .12 C1
Granville Pl **32** BH1 .121 C2
Granville Rd
　Bournemouth BH5 ...123 A4
　Poole BH12 ....120 A4
　Weymouth DT4 ......167 B1
Granville Way DT9 ...30 B4
Grasmere Cl
　Christchurch BH23 ...91 B2
　1 Salisbury SP2 ...213 A4
Grasmere Gdns BH25 ..95 A4

Grasmere Rd
　Bournemouth BH5 ....123 A4
　Poole BH13 ....147 A1
　Radipole DT3 ......167 B3
Grass Royal BA21 .....27 C3
Grass Royal Jun Sch
　BA21 ....27 C3
Gravel Hill BH18 .....87 B3
Gravel La
　Charlton Marshall DT11 .211 C3
　Ringwood BH24 ......55 A4
Gray Cl BH17 ....119 C4
Gray's Yd **23** BH15 ..119 B1
Graycot Cl BH10 .....89 B3
Grays DT4 ....167 A3
Grays Cl SP7 ....12 A4
Grayson Ct BA22 .....61 C2
Great Cnr BA21 ......26 C2
Great Down La DT10 ..21 A2
Great George St DT4 .167 B2
Great Head La DT2 ..206 F4
Great Hill BA9 ....1 A2
Great La SP7 ....12 C1
Great Owens Dr BH20 .142 B3
Great Pit La BA22 ....15 A1
Great Western Rd **11**
　DT1 ....107 C1
Great Western Terr
　Radipole DT4 ......167 B3
　Yeovil BA21 ....27 C3
Greaves Cl BH10 .....89 B2
Grebe Cl
　Broadstone BH17 ...118 C4
　2 Chickerell DT3 ..166 B3
　Christchurch BH23 ...125 A3
Green Acres BH23 ...124 C4
Green Acres Cl BH14 ..54 C3
Green Bottom BH21 ...60 A4
Green Cl
　Bere Regis BH20 ....81 A1
　Bradpole DT6 ......100 C4
　Charlton Marshall DT11 .211 D6
　Poole BH15 ....119 B1
　Sturminster Newton DT10 .35 B1
Green Dr SP6 ....42 B3
Green Gdns BH15 ....119 B1
Green La Ashmore SP5 ..39 B4
　Barton on Sea BH25 .127 A4
　Bournemouth BH10 ...89 B2
　Bridport DT6 ......100 C3
　Chickerell DT3 .....166 C3
　Crossways DT2 .....137 B3
　East Chinnock BA22 .192 E6
　Ferndown BH22 ......61 A1
　Hooke DT8 ....205 C2
　Kington Magna SP8 ...9 B2
　New Milton BH25 .....94 C4
　Ringwood BH24 ......55 B2
　Stour Provost SP7 ...22 B2
　Sturminster Marshall
　　DT11 ....56 A3
　Tatworth & Forton
　　TA20 ....202 A7
　West Coker BA22 ....193 B8
　Weymouth DT4 ......180 C4
Green Loaning **5** BH23 .124 C3
Green Mead BA21 ....26 C3
Green Pit Knapp DT6 ..65 A1
Green Pk BH1 ....122 C4
Green Rd
　Bournemouth BH9 ...122 A4
　Poole BH15 ....119 B1
Green St TA17 ......191 D7
Green The
　3 Hazelbury Bryan DT10 .197 A4
　Mappowder DT10 ....196 B1
　Puddletown DT2 .....78 A4
　Salisbury SP1 ......213 C2
　Sherborne DT9 ....30 A3
Greenacre
　Barton on Sea BH25 .127 A4
　Charminster DT2 ...107 C3
Greenacre Cl BH16 ..118 B3
Greenacres BH13 ....121 A4
Greenacres Cl BH10 ..89 C3
Green's Ct **7** SP1 ..213 B2
Greenclose La BH21 ..59 B2
Greencroft St SP1 ..213 B3
Greenfield Gdns BH25 .127 A4
Greenfield Rd
　3 Charlton Marshall
　　DT11 ....211 D6
　Poole BH15 ....119 C4
Greenfields BH21 ...120 C4
Greenfinch Cl BH17 ..86 C1
Greenfinch Wlk BH24 ..55 C2
Greenford CE Prim Sch
　DT2 ....72 C4
Greenford La
　Compton Valence DT2 ..104 A3
　Frome Vauchurch DT2 ..72 C4
Greenham La TA18 ..203 B7
Greenhayes
　Broadstone BH18 .....87 B1
　Charmouth DT6 ......96 C4
　2 Okeford Fitzpaine DT11 .197 F5
Greenhays Rise BH21 ..59 B3
Greenhill
　Blandford Forum DT11 .212 B3
　Radipole DT4 ......167 C4
　Sherborne DT9 ....30 A3
Greenhill Cl BH21 ....59 B3
Greenhill La BH21 ...59 B3
Greenhill Rd
　Wimborne Minster BH21 .59 B3
　Yeovil BA21 ....27 C4
Greenhill Terr **4** DT5 .186 C4
Greenings Ct DT1 ...108 A4

Greens Cross Dr 4 DT8 204 C4
Greenside Ct BH25 127 A3
Greensleeves Ave BH18 87 A3
Greensome Dr BH22 61 C3
Greenway
10 Child Okeford DT11 198 C7
Lyme Regis DT7 96 A3
Greenway Cl DT3 167 B4
Greenway Cres BH16 118 A4
Greenway La DT11 198 B7
Greenway Rd DT3 152 B1
Greenways
Christchurch BH23 125 C4
Easton/Weston DT5 186 C2
Greenways Ave BH8 90 B2
Greenways Ct BH22 61 C2
Greenwood Ave
Ferndown BH22 61 C3
Poole BH14 147 B4
Salisbury SP1 213 C3
Greenwood Copse BH24 54 A2
Greenwood Rd
Bournemouth BH9 121 C4
Yeovil BA21 26 C4
Greenwood Way BH24 54 A2
Greenwoods 32 BH25 95 A1
Grenfell Rd BH9 89 C2
Grenville Cl BH24 47 C1
Grenville Ct
6 Bournemouth BH4 121 B2
11 Poole BH15 119 B1
Grenville Rd BH21 59 B2
Gresham Rd BH9 90 A1
Grexy Cross DT2 205 E7
Grey Mare & Her Colts (Long Barrow) The* DT3 131 B2
Greyfriars Cl SP1 213 B2
Greys Bridge* DT1 108 B1
Greys Rd 7 TA16 191 F7
Greystoke Ave BH11 88 C3
Greystones Cl DT2 137 B3
Gribb View TA20 202 E6
Griffin Ct 12 BH21 59 B2
Griffins Ct 7 SP2 213 B3
Griffiths Gdns BH10 89 A3
Grimsey La SP8 4 C4
Grosvener Ct 19 BH1 122 A2
Grosvenor Cl BH24 53 C3
Grosvenor Cres DT1 135 A4
Grosvenor Ct
2 Bournemouth BH1 122 B2
Christchurch BH23 126 A4
Grosvenor Gdns BH1 122 C2
Grosvenor Rd
Bournemouth BH4 121 B2
Dorchester DT1 135 A4
Easton/Weston DT5 186 C2
Radipole DT4 167 B3
Shaftesbury SP7 12 C2
Stalbridge DT10 33 B4
Swanage BH19 179 B1
Grove Ave
Radipole DT4 167 B3
Yeovil BA20 27 A3
Grove Cty Inf Sch DT5 187 A3
Grove La
Abbotsbury DT3 149 A3
Bothenhampton DT6 101 A3
Portesham DT3 150 C3
Stalbridge DT10 33 B4
Grove La Cl DT10 33 B4
Grove Mans 21 BH1 122 A2
Grove Orch 3 DT6 128 A4
Grove Rd
Barton on Sea BH25 127 A4
Bournemouth BH1 122 A2
Burton Bradstock DT6 128 A4
Easton/Weston DT5 187 A3
Poole BH12 120 A3
Wimborne Minster BH21 59 B2
Grove Rd E BH23 124 A4
Grove Rd W BH23 123 C4
Grove The
Bournemouth BH9 89 C2
Christchurch BH23 91 C1
Dorchester DT1 107 C1
Ferndown BH22 61 B2
Verwood BH31 45 B3
Groveley Bsns Ctr BH23 124 C3
Groveley Rd
Bournemouth BH4 121 A1
Christchurch BH23 124 C3
Grovely Ave BH5 122 C2
Grower Gdns BH11 89 A2
Grugs La BH21 40 A4
Gryphon Leisure Ctr DT9 30 A4
Gryphon Sch The DT9 30 B4
Guard Ave BA22 26 B3
Guernsey Rd BH12 88 B1
Guernsey St 11 DT5 186 C4
Guest Ave BH12 121 A3
Guest Cl BH12 121 A3
Guest Rd BH16 118 A4
Guilder La SP1 213 B3
Guildford Ct BH4 121 B2
Guildhall Ct 4 BH15 119 A1
Guildhall Mus* BH15 119 A1
Guildhill Rd BH6 123 C2
Guinevere Cl BA21 26 C4
Gulliver Cl BH14 147 B4
Gulliver Ct 1 BH21 59 B3
Gullivers Orch DT6 101 B2
Gulway Mead 7 TA20 202 A8
Gundry La DT6 100 B3
Gundry Rd DT6 100 C4
Gunn La 3 DT11 198 B5
Gunners La BA22 26 B3
Gunville Cres BH9 90 A2
Gunville Down Rd DT11 199 F4
Gunville La
East Coker BA22 193 D8
Hermitage DT2 195 C2
Gunville Rd DT11 199 F4
Gurjun Cl BH16 118 A4
Gurney Rd BH21 86 C3
Gussage Rd BH12 120 C4
Gwenlyn Rd BH16 118 B3
Gwynne Rd BH12 120 C3
Gyllas Way SP8 5 C2
Gypshayes BH19 178 A1
Gypsy La
Easton/Weston DT5 186 C2
Ringwood BH24 55 B4
2 Weymouth DT4 167 B1

H

Haarlem Mews BH23 124 B4
Hackney DT2 205 A7
Hadden Rd BH8 122 B4
Haddon La DT10 19 C1
Haddons Dr BH21 52 C3
Hadley Way BH18 86 C2
Hadow Rd BH10 89 B2
Hadrian Cl BH22 61 B1
Hadrian Way BH21 86 C4
Hahnemann Rd BH2 121 C1
Haig Ave BH13 120 C1
Haimes La SP7 12 C2
Hainault Dr BH31 45 B3
Haines La DT8 203 A5
Hains La DT10 20 C3
Haking Rd BH23 124 B4
Halcyon Ct BH15 119 B3
Hale Ave BH25 95 A1
Hale Gdns BH25 95 A1
Hales Mdw BA21 14 A2
Halewood Way BH23 123 C4
Half Acre La DT8 204 C4
Half Acres DT9 30 A3
Half Hide Down SP5 188 B3
Half Moon St DT9 30 A3
Halfpenny La SP5 39 B4
Halifax Way BH23 125 A4
Hall Rd BH11 88 C2
Hallet Ct DT7 96 A3
Hallet Gdns BA20 27 B2
Halls Rd BH16 84 A1
Hallum Cl SP1 213 C4
Halsey Gn DT2 196 B3
Halstock Cl DT3 168 B4
Halstock Cres BH17 87 B1
Halter Path BH15 118 C2
Halter Rise BH21 60 B3
Halton Cl BH23 93 A4
Halves Cotts BH20 177 A4
Halves La BA22 193 B8
Ham La Ferndown BH21 60 C2
5 Gillingham SP8 6 A1
Marnhull DT10 20 B2
Trent DT9 15 A1
Ham Mdw DT10 20 B2
Hamble Rd BH15 120 A3
Hambledon Cl
Blandford Forum DT11 212 C2
Todber DT10 21 B2
Hambledon Gdns
Blandford Forum DT11 212 C2
Bournemouth BH6 123 B3
Hambledon Hill (Hill Fort)* DT11 198 D7
Hambledon View DT10 35 B1
Hambleton Rd BH7 123 A4
Hambro Rd DT5 186 C4
Hamcroft DT5 186 C2
Hamilton Cl
Bournemouth BH1 122 B3
Christchurch BH23 124 C2
Hamworthy BH15 118 C1
Radipole DT3 152 C1
Hamilton Cres BH15 118 C1
Hamilton Ct
10 Bournemouth BH8 122 A3
5 Wimborne Minster BH21 59 A3
Hamilton Rd
Bournemouth BH1 122 B2
Corfe Mullen BH21 86 C3
Hamworthy BH15 118 C1
Salisbury SP1 213 B3
Hamilton Way BH25 94 C1
Hamlands DT2 105 C1
Hamlon Cl BH11 89 A2
Hammett Cl DT2 79 B1
Hammond Ave DT4 167 A3
Hammond St DT10 196 E1
Hammonds Mead DT6 97 A4
Hampden La BH6 123 A3
Hampreston CE Fst Sch BH21 60 C2
Hampshire Cl BH23 91 C1
Hampshire Ct 26 BH2 121 C2
Hampshire Ctr The BH8 90 C1
Hampshire Hatches La BH24 55 A2
Hampshire House 25 BH2 121 C2
Hampshire Rd DT4 166 C2
Hampton DT3 132 A1
Hampton Cl 8 BA22 193 F8
Hampton Dr BH24 47 B1
Hampton Stone Circle* DT3 131 C1
Hamworthy Fst Sch BH15 118 C1
Hamworthy Mid Sch BH15 118 C1
Hamworthy Park* BH15 118 C1
Hamworthy Sta BH16 118 B2
Hanbury Rd 7 BH19 179 A1
Handley Ct BH24 55 A4
Handley Lodge BH12 120 C4
Hands La DT3 149 A4
Hanford House* DT11 198 D6
Hanford House Sch DT11 198 D6
Hanham Ct BH12 121 A4
Hanham Rd
Corfe Mullen BH21 86 B3
Wimborne Minster BH21 59 B3
Hankinson Rd BH9 122 A4
Hannam's Cl BH16 84 B2
Hannington Pl BH7 123 A3
Hannington Rd BH7 123 A3
Hanover Cl DT10 35 A1
Hanover Ct DT11 212 B2
Hanover Gn BH17 119 C4
Hanover House BH15 119 B2
Hanover La SP8 5 B1
Hanover Rd DT4 167 B3
Happy Island Way DT6 100 C4
Harbeck Rd BH8 90 B2
Harbin's Pk* DT11 199 D8
Harbour BA21 26 C3
Harbour Cl BH13 147 B3
Harbour Cres BH23 124 C3
Harbour Ct
Barton on Sea BH25 126 C4
Christchurch BH23 124 C3
Poole BH13 147 C3
Harbour Hill DT3 166 C4
Harbour Hill Cres BH15 119 C3
Harbour Hill Rd BH15 119 C3
Harbour Hospl The BH15 119 B2
Harbour Lights BH15 119 C2
Harbour Prospect BH14 147 B4
Harbour Rd
Bournemouth BH6 124 A2
Sherborne DT9 30 B4
Harbour View Cl BH14 120 A3
Harbour View Ct BH23 124 A3
Harbour View Rd
Fortuneswell DT5 186 C4
Poole BH14 120 A2
Harbour Watch BH14 147 B4
Harbour Way DT9 30 A4
Harbridge Dro BH24 42 C2
Harbridge Sch BH24 46 C4
Harcombe Cl BH17 87 C2
Harcombe Rd DT7 64 A2
Harcourt Mews 7 BH5 123 A3
Harcourt Rd BH5 123 A2
Harcourt Terr SP2 213 A2
Harding's La SP8 6 A1
Hardwick St 2 DT4 167 C2
Hardy Ave DT4 167 A1
Hardy Cl
2 Beaminster DT8 204 D4
Ferndown BH22 53 A1
Marnhull DT10 21 A2
Martinstown DT2 133 B3
New Milton BH25 94 C2
Hardy Cres
Stalbridge DT10 33 B4
Wimborne Minster BH21 59 B2
Hardy Ct 23 TA18 191 F4
Hardy Mon (National Trust)* DT2 132 B2
Hardy Rd Bridport DT6 100 C4
Ferndown BH22 53 A1
Poole BH14 120 B2
Wareham BH20 142 B1
Hardy's Birthplace (National Trust)* DT2 109 A3
Hardy's La DT8 203 D6
Hare La Cranborne BH21 40 C3
Hordle SO41 95 C2
Hare La Pottery* BH21 41 A3
Hares Gn BH7 123 A4
Harewood Ave BH7 123 A3
Harewood Cres BH7 122 C4
Harewood Gdns BH7 122 C4
Harewood Pl BH7 123 A3
Harford Rd BH12 120 B4
Hargrove La DT10 33 C2
Harkwood Dr BH15 118 C2
Harland Rd BH6 124 A2
Harleston Villas 17 BH21 59 B2
Harley Gap BH21 201 B8
Harley La BH21 201 A5
Harman's Cross Sta BH19 177 C3
Harness Cl BH21 60 A3
Harnham CE Jun & Inf Sch SP2 213 A1
Harnham Rd SP2 213 A2
Harnwood Rd SP2 213 A1
Harp Stone* BH20 175 C3
Harper Rd
21 Crewkerne TA18 191 F4
Salisbury SP2 213 A4
Harpitts La
Kington Magna SP8 9 C2
West Stour SP8 10 A2
Harpway La BH23 92 B3
Harrier Dr BH21 59 B1
Harriers Cl BH23 125 B4
Harrington Ct BH23 125 C4
Harris Way BH25 95 A3
Harrison Ave BH1 122 B3
Harrison Cl BH23 92 B2
Harrison Way BH22 53 A2
Harrow Cl BH23 93 A4
Harrow Rd BH23 93 A3
Harry Barrow Cl 1 BH24 55 B3
Harry Lodge's La SP8 5 A1
Hart Cl BH25 94 C2
Hart's La Holt BH21 51 B2
Nether Compton DT9 29 A3
Hartfoot Cl DT2 209 B5
Hartfoot La DT2 209 B5
Harting Rd BH6 123 B4
Hartington Rd SP2 213 A3
Hartley St DT2 195 B1
Hartmoor Hill SP8 9 B3
Hartnell Ct BH21 86 B3
Hartsbourne Dr BH7 123 A4
Harvard Cl 2 SP2 213 A1
Harvey Rd
Bournemouth BH5 123 A3
Oakley BH21 87 C4
Harveys Cl DT2 73 A4
Harwell Rd BH17 119 B4
Harwood Ct BH25 94 C2
Haselbury Plucknett VC Fst Sch TA18 192 C5
Haskells Rd BH12 120 A4
Haslemere Ave BH23 126 A4
Haslemere Pl BH23 126 A4
Hasler Rd BH17 87 B1
Haslop Rd BH21 60 A4
Hastings Rd
Bournemouth BH8 90 C1
Poole BH17 87 A1
Hatch Pond Rd BH17 119 B4
Hatches La SP1 213 C2
Hatfield Ct BH25 94 C2
Hatfield Gdns BH7 123 A4
Hathaway Cl SP1 213 A4
Hathaway Rd BH6 123 B2
Hatherden Ave BH14 119 C3
Hathermead Gdns BA21 27 C4
Havelins DT11 198 E4
Havelock Rd BH12 121 A3
Havelock Way BH23 93 B1
Haven Ct BH13 147 A2
Haven Gdns BH25 95 A1
Haven Rd
Corfe Mullen BH21 86 B3
Poole BH13 147 C4
Havenhurst BH13 147 C3
Haverstock Rd BH9 90 A2
Haviland Mews BH7 122 C3
Haviland Rd
Bournemouth BH1 122 C3
Ferndown BH21 61 A4
Haviland Rd E BH7 122 C3
Haviland Rd W 5 BH7 122 C3
Hawden Rd BH11 89 A1
Hawk Cl BH21 60 A4
Hawkchurch Gdns BH17 87 C1
Hawkchurch Prim Sch EX13 202 B3
Hawkchurch Rd EX13 202 B3
Hawkcombe La SP7 23 C1
Hawker Cl BH21 59 C1
Hawker's La SP7 22 A4
Hawkesdene SP7 12 C1
Hawkesdene La SP7 12 C1
Hawkesworth Cl DT3 153 A2
Hawkins Cl 2 BH24 47 C1
Hawkins Rd BH12 88 C1
Hawkins Way BA21 26 C3
Hawkmoor Hill EX13 202 E2
Hawksridge 5 SP2 213 B1
Hawkwood Rd BH5 122 C2
Haworth Cl BH23 92 A1
Hawthorn Ave SP8 5 C1
Hawthorn Cl
5 Dorchester DT1 107 C1
New Milton BH25 95 B2
Radipole DT4 167 A3
6 Salisbury SP2 213 A3
1 Shaftesbury SP7 13 A2
Hawthorn Dr BH17 86 C1
Hawthorn Rd
Bournemouth BH9 121 C4
Burton BH23 92 C2
Yeovil BA21 27 C4
Hawthorne Cl 15 TA18 191 F5
Hawthorne Rd DT1 107 C1
Hawthorns The
Christchurch BH23 124 C3
Stalbridge DT10 33 C4
Haxen La TA17 191 A8
Haycock Way 2 BH21 56 B2
Haycombe 4 DT11 198 E3
Haycrafts La BH19 177 C2
Haydon Hollow DT9 31 B3
Haydon La
Frome St Quintin DT2 206 D7
Lydlinch DT10 197 A6
Haydon Rd BH13 121 A1
Haye Cl DT7 96 A3
Haye La DT7 96 A3
Hayes Ave BH7 122 C3
Hayes Cl BH21 60 A2
Hayes La BH21 60 A3
Hayes The DT8 203 E5
Hayeswood Fst Sch BH21 60 A3
Hayeswood Rd BH21 60 A3
Haylands DT5 186 C2
Haymoor Ave DT3 167 C4
Haymoor Mid Sch BH17 87 C1
Haymoor Rd BH15 120 A4
Haynes Ave BH15 119 B2
Haysoms Cl BH25 95 A1
Hayters Way SP6 42 B3
Hayward Cres BH31 45 A3
Hayward La DT11 198 B7
Hayward Way BH31 44 C3
Haywards Ave DT3 167 B4
Haywards Farm Cl BH31 45 A3
Haywards La
Child Okeford DT11 198 C7
Corfe Mullen BH21 86 B4
Hazel Cl Alderholt SP6 42 B3
Christchurch BH23 93 B1
Hazel Ct
Bournemouth BH9 90 B2
27 New Milton BH25 95 A1
Hazel Dr Ferndown BH22 61 B4
2 Overcombe/Preston DT3 168 A4
Hazel La DT2 129 C4
Hazel View 11 TA18 191 F5
Hazeldene BH18 87 A2
Hazeldown Ave DT3 167 C4
Hazell Ave BH10 89 A1
Hazelton Cl BH7 123 A4
Hazelwood Ave BH25 94 C2
Hazelwood Dr BH31 45 B2
Hazlebury Rd BH17 119 A4
Hazlemere Dr BH24 54 A2
Hazzard's Hill BA12 3 A3
Head La SP8 10 B2
Head's La BH10 89 C3
Headland Cl 6 DT5 186 C1
Headlands Bsns Pk BH24 47 B1
Headless Cross BH10 89 B3
Heads Farm Cl BH10 89 C3
Headstock Rd TA20 202 B7
Headswell Ave BH10 89 C2
Headswell Cres BH10 89 C2
Headswell Gdns BH10 89 C2
Heanor Cl BH10 89 B1
Heath Ave BH15 119 B3
Heath Cl
Bovington Camp BH20 139 B4
Wimborne Minster BH21 60 A4
Heath Farm Cl BH22 61 B2
Heath Farm Rd BH22 61 B2
Heath Farm Way BH22 61 B2
Heath Gn Rd BH19 164 A1
Heath Rd
Christchurch BH23 94 A1
Hordle SO41 95 C2
St.Leonards BH24 53 C2
Heathcote Rd BH5 122 C2
Heather Cl
Bournemouth BH8 90 B2
Christchurch BH23 94 A1
Corfe Mullen BH21 86 C3
St.Leonards BH24 54 A2
Heather Dell BH16 118 A3
Heather Dr BH22 61 B4
Heather Fields 14 SP8 5 C2
Heather Lodge 2 BH25 95 A2
Heather Rd
Bournemouth BH10 89 B2
Yeovil BA21 27 C4
Heather View Rd BH12 120 C4
Heather Way
Ferndown BH22 61 B4
Yeovil BA22 26 B3
Heatherbank Rd BH4 121 B2
Heatherbrae La BH16 118 A3
Heatherdown Rd BH22 53 B1
Heatherdown Way BH22 53 B1
Heatherlands Fst Sch BH12 120 C3
Heatherlands Rise BH12 120 B3
Heatherlea Rd BH6 123 B2
Heathfield Ave BH12 121 A4
Heathfield Rd BH22 53 B1
Heathfield Way BH22 53 A1
Heathfields Way SP7 12 C2
Heathland Cl DT2 137 B3
Heathlands Ave BH22 61 B1
Heathlands Cl
Burton BH23 92 B2
Verwood BH31 45 B3
Heathlands Prim Sch BH11 89 A2
Heathwood Ave BH25 126 C4
Heathwood Rd
Bournemouth BH9 121 C4
Weymouth DT4 167 A2
Heathy Cl BH25 126 C4
Heaton Rd BH10 89 A1
Heavy Horse Ctr* BH21 40 C1

Heavytree Rd BH14 .....120 A2
Heber's La TA17 .....191 A5
Heckford La BH15 .....119 B2
Heckford Rd
  Corfe Mullen BH21 ....86 B3
  Poole BH15 .....119 B2
Heddington Dr DT11 ..212 B3
Hedgerley BH25 .....127 A4
Heights App BH16 .....118 B4
Heights Rd BH16 .....118 B4
Helen La 2 DT4 .....167 C1
Helena Rd BA20 ....26 C1
Helena Terr SP1 .....213 B3
Helic Ho 2 BH31 ....59 B3
Hell Cnr DT2 .....194 D1
Hell La DT6 ....99 A4
Helston Ct DT3 .....132 A1
Helyar Rd BH8 ....90 C1
Hembury Rd DT2 .....102 B4
Hemlet's Cl DT6 ....68 C1
Hemsbach Ct 6 BH20 ..142 C2
Henbest Cl DT11 ....60 B3
Henbury Cl
  Corfe Mullen BH21 ....86 B3
  Poole BH17 ....88 A1
Henbury Hall (English
  Heritage)★ BH21 .....56 C1
Henbury Rise BH21 .....86 B3
Henbury View Fst Sch
  BH21 ....86 B3
Henbury View Rd BH21 ..86 B3
Henchard Cl BH22 ....61 B1
Hendford 6 BA20 ....27 B2
Hendford Gdns BH10 ...89 B1
Hendford Gr BA20 ....27 B2
Hendford Hill BA20 ....27 A4
Hendford Rd BH10 ....89 B1
Hendrie Cl BH19 .....178 C1
Hengist Rd BH1 .....122 B2
Hengistbury Head Nature
  Reserve★ BH6 .....124 C1
Hengistbury Head Nature
  Trail★ BH6 .....124 B2
Hengistbury Rd
  Barton on Sea BH25 .....126 C4
  Bournemouth BH6 .....124 A2
Henhayes La 3 TA18 ..191 F4
Henley Gdns BH7 .....123 A4
Henley View 7 TA18 ..191 F3
Henning Way DT9 ....17 B2
Henning's Pk Rd BH15 ..119 C3
Henry Cl DT4 .....180 C4
Henry's Way DT7 ....96 B3
Henstridge CE VC Prim Sch
  BA8 ....19 A3
Henstridge Trad Est
  BA8 ....20 A3
Henville Rd 6 BH8 .....122 B3
Herbert Ave BH12 .....120 B4
Herbert Ct BH12 .....120 B4
Herbert Hospl BH4 .....121 A1
Herbert Rd
  Bournemouth BH4 .....121 A1
  New Milton BH25 ....95 A2
  Poole BH13 .....121 A1
Herberton Rd BH6 .....123 B3
Herblay Cl BA21 ....28 A3
Herbury La DT9 .....194 D4
Hercules Rd BH15 .....118 B2
Hereford Cres DT4 .....167 A2
Hereford Rd DT4 .....167 A2
Heritage Ct BH13 .....147 C4
Herm Rd BH12 ....88 B1
Hermitage La DT2 .....195 B1
Hermitage Rd BH14 .....120 A3
Hermitage St TA18 .....191 E4
Hermitage The BH14 ...120 A3
Hern La SP6 ....43 B3
Heron Cl
  3 Chickerell DT3 .....166 B3
  Overcombe/Preston
  DT3 .....168 A3
Heron Ct Rd BH3 .....122 A4
Heron Dr BH21 ....60 A4
Heronswood SP2 .....213 B1
Herringston Rd DT1 ..135 A4
Herrison Rd DT2 ....75 C1
Herston CE Sch BH19 ..178 C1
Herston Halt Sta
  BH19 .....178 C2
Herstone Cl BH17 ....87 C1
Hertford Ct 12 BH23 ..126 A4
Hertford Rd BA21 ....28 A4
Hesketh Cl BH24 ....54 B3
Hestan Cl BH23 ....91 B2
Heston Way BH22 ....52 C2
Hetherly Rd DT3 .....167 B4
Hewish La TA18 .....191 E4
Hewitt Rd BH15 .....118 C2
Hewlett's Dro DT10 ..197 C7
Heysham Rd BH18 ....87 A1
Heytesbury Rd BH6 ...123 B3
Hibberd Way BH10 ....89 B1
Hibberds Field BA21 ....40 A4
Hibbs Cl
  Northport BH20 .....142 C3
  Upton BH16 .....118 B4
Hickes Cl BH11 ....88 C2
Hickory Cl BH16 .....118 A4
High Brow BH22 ....61 B3
High Cl BH21 ....56 B2
High E St DT1 .....108 A1
High Howe Cl BH11 ....88 C2
High Howe Gdns BH11 ..88 C2
High Howe La BH11 ....88 C2

High Lea BA21 ....27 B4
High Lea Sch BH21 ....50 B4
High Marryats BH25 .....127 A4
High Mead BA22 ....61 A1
High Mead La BH22 ....61 A1
High Oaks Gdns BH11 ...88 C2
High Pines BH23 .....125 B4
High Pk Rd BH18 ....86 C2
High Ridge Cres BH25 ..95 B1
High St Ashmore SP5 ....39 B4
  Broadwindsor DT8 .....203 E5
  Burton Bradstock DT6 ...128 A4
  Child Okeford DT11 .....198 C7
  Christchurch BH23 .....124 A3
  Corscombe DT2 .....205 A8
  Cranborne BH21 ....40 A4
  Damerham SP6 .....190 F3
  East Chinnock BA22 ...192 E8
  13 Easton/Weston DT5 ..186 C1
  Fortuneswell DT5 .....186 C4
  Gillingham SP8 ....5 C1
  Hardington Mandeville
  BA22 .....193 A6
  Henstridge BA8 ....19 A2
  Hinton St George TA17 ..191 C7
  Lytchett Matravers BH16 ..84 A2
  Milborne Port DT9 ....17 B1
  Piddlehinton DT2 ....76 C4
  Poole BH15 .....119 B1
  Puddletown DT2 ....78 A1
  Rimpton BA22 ....15 A4
  Ringwood BH24 ....55 A4
  Salisbury SP1 .....213 B2
  Shaftesbury SP7 ....12 C1
  Shapwick DT11 ....48 B1
  Sixpenny Handley SP5 ..189 A4
  Spetisbury DT11 .....211 E5
  St.Leonards BH24 ....54 A3
  Stalbridge DT10 ....33 B4
  Sturminster Marshall
  BH21 ....56 B2
  Swanage BH19 .....178 A1
  Sydling St Nicholas DT2 ..207 A2
  Tarrant Monkton DT11 ..200 B3
  Thorncombe TA20 .....202 E5
  Toller Porcorum DT2 ....71 B4
  Weymouth DT4 .....180 B4
  Wimborne Minster DT2 ..59 A2
  Winfrith Newburgh DT2 ..156 C3
  Wool BH20 .....140 A1
  Yeovil BA20 ....27 B2
  Yetminster DT9 .....194 C5
  Zeale SP8 ....1 C2
High St Cl BH20 .....140 A1
High St Fordington
  DT1 .....108 A1
High St N BH15 .....119 B2
High Trees
  Broadmayne DT2 .....136 B1
  Poole BH13 .....147 D4
High Trees Wlk BH22 ...61 B4
High W St
  Dorchester DT1 .....107 C1
  Weymouth DT4 .....167 B1
High Way BH18 ....86 C2
Highacres DT6 ....69 B1
Highbridge Rd BH14 ..120 B2
Highbury Ave SP2 .....213 A3
Highbury Cl
  New Milton BH25 ....95 A1
  2 Salisbury SP2 .....213 A3
Highbury Fst Sch SP2 ..213 A3
Highcliff Rd DT7 ....96 A3
Highcliffe Castle★
  BH23 .....125 C4
Highcliffe Cnr BH23 ...126 A4
Highcliffe Jun Sch
  BH23 ....93 C1
Highcliffe Rd
  Christchurch BH23 .....125 B4
  Swanage BH19 .....179 B2
Highcliffe Sch BH23 ....93 B1
Highdown DT3 .....167 C4
Higher Barn Cl SP7 ....24 B3
Higher Beadon TA16 ..191 E7
Higher Blandford Rd
  Corfe Mullen BH18 ....86 C3
  Shaftesbury SP7 ....13 A1
Higher Bullen BA22 .....193 F8
Higher Cheap St DT9 ...30 A3
Higher Coombses
  TA20 .....202 A8
Higher Day's Rd BH19 ..178 C1
Higher Dro DT2 .....205 F2
Higher Easthams La
  TA18 .....192 A5
Higher End DT3 .....166 B3
Higher Eype Rd DT6 ....99 C3
Higher Filbank DT6 .....177 A4
Higher Gdns BH20 .....177 A4
Higher Gunville 5 DT9 ...17 B1
Higher Kingsbury DT9 ...17 B2
Higher Kingsbury Cl
  DT9 ....17 B2
Higher Kingston BA21 ...27 B3
Higher Mere Pk★ BA12 ..7 A4
Higher Merley La BH21 ..86 C2
Higher Ream BA21 ....26 C3
Higher Sea La DT6 ....97 A4
Higher Shaftesbury Rd
  DT11 .....212 B4
Higher St Bridport DT6 ...69 A1
  Iwerne Minster DT11 ....37 C1
  Lillington DT9 .....194 F7
  Merriott TA16 .....191 F8
  Morden BH20 ....83 B2
  Okeford Fitzpaine DT11 ..197 F5
  West Chinnock TA18 .....192 B8

Higher St La DT8 .....205 C3
Higher Westbury DT9 ...28 B1
Highfield TA18 .....192 B8
Highfield Ave BH24 ....55 B4
Highfield Cl
  Charminster DT2 .....107 B4
  Corfe Mullen BH21 ....86 C3
Highfield Dr BH24 ....47 B1
Highfield Gdns DT6 ...204 C2
Highfield House 12
  BH14 .....120 A2
Highfield Rd
  Bournemouth BH9 ....89 C1
  Corfe Mullen BH21 ....86 C3
  Ferndown BH22 ....53 A2
  Ringwood BH24 ....55 B4
  Salisbury SP2 .....213 A3
  Yeovil BA21 ....27 C3
Highfields DT11 .....212 C2
Highgate La DT2 .....136 B3
Highgrove SP8 ....5 C2
Highgrove Cl 5 DT1 ...135 A4
Highland Ave BH23 ....94 A1
Highland Rd
  Poole BH14 .....120 A3
  Weymouth DT4 .....167 B4
  Wimborne Minster BH21 ..59 B3
Highland View Cl BH21 ..59 B3
Highlands Cres BH10 ...89 B2
Highlands Rd
  Barton on Sea BH25 .....127 A4
  Salisbury SP2 .....213 B1
Highmoor Cl
  Corfe Mullen BH21 ....86 B3
  Poole BH14 .....120 A2
Highmoor Rd
  Bournemouth BH11 ....89 A1
  Corfe Mullen BH21 ....86 B3
  Poole BH14 .....120 A2
Hightown Gdns BH24 ...55 B3
Hightown Rd BH24 ....55 B3
Hightrees Ave BH8 ....90 C1
Highview Cl BH23 ....91 C2
Highview Gdns BH12 ..120 B4
Highwood Cl SP6 ....41 C3
Highwood La BH24 ....47 C1
Highwood Rd BH14 ...120 C2
Hilary Rd BH17 ....87 B1
Hilcot Way DT11 .....212 B3
Hilda Rd BH12 .....120 C4
Hiley Rd BH15 .....119 B3
Hilfield La DT2 .....194 F1
Hill Brow DT9 ....29 C2
Hill Cl Bransgore BH23 ...93 A4
  5 Bridport DT6 .....100 A1
Hill Crest Rd BA21 ....27 C3
Hill House Cl DT9 ....30 B4
Hill La Bransgore BH23 ...93 A4
  Burton BH21 ....92 C1
Hill Rd Lyme Regis DT7 ...96 A3
  Swanage BH19 .....179 A3
Hill Rise DT6 .....100 A1
Hill Rise Rd DT7 ....96 A3
Hill St BH15 .....119 B1
Hill View
  Bishop's Caundle DT9 ...196 A4
  Charminster DT2 .....107 B3
  5 Hazelbury Bryan DT10 .197 A4
  Maiden Newton DT2 ....73 A4
  Osmington DT3 .....169 A4
  Yeovil BA20 ....27 C3
Hill View Cl TA18 .....192 B7
Hill View Prim Sch
  BH10 ....89 C2
Hill View Rd
  Ferndown BH22 ....61 B4
  3 Salisbury SP1 .....213 B2
Hill Way BH24 ....54 A3
Hillard Ct 12 BH20 .....142 C2
Hillary Rd BH23 .....124 C4
Hillborne Gdns 4 BA21 ..26 C3
Hillbourne Fst & Mid Schs
  BH17 ....87 A1
Hillbourne Rd
  Poole BH17 ....87 A1
  11 Weymouth DT4 .....180 B4
Hillbrow Rd BH6 .....123 A3
Hillbury Rd SP6 ....42 B3
Hillcrest Ave BH22 ....61 B4
Hillcrest Cl
  Bournemouth BH9 ....90 A2
  Corfe Mullen BH21 ....86 B3
  Weymouth DT4 .....180 C4
Hillfort Cl DT1 .....134 C4
Hillgrove Ave BA20 ....27 A1
Hilling La DT2 .....207 F8
Hillingdon DT6 .....100 C4
Hillingdon Ct BA21 ....26 C3
Hillman Rd BH14 .....120 B3
Hillmeadow BH31 ....45 B2
Hillsea Rd BH19 .....179 A1
Hillside Cl BA12 ....2 C1
Hillside Cty Fst Sch
  BH31 ....45 B4
Hillside Dr BH23 ....91 B2
Hillside Gdns BH21 ....86 B2
Hillside Mews BH21 ....86 B2
Hillside Rd
  Blandford Camp DT11 ..199 E3
  Corfe Mullen BH21 ....86 B3
  Poole BH12 ....88 C1
  Verwood BH31 ....45 A4
  Woodlands BH21 ....44 B3

Hillside Rd continued
  6 Wool BH20 .....140 A1
Hillside Terr 4 BA20 ....27 C3
Hillside View 9 BA22 ..193 F8
Hilltop Cl BH22 ....61 A4
Hilltop Rd
  Corfe Mullen BH21 ....86 C3
  Ferndown BH22 ....61 A4
Hillview DT6 ....68 C3
Hillview Est 1 DT6 .....100 B4
Hillview Rd
  Bournemouth BH10 ....89 B2
  Swanage BH19 .....179 A1
Hilmar Dr SP8 ....5 C1
Hiltom Rd BH24 ....55 B4
Hilton Cl BH15 .....120 A3
Hilton Rd BH25 ....95 A2
Hilton Rd Cl DT11 ....79 C4
Hinchcliffe Cl BH15 .....118 C1
Hinchcliffe Rd BH15 ..118 C1
Hine Town La DT11 ..198 B6
Hine's Mead La DT2 ....103 B1
Hingsdon La DT6 .....204 B2
Hintock St DT1 .....107 B1
Hinton Admiral Mews
  BH23 ....93 C1
Hinton Admiral Sta
  BH23 ....93 C1
Hinton Cl
  Blandford Forum DT11 ..212 B3
  Hinton St George TA17 ..191 D7
Hinton Cross BA22 ....14 A3
Hinton La DT10 ....35 B4
Hinton Rd
  Bournemouth BH1 .....121 C2
  West Crewkerne TA18 ..191 E5
Hinton St George Prim Sch
  TA17 .....191 C7
Hinton St Mary Roman Villa
  (site of)★ DT10 ....35 A2
Hinton View DT10 ....35 A1
Hinton Wood BH1 .....122 A1
Hinton Wood Ave BH23 ..93 C1
Hintonwood La BH23 ...93 C1
Hitchen 3 TA16 .....191 F7
Hive Cl DT6 .....128 B4
Hive Gdns BH13 .....147 B3
Hoadley Gn SP1 .....213 C4
Hobart Rd BH25 ....94 C1
Hobbs Pk BH24 ....54 A2
Hobbs Rd BH12 .....120 B4
Hobgoblin DT11 ....37 C1
Hoburne DT23 ....93 B1
Hoburne Gdns BH23 ....93 B1
Hoburne La BH23 .....125 B4
Hoburne Rd BH19 .....179 A1
Hod Dr DT11 .....198 E5
Hod Hill (Roman Fort)★
  DT11 .....198 E5
Hod View 2 DT11 .....198 F4
Hodder's La DT7 ....64 A1
Hodges Cl BH17 .....119 C4
Hodway La DT11 .....198 D5
Hogarth Way BH8 ....91 A1
Hogshill St DT8 .....204 C4
Hogue Ave BH10 ....89 B3
Holbaek Cl DT1 .....135 A4
Holbury Cl BH8 ....90 C2
Holcombe Cl DT3 .....168 B4
Holcombe Mead DT2 ..208 A6
Holcombe Rd BH16 ...118 A3
Holdenhurst Ave BH7 ..123 B4
Holdenhurst Rd BH8 ....91 A2
Holditch Ct★ TA20 .....202 B5
Holditch Ct La TA20 ...202 A5
Holditch La TA20 .....202 A5
Holdscroft La DT6 .....202 E1
Hole House La DT10 ..197 D8
Holebrook La DT10 ..196 F7
Holes Bay Rd BH15 .....119 A2
Holes Cl SO41 ....95 C2
Holland Rd DT4 .....167 B2
Holland Way
  Blandford Forum DT11 ..212 B3
  Corfe Mullen BH18 ....86 C3
Hollands Cl BH20 .....176 C4
Hollands Mead Ave
  DT2 .....155 B4
Hollands Wood Dr
  BH25 ....95 A3
Holleys Cl 14 TA20 .....202 A8
Hollies The
  3 Crewkerne TA18 .....191 E3
  Yeovil BA21 ....27 C4
Hollis Way BA22 .....193 D3
Hollow Hill DT2 .....108 C2
Hollow La TA17 .....191 B7
Hollow Oak BH20 .....113 A4
Hollow Oak Rd BH20 ..142 C1
Hollow The
  Affpuddle DT2 .....112 A3
  Child Okeford DT11 .....198 C8
  Sixpenny Handley SP5 ..189 A4
Hollow Way BH10 ....90 B2
Holloway Ave BH11 ....88 C3
Holloway La DT11 .....198 C5
Holloway Rd DT1 .....108 A1
Hollows Cl SP2 .....213 A1
Holly Cl
  3 Dorchester DT1 .....107 C1
  2 Sandford BH20 .....116 A1
  1 St.Leonards BH24 ....53 C2
  Upton BH16 .....118 A4
Holly Ct BH15 .....119 B2
Holly Gdns BH23 ....92 B1
Holly Gn Rise BH11 ....88 C2
Holly Gr Merriott TA18 ..191 F5
  Verwood BH31 ....45 A3

Holly Hedge La BH17 ..119 B1
Holly La
  Broadwindsor DT8 .....203 D8
  Christchurch BH23 ....94 B1
  New Milton BH25 ....95 B2
Holly Lodge 13 BH12 ...121 A2
Holly Rd DT4 .....167 B2
Hollymoor Cl 8 DT8 ..204 D4
Hollymoor Comm La
  DT8 .....204 D4
Hollymoor Gdns 7 DT8 .204 D4
Hollymoor La DT8 .....204 D4
Holm Cl BH24 ....47 C1
Holm Hill La BH23 ....94 A4
Holm Oak Cl BH31 ....45 A4
Holme Cl DT3 .....167 A4
Holme La
  East Holme BH20 .....160 A4
  East Stoke BH20 .....141 A4
Holme Rd BH23 .....126 A4
Holmead Wlk DT1 .....107 B1
Holmes Rd BH19 .....178 C1
Holmfield Ave BH7 .....123 B4
Holmhurst Ave BH23 ...93 C1
Holmlea 1 DT11 .....212 C3
Holmwood Garth 4
  BH24 ....55 C3
Holnest Pk★ DT9 .....195 C4
Holnest Rd BH17 ....87 B1
Holt Heath National Nature
  Reserve★ BH21 ....52 B3
Holt Hill DT9 ....31 C1
Holt La
  Bishop's Caundle DT9 ..196 A8
  Holt BH21 ....51 A2
  Melbury Osmond DT2 ..194 A3
  South Perrott DT8 .....192 D1
  Stourton Caundle DT10 ..32 A1
Holt Rd Holt BH21 ....51 B3
  Horton BH21 ....52 C4
  Poole BH12 .....120 C3
  Wool BH20 .....139 B3
Holten's La BA22 .....192 E6
Holton Heath Sta
  BH16 .....116 B1
Holton Heath Trading Pk
  BH16 .....116 B1
Holton Rd BH16 .....116 B1
Holway TA20 .....202 A8
Holway La
  Cattistock DT2 .....206 A3
  Evershot DT2 .....205 F7
Holwell Dro DT9 .....195 F5
Holwell Prim Sch DT9 .196 B5
Holwell Rd DT10 .....196 C5
Holworth Cl BH11 ....88 C2
Holy Trinity Jun & Inf Sch
  DT4 .....167 B1
Holy Trintiy CE VA Prim Sch
  BA20 ....27 A2
Holyrood Cl BH17 .....119 A4
Holywell Cl BH17 ....87 B2
Home Dr BA21 ....27 A3
Home Farm Cl DT6 .....101 C4
Home Farm La BA22 ...15 A4
Home Farm Way BH31 ..45 A3
Home Rd BH11 ....89 A3
Homedale House BH2 .121 C2
Homedene House
  BH15 .....119 C3
Homefield
  6 Child Okeford DT11 ..198 C8
  Mere BA12 ....2 C3
  Milborne St Andrew DT11 ..79 C4
  Shaftesbury SP7 ....12 C1
Homefield House 13
  BH25 ....95 A1
Homefield Ind Prep Sch
  BH6 .....123 C3
Homefield Ind Senior Sch
  BH23 ....92 B3
Homelake House
  BH14 .....120 A2
Homelands Est BH23 ..123 C4
Homelands House
  BH22 ....61 B3
Homeleigh House 5
  BH8 .....122 A3
Homemill House 5
  BH25 ....95 A2
Homeoaks House
  BH2 .....121 C2
Homeside Rd BH9 ....90 A1
Homestour House 1
  BH23 .....124 A3
Homeview House
  BH15 .....119 B2
Homewood Cl BH25 ...95 B2
Honey Bun Mdw DT6 ..196 F4
Honeybourne Cres
  BH6 .....124 A2
Honeycombe Rise DT9 ..29 C2
Honeyfields 15 SP8 ....5 C2
Honeymead La DT10 ....35 A1
Honeysuckle Cl DT3 ...152 A1
Honeysuckle Gdns 2
  DT11 .....198 B3
Honeysuckle La BH17 ..86 C1
Honeysuckle Way
  BH23 .....125 A4
Honeywood House
  BH14 .....147 B3
Hood Cl BH10 ....89 A1
Hood Cres BH10 ....89 A1
Hooke Cl BH17 .....119 A4
Hooke Ct (School)★
  DT8 .....205 C3

Hooper's La
Barwick BA22 193 F7
Puncknowle DT2 129 C3
Hop Cl BH16 117 A4
Hope Bottom DT6 204 C2
Hope Cl DT2 137 B3
Hope Cross SP8 9 A3
Hopkins Cl BH8 91 A1
Hopmans Cl BH16 84 A2
Hopsfield DT11 79 C4
Horace Rd 10 BH5 122 C2
Hordle House Sch SO41 127 C3
Horn Hill View DT8 204 C4
Horn Pk★ DT8 204 B5
Hornbeam Cl DT4 167 A3
Hornbeam Way BH21 59 C3
Horncastles La 1 DT9 30 A3
Horning Rd BH12 120 C3
Horsa Cl BH6 123 C2
Horsa Ct BH6 123 C2
Horsa Rd BH6 123 C2
Horsecastles DT9 30 A3
Horsecastles La DT9 29 C3
Horsefields SP8 5 C2
Horsehill La DT8 204 A3
Horseponds SP7 12 B2
Horseshoe Cl BH21 60 A3
Horseshoe Ct 4 BH1 121 C2
Horseshoe Rd TA20 202 D7
Horseshoe The BH13 147 B2
Horsey Knap DT2 205 E7
Horsey La
East Chelborough DT2 205 E7
Yeovil BA20 27 B2
Horsford St DT4 167 C1
Horsham Ave BH10 89 B3
Horton Cl
Bournemouth BH9 90 B2
Yeovil BA21 26 C3
Horton Rd Horton BH21 44 B1
St Leonards & St Ives BH24 53 C3
St.Leonards BH24 54 B3
Wimborne St Giles BH21 40 A1
Woodlands BH21 201 F3
Horton Twr★ BH21 201 E1
Horton Way BH31 44 C3
Horyford Cl DT3 168 B4
Hosier's La 23 BH15 119 A1
Hosker Rd BH5 123 A3
Hospital La
Allington DT6 100 A4
Sherborne DT9 30 A3
Hotton Heath Nature Reserve★ BH16 116 C2
Houlton Rd BH15 119 C2
Hound St DT9 30 A3
Hounds Way BH21 60 A3
Houndstone Cl BA21 26 C3
Houndstone Ct 2 BA22 26 B3
Hounslow Cl BH15 118 C1
Howard Cl
Bothenhampton DT6 101 A4
Christchurch BH23 124 C3
Weymouth DT4 180 C4
Howard Rd
Bournemouth BH8 122 B4
Bridport DT6 100 C3
5 Swanage BH19 179 A1
Verwood BH31 45 A3
Yeovil BA21 28 A3
Howard's La BH20 142 C2
Howarth Cl 1 DT6 128 A4
Howe Cl
Christchurch BH23 124 C3
New Milton BH25 94 C2
Howe La BH31 45 A2
Howe's Eype La DT6 99 C3
Howell House BH21 59 C4
Howeth Cl BH10 89 B2
Howeth Rd BH10 89 B2
Howton Cl BH10 89 B3
Howton Rd BH10 89 B3
Hoxley Rd BH10 89 B2
Hoyal Rd BH15 118 B2
Hudson Cl Poole BH12 88 B1
Ringwood BH24 55 C4
Hudson Rd SP1 213 A4
Hughes Bsns Ctr BH23 125 A4
Huish BA20 27 B2
Huish CP Sch BA20 27 B3
Hull Cres BH11 88 C2
Hull Rd BH11 88 C2
Hull Way BH11 88 C2
Hulse Rd SP1 213 B3
Humber Chase BH20 142 B3
Humber Rd BH22 62 A3
Humpy La DT9 31 A1
Hundred Stone★ BA21 27 B4
Hundredstone Cl BA21 27 B4
Hunger Hill BH15 119 B1
Hungerford Hill SP6 43 C3
Hungerford Rd BH8 90 B2
Hunt Rd
Blandford Forum DT11 212 C3
Christchurch BH23 124 C4
Poole BH15 119 C2
Hunt's Hill DT10 21 C3
Hunter Cl
Christchurch BH23 125 A4
Wimborne Minster BH21 60 B3
Hunters Cl BH31 45 C3
Hunters Mead SP7 7 A1
Huntfield Rd BH9 90 A1
Huntick Rd
Lytchett Matravers BH16 84 C2

Huntick Rd *continued*
Lytchett Minster & Upton BH16 85 A1
Huntingdon Dr BH21 59 C1
Huntingdon Gdns BH23 92 A1
Huntley Down DT11 209 F1
Huntly Rd BH3 121 B4
Hunts Mead DT9 29 C2
Huntvale Rd BH9 90 A2
Hurdles The BH23 123 C4
Hurn Cl BH24 54 C3
Hurn Ct BH8 91 A2
Hurn Ct La BH23 90 C3
Hurn La BH24 54 C3
Hurn Rd
Christchurch BH23 91 B2
St Leonards & St Ives BH24 54 C2
Hurn Way BH23 91 B1
Hurricane Cl DT2 137 B3
Hursley Cl BH7 123 B4
Hurst Bridges★ DT2 111 B1
Hurst Cl
Barton on Sea BH25 126 B4
Christchurch BH23 94 B1
Hurst Ct 6 BH23 126 A4
Hurst Hill BH14 147 B4
Hurst Rd Moreton DT2 111 B1
Ringwood BH24 47 B1
Hurstbourne Ave BH23 93 C1
Hurstdene Rd BH8 90 B1
Hussar Cl BH23 123 C4
Hussey's DT10 20 C1
Hutchins Cl DT1 134 C4
Hyacinth Cl BH17 86 C1
Hyde CE Prim Sch SP6 43 C3
Hyde Cl BA21 26 C3
Hyde Gdns 6 DT11 199 D4
Hyde La SP6 43 C3
Hyde Rd
Bournemouth BH10 89 B3
Gillingham SP8 5 C2
Wool BH20 140 A1
Hyde The
New Milton BH25 94 C2
Swanage BH19 178 B1
Hydes La DT10 196 D7
Hynesbury Rd BH23 125 B4
Hythe Rd BH15 120 A4
Hythe The DT3 166 B3

I

Ibbertson Cl BH8 90 C1
Ibbertson Rd BH8 90 C1
Ibbertson Way BH8 90 C1
Ibbett Rd BH10 89 B2
Ibsley Cl BH8 122 B3
Ibsley Dro BH24 43 B1
Icen La Bincombe DT3 152 B2
Shipton Gorge DT6 101 C2
Icen Rd DT3 167 B4
Icen Way DT1 108 A1
Iddesleigh Rd BH3 122 A3
Iford Bridge Home Pk BH6 123 B4
Iford Cl BH6 123 C3
Iford Gdns BH7 123 B4
Iford La BH6 123 C3
Ilchester Rd
Weymouth DT4 167 B2
Yeovil BA21 27 A4
Ilminster Rd BH19 179 A1
Ilsington House★ DT2 78 B1
Ilsington Rd DT2 109 C2
Imber Dr BH23 125 A4
Imber Rd SP7 13 A2
Imbre Ct BH13 147 C4
Imperial Ct 4 BH13 147 C4
Incline Rd
Fortuneswell DT5 181 B1
Portland DT5 187 A3
India Ave SP2 213 A3
Ingarth 8 BH6 123 C2
Inglegreen Cl BH25 94 C1
Inglesham Way BH15 118 C2
Inglewood Ave BH8 90 C1
Inglewood Dr BH25 95 A1
Ingram Wlk 13 BH21 59 B2
Ingworth Rd BH12 121 A3
Inmosthay DT5 187 A3
Inner Breakwater Rd DT5 181 B1
Insley Cres BH18 86 C3
Institute Rd BH19 179 B1
Inveravon BH23 124 C2
Inverclyde House BH14 120 A2
Inverclyde Rd BH14 120 B2
Inverleigh Rd BH6 123 B3
Inverness Rd BH13 147 C4
Ipswich Rd BH4 121 A2
Iris Gdns 6 SP8 5 C1
Iris Rd BH9 89 C1
Irvine Way BH23 124 C4
Irving Rd BH6 123 B3
Isaacs Cl BH12 121 A4
Island View Ave BH23 125 A3
Island View Rd BH25 126 B4
Isle of Purbeck Golf Club BH19 178 C4
Isle Rd DT5 186 C2
Isles La BA22 193 D6
Ivamy Pl BH11 88 C1
Ivel Ct BA20 27 C2
Ivelway 14 TA18 191 F4
Ivers Coll DT10 20 C2

Ivor Rd
Corfe Mullen BH21 86 B2
Poole BH15 119 A1
Ivy Cl 4 Gillingham SP8 5 B1
St.Leonards BH24 53 C2
Ivy La BH24 47 B2
Ivy Mead BA12 3 A3
Ivy Rd BH21 87 B4
Ivy St SP1 213 B2
Iwerne Cl BH9 90 A2

J

Jack Paul Cl BA12 3 A3
Jack the Treacle Eater (Folly)★ BA22 27 C1
Jack's Hedge Cnr BH21 189 F2
Jacklin Ct BH18 87 A3
Jackson Gdns BH12 120 B3
Jackson Rd BH12 120 B3
Jacmar Ct 8 BH25 95 A1
Jacobean Cl BH23 94 A1
Jacobs Ladder 2 DT11 198 C7
Jacobs Rd BH15 118 C1
Jacqueline Rd BH12 120 B4
James Cl DT11 212 C3
James Cross La BH21 201 A6
James Day Mead BH19 179 A3
James Rd
Dorchester DT1 134 C4
Poole BH12 121 A3
James St Salisbury SP2 213 A3
Weymouth DT4 167 B1
Jameson Rd BH9 89 C1
Janred Ct BH25 126 C4
Jarvis Cl DT10 33 B4
Jarvis Way DT10 33 B4
Jasmine Cl
Crewkerne TA18 191 F5
Yeovil BA22 26 B3
Jasmine Way 2 DT4 180 A4
Jaundrells Cl BH25 95 B2
Jay's Ct BH23 126 A4
Jeanneau Cl 8 SP7 12 C2
Jefferson Ave BH1 122 B3
Jellicoe Cl BH14 119 C3
Jellicoe Dr BH23 124 C3
Jenner Way DT3 152 B2
Jennings Rd BH14 120 B1
Jennys La BH16 84 A2
Jephcote Rd BH11 88 C2
Jeremy Cl BH20 140 A1
Jersey Cl BH12 88 B1
Jersey Rd BH12 88 B1
Jesmond Ave BH23 125 C4
Jesop Cl 1 SP8 5 C1
Jessica Ave BH31 44 C4
Jessop Cl BH10 89 C2
Jessop Rd BH21 60 A3
Jessopp Ave DT6 100 C4
Jessopp House 6 BH21 59 B3
Jesty's Ave DT3 152 B2
Jewell Cl SP1 213 C4
Jewell Rd BH8 91 A1
Jimmy Brown Ave BH21 53 A3
Johns Rd BH20 142 B3
Johnson Rd BH21 61 A4
Johnston Rd BH15 119 B4
Johnstone Rd BH23 124 C3
Jolliffe Ave BH15 119 B2
Jolliffe Rd BH15 119 B2
Jopps Cnr BH23 92 B2
Jordan Hill Roman Temple★ DT3 168 A4
Jordan Way 5 DT3 152 B2
Joshua Cl BH15 118 C1
Journeys End DT6 100 A3
Jowitt Dr BH25 94 C1
Joyce Dickson Cl 6 BH24 55 B3
Joys Rd BH21 53 A4
Juan's La SP8 9 B1
Jubilee Cl
Corfe Mullen BH21 86 C4
Radipole DT4 167 B2
Ringwood BH24 55 C4
Jubilee Cres BH12 120 B3
Jubilee Cross BH16 85 A2
Jubilee Ct 5 SP2 213 A3
Jubilee Gdns
Bournemouth BH10 89 B1
Corfe Castle BH20 177 A4
Jubilee Rd
Corfe Mullen BH21 86 C4
Poole BH12 120 B3
Swanage BH19 178 C1
Jubilee Way DT11 212 B3
Julia Cl BH23 125 C4
Julian's Rd BH21 59 A2
Julyan Ave BH12 121 A4
Jumpers Ave BH23 123 C4
Jumpers Rd BH23 123 C4
Junction Rd
Bournemouth BH9 121 C4
Hamworthy BH16 118 B2
Juniper Cl
Ferndown BH22 61 B4
Three Legged Cross BH21 53 A4
Yeovil BA20 27 A2
Juniper Flats BH23 123 C4
Juniper Gdns 7 SP8 5 C1
Juniper Way DT3 152 B2
Jupiter Way BH21 86 C4
Justin Gdns BH10 89 C2

K

Kamptee Copse BH25 95 A3
Kangaw Pl BH15 118 B1
Katherine Chance Cl BH23 92 B2
Katterns Cl BH23 91 C1
Kay Cl BH23 124 C3
Kayes Cl DT4 180 B4
Keats House 17 BH25 95 A1
Keeble Cl BH10 89 B3
Keeble Cres BH10 89 B3
Keeble Rd BH10 89 B3
Keepers La BH21 60 C2
Keighley Ave BH18 86 C1
Keith Rd BH3 121 B4
Kellaway Rd BH17 119 C4
Kellaway Terr DT4 167 B2
Kelly Cl BH17 119 C4
Kelsall Gdns BH25 95 A2
Kelsey Rd SP1 213 B3
Kemp Rd BH9 121 C4
Kemp Welch Ct BH12 121 A4
Kempston Rd DT4 167 B1
Ken Rd BH6 123 C2
Kendalls La SP8 5 C3
Kenilworth DT4 167 A3
Kenilworth Cl BH25 95 A2
Kenilworth Ct
2 Christchurch BH23 124 A4
11 Poole BH13 147 C4
Kenmoor Cl DT3 167 C4
Kenmore Dr BA21 27 B3
Kennard Ct BH25 94 C2
Kennard Rd BH25 94 C2
Kennart Rd BH17 119 A4
Kennel La DT2 206 C2
Kennels La DT9 195 E2
Kenneth Ct 15 BH23 126 A4
Kennington Rd BH17 119 B4
Kennington Sq 5 BH20 142 C2
Kensington Dr BH2 121 B2
Kensington Rd 3 SP2 213 A3
Kent Cl DT4 166 C2
Kent House 20 BH4 121 B2
Kent La BH24 43 A1
Kent Rd Poole BH12 120 C3
Salisbury SP2 213 A1
10 Tatworth TA20 202 A8
Kentisworth Rd DT10 20 C1
Kents La 8 TA20 202 A8
Kenwyn Rd DT6 100 C4
Kenyon Cl BH15 119 C4
Kenyon Rd BH15 119 C4
Keppel Cl BH24 55 B4
Kerley Rd BH2 121 C1
Kestrel Cl
Ferndown BH22 61 A4
Upton BH16 118 A4
Kestrel Ct BH24 55 B4
Kestrel Dr BH23 125 A3
Kestrel View DT3 152 B2
Kestrel Way SP6 42 B3
Keswick Ct BH25 95 A3
Keswick Rd
Bournemouth BH5 123 A2
New Milton BH25 95 A3
Keswick Way BH31 45 A3
Keverstone Ct BH1 122 B2
Key La 21 BH15 119 A1
Keyes Cl
Christchurch BH23 124 C3
Poole BH12 88 C1
Keynston Down Rd 7 DT11 199 E2
Keysworth Ave BH25 126 C4
Keysworth Dr BH20 143 A4
Keysworth Rd BH16 118 B2
Khartoum Rd DT4 180 C4
Khyber Rd BH12 120 B3
Kiddles BA21 27 C3
Kidmore Cl 2 DT6 97 A4
Kilbride 11 BH12 121 A2
Killicks Hill DT5 186 C4
Killock 6 BH13 147 C4
Kilmarnock Rd BH9 89 C1
Kilmington Way BH23 125 C4
Kiln Cl BH21 86 B2
Kimber Rd BH11 88 C2
Kimberley Cl
Christchurch BH23 123 C4
1 Radipole DT3 152 C1
Kimberley Rd
Bournemouth BH6 123 B3
Poole BH14 120 A2
Kimmeridge Ave BH12 120 B4
Kimmeridge Cl DT3 167 A4
Kine Bush La SP8 10 A4
King Alfred's Mid Sch SP7 13 A2
King Arthur Dr BA21 26 C4
King Barrow (Tumulus)★
Alderholt SP6 41 B3
Studland BH19 164 C1
King Charles Way DT6 100 C4
King Cl BH24 54 A2
King Down Dro BH21 49 B2
King Down Rd DT11 199 F3
King Edmund Ct SP8 5 C1
King Edward Ave BH9 90 A1
King Edward Ct BH9 89 C1
King Edward's Dr DT11 209 F5
King Fisher Way BH23 125 A3
King George Ave BH9 89 C1

King George Mobile Home Pk BH25 94 C1
King George St 7 BA20 27 B2
King George V Rd BH20 139 C4
King John Ave BH11 88 B3
King John Cl BH11 88 B3
King John's House★ SP5 188 B4
King Richard Dr BH11 88 B3
King St Bridport DT6 100 B3
Fortuneswell DT5 186 C4
Radipole DT4 167 B2
Wimborne Minster BH21 59 A2
Yeovil BA21 27 B3
King's Ave BH23 123 C3
King's Barrow★ BH20 160 C4
King's Cres BH14 120 C1
King's Ct Pal★ SP8 6 A1
King's House★ SP2 213 A2
King's La DT6 70 B3
King's Mill Rd DT10 34 A3
King's Pk Athletic Ctr BH7 122 C3
King's Pk Dr BH7 122 C3
King's Pk Rd BH7 122 C3
King's Pk Sch BH1 122 C3
King's Rd
Blandford Forum DT11 212 B3
Bournemouth BH3 122 A4
Salisbury SP1 213 B3
Thornford DT9 194 D7
King's St BH21 56 B3
Kingcombe Cross Roads DT2 205 E3
Kingcombe La DT2 205 E3
Kingcombe Rd DT8 205 C3
Kingcome Nature Reserve★ DT2 205 D1
Kingcup Cl BH18 86 C1
Kingfisher Cl
Bournemouth BH6 123 C3
Ferndown BH22 53 A1
Salisbury SP2 213 B1
Weymouth DT4 180 B3
Kingfisher Pk Homes 3 BH10 89 C2
Kingfisher Way BH24 47 B1
Kingfishers 9 BH23 124 A3
Kingfishers The BH31 45 B3
Kinghton Heath Ind Est BH11 88 C2
Kingland Cres BH15 119 B1
Kingland Rd BH15 119 B1
Kings Arms La BH24 55 A4
Kings Arms Row BH24 55 A4
Kings Ave BH14 120 B1
Kings Cl Ferndown BH22 53 A1
Longburton DT9 195 B8
Kings Cres DT9 30 A4
Kings Hill 2 SP7 12 C2
Kings La BH21 201 F4
Kings Mead DT2 78 A1
Kings Pk Com Hospl BH7 122 C3
Kings Rd
Dorchester DT1 108 A1
New Milton BH25 95 B2
Radipole DT3 167 B4
Sherborne DT9 30 A4
Kings Rd E BH19 179 A1
Kings Rd W BH19 179 A1
Kingsbere Ave BH10 89 A1
Kingsbere Cres DT1 135 A4
Kingsbere Gdns BH23 126 A4
Kingsbere La SP7 13 A2
Kingsbere Rd
Overcombe/Preston DT3 168 A4
Poole BH15 119 C3
Kingsbridge Rd BH14 120 B2
Kingsbury's La BH24 55 A4
Kingscourt Cl 6 SP8 6 A1
Kingscourt Rd SP8 6 A1
Kingsfield BH24 55 B4
Kingsland Ct BH13 147 C4
Kingsland Rd SP2 213 A3
Kingsleigh Fst Sch BH10 89 B2
Kingsleigh Jun Sch BH10 89 B2
Kingsleigh Sec Sch BH10 89 B2
Kingsley Ave BH6 124 A2
Kingsley Cl BH6 124 A2
Kingsman La SP7 12 C1
Kingsmead Ct 9 BH21 59 A3
Kingsmill Rd BH17 119 C4
Kingsnorth Cl DT6 100 C4
Kingston BA20 27 B3
Kingston Cl DT11 212 B3
Kingston Hill BH20 176 C2
Kingston La DT10 196 F4
Kingston Lacy House (NT)★ BH21 58 A4
Kingston Maurward Agricultural Coll DT2 108 C2
Kingston Maurward Gdns & Animal Pk★ DT2 108 C2
Kingston Rd BH15 119 B2
Kingston Russell House★ DT2 131 A4
Russell Stone Circle★ DT3 131 A2

Kingston View BA21 ....27 B3
Kingsway
　Ferndown BH22 ....61 B4
　Lyme Regis DT7 ....96 B3
Kingsway Cl BH23 ......91 C1
Kingswell Cl BH10 ......89 B1
Kingswell Gdns BH10 ...89 A1
Kingswell Gr BH10 ......89 A1
Kingswell Rd BH10 ......89 B1
Kingswood BH4 ....121 B1
Kingswood Cl 6 BH19 .178 C1
Kingswood Rd 6 TA18 .191 F3
Kinross Rd BH3 ....121 C3
Kinsbourne Ave BH10 ..89 B1
Kinson Ave BH15 ......120 A4
Kinson Gr BH10 ....89 B3
Kinson Pk Rd BH10 .....89 B3
Kinson Pottery Ind Est
　BH14 ....120 A3
Kinson Prim Sch BH11 .89 A3
Kinson Rd BH10 ....89 B2
Kiosks The 20 BH15 ...119 B1
Kipling Rd BH14 ......120 A3
Kirby Cl BH15 ....119 C3
Kirby Way BH6 ....123 B2
Kirkham Ave BH23 ......92 B2
Kirkleton Ave DT4 ....167 B3
Kirkway BH18 ....87 A2
Kit La DT2 ....155 B4
Kitchener Cres BH17 ...87 A1
Kitchener Rd DT4 .....167 A2
Kite's Nest La SP8 ......1 C1
Kitford La DT11 ....197 C3
Kitscroft Rd BH10 .....89 B3
Kitt Hill DT9 ....30 A3
Kittiwake Cl BH6 ......123 C3
Kivel Ct SP2 ....213 B3
Kiwi Cl BH15 ....119 C2
Knacker's Hole La
　TA20 ....202 F4
Knap Barrow (Long
　Barrow)★ SP6 ....190 D6
Knapp Cl BH23 ....124 A4
Knapp Mill Ave BH23 .124 A4
Knapp The
　Chickerell DT3 ....166 B3
　Fontmell Magna SP7 ...37 C3
　Hilton DT11 ....209 D6
　Shaftesbury SP7 ......12 B2
Knapps DT11 ....198 B6
Knighton Heath Cl
　BH11 ....88 C2
Knighton Heath Rd
　BH11 ....88 C2
Knighton House Sch
　DT11 ....198 E3
Knighton La
　Broadmayne DT2 .....136 B1
　Oakley BH21 ....88 B4
Knighton Pk BH25 ....126 C4
Knights Cl 5 DT11 ....212 B1
Knights Rd BH11 ....88 B3
Knightsbridge Ct BH2 121 C1
Knightsdale Rd DT4 ..167 A1
Knightsdale Rd Swimming
　Pool BH22 ....167 A1
Knightstone Ct 14 BH20 142 C2
Knightstone Rise DT6 ..68 C1
Knightwood Cl BH23 .125 B4
Knobcrook Rd 3 BH21 ..59 A3
Knole Ct 5 BH1 ....122 B2
Knole Gdns BH1 ......122 B2
Knole Rd BH1 ....122 B2
Knoll Gdns★
　Ferndown BH21 ....60 C2
　St.Leonards BH24 .....54 A2
Knoll La BH21 ....86 A4
Knoll Manor BH2 .....121 C3
Knoll Pl SP8 ....5 C2
Knoll Rise DT3 ....152 C1
Knollsea Cl 8 BH19 ..179 B1
Knotts Cl 7 DT11 .....198 C7
Knotts Paddock DT9 ...30 B3
Knowl La DT6 ....101 B4
Knowle Cross DT8 ....203 D6
Knowle Hill BH20 ....140 A1
Knowle La TA18 ......191 F1
Knowle Wood Knap 4
　BH20 ....140 A1
Knowles Cl BH23 .....124 C4
Knowlton Church (remains
　of)★ BH21 ....201 D5
Knowlton Circles★
　BH21 ....201 D5
Knowlton Gdns BH9 ...90 A2
Knowlton Rd BH17 .....87 C1
Knyeton House BH1 ...122 A2
Knyveton Rd BH1 .....122 B2
Kyrchil La DT11 ....59 C3
Kyrchil Way BH21 .....59 C4

L

La Retraite Sch SP1 ...213 B3
Labrador Dr BH15 ....119 B1
Laburnam Way SP8 .....5 B1
Laburnum Cl
　Ferndown BH22 ....61 A3
　Radipole DT4 ....167 A3
　1 Sandford BH20 ....116 A1
　Verwood BH31 ....45 C3
Laburnum Cres 19 TA18 .191 F5

Laburnum House 8
　BH10 ....89 C2
Laburnum Way BA20 ...26 C1
Lacey Cres BH15 .....120 A3
Lackington Dro DT2 ..208 B1
Lacy Cl BH21 ....59 B3
Lacy Dr BH21 ....59 B3
Lady Baden Powell Way
　DT11 ....212 C3
Lady Caroline's Dr
　DT11 ....210 D7
Lady Mead Cl 3 DT5 ..187 A2
Lady's Well★ DT2 ....195 C1
Ladygado DT11 ....147 B4
Ladysmith Rd BH23 ..124 C4
Lagado Cl BH14 ......147 B4
Lagland Ct 12 BH15 ..119 B1
Lagland St BH15 .....119 B1
Lagoon Cl BH14 ......147 A4
Lagoon Rd BH14 .....147 A4
Laidlaw Cl BH12 .....121 A4
Lake Ave
　Bournemouth BH11 ....89 A3
　Hamworthy BH15 .....118 C1
　Verwood BH31 ....45 B2
Lake View Manor BH25 .95 A2
Lakefields BA22 ......193 B7
Lakegate La DT9 .....194 A5
Lakeside BH4 ....55 C3
Lakeside Gdns DT3 ..167 A4
Lakeside Pines BH25 ..95 A4
Lakeside Rd BH13 ...121 A1
Lakewood Rd BH23 ....93 C1
Lakeview Dr BH24 .....55 C3
Lamb Plot DT9 ....194 D2
Lambert Cl 13 DT9 ....17 B1
Lambert's Castle (Fort)★
　DT6 ....202 E2
Lambourne Ct TA18 ..191 F5
Lambs Cl BH17 ....87 B1
Lambs La BH21 ....56 B2
Lambsfield DT9 ....30 B4
Lambsgreen La BH21 ..58 C1
Lammas Cl SP8 ....5 C2
Lampton Cl BH20 ....139 C1
Lampton Gdns BH9 ...89 C1
Lancaster Cl
　Christchurch BH23 ...125 B4
　Corfe Mullen BH18 ...86 C3
Lancaster Dr
　Corfe Mullen BH18 ...86 C3
　Verwood BH31 ....45 A3
Lancaster Rd
　Dorchester DT1 .....108 A1
　Ferndown BH21 ....61 A4
　Radipole DT3 ....152 A1
Lancer Cl BH23 ......123 C4
Lanchards 4 DT11 ...198 B6
Lanchards La DT11 ..198 B5
Lander Cl BH15 ......119 B1
Landers Reach BH16 ..84 B1
Landford Gdns BH8 ...90 B1
Landford Way BH8 ...90 B1
Landscombe Vale
　DT2 ....208 A8
Landseer Rd 13 BH4 .121 B2
Landshire La
　Fifehead Magdalen SP8 ..20 B3
　Henstridge BA8 ......18 C1
　Stalbridge BA8 ......19 B2
Lane Cl DT11 ....212 C3
Lane End DT11 ....79 C4
Lane The
　4 Bournemouth BH8 .122 B3
　Corfe Castle BH20 ..176 C2
Lanehouse Rocks Rd 1
　DT4 ....180 B4
Lanes The BH25 ......95 A3
Lane-side SP7 ....12 C2
Lang Rd TA18 ....191 E3
Langdon Cl BH14 ....120 B2
Langdon La
　Beaminster DT8 .....204 E4
　Chideock DT6 ....98 C4
Langdon Rd BH14 ...120 B2
Langdons DT9 ....30 B4
Langdons Way 11 TA18 .202 A8
Langfords La SP7 .....12 B1
Langham Ct BH23 .....91 C1
Langham La SP8 ....4 C1
Langley Chase BH24 ..54 A3
Langley Rd
　Christchurch BH23 ...93 C1
　Poole BH14 ....120 C2
Langmead Pl 3 TA18 .191 F3
Langmead Rd TA18 ..191 F3
Langmead Sq 11 TA18 .191 F3
Langmoor La EX13 ...202 A2
Langside Ave BH11 ..121 A4
Langside Sch BH12 ..121 A4
Langton Ave BH10 ...180 B3
Langton Cl BH25 ....127 A4
Langton Cross★ DT11 .150 C1
Langton Cres DT11 ..212 C2
Langton Dene 27 BH4 .121 B2
Langton Matravers Mus★
　BH19 ....178 A2
Langton Matravers Prim Sch
　BH19 ....178 A1
Langton Rd
　Blandford Forum DT11 .212 C2
　Bournemouth BH7 ...122 C3
Lansdell Ct 6 BH15 ..119 C2
Lansdowne Cres BH1 .122 A4

Lansdowne Gdns BH1 .122 A2
Lansdowne House 13
　BH1 ....122 A2
Lansdowne Rd
　Bournemouth BH1 ...122 A3
　Bridport DT6 ....100 B3
Lansdowne Sq DT4 ..167 B1
Lansdowne The BH1 .122 A2
Lapwing Rd BH21 .....60 A4
Lara Cl BH8 ....90 B2
Larch Cl
　Broadstone BH17 .....86 C1
　Hordle SO41 ....95 C2
　Sandford BH20 ......143 A4
　St.Leonards BH24 ....54 B2
Larch Way BH22 ......61 B4
Larcombe La DT6 ......69 B3
Lark Rd BH23 ....125 C3
Larkhill Rd Yeovil BA21 ..27 A3
　Yeovil Without BA21 ..26 C4
Larks Cl BH22 ....61 A4
Larks Rise BH22 ......61 A4
Larksfield Ave BH9 ...90 B2
Larkshill Cl BH25 .....95 A2
Larksmead DT11 .....212 C3
Larkspur Cl DT4 .....167 C3
Larkspur Cres BA21 ..26 C4
Larmer Tree Victorian
　Pleasure Gdn★ SP5 .188 B3
Lascelles Cl 1 BH7 ..123 A4
Lascelles Rd BH7 ....123 A3
Latch Farm Ave BH23 124 A4
Latimer Rd BH9 ......121 C4
Latimers Cl BH23 .....93 C1
Launches The BH20 .172 B3
Laundry La SP7 ....12 B1
Laurel Ave BH20 .....116 A1
Laurel Cl 1 Bridport DT6 100 A4
　Christchurch BH23 ...93 B1
　Corfe Mullen BH21 ...86 B3
　Hordle SO41 ....95 C2
Laurel Dr BH18 ....87 B2
Laurel Gdns BH18 ....87 B2
Laurel La BH24 ....54 A2
Laurels The
　7 Crewkerne TA18 ..191 F5
　Ferndown BH22 ......61 B4
　8 Gillingham SP8 .....5 C1
　Iwerne Courtney or Shroton
　DT11 ....198 E7
Lavender Cl BH31 .....45 C3
Lavender Rd
　Bournemouth BH8 ....90 B2
　Hordle SO41 ....95 C2
Lavender Villas 1
　BH23 ....126 A4
Lavender Way BH18 ..86 B2
Laver's La TA20 .....202 C2
Laverstock BH7 ......122 C2
Laverstock Pk SP1 ...213 C3
Laverstock Pk W SP1 213 C3
Laverstock Rd SP1 ...213 C3
Lavinia Rd BH12 .....120 B4
Lawford Rd BH9 ......90 A2
Lawn View BH25 ...94-B3
Lawns Cl BH21 ....60 B3
Lawns Rd BH21 ....60 B3
Lawns The
　Charmouth DT6 ....97 A4
　Christchurch BH23 ..126 A4
Lawrence Ct BH8 ....122 B3
Lawrence Dr
　Crossways DT2 .....137 B3
　Poole BH13 ....120 C1
Lawrence La Hyde SP6 ..43 B2
　Witchampton BH21 ..201 A2
Lawrence of Arabia's
　Cottage★ BH20 ....112 B1
Lawrence of Arabia's Grave★
　DT2 ....138 C4
Lawrence Rd BH24 ...47 C1
Lawson Rd BH12 ....120 A3
Layard Dr BH21 ......59 B1
Laymoor La BH21 .....60 B3
Layton Cl BH12 ......120 B3
Layton La SP7 ....12 C1
Layton Rd BH12 .....120 B3
Le Neubourg Way SP8 ..5 C1
Le Patourel Cl BH23 .124 B4
Lea Cl BA21 ....27 B4
Lea Rd DT4 ....180 A4
Lea The BH31 ....45 B3
Lea Way BH11 ....88 C2
Leaden Hall Sch SP2 213 B2
Leamington Rd
　Bournemouth BH9 ...122 A4
　Weymouth DT4 .....166 C1
Leaphill Rd BH7 .....123 A3
Learoyd Rd BH17 ....119 C4
Leaze La BA21 ....28 A2
Lecher La DT8 ....192 B1
Lechlade Gdns BH7 ..123 A4
Ledbury Rd BH23 ....124 C3
Ledgard Cl BH14 ....120 A2
Lee Ct BH22 ....61 B2
Lee La DT6 ....101 A4
Leedam Rd BH10 .....89 B2
Leeds Cres DT4 .....166 C1
Lees Cl BH23 ....91 B2
Leeson Cl 2 BH19 ..178 C1
Leeson Dr BH22 ......61 A4
Leeson House Field Studies
　Ctr★ BH19 ....178 B1
Leeson Rd BH7 ......122 C4
Leet Cl 1 DT5 ....181 A1
Leet Ct DT9 ....29 C2

Legg La BH21 ....59 B2
Legion Cl
　Dorchester DT1 .....134 C4
　Hamworthy BH15 ...118 C1
Legion Rd
　Hamworthy BH15 ...118 C1
　Yeovil BA21 ....27 A3
Leicester Rd BH13 ..120 C2
Leigh Comm BH21 ...59 C3
Leigh Gdns BH21 .....59 B2
Leigh La Halstock BA22 .193 C3
　Ibberton DT11 ......197 D3
　Wimborne Minster BH21 ..59 C3
　Winsham TA20 .....202 D8
Leigh Rd
　New Milton BH25 ....95 A2
　Wimborne Minster BH21 ..59 C2
Leigham Vale Rd BH6 123 B2
Lennox St DT4 ....167 B2
Lentham Cl BH17 .....87 B1
Lenthay Cl DT9 ......29 C2
Lenthay Rd DT9 .....29 C2
Lerrett Cl DT3 ....166 B3
Leslie Rd
　Bournemouth BH9 ...121 C4
　Poole BH14 ....120 A2
Lessingham Ave BH8 .180 B3
Letton Cl DT11 ....212 C4
Letton Pk★ DT11 ...212 C3
Leven Ave BH11 .....121 B3
Leven Cl BH4 ....121 B2
Levet's La 5 BH15 ..119 A1
Lewell Way DT2 ......136 B2
Lewens Cl BH21 ......59 B2
Lewens La BH21 ......59 B2
Lewesdon Cl 6 DT8 ..204 C4
Lewesdon Dr BH18 ..86 C2
Lewesdon Hill (National
　Trust)★ DT8 ....203 E4
Leybourne Ave BH10 ..89 B2
Leybourne Cl BH10 ..89 B3
Leydene Ave BH8 ....90 C1
Leydene Cl BH8 ......90 C1
Leyland Rd BH12 ....88 C1
Leyside BH23 ....124 C3
Leyton Conyers 16
　BH13 ....147 C4
Liberty Cl BH21 ......53 B3
Liberty Ct BH23 .....123 C4
Library Mews BH12 ..120 B3
Library Rd
　Bournemouth BH9 ...89 C1
　Ferndown BH22 ......61 B1
　Poole BH12 ....120 C3
Lichfield Rd DT4 ....167 A1
Liddington Cres DT11 212 B3
Liddon Hill TA18 ....191 C5
Lighthouse Rd BH19 .185 B4
Lilac Cl BH24 ....55 B4
Lilliput CE Fst Sch
　BH14 ....147 B4
Lilliput Ct BH14 ....120 A2
Lilliput Rd BH14 ....147 B4
Limber Rd BA22 .....26 B3
Lime Cl Dorchester DT1 .134 C4
　Poole BH15 ....119 C3
Lime Hill DT6 ....70 A4
Lime Kiln BA21 ......26 C3
Lime Kiln La BA8 ....19 A2
Lime Kiln Rd BH16 ..84 B2
Lime Kiln Way SP2 ..213 B1
Lime Tree Ave BA20 ..27 A1
Lime Tree Cl BH25 ...42 A3
Limekiln Cl 2 DT5 ..186 C1
Limerick Cl BH23 ....17 B1
Limes The SP7 ......12 A1
Limited BH9 ....90 A1
Lin Brook Dr BH24 ..47 C1
Linclieth Rd 3 BH20 .140 A1
Lincoln Ave
　Bournemouth BH1 ...122 B3
　Christchurch BH23 ..91 C1
Lincoln Rd Poole BH12 120 B4
　2 Weymouth DT4 ..166 C1
Lindbergh Rd BH21 ..61 A4
Linden Ave DT1 .....108 A1
Linden Cl
　Ferndown BH22 ......61 B1
　Salisbury SP1 ......213 C3
Linden Gdns 1 BH24 .55 A4
Linden Pk SP7 ....13 A1
Linden Rd
　Bournemouth BH9 ...90 A2
　Ferndown BH22 ......61 B1
　Poole BH12 ....120 B3
　Swanage BH19 .....179 A1
Lindens The BH23 ...92 B2
Lindford Rd BH24 ...47 C1
Lindlar Cl SP7 ....12 C2
Lindsay Manor 10 BH12 121 A2
Lindsay Pk 15 BH13 .121 A2
Lindsay Rd BH13 ....121 A2
Lindum Ct 3 BH12 ..121 A2
Lineside BH23 ....124 B4
Linford Cl BH25 .....95 A2
Linford Rd BH24 ....47 C1
Ling Rd BH12 ....88 A1
Lingdale Rd BH6 ....123 B3
Lingfield Ave BA21 ..27 C4
Lingfield Grange BH4 121 B2
Lington Cl DT2 .....137 B3
Lingwood Ave BH23 .124 C3
Linhorns La BH25 ....95 A3
Link Rd BH24 ....47 C1
Link Rise BH21 ......86 C3
Link Way SP1 ....213 C3
Linkhay 12 TA20 ....202 A8

Linkhay Cl 11 TA20 ..202 A8
Links Dr BH23 ....91 B1
Links Rd Poole BH14 ..120 B1
　Weymouth DT4 .....167 A4
Links View Ave BH14 120 C1
Linkside Ave BH8 ...122 C4
Linmead Dr BH11 ....89 A3
Linnet Cl Radipole DT3 .152 B2
　Ringwood BH24 .....55 C3
Linnet Ct BH25 ......94 C2
Linnet La DT2 ......205 D5
Linnet Rd BH17 .....118 C4
Linnetsdene 7 SP2 ..213 B1
Linsay Rd BH20 .....139 C3
Lintern La SP8 ....11 A3
Linthorpe Rd BH15 .119 C2
Linwood Mix Sch BH9 122 A4
Linwood Rd BH9 ....122 A4
Lionheart Cl BH11 ...88 B3
Lions Hill Way BH24 .53 C2
Lions La BH24 ....53 C2
Lions Wood BH24 ...54 A2
Liscombe Cl DT1 ...107 B1
Litchford Rd BH25 ..95 B2
Little Barrs Dr BH25 ..95 A2
Little Britain DT1 ...108 B1
Little Content La SP7 ..2 C2
Little Croft Rd BH12 .120 A3
Little Ct BH4 ....147 B4
Little Dewlands BH31 ..44 C3
Little England DT11 ..79 C4
Little Forest Mans 10
　BH1 ....122 A2
Little Forest Rd BH4 121 C3
Little Fosters BH13 .147 C3
Little La DT11 ......198 A6
Little Lonnen BH21 ..59 C4
Littlecroft Ave BH9 ..90 A2
Littledown SP7 ......12 C3
Littledown Ave BH7 .122 C4
Littledown Dr BH7 ..122 C4
Littlefield DT9 ....29 C2
Littlefield La SP5 ...189 A4
Littlemead
　Broadmayne DT2 ...136 A1
　Radipole DT3 ......152 A2
Littlemead Cl BH17 .119 A4
Littlemill La SP6 ....190 F3
Littlemoor Ave BH11 .88 B2
Littlemoor CP Sch
　DT3 ....152 B2
Littlemoor Rd
　Overcombe/Preston
　DT3 ....168 A4
　Radipole DT3 ......152 B2
Littleton Dro DT11 ..211 B6
Littletowns DT11 ...212 B3
Littleview Rd DT4 ..166 C1
Litton Hill DT2 .....103 A1
Litton Cl
　Askerswell DT2 .....102 C3
　Litton Cheney DT2 .103 A1
　Puncknowle DT2 ...129 C4
Liverpool Rd 3 DT4 166 C1
Livingstone Rd BH12 .120 B3
Livingstone Rd
　Bournemouth BH5 ..123 A4
　Christchurch BH23 ..124 B4
　Wimborne Minster BH21 ..59 C2
Llewellin Cl BH16 ..118 B4
Llewellin Ct BH16 ..118 B4
Load La DT2 ....194 B4
Loaders Cl BH9 .....122 A4
Locarno Rd BH19 ...179 A1
Loch Rd BH14 ....120 C3
Lockeridge Cl DT11 .212 B3
Lockett's La DT2 ....207 C3
Locks La
　Glanvilles Wootton DT9 .195 C3
　Loders DT6 ....101 C3
　Stratton DT2 ......106 C4
Locksley Dr BH22 ...61 B2
Lockwood Terr SP8 ...11 A4
Lockyer's Mid Sch
　BH21 ....86 B4
Lockyer's Rd BH21 ..86 C4
Lockyer's Way BH16 .84 B2
Lockyers Dr BH22 ...61 C3
Lodbourne Gdns 6 SP8 .5 C2
Lodbourne Gn 7 SP8 ..5 C2
Lodbourne Terr 5 SP8 ..5 C2
Lodden View SP8 ....11 A4
Loders CE Prim Sch
　DT6 ....69 B1
Loders Cl BH17 ......87 B2
Loders La DT6 ......101 C2
Lodge Cl BH14 ......120 C2
Lodge Ct BH14 .....120 C2
Lodge Rd
　Christchurch BH23 .123 C4
　Holt BH21 ....51 A3
Lodge The BH2 .....121 C2
Lodge Way DT4 .....180 B4
Lodmoor Ave DT3 ..167 B4
Lodmoor Ctry Pk★
　DT3 ....167 C4
Loewy Cres BH12 ...88 B1
Lombard Ave BH6 ..123 B3
Lombardy Cl BH31 ..45 B3
Lomer La SP6 ....42 C2
Lomond Dr DT4 .....167 B1
London Cl
　20 Dorchester DT1 .108 A1
　Piddlehinton DT2 ...76 C4
London La BH23 ....63 C1
London Rd
　Dorchester DT1 ....108 A1
　Milborne Port DT9 ..17 C1

London Rd continued
Salisbury SP1 ....213 C4
London Row DT2 ....76 C4
Lone Pine Dr BH22 .....61 C2
Lone Pine Way BH22 ...61 C1
Long Acre DT5 ....187 A2
Long Ash La
Cattistock DT2 ....206 E2
Frampton DT2 ....74 A2
Frome St Quintin DT2 ..206 D6
Maiden Newton DT2 ......73 C3
Long Barrow La DT8 ..204 B3
Long Bredy Hut La
DT2 ....103 C1
Long Cl BA21 ....26 C3
Long Cross SP7 ....12 C2
Long Entry DT7 ....96 B3
Long Furlong La BA22 .193 C8
Long Hill BA12 ....2 C3
Long La
Bothenhampton DT6 .....100 C2
Bourton SP8 ....1 A1
Cann SP7 ....24 A4
Colehill BH21 ....51 A1
Cucklington BA9 ....4 A1
Puddletown DT2 ....78 A1
Ringwood BH24 ....55 B2
Whitchurch Canonicorum
DT6 ....65 B4
Wimborne Minster BH21 ..59 C4
Long Mdw BH21 ....195 A2
Long Mead BA21 ......26 C3
Long Rd BH10 ....89 B3
Long St
Cerne Abbas DT2 ......207 D4
Sherborne DT9 ....30 B3
Longacre Dr BH22 .....61 B2
Long's La DT6 ....100 C4
Longbarrow Cl BH8 ....91 A1
Longbury Hill La SP8 ...5 A2
Longcroft Rd
Weymouth DT4 ....167 A2
Yeovil BA21 ....27 B3
Longdown Rd DT9 ....194 D7
Longespee Rd BH21 ...87 C4
Longfield Dr
Bournemouth BH11 ......89 A3
Ferndown BH22 ....89 C4
Longfield Rd DT4 ....167 B1
Longfleet CE Comb Sch
BH15 ....119 B2
Longfleet Rd BH15 ....119 C2
Longford Rd DT9 .....194 C7
Longforward Hill
TA17 ....191 A8
Longforward La TA17 ..191 B8
Longhayes Ave DT6 ...100 A4
Longhill Dr 11 SP2 ...213 B1
Longland SP2 ....213 A3
Longland's La
Littlebredy DT2 ....131 C4
Winterbourne Abbas
DT2 ....105 A1
Longlands La BA22 ....193 C8
Longleat Gdns BH25 ...94 C2
Longman's Rd BH21 ...201 A3
Longmead SP7 ....12 C2
Longmeadow La BH17 ..118 C4
Longspee Sch BH17 ...119 B4
Lonnen Rd BH21 ....51 B1
Lonnen Wood Cl BH21 .60 A4
Lonsdale Rd BH3 .....121 C3
Looke La DT2 ....129 C3
Lopen Rd TA13 ....191 D8
Loraine Ave BH23 ....126 B4
Lord Cl BH17 ....119 C4
Lordsmead Rd BA12 ....3 A2
Lorne Pk Rd BH1 .....122 A2
Lorne Rd DT1 ....107 C1
Lorton La DT3 ....152 A2
Loscombe's Well Rd
DT6 ....66 B1
Lotmoor Hill SP8 ......10 B1
Louise Rd DT1 ....107 C1
Louse La DT11 ....211 E4
Louviers Rd DT3 .....152 C1
Love La Marnhull DT10 .21 B3
Salisbury SP1 ....213 B2
Shaftesbury SP7 ....12 B1
Love's La DT6 ....66 B1
Lovelands DT2 ....193 A1
Lovells Mead DT10 ....20 C2
Loveridge La 16 TA20 ..202 A8
Loverley La BH21 .....201 B3
Lovett Gn SP1 ....213 C4
Low's Hill La DT9 .....29 B3
Lower Acreman St DT9 .30 A3
Lower Ashley Rd BH25 ..95 B1
Lower Beadon TA16 ...191 F7
Lower Blandford Rd
Broadstone BH18 ....87 C1
Cann SP7 ....24 A4
1 Shaftesbury SP7 .....12 C1
2 Shaftesbury SP7 .....13 C1
Lower Boyston La SP7 ..16 C2
Lower Catherston Rd
DT6 ....65 A1
Lower Comm La BH21 ..53 B4
Lower Comm La DT11 ..36 B1
Lower Coombses
TA20 ....202 A8
Lower E Coker Rd
BA20 ....27 A1
Lower Fairmead Rd
BA21 ....27 C4
Lower Golf Links Rd
BH18 ....87 A3

Lower Gunville 4 DT9 ..17 B1
Lower Hillside Rd
BH20 ....140 A1
Lower Kingsbury DT9 ..17 B2
Lower N Rd SP5 ......188 C5
Lower Odcombe BA22 ..26 A2
Lower Putton La DT3 ..166 B3
Lower Rd Britford SP5 ..213 C1
Stalbridge DT10 ....33 C4
Toller Porcorum DT2 ....71 C4
Lower Ream BA21 .....26 C3
Lower S Rd SP5 ......188 C4
Lower Sch 2 DT11 ....212 B1
Lower Sea La DT6 .....97 A4
Lower St Lillington DT9 .194 F7
Merriott TA16 ....191 F7
Morden BH21 ....83 B1
Okeford Fitzpaine DT11 ..197 F6
Salisbury SP2 ....213 A2
West Chinnock TA18 ...192 B8
Witchampton BH21 .....200 F1
Lower St Alban St 4
DT4 ....167 B1
Lower St Edmund St 5
DT4 ....167 B1
Lower Steppes BH19 ..178 B1
Lower Townsend TA16 .128 A4
Lower Turners Barn La
BA20 ....27 A1
Lower Walditch La
DT6 ....100 C3
Lower Way DT3 ....166 B3
Lower Wraxhill Rd
BA20 ....27 A1
Lowesmore Ct BH14 ..120 B2
Lowther Gdns 3 BH8 ..122 B3
Lowther Rd
Bournemouth BH8 .....122 A3
Yeovil BA21 ....28 A4
Lox La SP7 ....11 C2
Lubbecke Way DT1 ...108 B1
Lucas Rd BH15 ....119 A1
Lucerne Ave BH6 .....123 B3
Lucetta La DT1 ....135 A4
Luckham Cl BH9 ....90 A1
Luckham Gdns BH9 ....90 B1
Luckham Pl BH9 ....90 A1
Luckham Rd BH9 ......90 A1
Luckham Rd E BH9 ....90 A1
Ludbourne Rd DT9 .....30 B3
Ludlow Rd DT4 ....166 C1
Ludney La TA17 ......191 A7
Lufton Manor Coll
BA22 ....26 A4
Lufton Trad Est BA22 ..26 B4
Lufton Way BA22 ......26 B3
Lulworth Ave BH15 ...118 C1
Lulworth Castle★
BH20 ....158 B1
Lulworth Cl BH15 .....118 C1
Lulworth Cove Heritage Ctr★
BH20 ....172 B3
Lulworth Cres BH15 ...118 C1
Lulworth Rd BH20 ....140 A1
Lumber La BH21 ......201 C5
Lumby Dr BH24 ....55 B4
Lumby Dr Pk BH24 ....55 B4
Lurmer St SP7 ....37 C3
Luscombe Rd BH14 ...120 B1
Luther Rd BH9 ....121 C4
Luton Down Rd 3 DT11 .199 E2
Maitlands The DT2 ....121 B1
Major's Comm DT2 ...208 A7
Majorca Mans 11 BH2 ..121 C2
Malan Cl BH17 ....119 C4
Malcomb Cl BH6 .....124 A2
Mallams DT5 ....186 C4
Mallard Bldgs 6 BH25 ..95 A2
Mallard Cl
Bournemouth BH8 ....90 B1
Christchurch BH23 .....125 A3
Salisbury SP2 ....213 A2
Mallard Rd
Bournemouth BH8 ....90 B1
Wimborne Minster BH21 ..60 A4
Mallory Cl BH23 .....124 C4
Mallow Cl
Broadstone BH18 ....86 C2
Christchurch BH23 .....125 B4
Mallows The BH25 .....95 B2
Malmesbury Ct BH8 ...122 B3
Malmesbury Pk Pl 7
BH8 ....122 B3
Malmesbury Pk Prim Sch
BH8 ....122 A3
Malmesbury Pk Rd
BH8 ....122 A3
Malmesbury Rd BH24 ..54 A2
Malmesbury Way BA21 .26 C3
Maloren Way BH22 ....53 B1
Malta Cl 2 DT1 ......107 C1
Malthouse BH15 .....119 B1
Malthouse La
8 Salisbury SP2 ....213 B3
Trent DT9 ....14 C1
Malthouse Mdw 4 DT3 .150 A4
Maltings The
Bournemouth BH11 ......88 C3
Cerne Abbas DT2 ......207 D4
Poole BH15 ....119 C2
Salisbury SP2 ....213 B3
Weymouth DT4 ....167 B1
Malvern Cl BH9 ....90 A2
Malvern Ct
4 Bournemouth BH9 ....90 A1
2 Christchurch BH23 ...124 C4
7 Yeovil BA21 ....26 C3
Malvern Rd BH9 ....90 A1
Malvern Terr DT4 ....167 A1

Mampitts La SP7 ......13 A1
Mampitts Rd SP7 .....13 A1
Mandalay Cl BH31 ....45 A3
Mandale Cl BH11 ......89 C2
Mandale Rd BH11 .....88 C2
Mandeville Cl DT4 ....180 A4
Mandeville Rd DT4 ...180 A4
Mandeville Stoke La
DT6 ....66 A4
Mangerton La DT6 ....69 A2
Mangerton Water Mill★
DT6 ....69 B2
Mangle Cave Hill
TA18 ....191 C5
Manning Ave BH23 ....93 B1
Manning's Heath Rd
BH12 ....88 A1
Manningford Rd DT11 .212 B3
Mannings Heath Works
BH12 ....88 A1
Mannington Pl 19 BH2 .121 C2
Mannington Way BH22 .52 C1
Manor Ave
Lyme Regis DT7 ....96 A3
Poole BH12 ....88 B1
Manor Cl
Bradford Abbas DT9 ....28 B1
Dewlish DT2 ....209 A4
Ferndown BH22 ....61 C3
1 Portesham DT3 ......150 A4
South Perrott DT8 .....192 C1
Stratton DT2 ....106 C4
Templecombe BA8 ......18 A4
Manor Ct
Ringwood BH24 ....55 B4
Verwood BH31 ....45 A3
Manor Dr
Litton Cheney DT2 ....103 B1
New Milton BH25 ....94 C1
Manor Farm Cl DT2 ..133 C2
Manor Farm Rd
Bere Regis BH20 ....81 A3
Bournemouth BH10 .....89 A4
Manor Farmyard BH8 ..91 A2
Manor Fields DT6 ....100 C3
Manor Gdns
12 Beaminster DT8 ....204 D4
2 Ringwood BH24 .....55 A4
Verwood BH31 ....45 A3
Manor Gr DT2 ....133 B3
Manor La
Bradford Peverell DT2 ..106 C3
Verwood BH31 ....45 A3
Manor Pk BH15 ......119 A3
Manor Pk CE Fst Sch
DT1 ....135 A4
Manor Rd
Bournemouth BH1 .....122 B2
Christchurch BH23 ....124 A3
Dorchester DT1 ....135 A4
Gussage St Michael
BH21 ....200 F6
Mere BA12 ....2 C4
Milborne Port DT9 .....17 B2
New Milton BH25 ....95 A4
Radipole DT3 ....167 A4
Ringwood BH24 ....55 B4
Salisbury SP1 ....213 C3
Stourpaine DT11 ......198 F4
Studland BH19 ....164 B1
Swanage BH19 ....179 A1
Verwood BH31 ....45 A3
Yeovil BA21 ....27 B2
Manor St BA22 ....193 B8
Manor Vale 3 DT8 ....204 A8
Manor View TA18 .....191 F3
Manor Way BH31 .....45 A3
Mansard Ct BH13 ....147 A2
Manscombe Abbey★
DT6 ....66 A1
Mansel Cl BH12 ......121 B2
Mansfield Ave BH14 ...120 B2
Mansfield Cl
Ferndown BH22 ....61 C3
Poole BH14 ....120 B2
Mansfield Rd
Bournemouth BH9 ......89 C1
Poole BH14 ....120 B2
Ringwood BH24 ....55 A4
Manshay La DT6 ......203 A1
Manston Rd DT10 .....35 B1
Manton Cl BH15 .....118 C2
Manton Rd BH15 .....118 C2
Manwell Dr BH19 ....179 A1
Manwell Rd BH19 ....179 A1
Manwell's La 14 BH19 .179 A1
Maple Cl
Barton on Sea BH25 ...127 A4
Christchurch BH23 ....125 C4
4 Overcombe/Preston
DT3 ....168 A4
Sandford BH20 ....143 A4
Shaftesbury SP7 ....12 C2
Maple Dr
12 Crewkerne TA18 ....191 F5
Ferndown BH22 ....61 B4
Yeovil BA20 ....27 A4
Maple Gdns DT6 .....100 B3
Maple Lodge BH16 ...118 B4
Maple Rd
Bournemouth BH9 .....121 C4
Poole BH15 ....119 C2
Maple Way SP8 ....5 B1
Maplecroft 4 SP2 ....213 B1

Mapperton Cl BH17 ...87 C1
Mapperton Hill SP8 .....2 C1
Mapperton House★
DT8 ....204 F2
Mappowder Ct★ DT10 .208 F8
Marabout Cl DT3 ......69 A4
Marchwood Rd BH10 ...89 B2
Margards La BH31 .....45 A3
Margaret Pl DT1 .....107 C2
Marian Cl BH21 ....86 B2
Marian Rd BH21 ......86 B2
Marianne Rd
Poole BH12 ....121 B4
Wimborne Minster BH21 ..60 B1
Marie Cl BH12 ....120 B4
Marie Rd DT1 ....107 C2
Marina Ct
21 Bournemouth BH5 ..122 C2
Christchurch BH23 ....126 A4
Marina Dr BH14 .....120 A1
Marina Gdns DT4 ....167 A1
Marina Rd SP1 ......213 C2
Marina The BH5 .....122 C2
Marina Twrs 24 BH5 ..122 C2
Marina View 6 BH23 ..124 A3
Marine Cl BH25 .....126 B4
Marine Dr BH25 .....126 C4
Marine Dr E BH25 ...127 A3
Marine Dr W BH25 ...126 C4
Marine Par DT7 ......96 A2
Marine Rd BH6 ......123 B2
Mariners Ct BH23 ...125 A3
Mariners Dr BH19 ...179 A1
Mariners Way DT3 ...166 B3
Marion Ct BH23 .....124 A4
Mark's La BH25 ......95 A3
Market Cl BH15 .....119 B1
Market Pl
Blandford Forum DT11 .212 B2
Ringwood BH24 ....55 A4
Sturminster Newton DT10 .35 A1
Market St
Abbotsbury DT3 ....149 A4
Poole BH15 ....119 A1
Radipole DT4 ....167 B1
Yeovil BA20 ....27 B3
Market Way BH21 .....59 B2
Markets La DT6 .....101 C2
Markham Ave
Bournemouth BH10 .....89 B4
Weymouth DT4 ....167 A1
Markham Cl BH10 .....89 B3
Markham Rd BH9 ....122 A4
Marks Rd BH9 ....89 C2
Marl Cl BA21 ....27 A4
Marl La DT9 ....28 B3
Marlborough Ave DT4 .180 B4
Marlborough Ct
21 Bournemouth BH4 ..121 B2
2 Poole BH12 ....121 A2
3 Wimborne Minster BH21 59 B3
Marlborough Mans 2
BH7 ....123 A3
Marlborough Pl BH21 ..59 B3
Marlborough Rd
Bournemouth BH4 .....121 B2
Poole BH14 ....120 B2
Salisbury SP1 ....213 B3
Yeovil BA21 ....28 A3
Marler House BH4 ....121 A2
Marley Ave BH25 ....94 C2
Marley Cl
New Milton BH25 ......94 C2
Overcombe/Preston
DT3 ....153 B2
Marline Rd DT3 .....153 B2
Marlott Rd Gillingham SP8 .5 C4
Poole BH15 ....119 B3
Marlow Dr BH23 .....91 C2
Marlow Rd DT4 ......167 B1
Marlpit Dr BH25 .....94 A1
Marlpit La BH25 ......95 A4
Marmion Gn BH23 ...124 C4
Marnhull Rd
Hinton St Mary DT10 ...35 A3
Poole BH15 ....119 B3
Marpet Cl BH11 ......88 C3
Marquis Cl DT4 .....166 C1
Marquis Way BH11 ...88 B3
Marriage La DT10 ....35 A3
Marrowbone La DT6 ..100 C2
Marryat Ct
Christchurch BH23 ....126 A4
New Milton BH25 ....94 C2
Marryat Rd BH25 ....94 C2
Marsh Gate DT6 .....100 B2
Marsh La
Christchurch BH23 .....91 C1
Hazelbury Bryan DT10 ..196 F2
Henstridge BA8 ....19 B3
Ibberton DT11 ....197 D3
Pen Selwood BA9 ....1 A2
Salisbury SP2 ....213 A3
Upton BH16 ....118 A4
Wincanton BA9 ....8 C4
Winterborne Kingston
DT11 ....81 C4
Yeovil BA21 ....27 A4
Marsh Rd DT4 ......167 B1
Marsh The DT9 .....194 E3
Marsh Way
15 Pimperne DT11 ....199 D4
Swanage BH19 ....178 C1
Marshal Rd BH17 .....87 A1

Marshall Row 5 BH19 ..179 B1
Marshallsay Rd DT3 ..166 B3
Marshfield BH21 ....59 C4
Marshlands Cl BH23 ..124 B3
Marshwood Ave BH17 ..87 C2
Marshwood CE Prim Sch
DT6 ....202 F2
Marston Cl
Blandford Forum DT11 ..212 B3
New Milton BH25 ....95 A3
Marston Gr BH23 ......93 C1
Marston Rd
Castleton DT9 ....29 C4
New Milton BH25 ....95 A3
2 Poole BH15 ....119 A1
Sherborne DT9 ....30 A4
Martel Cl DT2 ....136 A1
Martello House 10
BH13 ....147 C4
Martello Pk BH13 ....147 C4
Martello Rd BH13 ....120 C1
Martello Rd S BH13 ..147 C4
Martello Twrs BH13 ..147 C4
Martells The BH25 ..127 A4
Martin Cl BH17 ......118 C4
Martin Dro End SP6 ..190 A7
Martin Kemp-Welch Sch The
BH12 ....120 B4
Martin's La SP8 ....5 A4
Martin's St SP7 ......12 C1
Martindale Ave BH21 ..60 A3
Martingale Cl BH16 ..118 B4
Martins Cl
Ferndown BH22 ....61 C4
3 Salisbury SP2 ......213 B1
Martins Dr BH22 ......61 C4
Martins Hill Cl BH23 ..92 B1
Martins Hill La BH23 ..92 B1
Martins Way BH22 ....61 C4
Martinscroft Rd 4 DT5 ..186 C2
Martleaves Cl 6 DT4 ..180 B4
Martyr DT1 ....134 C4
Marwell Cl BH7 ......123 C4
Mary Cossins Cl DT11 ..212 B3
Mary Gdns 4 DT11 ..197 F6
Mary La BH22 ....52 C1
Mary St BA21 ....27 B3
Maryland Rd BH16 ....118 B3
Maskew Cl DT3 ......166 B3
Mason's La DT8 ......204 A4
Masters Ct BH4 ......121 B2
Masterson Cl BH23 ..124 B4
Matchams Cl BH24 ....63 A4
Matchams La BH24 ....63 A2
Matlock Rd BH22 ......61 B2
Matthews Rd BA21 ....27 C3
Maud Rd DT1 ....107 C1
Maudlin Cross TA20 ..202 E8
Maudlin La TA20 ....202 F8
Maumbury Rd DT1 ..107 C1
Maumbury Rings★
DT1 ....135 A4
Maundeville Cres
BH23 ....123 B4
Maundville Rd BH23 ..123 C4
Maunsell Ave DT3 ..153 A2
Maureen Cl BH12 ....120 A4
Maurice Rd BH8 ......122 B4
Mavis Rd BH9 ....90 A1
Max Gate (NT)★ DT1 ..135 B4
Maxwell Rd
Bournemouth BH9 ......122 A4
Broadstone BH18 ....86 C2
Poole BH13 ....147 C4
May Gdns
Bournemouth BH11 ......88 C2
Christchurch BH23 ......94 A1
May Gr DT11 ....211 B4
May La DT11 ....199 D7
May Terr Gdns DT3 ..166 B3
Maycroft Rd DT4 ....167 B1
Mayfair BH4 ....121 B1
Mayfair Gdns BH11 ....89 A2
Mayfair Rd SP1 ......213 C3
Mayfield Ave BH14 ..120 C2
Mayfield Cl
Ferndown BH22 ....61 B3
Radipole DT4 ....167 A3
Mayfield Dr BH22 ......61 B3
Mayfield Rd
Bournemouth BH9 ......90 A1
Yeovil BA21 ....27 C3
Mayfield Way BH22 ....61 B3
Mayford Rd BH12 ....121 A3
Maylyn Rd BH16 ......85 A1
Mc Creery Rd DT9 ....30 A4
Mcintyre Rd BH23 ....91 A4
Mckay Way DT4 ......166 C1
Mckinley Rd BH4 ....121 B1
Mcwilliam Cl DT11 ..121 B4
Mcwilliam Rd 2 BH9 ..90 A1
Mead Ave BA22 ....26 B3
Mead Bower DT5 ....186 C1
Mead Cl BH18 ....87 A1
Mead La Allington DT4 ..100 A4
Gussage All Saints BH21 ..201 A5
Mead Rd
Corfe Castle BH20 ....177 A4
Radipole DT4 ....167 A3
Meadow Cl
Bransgore BH23 ....93 A4
Cattistock DT2 ....206 C2
Chickerell DT3 ....166 B3
Ferndown BH22 ....61 B1
Henstridge BA8 ....19 A3

Meadow Cl continued
Ringwood BH24 ....55 B4
Sopley BH23 ....92 A4
Stalbridge DT10 ....33 B4
Meadow Ct
6 Bournemouth BH9 ....90 A2
15 Wimborne Minster BH21 59 B2
Meadow Ct Cl BH9 ....90 A2
Meadow Farm La BH21 ..86 B4
Meadow Gr BH31 ......45 B3
Meadow La Burton BH23 ..92 B1
Wool BH20 ....140 A1
Meadow Rd (South) 10
SP2 ....213 A3
Meadow Rise
5 Charlton Marshall
DT11 ....211 D6
New Milton BH25 ....95 A4
Ringwood BH24 ....55 B4
8 Salisbury SP2 ......213 A3
Yeovil BA21 ....27 C4
Meadow Rise BH8 ......86 C3
Meadow View
7 Blandford Forum DT11 ..212 B2
Bradford Peverell DT2 ..107 A3
Cattistock DT2 ....206 B2
Charminster DT2 ......107 B3
7 Stofold BA22 ....193 F8
Meadow View Cl
BH20 ....142 C2
Meadow View Rd
Bournemouth BH11 ......88 C2
Radipole DT3 ....152 B2
Meadow Way
Barton on Sea BH25 ..127 A4
Charmouth DT6 ....97 A4
Ringwood BH24 ....55 B4
Verwood BH31 ....45 B2
Meadowbank BH16 ..118 B4
Meadowcroft SP8 ......11 A4
Meadowland BH23 ..124 C3
Meadowlands DT6 ..100 B1
Meadows Cl BH16 ..118 B4
Meadows Dr BH16 ..118 B4
Meadows The
Gillingham SP8 ....11 A4
Salisbury SP1 ....213 C2
Meadowside 4 DT8 ..204 A7
Meadowsweet Rd
BH17 ....118 C4
Meads Cl DT2 ....194 A2
Meads The DT9 ....17 B1
Meadus's La BH20 ..162 B2
Meadway DT4 ....100 A1
Meadway The BH23 ....93 B1
Medbourne Cl DT11 ..212 B3
Medina Way BH23 ..125 B3
Medlar Cl BH23 ....92 B1
Medway Dr DT3 ......168 A4
Medway Rd BH22 ......62 A3
Meech Cl DT6 ....100 B2
Meech Way DT6 ....75 C1
Meerhay La DT6 ....65 A2
Meerhay Manor★
DT8 ....204 D5
Meeting House La
BH24 ....55 A4
Melancholy La BH20 ..142 C1
Melboure Rd BH23 ....91 C1
Melbourne Rd BH8 ..122 B3
Melbourne St DT4 ..167 A2
Melbury Abbas Mill★
SP7 ....24 A3
Melbury Ave BH12 ..120 C4
Melbury Cl BH22 ......61 B2
Melbury Down★ SP5 ..24 C2
Melbury House★ DT2 ..194 A1
Melbury Pk★ DT2 ....194 A1
Melbury Rd
Weymouth DT4 ....167 B2
Yetminster DT9 ....194 C5
Melbury St SP7 ....24 B2
Melbury Way SP7 ......13 A2
Melchester Cl 11 SP8 ..5 C2
Melcombe Ave DT4 ..167 C3
Melcombe Pl 1 DT4 ..167 C2
Melford Ct BH1 ......122 A2
Mellstock Ave DT1 ..135 A4
Mellstock Cres BH20 ..142 B3
Mellstock Rd BH15 ..119 B3
Melplash Ct★ DT6 ..204 D1
Melrose Ave DT3 ....168 A4
Melrose Rd BA21 ......27 B3
Melstock Ave DT3 ..168 A4
Melton Ct BH13 ......120 C2
Melverley Gdns BH21 ..59 B3
Melville Rd BH9 ......121 C4
Melvin Cl SP1 ....213 C3
Melway Gdns 11 DT11 ..198 C7
Melway La DT11 ......198 C7
Memorial Ave 19 TA18 ..191 F4
Memorial Rd BA22 ....26 B3
Mendip Cl
New Milton BH25 ......95 B1
Verwood BH31 ....45 A3
Mendip Ct 4 BH23 ..124 C4
Mendip Rd BH31 ......45 A3
Menin Rd BH20 ......139 B3
Mentone Rd 2 BH14 ..120 C2
Meon Rd BH7 ....123 A4
Mercery Rd DT3 ....167 B4
Mere Castle★ BA12 ....2 C3
Mere Fst Sch BA12 ......3 A3
Meredith Cl
Christchurch BH23 ....124 B4
Halstock BA22 ....193 C3
Meriden Cl BH13 ....147 C4
Meridians The BH23 ..123 C3

Merino Way BH22 ....53 A1
Merlewood Cl BH2 ..121 C2
Merlewood Ct 19 BH25 ..95 A2
Merley Dr BH23 ......126 A4
Merley Fst Sch BH21 ..59 B1
Merley Gdns BH21 ....59 C1
Merley House BH21 ..59 A1
Merley House La BH21 ..59 B1
Merley House Mus★
BH21 ....59 A1
Merley La BH21 ....59 C1
Merley Pk Rd
Corfe Mullen BH21 ......86 C4
Wimborne Minster BH21 ..59 B1
Merley Rd DT4 ......180 B3
Merley Ways BH21 ....59 B1
Merlin Ave N DT3 ....152 A2
Merlin Ave S DT3 ....152 A2
Merlin Cl BH24 ....55 C3
Merlin Way BH23 ....125 A3
Mermaid Ct 22 BH5 ..122 C2
Mermond Pl BH19 ....179 B1
Merredin Cl DT3 ....152 B2
Merriefield Ave BH18 ..87 A3
Merriefield Cl BH18 ..87 A3
Merriefield Dr BH18 ..87 A3
Merrifield BH21 ......59 C4
Merriott Fst Sch TA16 ..191 F7
Merriott Rd
Hinton St George TA17 ..191 D7
Merriott TA18 ....191 F6
Merritown La BH23 ....90 B4
Merrivale Ave BH6 ..123 C3
Merrow Ave BH12 ..121 A4
Merrow Chase 1 BH13 ..147 C4
Merryfield Cl
Bransgore BH23 ....93 A4
Verwood BH31 ....45 A4
Merryfield Ct BH10 ..89 B2
Merryfield La BH10 ..89 B2
Merton Ct
8 Christchurch BH23 ..126 A4
3 Poole BH15 ....119 C2
Merville Gdns BH9 ..121 C4
Methuen Cl 2 BH8 ..122 B3
Methuen Dr 1 SP1 ..213 C2
Methuen Rd
Bournemouth BH8 ....122 A3
Poole BH17 ....87 A1
Mews The 1 BH2 ....121 B2
Meyrick Ave SP2 ....213 B1
Meyrick Cl BH23 ......93 A4
Meyrick Pk Cres BH3 ..121 C3
Meyrick Pk Mans 5
BH2 ....121 C2
Meyrick Rd BH1 ......122 A2
Michelgrove Rd BH6 ..122 C2
Michelmersh Gn BH8 ..90 B1
Mickleham Cl BH12 ..121 A4
Middle Brook BH11 ..89 A3
Middle Field La DT9 ..15 B3
Middle Gn 1 DT8 ....204 D4
Middle La Martin SP6 ..190 A7
Ringwood BH24 ....55 B4
Middle Path TA18 ..191 E4
Middle Rd
Bournemouth BH10 ......89 B3
Lytchett Matravers BH16 ..84 A1
New Milton SO41 ....95 C4
Poole BH15 ....119 C3
Sturminster Marshall
BH21 ....56 C3
Sway SO41 ....95 C4
Middle St Bridport DT6 ..69 A1
Burton Bradstock DT6 ..128 A4
Crewkerne TA18 ......192 A3
Dewlish DT2 ....209 C1
Rimpton BA22 ....15 A4
Salisbury SP2 ....213 A3
3 Yeovil BA20 ....27 C2
Middlebere Cres
BH16 ....118 B2
Middlebere Dr BH20 ..142 B3
Middlefield BH20 ....141 A2
Middlefield La TA13 ..191 F8
Middlehill Dr BH21 ....60 A3
Middlehill Rd BH21 ....60 A3
Middlemarsh St DT1 ..107 B1
Middleton Rd
Bournemouth BH9 ......89 C1
Ringwood BH24 ....55 B4
Salisbury SP2 ....213 A3
Midland Rd BH9 ......89 C1
Midleaze DT9 ....29 C3
Midney La SP8 ....4 A4
Midway Path BH13 ..147 B2
Midwood Ave BH8 ....90 C1
Milborne Cres BH12 ..120 C4
Milborne Port CP Sch
DT9 ....17 B2
Milborne St Andrew C Fst
Sch DT11 ....79 C4
Milbourne Rd BH22 ....61 B3
Milburn Cl 12 BH4 ..121 B2
Milburn La DT9 ......196 A7
Milburn Rd BH4 ......121 A2
Miles Ave BH20 ......142 C4
Miles Gdns DT3 ......152 A3
Milestone Rd BH15 ..119 B3
Milestone Way SP8 ....5 B1
Milford Cl BH22 ......53 A1
Milford Ct SP8 ....5 B1
Milford Cty Jun Sch
BA21 ....27 B4
Milford Dr BH11 ......88 C3
Milford Hill SP1 ......213 B3
Milford Hollow 6 SP1 ..213 C2
Milford Ind Est SP1 ..213 C2

Milford Manor Gdns
SP1 ....213 C2
Milford Mill Rd SP1 ..213 C2
Milford Pk SP1 ......213 C2
Milford Rd
Barton on Sea BH25 ..127 A4
Dorchester DT1 ....107 C1
Yeovil BA21 ....27 B3
Milford St SP1 ......213 B2
Military St DT10 ....197 A4
Mill Cl BA22 ....193 C8
Mill End SP6 ....190 F2
Mill Gn DT7 ....96 B3
Mill Hill Cl BH14 ....120 A2
Mill Hollow La SP7 ....24 C3
Mill House Cider Mus★
DT2 ....137 C2
Mill La Bourton SP8 ....1 C1
Bradford Abbas DT9 ....28 B1
Cann SP7 ....24 A3
Cattistock DT2 ....206 B2
Cerne Abbas DT2 ......207 D4
Charminster DT2 ......107 B4
Chetnole DT9 ....194 D2
Chideock DT6 ....99 A2
Christchurch BH23 ....126 A4
Cranborne BH21 ....40 B3
Crewkerne TA18 ......191 F3
Durweston DT11 ......198 E3
East Coker BA22 ......193 C7
Edmondsham BH21 ......40 C2
Halstock BA22 ....193 C3
Hawkchurch EX13 ....202 C3
Hurn BH23 ....91 A3
Ibberton DT11 ....197 D3
Kingstone TA17 ......191 B8
Lyme Regis DT7 ....96 A4
Lyme Regis DT7 ....96 B3
Marnhull DT10 ....20 C2
Mere BA12 ....3 A3
Misterton TA18 ....192 B3
Poole BH14 ....120 A2
Shapwick DT11 ....56 C3
Stour Provost SP8 ....21 B4
Stratton DT2 ....106 C4
Symondsbury DT6 ......99 C4
Trent DT9 ....14 C1
Wareham BH20 ....142 C2
West Coker BA22 ......193 B8
Wimborne Minster BH21 ..59 A3
Winterbourne Abbas
DT2 ....132 C4
Yeovil BH23 ....27 B2
Yetminster DT9 ......194 C5
Zeale SP8 ....1 C1
Mill Rd
Christchurch BH23 ....124 A4
Salisbury SP2 ....213 A2
Mill Rd N BH8 ....90 B2
Mill Rd S BH8 ....90 B1
Mill Rise SP8 ....1 C1
Mill St
Blandford Forum DT11 ..212 B2
Broadstone BH21 ......58 A1
Burton Bradstock DT6 ..128 A4
Corfe Mullen BH21 ......57 A1
Dorchester DT1 ......108 A1
Fontmell Magna SP7 ....37 C3
Puddletown DT2 ....78 A1
Radipole DT3 ....152 A2
Rimpton BA22 ....15 A4
Mill Stream App SP2 ..213 B3
Millbank House 5 BH21 ..59 B3
Millbrook
Salisbury SP1 ....213 C3
17 Yeovil BA20 ....27 B2
Millbrook Cl 2 DT11 ..198 C8
Millbrook Ct 3 DT11 ..198 C8
Milldown CE Fst Sch
DT11 ....212 B3
Milldown CE Mid Sch
DT11 ....212 A3
Milldown Rd DT11 ..212 A3
Millennium Way SP2 ..213 B1
Miller Cl BH25 ....95 B2
Miller Rd BH23 ......124 B4
Miller's Cl DT1 ......107 C2
Miller's Hill DT9 ......17 A3
Miller's La
Farnham DT11 ....200 D8
Sixpenny Handley DT11 ..188 D1
Millers Cl DT3 ......153 B2
Millfield
Beaminster DT8 ......204 D5
Broadstone BH17 ......119 A4
New Milton BH25 ......94 C2
Millhams Cl BH10 ....89 A3
Millhams Dr BH10 ....89 A3
Millhams Rd BH10 ....89 A3
Millhams St BH23 ....124 A3
Millhams St N BH23 ..124 A3
Mills Rd DT3 ....169 B4
Mills The BH12 ......120 C4
Millstream Cl
Broadstone BH17 ......119 A4
Wimborne Minster BH21 ..59 B2
Millyford Cl BH25 ..126 B4
Milne Rd BH17 ....87 A1
Milner Rd BH4 ......121 B1
Milom La
Athelhampton DT2 ....110 B4
Puddletown DT2 ....78 B1
Milton Abbas CE Prim Sch
DT11 ....209 F5
Milton Abbey Sch
DT11 ....209 E5
Milton Cl Poole BH14 ..120 B2

Milton Cl continued
Radipole DT4 ....167 B3
Yeovil BA21 ....26 C3
Milton Cres DT3 ....167 B3
Milton Ct BH22 ....61 B3
Milton Gr BH25 ....95 A1
Milton La DT11 ......198 D2
Milton Mead BH25 ....94 C3
Milton Rd
Bournemouth BH8 ....122 A4
Milborne St Andrew DT11 ..79 C4
Poole BH14 ....120 B2
Salisbury SP2 ....213 B1
Weymouth DT4 ....167 B2
Wimborne Minster BH21 ..59 B3
Milton Terr DT4 ....167 B3
Milton Villas BH8 ..122 A4
Milvers La DT6 ......101 A2
Milverton Cl BH23 ....93 C1
Mimosa Ave BH21 ....87 C4
Minerva Cl DT1 ......134 C4
Minstead Rd BH10 ....89 B2
Minster St 11 SP1 ..213 B3
Minster View BH21 ..59 B3
Minster Way BH16 ..118 A4
Minterne Gdns★ DT2 ..207 D6
Minterne Grange
BH14 ....147 B4
Minterne Rd
3 Bournemouth BH9 ..90 A1
Christchurch BH23 ....124 C3
Poole BH14 ....147 B4
Minton Mews BH2 ..121 C3
Mission Hall La DT3 ..153 B2
Mission Rd BH18 ......87 A1
Misterton Sch TA18 ..192 A2
Mistover Cl DT1 ....135 A4
Mistover Rd BH20 ..142 B3
Mitchell Cl BH25 ....127 A4
Mitchell Rd
Ferndown BH21 ....61 A4
Poole BH17 ....119 C4
Mitchell St 1 DT4 ..167 C1
Mitchelmore Rd BA21 ..27 B3
Mithras Cl DT1 ......134 C4
Miz Maze★ DT9 ......194 F3
Moat Ct BH4 ....121 B3
Moat La BH25 ....126 C4
Moats Cotts DT2 ....209 C1
Moberly Rd SP1 ....213 B4
Mockbeggar La BH24 ..47 B4
Modbury Village★
DT6 ....129 A4
Moffat Rd BH23 ....124 B4
Mohun Castle★ DT8 ..192 C1
Mohune Way DT3 ....166 B3
Mohuns Pk★ BA8 ....19 B4
Moigne Ct★ DT2 ....155 C4
Molyneux Rd BH25 ....95 B2
Mompesson House★
SP1 ....213 B2
Monaco Ct BH9 ......122 A4
Moneyfly Rd BH31 ....45 B3
Monkey World★
BH20 ....140 A3
Monks Cl BH22 ....62 A4
Monks Dale BA21 ....26 C4
Monks Way BH11 ....88 B3
Monkshood Cl BH23 ..93 A1
Monkton Cl BH22 ....61 B3
Monkton Cres BH12 ..120 C4
Monkton Down Rd 5
DT11 ....199 E2
Monkton Dro BH21 ..189 D1
Monkton Hill DT2 ..134 C3
Monkton Wyld Cross
DT6 ....64 A4
Monkton Wyld La DT6 ..64 B3
Monkwood La DT6 ..203 E2
Monkworthy Dr BH24 ..54 A3
Monmouth Ave DT3 ..167 B4
Monmouth Cl BH31 ..45 B2
Monmouth Dr BH31 ..45 B2
Monmouth Gdns DT8 ..204 C4
Monmouth Rd
Dorchester DT1 ......108 A1
Wareham BH20 ....142 B2
Yeovil BA21 ....27 C4
Monmouth St 5 DT7 ..96 B3
Monsal Ave BH22 ....61 B2
Montacute Sch BH17 ..87 B1
Montacute Way BH21 ..87 C4
Montagu Pk BH23 ..126 A4
Montagu Rd BH23 ..126 A4
Montague Rd BH5 ..123 A2
Monterey Dr SO41 ..95 C2
Montgomery Ave BH11 ..89 A2
Montgomery Gdns
SP2 ....213 A3
Montrose Cl
1 Easton/Weston DT5 ..186 C2
Verwood BH31 ....45 A3
Montrose Dr BH10 ....89 A1
Montrose Rd BA21 ....28 C4
Moonrakers BH13 ..147 C4
Moonrakers Way BH23 ..93 C1
Moor Rd
Broadwinsor DT8 ....203 B6
Buckhorn Weston SP8 ....4 B1
East Coker BA22 ......193 D7
Gillingham SP8 ....9 A4
Hardington Mandeville
BA22 ....193 A7
Sturminster Marshall
BH21 ....56 B2
Moor Rd
Broadstone BH18 ......87 A3

Moor Rd continued
Swanage BH19 . . . . 179 A3
Moor The DT2 . . . . 78 A1
Moor View Rd BH15 . . . . 119 C4
Moorcombe Dr DT3 . . . 153 A2
Moordown Ave DT3 . . . 167 C4
Moordown Cl BH9 . . . . . . 90 A2
Moordown St John's CE Prim Sch BH9 . . . . . . 89 C1
Moore Ave BH11 . . . . 89 A2
Moore Cl BH25 . . . . 94 C1
Moorfield Gr BH9 . . . . . . 89 C1
Moorfield Rd DT5 . . . . . 187 A2
Moorfields Rd BH13 . . . 147 C4
Moorhaven BH22 . . . . . . 61 B3
Moorhills 14 BH21 . . . . . 59 B2
Moorings Cl BH15 . . . . . 118 C1
Moorings The 7 BH23 . . 124 A3
Moorland Ave BH26 . . . 126 C4
Moorland Cres BH16 . . 118 A4
Moorland Gate BH4 . . . . 55 B3
Moorland Par BH16 . . . 118 A4
Moorland Rd BH1 . . . . . 122 B2
Moorland Way BH16 . . 118 A4
Moorlands Coll BH23 . . . 92 A3
Moorlands Rd
 Ferndown BH22 . . . . 53 A2
 Merriott TA18 . . . . 191 E6
 Verwood BH31 . . . . 45 A4
Moorlands Rise BH22 . . 53 A2
Moorlea 11 BH8 . . . . 122 A3
Moors Cl BH23 . . . . 91 A4
Moors Valley Ctry Pk★ BH24 . . . . 46 A1
Moorside Ave DT4 . . . . 167 C4
Moorside Cl BH11 . . . . . 89 A2
Moorside Rd
 Bournemouth BH11 . . . . . 89 A2
 Corfe Mullen BH21 . . . . . 86 B3
 Ferndown BH22 . . . . 53 A1
Moortown Dr BH21 . . . . . 88 A4
Moortown House BH24 . . 55 B3
Moortown La BH24 . . . . . 55 B2
Moorvale Rd BH9 . . . . . . 90 A1
Moorway La DT9 . . . . . . 15 C2
Morant Ct 14 BH25 . . . . . 95 A2
Morant Rd BH24 . . . . 47 B1
Moray Ct 14 BH22 . . . . . 59 A3
Morden Ave BH22 . . . . . 61 B2
Morden La BH20 . . . . . . 82 B2
Morden Rd
 Bournemouth BH9 . . . . . . 89 C1
 Sandford BH20 . . . . 142 C4
 Wareham St Martin BH20 . . . . 115 C2
Moreton Dr
 Moreton DT2 . . . . 138 C4
 Turners Puddle DT2 . . . . 112 A1
Moreton House★ DT2 . 138 C4
Moreton Pk★ DT2 . . . . 138 C3
Moreton Rd
 Bournemouth BH9 . . . . . . 90 A2
 Crossways DT2 . . . . 137 C3
Moreton Sta DT2 . . . . . 137 C4
Moreton's La BH20 . . . . 142 C2
Morgan's La SP5 . . . . . 189 E5
Moriconium Quay BH15 . . . . 118 B1
Morington Ct 8 BH8 . . . 122 A3
Morley Cl
 Bournemouth BH5 . . . . . 123 A3
 Burton BH23 . . . . 92 B2
Morley Rd BH5 . . . . 123 A3
Morley Way BH22 . . . . . 61 C2
Mornish Rd BH13 . . . . . 120 C1
Morris Rd Poole BH17 . . 119 B4
 Wool BH20 . . . . 139 C3
Morrison Ave BH12 . . . 120 C3
Morrison Rd BH19 . . . . 179 A1
Morston DT9 . . . . 194 D8
Mortain Cl DT11 . . . . . . 212 B3
Mortimer Cl BH23 . . . . . 125 A3
Mortimer Rd BH8 . . . . . . 90 A1
Mossley Ave BH12 . . . . . 89 A1
Mosterton Down La
 Misterton TA18 . . . . . . 191 F1
 Mosterton DT8 . . . . 192 A1
Motcombe CE Sch SP7 . 12 A4
Motcombe Grange Prep Sch SP7 . . . . 7 A1
Motcombe Rd
 Poole BH13 . . . . 121 A1
 Shaftesbury SP7 . . . . 12 C2
Mount Ave BH25 . . . . . . 95 A1
Mount Cl BH25 . . . . 95 A1
Mount Grace Dr BH14 . 147 B4
Mount Heatherbank 30 BH1 . . . . 121 C2
Mount Joy DT6 . . . . 100 B4
Mount La DT6 . . . . 99 C2
Mount Pleasant
 Bridport DT6 . . . . 100 B4
 Christchurch BH23 . . . . 125 A3
 East Lulworth BH20 . . . 158 C1
 Ringwood BH24 . . . . 55 B4
 Wareham Town BH20 . . . 142 C2
 Yeovil BA21 . . . . 27 C3
Mount Pleasant Ave N DT3 . . . . 167 A4
Mount Pleasant Ave S DT3 . . . . 167 B4
Mount Pleasant Dr BH8 . . . . 90 C1
Mount Pleasant La 3 BH19 . . . . 179 B1
Mount Pleasant Rd BH15 . . . . 119 B1

Mount Rd
 Bournemouth BH11 . . . . . 89 A2
 Poole BH14 . . . . 120 A3
Mount Scar BH19 . . . . . 179 A1
Mount Skippet Way DT2 . . . . 137 B3
Mount The
 8 Blandford Forum DT11 . 212 B2
 Ringwood BH24 . . . . 55 C4
Mountain Ash Rd 4 DT1 . . . . 107 C1
Mountbatten Cl
 Christchurch BH23 . . . . 125 A3
 Weymouth DT4 . . . . 180 A4
Mountbatten Ct BH25 . . 94 C2
Mountbatten Dr BH22 . . 61 B3
Mountbatten Gdns BH8 . 90 C1
Mountbatten Rd BH13 . 121 A1
Mounters Cl DT10 . . . . . 20 C1
Mountjoy Cl DT1 . . . . . . 59 C1
Mountjoy Sch DT6 . . . . 100 B2
Mower La DT11 . . . . 37 C1
Mowes La DT10 . . . . 34 C4
Mowleaze 1 BA22 . . . . 193 F8
Moynton Cl DT2 . . . . . . 137 B3
Muchelney Way BA22 . . 26 C4
Muddox Barrow La BH20 . . . . 81 A3
Muddyford La DT6 . . . . . 98 B4
Mude Gdns BH23 . . . . . 125 A3
Mudeford BH23 . . . . . . 125 A3
Mudeford Cty Inf Sch BH23 . . . . 124 C3
Mudeford Cty Jun Sch BH23 . . . . 124 C3
Mudeford Gn Cl BH23 . 124 C3
Mudeford La BH23 . . . . 124 C3
Mudford Rd BA21 . . . . . 27 B4
Mudros Rd DT11 . . . . . . 199 E3
Mulberry Ct
 4 Christchurch BH23 . . 124 A4
 Sixpenny Handley SP5 . . 189 B4
Mulberry Gdns
 16 Crewkerne TA18 . . . 191 F4
 Fordingbridge SP6 . . . . . 43 A4
Mullins Cl BH12 . . . . . . 121 B4
Munden's La DT9 . . . . . 31 A1
Munks Cl 3 SP2 . . . . . 213 A2
Munster Rd BH14 . . . . . 120 B2
Murley Rd BH9 . . . . 122 A4
Murray-Smith Dr BA22 . 26 B3
Musbury Cl DT4 . . . . 20 C2
Musbury La DT10 . . . . . 20 C2
Muscliffe La BH9 . . . . . . 90 A3
Muscliffe Prim Sch BH9 . 90 B2
Muscliffe Rd BH9 . . . . . . 89 C1
Museum of Childhood★ BH8 . . . . 122 C3
Museum of Electricity★ BH23 . . . . 124 A4
Museum of S Somerset★ BA20 . . . . 27 B2
Musgrave Pl 4 DT4 . . . 167 C2
Muston La DT11 . . . . 82 A4
Mustons La 4 SP7 . . . . 12 C2
Mutton St DT6 . . . . 203 A1
Myrtle Cl
 10 Beaminster DT8 . . . 204 C4
 Hordle SO41 . . . . 95 C2
Myrtle Rd BH8 . . . . 122 B3

N

Nada Rd BH23 . . . . 93 B1
Nag's La TA18 . . . . 191 B1
Nairn Ct BH3 . . . . 121 C4
Nairn Rd
 Bournemouth BH3 . . . . . 121 C3
 Poole BH13 . . . . 147 C4
Naish Holiday Village★ BH25 . . . . 126 B4
Naish Rd BH25 . . . . 126 C4
Nallers La DT2 . . . . 102 C3
Namu Rd BH9 . . . . 89 C1
Nansen Ave BH15 . . . . . 119 B3
Napier Cres SP1 . . . . . . 213 C3
Napier Rd BH15 . . . . . . 118 B2
Napiers Way DT11 . . . . 37 C2
Narrow La BH24 . . . . . . 47 C1
Naseby Rd BH9 . . . . 90 A1
Nash Ct★ DT10 . . . . . . 21 A2
Nash La
 Chillington TA17 . . . . . . 191 A6
 East Coker BA20 . . . . . . 193 C8
 Marnhull DT10 . . . . 21 A2
 Marshwood DT6 . . . . . . 202 E2
 Yeovil BA20 . . . . 26 C1
Nathan Cl BA21 . . . . 27 B4
Nathen Gdns BH15 . . . 118 B2
Nations Rd SP8 . . . . 10 A3
Navarac Ct BH14 . . . . . 120 B2
Nea Cl BH23 . . . . 125 B4
Nea Dr BH24 . . . . 46 C2
Nea Rd BH23 . . . . 125 C4
Neacroft Cl BH25 . . . . . 126 B4
Neal's La DT9 . . . . 194 D2
Neathem Rd BA21 . . . . . 27 C4
Neighbourhood Ctr BH17 . . . . 87 C1
Nelson Cl BH23 . . . . 94 C2
Nelson Ct 10 BH15 . . . . 119 B1
Nelson Dr BH23 . . . . . . 124 C1
Nelson Rd
 Bournemouth BH4 . . . . . 121 A2
 Salisbury SP2 . . . . 213 B3
 Tarrant Monkton DT11 . . 199 F3
Nether Abber Village (site of)★ BA22 . . . . 14 B4
Nether Mead 1 DT11 . . 197 F6
Netheravon Rd SP1 . . . 213 B3
Netherby La DT8 . . . . . 204 A3
Nethercoombe La DT9 . 30 A4
Netherhall Gdns BH4 . . 121 B2
Netherhay La DT8 . . . . 203 C8
Netherstoke La BA22 . . 193 C3
Netherton La BA22 . . . . 193 F6
Netherton Rd
 Weymouth DT4 . . . . 167 B1
 Yeovil BA21 . . . . 27 B3
Netherwood Pl BH21 . . . 59 A3
Netley 8 BA21 . . . . 26 C3
Netley Cl BH15 . . . . 120 A4
Netmead La DT11 . . . . 198 B8
Nettlebed Nursery SP7 . 12 C1
Nettlecombe SP7 . . . . . 13 A2
Nettleton Cl BH17 . . . . . 119 C4
Neville Cl SP1 . . . . 213 C4
New Barn Rd DT3 . . . . . 149 A4
New Bond St DT4 . . . . . 167 B2
New Borough Rd BH21 . 59 B2
New Bridge Rd SP1 . . . 213 B3
New Canal SP1 . . . . 213 B2
New Cl Bourton SP8 . . . . . 1 C1
 Haselbury Plucknett TA18 . . . . 192 B5
New Cl Gdns DT4 . . . . . 167 B1
New Cotts BH21 . . . . 60 C1
New Cross Gate DT11 . 198 A7
New Cut BA12 . . . . 3 A3
New Field La DT11 . . . . 198 D8
New Fields Bsns Pk BH17 . . . . 119 B4
New Gd DT5 . . . . 187 A4
New Harbour Rd BH15 . . . . 119 A1
New Harbour Rd S BH15 . . . . 146 A4
New Harbour Rd W BH15 . . . . 119 A1
New Harnham Rd SP2 . 213 B1
New Inn La DT6 . . . . . . 204 C2
New La Cann SP7 . . . . . 13 A1
 Caundle Marsh DT9 . . . . 195 E8
 Haselbury Plucknett TA18 . . . . 192 C6
 Morden BH20 . . . . 83 B2
 Motcombe SP7 . . . . 12 A4
 New Milton BH25 . . . . . 94 C3
 Stour Provost SP8 . . . . . 11 A3
New Line DT10 . . . . 161 B2
New Merrifield BH21 . . . 59 C4
New Milton Inf Sch BH25 . . . . 95 A1
New Milton Jun Sch BH25 . . . . 95 A1
New Milton Sta BH25 . . 95 A2
New Orch BH15 . . . . . . 119 A1
New Par BH10 . . . . 89 C2
New Pk Rd BH6 . . . . . . 123 B2
New Quay Rd BH15 . . . 119 A1
New Rd Arne BH20 . . . . 143 A1
 Bournemouth BH10 . . . . . 89 C3
 Bovington Camp BH20 . . 139 B4
 Bryanston DT11 . . . . . . 212 A2
 Brympton BA22 . . . . 26 B3
 Castleton DT9 . . . . 30 A2
 Corfe Castle BH20 . . . . 162 C1
 Ellingham Harbridge & Ibsley BH24 . . . . 47 B3
 Ferndown BH22 . . . . 61 C2
 Gillingham SP8 . . . . 6 A1
 Haselbury Plucknett TA18 . . . . 192 C5
 Hinton St George TA17 . . 191 C7
 Loders DT6 . . . . 101 C4
 Lytchett Minster & Upton BH16 . . . . 116 C4
 Odcombe BA22 . . . . 26 A3
 Poole BH12 . . . . 120 B3
 Portesham DT3 . . . . 150 A4
 Portland DT5 . . . . 186 C3
 Radipole DT4 . . . . 167 B2
 Shaftesbury SP7 . . . . 12 B2
 Shapwick DT11 . . . . 48 B1
 Stalbridge DT10 . . . . 33 B4
 Stoborough Green BH20 . 160 C4
 Stofold BA22 . . . . 193 F8
 Sturminster Newton DT10 . 197 D7
 West Crewkerne TA18 . . 191 B4
 Weymouth DT4 . . . . 167 B1
 Winsham TA20 . . . . 202 C8
 Winterborne Stickland DT11 . . . . 198 B1
 Woodlands BH21 . . . . . . 44 B4
 Wool BH20 . . . . 139 C1
 Zeale SP8 . . . . 2 A2
New St
 9 Dorchester DT1 . . . . 108 A1
 Easton/Weston DT5 . . . 187 A2
 Marnhull DT10 . . . . 20 C1
 North Perrott TA18 . . . . 192 C4
 9 Poole BH15 . . . . 119 A1
 Puddletown DT2 . . . . 78 A1
 Radipole DT4 . . . . 167 C1
 Ringwood BH24 . . . . 55 B3
 Salisbury SP1 . . . . 213 B2
 Wareham BH20 . . . . 142 C2
New St La Loders DT6 . . . 69 B1
 Symondsbury SP6 . . . . . 99 C3
Newberry Gdns 8 DT4 . 167 C1
Newberry Rd DT4 . . . . . 167 B1
Newbery La TA18 . . . . . 192 A3
Newbury SP8 . . . . 6 A1
Newbury Dr BH10 . . . . . 89 B1

Newchester Cross TA16 . . . . 191 E7
Newcombe La DT2 . . . . 108 C2
Newcombe Rd
 Bournemouth BH6 . . . . . 123 C3
 Ferndown BH22 . . . . 53 A2
Newcroft Gdns BH23 . . 124 A4
Newell DT9 . . . . 30 A3
Newell House Sch DT9 . 30 A3
Newfield Rd DT11 . . . . . 199 D5
Newfoundland Cl BH19 . . . . 183 B4
Newfoundland Dr BH15 . . . . 119 B1
Newhaven DT2 . . . . 105 C1
Newland DT9 . . . . 30 B3
Newland La DT9 . . . . . . 195 F3
Newlands
 Bournemouth BH7 . . . . . 123 A3
 Christchurch BH23 . . . . 124 C4
 New Milton BH25 . . . . . 95 A1
Newlands Way BH18 . . . 86 B2
Newlyn Way BH12 . . . . 120 C4
Newman Cl 3 DT11 . . . 212 C3
Newman's La BA22 . . . . 52 C3
Newmans Cl BH22 . . . . . 53 A2
Newmorton Rd BH9 . . . . 90 A2
Newport Cl BH20 . . . . . . 82 B1
Newstead Rd
 Bournemouth BH6 . . . . . 123 B2
 Weymouth DT4 . . . . 167 B2
Newton Cl Gillingham SP8 . 5 C1
 Sturminster Newton DT10 . . . . 197 D8
Newton Hill DT10 . . . . . 197 D8
Newton Manor Cl 2 BH19 . . . . 179 A1
Newton Morrell BH14 . . 120 B2
Newton Rd
 Barton on Sea BH25 . . . 127 A4
 Barwick BA22 . . . . 27 C2
 Maiden Newton DT2 . . . . 73 A4
 Poole BH14 . . . . 147 C4
 Stofold BA22 . . . . 193 F8
Newton Rise 4 BH19 . . 179 A1
Newton Surmaville★ BA20 . . . . 27 C2
Newton's Rd DT4 . . . . . 167 C1
Newtown DT8 . . . . 204 C4
Newtown Bsns Ctr BH12 . . . . 120 A4
Newtown Hill BH20 . . . . 157 C2
Newtown La
 Corfe Mullen BH21 . . . . . 86 B4
 Ellingham Harbridge & Ibsley BH24 . . . . 43 C1
 Verwood BH31 . . . . 45 B3
Newtown Rd BH31 . . . . . 45 B3
Nicholas Cl BH23 . . . . . 94 A1
Nicholas Gdns BH10 . . . 89 B1
Nichole Ct BH12 . . . . . . 120 A4
Nicholson Cl BH17 . . . . 119 C4
Nightingale Cl BH31 . . . 45 B3
Nightingale Dr DT3 . . . . 152 B2
Nightingale La 4 BH15 . 119 B1
Nightjar Cl BH17 . . . . . . 118 C4
Nimrod Way BH21 . . . . . 60 C3
Nine Stones (Stone Circle)★ DT2 . . . . 105 B1
Noade St SP5 . . . . 25 B1
Noah Henville Cnr 4 DT11 . . . . 81 C4
Noake Rd DT9 . . . . 29 C3
Noble Cl BH11 . . . . 88 C1
Noel Rd BH10 . . . . 89 A1
Noel The BH25 . . . . 95 B2
Nonesuch Cl 3 DT1 . . . 135 A4
Noon Gdns BH31 . . . . . . 45 B3
Noon Hill Dr BH31 . . . . . 45 B3
Noon Hill Rd BH31 . . . . . 45 B3
Norburton DT6 . . . . 128 A4
Norcliffe Cl BH10 . . . . . . 89 A2
Norden Dr BH20 . . . . . . 142 B3
Norden La DT2 . . . . 72 C4
Norden Sta BH20 . . . . . 161 C1
Nordon Rd DT11 . . . . . . 212 B3
Nordons DT6 . . . . 100 C3
Norfolk Ave BH23 . . . . . 91 C4
Norfolk Rd
 Salisbury SP2 . . . . 213 A2
 Weymouth DT4 . . . . 167 A2
Norleywood BH23 . . . . . 125 C4
Norman Ave BH12 . . . . 121 A3
Norman Cl DT6 . . . . 100 C4
Norman Gdns BH12 . . . 121 A3
Normandy Dr BH23 . . . 124 B4
Normandy Way
 Dorchester DT1 . . . . . . 107 C1
 Hamworthy BH15 . . . . . 118 B1
Normanhurst Ave BH8 . . 90 C1
Normanton Cl BH21 . . . . 91 C1
Norris Cl DT4 . . . . 54 A2
Norris Gdns BH25 . . . . . 95 A1
Norrish Rd BH12 . . . . . . 120 B3
North Allington DT6 . . . 100 B4
North Ave
 Bournemouth BH10 . . . . . 89 B3
 Lyme Regis DT7 . . . . 96 A3
North Bestwall Rd BH20 . . . . 142 C2
North Bowood La DT6 . 203 F2
North Bridge★ BH20 . . 142 B2

North Cres DT9 . . . . 17 B2
North Cswy DT9 . . . . . . 17 C3
North Dorset Leisure Ctr SP8 . . . . 6 A1
North End DT9 . . . . 194 F3
North End La SP6 . . . . . 42 C2
North Gr DT11 . . . . 199 E3
North Hill Cl DT6 . . . . . 128 A4
North Hill Way DT6 . . . 100 B2
North La
 Hardington Mandeville BA22 . . . . 193 A7
 Yeovil BA20 . . . . 27 B3
North Lodge Rd BH14 . 120 C2
North Mills Rd DT6 . . . 100 B4
North Perrott Rd TA18 . . . . 192 C5
North Pk DT2 . . . . 73 C2
North Pl DT11 . . . . 212 B2
North Poulner Rd BH24 . 47 B1
North Quay DT4 . . . . . . 167 B1
North Rd Ashmore SP5 . . 25 B1
 Bournemouth BH7 . . . . . 122 C3
 Chideock DT6 . . . . 99 A4
 Mere BA12 . . . . 3 A3
 Poole BH14 . . . . 120 A2
 Sherborne DT9 . . . . 30 B4
 Weymouth DT4 . . . . 180 A4
North Rew La DT2 . . . . 106 A1
North Sq Chickerell DT3 . 166 B3
 2 Dorchester DT1 . . . . 108 A1
North St
 Beaminster DT8 . . . . . . 204 D4
 Bere Regis BH20 . . . . . . 81 A1
 Bradford Abbas DT9 . . . . 28 B1
 Bridport DT6 . . . . 100 B4
 Charminster DT2 . . . . . . 75 B1
 Crewkerne TA18 . . . . . . 191 F5
 Fontmell Magna SP7 . . . . 37 C4
 Haselbury Plucknett TA18 . . . . 192 C6
 Langton Matravers BH19 . . . . 178 A1
 Mere BA12 . . . . 3 A3
 Milborne Port DT9 . . . . . 17 B1
 Poole BH19 . . . . 119 B1
 Salisbury SP2 . . . . 213 A3
 Wareham BH20 . . . . 142 C2
 Winterborne Kingston DT11 . . . . 81 C4
 Winterborne Stickland DT11 . . . . 210 C7
North Terr BA21 . . . . 27 C3
North Walls BH20 . . . . . 142 C2
North Wlk SP1 . . . . 213 B2
Northay La EX13 . . . . . 202 C3
Northbourne Ave BH10 . 89 B3
Northbourne Gdns BH10 . . . . 89 C3
Northbourne Pl 3 BH10 . 89 B3
Northbrook Rd
 Broadstone BH18 . . . . . . 87 A1
 Swanage BH19 . . . . 179 A1
 Yeovil BA21 . . . . 27 C4
Northcote Rd BH1 . . . . 122 A2
Northernhay 1 DT1 . . . 108 A1
Northey Rd BH6 . . . . . . 123 C3
Northfield La TA17 . . . . 191 B8
Northfield Rd BH24 . . . . 47 B1
Northleigh La BH21 . . . . 59 C3
Northmead Dr BH17 . . . 118 C4
Northmere Dr BH12 . . . 120 C4
Northmere Rd BH12 . . . 120 C4
Northmoor Way BH20 . 142 B3
Northover BH3 . . . . 121 C3
Northover Cl
 Burton Bradstock DT6 . . 128 B4
 Piddletrenthide DT2 . . . 208 B2
Northover La SO41 . . . . 95 C4
Northport Dr BH20 . . . . 142 C4
Northtoft Rd BH8 . . . . . 122 A3
Norton Cl BH23 . . . . . . 124 B4
Norton La
 Durweston DT11 . . . . . . 198 D3
 Netherbury DT6 . . . . . . 204 C2
Norton Rd BH9 . . . . 121 C4
Norway Cl 3 BH9 . . . . . 89 C1
Norway La DT8 . . . . 203 F4
Norwich Ave BH2 . . . . . 121 B2
Norwich Ave W BH2 . . . 121 B2
Norwich Ct 12 BH2 . . . 121 B2
Norwich Mans 4 BH2 . . 121 B2
Norwich Rd
 Bournemouth BH2 . . . . . 121 C2
 Weymouth DT4 . . . . 167 B1
Norwood Pl BH5 . . . . . . 123 A3
Nothe Fort★ DT4 . . . . . 167 C1
Nothe Par DT4 . . . . 167 C1
Nottington La
 Chickerell DT3 . . . . 151 B1
 Radipole DT3 . . . . 152 A1
Nouale La BA20 . . . . 55 C4
Noyce Gdns BH8 . . . . . . 91 A1
Nuffield Hospl BH15 . . . 122 C2
Nuffield Ind Est BH17 . . 119 B4
Nuffield Rd BH17 . . . . . 119 B4
Nugent Rd BH6 . . . . 124 C3
Nundico BH20 . . . . 142 C2
Nursery Gdns
 Bridport DT6 . . . . 100 C4
 Mere BA12 . . . . 3 A3
Nursery Rd
 Blandford Forum DT11 . . 212 B2
 Bournemouth BH9 . . . . . . 90 A2
 Ringwood BH24 . . . . 55 B3

Nursery Rd continued
Salisbury SP2 ....213 A3
Yeovil BA20 ....27 B2
Nursling Gn BH8 ......90 B1
Nutcombe Cl DT6 .....97 A4
Nutcrack La BH20 ....142 C1
Nutgrove Ave DT4 ...166 C1
Nuthatch Cl
Broadstone BH17 .....118 C4
Ferndown BH22 ....61 A4
Radipole DT3 ....152 B2
Nutley Cl BH11 ......88 C2
Nutley Way BH11 .....88 C2
Nutmead Cl 4 DT11 ...198 C8
Nyland La SP8 ....8 B1

O

Oak Ave
Christchurch BH23 ....123 B4
Holton Heath BH20 ...116 A2
Oak Cl Corfe Mullen BH21 .86 B3
Ferndown BH22 ....61 C1
Oak La Corscombe DT2 ..205 C6
Ringwood BH24 ....55 B4
Oak Mews BH12 ......120 B3
Oak Rd Alderholt SP6 ...42 A3
Bournemouth BH8 ....122 B3
New Milton BH25 .....95 B2
Upton BH16 ....118 B3
Oak Vale La BA8 ......19 A2
Oakbury Dr DT3 ......168 A4
Oakdale Rd BH15 .....119 C3
Oakdale S Rd Mid Sch
BH15 ....119 B3
Oakdene Cl BH21 .....59 B3
Oakdene Rd BH20 ....139 C1
Oakfield Rd BH15 .....119 B3
Oakfield St DT11 .....212 B2
Oakford Ct BH8 ......90 B2
Oakham Grange BH22 ..61 C3
Oakhurst Cl BH22 ....53 A1
Oakhurst La BH22 ....53 A1
Oakhurst Rd BH22 ....53 A1
Oakland Wlk BH21 ....61 C1
Oaklands Cl BH31 ....45 A3
Oaklands La BA21 ....27 C4
Oakleigh 4 BA20 .....26 C1
Oakleigh Way BH23 ...125 C4
Oakley Gdns BH16 ....118 A4
Oakley Hill BH21 .....59 B1
Oakley La
Farnham DT11 ....188 D2
Oakley BH21 ....59 C1
Oakley Pl DT4 ....167 B1
Oakley Rd BH21 .....59 B1
Oakley Straight BH21 .59 C1
Oakmead Coll of Tech
BH11 ....88 C2
Oakmead Gdns BH11 ..88 C2
Oakmead Rd BH17 ....118 C4
Oaks Dr BH24 ....53 C2
Oaks Mead BH31 .....45 A3
Oaks The Gillingham SP8 ..5 C1
Verwood BH31 ....45 A4
Oaktree Cl BH20 .....142 C1
Oakwood
Bournemouth BH3 ....121 C4
West Knighton DT2 ...136 B2
Oakwood Ave BH25 ...95 B2
Oakwood Cl BH9 .....90 A1
Oakwood Ct BH25 ....95 A2
Oakwood Dr 5 DT11 ..37 C1
Oakwood Rd
Bournemouth BH9 ....90 A1
Christchurch BH23 ....93 C1
Oasis Mews BH16 ....118 A4
Oasis The 12 BH12 ...121 A2
Oates Rd BH9 ....89 C1
Oathill La
Broadwinsor TA18 ....203 A7
West Crewkerne TA18 .191 B1
Oban Rd BH3 ....121 C4
Oborne Rd DT9 ......30 B4
Ocean Hts 28 BH5 ....122 C2
Octagon Theatre ★
BA20 ....27 B2
Odcombe Hollow
BA22 ....192 E8
Odstock Rd SP2 .....213 B1
OK Mobile Home Pk
BH23 ....125 A4
Okeford Fitzpaine CE Prim
Sch DT11 ....197 F5
Okeford Rd BH18 .....87 B2
Old Bakery Cl 4 DT11 .199 D3
Old Bakery The DT8 ..203 E5
Old Barn Cl
Christchurch BH23 ....91 B1
Ringwood BH24 ......55 B4
Old Barn Farm Rd
BH21 ....53 B3
Old Barn Rd
Bere Regis BH20 .....81 A1
Christchurch BH23 ....91 B1
Old Barn Way BA20 ...27 A1
Old Bincombe La DT3 .153 B2
Old Blandford Rd SP2 .213 A1
Old Bound Rd BH16 ...118 B3
Old Boundary Rd SP7 .12 C1
Old Bowden Way DT9 .17 B2
Old Brickfields DT2 ..136 B2
Old Bridge Rd BH6 ...123 B4
Old Cann Sch SP7 ....13 C1

Old Castle Rd DT4 ...180 C4
Old Chalk Pit BH20 ...81 A1
Old Chapel Dr BH25 ..84 B2
Old Christchurch La 35
BH1 ....121 C2
Old Christchurch Rd
BH1 ....121 C2
Old Church Rd DT6 ...100 C2
Old Church Sch DT8 ..204 D4
Old Coastguard Rd
BH13 ....147 A2
Old Ct Mews BH14 ...120 A2
Old Depot Rd DT5 ....181 B1
Old Farm Cl BH24 ....47 C1
Old Farm Gdns DT11 .212 B3
Old Farm Rd BH15 ...119 C3
Old Farm Way DT2 ...137 B3
Old Forge Cl BH16 ...116 C3
Old Forge Rd BH21 ...60 C3
Old Furzebrook Rd
BH20 ....160 C4
Old Generator House The
BH12 ....121 A3
Old Granary Cl DT3 ..153 B2
Old Ham La BH21 ....60 B2
Old Highway Mews
BH21 ....59 B2
Old Hitchen 4 TA16 ..191 F7
Old Hollow BA12 .....3 A3
Old Kiln Rd
Ridge BH20 ....143 A1
Upton BH16 ....118 B3
Old Lifeboat House (Mus) ★
BH15 ....119 B1
Old Lyme Hill DT6 ...96 C4
Old Lyme Rd DT6 ....96 C4
Old Manor Cl BH21 ..59 B2
Old Manor Hospl SP2 .213 A3
Old Mdws Wlk SP2 ...213 A2
Old Mill La DT10 ....21 A2
Old Mills DT2 ....71 C4
Old Milton Gn BH25 ..94 C1
Old Milton Rd BH25 ..95 A1
Old Mkt Rd BH21 ....85 A4
Old Mulberry Cl BH10 .89 A1
Old Oak Way DT11 ...210 C3
Old Orch BH15 ......119 B1
Old Orch Cl DT10 ....196 F8
Old Parish La DT4 ...167 A2
Old Pines Cl BH22 ...61 C2
Old Pound Cl BH16 ..84 B2
Old Pound Ct SP8 ...1 B1
Old Priory Rd BH6 ...123 C2
Old Rd Odcombe BA22 ..26 A2
Wimborne Minster BH21 .59 A3
Old Rd The DT9 .....18 A1
Old Rectory Cl
4 Charmouth DT6 ....97 A4
Corfe Mullen BH21 ...86 B4
Old Rectory La DT9 ..195 E3
Old Rope Wlk The
BH15 ....118 C1
Old Ropewalk BH15 ..119 A1
Old Sandpit La BH16 ..86 A1
Old Sawmill Cl BH31 ..45 A4
Old Sch Cl
Ferndown BH22 ......61 B3
Folke DT9 ....31 A1
Poole BH14 ....120 A2
Old Sch La
Hinton St Mary DT10 .35 A3
Iwerne Minster DT11 ..37 C1
Old Sch The DT2 ....72 C4
Old St Salisbury SP2 .213 B1
Sturminster Marshall
BH21 ....56 C2
Old St John's Mews
BH9 ....89 C2
Old Sta Gdns BA8 ...19 A3
Old Sta Rd
Radipole DT3 ....152 A2
4 Yeovil BA20 ....27 C2
Old Stacks Gdns 1 BH24 55 C3
Old Town Mews 5
BH15 ....119 B1
Old Vicarage Cl BH10 .89 C3
Old Vicarage Gdn DT7 .96 A3
Old Wareham Rd
Corfe Mullen BH21 ...86 A2
Poole BH12 ....120 A4
Olga Rd DT1 ....107 C1
Olivers Mead 1 DT11 .198 C8
Olivers Rd BH21 .....60 A3
Olivers Way BH21 ...60 A3
Onslow Gdns BH21 ..59 B3
Onslow House BH21 ..59 B3
Ophir Gdns 1 BH8 ...122 B3
Ophir Rd BH8 ....122 A3
Oratory Gdns BH13 ..147 C4
Orchard Ave
Bridport DT6 ....100 B4
Poole BH14 ....119 C1
Orchard Chase 2 DT11 .199 F7
Orchard Cl
3 Charmouth DT6 ....97 A4
Cheselbourne DT2 ...209 A3
Christchurch BH23 ...124 A3
Corfe Mullen BH21 ...86 B4
Ferndown BH22 ......61 C3
Fontmell Magna SP7 ..37 C3
Lytchett Minster & Upton
BH16 ....116 C3
3 Okeford Fitzpaine DT11 197 F6
Ringwood BH24 ......55 B4
4 Stourpaine DT11 ..198 F4
Sturminster Newton
DT10 ....197 C8
Sydling St Nicholas DT2 .207 A3

Orchard Cl continued
4 West Coker BA22 ..193 A8
Orchard Cres DT6 ...100 B4
Orchard Ct
10 New Milton BH25 ..95 A2
Verwood BH31 ....45 B3
Orchard Dr DT3 .....168 A4
Orchard Gr BH25 ....95 A1
Orchard La
Corfe Mullen BH21 ...86 B4
2 Crewkerne TA18 ...191 F4
Thorncombe TA20 ...202 E6
7 Winterborne Kingston
DT11 ....81 C4
Orchard Leigh 6 BH25 .95 A1
Orchard Mead DT8 ...203 E5
Orchard Mews
2 Christchurch BH23 .124 A3
7 Gillingham SP8 ....5 B1
Orchard Rd
Gillingham SP8 ......5 C1
Milborne Port DT9 ...17 B1
Orchard Rise
7 Crewkerne TA18 ...191 F4
Milborne St Andrew DT11 .79 C4
Orchard St
Blandford Forum DT11 .212 B2
Bournemouth BH2 ...121 C2
Dorchester DT1 ......108 A1
Yeovil BA20 ....27 A2
Orchard The
Blandford Forum DT11 .212 B3
Bournemouth BH11 ..88 B3
Bransgore BH23 .....93 B4
Hazelbury Bryan DT10 .196 F3
Radipole DT3 ....152 A2
Sixpenny Handley SP5 .189 B4
Winfrith Newburgh DT2 .156 C3
Orchard Way
Misterton TA18 ......192 A2
2 Mosterton DT8 ....204 A8
Orchard Wlk
22 Bournemouth BH2 .121 C2
Milborne Port DT9 ...17 B1
Orchardleigh BA22 ...192 E8
Orcheston Rd BH8 ...122 B3
Orchid Way DT1 .....124 B4
Orestes Gate BH23 ..125 A3
Orford Cl BH23 ......91 B2
Orford St DT2 ....78 A1
Organford Rd BH16 ..116 B2
Orion Rd DT4 ....167 B1
Ormonde Rd BH13 ...121 A1
Osborne Rd
Bournemouth BH9 ...121 C4
New Milton BH25 ....95 A2
Poole BH14 ....120 A2
Swanage BH19 ......179 A1
Wimborne Minster BH21 .59 B2
Yeovil BA20 ....27 B3
Osbourne House 4
BH25 ....95 A2
Osbourne Rd DT6 ...100 B4
Osmay Rd BH19 .....185 B4
Osmington Dro DT2 ..136 A1
Osmington White Horse ★
DT3 ....153 C2
Osprey Cl BH23 .....125 A3
Osprey Dr DT4 ......180 B3
Ossemsley Manor House
BH23 ....94 B3
Ossemsley S Dr BH25 .94 C4
Oswald Cl BH9 ......89 C1
Oswald Rd BH9 .....89 C1
Otter Cl Upton BH16 .118 A3
Verwood BH31 ......45 B3
Otter Rd BH15 ......119 C3
Otters Wlk BH25 ....95 B3
Ottery La DT9 ......30 A3
Oval Gdn DT20 .....160 C4
Oval The BH20 ......172 C4
Over Links Dr BH14 ..120 B1
Overbury Cl DT4 ....166 C1
Overbury Rd BH14 ..120 B2
Overcliffe Mans BH1 .122 B2
Overcombe BA8 .....18 B4
Overcombe Cl BH17 ..87 C1
Overcombe Dr DT3 ..168 A4
Overlands Rd DT4 ...180 A4
Overton Cl DT7 .....96 B4
Ovington Ave BH7 ...123 B4
Ovington Gdns BH7 ..123 B4
Owermoigne CE Prim Sch
DT2 ....155 B4
Owl Sanctuary ★ BH24 .55 C3
Owls Rd
Bournemouth BH5 ...122 C2
Verwood BH31 ......45 B3
Owlshotts BH13 .....147 C4
Owlswood 10 SP2 ...213 B1
Ox Dro
Berwick St John SP5 ..188 B7
Bower Chalke SP5 ...189 A8
Oxen Rd 5 TA18 .....191 F4
Oxencroft 12 SP7 ....12 C2
Oxey Cl BH25 ....95 A1
Oxford Ave BH6 .....123 A3
Oxford La BH11 .....89 A3
Oxford Rd
Bournemouth BH1 ...122 A2
Yeovil BA21 ....28 A4
Oxhayes DT8 ....203 C8
Ozone Terr DT7 .....96 A2

P

Paceycombe Way DT1 .107 B1

Packers' Way 1 TA18 .192 B3
Paddington Cl BH11 ..88 B2
Paddington Gr BH11 ..88 B2
Paddock Cl
Ferndown BH21 .....61 A3
Lytchett Matravers BH16 .84 B2
Shaftesbury SP7 ....13 A1
Sixpenny Handley SP5 .189 A3
St.Leonards BH24 ...54 A2
Paddock Gr BH31 ....45 B3
Paddock The DT2 ....136 A4
Paddock Wlk DT9 ...17 B1
Paddock's Cross DT6 .67 A4
Paddock's La DT6 ...67 A4
Paddocks Cl BH12 ...120 A4
Paddocks The
Bournemouth BH8 ...89 B2
1 Iwerne Minster DT11 .37 C1
5 Mosterton DT8 ....204 A8
Thornford DT9 ......194 D8
Padfield Cl BH6 .....123 C3
Padget Rd BH24 ....47 C1
Padstow Pl SP6 .....43 A4
Pageant Dr DT9 ....30 A3
Pageants Cl DT6 ....68 C1
Paget Cl BH21 ......60 A4
Paget Rd BH11 .....89 A2
Paisley Rd BH6 .....123 B3
Palfrey Rd BH10 ....89 B3
Palma Ct BH23 .....126 A4
Palmer Pl BH25 .....95 A2
Palmer Rd Poole BH15 .119 B3
Salisbury SP2 ....213 A3
Palmers La DT11 ....211 D7
Palmers Orch BH21 ..84 B2
Palmerston Ave BH24 .124 B3
Palmerston Cl BH16 ..118 B4
Palmerston Rd
Bournemouth BH1 ...122 C3
Poole BH14 ....120 B2
Upton BH16 ....118 B4
Pamphill CE Fst Sch
BH21 ....58 C3
Panorama Rd
Poole BH13 ....147 A2
Swanage BH19 ......179 A1
Pans Cnr BH22 .....61 C2
Parade The
Barton on Sea BH25 ..94 C1
5 Bournemouth BH6 .123 C2
New Milton BH25 ....95 B2
Poole BH17 ....87 A1
Paradise La BH24 ...83 B2
Paradise Rd BH21 ...51 C4
Paradise St 17 BH15 .119 A1
Parcroft Gdns BA20 ..27 A3
Pardys Hill BH21 ....86 B4
Parfields BA20 ......27 A3
Parham Cl BH25 ....94 C2
Parham Rd BH10 ...89 B1
Parish Rd BH15 .....119 C3
Park Ave BH10 .....89 B3
Park Cl Burton BH23 .92 B2
New Milton BH25 ....95 B3
Salisbury SP1 ....213 B4
3 Stourpaine DT11 ..198 F4
Park Cnr BH20 .....115 B4
Park Dr
Holton Heath BH20 ..116 A2
Verwood BH31 ......45 A4
Park Est Rd DT5 ....186 C2
Park Gate Mews 14
BH2 ....121 C2
Park Gdns
Christchurch BH23 ...124 C4
Yeovil BA20 ....27 B3
Park Gr DT10 ......33 B4
Park Hill DT11 ......211 C6
Park Homer Dr BH21 .60 A3
Park Homer Rd BH21 .59 C3
Park La Alderholt SP6 .42 A3
Bournemouth BH10 ..89 C2
Evershot DT2 ....206 A7
Glanvilles Wootton DT9 .195 F2
Henstridge BA8 .....19 A4
Melbury Sampford DT2 .194 A1
Radipole DT4 ....167 B3
Salisbury SP1 ....213 B4
Shapwick DT11 .....48 B1
Thorncombe TA20 ...202 D7
Wayford TA18 ....191 B1
Wimborne Minster BH21 .59 B2
Wimborne St Giles BH21 .201 E7
Woodlands BH21 ....44 A3
Park La Rd BH15 ...119 C1
Park Lands DT11 ....212 B3
Park Mead Rd DT4 ..180 B4
Park Pl BH14 ....119 C2
Park Rd
Barton on Sea BH25 ..94 C1
Blandford Forum DT11 .212 B2
Bournemouth BH8 ...122 A4
Bridport DT6 ....100 B4
Easton/Weston DT5 ..187 A4
Henstridge BA8 .....19 A4
New Milton BH25 ....95 B3
Poole BH14 ....119 C2
Stalbridge DT10 ....33 B4
Swanage BH19 ......179 A1
Yeovil BA20 ....27 B3
Park St Radipole DT4 .167 B2
Salisbury SP1 ....213 B4
Yeovil BA20 ....27 B2
Park The
Barton on Sea BH25 ..126 B4
Yeovil BA20 ....27 B3

Park View
Crewkerne TA18 .....191 ?
New Milton BH25 ....95 A
9 Poole BH15 ....119 C
Park View Mews BH25 .95 A
Park Way BH22 .....53 A
Park Wr La DT8 .....203 C
Park's La DT2 ......130 E
Parkelea 3 BH21 ....56 E
Parker Rd BH9 .....121 C
Parkers Cl BH24 ....47 C
Parkland Cl BH25 ...45 C
Parkland Dr BH25 ...126 C
Parkland Pl BH25 ...95 A
Parkside
Christchurch BH23 ...93 E
Ringwood BH24 .....55 A
Parkside Gdns BH10 .89 C
Parkside Rd BH14 ...120 E
Parkstone Ave BH14 .120 E
Parkstone Gram Sch
BH17 ....87 A
Parkstone Hts BH14 ..119 C
Parkstone Rd BH15 ..119 C
Parkstone Sta BH14 ..120 A
Parkview DT2 ....121 C
Parkway DT6 ....97 A
Parkway Dr BH22 ...122 C
Parkwood La 14 BH5 .123 A
Parkwood Rd
Bournemouth BH5 ...123 A
Wimborne Minster BH21 .59 E
Parley Cl BH22 .....61 C
Parley Cross BH22 ..89 C
Parley Fst Sch BH22 ..61 E
Parley La BH23 .....90 E
Parley Rd BH9 ......90 A
Parmiter Dr BH21 ...59 C
Parmiter Rd BH21 ...59 C
Parmiter Way BH21 ..59 C
Parnham House ★
DT8 ....204 C
Parr Gr 5 DT11 .....199 C
Parr House 5 BH14 ..120 A
Parr St BH14 ....120 A
Parrett & Axe CE Prim Sch
DT8 ....204 A
Parrett Mead DT8 ...192 C
Parricks La EX13 ....202 A
Parsonage Barn La
BH24 ....55 E
Parsonage Ct 9 BH8 .122 A
Parsonage Gn BH21 .213 A
Parsonage Hill BH21 .200 F
Parsonage La BH21 ..201 E
Parsonage Rd
Bournemouth BH1 ...122 A
Bridport DT6 ....100 E
Parsonage St SP7 ...37 C
Parsonage The SP5 ..189 E
Parsons Cl BH19 ....179 A
Parsons La DT2 .....102 C
Parsons Pool 3 SP7 ..12 C
Partridge Cl BH23 ...125 A
Partridge Dr BH14 ..120 E
Partridge Gr BH25 ...95 A
Partridge Wlk BH14 ..120 A
Partway DT10 ......196 F
Partway La
Hardington Mandeville
BA22 ....192 F
Hazelbury Bryan DT10 .196 F
Thorncombe TA20 ...202 C
Pascoe Cl BH14 ....120 A
Pasture Way DT6 ...100 E
Patchins Rd BH16 ...118 A
Patchins The BH14 ..147 E
Patson Hill La DT9 ..15 E
Pattinson Cl BA21 ...27 A
Paul's Mead DT5 ...186 C
Pauls Way DT11 ....137 E
Pauncefote Rd BH5 ..123 A
Pauntley Rd BH23 ...124 C
Pavan Gdns BH10 ...89 E
Pavilion Theatre ★
DT4 ....167 C
Pavyotts La BA22 ...193 E
Payne Cl BH21 .....53 A
Payne's Hill 5 SP1 ..213 E
Paynes Cl DT2 .....76 C
Peace Cl BH23 .....93 A
Peaceful La DT10 ...196 F
Peacemarsh Farm Cl 12
SP8 ....5 C
Pear Cl BH12 ......121 A
Pear Tree Cl
Alderholt SP6 ....42 A
Bransgore BH23 .....93 A
Pearce Ave BH14 ...120 A
Pearce Gdns BH14 ..120 A
Pearce Rd BH16 ....118 A
Pearce-Smith Ct
BH25 ....126 C
Pearl Gdns BH10 ...89 E
Pearl Rd BH10 .....89 E
Pearson Ave BH14 ..120 A
Pearson Gdns BH10 .89 E
Peatons La BH16 ...84 A
Peckham Ave BH25 ..95 A
Peeks Mews BH6 ...123 C
Peel Cl
Blandford Forum DT11 .212 E
Poole BH12 ....120 E
Pegasus Ct
Bournemouth BH1 ...122 A
8 New Milton BH25 ..95 A
Pegasus Lodge BH22 .61 E

eggy's La TA18 ......192 C5
elham Cl BH23 ......124 B3
elican Mead BH4 .....55 C3
emberton Cl DT3 ....152 B2
embroke Cl BA21 .....28 A4
embroke Ct 11 BH23 ..126 A4
embroke Rd
  Bournemouth BH4 ....121 A1
  Poole BH12 ....120 B4
en Mill City Inf Sch
  BA21 ....27 C3
en Mill Hill BA9 ......1 C2
en Mill Trading Est
  BA21 ....28 A3
encraig BH13 ....121 A2
endomer Rd BA22 ....193 B5
enelope Ct 18 BH23 ..126 A4
engelly Ave BH10 .....89 C3
enmore Rd DT9 ....15 B3
enn Cl BH25 ....94 C1
enn Cross DT6 ....64 B1
enn Hill DT20 ....27 B2
enn Hill Ave BH14 ...120 B2
enn Hill Pk BH20 .....27 B2
enn House Day Hospl
  BA20 ....27 B2
enn La BA22 ....193 A6
ennant Way BH23 ....124 C4
enney's Hill DT4 .....204 D8
ennine Ct 8 BH23 ...124 C4
ennine Way BH31 .....45 A3
ennington Cl BH22 ...52 C1
ennington Cres BH22 .52 C1
ennington Rd BH22 ...52 C1
ennsylvania Rd DT5 .187 A2
enny Hedge BH25 ....127 A4
enny La 6 BH7 ......122 C2
enny Plot DT7 ....96 A3
enny St Radipole DT4 .167 B2
1 Sturminster Newton
  DT10 ....197 D8
enny Way BH23 ......125 B3
enny's Cnr SO41 .....95 C2
enny's La BH21 ......40 A4
enny's Mead BH21 ...40 A4
enny's Wlk BH22 .....61 B2
ennyfarthing St SP1 .213 B3
ennywell Gdns BH25 ..95 B2
enrith Cl BH31 ....45 A3
enrith Rd BH5 ......123 A2
enrose Cl BH14 ......84 B1
enrose Rd BH22 .....61 B1
entons Hill BH9 ......43 C3
entridge La DT10 .....34 B2
epper Hill DT11 .....198 B5
ercy Gdns DT11 .....212 B2
ercy Rd
  Bournemouth BH5 ...122 C2
  Yeovil BA21 ....27 C3
eregrine Rd BH23 ...125 A3
ergin Cres BH17 ....119 A4
ergin Way BH17 .....119 A4
errott Hill Sch TA18 .192 B4
erry Gdns BH15 .....119 B1
erry St TA20 ....202 A7
erryfield Gdns BH7 ..123 A4
ersley Rd BH10 ......89 C2
erth Cl BH23 ....91 C1
erth St DT4 ....167 A2
Peter Grant Way BH22 .61 B3
Peter St 3 BA20 .....27 B2
Peters Cl BH16 ......118 B3
Peters Rd BH22 ......61 C2
Petersfield Pl BH7 ...123 A4
Petersfield Rd BH7 ..123 A4
Petersham La BH21 ..51 A2
Petersham Rd BH17 .119 A4
Petit Rd BH9 ....90 A2
Petter's Way BA20 ...27 B2
Pettitts Cl DT9 ......28 B1
Pettridge La BA12 ....3 A3
Pettycrate La DT6 ...98 C3
Petwyn Cl BH22 .....62 A3
Peverell Ave E DT1 ..107 B1
Peverell Rd BH16 ...118 A4
Peveril Cl BH24 ......54 A3
Peveril Point Rd BH19 179 B1
Peveril Rd BH19 ....179 B1
Phelipps Rd BH21 ...86 C3
Philip Rd DT11 ......212 C3
Phillips Rd BH16 .....21 A1
Phyldon Cl BH12 ....120 A3
Phyldon Rd BH12 ...120 A3
Piccadilly La DT11 ...56 B4
Pickard Rd DT1 .....61 C4
Pickering Cl BH18 ...87 A1
Picket La DT8 ....192 C1
Pickett La BA21 .....27 B4
Pickford Rd BH9 ....89 C1
Picketts Cross DT2 ..74 A2
Piddle La DT2 ....207 D3
Piddle Valley Fst Sch
  DT2 ....208 B2
Pidney Hill DT10 ....196 F3
Piece Cl DT9 ....17 B2
Piece The 2 TA16 ...191 F7
Pierston Fields SP8 ...5 B3
Pig Hill BA22 ....193 A7
Pig Shoot La BH23 ...90 C3
Pigeon Cl
  Blandford Forum DT11 212 B1
  Winfrith Newburgh DT2 156 C3
Pikes La BH19 ......183 B4
Pile La DT10 ....32 C3
Pilford Heath Rd BH21 60 C4
Pilford La BH21 .....51 B1
Pilgrim Pk BH24 ....55 C4

Pilgrim's Cl BH25 ....95 B2
Pilgrims Way
  Broadstone BH17 ...119 A4
  4 Radipole DT4 ....167 C1
Pill Mdw SP8 ....9 B2
Pilot Hight Rd BH11 ..89 A2
Pilsdon Cl 7 DT8 ....204 C4
Pilsdon Dr BH17 .....87 C2
Pilsdon La DT6 ......203 C3
Pilsdon Manor* DT6 .203 C2
Pilsdon Pen (Hill Fort)*
  DT6 ....203 C4
Pilwell DT10 ....21 A2
Pimperleaze Rd BA12 .3 C1
Pimpern Cl BH17 .....87 C1
Pimperne CE VC Fst Sch
  DT11 ....199 D4
Pimpernel Ct 6 SP8 ..5 B1
Pine Ave
  Bournemouth BH6 ..123 B2
  Poole BH12 ....120 C3
Pine Cl
  Barton on Sea BH25 .126 A3
  Corscombe DT2 ....205 B8
  Ferndown BH22 .....61 B4
Pine Cres
  Christchurch BH23 ..125 C4
  Holton Heath BH20 .116 A2
Pine Dr Poole BH13 .120 C2
  St.Leonards BH24 ...54 A2
Pine Glen Ave BH22 ..61 B4
Pine Grange 4 BH1 .122 B3
Pine House BH25 .....95 A2
Pine Lodge 15 BH13 .147 C4
Pine Manor Rd BH24 .53 C3
Pine Mans 3 BH1 ...122 B2
Pine Pk Mans 16 BH13 121 A1
Pine Rd Alderholt SP6 42 A3
  Bournemouth BH9 ..122 A4
  Broadstone BH21 ...58 C1
Pine Ridge DT7 ......96 B4
Pine Tree Ave BA20 ..27 A2
Pine Tree Cl BH21 ...59 B3
Pine Tree Glen BH4 .121 B2
Pine Vale Cres BH10 .89 C2
Pine View DT6 ......100 A3
Pine View Cl
  Upton BH16 ....118 B3
  Verwood BH31 ......44 C4
Pine View Rd BH31 ..44 C4
Pine Wlk
  Lyme Regis DT7 ....96 A2
  Verwood BH31 ......45 B3
Pineapple La DT6 ....68 B3
Pinebeach Ct BH13 .147 D4
Pinecliffe Ave BH6 .123 B3
Pinecliffe Rd BH25 .126 B4
Pineholt Cl BH24 .....54 B3
Pinehurst Ave BH23 .124 C3
Pinehurst Rd BH22 ..53 A1
Pinemoor Cl DT6 ....167 C4
Pines Mews 11 DT8 .204 D4
Pines The BH13 .....121 A1
Pineside BH9
  122 A4
Pinesprings Dr BH18 .86 C1
Pinetree Wlk BH17 .118 C4
Pinewood Ave BH10 ..89 B3
Pinewood Cl
  Bournemouth BH10 .89 B3
  Christchurch BH23 ...94 A1
  Upton BH16 ....118 A4
Pinewood Gdns BH22 61 B4
Pinewood Rd
  Christchurch BH23 ...93 C1
  Ferndown BH22 .....61 B4
  Hordle SO41 ....95 A4
  Poole BH13 ....121 A1
  St.Leonards BH24 ...54 A2
  Upton BH16 ....118 A4
Pinford La DT9 ......30 C3
Pink End DT2 ....61 C2
Pink Knoll Hollow DT9 15 C4
Pipers Ash 2 BH24 ..55 C4
Pipers Dr BH23 .....125 A4
Pipit Cl DT3 ....152 B2
Pippin Cl BH23 ......91 C1
Pirates La DT4 ......180 A4
Pit Hill TA17 ....191 B7
Pit Rd TA17 ....191 B7
Pitcher Cl 3 DT11 ...81 C4
Pitchers DT6 ....68 A3
Pitfield Cnr BA22 ....15 A3
Pitman's La DT6 .....66 A1
Pitt Cl DT11 ....212 B1
Pitt La DT6 ....65 C2
Pitt's Dro BH21 .....49 C1
Pittmore Rd BH23 ...92 B1
Pitts La
  Melbury Abbas SP7 ..23 C3
  Sedgehill And Semley SP7 7 B3
Pitts Orch DT10 .....35 A1
Pitts Pl BH25 ....95 B1
Pitwines Cl BH15 ...119 B1
Pix Mead Gdns SP7 ..13 A1
Place Mill* BH23 ...124 A3
Placket La BA20 .....27 A1
Plain The DT2 ......109 A3
Plaisters La DT3 ....153 B2
Plant Pk Rd BH24 ...54 C1
Plantaganet Chase
  BA20 ....27 A1
Plantaganet Cres BH11 88 B3
Plantaganet Pk BA20 .27 A2
Plantaganet Way 8 SP8 5 B1
Plantation Ct BH17 ...87 B1
Plantation Dr BH23 ..94 A1
Plantation Rd BH17 ..87 B1

Plassey Cl DT1 ......107 C1
Plassey Cres BH10 ..89 B3
Playfield Cl BA8 ......19 A4
Playfields Dr BH12 ..120 C3
Pleasance Way BH25 .94 C2
Pleck Hill DT10 .....196 E3
Pleck La DT2 ....209 B7
Plecy Cl DT2 ....61 B1
Plemont Cl BH12 .....88 C1
Plocks The DT11 ....212 B2
Plot La DT9 ....14 C1
Plott La BA8 ....19 B3
Plough Est DT11 ....212 B3
Plover Cl 11 DT9 ....17 B1
Plover Cl BA21 ......26 C3
Plover Dr DT3 ......166 B3
Plover Rd DT9 ......17 B1
Plowman Cl DT10 ...21 A2
Plum Orch DT9 .....28 C4
Plumbley Mdws 6 DT11 81 C4
Plumer Rd BH17 .....87 A1
Podington Mdws DT3 .166 B3
Pokesdown Com Prim Sch
  BH5 ....123 A3
Pokesdown Sta BH7 .123 A3
Polans DT11 ....194 D2
Polden Rd 7 SP1 ...213 C2
Policemans La BH16 .117 A4
Pollards La DT2 .....155 B4
Pomona Cl BH22 .....61 B3
Pompey's Cnr BH21 ..61 A2
Pompey's La BH22 ...61 A1
Pond Cl Henstridge BA8 19 A2
  New Milton BH25 ....95 A2
Pond Head BH21 .....51 B3
Pond Wlk DT10 .....33 B4
Ponsonby Rd BH14 ..120 B2
Pony Dr BH16 ......118 B4
Poole Aquarium &
Serpentarium*
  BH15 ....119 B1
Poole Commerce Ctr
  BH12 ....120 C3
Poole Gram Sch BH17 87 B1
Poole High Sch BH15 119 B2
Poole Hill BH2 ......121 C2
Poole Hospl BH15 ...119 B2
Poole La BH11 ......89 A3
Poole Rd
  Bournemouth BH2 ..121 B2
  Lytchett Matravers BH16 84 C3
  Poole BH12 ....121 A2
  Sturminster Marshall
    BH21 ....56 B1
  Upton BH16 ....118 B4
  Wimborne Minster BH21 59 B2
Poole Sta BH15 .....119 B2
Poole's Ct 4 DT7 ....96 B3
Poop Hill TA18 ......192 C8
Poop Hill La TA18 ...192 C8
Poorhouse La DT6 ...66 B4
Pope's Hill DT2 .....205 F1
Pope's La DT9 ......17 B1
Popes St BH23 .....119 B3
Poplar Cl
  Bransgore BH23 ....93 B4
  Christchurch BH23 ..126 A4
  6 Poole BH15 .....119 A1
  Wimborne Minster BH21 59 B3
Poplar Cres BH24 ...55 B4
Poplar Hill 3 DT11 ..198 B6
Poplar La BH23 ......93 B4
Poplar Rd BH25 .....95 B2
Poplar Way BH24 ....55 B4
Pople's Well TA18 ..191 E4
Poppy Cl
  Christchurch BH23 ..125 B4
  Upton BH16 ....117 A4
  Yeovil BA22 ....26 B3
Poppyfields SP8 ......5 C2
Porchester Ct 12 BH1 122 A3
Porchester Pl BH8 ..122 A3
Porchester Rd BH8 ..122 A3
Port La DT6 ....101 B2
Port Regis Sch SP7 ..12 A3
Portarlington Cl BH2 121 B1
Portarlington Rd BH4 121 B1
Portchester Boys Sch
  BH7 ....123 A4
Portelet Cl BH12 .....88 B1
Porter Rd BH17 .....119 A4
Porters La BH21 .....60 B3
Portesham CE Prim Sch
  DT3 ....150 A4
Portesham Gdns BH9 .90 A2
Portesham Hill DT3 .132 A1
Portesham Way BH17 .87 C2
Portfield Cl BH23 ...124 A4
Portfield Rd BH23 ..124 A3
Portfield Sch BH23 .124 A3
Portiere House BH11 .89 A2
Portland Ave SP2 ...213 A4
Portland Beach Rd
  DT4 ....180 C2
Portland Castle* DT5 181 A1
Portland Cres DT4 ..167 A1
Portland Ct DT7 .....96 A3
Portland Hospl DT5 .181 A1
Portland Mus* DT5 .187 A2
Portland Pl BH2 ....121 C2
Portland Port DT5 ..181 B1
Portland Rd
  Bournemouth BH9 ..122 A4
  Weymouth DT4 .....180 B4
Portland Tophill Jun Sch
  DT5 ....187 A2
Portman Cres BH5 ..123 A4
Portman Ct BA22 ...192 E8

Portman Dr 5 DT11 ..198 C8
Portman Rd
  Bournemouth BH7 ..122 C4
  11 Pimperne DT11 .199 D4
Portman Terr BH5 ..123 A2
Portman Rd BH5 ....123 A2
Portmore BH18 ......87 B3
Portmore Gdns DT4 .167 B1
Portnell's La BH12 ...1 C2
Portreeve Dr BA21 ..27 B3
Portswood Dr 2 BH9 .90 A2
Portway DT2 ....102 B3
Portway Cl DT1 .....107 C1
Possessions Cnr SP5 .25 A2
Post Gn Rd BH16 ...116 C4
Post Office Bldgs BH9 121 C4
Post Office La
  6 Poole BH15 ......119 B1
  St.Leonards BH24 ...54 B3
Post Office Rd
  41 Bournemouth BH1 121 C2
  Gillingham SP8 ......5 B3
Potterne Way BH21 ..45 B2
Potters Way
  Poole BH14 ....120 B1
  Salisbury SP1 ......213 C2
Pottery Cl DT4 ......167 B2
Pottery Lines BH20 .142 C4
Pottery Rd BH14 ...120 A1
Poulner Hill BH24 ...55 C4
Poulner Jun & Inf Sch
  BH24 ....47 C1
Poulner Pk BH24 ....47 C1
Pound Cl
  Charminster DT2 ...107 B3
  Poole BH15 ....119 C2
  Ringwood BH24 ....55 B4
  Stalbridge DT10 ....33 B4
  Yeovil BA21 ....26 C3
Pound Cottage Visitor Ctr*
  DT2 ....205 E2
Pound Hill
  Corscombe DT2 ....205 B7
  Witchampton DT11 .200 F1
Pound La
  Bishop's Caundle DT9 196 A7
  Burstock DT8 ......203 D5
  3 Christchurch BH23 124 A3
  Damerham SP6 .....190 E3
  Dewlish DT2 ....209 C1
  21 Dorchester DT1 .108 A1
  Gillingham SP8 ......5 B1
  5 Okeford Fitzpaine DT11 197 F5
  Poole BH15 ....119 C3
  Shaftesbury SP7 ....13 A2
  Wareham BH20 ....142 C2
  Wootton Fitzpaine DT6 64 A3
Pound Piece
  Easton/Weston DT5 .186 C2
  Maiden Newton DT2 .72 C4
Pound Rd
  Hawkchurch EX13 ..202 C2
  Lyme Regis DT7 ....96 A3
  Thornford DT9 .....194 D8
Pound St DT7 ....96 A3
Poundbury Cres DT1 .107 C1
Poundbury Rd DT1 ..107 C1
Poundbury W Ind Est
  DT1 ....107 C1
Povington Barrow*
  BH20 ....159 B1
Powell Rd BH14 ....120 A3
Powerscourt Rd BH25 126 C4
Powis Cl BH25 ......95 A2
Powys Cl DT1 ......134 C4
Poxwell Dro DT2 ....154 A3
Poxwell Manor* DT2 154 C2
Prankerds Rd 12 DT9 17 B1
Preetz Way BH16 ...212 C3
Preston Cl BH16 ....118 B4
Preston Cty Comp Sch
  BA21 ....26 C3
Preston Gr BA20 ....27 A3
Preston La BH23 .....92 B2
Preston Rd
  Overcombe/Preston DT3 153 B2
  Poole BH15 ....119 B3
  Radipole DT3 ......167 C3
  Yeovil BA22 ....26 B3
Preston VC Prim Sch
  BA21 ....27 A3
Preston Way BH23 ..125 B4
Prestwood Cl BH25 ..94 C1
Pretoria Terr DT4 ...167 B1
Priest La 2 DT4 .....92 A4
Priest's House Mus & Gdns*
  BH21 ....59 A2
Priest's Rd BH19 ...179 A1
Priest's Way BH19 ..178 C1
Priestlands DT9 .....30 A4
Priestlands La DT9 ..30 A4
Priestley Rd BH10 ...89 A1
Prime La DT6 ....65 C4
Primrose Cl 3 SP8 ...5 B1
Primrose Gdns BH17 .86 C1
Primrose Hill BA21 .193 B7
Primrose La BA21 ....14 A1
Primrose Way
  Christchurch BH23 .125 B4
  Corfe Mullen BH21 ..86 C4
Primula Cl DT3 .....152 C1
Prince of Wales Rd
  Bournemouth BH4 .121 B2
  Dorchester DT1 ....108 A1
  3 Weymouth DT4 ..167 B1
Prince of Wales Sch The
  DT1 ....134 B4
Prince's Dr DT4 ....167 B3
Prince's Pl BH25 .....95 B2

Prince's St DT1 .....108 A1
Princes Cl BH22 .....61 B3
Princes Ct 6 BH12 ..121 A2
Princes St BA20 .....27 B2
Princess Ave BH23 .124 A3
Princess Rd
  Bournemouth BH4 .121 A2
  Bridport DT6 ......100 B3
  Poole BH12 ....121 A2
  Swanage BH19 ....179 A1
Pringles Cl BH22 ....61 C3
Pringles Dr BH22 ...61 C3
Priors Cl BH23 .....125 B4
Priors Cnr 2 BH21 ..201 D1
Priors Rd BH17 ....119 A4
Priors Wlk 7 BH7 ...59 A3
Priory CE Prim Sch The
  BH23 ....124 A3
Priory Cl DT3 ....26 C1
Priory Gdns
  3 Pimperne DT11 ..199 D3
  3 Spetisbury DT11 .211 E5
  West Moors BH22 ..62 A4
Priory Glade BA21 ...26 C3
Priory House BH23 .124 B3
Priory Ind Pk BH23 .125 A4
Priory La DT6 ....100 B3
Priory Quay BH23 ..124 B3
Priory Rd
  Bournemouth BH2 .121 C1
  Portland DT5 ......186 B3
  West Moors BH22 ..62 A4
Priory Sq 9 SP2 ....213 B3
Priory View Ct 5 BH23 124 A3
Priory View Pl 7 BH9 .90 A2
Priory View Rd
  Bournemouth BH9 ..90 A2
  Burton BH23 ....92 B1
Privet Rd BH9 ......121 C4
Promenade BH23 ...125 A3
Prospect Cl 2 SP8 ...6 A1
Prospect Cres BH19 .179 A2
Prospect Pl Mere BA12 .2 C3
  9 Weymouth DT4 ..167 B1
Prospect Rd
  Dorchester DT1 ....107 C1
  Lytchett Matravers BH16 84 B2
Prosperous St 14 BH15 119 B1
Prout Hill 9 DT8 ....204 D4
Prunus Cl BH22 .....61 A4
Prunus Dr BH22 ....61 A4
Pryors Wlk BH16 ....84 B1
Pud Brook 9 DT9 ...17 B1
Puddledock La DT3 .153 B2
Puddletown CE Fst Sch
  DT2 ....78 A1
Puddletown Cres BH17 87 C1
Puddletown Rd
  Arne BH20 ....142 A2
  Bere Regis BH20 ...140 C4
  East Stoke BH20 ...113 A4
Pugmill La DT3 .....166 B3
Pullman Ct BH22 ....52 C1
Pullman Way BH24 ..55 B2
Pulmans La 4 TA18 .191 F4
Purbeck Ave BH15 ..118 C3
Purbeck Cl Loders DT6 101 C4
  Lytchett Matravers BH16 84 B2
  Upton BH16 ....118 A4
  Weymouth DT4 ....167 A1
Purbeck Ct
  Bournemouth BH5 .123 A2
  3 Christchurch BH23 124 C4
Purbeck Dr BH31 ...45 A3
Purbeck Gdns BH14 119 C3
Purbeck Hts BH14 .120 A3
Purbeck Information &
  Heritage Ctr* BH20 142 C2
Purbeck Rd
  Barton on Sea BH25 126 A3
  Bournemouth BH2 .121 C1
  Lytchett Matravers BH16 84 B2
Purbeck Sch The
  BH20 ....142 B1
Purbeck Sports Ctr
  BH20 ....142 B1
Purbeck Terr Rd
  BH19 ....179 B1
Purbeck Toy Mus*
  BH20 ....144 B2
Purbeck View 13 BH19 178 C1
Purbeck View Sch
  BH19 ....179 B1
Purchase Rd BH12 .121 B4
Purewell BH23 .....124 B3
Purewell Cl BH23 ..124 C3
Purewell Cross BH23 124 C3
Purewell Cross Rd
  BH23 ....124 B4
Purewell St 11 BH23 124 C4
Purns Mill La SP8 ...5 C3
Pussex La BH23 .....91 A4
Putt's La DT9 ......16 A4
Putton La DT3 .....166 B3
Puxey La
  Shillingstone DT11 .198 B5
  Sturminster Newton
    DT10 ....197 B3
Pye Cl BH21 ....86 C4
Pye Cnr BH21 ......59 A2
Pye La Cranborne BH21 41 A3
  Tatworth & Forton
    TA20 ....202 B8
  Wimborne Minster BH21 59 A2
Pymore La DT6 .....68 B2

Pymore Rd
Bradpole DT6 ....68 C1
Bridport DT6 ....100 B4

Q

Quantock Ct **7** BH23 ...124 C4
Quar Cl DT10 ....196 E1
Quarr Dr DT9 ....30 A4
Quarr Hill Morden BH20 ..83 B1
Wool BH20 ....140 A1
Quarr La Sherborne DT9 ..30 A4
Symondsbury DT6 ....99 B3
Quarry Chase **7** BH4 ..121 B2
Quarry Cl
Shipton Gorge DT6 .....101 B3
Stour Provost SP8 ......21 B4
Sturminster Newton DT10 ..35 A1
12 Swanage BH19 ....178 C1
Wimborne Minster BH21 ..60 A4
Quarry Dr BH21 ....60 A4
Quarry Fields Ind Est
BA12 ....2 C3
Quarry La
Bothenhampton DT6 ....100 C2
Bradford Abbas DT9 .....28 B2
Longburton DT9 ....195 B8
Melbury Abbas SP7 ......24 A3
Quarry Rd BH21 ....60 A4
Quarterjack Mews 1
BH21 ....59 B2
Quay Point **19** BH15 ...119 B1
Quay Rd BH23 ....124 A3
Quay The Poole BH15 ...119 B1
8 Wareham Town BH20 ..142 C2
Quayle Dr BH11 ....88 C3
Quayside DT6 ....100 B1
Quebec Pl **7** DT4 .....167 B2
Queen Anne Dr BH21 ....87 C4
Queen Elizabeth Ct
BH21 ....59 A2
Queen Elizabeth's Sch
BH21 ....58 C3
Queen Manor Rd SP1 ...213 C2
Queen Mary Ave BH9 ....89 C1
Queen St Gillingham SP8 ..5 C1
Radipole DT4 ....167 C2
Salisbury SP1 ....213 B3
4 Yetminster DT9 ......194 C5
Queen's Ave
Christchurch BH23 .....124 C4
Dorchester DT1 ....134 C4
Queen's Copse La BH21 ..51 B4
Queen's Pk Ave BH8 ...122 B4
Queen's Pk Gdns BH8 ..122 B4
Queen's Pk Rd BH8 ....122 B4
Queen's Pk S Dr BH8 ..122 B4
Queen's Pk W Dr BH8 ..122 B4
Queen's Rd
Blandford Forum DT11 ..212 C2
Bournemouth BH4 ......121 B2
Christchurch BH23 .....124 C3
Corfe Mullen BH21 ......86 B3
Poole BH14 ....120 B2
Swanage BH19 ....179 A1
Queens Cl BH22 ....52 C2
Queens Ct
5 Bournemouth BH4 ...121 B2
New Milton BH25 ....95 B2
Queens Gdns BH2 ......121 B2
Queens Gr
New Milton BH25 ....95 B2
Pen Selwood BA9 ....1 B2
Queens Mead **16** BH19 ..179 A1
Queens Rd
Bradford Abbas DT9 .....28 B1
Bridport DT6 ....100 B3
Ferndown BH22 ....61 B4
Fortuneswell DT5 ......186 C4
Mere BA12 ....3 A3
Radipole DT3 ....167 A4
Salisbury SP1 ....213 B3
Queens Wlk DT7 ....96 A3
Queensbury Rd SP1 ....213 C2
Queensbury Mans 7
BH1 ....122 A2
Queensland Rd
Bournemouth BH5 ......123 A3
Weymouth DT4 ....167 A2
Queensmead **4** BH21 ..59 B3
Queensway
New Milton BH25 ....94 C2
Ringwood BH24 ....55 B4
Yeovil BA20 ....27 B3
Queenswood Ave BH8 ...90 C1
Queenswood Dr BH22 ...61 B4
Queenwell DT6 ....68 C1
Quibo La DT4 ....167 A2
Quince La BH21 ....59 C3
Quinton Cl BH23 ....125 C4
Quomp The BH24 ....55 B4

R

R L Stevenson Ave
BH4 ....121 A2
Rabin Hill DT10 ....35 A1
Rabling La BH19 ....179 A2
Rabling Rd BH19 ....179 A2
Racedown Rd DT11 ....199 E3
Rachel Cl BH12 ....120 B4
Radcliffe Rd SP2 ......213 B1

Radipole La
Chickerell DT4 ....166 C2
Radipole DT4 ....167 A3
Radipole Lake Nature
Reserve★ DT4 ......167 B2
Radipole Pk Dr DT4 ...167 B3
Radipole Prim Sch
DT3 ....167 A4
Radipole Rd BH17 ......88 A1
Radnor Rd SP1 ....213 B4
Raglan Gdns BH11 ......89 A1
Raglan Terr BA21 ....27 A4
Railway Dr BH21 ....56 B2
Railway Terr **4** SP8 ....6 A1
Raleigh Cl
Christchurch BH23 .....124 C3
New Milton BH25 ....94 C2
3 Ringwood BH24 ......55 C4
Raleigh Rd Poole BH12 ..88 C1
Stalbridge DT10 ....33 C4
Ralph Rd BH21 ....86 C4
Ram La DT11 ....48 B1
Ram's Hill DT10 ....21 C1
Rampant Wlk DT1 .....134 C4
Rampart Rd SP1 ....213 B3
Rampisham Hill DT8 ...205 C2
Ramsbury DT10 ....196 D5
Ramsbury Cl DT11 ....212 B3
Ramsbury Ct DT11 ....212 B3
Ramsey Ct BH25 ....94 C2
Randall Cl DT3 ....166 B3
Randalls Hill BH16 ......85 A1
Randolph Rd
2 Bournemouth BH1 ..122 C2
Poole BH14 ....120 B3
Ranelagh Ct BH23 ....125 C4
Ranelagh Rd
Christchurch BH23 .....125 C4
Radipole DT4 ....167 B2
Rashley Rd DT3 ....166 B3
Raspberry La SP7 ......12 B1
Ratcliff's Gdn SP7 ......12 B1
Ratleigh La DT9 ....29 A3
Ravana Ct 4 BH8 ....122 A3
Raven Way BH23 ....125 A3
Ravenscourt Rd BH6 ..123 B3
Ravenscroft **8** SP2 ...213 B1
Ravensdale Cl BH12 ...120 B3
Ravenshall BH21 ....121 B1
Ravine Cl BH13 ....147 C4
Ravine Gdns **5** BH13 ..147 C4
Ravine Rd
Bournemouth BH5 .....123 A2
Poole BH13 ....147 C4
Rawles Way DT6 ......100 B4
Rawlsbury Camp★
DT11 ....209 B8
Rawston Down Rd **6**
DT11 ....199 E2
Rax La DT6 ....100 B4
Raymond Cl BH31 ......45 B3
Raymond Rd DT4 .....166 C1
Rayners Dr BH12 ......120 B3
Reap La DT5 ....186 C4
Rebbeck Rd BH7 ......123 A3
Reckleford BA20 ....27 B3
Reckleford Cty Inf Sch
BA21 ....27 C3
Recreation Rd BH12 ...120 C3
Rectory Ave BH11 ......58 B1
Rectory Cl DT2 ....136 A1
Rectory Gdns DT11 ...198 F7
Rectory La
Child Okeford DT11 ...198 C7
Hardington Mandeville
BA22 ....193 A7
Puncknowle DT2 ......129 C3
Studland BH19 ....164 B1
West Stafford DT2 ....136 A4
Rectory Rd
Broadmayne DT2 .....136 A1
Piddlehinton DT2 ......76 C4
Poole BH15 ....119 B3
Salisbury SP2 ....213 A2
Rectory Way DT4 .....167 B1
Red Horn Cl BH16 .....118 B2
Red House Mus & Gdns★
BH23 ....124 A3
Red La
Corfe Mullen BH21 .....86 A4
Seaborough DT8 ......191 E1
Sixpenny Handley SP5 .189 A3
Todber DT10 ....21 B2
Red Lion Cl **3** DT10 ..197 D8
Red Oaks Cl BH22 .....61 A4
Red Post Bloxworth DT11 ..82 B4
Poyntington DT9 ....16 B2
Red Roofs DT2 ....61 C2
Red Wing Rd DT9 ......17 B1
Redan Cl BH23 ....125 C4
Redbreast Rd BH9 .....90 A2
Redbreast Rd N BH9 ...90 A2
Redbridge La DT2 .....137 C3
Redbridge Rd DT2 ....137 C3
Redcliff View DT4 .....167 C1
Redcliffe Cl BH23 ......92 B2
Redcliffe Rd BH19 ....179 A3
Redcotts La BH21 ......59 A3
Redcotts Rd BH21 .....59 A3
Redford Cl SP1 ....213 C4
Redgate Pk TA18 .....191 E5
Redhill Ave BH9 ....89 C2
Redhill Cl BH10 ....89 C2
Redhill Cres BH9 ....89 C2
Redhill Dr BH10 ....89 C2
Redhill Pk Homes 1
BH10 ....89 C2

Redhoave Rd BH17 .....87 C1
Redhole La
Castleton DT9 ....16 A1
Sherborne DT9 ....30 A4
Redlands
Christchurch BH23 .....125 A4
Poole BH12 ....120 C3
Redlands La DT8 ......203 F5
Redmans View BH31 ...45 A3
Redmans La SP7 ....24 A3
Redpoll Cl **1** DT3 ....152 B2
Redsails BH13 ....147 A2
Redshank Cl BH17 .....86 C1
Redvers Rd BH23 .....124 C4
Redwood Cl BH24 ......55 B4
Redwood Dr BH22 .....61 B4
Redwood Rd
Upton BH16 ....118 A4
Yeovil BA21 ....28 A4
Reed View Cl DT4 ....167 A3
Reedling Cl DT3 ......152 B2
Reeves Orch DT11 .....56 B3
Reforne DT5 ....186 C2
Reforne Cl **1** DT5 ....187 A2
Regency Cres BH23 ...123 C4
Regency Dr **7** DT3 ...152 B2
Regent Dr BH7 ....122 C4
Regent Way BH23 ....124 A3
Regents The **2** BA21 ..26 C3
Regimental Mus★
SP1 ....213 B2
Reid St BH23 ....124 A4
Rempstone Rd
Oakley BH21 ....87 B4
Swanage BH19 ....179 A2
Remus Cl DT1 ....134 C4
Renault Dr BH18 ....87 A1
Renfrew Cl DT1 ....135 B4
Renscombe Rd BH19 ..183 A4
Restharrow BH1 ......122 A2
Retreat Rd BH21 ....59 B2
Revels Hill DT2 ....207 E7
Rew La DT3 ....208 A8
Rex La DT3 ....166 B3
Rex's La BA22 ....27 C1
Reynard Ct BH15 .....119 C2
Reynards Way DT3 ...153 B2
Rhine Rd BH20 ....139 C3
Rhode La DT7 ....64 A1
Rhosewood Dr DT3 ...153 A2
Rhydderch Way **9** TA18 ..191 F4
Ribble Cl BH31 ....87 A1
Ribbonwood Hts
BH14 ....120 A2
Ricardo Cres BH23 ...125 A3
Rice Gdns BH16 ......118 B2
Rice Terr BH16 ....118 B2
Richard Cl BH16 ......118 A4
Richards Way SP2 ....213 A2
Richmond Cl DT9 ......30 A3
Richmond Ct
15 Bournemouth BH5 ..122 C2
7 New Milton BH25 ....95 A2
Richmond Gdns BH1 ..121 C2
Richmond Gn DT9 .....30 A3
Richmond Hill BH2 ...121 C2
Richmond Hill Dr BH2 ..121 C2
Richmond Pk Ave
BH8 ....122 B4
Richmond Pk Cl BH8 ..122 B4
Richmond Pk Cres
BH8 ....122 B4
Richmond Pk Rd BH8 ..122 B4
Richmond Rd
4 Blandford Forum DT11 ..212 C3
Poole BH14 ....120 B2
4 Salisbury SP2 ......213 A3
Sherborne DT9 ....30 A3
Swanage BH19 ....179 A1
Wimborne Minster BH21 ..59 B2
Yeovil BA20 ....27 B2
Richmond Rise BH23 ..122 B3
Richmond Way BA21 ...26 C3
Richmond Wood Rd
BH8 ....122 B4
Ricketts La DT10 ....35 A1
Rickhay Rise TA18 ...192 B8
Ridge Dro DT10 ......196 F5
Ridge La
Hazelbury Bryan DT10 ..196 D5
West Coker BA22 .....193 A8
Ridge The DT9 ....16 C3
Ridge Way
Puddletown DT2 ....76 C1
Shaftesbury SP7 ....12 C2
Ridgeback La DT6 ......69 C4
Ridgefield Gdns BH23 ..125 B4
Ridgemead **5** BA20 ...26 C1
Ridgemount Gdns
BH15 ....118 C2
Ridgeway Bradpole DT6 ..68 C1
Broadstone BH18 ......87 A2
Corfe Mullen BH21 .....86 B4
Ferndown BH22 ....89 C4
3 Sherborne DT9 ......30 A3
Ridgeway La
Child Okeford DT11 ...198 C8
Hinton St Mary DT10 ...35 A2
Ridgeway Rd SP1 .....213 B3
Ridgway TA18 ....192 B8
Ridley Rd BH9 ....121 C4
Ridout Cl DT1 ....134 C4
Ridwood DT6 ....99 A3
Rigg La DT9 ....14 C1
Riggs Gdns BH11 ......88 C1
Rigler Rd BH15 ....119 A1
Rimbrow Cl DT3 ......153 B2
Rimbury Way BH23 ...124 A4

Ring St DT10 ....33 B4
Ringmoor (Settlement &
Field System)★
DT11 ....197 F3
Rings The DT11 ....79 C4
Ringstead Cres DT3 ..168 A3
Ringwood CE Inf Sch
BH24 ....55 B4
Ringwood Cty Jun Sch
BH24 ....55 B4
Ringwood La BH21 ....201 E7
Ringwood Rd
Alderholt SP6 ....42 B3
Bournemouth BH11 ....88 C2
Bransgore BH23 ....93 B3
Christchurch BH23 .....94 A1
Ferndown BH22 ....61 B2
Fordingbridge SP6 .....43 B3
Hyde SP6 ....43 C2
Poole BH12 ....120 A4
Sopley BH23 ....92 A4
St.Leonards BH24 .....53 C1
Three Legged Cross BH21 ..52 C4
Verwood BH31 ....45 B3
Ringwood Recn Ctr
BH24 ....55 B4
Ringwood Ret Pk BH11 ..88 C2
Ringwood Sch BH24 ...55 B4
Rip Croft DT5 ....186 C1
Ripon Rd BH9 ....90 A1
Ripp's La DT2 ....207 F4
Rise The DT4 ....167 A3
Ritchie Pl BH22 ....52 C2
Ritchie Rd
Bournemouth BH11 ....89 A2
Yeovil BA22 ....26 B3
River Cl BH21 ....59 B3
River La **2** DT11 ......211 D6
River Pk BH23 ....123 C3
River View SP8 ....5 C1
River Way
Charmouth DT6 ....97 A4
Christchurch BH23 .....91 B1
Riverbourne Rd SP1 ..213 C2
Riverdale La BH23 ....124 A3
Riverlea Rd BH23 .....124 A3
Rivermead Gdns BH21 ..91 C1
Rivers Mead DT10 .....35 B1
Rivers Rd BA21 ....27 C4
Riversdale **8** BH21 ...59 B2
Riversdale Rd BH6 ...124 A2
Riversdene DT11 ......48 A3
Riverside
3 Beaminster DT8 ....204 D4
4 Bournemouth BH10 ..89 C2
Ringwood BH24 ....55 A3
Riverside Ave BH7 ....91 B1
Riverside Cl SP1 ......213 C3
Riverside La BH6 .....123 C3
Riverside Pk BH23 ...124 A3
Riverside Pk Ind Est
BH21 ....59 B2
Riverside Rd
Blandford Forum DT11 ..212 C2
Bournemouth BH6 ....123 C3
Ferndown BH22 ....89 C4
Salisbury SP1 ....213 C3
Riverslea Mews BH23 ..124 B3
Riversmeet Ct BH23 ..124 B3
Rivervale DT6 ....100 B4
Riviera Ct
3 Bournemouth BH2 ..121 B2
3 Poole BH13 ....147 C4
Rivirea **22** BH1 ......122 A2
Rixon Cl DT10 ....35 B1
Rixon Hill DT10 ....35 B1
Roberts La BH17 ......119 A4
Roberts Pl DT11 ......107 C1
Roberts Rd
Bournemouth BH7 ....123 A3
Poole BH17 ....87 A1
Robertson Rd BH20 ...139 B4
Robin Cl **2** DT3 ......152 B2
Robin Cres BH25 ......94 B3
Robin Gr BH25 ....94 C1
Robins Ct **7** BH21 ....59 B2
Robins Garth DT1 ....108 A1
Robins Gdn DT2 ......209 A2
Robins Way BH23 ....125 A3
Robinson Hts DT10 ...33 B4
Robinsondor Dr BH22 ..61 B4
Robsall Cl DT1 ....120 C4
Robville Ct BH6 ......123 A3
Rochester Rd DT1 ....89 A2
Rockbourne Gdns
BH25 ....126 B4
Rockbourne La SP6 ...190 F3
Rockford Cl BH6 .....123 C2
Rockhampton Cl DT3 ..152 B2
Rockley Rd BH15 .....118 C1
Rocks La DT2 ....206 A7
Rockway DT6 ....101 B2
Rocky Knap DT3 ......167 B4
Rod Hill La DT2 ....78 A1
Rodden Cl **2** DT3 ....152 B2
Rodden House★ DT3 ..150 B3
Rodden La DT3 ....150 B3
Rodden Row DT3 .....149 A4
Rodgett Cres BH20 ...142 C4
Rodney Cl BH12 ......121 A4
Rodney Ct
Christchurch BH23 ...125 A3
Poole BH15 ....119 B1
Rodney Dr BH23 .....124 C3
Rodway DT11 ....59 B2
Rodwell Ave DT4 .....167 B1
Rodwell Cl BH10 ......89 B3
Rodwell Rd DT4 .....167 B1

Rodwell St DT4 ....167 B1
Roe Ave BA22 ....26 B3
Roe La BA21 ....15 A4
Roebuck Cl BH25 ......95 A4
Roeshot Cres BH23 ....93 C1
Roeshot Hill BH23 .....93 B1
Roke Rd BH20 ....80 C2
Rolfe Cres DT3 ......167 B4
Rollestone St **12** SP1 ..213 B3
Rolls Bridge La SP8 .....5 C1
Rolls Bridge Way SP8 ...5 B1
Rolls Dr BH6 ....124 A2
Rolls Mill Bridge★
DT10 ....197 C8
Roman Cl DT3 ....167 B4
Roman Hts BH21 ......86 C4
Roman Rd
Corfe Mullen BH18 ....86 C3
Dorchester DT1 ......134 C4
Osmington DT3 ......154 A4
Radipole DT3 ....167 B4
Roman Way DT1 ....58 B3
Romer Rd SP2 ....213 B1
Romney Cl BH10 ....89 C2
Romney Rd BH10 .....89 C2
Romsey Rd BA21 ......28 A4
Romulus Cl DT1 ......134 C4
Rook Hill Rd BH23 ...125 B3
Rook La DT11 ....210 C2
Rook St BA12 ....3 A2
Rookery Cl
7 Gillingham SP8 ......6 C1
Gillingham SP8 ....11 A4
Rookery La
Burstock DT8 ....203 C6
Uplyme DT7 ....64 A1
Rookery The DT2 ....130 C4
Roosevelt Cres BH11 ..89 A3
Rope Walks DT6 ......100 B3
Roper's La BH16 ......142 C2
Ropers La BH16 ......118 B4
Roping Rd BA21 ....27 B3
Ropley Rd BH7 ....123 B4
Rosamond Ave BH11 ..101 B2
Rosamund Ave BA21 ..59 C1
Roscrea Cl BH6 ......124 A2
Roscrea Dr BH6 ......124 A2
Rose Cres BH15 .....119 C3
Rose Ct **3** Gillingham SP8 ..6 A1
Poole BH15 ....119 C2
Rose Gdn The BH23 ...91 B3
Rose Gdns BH9 ....90 A2
Rose La **1** TA18 .....191 E4
Rose's La DT3 ....150 B1
Rosebank La BH11 ....212 B1
Roseberry Gdns **3** SP8 ..5 C3
Rosebery Cl BH31 .....45 C3
Rosebery Rd BH5 ....123 A3
Rosebud Ave **1** BH9 ..90 A1
Rosecrae Cl BH25 .....94 C2
Rosecroft Rd DT4 ....166 C1
Rosedale Cl **3** BH23 ..124 C4
Rosefields **6** DT11 ...212 B1
Roselyn Cres DT9 .....31 A1
Rosemary Cl SP1 ....213 C3
Rosemary Ct **14** BH23 ..126 A4
Rosemary Gdns BH12 ..124 A2
Rosemary La
Abbotsbury DT3 ....149 A4
1 Salisbury SP1 ......213 B2
Rosemary Rd BH12 ...120 B2
Rosemary St DT9 ......17 B1
Rosemount Rd BH4 ...121 A1
Rosewood Gdns BH25 ..94 C2
Roslin Gdns BH3 .....121 B4
Roslin Rd BH3 ....121 B4
Roslin Rd S BH3 ......121 C4
Ross Cl BH20 ....139 C3
Ross Gdns BH11 ......88 B3
Ross Glades BH3 .....121 C3
Ross Rd BH24 ....47 C1
Rossiters Quay BH23 ..124 B3
Rossley Cl BH23 ......93 C1
Rossmore Par BH12 ..120 A4
Rossmore Rd BH12 ...120 B4
Rotary Cl BH21 ....59 C4
Rotherfield Rd
Bournemouth BH5 ....123 A4
Christchurch BH23 .....94 A1
Rotherham Rd DT5 ..181 B1
Rothesay Dr BH23 ...125 C4
Rothesay Rd
Bournemouth BH4 ....121 B2
Dorchester DT1 ......135 A4
Rotterdam Dr BH23 ..124 B4
Rougemont Cl SP1 ...213 B3
Rough Down La DT6 ...65 A1
Rough Height BH19 ...179 A4
Roumelia La BH5 .....122 C2
Roundham Gdns
Bridport DT6 ....100 B2
Weymouth DT4 ......167 A4
Roundhaye Rd BH11 ...88 C3
Roundhayes Cl DT4 ..167 A1
Roundways★ BH11 ...88 C2
Row The DT10 ....35 A1
Rowan Cl
Christchurch BH23 ...125 B4
Radipole DT4 ....167 A3
St Leonards & St Ives
BH24 ....53 C2
Sandford BH20 ......143 A4
Rowan Dr
Broadstone BH17 ......86 C4
Christchurch BH23 ...125 B4
Verwood BH31 ....45 B2

Row - San 237

Rowan Way BA20 ....27 A2
Rowbarrow Cl
Poole BH17 ....87 C1
Salisbury SP2 ....213 B1
Rowbarrow Hill DT9 ....14 C2
Rowbarrow La BH21 ...200 F2
Rowden Mill La DT10 ...32 C1
Rowena Rd BH6 ......123 C3
Rowland Ave BH15 ....119 C3
Rowlands Hill BH21 .....59 B3
Rowlands Rd 5 DT11 ..198 F4
Rowls La BA9 ....4 A2
Rownhams Rd BH8 .....90 B2
Royal Arc 5 BH7 ......122 C2
Royal Armoured Corps Tank Mus★ BH20 ....139 C3
Royal Bournemouth Gen Hospl The BH7 ....91 A1
Royal Manor Sch DT5 .186 C2
Royal Oak Rd BH10 .....89 B3
Royal Signals Mus★ DT11 ....199 E3
Royal Victoria Hospl BH4 ....121 B2
Royster Cl BH17 ....87 B1
Royston Dr BH21 ....59 B3
Royston Pl BH25 ......127 A4
Rozel Manor BH13 .....121 A1
Rozelle Rd BH14 ......120 B2
Ruben Dr BH15 ....118 B1
Rubens Cl BH25 ....95 A2
Ruddock Cl BA22 ......193 B8
Ruddock Way BA22 ....193 A8
Rue La DT9 ....31 C2
Rufford Gdns BH6 .....123 C3
Rufus Castle★ DT5 ....187 A2
Rufus Way DT5 ....187 A3
Rugby Rd BH17 ....87 A1
Ruins La DT6 ....99 A3
Runnymede Ave BH11 ..88 C3
Runnymede Rd BA21 ...27 C4
Runton Rd BH12 ......120 C3
Runway The BH23 ....125 A4
Rural La DT2 ....73 C2
Ruscombe La DT6 ......69 C3
Rushall La BH21 ....86 A3
Rushcombe Fst Sch BH21 ....86 B3
Rushcombe Way BH21 ..86 C3
Rushetts Cl 7 DT5 .....186 C1
Rushford Warren BH23 ....124 C2
Rushmere Rd BH6 .....123 B4
Rushmore Golf Club SP5 ....188 C5
Rushmore Pk★ SP5 ....188 C5
Rushton Cres BH3 ....121 C3
Ruskin Ave BH9 ....90 A2
Russel Rd BH10 ....89 B3
Russell Ave
Swanage BH19 ....179 A1
Weymouth DT4 ....167 A1
Russell Cotes Art Gall & Mus★ BH1 ....122 A1
Russell Cotes Rd BH1 .122 A1
Russell Ct 3 BH25 ......95 A2
Russell Dr
Christchurch BH23 ......124 B3
Swanage BH19 ....179 A1
Russell Gdns
Hamworthy BH16 ....118 B2
St.Leonards BH24 ....54 B3
Russell Rd SP2 ....213 A3
Russet Cl BH22 ....61 B3
Russet Way BA20 ....26 C1
Rutland Manor 9 BH12 121 A2
Rutland Rd
Bournemouth BH9 ......122 A4
Christchurch BH23 ....91 C1
Weymouth DT4 ....167 A2
Ryall Rd Poole BH17 .....87 B1
Whitechurch Canonicorum DT6 ....66 B1
Ryall's La DT9 ....196 A7
Ryan Cl Ferndown BH22 ..61 B4
Northport BH20 ....142 C3
Ryan Gdns
Bournemouth BH11 ....89 A3
Ferndown BH22 ....61 B4
Rydal Cl BH23 ....91 B2
Rydal Mews BH21 ....59 B3
Rye Gdns BA20 ....26 C1
Rye Hill BH20 ....81 A1
Rye Hill Cl BH20 ....81 A1
Rye Wr La TA18 ....193 A1
Ryecroft Ave BH11 ....88 C3
Ryefields Cl BA22 .....193 B8
Ryemead La DT4 ......180 B3
Ryland's La DT4 ......180 B4
Rymbury DT3 ....153 B2
Ryme Rd DT9 ....194 B5

S

Sackmore Gn DT10 .....20 C2
Sackmore La DT10 ......20 C2
Sackville St DT11 ....81 C4
Sadborow La TA20 ....202 E5
Saddle Cl BH21 ....60 B3
Saffron Ct BH11 ....88 B2
Saffron Dr BH23 ....125 A4
Saffron Way BH11 ....88 B2
St Adlem's CE Comb Sch BH12 ....121 A3
St Alban St DT4 ....167 B1
St Alban's Ave BH8 ...122 B4
St Alban's Cres BH8 ...122 A4
St Alban's Rd BH8 ....122 A4
St Aldhelm's BH14 ....120 C2
St Aldhelm's Chapel★ BH19 ....183 A2
St Aldhelm's Cl BH13 ..120 C2
St Aldhelm's Rd
Poole BH13 ....120 C2
Sherborne DT9 ....30 A4
St Andrew's Cl DT9 ....194 E3
St Andrew's Rd DT6 ....68 C1
St Andrews BH23 ......124 A3
St Andrews Ave DT3 ..167 B4
St Andrews CE Prim Sch
Overcombe/Preston DT3 ....168 A4
Yetminster DT9 ....194 C6
St Andrews Cl 4 DT1 ..135 A4
St Andrews Dr DT6 .....97 A4
St Andrews Ind Est DT6 ....100 C4
St Andrews Mdw DT7 ...96 A3
St Andrews Rd
Broadstone BH18 ....87 A3
Yeovil BA20 ....27 A3
St Andrews View SP7 ...37 C4
St Ann Pl SP1 ....213 B2
St Ann St SP1 ....213 B2
St Ann's Ct 1 BH1 ....122 C3
St Ann's Hospl BH13 ..147 C3
St Anne's Ave BH6 ....123 C3
St Anne's Gdns BA21 ...27 A3
St Anne's Rd
Upton BH16 ....118 A4
Weymouth DT4 ....180 C4
St Annes Cl SP7 ....23 A3
St Anthony's Rd BH2 ..121 C3
St Antonys Leweston Sch DT9 ....195 A7
St Aubyns Ct 3 BH15 ..119 A1
St Augustin's Rd BH2 ..121 C3
St Augustines RC Prim Sch DT4 ....167 A1
St Bartholomews CE VC Fst Sch TA18 ....191 F4
St Brelades BH14 ......120 B1
St Brelades Ave BH12 ...88 B1
St Catharines Rd BH19 ....185 B4
St Catherine's Chapel★ DT11 ....209 F5
St Catherine's Cres 2 DT9 ....30 A3
St Catherine's Par BH23 ....91 C1
St Catherine's RC Prim Sch BH21 ....60 A3
St Catherine's Rd BH6 .123 C2
St Catherine's Way BH23 ....91 B2
St Catherines BH21 .....59 B2
St Catherines Chapel★ DT3 ....149 A3
St Catherines RC Sch DT6 ....100 B4
St Clair Rd Poole BH13 .147 C4
Salisbury SP2 ....213 B1
St Cleeves Way BH22 ...61 B2
St Clement & St John CE Inf Sch BH8 ....122 B3
St Clement's Gdns BH1 ....122 B3
St Clement's Rd BH8 ..122 B3
St Clements La BH15 ..119 A1
St Clements Rd BH15 ..120 A4
St David's Cres BA21 ...27 B4
St David's Ct 3 BH1 ...122 C3
St David's Rd
Upton BH16 ....118 A4
Weymouth DT4 ....180 B4
St Denys 28 BH25 ......95 A1
St Edmund St 6 DT4 ...167 B1
St Edmund's Church St 13 SP1 ....213 B3
St Edward's Sch BH15 .119 C4
St Edwards 5 SP7 ....12 C2
St Edwards Cl BH20 ...177 A4
St Francis Rd SP1 .....213 B4
St Gabriel's Cl DT6 .....98 B4
St George's Almshos 11 BH15 ....119 A1
St George's Ave
Bournemouth BH8 ......122 B4
Poole BH12 ....120 A4
Radipole DT4 ....167 C3
Yeovil BA21 ....27 B4
St George's Cl
Bournemouth BH8 ......122 B4
Christchurch BH23 .....125 B4
Langton Matravers BH19 ....178 A1
St George's Ct 2 BH1 ..122 C3
St George's Dr BH22 ...61 B2
St George's Rd
Portland DT5 ....186 C2
Shaftesbury SP7 ....12 C1
St Georges Cl
Bransgore BH23 ....93 A4
Dorchester DT1 ....108 B1
St Georges Cty Inf Sch DT5 ....186 C2
St Georges Est Rd DT5 ....186 C2
St Georges Hill DT7 ....96 A3
St Georges Mans 18 BH5 ....122 C2
St Georges Rd DT1 ....108 B1
St Gildas Sch BA21 .....27 B3
St Giles Cl DT6 ....99 A4
St Giles's House★ BH21 ....201 E6
St Gregorys CE Prim Sch DT10 ....20 C1
St Helen's La DT2 .....206 B2
St Helen's Rd
Dorchester DT1 ....107 C1
Sandford BH20 ....143 A4
Weymouth DT4 ....166 C1
St Helier Ave DT3 .....152 A2
St Helier Rd BH12 ......88 B1
St Ives CP Sch BH24 ....54 B3
St Ives End La BH24 ....54 B2
St Ives Gdns BH2 .....121 C3
St Ives Pk BH24 ....54 B3
St Ives Wood BH24 .....54 B3
St James DT8 ....204 C4
St James CE Fst Sch SP6 ....42 B3
St James CE Prim Sch BH7 ....123 A3
St James Cl 7 BH15 ...119 A1
St James Fst Sch BH21 .51 A3
St James Pk DT6 ....69 A1
St James Rd BH22 ......61 A3
St James St SP7 ....12 C1
St James's 20 BH5 .....122 C2
St James's Cl BA21 .....26 C3
St James's Pk BA21 ....26 C3
St James's Sq BH5 ....123 A3
St John's Cl
9 Salisbury SP1 ....213 C2
Wimborne Minster BH21 ..59 B2
St John's Ct 4 BH1 ....122 C3
St John's Gdns 3 BH9 ..89 C1
St John's Hill
Shaftesbury SP7 ....12 B1
Wareham BH20 ....142 C2
Wimborne Minster BH21 ...59 B3
St John's Rd
Bournemouth BH5 ......122 C2
Christchurch BH23 .....124 A3
Poole BH15 ....119 B2
Yeovil BA21 ....27 C4
St John's St SP1 ......213 B2
St Johns CE Fst Sch BH21 ....59 B2
St Johns CE Prim Sch DT4 ....167 C3
St Johns Rd BH25 ......95 A4
St Joseph's RC Comb Sch BH12 ....120 C4
St Joseph's RC Prim Sch BH23 ....125 A4
St Judes Cl SP1 ....213 C4
St Julien Cres DT3 ....152 A2
St Julien Rd BH20 .....139 B4
St Just Cl BH22 ....61 B2
St Juthware Cl BA22 ..193 C3
St Katharine's CE Prim Sch BH6 ....124 A2
St Katherine's Ave DT6 ....100 C4
St Katherine's CE Prim Sch BH6 ....123 A2
St Katherine's Dr DT6 .100 C4
St Lawrence 4 DT6 ....128 A4
St Lawrence Cres SP7 ..12 C2
St Lawrence Rd DT3 ..152 B3
St Ledger's Pl BH1 ....122 B3
St Ledger's Rd BH8 ...122 B3
St Leonard's Ave DT11 ....212 C2
St Leonard's Rd
Bournemouth BH8 ......122 A3
Weymouth DT4 ....167 B1
St Leonards Cty Mid Sch DT11 ....212 C2
St Leonards Hospl BH24 ....53 C1
St Leonards Way BH24 ..53 C3
St Luke's CE Prim Sch BH9 ....121 C4
St Luke's Ct 2 DT6 ....100 A4
St Luke's Rd BH3 .....121 C4
St Margaret's Almshouses BH21 ....59 A3
St Margaret's Ave BH23 ....124 A3
St Margaret's Cl 2 SP1 213 C2
St Margaret's Rd
Bournemouth BH10 ....89 B1
Poole BH15 ....119 B2
St Margarets BH2 ......121 C3
St Margarets Cl BH21 ...59 A3
St Margarets Hill BH21 .59 A3
St Mark's Ave SP1 .....213 B4
St Mark's CE Prim Sch BH10 ....89 B1
St Mark's Rd
Bournemouth BH11 ....89 A2
Salisbury SP1 ....213 B3
St Marks CE Jun Sch SP1 ....213 B4
St Martin's 6 SP1 ......213 B2
St Martin's Cl 1 BH20 .142 C2
St Martin's La BH20 ..142 C2
St Martin's Rd
12 Fortuneswell DT5 ....186 C4
Sandford BH20 ....143 A4
Weymouth DT4 ....180 C4
St Martin's Sq SP8 ......5 C1
St Martins CE Inf Sch SP1 ....213 B2
St Martins CE Jun Sch SP1 ....213 C2
St Martins Ch★ DT11 ..212 A2
St Martins Cl DT2 .....136 A1
St Martins Field DT2 ..133 B4
St Martins Rd BH16 ...118 A4
St Martins Sch TA18 ..191 E4
St Mary St 7 DT4 .....167 B1
St Mary Well St 11 DT8 .204 C4
St Mary's Church (remains of)★ SP7 ....24 A1
St Mary's Cl
Northport BH20 ....142 B3
Sixpenny Handley SP5 ..189 A4
3 Winterborne Whitechurch DT11 ....210 C3
St Mary's Cres BA21 ....27 C4
St Mary's Ct BH6 ......123 C2
St Mary's Gdns 3 DT8 .204 C4
St Mary's Maternity Hospl BH15 ....119 B2
St Mary's Mews BH22 ..61 B2
St Mary's Rd
Bournemouth BH1 ......122 B3
Ferndown BH22 ....61 B3
Poole BH15 ....119 C2
Salisbury SP2 ....213 A2
Sherborne DT9 ....29 C3
St Marys Cath Fst Sch DT1 ....135 A4
St Marys CE Mid Sch DT2 ....78 A1
St Marys CE Prim Sch DT6 ....100 B3
St Marys Cl BH23 ....93 B4
St Marys Fst Sch BH22 ..52 C2
St Marys Prim Sch DT8 ....204 C4
St Marys RC Fst Sch BH19 ....179 A1
St Marys RC Prim Sch BH20 ....140 A1
St Marys RC Sch DT10 ..21 A3
St Marys Sch
Donhead St Mary SP7 .....13 B1
Thorncombe TA20 ....202 E6
St Merrin's Cl BH10 .....89 B2
St Michael's 2 BH2 ....121 B2
St Michael's Ave BA21 ..27 C4
St Michael's CE Mid Sch BH21 ....59 C4
St Michael's CE Prim Sch BH2 ....121 B2
St Michael's La DT6 ...100 B3
St Michael's Mews 16 BH2 ....121 C2
St Michael's Pl 18 BH2 .121 C2
St Michael's Rd
Bournemouth BH2 ......121 C1
11 Wareham BH20 ......142 C2
Yeovil BA21 ....27 C3
St Michael's Trading Est DT6 ....100 B3
St Michaels DT7 ....96 B3
St Michaels Cl
Hamworthy BH15 ....118 C1
Over Compton DT9 ....28 C4
Verwood BH31 ....45 A3
St Michaels Ct
1 Bournemouth BH6 ....123 B2
Weymouth DT4 ....167 B1
St Michaels Rd BH31 ...45 A2
St Michaels VC Inf Sch DT7 ....96 B3
St Nicholas & St Laurence CE Prim Sch DT3 ....152 B1
St Nicholas CE Prim Sch DT11 ....198 C7
St Nicholas Cl
3 Henstridge BA8 ....19 A2
11 Yeovil BA20 ....27 B2
St Nicholas Ct 5 DT11 .198 C7
St Nicholas Gdns 2 DT11 ....198 E3
St Nicholas St DT4 ....167 B1
St Nicholas' Rd SP1 ...213 B2
St Osmonds Sch SP1 ..213 B2
St Osmund Cl 3 DT9 ..194 C5
St Osmund's Rd BH14 .120 B2
St Osmunds CE Mid Sch DT1 ....135 A4
St Patrick's Rd BA21 ...26 C4
St Patricks Ave DT4 ...166 C1
St Paul's Cl DT9 ....30 B4
St Paul's Gn DT9 ....30 B4
St Paul's La BH1 ......122 A2
St Paul's Pl BH1 ......122 A2
St Paul's Rd
Bournemouth BH1 ......122 A2
13 Fortuneswell DT5 ...186 C4
Salisbury SP2 ....213 A3
St Peter's Abbey★ DT3 ....149 A4
St Peter's Cl 1 DT11 ..199 D4
St Peter's Cres 36 BH1 121 C2
St Peter's Ct 7 BH14 ..120 A2
St Peter's RC Comp Sch BH6 ....123 C2
St Peter's RC Sch BH7 123 A4
St Peter's Rd
Bournemouth BH1 ......122 A2
Poole BH14 ....120 A2
St Peter's Wlk 38 BH1 .121 C2
St Peters Ct BH1 ......122 A2
St Rayn Hill TA18 .....191 A4
St Richards Cl DT11 ..211 F7
St Rumbold's Rd SP7 ...12 C1
St Saviors Cl BH7 .....123 B4
St Stephen's Ct 6 BH2 .121 C2
St Stephen's Rd BH2 ..121 C2
St Stephen's Way 27 BH2 ....121 C2
St Stephens La BH31 ...45 B3
St Swithin's Rd DT9 ....30 B3
St Swithins Ave DT6 ...100 B4
St Swithins Cl DT9 .....30 B3
St Swithins Rd DT6 ...100 B4
St Swithun's Rd BH1 ..122 A2
St Swithun's Rd S BH1 ....122 A2
St Thomas Cross 1 BA21 ....27 C3
St Thomas Garnet's RC Sch BH5 ....123 A3
St Thomas Rd DT1 ....107 C1
St Thomas St DT4 .....167 B1
St Thomas's Cl BH10 ...89 C1
St Valerie Rd BH2 .....121 C3
St Vast's Rd BH19 .....179 B1
St Walburga's RC Prim Sch BH9 ....90 A1
St Winifred's Rd BH2 ..121 C3
Salerno Pl BH15 ....118 B1
Salisbury & S Wiltshire Mus★ SP2 ....213 A2
Salisbury Arts Ctr★ SP1 ....213 B3
Salisbury Bsns Pk SP1 ....213 C2
Salisbury Cath★ SP1 ..213 B2
Salisbury Cath Sch SP1 ....213 B2
Salisbury Coll of Tech SP1 ....213 B2
Salisbury Cres DT11 ..212 B3
Salisbury Leisure Ctr SP1 ....213 A4
Salisbury Rd
Blandford Forum DT11 ..212 C3
Bournemouth BH1 ......122 C2
Burton BH23 ....92 B2
Donhead St Mary SP7 ....13 B1
Ellingham Harbridge & Ibsley SP6 ....43 B1
Pimperne DT11 ....199 E4
Poole BH14 ....120 B3
Shaftesbury SP7 ....12 C1
Sopley BH23 ....92 A3
9 Swanage BH19 ......179 B1
Weymouth DT4 ....167 B2
Salisbury Sch of English SP1 ....213 B2
Salisbury St
Cranborne BH21 ....40 A4
Dorchester DT1 ....108 A1
Marnhull DT10 ....21 A1
Mere BA12 ....3 A3
Shaftesbury SP7 ....12 C1
Salisbury Sta SP2 .....213 A3
Salisbury Street DT11 .212 B2
Salisbury Swimming Baths SP1 ....213 B3
Sally Kings La SP7 .....12 B2
Sally Lovell's La BA8 ...18 C4
Salt La SP1 ....213 B3
Salter Rd BH13 ....147 B2
Salterns Ct BH14 ......147 A4
Salterns Point BH14 ...147 A4
Salterns Quay BH14 ...147 A4
Salterns Rd BH14 .....120 A2
Salterns Way BH14 ....147 A4
Salthouse La BA20 .....27 B2
Saltings Rd BH16 .....118 A3
Salway Dr DT6 ....68 A3
Salwayash Prim Sch DT6 ....68 A4
Sammy Miller's Motorcycle Mus★ BH25 ....94 C3
Samphire Cl DT4 ......167 B3
Samples Way BH17 ...119 C4
Samson Rd BH15 ......118 B1
Samways Cl BA22 ....26 B3
San Remo Twrs 23 BH5 .122 C2
Sancreed Rd BH12 .....120 C4
Sancroft BH21 ....60 A1
Sandbanks Bsns Ctr BH13 ....147 A2
Sandbanks Rd BH14 ...120 A1
Sandbourne Ave DT11 .212 C3
Sandbourne Cl 11 BH19 178 C1
Sandbourne Rd
Bournemouth BH4 ....121 B1
Overcombe/Preston DT3 ....168 A4
Poole BH15 ....119 B2
Sandecotes Rd BH14 ..120 B2
Sanderling 6 DT3 ......152 B2
Sanderlings 3 BH24 ....55 C3
Sanders Gn 4 DT11 ...210 C3
Sandford Cl BH9 ....90 B2
Sandford Dr BH20 .....116 A1
Sandford La BH20 .....142 C3
Sandford La Ind Est BH20 ....142 C3
Sandford Mid Sch BH20 ....116 A1
Sandford Orcas Rd
Castleton DT9 ....15 C2
Sandford Orcas DT9 ......15 C2
Sandford Rd
Northport BH20 ....142 C3
Wareham St Martin BH20 ....116 A1
Sandford St Martin CE Fst Sch BH20 ....143 A4
Sandford Way BH18 .....86 C1
Sandhills Cl BH17 ......87 B1

Sandhills Cres BH20 . . . . .**139** C1
Sandhurst Dr BH21 . . . . .**53** B4
Sandhurst Rd BA20 . . . . .**27** A1
Sandilands Cl SP8 . . . .**10** C2
Sandleheath Rd SP6 . . . . .**42** A4
Sandlewood Cl BA21 . . . . .**28** A4
Sandmartin Cl BH25 . . . .**126** C4
Sandown Cl BA20 . . . .**27** B3
Sandown Pl 14 SP2 . . .**213** A3
Sandown Rd BH23 . . . . . .**124** C3
Sandpiper Cl BH17 . . . . . .**86** C1
Sandpiper Way DT4 . . .**180** B3
Sandpit La BH15 . . . .**119** B2
Sandringham Cl BH9 . . . .**90** A2
Sandringham Ct
  Bournemouth BH8 . . . . .**122** B3
  1 Dorchester DT1 . . . .**135** B4
Sandringham Gdns
  BH9 . . . .**90** A2
Sandringham Rd
  Poole BH14 . . . .**120** B2
  Yeovil BA21 . . . .**28** A3
Sandringham Sports Ctr
  DT1 . . . .**108** A1
Sandroyd Sch SP5 . . . . .**188** C5
Sandsfoot Castle ★
  DT4 . . . .**180** C4
Sandy BH21 . . . .**60** A4
Sandy Hill La BH20 . . . .**162** A4
Sandy Hole TA16 . . . . .**191** F8
Sandy La
  Bournemouth BH6 . . . . .**123** A3
  Christchurch BH23 . . . . . .**91** C1
  Lytchett Matravers BH16 . . .**84** C3
  Minterne Magna DT2 . . . .**207** C7
  Pamphill BH21 . . . .**58** A3
  St.Leonards BH24 . . . .**54** B3
  Upton BH16 . . . .**118** A3
  Verwood BH21 . . . .**45** A1
  Whitechurch Canonicorum
   DT6 . . . .**65** A4
  Wimborne Minster BH21 . . .**60** A4
Sandy Mead Rd BH8 . . . .**90** C1
Sandy Plot BH23 . . . . . .**124** B4
Sandy Way BH10 . . . .**89** C2
Sandyhurst Cl BH17 . . . . .**87** B1
Sansome's Hill 6 DT9 . . .**17** B1
Santoy BH13 . . . .**147** B3
Sarah Cl DT4 . . . .**167** B4
Sarah Sands Cl BH23 . . .**124** B4
Sark Rd BH12 . . . .**120** B4
Sarum 3 DT9 . . . .**194** D8
Sarum Ave BH22 . . . .**53** A2
Sarum Cl SP2 . . . .**213** A4
Sarum Coll SP1 . . . .**213** B2
Sarum Ct BH14 . . . .**120** B2
Sarum St 14 BH15 . . . . .**119** A1
Sarum St Pauls CE Sch
  SP2 . . . .**213** A4
Saulfland Dr BH23 . . . . .**125** B4
Saulfland House BH23 . . .**125** B4
Saulfland Pl BH23 . . . . . .**125** B4
Saville Ct 9 BH21 . . . . . .**59** B2
Sawyers La DT2 . . . .**106** C4
Saxon Hts BH6 . . . .**123** C3
Saxon King Gdns BH6 . .**124** A2
Saxon Mead Cl SP8 . . . . . .**5** C2
Saxon Rd SP2 . . . .**213** A1
Saxon Rise DT11 . . . . . .**210** C7
Saxon Spur SP7 . . . .**12** C2
Saxon Sq Sh Ctr 4
  BH23 . . . .**124** A3
Saxon Way SP6 . . . .**42** B3
Saxonbury Rd BH6 . . . . .**123** C3
Saxonford Rd BH23 . . . .**125** B4
Saxonhurst Cl BH10 . . . . .**89** C1
Saxonhurst Gdns BH10 . .**89** C2
Saxonhurst Rd BH10 . . . .**89** C2
Scadden's Cnr DT6 . . . . .**66** A4
Scamell's Rd SP2 . . . . .**213** B3
Scaplen's Ct Mus ★
  BH15 . . . .**119** A1
Scarf Rd BH17 . . . .**119** C4
Schelin Way 6 DT11 . . .**198** B5
School Cl
  Chickerell DT3 . . . .**166** B3
  4 Tarrant Gunville DT11 . .**199** F7
  Verwood BH31 . . . .**45** B4
School Hill
  Chickerell DT3 . . . .**166** B3
  Cucklington BA9 . . . .**4** A2
  Powerstock DT6 . . . .**70** A3
  South Perrott DT8 . . . . . .**192** C1
School House La DT2 . .**103** A1
School La
  Askerswell DT2 . . . .**102** B4
  4 Blandford Forum DT11 .**212** B1
  Bournemouth BH11 . . . . . .**89** A3
  Broadwindsor DT8 . . . . . .**203** B6
  Chetnole DT9 . . . .**194** D3
  9 Dorchester DT1 . . . . .**107** C1
  Gillingham SP8 . . . .**6** A1
  4 Pimperne DT11 . . . . .**199** D4
  Poole BH15 . . . .**119** B3
  Ringwood BH24 . . . .**55** B4
  St.Leonards BH24 . . . .**54** B3
  Studland BH19 . . . .**164** B1
  3 Tarrant Gunville DT11 .**199** F7
  Toller Porcorum DT2 . . . . .**71** C4
  Verwood BH31 . . . .**53** A4
  West Lulworth BH20 . . . .**172** B3
  Wimborne Minster BH21 . . .**59** A3
  Winfrith Newburgh DT2 . .**156** C3
  Woodsford DT2 . . . .**110** B1
School Rd SP8 . . . .**5** C1

School St 11 DT4 . . . . .**167** B2
Schoolhouse La DT10 . . .**21** A1
Scotchey Hill SP8 . . . . . .**10** B1
Scotchey La SP8 . . . .**10** C1
Scots La SP1 . . . .**213** B3
Scott Cl Poole BH12 . . . . .**88** C1
  Stoborough Green BH20 . .**160** C4
Scott Rd BH12 . . . .**88** C1
Scott's Gn BH23 . . . . . .**124** C4
Scott's La DT6 . . . .**64** A3
Scotter Rd BH7 . . . .**123** A4
Scotton Way The DT2 . .**137** B3
Scotts Hill La BH23 . . . .**124** B4
Scotts Way TA18 . . . . . .**192** A8
Scouse La EX13 . . . .**202** B2
Scrubbity Barrows ★
  SP5 . . . .**188** B4
Scutts Cl BH16 . . . .**84** B2
Sea Hill La DT6 . . . .**99** A3
Sea King Rd BA20 . . . . . .**26** C2
Sea Life Pk & Model
  Village ★ DT4 . . . .**167** C3
Sea Point 8 BH13 . . . . .**147** C4
Sea Rd
  Barton on Sea BH25 . . . .**126** C4
  Bournemouth BH5 . . . . . .**122** C2
Sea Rd N DT6 . . . .**100** C4
Sea Rd S DT6 . . . .**100** B3
Sea View 7 DT5 . . . . . .**186** C4
Sea View Rd
  Poole BH12 . . . .**120** A3
  Upton BH16 . . . .**118** A4
Sea Vixen Ind Est
  TA18 . . . .**191** F3
Seabank Cl BH16 . . . . . .**118** A4
Seaborough View
  TA18 . . . .**191** F3
Seabourne Pl 12 BH5 . .**123** A3
Seabourne Rd BH5 . . . . .**123** A3
Seacombe Rd BH13 . . . .**147** A2
Seacroft Ave BH25 . . . .**126** C4
Seafield Cl BH25 . . . . . .**126** C4
Seafield Dr BH6 . . . .**123** C3
Seafield Rd
  Barton on Sea BH25 . . . .**126** C4
  Bournemouth BH6 . . . . . .**123** B2
  Christchurch BH23 . . . . . .**125** B4
Seagull Rd BH8 . . . .**90** B1
Seamoor Cl DT3 . . . . . .**167** C4
Seamoor La BH4 . . . . . .**121** A2
Seamoor Rd BH4 . . . . . .**121** A2
Seaton Cl BH23 . . . .**126** A4
Seaton Rd
  Christchurch BH23 . . . . . .**126** A4
  Yeovil BA20 . . . .**27** A2
Seatown Rd BH17 . . . . . .**88** A1
Seaview Rd
  Barton on Sea BH25 . . . .**126** B4
  Christchurch BH23 . . . .**94** B1
Seaward Ave BH25 . . . .**126** C4
Seaward Gdns DT6 . . . .**100** B1
Seaward Rd BH19 . . . . .**179** A2
Seaway BH25 . . . .**127** A4
Seaway Ave BH23 . . . . .**125** B4
Second Cliff Wlk 2
  DT6 . . . .**100** A1
Second Marine Ave
  BH25 . . . .**127** A3
Sedgefield Cl DT4 . . . . .**167** B2
Sedgemoor Cl BA21 . . . .**27** C3
Sedgley Rd BH9 . . . .**121** C4
Seed Warehouse The 15
  BH15 . . . .**119** B1
Selby Cl BH18 . . . .**87** A2
Seldown BH15 . . . .**119** B2
Seldown Bridge BH15 . .**119** B1
Seldown La BH15 . . . . . .**119** B2
Seldown Rd BH15 . . . . . .**119** B2
Self Rd BH15 . . . .**119** A1
Selfridge Ave BH6 . . . . .**124** A2
Selfridge Cl BH6 . . . . . .**124** A2
Seliot Cl BH15 . . . .**119** B3
Selkirk Cl BH21 . . . .**59** C1
Selle Rd BH20 . . . .**139** C3
Sellwood Way BH25 . . . .**126** B4
Selwood Cl DT10 . . . .**35** B1
Selwood Pk BH10 . . . . . .**89** B4
Selworthy Cl BH14 . . . . .**120** A1
Selwyn Cl DT3 . . . .**152** B2
Senior Dr SP2 . . . .**213** B1
Sentinal Ct BH15 . . . . . .**119** C2
Sentry Rd BH19 . . . .**179** B1
Serpentine Rd BH15 . . . .**119** B2
Serrells Mead BH19 . . . .**178** B1
Seth Ward Dr SP1 . . . . .**213** C4
Setley Gdns BH8 . . . .**90** C2
Seven Acres 9 DT5 . . . .**186** C1
Seven Acres Rd DT3 . . .**153** B2
Seven Ash Comm Rd
  DT9 . . . .**195** B4
Seven Barrows Rd
  BH20 . . . .**142** B3
Sevenoaks Dr BH7 . . . .**123** A4
Severalls Pk Ave 17
  TA18 . . . .**191** F4
Severn Rd BH22 . . . .**62** A3
Seward Ave BH6 . . . . . .**123** B2
Sewell Rd BH20 . . . .**139** B4
Seymer Rd BH19 . . . . . .**179** B1
Seymour Rd BH24 . . . . . .**47** B1
Shadrack DT6 . . . .**128** A4
Shadrack St 2 DT8 . . . .**204** C4
Shady Bower SP1 . . . . . .**213** C4
Shaftesbury Cl BH22 . . .**53** A1
Shaftesbury Fst Sch
  SP7 . . . .**13** A1
Shaftesbury Mus ★ SP7 .**12** C1

Shaftesbury Rd
  Child Okeford DT11 . . . .**198** C8
  Ferndown BH22 . . . .**53** A1
  Gillingham SP8 . . . .**6** A1
  Henstridge BA8 . . . .**19** B3
  Kington Magna SP8 . . . . . .**20** A4
  Mere BA12 . . . .**3** A2
  Poole BH15 . . . .**119** B2
Shaftesbury Upper Sch
  SP7 . . . .**12** C1
Shaftsbury Rd BH18 . . .**122** B3
Shakespeare Rd
  Bournemouth BH6 . . . . . .**123** B4
  Salisbury SP1 . . . .**213** A4
  Wimborne Minster BH21 . . .**59** B3
Shamrock Ct 2 BH21 . . .**59** B2
Shapland Ave BH11 . . . . .**88** C3
Shapwick Rd BH15 . . . . .**119** A1
Shard Cl BH31 . . . .**45** B3
Sharford Bridge ★
  BH20 . . . .**162** A3
Sharlands Cl BH18 . . . . . .**87** A2
Sharp Rd BH12 . . . .**121** A4
Shaston Cl 10 BH19 . . .**178** C1
Shaston Cres DT1 . . . . .**135** A4
Shaston Rd DT11 . . . . . .**198** F4
Shatcombe La DT2 . . . . .**71** B2
Shatter's Hill BH20 . . . .**142** C2
Shave Cross DT6 . . . . . .**203** C1
Shave Hill SP8 . . . .**9** A4
Shave La Todber DT10 . . .**21** B3
  West Crewkerne TA18 . . . .**191** E3
Shaves La BH25 . . . .**95** A3
Shaw Cl DT11 . . . .**212** B3
Shaw Dr BH20 . . . .**142** C4
Shaw Rd BH24 . . . .**47** C1
Shawford Gdns BH8 . . . .**90** B1
Shawford Rd BH8 . . . . . .**90** B2
Shear Plot DT6 . . . .**99** C4
Shears Rd DT4 . . . .**167** B4
Shearstones DT9 . . . . . .**194** D5
Sheasby Cl SP5 . . . .**189** A3
Shedbush La DT6 . . . . . .**98** B4
Shedrick Hill TA20 . . . . .**202** E8
Sheep Mkt Hill 4 DT11 .**212** B1
Sheepcroft La BH21 . . . .**51** B2
Sheephouse Dro
  BH21 . . . .**200** E2
Sheeplands La DT9 . . . . .**29** C3
Sheeplands The DT9 . . . .**29** C4
Sheepspine La TA20 . . . .**202** C5
Sheepwash La
  Burstock DT8 . . . .**203** D5
  Tatworth & Forton
   TA20 . . . .**202** A6
Shelbourne Cl BH8 . . . .**122** B3
Shelbourne Rd BH8 . . . .**122** A3
Sheldrake Rd BH23 . . . .**125** A3
Shell Bay Sailing Ctr ★
  BH19 . . . .**147** A1
Shelley Cl
  Bournemouth BH1 . . . . . .**122** C3
  Christchurch BH23 . . . . . .**125** B4
  St.Leonards BH24 . . . .**53** C3
  Yeovil BA21 . . . .**26** C3
Shelley Ct BH22 . . . .**61** B3
Shelley Dr SP1 . . . .**213** A4
Shelley Gdns BH1 . . . . .**122** C3
Shelley Hamlets BH23 . .**125** B4
Shelley Hill BH23 . . . . . .**125** B4
Shelley House 16 BH9 . . .**95** A1
Shelley Pk (Bournemouth &
  Poole Coll) BH5 . . . . .**122** C2
Shelley Rd
  Bournemouth BH1 . . . . . .**122** C3
  Poole BH12 . . . .**120** B3
Shelley Rd E BH7 . . . . . .**122** C3
Shelton Rd BH6 . . . .**123** B3
Shenstone Ct 18 BH25 . .**95** A1
Shepherd Cl BH23 . . . . . .**93** C1
Shepherd's Hill SP8 . . . . . .**9** B4
Shepherds Croft DT5 . . .**187** B3
Shepherds Hill BH24 . . . .**46** C3
Shepherds La BH24 . . . . .**46** B3
Shepherds Way
  Bournemouth BH7 . . . . . .**123** A4
  West Lulworth BH20 . . . .**172** B3
Sheppards Field 4 BH21 .**59** A3
Sherborn Cres BH17 . . . . .**88** C1
Sherborne Abbey ★ DT9 .**30** A3
Sherborne Castle ★
  DT9 . . . .**30** B3
Sherborne CP Sch DT9 . .**30** B4
Sherborne Cswy SP7 . . .**11** C2
Sherborne Dr BH22 . . . . .**61** B2
Sherborne Golf Club
  DT9 . . . .**16** A2
Sherborne Hill DT9 . . . . .**30** B2
Sherborne Mus ★ DT9 . .**30** B3
Sherborne Rd
  Henstridge BA8 . . . .**18** C2
  Milborne Port DT9 . . . . . .**17** B1
  Purse Caundle DT10 . . . . .**18** B1
  Yeovil BA21 . . . .**27** C3
Sherborne Sch DT9 . . . . .**30** A3
Sherborne Sta DT9 . . . . .**30** A3
Sherbourne La 3 DT7 . . .**96** B3
Sherbourne Old Castle ★
  DT9 . . . .**30** B3
Sherfield Cl BH8 . . . .**90** B1
Sherford Cl BH20 . . . . . .**142** B3
Sherford Dr BH20 . . . . . .**142** C3
Sheridan Cl DT2 . . . .**73** C2
Sheriden Way 5 BH21 . . .**56** B2
Sheringham Rd BH12 . . .**120** C3
Sherlands 1 TA16 . . . . .**191** F7
Sherren Ave DT2 . . . .**75** C1
Sherrin Cl BH15 . . . .**119** B3

Sherwood Ave
  Ferndown BH22 . . . .**61** B2
  Poole BH14 . . . .**120** A2
Sherwood Dr BH31 . . . . .**45** B3
Shetland View BH31 . . . . .**45** B3
Shiller's La DT9 . . . .**15** C3
Shillingstone CE Prim Sch
  DT11 . . . .**198** B6
Shillingstone Dr BH9 . . . .**90** A2
Shillingstone Gdns
  BH12 . . . .**120** C4
Shillingstone La DT11 . .**197** F5
Shillito Rd BH12 . . . .**120** C3
Ship Knapp DT6 . . . .**66** A1
Shipney La DT10 . . . .**19** C1
Shipstal Cl BH16 . . . . . .**118** B2
Shipstal Nature Trail ★
  BH20 . . . .**144** B2
Shipton La
  Burton Bradstock DT6 . . .**101** B3
  Loders DT6 . . . .**101** C3
Shipton Rd DT6 . . . .**101** B2
Shirecroft Rd DT4 . . . . .**167** A2
Shiremoor Hill TA16 . . .**191** F7
Shires Cl BH24 . . . .**55** B2
Shires Copse BH6 . . . . .**123** C2
Shires Mead BH31 . . . . . .**45** B3
Shirley Cl
  Ferndown BH22 . . . .**53** A1
  Swanage BH19 . . . .**178** C1
Shirley Rd
  Bournemouth BH9 . . . . . .**90** A1
  Poole BH12 . . . .**120** A3
  Upton BH16 . . . .**118** B4
  Wareham BH20 . . . .**142** B2
Shoe La DT6 . . . .**100** C4
Shoot Hill TA17 . . . .**191** C8
Shop La DT3 . . . .**150** B1
Shore Ave BH16 . . . .**118** B3
Shore Cl BH16 . . . .**118** A3
Shore Gdns BH16 . . . . . .**118** A3
Shore La BH16 . . . .**118** B3
Shore Rd Poole BH13 . . .**147** B3
  Swanage BH19 . . . .**179** B2
Shoreacres BH13 . . . . . .**147** B2
Shoredown La DT9 . . . . . .**17** B3
Short Cl BH12 . . . .**121** A4
Short Cross DT2 . . . . . .**206** C6
Short Rd DT4 . . . .**167** A2
Short's La DT11 . . . .**212** B2
Shortedge DT10 . . . .**35** B1
Shortlake La DT3 . . . . . .**169** A4
Shortlands DT5 . . . .**186** C2
Shortlands Rd DT3 . . . .**152** A3
Shortmarsh La TA18 . . .**192** F4
Shorts Cl BH23 . . . .**92** B1
Shorts Gn La SP7 . . . . . .**12** A4
Shottsford Cl 7 BH19 . .**178** C1
Shottsford Rd BH15 . . . .**119** B3
Shreen Cl 9 SP8 . . . .**5** C2
Shreen Way SP8 . . . .**5** C2
Shrubbery La DT7 . . . . .**180** B4
Shute La DT11 . . . .**37** C1
Shute Lake La 11 TA18 .**191** F4
Shute's La SP8 . . . .**9** B4
Sidmouth Rd DT7 . . . . . .**96** A3
Sidney Gdns 11 BH9 . . . .**90** A2
Sidney Smith Ct BH17 . . .**87** C1
Sidney St SP2 . . . .**213** A3
Silchester Cl BH2 . . . . . .**121** C3
Silk House Barton
  DT10 . . . .**33** B4
Sillen La SP6 . . . .**190** B6
Silton Rd SP8 . . . .**1** C1
Silver Birch Cl BH12 . . .**121** A2
Silver Bsns Pk BH23 . . . .**124** C4
Silver St
  Christchurch BH23 . . . . . .**124** A3
  Crewkerne TA18 . . . .**192** B3
  Lyme Regis DT7 . . . .**96** A3
  Overcombe/Preston
   DT3 . . . .**153** B2
  Salisbury SP1 . . . .**213** B2
  4 Stofold BA22 . . . .**193** F8
  Yeovil BA20 . . . .**27** B3
Silver Way BH23 . . . . . .**125** C4
Silverdale BH25 . . . .**127** A4
Silverdale Cl BH18 . . . . .**86** C2
Silverdale Cres SP6 . . . .**42** B3
Silverwood Cl BH21 . . . . .**59** B1
Simmonds Cl BH15 . . . .**119** B3
Simons Rd DT9 . . . .**30** A4
Sinclair Cl 8 BH14 . . . . .**120** A2
Singleton Dr BH10 . . . . . .**89** B1
Sir John Colfox Sch
  DT6 . . . .**68** C1
Sir Richard Hull Rd
  BH20 . . . .**139** B3
Siskin Cl BH22 . . . .**61** A4
Sitterton Cl BH20 . . . . . .**81** A2
Six Ways Cross BH21 . .**200** E3
Sixpenny Cl BH12 . . . . .**120** C4
Sixpenny Handley Cty Fst Sch
  SP5 . . . .**189** A4
Skilling Hill Rd DT6 . . . .**100** B3
Skilling La DT6 . . . .**100** A3
Skinner St BH15 . . . .**119** B1
Skipton Cl BH18 . . . .**87** A1
Slade La BA22 . . . .**15** C3
Slade's La BH10 . . . .**121** B4
Slades Farm Rd BH10 . . .**89** B1
Slades Farm Specl Sch
  BH10 . . . .**89** B1
Slades Gn DT6 . . . .**100** C3
Slape Hill DT6 . . . .**68** B4
Slape Manor ★ DT6 . . . .**204** C1
Sleepbrook Cl BH31 . . . . .**45** B3
Sleight Cl BA21 . . . .**26** C3

Sleight La BH21 . . . .**86** B3
Slepe Cres BH12 . . . . . .**120** C4
Slinn Rd BH23 . . . .**124** C4
Slip Way BH15 . . . .**119** A_
Slodbrook La SP8 . . . .**2** B_
Slopers Mead 2 DT11 . .**211** E_
Slough Dro DT2 . . . .**205** E_
Slough La Horton BH21 . . .**44** A_
  Lytchett Minster & Upton
   BH16 . . . .**117** A_
  Upton BH16 . . . .**118** A_
  Woodlands BH21 . . . .**44** A_
Slyer's La
  Puddletown DT2 . . . .**76** C_
  Stinsford DT2 . . . .**108** B_
Smacombe La DT6 . . . . .**101** B_
Smallmouth Cl DT4 . . . .**180** B_
Smeaton Rd SP2 . . . . . .**213** A_
Smedmore House ★
  BH20 . . . .**175** C_
Smishops La DT6 . . . .**69** B_
Smith's Hill TA18 . . . . . .**192** B_
Smith's La DT2 . . . .**208** B_
Smith's Terr BA21 . . . . . .**27** C_
Smithfield Pl BH9 . . . .**89** C_
Smithson Cl BH12 . . . . .**121** B_
Smithy La BH25 . . . .**94** C_
Smokey Hole La 3 DT1 .**135** B_
Smugglers La BH21 . . . . .**59** C_
Smugglers La N BH23 . . .**93** C_
Smugglers La S BH23 . .**125** C_
Smugglers Reach
  BH23 . . . .**125** A_
Smugglers Wood Rd
  BH23 . . . .**93** B_
Smuggler's' La
  Colehill BH21 . . . .**50** C_
  Stourpaine DT11 . . . .**199** A_
Snag La DT11 . . . .**79** C_
Snail's La BH24 . . . .**47** B_
Snails La BH24 . . . .**47** B_
Snow Down Rd 1 DT11 .**199** E_
Snow Hill BH20 . . . .**81** A_
Snow Hill La BH20 . . . . . .**81** A_
Snowdon Rd BH4 . . . . . .**121** B_
Snowdrop Gdns BH23 . . .**93** A_
Soberton Rd BH8 . . . . . .**122** B_
Sodern La DT2 . . . .**107** B_
Sodom La DT10 . . . .**21** A_
Solar Ct BH13 . . . .**147** B_
Soldiers Rd BH20 . . . . . .**143** B_
Solent Dr BH25 . . . .**127** A_
Solent Lodge 21 BH25 . . .**95** A_
Solent Rd
  Barton on Sea BH25 . . . .**126** B_
  Bournemouth BH6 . . . . . .**124** A_
  Christchurch BH23 . . . .**94** A_
  Swanage BH19 . . . .**185** B_
Solent View BH6 . . . . . .**124** A_
Solly Cl BH12 . . . .**120** C_
Solomon Way BH15 . . . .**118** B_
Somerby Rd BH15 . . . . .**119** B_
Somerford Ave BH23 . . .**125** A_
Somerford Bsns Pk
  BH23 . . . .**125** A_
Somerford Ct BH23 . . . .**125** C_
Somerford Cty Inf Sch
  BH23 . . . .**124** C_
Somerford Cty Jun Sch
  BH23 . . . .**124** C_
Somerford Rd BH23 . . . .**124** C_
Somerford Way BH23 . . .**124** C_
Somerley Pk ★ BH24 . . . .**46** C_
Somerley Rd BH9 . . . . . .**122** A_
Somerley View BH24 . . . .**55** A_
Somers Rd DT7 . . . .**96** A_
Somerset Cl SP8 . . . .**5** C_
Somerset Rd
  Bournemouth BH7 . . . . . .**123** A_
  Salisbury SP1 . . . .**213** B_
  Weymouth DT4 . . . .**167** A_
Somerton Cl BH25 . . . . . .**95** B_
Somerville Ct BH25 . . . . .**94** C_
Somerville Rd
  Bournemouth BH2 . . . . . .**121** B_
  Ringwood BH24 . . . .**55** C_
Sonning Way BH8 . . . . . .**90** A_
Soper's La BH23 . . . . . .**124** A_
Sopers La BH17 . . . .**87** A_
Sopley Cl BH25 . . . .**126** B_
Sopley Farm Bldgs
  BH23 . . . .**92** A_
Sopwith Cl BH23 . . . . . .**125** A_
Sopwith Cres BH21 . . . . .**59** C_
Sorrel Cl DT4 . . . .**167** C_
Sorrel Gdns BH18 . . . . . .**86** C_
Sorrel Way SP8 . . . .**5** B_
Sorrell Ct BH23 . . . .**125** A_
Sorrell Way BH23 . . . . . .**125** A_
Souter Way DT3 . . . .**167** B_
South Annings 2 DT6 . . .**128** A_
South Ave
  Lyme Regis DT7 . . . .**96** A_
  New Milton BH25 . . . .**95** A_
  Sherborne DT9 . . . .**29** C_
South Bridge ★ BH20 . .**142** C_
South Cliff Rd
  Bournemouth BH2 . . . . . .**121** C_
  Swanage BH19 . . . .**179** B_
South Cres DT11 . . . . . .**199** E_
South Cswy BH20 . . . . .**142** C_
South Ct DT9 . . . .**29** C_
South Ct Ave DT1 . . . . .**135** A_
South Dr DT2 . . . .**206** C_
South Dro DT2 . . . .**135** C_
South Farm Cl DT11 . . .**200** A_
South Haven Cl BH16 . .**118** A_

South Hill SP6 ....42 B3
South Holme DT11 ....198 F4
South Instow BH19 ....177 C3
South Kinson Dr BH11 ..89 A2
South Lawns DT6 .....100 B3
South Mead BH20 ......81 A1
South Mill La DT6 ....100 B3
South Par 3 DT4 ....167 C1
South Pk Rd BH12 ...121 A4
South Rd
  Bournemouth BH1 .....122 C3
  Corfe Mullen BH21 .....86 C3
  Poole BH15 ....119 B1
  Swanage BH19 ....179 A1
  Weymouth DT4 ....180 B3
South Rd Comb Sch
  BH15 ....119 B1
South St Arne BH20 ...142 C2
  Bridport DT6 ....100 B3
  Corfe Castle BH20 ...176 C2
  Crewkerne TA18 .....191 F4
  Dorchester DT1 ......108 A1
  11 Gillingham SP8 .....5 C1
  Hinton St George TA17 .191 D7
  Kington Magna SP8 .....9 B1
  Leigh DT9 ....194 E3
  Milborne Port DT9 .....17 B1
  15 Salisbury SP2 ....213 A3
  Sherborne DT9 ....30 A3
  Yeovil BA20 ....27 B2
South View
  Bournemouth BH2 .....121 C3
  Bradford Abbas DT9 ...28 B1
  Piddletrenthide DT2 ...208 C1
South View Pl 17 BH2 .121 C3
South View Rd
  Christchurch BH23 ....124 A3
  Milborne Port DT9 .....17 B1
South Walks Rd DT1 ..108 A1
South Way DT5 ....186 B1
South Western Cres
  BH14 ....120 A1
South Western Rd
  SP2 ....213 A3
South Wilts Gram Sch For
  Girls SP2 ....213 B4
South Wlk DT6 ....100 B3
Southampton Rd
  Ringwood BH24 ....55 A4
  Salisbury SP1 ....213 C2
Southbourne Coast Rd
  BH6 ....123 C2
Southbourne Cross Roads 6
  BH6 ....123 C2
Southbourne Gr BH6 ..123 B2
Southbourne Overcliff Dr
  BH6 ....123 B2
Southbourne Rd BH5 .123 B2
Southbourne Sands
  BH6 ....123 B2
Southbrook
  Bere Regis BH20 ......81 A1
  Mere BA12 ....3 B2
Southbrook Cl BH17 ...88 A1
Southbrook Gdns BA12 ..3 B2
Southcliffe Rd
  Barton on Sea BH25 ..126 B4
  Christchurch BH23 ....125 B3
Southcote Rd BH1 ....122 B2
Southdown Ave DT3 ..167 C4
Southdown Rd DT4 ...180 C4
Southdown Way BH22 ..53 A1
Southern Ave BH22 ....53 B1
Southern La BH25 ....126 C4
Southern Oaks BH25 ..94 C1
Southern Rd BH6 .....123 B2
Southernhay BH31 .....45 B3
Southey Rd BH23 .....124 C4
Southfield Ave DT4 ...167 B3
Southfield Mews 4
  BH24 ....55 B3
Southill Ave BH12 ....120 B4
Southill CP Sch DT4 ..167 A4
Southill Gdn Dr DT4 ..167 A3
Southill Gdns BH9 ....90 A1
Southill Rd
  Bournemouth BH9 .....90 A1
  Poole BH12 ....120 B4
Southlands Ave
  Bournemouth BH6 ....123 C2
  Corfe Mullen BH21 ....86 C3
Southlands Cl BH21 ...86 B3
Southlands Dr BH18 ...87 A2
Southlands Rd DT4 ...180 C4
Southlawns Wlk BH25 ..94 C1
Southlea Ave BH6 ....123 C2
Southmead Cres 20
  TA18 ....191 F4
Southmead La BA8 .....19 A2
Southover DT6 ....128 A4
Southover Cl DT11 ....212 B1
Southover La DT1 .....79 B1
Southview Rd DT4 ....167 A4
Southville BA21 ......27 C3
Southville Rd BH5 ....123 A3
Southway Cl BA21 ....27 A4
Southway Cres BA21 ..27 A3
Southway Dr BA21 ....27 A4
Southwell Prim Sch
  DT5 ....186 C1
Southwell Rd
  12 Easton/Weston DT5 .186 C1
  Portland DT5 ....187 A1
Southwick Pl BH6 ....123 B4
Southwick Rd BH6 ....123 B3

Southwood Ave
  Bournemouth BH6 ....123 B2
  Christchurch BH23 ....94 A1
Southwood Cl
  Christchurch BH23 ....94 A1
  Ferndown BH22 ....61 B3
Southwood Ct BH23 ...94 A1
Southwoods BA20 .....27 B2
Sovereign Bsns Ctr
  BH15 ....119 A3
Sovereign Cl BH7 ....122 C4
Sovereign Ctr BH1 ...122 C3
Sovereign Sq 8 BH7 ..122 C2
Spa Ave DT3 ....167 B4
Spa Rd DT3 ....167 A4
Sparacre Gdns DT6 ..100 B4
Sparkford Cl DT7 ....123 A4
Sparrow Rd BA21 .....27 B3
Spearhay La TA20 ...202 B4
Specket La DT2 .....203 A5
Speedwell Dr BH23 ..125 A4
Speke Cl 10 TA16 ....191 F7
Spence La DT6 ....64 C3
Spencer Ct 5 BH25 ..95 A1
Spencer Gdns DT11 ..198 C5
Spencer Rd
  Bournemouth BH1 .....122 B2
  New Milton BH25 ......95 A1
  Poole BH13 ....147 C4
Spetisbury CE Prim Sch
  DT11 ....211 D5
Spetisbury Cl BH9 ....90 A2
Spettisbury Rings ★
  ....211 E5
Spicer La BH11 ....88 C3
Spiller Rd DT3 ......166 B3
Spinacre BH25 ....127 A4
Spindle Cl BH11 ......86 C1
Spindlewood Cl 26 BH25 .95 A1
Springfield Rd BA12 ....3 A3
Spinners Cl BH22 .....53 A1
Spinners Way BA12 ....3 A3
Spinners' La BH11 ...101 A3
Spinney Cl 2 BH24 ...53 C2
Spinney The
  Broadmayne DT2 .....136 A1
  Lytchett Matravers BH16 ..84 B1
  Radipole DT3 ....152 A1
  St.Leonards BH24 .....54 A3
  7 Yeovil BA20 ....26 C1
Spinney Way BH25 ....95 A3
Spinneys La BH22 ....61 B3
Spitfire Cl DT2 ......137 B3
Spittlefields BH24 ....55 B4
Spittles La DT7 ....96 B3
Spread Eagle Hill SP7 ..24 B2
Spring Ave DT4 .....167 B3
Spring Cl 4 Bridport DT6 ..68 C1
  Verwood BH31 ....45 A3
Spring Ct BH12 .....120 B3
Spring Gdns
  10 Fortuneswell DT5 ..186 C4
  Poole BH12 ....120 B3
  West Knighton DT2 ...136 B2
  Weymouth DT4 ....167 B1
Spring Gr DT2 ......196 A1
Spring La
  Longburton DT9 .....195 B7
  New Milton BH25 ......95 B1
  Sandford Orcas DT9 ...15 C3
Spring Rd
  Bournemouth BH1 .....122 B3
  6 Weymouth DT4 .....167 C1
Spring St BH20 .....140 A1
Springbank Rd BH7 ..122 C4
Springbourne Ct BH1 .122 B3
Springbourne Mews
  BH1 ....122 B3
Springbrook Cl BH20 .177 C3
Springdale Ave BH5 ..86 C3
Springdale Fst Sch
  BH18 ....86 C2
Springdale Gr BH21 ..86 C2
Springdale Rd BH18 ..86 C2
Springfield
  East Chinnock BA22 ..192 E8
  Puncknowle DT2 .....129 C3
Springfield Ave
  Bournemouth BH6 ....124 A2
  Christchurch BH23 ....91 B1
Springfield Cl
  2 Shaftesbury SP7 ....13 A2
  Verwood BH31 ....45 A3
Springfield Cres
  Poole BH14 ....120 A2
  Radipole DT3 ....152 A2
  5 Sherborne DT9 .....30 A3
Springfield Gdns BH25 .95 B1
Springfield Pl BA21 ...27 A4
Springfield Rd
  Milborne Port DT9 .....17 B2
  Poole BH14 ....120 A2
  Radipole DT3 ....152 A2
  10 Swanage BH19 ....179 A1
  Verwood BH31 ....45 A3
  Yeovil BA21 ....27 A4
Springfields Holt BH21 .51 A2
  Stalbridge DT10 ......33 C4
Springhill Gdns DT7 ...96 A3
Springvale Ave BH7 ..123 A4
Springwater Cl BH11 .89 A2
Springwater Ct BH23 .124 B3
Springwater Dr BH23 .124 B3
Springwater Rd BH11 .89 A2
Springwell Cl BH20 ..177 A4
Spruce Cl BH17 ......86 C1
Spur Cl BH21 ....60 B3
Spur Hill Ave BH14 ..120 B2

Spur Rd BH14 ....120 B2
Spurgeon Rd BH7 ...123 A3
Spy Cl BH7 ....84 B2
Spyway Rd DT2 .....102 B4
Square The
  Bournemouth BH2 ...121 C2
  Cattistock DT2 .....206 C2
  Corfe Castle BH20 ...162 A1
  Cranborne BH21 ......40 A4
  12 Gillingham SP8 .....5 C1
  Langton Herring DT3 ..150 B1
  Mere BA12 ....3 A3
  Milborne St Andrew DT11 .79 C4
  Powerstock DT2 ......70 A2
  Puddletown DT2 ......78 A1
  Wimborne Minster BH21 .59 A3
Squirrel's Cl BH23 ....91 B1
Squirrel's Cnr BH21 ..189 D1
Srringfield DT2 ......207 D4
Stables The BH23 ...123 C4
Stacey Cl BH12 .....120 B4
Stacey Gdns BH8 .....90 C1
Stafford Cl DT2 .....136 B2
Stafford Gdns DT2 ..136 A4
Stafford House ★ DT2 .136 A4
Stafford Rd
  Bournemouth BH1 .....122 A2
  Swanage BH19 ....179 B1
Stag Cl BH25 ....94 C2
Stag Gate ★ DT11 ...211 F2
Stagg's Folly ★ DT2 ..206 E3
Stagswood BH31 ......44 C3
Stainers Mead SP7 .....7 A1
Stainforth Cl DT4 ...166 C2
Stake Ford Cross DT9 .194 E4
Staker's Cross TA18 ..191 B2
Staker's Cross La
  TA18 ....191 B2
Stakes La DT9 ......195 E6
Stalbridge CE Prim Sch
  DT10 ....19 B1
Stalbridge Cl DT10 ...33 B4
Stalbridge Dr BH22 ...61 B2
Stalbridge La DT10 ...34 B2
Stalbridge Pk ★ DT10 ..19 B1
Stalbridge Rd
  Broadstone BH17 ....119 A4
  Henstridge BA8 ......19 A4
  Stalbridge DT10 ......32 C2
Stalham Rd DT2 ....120 C3
Stallards La BH24 .....55 A4
Stamford Rd BH6 ...123 B3
Stammery Hill EX13 ..202 A1
Stanbarrow Cl DT2 ....81 A1
Standpitts La SP8 .....10 C3
Stanfield Cl BH12 ...120 B4
Stanfield Rd
  Bournemouth BH9 ....121 C4
  Ferndown BH22 ......61 B3
  Poole BH12 ....120 B4
Stanier Rd DT3 .....153 A2
Staniforth Ct BH23 ..124 B3
Stanley Cl BH31 ......45 B3
Stanley Ct
  Bournemouth BH1 .....122 B3
  Poole BH15 ....119 B3
Stanley Gn Cres BH15 .119 B3
Stanley Gn Fst Sch
  BH15 ....119 B3
Stanley Gn Ind Est
  BH15 ....119 B3
Stanley Gn Rd BH15 ..119 B3
Stanley Pearce House
  BH17 ....87 B1
Stanley Rd
  Bournemouth BH1 .....122 B3
  Christchurch BH23 ...126 A4
  Poole BH15 ....119 B1
Stanley St 1 DT4 ...167 B2
Stannington Cl BH25 ..95 A1
Stanpit BH23 ....124 C3
Stanpit Marsh Nature
  Reserve ★ 124 B3
Stanstead Rd DT2 ....73 A4
Stanton Cl DT11 ....212 B3
Stanton Lacy 17 BH13 .147 C4
Stanton Rd BH10 .....89 B1
Stapehill Cres BH21 ..60 B3
Stapehill Mus & Gdns ★
  BH21 ....60 C3
Stapehill Rd BH21 ....60 C2
Staple Cl La BH15 ...119 B1
Staple Cross BH23 ..124 C4
Staplecross La DT2 ..124 B4
Stapleford Ave BH22 ..61 C3
Staples Mdw 4 TA20 .202 A8
Staples Terr DT7 .....96 B3
Star Cottage Gdn ★
  BH21 ....58 B3
Star La DT6 ....98 B4
Starlight Farm Cl BH31 .45 B4
Stars La BA20 ....27 B2
Station App
  Broadstone BH18 .....87 A2
  Dorchester DT1 .....108 A1
Station Pl 1 BH19 ..179 A1
Station Rd Alderholt SP6 .42 A3
  Child Okeford DT11 ..198 C7
  Christchurch BH23 ....93 C1
  2 Easton/Weston DT5 .187 A2
  Edmondsham BH31 ....44 C4
  Ferndown BH22 ......52 C1
  Gillingham SP8 ....5 C1
  Hamworthy BH15 ....119 A1
  Henstridge BA8 ......19 A3
  Holton Heath BH20 ..116 B2
  Maiden Newton DT2 ...72 C4
  Milborne Port DT9 ....17 B2

Station Rd continued
  Misterton TA18 ......192 A1
  Moreton DT2 ....138 A4
  New Milton BH25 ......95 A1
  Poole BH14 ....120 A2
  Sherborne DT9 ....30 A3
  2 Shillingstone DT11 .198 B6
  Stalbridge DT10 ......19 B1
Sturminster Marshall
  BH21 ....56 B2
Sturminster Newton DT10 .35 A1
  Swanage BH19 ....179 A1
Tatworth & Forton
  TA20 ....202 A8
  Verwood BH31 ....45 A4
Wareham St Martin
  BH16 ....116 B1
  Wimborne Minster BH21 .59 B2
  Wool BH20 ....140 A1
Station Terr
  13 Salisbury SP2 ....213 A3
  Wimborne Minster BH21 .59 B2
Station Yd SP6 ....42 A3
Staunton DT2 ....121 C1
Stavordale Rd DT4 ...167 B2
Stearts La DT11 ......35 A3
Stedman Rd BH5 ....123 A3
Steel Well La BA8 .....19 A2
Steel's La BH20 ......20 A2
Steels La SP6 ....190 F1
Steep St BA12 ....3 A3
Steepdene BH14 ....120 A2
Steeple Cl Poole BH17 ..87 B2
  Radipole DT3 ....167 A4
Steepleton Rd BH18 ..87 B1
Steer Rd BH19 ......178 C1
Stella Ct 19 BH23 ...126 A4
Stem La BH25 ....94 C2
Stenhurst Rd BH15 ..119 C3
Stephen Langton Dr
  BH11 ....88 B3
Stephen's Castle (Tumulus) ★
  BH31 ....45 B4
Stephens Cl
  Netherbury DT6 .....204 B1
  1 Salisbury SP2 ....213 A2
Stephenson Rd SP2 ..213 A2
Stepleton House ★
  DT11 ....198 F6
Stepnell Reach BH16 .118 B3
Steppes BH19 ......178 C1
Steppes Hill BH19 ..178 B1
Sterte Ave BH15 ....119 A2
Sterte Ave W BH15 ..119 A2
Sterte Cl BH15 .....119 B2
Sterte Ct BH15 .....119 A2
Sterte Espl BH15 ...119 A2
Sterte Ind Est BH15 .119 A2
Sterte Rd BH15 ....119 B2
Stevens Cl 2 DT11 ..212 C3
Stevenson Cres BH14 .120 C2
Stevenson Rd BH6 ..124 A3
Stevensons Cl 3 BH21 .59 B2
Steward's La DT11 ....56 A4
Stewart Cl 5 BH8 ...122 B4
Stewart Rd BH8 .....122 A3
Stewarts Way BH22 ..61 C3
Stibles La DT11 ....197 D3
Stiby Rd BA21 ....27 A4
Stickland Sch DT2 ..206 A7
Stile La DT7 ....96 A2
Stile Way DT2 ......206 E6
Stileham Bank DT11 ..79 C4
Stillmore Rd BH11 ....88 B2
Stinford La DT8 ....204 D6
Stinsford Cl BH9 .....90 A2
Stinsford Hill DT2 ...108 B2
Stinsford La BH17 ...119 B4
Stinsford Rd BH17 ....87 B1
Stinsford View DT11 ..108 B1
Stirling Cl BH25 .....95 A2
Stirling Ct
  Bournemouth BH4 ...121 B3
  21 New Milton BH25 ..95 A2
Stirling Rd
  Bournemouth BH3 ...121 C4
  Radipole DT3 ....167 B4
Stirling Way BH23 ...125 A4
Stirrup Cl Upton BH16 .118 B4
  Wimborne Minster BH21 .60 B3
Stoborough Cl DT3 ..167 A4
Stoborough Dr BH18 ..87 A1
Stoborough Mdw
  BH20 ....142 C1
Stoborough Sch BH20 .142 C1
Stock Hill La DT9 ...195 F4
Stock La SP8 ....5 A1
Stockbridge Cl BH17 ..88 A1
Stockley Rd BH20 ...142 B3
Stockwood Cl SP1 ...213 C4
Stoke La
  Mappowder DT10 ....196 F1
  Stoke Wake DT11 ...209 A8
Stoke Rd
  Beaminster DT8 ....204 C4
  Weymouth DT4 .....180 B4
Stoke Wood Rd BH1 .121 C3
Stokehouse St DT1 ..107 B1
Stokes Ave BH15 ...119 B2
Stokes La DT10 ......32 C1
Stonage La TA18 ...192 C5
Stone Gdns BH8 .....91 A1
Stone La
  Wimborne Minster BH21 .59 A3
  Yeovil BA21 ....27 B4
Stone La Ind Est BH21 .59 A3

Stonebarrow La
  Charmouth DT6 ......97 B4
  Hawkchurch EX13 ...202 C2
  Stanton St Gabriel DT6 .97 C4
Stonechat Cl
  Ferndown BH22 ......61 A4
  3 Radipole DT3 .....152 B2
Stonechat Ct BH23 ..124 C4
Stonecrop Cl BH18 ...86 C1
Stonedene DT9 ......30 A4
Stoneleigh 18 BH13 ..147 C4
Stoneleigh Ave SO41 .95 C2
Stoney La BA22 .....193 D6
Stoney Lawn DT11 ...81 B4
Stoneylawn DT10 .....21 A1
Stony Down La DT6 ..65 A2
Stony La
  Bishop's Caundle DT9 .196 A8
  Burton BH23 ....92 B1
  Damerham SP6 .....190 E2
  Holwell DT10 ......196 C6
Stony La S BH23 ....124 B3
Stony Weir ★ BH20 ..140 B2
Stonyacres DT9 .....194 C6
Stopples La SO41 ....95 C2
Story La BH18 ....87 A2
Stottingway St DT3 ..152 A3
Stour Cl East Stour SP8 .10 B1
  Ferndown BH21 ......60 B1
  Shillingstone DT11 ..198 C5
Stour Dr BH20 ....142 B3
Stour Gdns SP8 ......5 C1
Stour Hill SP8 ....9 C1
Stour Hill Pk SP8 .....9 C1
Stour La SP8 ....21 C4
Stour Mdws SP8 ......5 C1
Stour Pk BH10 ....89 C3
Stour Rd
  Blandford Forum DT11 .212 C2
  Bournemouth BH8 ...122 B3
  Christchurch BH23 ...124 A3
Stour View Cl DT10 ...35 A1
Stour View Gdns BH21 .58 C1
Stour Way BH23 .....91 B1
Stour Wlk
  Bournemouth BH8 ...122 B3
  11 Wimborne Minster BH21 59 B2
Stourbank Rd BH23 ..124 A3
Stourcliffe Ave BH6 ..123 B2
Stourcroft Dr BH23 ...91 C1
Stourfield Fst & Jun Schs
  BH6 ....123 B3
Stourfield Rd BH5 ...123 A2
Stourpaine Rd BH17 ..87 B1
Stourton Ct 17 BH4 ..121 B2
Stourton Way BA21 ...26 C4
Stourvale Ave BH23 ..123 B4
Stourvale Pl 10 BH5 .123 A3
Stourvale Rd BH5 ...123 B3
Stourwood Ave BH6 ..123 B2
Stourwood Mans 4
  BH6 ....123 B2
Stourwood Rd BH6 ..123 B2
Stowcastle St 9 DT1 ..107 B1
Stowell Cres BH20 ..142 B1
Stowell 15 TA20 ....202 A8
Stower Provost CP Sch
  SP8 ....21 C4
Stowey St DT1 ......107 B1
Straits DT5 ....187 A2
Strand St DT4 ......119 B1
Stratfield Pl BH25 ....94 C2
Stratford Rd
  Salisbury SP1 ....213 B4
  Yeovil BA21 ....26 C3
Strathmore Dr BH31 ..45 B3
Strathmore Rd BH9 ..90 A2
Stratton Rd BH9 .....90 B2
Straw Barrow ★ DT11 ..48 B2
Streche Rd
  Swanage BH19 ....179 B3
  Wareham BH20 .....142 B2
Street La
  Longburton DT9 .....195 C6
  Sedgehill And Semley SP7 ..7 C2
Street The
  Charmouth DT6 ......97 A4
  Moreton DT2 ....138 C4
  Motcombe SP7 ....7 A1
  Sutton Waldron DT11 ..37 B3
  Winterborne Zelston
  DT11 ....82 C4
Streets La DT11 ......55 C2
Streetway La DT2 ...209 B3
Strete Mount 10 BH23 .124 C4
Stretton Ct BH14 ...120 C2
Strides La BH24 ......55 A4
Strode Gdns BH24 ....54 B3
Strodes La DT2 ......75 B1
Strongate La DT6 .....68 A4
Stroud La BH21 ......60 A3
Stroud Gdns 4 BH23 .124 C3
Stroud La DT2 ......124 C4
Stroud Pk Ave BH23 .124 C3
Strouden Ave BH8 ...122 B4
Strouden Rd BH9 .....90 A1
Stroudley Cres DT3 ..153 B2
Struan Cl BH24 ......54 B3
Struan Dr BH24 ......54 B3
Struan Gdns BH24 ...54 A3
Stuart Cl BH16 .....118 C4
Stuart La SP8 ....5 B1
Stuart Rd BH23 .....126 A4
Stuart Way DT6 .....100 C4

Stubhampton Bottom
DT11 .38 C3
Stuckton Rd SP6 .43 B4
Student Village BH12 .121 B4
Studland Heath (National Nature Reserve)★
BH19 .164 A3
Studland Rd BH4 .121 B1
Studland Way DT3 .167 A4
Studley Cl BH23 .126 B4
Studley Ct BH25 .126 B4
Sturminster Marshall Fst Sch
BH21 .56 C2
Sturminster Newton High Sch DT10 .35 A2
Sturminster Newton Leisure Ctr DT10 .35 A2
Sturminster Newton Mill & Mus★ DT10 .35 A1
Sturminster Rd 10 BH9 .90 A2
Sturt La BH20 .81 B2
Styles Cl 9 DT8 .204 C4
Styles La DT2 .78 A1
Sudan Rd DT4 .180 C4
Suffolk Ave BH23 .91 C1
Suffolk Cl BH21 .60 B3
Suffolk Rd
Bournemouth BH2 .121 B2
Salisbury SP2 .213 A1
Suffolk Rd S BH2 .121 B2
Sugar Hill
Bere Regis BH20 .113 C4
Bloxworth BH20 .114 A3
Summer Field Cl BH21 .60 A2
Summer Fields BH31 .45 A2
Summer Hill TA17 .191 D7
Summer House Terr
BA20 .27 B2
Summer La
Evershot DT2 .206 A7
Hinton St George TA17 .191 D8
Summerbee Comp Sch
BH8 .90 B1
Summerbee Fst Sch
BH8 .90 B1
Summerbee Jun Sch
BH8 .90 B1
Summercroft Way
BH22 .53 A2
Summerfield Cl BH23 .92 B1
Summerfields
Bournemouth BH7 .122 C4
Henstridge BA8 .19 A3
Summerhill Rd DT7 .96 B3
Summerhouse View
BA21 .27 C3
Summerlands
Ferndown BH22 .61 B3
Yeovil BA21 .27 A3
Summerlands Hospl
BA21 .27 A3
Summerleaze Pk BA20 .27 A3
Summerlock App 6
SP2 .213 B3
Summers Ave BH11 .89 A3
Summers La BH23 .92 B1
Summertrees Ct BH25 .95 B2
Sun La
Piddletrenthide DT2 .208 B1
Whitechurch Canonicorum
DT6 .98 B4
Sunbury Cl BH11 .89 A3
Sunbury Ct 8 BH2 .121 C2
Sunderland Dr BH23 .125 A4
Sundew Cl
Christchurch BH23 .93 B1
New Milton BH25 .95 B2
Radipole DT4 .167 C4
Sundew Rd BH18 .86 C1
Sunningdale
Christchurch BH23 .123 C3
8 Poole BH15 .119 C2
Sunningdale Cres BH10 .89 B2
Sunningdale Gdns
BH18 .87 A3
Sunningdale Rd BA21 .27 C3
Sunny Hill Ct BH12 .120 B3
Sunny Hill Rd BH12 .120 B3
Sunnybank Dr BH21 .60 A3
Sunnybank Rd BH21 .60 A3
Sunnybank Way BH21 .60 A3
Sunnyfield Rd BH25 .127 A4
Sunnyfields DT3 .153 B2
Sunnyhill Rd
Bournemouth BH6 .123 B3
Salisbury SP1 .213 B4
Sunnylands Ave BH6 .123 C2
Sunnymoor Rd BH11 .89 A1
Sunnyside Ridge BH20 .143 A1
West Lulworth BH20 .172 B3
Sunnyside Rd
Poole BH12 .120 B3
Weymouth DT4 .180 B4
Sunridge Cl
Poole BH12 .121 A3
Swanage BH19 .179 A1
Sunrise Bsns Pk DT11 .212 C4
Sunrise Ct BH22 .61 B3
Sunset Lodge BH13 .121 A1
Surrey Cl
Christchurch BH23 .91 C1
Weymouth DT4 .166 C2
Surrey Gdns BH4 .121 B2
Surrey Rd BH2 .121 A2
Surrey Rd S BH4 .121 B2
Sussex Cl BH9 .90 A2
Sussex Farm Way 8
DT9 .194 C5
Sussex Rd
Salisbury SP2 .213 A1
Weymouth DT4 .167 A2
Sutcliffe Ave DT4 .167 A3
Sutherland Ave BH18 .86 C3
Sutton Cl 4 Gillingham SP8 5 C1
Overcombe/Preston
DT3 .153 B2
Poole BH17 .88 A1
Sutton Ct Lawns DT3 .153 B2
Sutton Grange BA21 .26 C3
Sutton Hill BA22 .193 D6
Sutton Pk DT3 .153 B2
Sutton Rd
Bournemouth BH9 .90 A1
Overcombe/Preston
DT3 .153 B2
Swaffield Gdns 5 DT4 .180 B4
Swainson Rd DT11 .199 E4
Swallow Cl BH17 .118 C4
Swallow Way BH21 .60 A4
Swallowcliffe Gdns
BA20 .27 B3
Swallowfields 13 SP8 .5 C2
Swallowmead 2 SP2 .213 B1
Swan Cl SP2 .213 B1
Swan Gn 8 BH23 .124 A3
Swan Hill TA18 .192 B5
Swan La DT2 .208 B1
Swan Mead BH24 .55 C3
Swan St BH21 .40 A4
Swanage Cty Mid Sch
BH19 .178 C2
Swanage Her Ctr★
BH19 .179 B1
Swanage Hospl BH19 .179 A1
Swanage Rd BH19 .164 B1
Swanage Rly★ BH20 .177 B3
Swanmore Cl BH7 .123 A4
Swanmore Rd BH7 .123 A4
Swansbury Dr BH8 .91 A1
Sway Gdns BH8 .90 B1
Sway Rd BH25 .95 B3
Swaynes Cl 3 SP1 .213 B3
Sweep The BH24 .55 A4
Sweet Hill La DT5 .186 C1
Sweet Hill Rd DT5 .186 C1
Sweetmans Rd SP7 .12 C2
Swift Cl BH17 .118 C4
Swiftdown 6 SP2 .213 B1
Swilletts La DT6 .203 D4
Swinton Ave BH20 .139 B4
Swordfish Dr BH23 .125 A4
Swyre Rd DT2 .129 C1
Sycamore Ave BH20 .116 A2
Sycamore Cl
Broadstone BH17 .86 C1
Christchurch BH23 .123 B4
Sandford BH20 .143 A4
Sixpenny Handley SP5 .189 A4
Sycamore Dr
14 Crewkerne TA18 .191 F5
Yeovil BA20 .27 A1
Sycamore Pl BH21 .60 B3
Sycamore Rd
Hordle SO41 .95 C2
Radipole DT4 .167 A3
Sycamore Way SP8 .5 B1
Sydenham Cres BH20 .139 C1
Sydenham Rd BH19 .178 C1
Sydenham Way 17 DT1 .108 A1
Sydling Cl BH17 .88 A1
Sydling Rd
Cerne Abbas DT2 .207 C3
Yeovil BA21 .27 C3
Sydney Pl 3 SP8 .5 C1
Sydney Rd
Broadstone BH18 .87 A2
Christchurch BH23 .91 C1
Sydney St DT4 .167 A2
Sylmor Gdns BH9 .90 A1
Sylvan Cl 4 Gillingham SP8 .5 C2
St.Leonards BH24 .53 C2
Sylvan Fst Sch BH12 .120 A3
Sylvan Rd BH12 .120 A3
Sylvan Way SP8 .5 C2
Symes Cl TA18 .192 C4
Symes Rd BH15 .118 C2
Symonds Cl DT3 .167 B4
Symondsbury Prim Sch
DT6 .99 C4
Syward Cl DT1 .108 B1
Syward Rd DT1 .108 B1

T

Tabbit's Hill La BH20 .177 C3
Tabernacle La 8 BA20 .27 B2
Tadden Cotts BH21 .58 B4
Tadden Wlk BH18 .86 C1
Tadnoll Barrow★ DT2 .138 B2
Tail Mill TA16 .191 F7
Tait Cl BH17 .119 C4
Talbot Ave BH3 .121 C4
Talbot Cl SP1 .213 C4
Talbot Comb Sch
BH12 .121 A4
Talbot Ct BH9 .89 C1
Talbot Dr
Christchurch BH23 .93 C1
Poole BH12 .121 A4
Talbot Heath Sch BH4 .121 B3
Talbot Hill Rd BH9 .121 B4
Talbot House Prep Sch
BH9 .121 C4
Talbot Manor BH3 .121 B4
Talbot Mdws BH12 .121 A4
Talbot Mews BH10 .89 A1
Talbot Rd
Bournemouth BH9 .121 C4
Lyme Regis DT7 .96 A4
Talbot Rise BH10 .89 B1
Talbothays Rd DT1 .135 A4
Tall Trees BH14 .120 A3
Tallidge Cl DT3 .168 B4
Tamar Cl BH22 .62 A3
Tamlin St BH20 .143 A4
Tamworth Rd BH7 .122 C3
Tan Howse Cl BH7 .123 A4
Tan La SP8 .2 A1
Tanglewood Ct 11 BH25 .95 A2
Tanglewood Lodge
BH17 .118 C4
Tangmere Cl BH23 .125 A3
Tangmere Pl BH17 .119 C4
Tanner's La 10 BH20 .142 C2
Tannery Rd DT6 .100 B3
Tansee Hill TA20 .202 E6
Tantinoby La BH20 .142 B3
Tanyard DT2 .206 A7
Tanyard La SP7 .12 B1
Tanzey La DT10 .21 A2
Taphouse La DT6 .66 B4
Tapper Ct BH21 .59 C2
Tark's Hill DT9 .194 C5
Tarn Dr BH17 .118 C4
Tarrant Abbey House★
DT11 .211 F6
Tarrant Cl BH17 .87 C1
Tarrant Dr BH20 .142 B3
Tarrant Rd BH9 .90 A2
Tarratt La BA20 .27 A1
Tarratt Rd BA20 .27 A1
Tasman Cl BH23 .123 C4
Tatnam Rd BH15 .119 B2
Tattershall Gdns 4 BH21 56 B2
Tatum Cres BH15 .119 B2
Taunton Rd BH19 .179 B1
Taverner Cl BH15 .119 B1
Taylor Dr BH8 .90 B2
Taylor Way BH31 .45 B3
Taylor's Bldgs 21 BH15 .119 B1
Taylor's La
Mappowder DT10 .196 E1
Whitechurch Canonicorum
DT6 .66 A1
Teal Ave DT3 .166 B3
Teasel Way BH22 .53 A1
Tecan Way DT4 .166 C2
Technology Rd BH17 .119 A4
Tedder Cl BH11 .89 A2
Tedder Gdns BH11 .89 A2
Tedder Rd BH11 .89 A2
Teeling Rd DT3 .167 B4
Telegraph St DT11 .198 E8
Telford Cl DT3 .168 A4
Telford Rd
Ferndown BH21 .61 A4
Salisbury SP2 .213 A2
Temple Cl DT1 .134 C4
Temple La BA8 .8 A1
Temple Mews BH1 .122 B3
Templecombe La SP8 .8 C3
Templer Cl BH11 .88 C1
Ten Acres SP7 .12 C2
Tennyson Rd
Bournemouth BH9 .89 C1
1 Poole BH14 .120 A2
Weymouth DT4 .167 B1
Wimborne Minster BH21 .59 B3
Tensing Rd BH23 .124 C4
Terence Ave BH17 .87 B1
Terence Rd BH21 .86 B3
Termare Cl BA22 .26 B3
Terminus St 3 DT4 .167 B2
Tern Ct BH6 .123 B3
Terrace Rd BH2 .121 C2
Terrington Ave BH23 .93 C1
Tewkesbury 9 BA21 .26 C3
Thames Alley 18 BH15 .119 A1
Thames Cl BH22 .62 A3
Thames Mews 12 BH15 .119 A1
Thames St BH15 .119 A1
Thatcham Ct BA21 .27 A4
Thatcham Pk BA21 .27 A4
Thatcham Pk Cl BA21 .27 A4
Theobold Rd BH23 .91 A4
Thessaly Ct 17 BH5 .122 C2
Thetchers Cl BH25 .95 A3
Thetford Rd BH12 .120 C3
Thickthorn Cross
BH21 .200 D7
Thickthorn La DT10 .197 A2
Third Cliff Wlk 3 DT6 .100 A1
Thistlebarrow Rd
Bournemouth BH7 .122 C3
Salisbury SP1 .213 B4
Thomas Hardy Cl DT10 .35 A1
Thomas Hardy Dr SP7 .13 A2
Thomas Hardye Leisure Ctr
DT1 .134 B4
Thomas Hardye Sch
DT1 .134 C4
Thomas's London Day Schs
BH24 .55 A4
Thompson Cl
Britford SP2 .213 A1
Puddletown DT2 .78 A1
Thomson Dr 10 TA18 .191 F4
Thoresby Ct BH25 .94 C2
Thorn Rd BH17 .87 B2
Thornbury 15 BH4 .121 B2
Thornbury Rd BH6 .124 A2
Thorncombe Beacon★
DT6 .99 B2
Thorncombe Cl
Bournemouth BH9 .90 A2
Poole BH17 .87 C1
Thorne Cl BH31 .45 A4
Thorne Gdns BA21 .26 C4
Thorne La
Brympton BA21 .26 C4
Yeovil BA21 .27 A4
Thorners CE Prim Sch
DT2 .103 B1
Thornfield Dr BH23 .93 C1
Thornford CE Prim Sch
DT9 .194 D8
Thornford Rd DT9 .194 C6
Thornford Sta DT9 .194 C7
Thornham Rd BH25 .95 B2
Thornhill Cl DT1 .134 C4
Thornhill Cres DT4 .167 B2
Thornhill Rd DT10 .33 B4
Thornicks DT2 .156 C3
Thornley Rd BH10 .89 B2
Thornlow Prep Sch
DT4 .167 B1
Thornton Cl BH21 .86 B3
Thornton Rd BA21 .26 C4
Thorny La BA22 .14 B4
Thorogood Ct 4 BH15 .119 C2
Thrasher's La BH20 .162 A2
Three Acre Dr BH25 .126 C4
Three Acre La BH19 .178 B1
Three Acres DT2 .207 A2
Three Barrows★
BH20 .161 A3
Three Cnr Mead 5 BA21 26 C3
Three Cross Rd BH21 .53 A3
Three Legged Cross Fst Sch
BH21 .45 A1
Three Lions Ct 12 BH21 .59 A3
Three Lords' Barrow★
BH20 .160 B3
Three Yards Cl DT5 .186 C4
Thrift Cl DT10 .33 C4
Throop Cl BH8 .91 A1
Throop Hollow DT2 .112 B3
Throop Rd
Abbas & Templecombe
BA8 .8 A2
Bournemouth BH8 .90 C2
Throopside Ave BH9 .90 B2
Thrush Rd BH12 .88 B1
Thursby Rd BH23 .93 C1
Thwaite Rd BH12 .121 A3
Tidemill Ct BH23 .124 A4
Tiffany Cl SO41 .95 C2
Tilburg Rd BH23 .124 B4
Tilbury Mead BH20 .177 A4
Tiley Knap DT2 .207 E8
Tilly Whim Caves★
BH19 .185 B3
Tilly Whim La DT2 .106 C2
Tillycombe Rd DT5 .187 A4
Timber Hill DT7 .96 B4
Timothy Cl BH10 .89 B3
Tin Pot La DT11 .212 B3
Tincleton Cross DT2 .110 B3
Tincleton Gdns BH9 .90 A2
Tinker's Barrow★
DT2 .137 C2
Tinker's La
Cucklington BA9 .4 A3
Wareham Town BH20 .142 C2
Tinneys La DT9 .30 B3
Tintagel Rd BA21 .26 C4
Tintern BA21 .26 C3
Tintinhull Rd
Yeovil BA21 .27 A4
Yeovil Without BA21 .26 C4
Tiptoe Prim Sch SO41 .95 B4
Tithe Barn Children's Farm★
DT3 .149 B4
Tithe Barn Mus★
BH19 .179 A1
Tiverton Ct 24 BH4 .121 B2
Tizard's Knap DT6 .66 A1
Toby's Cl DT5 .186 C2
Tobys Ct SP7 .12 C2
Todber Cl BH11 .88 C2
Tollard Cl BH12 .120 C4
Toller La DT2 .72 A4
Tollerdown Rd 4 DT4 .166 C1
Tollerford Rd BH17 .87 B1
Tollgate Pk SP7 .12 C3
Tollgate Rd SP1 .213 B2
Tolpuddle Gdns BH9 .90 A2
Tolstoi Rd BH14 .120 A3
Tomlins La SP8 .5 C1
Toms Field Rd BH19 .178 A1
Tonge Rd BH11 .89 A3
Toose The BA21 .26 C3
Top La Ringwood BH24 .55 B4
Stourton with Gasper BA12 .1 B4
Torbay Rd BH14 .120 B2
Torre The BA21 .26 C3
Totmel Rd BH17 .88 A1
Tourney Rd BH11 .88 C3
Tout Hill
East Stoke BH20 .140 A2
Shaftesbury SP7 .12 B2
Tout Hill La DT2 .104 C3
Tout Quarry Nature Reserve★ DT5 .186 C3
Tout Quarry Sculpture Pk★
DT5 .186 C3
Towans The BH13 .147 B2
Tower Cl 1 BH21 .201 D1
Tower Ct BH2 .121 C1
Tower Hill
Bere Regis BH20 .81 A1
Iwerne Minster DT11 .37 C1
Netherbury DT6 .204 B2
Tower Hill Rd 6 TA18 .191 E4
Tower La BH21 .59 B3
Tower Mews SP1 .213 B3
Tower Rd
Bournemouth BH1 .122 C3
Poole BH13 .121 A1
Yeovil BA21 .27 B4
Tower Rd W BH13 .121 A1
Towers Farm BH21 .86 B4
Towers Way BH21 .86 B4
Town Farm Pl SP5 .189 B4
Town Hall La BH19 .179 A1
Town Path SP2 .213 A2
Towngate Bridge
BH15 .119 B2
Towngate Sh Ctr 1
BH15 .119 B1
Townsend BH21 .56 B2
Townsend Cl
Bournemouth BH11 .89 A3
Mere BA12 .2 C3
Townsend Gn BA8 .19 A2
Townsend La SP6 .190 A6
Townsend Mead
BH20 .177 A4
Townsend Orch TA16 .191 F8
Townsend Prim & Com Sch
BH8 .91 A1
Townsend Rd
Corfe Castle BH20 .177 A4
Swanage BH19 .179 A1
Townsend Way DT6 .68 C1
Townsville Rd BH9 .90 A1
Tozer Cl BH11 .88 C1
Tracey Ct BH23 .126 A4
Tradecroft DT5 .186 C3
Trafalgar Ct BH23 .124 C3
Trafalgar Rd BH9 .121 C4
Tree Hamlets BH16 .118 B3
Treebys Cl BH23 .92 B1
Treeside BH23 .93 B1
Treetops 9 BH13 .147 C4
Trefoil Way BH23 .125 B4
Tregonwell Rd BH2 .121 C1
Trellech Ct 1 BA22 .26 C3
Treloen Ct 3 BH8 .122 A3
Trenchard Mdw BH16 .84 B2
Trenchard Way DT3 .166 B3
Trendle St DT9 .30 A3
Trent Cl Tolpuddle DT2 .79 B1
Yeovil BA21 .28 A4
Trent Dr BH20 .142 B3
Trent Path La DT9 .29 C3
Trent Way BH22 .62 A3
Trent Youngs CE Prim Sch
DT9 .14 C1
Trentham Ave BH7 .123 A4
Trentham Cl BH7 .123 A4
Tresco Spinney BA21 .26 C3
Tresillian Cl BH23 .94 A1
Tresillian Way BH23 .94 A1
Treves Rd DT1 .134 C4
Trevone 15 BH25 .95 A2
Triangle The
Bournemouth BH2 .121 C2
Upton BH16 .118 A4
Tricketts La BH22 .61 C3
Trigon Rd BH15 .119 B4
Trill La DT9 .194 B7
Trinidad Cres BH12 .120 B4
Trinidad Fst Sch BH12 .120 B4
Trinidad House BH12 .120 B4
Trinity 2 BH1 .122 A2
Trinity Ind Est BH21 .59 C2
Trinity La BH20 .142 C2
Trinity Rd
Bournemouth BH1 .122 A2
Weymouth DT4 .167 B1
Trinity St
Dorchester DT1 .108 A1
Salisbury SP1 .213 B2
7 Weymouth DT4 .167 C1
Trinity Terr DT4 .167 B1
Trinity Way DT6 .68 C1
Troak Cl BH23 .124 C4
Troon Rd BH18 .87 A3
Trotters La BH21 .60 A3
Truman Rd BH10 .89 A3
Truscott Ave BH9 .122 A4
Trusthams DT8 .203 E5
Trustin Cl 6 DT6 .100 B4
Trystworthy 10 BH2 .121 C2
Tuckers La BH15 .118 C1
Tuckers Mill Cl BH20 .160 C4
Tucks Cl BH23 .93 A4
Tuckton Cl BH6 .123 B2
Tuckton Rd BH6 .123 C2
Tudor Cl SP6 .42 B3
Tudor Ct
Bournemouth BH1 .122 A3
Poole BH15 .119 C3
Tudor Gdns DT11 .212 C3
Tudor Rd BH18 .87 A2
Tulse Hill Zeale BA12 .2 A2
Zennor BA12 .1 C2
Tuncombe La TA18 .191 D4
Tunnel Rd DT8 .204 C5
Turbary Ct
Bournemouth BH12 .89 A1
Ferndown BH22 .61 C3
Upton BH16 .118 B4
Turbary Hts BH11 .88 C1

Turbary Pk Ave BH11 ...89 A1
Turbary Rd BH22 ....61 C3
Turbary Ret Pk BH11 ...88 C2
Turberville Rd BH20 ....81 A1
Turbetts Cl BH16 ......84 B2
Turbury Cl BH12 ......120 B4
Turbury Rd BH12 ......120 B4
Turf Croft BH23 ....94 A1
Turk's La BH14 ....120 A1
Turlin Moor Fst Sch
  BH16 ....118 B2
Turlin Moor Mid Sch
  BH16 ....118 B2
Turlin Rd BH16 ....118 B2
Turnberry Rd BH23 ....123 C3
Turner Cl 2 SP2 ......213 A2
Turner's Barn La BA20 ..27 A1
Turner's La
  Marshwood DT6 ......202 E2
  Tarrant Monkton DT11 ..200 B4
Turners La SP8 ....5 C1
Turnpike Cl 2 TA18 ...192 B3
Turnpike Gn 3 TA18 ...192 B3
Turnstone Cl DT3 .....152 B2
Turnworth Cl BH18 .....87 B2
Turton St 8 DT4 ......167 B2
Tut Hill DT9 ....31 C1
Tweedale Rd BH9 ....90 B2
Twemlow Ave BH14 ....119 C2
Twin Oaks Cl BH18 .....87 A2
Twinways La DT6 ....69 A4
Two Droves DT2 ....109 C4
Two Elms BA22 ....14 B4
Two Riversmeet Leisure Ctr
  BH23 ....124 B3
Two Twr La BA22 ....27 B1
Twyford Cl BH8 ....90 B1
Twyford Way BH17 .....88 A1
Twynham Ave BH23 ....124 A4
Twynham Rd BH6 ......123 C2
Twynham Sch BH23 ....124 A3
Tynedale Cl BH9 ......90 A2
Tyneham Ave BH12 ....120 B4
Tyneham Cl
  Radipole DT3 ....167 A4
  Sandford BH20 ......143 A4
Tyneham House (remains
  of)* BH20 ....174 B3
Tyneham Mus* BH20 ..174 B3
Tyrrell Gdns BH8 ......91 A1
Tytherley Gn BH8 ......90 B1

U

Ubsdell Cl BH25 ....95 A2
Uddens Dr
  Ferndown Town BH21 ...51 C1
  Wimborne Minster BH21 ..60 B4
Uddens Trad Est BH21 ..60 C3
Ullswater Cres DT3 ...167 A4
Ullswater Rd BH21 .....59 B1
Ulwell Rd BH19 ....179 A3
Umbers Hill SP7 ....12 B1
Undercliff Dr BH1 ....122 B1
Undercliff Rd BH5 ....122 C2
Underdown Hollow
  DT9 ....28 B2
Underhedge Gdns
  DT5 ....186 C1
Underhill Mere BA12 ...2 C1
Pen Selwood BA9 ....1 A1
Underhill Jun Sch
  DT5 ....186 C4
Underwood Cl BH17 ....87 A1
Union St 2 BA20 ......27 B2
Unity La 4 TA18 .....192 A3
Upland Cl DT10 ......197 D7
Uplands
  Bothenhampton DT6 ...101 A3
  2 Yetminster DT9 ...194 C3
Uplands Ave BH25 ....127 A4
Uplands Cl BH22 ......62 A4
Uplands Rd
  Bournemouth BH8 .....90 B1
  Ferndown BH22 ......53 A1
Uplands Sch BH14 ....120 B2
Uplyme Cl BH17 ....88 A1
Uplyme Rd DT7 ....96 A3
Upper Fairfield Rd
  18 Dorchester DT1 ...107 C1
  12 Dorchester DT1 ...108 A1
Upper Golf Links Rd
  BH18 ....87 A3
Upper Gordon Rd BH23 ..94 A1
Upper Hinton Rd BH1 ..121 C2
Upper Linhay DT2 .....205 A8
Upper N Rd SP5 ......188 C5
Upper Norwich Rd 18
  BH2 ....121 C2
Upper Rd BH12 ....120 B3
Upper Sch La 1 DT11 ..212 B1
Upper St 4 DT11 .....198 C7
Upper Terr Rd BH2 ...121 C2
Upper Westhill Rd DT7 ..96 A3
Upper Wr St BA12 ......3 A1
Uppington Cl 2 BH21 ..201 C1
Uppleby Rd BH12 .....120 B3
Upton Cl BH16 ....118 A4
Upton Cross Mobile Home Pk
  BH16 ....118 B4
Upton Cl BH16 ....118 B4
Upton Ctry Pk* BH17 ..118 C3
Upton Heath Est BH16 ..118 B4
Upton Inf Sch BH16 ...118 B4
Upton Inf Sch BH16 ...118 A4
Upton Jun Sch BH16 ...118 A4

Upton Rd
  Broadstone BH17 .....119 A4
  Poole BH14 ....118 C4
Upton Way BH18 ....86 C2
Upway St 2 DT4 ......167 B2
Upway Ave BH15 ......118 C2
Upwey Ave BH15 ......118 C2
Upwey Sta DT3 ....152 B2
Utrecht Ct BH23 .....124 B4

V

Vaggs La SO41 ....95 C3
Vale Cl
  4 Crewkerne TA18 ...191 F3
  Poole BH14 ....120 C2
Vale Lodge BH1 ......122 B3
Vale Mans 4 BH1 .....122 B2
Vale Pk DT11 ....212 B1
Vale Rd
  Bournemouth BH1 ....122 B2
  Poole BH14 ....120 C2
  Stalbridge DT10 .....33 B4
  West Lulworth BH20 ..172 C3
  Yeovil BA21 ....28 A3
Vale St BA8 ....19 A2
Vale View Pk SO41 ....95 C4
Valencia Cl BH23 .....91 B2
Valette Rd BH9 ....90 A2
Valiant Way BH23 ....125 A4
Valley Bladen DT2 ...112 A4
Valley Cl
  Christchurch BH23 ...91 C2
  Yeovil BA21 ....27 B3
Valley Rd
  Blandford Camp DT11 ..199 E3
  Bournemouth BH8 .....90 C2
  Bridport DT6 ....100 B2
  2 Crewkerne TA18 ...191 F3
  Langton Matravers
    BH19 ....178 A3
  Worth Matravers BH20 ..177 B3
Valley View BH12 ....121 A4
Vallis BH15 ....119 B1
Vanessa Ave SP1 .....213 C3
Vanguard Ave DT4 ...166 C1
Vanguard Rd
  Bournemouth BH8 .....90 C1
  Poole BH15 ....119 B1
Veals La DT10 ....35 A3
Vearse Cl DT6 ....100 A3
Vecta Cl BH23 ....125 B3
Vectis Rd BH25 ......126 B4
Velvet Lawn Rd BH25 ..94 C2
Venator Pl BH21 ......59 B3
Venn Hill TA20 ......202 F6
Venn La Chideock DT6 ..66 C1
  Stoke Abbott DT8 ...203 D2
Venn The SP7 ....12 C2
Venning Ave BH11 .....88 C3
Ventnor Rd DT5 .....186 C4
Ventry Cl Poole BH13 ..120 C2
  2 Salisbury SP1 ....213 B3
Ventry The 1 SP1 ....213 B3
Ventura Ctr The BH16 ..118 B3
Ventura Pl BH16 ....118 B3
Verity Cres BH17 .....88 A1
Verlands Rd DT3 .....153 B2
Vermin La BH20 ....83 A4
Vernalls Cl BH10 .....89 B3
Vernalls Cl BH25 .....95 B3
Vernalls Gdns BH10 ...89 B3
Vernalls Rd DT9 ......30 A4
Verne Cl DT4 ....167 B1
Verne Comm Rd DT5 ..186 C4
Verne Hill Rd DT5 ...187 A4
Verne Rd Verwood BH31 ..45 B3
  Weymouth DT4 ......167 B1
Verne Way DT4 ......167 B1
Verney Cl BH11 ....89 A2
Verney Rd BH11 ......89 A2
Verno La BH23 ....93 B1
Verona Ave BH6 .....123 B3
Verona Rd SP1 ......213 A4
Verriott's La DT6 ....66 B1
Verulam Pl 31 BH1 ...121 C2
Verulam Rd BH11 ....119 C2
Verwood CE Fst Sch
  BH31 ....45 A3
Verwood Cres BH6 ...124 A2
Verwood Ind Est BH31 ..45 B3
Verwood Leisure Ctr
  BH31 ....45 A3
Verwood Rd
  Ellingham Harbridge & Ibsley
    BH24 ....46 B1
  St Leonards & St Ives
    BH24 ....54 C4
  Three Legged Cross BH21 ..45 A1
  Verwood BH21 ....53 A4
  Woodlands BH21 .....44 B4
Verwood Sports Ctr
  BH31 ....45 B3
Vespasian Way DT1 ...134 C4
Vetch Cl BH23 ....125 B4
Vian Ct BH25 ....94 C2
Vicarage Cl 5 BH20 ..140 A1
Vicarage Cotts BH8 ...90 C2
Vicarage Ct 4 DT6 ...100 B4
Vicarage La DT2 .....107 C3
Vicarage Rd
  Bournemouth BH9 .....89 C1
  Poole BH15 ....119 B3
  Verwood BH31 ....45 A3
Vicarage Way BH23 ....92 B1
Vickers Cl BH8 ....91 A1
Vickery Way BH23 ...124 B4

Victoria Ave
  Bournemouth BH9 .....89 C1
  Radipole DT3 ....152 A3
  1 Swanage BH19 ....178 C1
Victoria Ave Ind Est
  BH19 ....178 C2
Victoria Cl
  Corfe Mullen BH21 ...86 B3
  Wool BH20 ....139 B3
  Yeovil BA21 ....27 C3
Victoria Cres BH12 ..120 B3
Victoria Ct SP1 .....213 B4
Victoria Gdns
  Ferndown BH22 ......61 B3
  Ringwood BH24 ......55 B3
Victoria Gr DT6 .....100 B4
Victoria Hospl DT4 ...59 A3
Victoria Pk Rd BH9 ...89 C1
Victoria Pl
  Bournemouth BH1 ....122 B2
  Easton/Weston DT5 ..187 A4
  Wimborne Minster BH21 ..59 A3
Victoria Rd
  Blandford Forum DT11 ..212 A3
  Bournemouth BH1 ....122 B3
  Christchurch BH23 ...124 C3
  Dorchester DT1 .....107 C1
  Easton/Weston DT5 ..187 A3
  Ferndown BH22 ......61 B3
  Gillingham SP8 ......6 A1
  Poole BH12 ....120 B3
  Salisbury SP1 ......213 B3
  Swanage BH19 ......179 B3
  Weymouth DT4 ......180 B4
  Wimborne Minster BH21 ..59 A3
  Yeovil BA21 ....27 C3
Victoria Sq DT5 .....186 C4
Victoria St
  Radipole DT4 ....167 C2
  Shaftesbury SP7 .....12 C2
Victory Cl BH21 ......53 B3
Victory Rd DT5 .....186 C4
View Rd DT7 ....96 A3
Viewside Cl BH21 .....86 B3
Viking Cl BH6 ....124 A2
Viking Way
  Bournemouth BH6 ...124 A2
  Christchurch BH23 ...125 A4
  Salisbury SP2 ......213 B1
Village Rd DT6 ....68 C1
Villette Cl BH23 .....92 A1
Vince Cl BH11 ....89 A3
Vincent Cl 2 BH25 ...95 A1
Vincent Pl BA20 ......27 B3
Vincent Rd 1 BH25 ...95 A1
Vincents Cl DT9 ......31 A1
Vine Cl BH7 ....123 A4
Vine Farm Cl BH12 ...121 A4
Vine Farm Rd BH12 ..121 A4
Vine Hill DT6 ....58 C3
Vineries Cl BH21 .....59 C3
Vineries The BH21 ....59 C3
Vinery The BH25 ......95 A1
Vineyard Cl BH16 .....84 B2
Vinney Cross DT6 ....102 A3
Vinneys Cl BH23 ......92 B1
Violet Cl BH18 ....86 B3
Violet Farm Cl BH21 ..86 B4
Violet La BH25 ....95 A2
Virginia Cl
  1 Henstridge BA8 ...19 A2
Viscount Ct BH11 .....88 B3
Viscount Dr BH23 ....125 A3
Viscount Rd DT4 ....166 C1
Viscount Wlk BH11 ...88 B3
Vista Marina BH13 ...147 B3
Vivian Pk BH6 ......179 A2
Vixen Wlk BH25 ......95 A3
Voss's La DT2 ......206 A3
Vulcan Cl DT4 ......166 C1
Vulcan Way BH23 ...125 A4

W

W Burton Medieval Village
  of* DT2 ....139 B1
Waddock Dro DT2 ....111 C2
Waddon Hill (Roman Fort)*
  DT8 ....203 F4
Waddon House* DT3 ..150 C4
Waddon Way DT6 .....69 B1
Wadham Com Sch
  TA18 ....191 F5
Wadmore La BH19 ....164 B1
Wagtail Dr BH25 ......94 C1
Wain Rd BH20 ....139 B4
Wain-a-long Rd SP1 ..213 C3
Wainwright Cl DT3 ..153 A2
Wakefield Ave BH10 ...89 C3
Wakeham DT5 ....187 A2
Wakely Gdns BH11 ....89 A3
Wakely Rd BH11 ......89 A3
Walcheren Pl BH15 ..118 B2
Walcott Ave BH23 ....91 C1
Walditch Gdns BH17 ..87 C1
Walditch Rd DT6 ....100 C3
Waldren Cl BH15 ....119 C1
Waldrons The 5 DT9 ..194 D8
Walford Cl BH21 .....59 B3
Walford Gdns BH21 ...59 A3
Walford Mill Craft Ctr*
  BH21 ....59 A3
Walker Cres DT4 ....180 B3
Walkford La BH25 ....94 B2
Walkford Rd BH23 ....94 B1
Walkford Way BH23 ...94 A1
Walkingfield La BH15 ..119 B1

Walkwood Ave BH7 ...123 A4
Wall La DT6 ....203 D4
Wallace Rd BH18 .....87 A2
Wallis Rd BH10 ......89 A1
Walliscott Rd BH11 ...89 A1
Wallisdown Rd BH10 ..121 B4
Walls View Rd BH20 ..142 B3
Wallsend Cl 3 DT5 ..186 C1
Walnut Ave DT11 ....212 A3
Walnut Cl BH25 ......94 C2
Walnut Orch 3 DT3 ..150 A4
Walpole Rd BH1 .....122 C3
Walpole St DT4 .....167 B2
Walrond Rd BH19 ....179 A2
Walsford Rd BH4 ....121 B3
Walsingham Dene
  BH7 ....122 C4
Walters Dr 18 DT11 ..199 D4
Waltham Rd BH7 .....123 A3
Walton Elm Hill DT10 ..35 A4
Walton Rd
  Bournemouth BH10 ...89 B1
  Poole BH15 ....120 A3
Wanchard La DT2 ....107 B4
Wanderwell DT6 .....100 B2
Wanderwell Farm La
  DT6 ....100 B2
Wanstead Cl 3 BH23 ..47 B1
Warbler Cl BH16 ....118 A4
Warburton Rd BH17 ..119 C4
Wardcliffe Rd DT4 ..167 B2
Wardstone Barrow*
  DT2 ....171 B4
Ware La DT7 ....96 A2
Wareham Ct BH7 ....123 A3
Wareham Golf Club
  BH20 ....142 C3
Wareham Hospl DT4 ..142 B2
Wareham Lady St Mary CE
  Fst Sch BH20 ......142 B2
Wareham Mid Sch
  BH20 ....142 B2
Wareham Mus* BH20 .142 C2
Wareham Rd
  Corfe Mullen BH21 ...86 B3
  Hawkchurch EX13 ...202 B2
  Lytchett Matravers BH16 ..84 B1
  Lytchett Minster & Upton
    BH16 ....116 A3
  Owermoigne DT2 ....155 C4
  Wareham St Martin
    BH16 ....116 B2
  Wareham Sta BH20 ..142 B3
Wares Cl 5 DT11 .....81 C2
Warland Way BH21 ...86 C4
Warmwell Cl
  9 Bournemouth BH9 ..90 A2
  Poole BH17 ....87 C1
Warmwell Dro DT2 ...154 B4
Warmwell House*
  DT2 ....155 A4
Warmwell Rd DT2 ...137 B3
Warne Hill DT6 .....100 C4
Warnford Rd BH6 ...123 B4
Warren Ave BH23 ...124 C3
Warren Cl
  St.Leonards BH24 ...54 C3
  Weymouth DT4 .....166 C1
Warren Dr BH24 .....54 C3
Warren Edge Cl BH6 .123 C2
Warren Edge Ct BH6 .123 C2
Warren Edge Rd BH6 .123 C2
Warren Hill DT2 .....78 B4
Warren La BH24 .....54 C3
Warren Rd
  Bere Regis BH20 ...113 B2
  Bournemouth BH4 ...121 B2
  Poole BH14 ....120 B2
  Puddletown DT2 .....78 A3
Warren Way BH16 ...116 B1
Warren Wlk BH22 ....61 A4
Warwick Ave BH25 ...95 A2
Warwick Cl SP1 .....213 A4
Warwick Ct 14 BH5 ..122 C2
Warwick Pl 3 BH7 ..123 A3
Warwick Rd
  Bournemouth BH7 ...123 A3
  Poole BH14 ....120 B2
Washington Ave BH8 .122 B3
Washpond La BH19 ..178 C3
Watcombe Rd BH6 ..123 B3
Water Barrows*
  BH20 ....173 C4
Water Knap DT10 ...196 F3
Water La
  Bournemouth BH6 ...123 B4
  Durweston DT11 ....198 E3
  Swyre DT6 ....129 B4
  Winfrith Newburgh DT2 ..156 C4
  Winterborne Stickland
    DT11 ....210 B7
Water La Farm BH10 ..89 C3
Water Mdw La BH20 .139 C1
Water St
  Cranborne BH21 .....40 A4
  Mere BA12 ....3 A1
Water Twr Rd BH18 ..87 B2
Watercombe Hts BA20 ..26 C1
Watercombe La BA20 ..26 C1
Watercombe Pk BA20 ..26 C2
Waterditch Rd BH23 ...93 A2
Waterford Cl BH14 ..120 A1
Waterford Gdns BH23 ..126 A4
Waterford Lodge
  BH23 ....125 A3
Waterford Pl BH23 ..126 A4

Waterford Rd
  Christchurch BH23 ..126 A4
  New Milton BH25 .....95 B2
Waterfront Mus*
  BH15 ....119 A1
Watergates La DT2 ..136 B2
Waterlake Rd TA20 ..202 A8
Waterloo House BH17 ..87 A1
Waterloo La Silton SP8 ..5 A4
  Stourton Caundle DT10 ..33 A1
Waterloo Rd
  Bournemouth BH9 ...121 C4
  Broadstone BH17 ...119 B4
  Corfe Mullen BH21 ...86 A3
  Salisbury SP1 ......213 C2
Waterloo Way 3 BH24 ..55 B3
Watermead
  Christchurch BH23 ..124 A3
  3 Tatworth TA20 ...202 A8
Watermill Rd BH23 ..124 A4
Waterpot Hill DT6 ..204 C2
Waters Edge BH13 ..147 B3
Waters Rd SP1 .....213 B4
Watership Dr BH24 ...55 C3
Waterside BH23 .....124 C2
Waterside Cl BH23 ...47 B1
Watersmeet Rd SP2 ..213 B1
Waterston Cl BH17 ...87 B1
Waterston La DT2 ....77 B2
Waterston Manor*
  DT2 ....77 B2
Watery La
  Christchurch BH23 ..125 A4
  Donhead St Mary SP7 ..24 C1
  Halstock BA22 .....193 D2
  Iwerne Minster DT11 ..37 C1
  Lytchett Minster & Upton
    BH16 ....117 A3
  Radipole DT3 ......152 A2
  Shaftesbury SP7 .....12 C1
  Studland BH19 .....164 B1
  Tincleton DT2 .....110 B2
  Upton BH16 ....118 A4
  West Crewkerne TA18 ..191 D2
Watford La DT6 ......68 C1
Watkin Rd 19 BH5 ..122 C2
Watton Cl BH8 ....91 A1
Watton Cross DT6 ..100 A3
Watton Gdns DT6 ...100 C4
Watton La DT6 .....100 A3
Watton Pk DT6 .....100 B3
Wavell Ave BH17 .....87 A1
Wavell Rd
  Bournemouth BH11 ...89 A2
  Salisbury SP2 ......213 B1
Wavendon Ave BH26 ..126 C4
Wavering La SP8 ......5 A2
Waverley Cres BH15 ..119 B3
Waverley House 12 BH25 ..95 A1
Waverley Rd
  New Milton BH25 .....95 A1
  Radipole DT3 ......167 B3
Wayclose La
  Buckhorn Weston SP8 ..9 A4
  Cucklington SP8 .....4 A1
Wayford Hill TA18 ...191 B1
Wayground Rd BH21 ..58 C1
Wayman Rd BH21 .....86 C3
Wayne Rd BH12 .....120 B3
Wayside Rd
  Bournemouth BH6 ...123 C2
  St Leonards BH24 ...62 C4
  St.Leonards BH24 ...53 C1
Waytown Cl BH17 ....87 B1
Weare Cl DT5 ......186 C4
Weatherbury Way
  DT1 ....135 A4
Weatherby Castle (Fort)*
  BH20 ....79 C3
Weavers Cl
  Crewkerne TA18 ....191 F4
  Ferndown BH22 .....53 B1
Webb La DT10 ......196 E8
Webb's Way BH11 ....88 C1
Webbers Cl BH20 ...176 C4
Webbers Piece DT2 ..206 C1
Webbs Cl BH24 ......53 C3
Webster Rd BH9 .....90 A2
Wedgwood Dr BH14 ..120 A1
Weiner Cl DT11 ....199 E2
Weir The DT3 ......153 B2
Weir View DT2 .....107 B3
Welbeck Rd BA21 ....28 A4
Weldon Ave BH11 ....88 C3
Well Cl
  Bradford Abbas DT9 ..28 A1
  New Milton BH25 .....94 C1
Well La Poole BH15 ..119 B2
  Powerstock DT6 .....70 A2
  Shaftesbury SP7 .....12 B2
Well Plot DT6 ......101 B4
Welland Rd
  Wimborne Minster BH21 ..59 B2
  Yeovil BA21 ....27 C4
Wellbridge Cl DT1 ..135 A4
Wellesley Ave BH23 ..125 B4
Wellfield Hill EX13 ..202 E2
Wellfields Dr DT6 ...100 C4
Wellington Ave BH23 ..125 B4
Wellington Ct
  7 Bournemouth BH8 ..122 A3
  New Milton BH25 .....95 A1
Wellington Rd
  Bournemouth BH1 ...122 A3
  Poole BH14 ....120 B2

Wellstead Rd BH20 ....142 B3
Wendover Cl BH25 ......94 C1
Wendy Cres BH22 ....61 C2
Wenlock Ct **9** BH23 ...124 C4
Wentwood Gdns BH25 ...95 B1
Wentworth BH14 ....147 B4
Wentworth Ave BH5 ..123 A2
Wentworth Cl
  Bournemouth BH5 .....123 A2
  Radipole DT3 ....152 C1
Wentworth Coll BH5 ..123 A2
Wentworth Dr
  Broadstone BH18 ....87 A3
  Christchurch BH23 ....123 C3
Wentworth Rd BA21 .....28 A4
Wescott Way BH11 ......88 C2
Wesley Cl
  8 Bournemouth BH8 ...122 B3
  Charmouth DT6 ....97 A4
Wesley Grange **33** BH4 .121 B2
Wesley Rd Poole BH12 ..120 B3
  Wimborne Minster BH21 ..59 C3
Wessex Ave
  New Milton BH25 ....95 A4
  4 Shillingstone DT11 ..198 B5
Wessex Cl BH23 ....125 C4
Wessex Dr DT9 ....28 B1
Wessex Est BH24 ....55 B4
Wessex Gate Ret Pk
  BH17 ....119 A3
Wessex Oval BH20 .....142 B3
Wessex Rd
  Dorchester DT1 ......107 B1
  Poole BH14 ....120 A2
  Ringwood BH24 ....55 B4
  Salisbury SP1 ....213 C3
  Stalbridge DT10 ......33 B4
  Weymouth DT4 ....167 A2
  Yeovil BA21 ....26 C4
Wessex Trad Ctr
  BH12 ....120 A4
Wessex Way
  Bournemouth BH8 .....122 B3
  Dorchester DT1 ......107 B1
  Gillingham SP8 ....5 C2
  Swanage BH19 ....179 A2
West Allington DT6 ...100 A4
West Ave BH21 ....53 A4
West Bay Cres DT4 ....180 B4
West Bay Rd DT6 ......100 B1
West Borough BH21 .....59 A3
West Bourton Rd SP8 ....1 B1
West Brook BA21 ....26 C3
West Butts St **1** BH15 ..119 A1
West Chinnock Prim Sch
  TA18 ....192 B8
West Cl Chickerell DT3 .166 B3
  Verwood BH31 ....44 C3
West Cl Ct BH6 ....124 C4
West Cl House BH6 ....124 A2
West Cliff Cotts BH2 ..121 C1
West Cliff Gdns BH2 ..121 C1
West Cliff Mews BH2 ..121 C1
West Cliff Rd
  Bournemouth BH2 .....121 B1
  Bridport DT6 ....100 A1
West Coker Rd
  East Coker BA20 ......26 C1
  Yeovil BA20 ....27 A1
West Coker VC Prim Sch
  BA22 ....193 A8
West Dr **3** BH19 .....179 A1
West Durlston La
  BH19 ....179 A1
West End DT2 ....206 B3
West Gables Cl DT6 ...100 A4
West Hall* DT9 ......195 C7
West Hendford BA20 ...27 A2
West Hill
  Charminster DT2 .....107 B3
  Evershot DT2 ....205 F7
  Milborne Port DT9 .....17 B1
West Hill Pl **15** BH2 ..121 C2
West Hill Rd
  Bournemouth BH2 .....121 C1
  Lyme Regis DT7 ....96 A3
West Howe Cl BH11 .....89 A2
West Howe Ind Est
  BH11 ....88 C2
West La Arne BH20 ....142 C1
  Hazelbury Bryan DT10 .196 E4
  Melbury Abbas SP7 ....24 A3
  Mosterton DT8 ....203 F8
  North Wootton DT9 .....30 C1
West Lulworth CE Fst Sch
  BH20 ....172 C4
West Mans **8** BH4 ...121 B2
West Mead DT6 ....100 A4
West Mill Cres BH20 ..142 B3
West Mill La
  Castleton DT9 ....30 A2
  Stalbridge DT10 ......20 A2
West Mills Rd DT1 ....107 C2
West Moors Mid Sch
  BH22 ....53 A1
West Moors Rd
  Ferndown BH22 ....61 B4
  Three Legged Cross BH21 .53 A4
  West Moors BH22 ......52 C2
West Overcliff Dr BH4 .121 B1
West Pk BA20 ....27 A3
West Pk Dr SP6 ....190 F3
West Pk La SP6 ....190 F3
West Quay Rd BH15 ...119 A1

West Rd
  Bournemouth BH5 .....123 A2
  Bransgore BH23 ....93 A4
  Symondsbury DT6 ......99 B3
  West Lulworth BH20 ..172 B3
West Row BH21 ....59 A2
West Row Mews BH21 ...59 A2
West St
  Abbotsbury DT3 ......149 A4
  Bere Regis BH20 ......81 A2
  Blandford Forum DT11 .212 B2
  Bridport DT6 ....100 B3
  Broadwindsor DT8 ....203 E5
  Chickerell DT3 ......166 B3
  Corfe Castle BH20 ...162 A1
  Crewkerne TA18 ......191 E4
  Fontmell Magna SP7 ...37 C3
  Hinton St George TA17 .191 C7
  Kington Magna SP8 ....9 B1
  Poole BH15 ....119 A1
  Radipole DT4 ....167 B1
  Ringwood BH24 ....55 A4
  Salisbury SP2 ....213 A3
  Shapwick DT11 ....56 A4
  Templecombe BA8 .....18 B4
  Wareham BH20 ....142 C2
  Wimborne Minster BH21 .59 A3
  Winterborne Kingston
    DT11 ....81 B4
  Winterbourne Stickland
    DT11 ....210 C7
  Yeovil BA20 ....27 A2
West St **11** BH21 ....59 A3
West Sta Terr BH4 ....121 B2
West View SP7 ....37 C3
West View Rd
  Christchurch BH23 ...124 C3
  Poole BH15 ....119 A2
West Walks Rd **8** DT1 .108 A1
West Walls BH20 ......142 B2
West Way
  Bournemouth BH9 ......90 A1
  Broadstone BH18 ......87 A1
  Easton/Weston DT5 ...186 C1
  Winterbourne Abbas
    DT2 ....105 B1
West Ways Cl BH9 ......90 A1
West Ways BA22 ....192 D8
West Wlk Bridport DT6 .100 A1
  Salisbury SP1 ....213 B2
West Wools DT5 ....186 C1
Westbourne Cl
  Bournemouth BH4 .....121 B2
  Salisbury SP1 ....213 C2
  Yeovil BA20 ....27 A3
Westbourne Gr BA20 ...27 A3
Westbourne Pk Rd
  BH4 ....121 A1
Westbourne Rd DT4 ...167 B3
Westbridge Pk DT9 ....29 C2
Westbrook Cl BH10 .....89 B1
Westbrook Rd SP8 ......5 A1
Westbury
  Bradford Abbas DT9 ...28 B1
  Sherborne DT9 ....30 A2
Westbury Cl
  Barton on Sea BH25 ..127 A4
  Bransgore BH23 ....93 A4
Westbury Ct **10** BH14 .120 A2
Westbury Rd BH24 ......55 B4
Westby Rd BH5 ....122 C2
Westcliff Rd
  Charmouth DT6 ....96 C4
  Easton/Weston DT5 ...186 C2
Westcroft Par **10** BH25 ..95 A1
Westcroft Pk BH18 ....87 B2
Westdown Rd BH11 .....89 A3
Westdowne Cl DT4 ....167 A1
Westerhall Rd DT4 ....167 C3
Westerham Rd BH4 ....121 A2
Westerleigh BH4 .....121 B1
Western Ave
  Barton on Sea BH25 ..126 B4
  Bournemouth BH10 ....89 B2
  Poole BH13 ....120 C1
  Yeovil BA22 ....28 B4
Western Cl BH10 ....89 B3
Western Downland Prim Sch
  SP6 ....190 F2
Western Rd BH13 .....121 A1
Western St DT9 ....28 B4
Westerngate BH13 ....121 A2
Westfield
  2 Portesham DT3 ...150 A4
  Sherborne DT9 ....29 C2
  13 Wimborne Minster BH21 .59 A3
Westfield Ave BA21 ....27 A3
Westfield Cl BA21 .....59 A3
Westfield Com Sch
  BA21 ....27 A3
Westfield Cres BA21 ...27 A3
Westfield Est BA12 ...1 C2
Westfield Gdns BH23 ...93 A1
Westfield Gr BA21 .....27 A4
Westfield Inf Sch BA21 ..27 A3
Westfield Pl BA21 .....27 A4
Westfield Rd
  Bournemouth BH6 .....123 C2
  Yeovil BA21 ....27 A3
Westfield Sch DT3 ....153 A2
Westgate Pk BH4 .....121 A2
Westham Cl BH17 .....87 C2
Westham Rd DT4 ......167 B2
Westhaven DT4 ....167 A1
Westhaven Cty Inf Sch
  DT4 ....167 A2
Westhaven Cty Jun Sch
  DT4 ....167 A2

Westhaven Hospl DT4 .167 A2
Westheath Rd BH18 ....87 A2
Westhill Cl **5** DT4 ...180 A4
Westhill Rd DT4 .....180 B4
Westlake Cl DT3 .....152 A2
Westland Rd BA20 .....27 A2
Westlands Ct BH23 ....93 A4
Westlands Dr BH13 ...147 C4
Westleaze DT2 ....107 C3
Westleaze Cl DT2 ....107 C3
Westminster BA22 .....26 B3
Westminster Cl **10** SP7 .12 C2
Westminster St BH25 .126 C4
Westminster Meml Hospl
  SP7 ....12 C1
Westminster Rd
  Northport BH20 ......142 B3
  Poole BH13 ....121 A1
  Salisbury SP2 ....213 A3
Westminster Rd E
  BH13 ....121 A1
Westminster Rd Ind Est
  BH20 ....142 B3
Westminster St **10** BA20 .27 B2
Westmoreland Ct SO41 .95 C2
Weston Cl BA22 ......192 E8
Weston Dr BH1 ....122 A2
Weston Hill SP8 ....9 A3
Weston La
  Closworth BA22 ......193 E5
  Corscombe DT2 ....192 F1
Weston Rd
  Easton/Weston DT5 ...186 C2
  Weymouth DT4 ....167 B1
  Wimborne Minster BH21 .59 C4
  Worth Matravers BH19 .183 B4
Weston St
  East Chinnock BA22 ..192 E8
  Easton/Weston DT5 ...187 A1
Westons La **8** BH15 ..119 B1
Westover Hill DT6 ....64 C1
Westover La BH24 .....54 C4
Westover Rd
  Bournemouth BH1 ....121 C2
  14 Dorchester DT1 ....107 C1
Westport Rd BH20 ....142 B2
Westray Hall BH1 ....121 B1
Westridge **6** DT9 ....30 A3
Westville BH21 ....27 C3
Westwey Rd DT4 .....167 B1
Westwood Ave BH22 ...61 B1
Westwoods & Glendene Pk
  BH25 ....94 B3
Wet La BA12 ....3 B1
Wetherbury Cl DT11 ..212 C3
Wetherby Cl
  Broadstone BH18 ......87 A1
  Milborne St Andrew DT11 .79 C4
Wey Valley Sch The
  DT3 ....152 B1
Weyman's Ave BH10 ...89 B3
Weymans Dr BH10 .....89 B3
Weymouth & Portland Sailing
  Acad* DT5 ....181 A1
Weymouth Ave
  10 Dorchester DT1 ...108 A1
  Dorchester DT1 ......134 C4
Weymouth Bay Ave
  DT4 ....167 B4
Weymouth Coll
  Dorchester DT1 ......107 B1
  Radipole DT4 ....167 C3
Weymouth Com Hospl
  DT4 ....167 C3
Weymouth Golf Club
  DT4 ....167 A2
Weymouth Mus* DT4 .167 C1
Weymouth Rd
  Dorchester DT1 ......134 C4
  Poole BH14 ....120 B3
  Winterborne Monkton
    DT2 ....134 C3
Weymouth Rugby Football
  Club DT3 ....167 C4
Weymouth Sports Club
  DT3 ....152 A1
Weymouth Sta DT4 ...167 B2
Weymouth Way DT4 ..167 A3
Weyview Cres DT3 ....152 A2
Wharf Cl BH12 ......120 C3
Wharfdale Rd
  Bournemouth BH4 ....121 B2
  Poole BH12 ....120 C3
Wharncliffe Ct BH23 .125 C4
Wharncliffe Gdns
  BH23 ....126 A4
Wharncliffe Rd
  Bournemouth BH5 ....122 B2
  Christchurch BH23 ...126 A4
Whatcombe Rd DT11 ..210 D4
Whatleigh Cl BH15 ...119 B1
Whatley La TA20 .....202 C8
Wheat Cl **4** DT10 ...197 A4
Wheat Farland DT3 ...166 B3
Wheatear Cl **4** DT3 .152 B2
Wheathill Cl **1** DT9 ..17 B1
Wheathill La DT9 ....17 C2
Wheathill Way DT9 ...17 B1
Wheatlands DT5 .....186 C1
Wheaton Grange BH4 .121 B2
Wheaton Rd BH7 .....123 A4
Wheatplot Pk Homes **2**
  BH10 ....89 C2
Wheel House La TA20 .202 E7
Wheelers La BH11 .....88 B3
Wheelwright's Cl SP5 .189 A4
Whetham Mill La DT8 .203 C6
Whetland's La DT6 ....69 B1

Whimbrel Ct BH23 ....125 A3
Whincroft Cl BH22 ....61 C4
Whincroft Dr BH22 ....61 C3
Whitby Ave BH18 ......87 A1
Whitby Cl BH23 ....91 B2
Whitby Cres BH18 .....87 A1
Whitchurch Ave BH18 ..87 B2
Whitchurch La BA8 ....19 A3
Whitcombe Rd DT8 ...204 D3
Whitcross **2** BA22 ..193 F8
White Cl **3** Bridport DT6 .68 C1
  Poole BH15 ....120 A4
White Cliff DT11 ....212 B2
White Farm Cl BH10 ..121 B4
White Hart Cl DT10 ..196 D5
White Hart La SP7 ....12 C1
White Hill
  5 Puddletown DT2 .....78 A1
  Tolpuddle DT2 ....79 B1
White Hill La DT2 ....79 B1
White Horse Dr
  Overcombe/Preston
    DT3 ....153 B2
  Poole BH15 ....119 B3
White Horse La
  Hinton St Mary DT10 ..35 A3
  Overcombe/Preston
    DT3 ....153 B2
White Horse Mews
  DT2 ....72 C4
White Horses BH25 ..126 C4
White House La DT9 ..195 A4
White Knights BH25 ..126 C4
White La DT2 ....205 C8
White La Cl DT10 .....35 A1
White Lodge BH15 ...119 C2
White Lovington BH20 ..81 A1
White Mead BA21 .....26 C3
White Mill Bridge*
  BH21 ....56 C3
White Pit DT11 ......198 B5
White Pit La SP7 ....24 B2
White Way
  Buckland Newton DT2 .208 B6
  Litton Cheney DT2 ...103 B2
White Way La DT10 ...21 C1
Whitebeam Way BH31 ..45 B3
Whitebridge Rd SP1 ..213 C3
Whitecliff Cres BH14 .120 A1
Whitecliff Gdns DT11 .212 B2
Whitecliff Rd
  Poole BH14 ....119 C1
  Swanage BH19 ....179 A3
Whitecross Cl BH17 ...87 C2
Whitecross Dr DT4 ..180 C4
Whitefield Dr SP8 ....10 B2
Whitefield Lodge **1**
  BH25 ....95 A2
Whitefield Rd
  New Milton BH25 ......95 A1
  Poole BH14 ....120 A1
Whitefriars Rd **9** SP1 .213 B2
Whitehall BH24 ....55 C4
Whitehall Ct **3** TA18 .191 F5
Whitehart Fields **1**
  BH24 ....55 C4
Whitehayes Cl BH23 ...92 B1
Whitehayes Rd BH23 ..92 B1
Whitehead Dr DT4 ...180 B3
Whitehouse Rd BH21 ..59 B1
Whitelegg Way BH10 ..89 C3
Whitemarsh BA12 ......3 A2
Whites Cl DT2 ....76 C4
Whiteway Hill BH21 ..201 B4
Whiteways BH21 ......59 C3
Whitfield Pk BH24 ....54 B3
Whitfield Rd DT1 ....107 B1
Whithay La DT6 ....68 A4
Whitingham Ct **8** BH5 .123 A3
Whitley Way BH25 .....95 A3
Whitmore La BH21 ....44 A4
Whitsbury Cl BH8 .....90 B1
Whittle Rd BH21 ......60 C4
Whittles Way BH15 ...119 A1
Whynot Way DT3 .....166 B2
Wick 1 Ind Est BH25 ..94 C1
Wick 2 Ind Est BH25 ..94 C1
Wick Cl BH25 ....94 C1
Wick Dr BH25 ....94 C1
Wick Farm BH6 ......124 A3
Wick Hill DT9 ....17 A3
Wick La BH6 ....124 A3
Wick Rd DT9 ....17 B2
Wicket Rd BH10 ......89 B3
Wicketsbeer Rd BA22 .193 C6
Wickfield Ave BH23 ..124 A3
Wickfield Cl BH23 ...124 A3
Wickford House BH23 .124 A3
Wickham Ct BH22 .....61 C3
Wickham Dr BH21 .....86 B2
Wickham Rd BH7 .....123 A4
Wicklea Rd BH6 .....124 A3
Wickmeads Rd BH6 ..124 A3
Widdicombe Ave
  BH14 ....120 C1
Wide St DT5 ....186 C3
Widget Cl BH11 ......89 A1
Widworthy Dr BH18 ...86 C3
Wight Wlk BH22 ......61 C1
Wightman's Orch DT2 .208 B2
Wilderness The DT9 ...30 B3
Wilderton Rd BH13 ..120 C2
Wilderton Rd W BH13 .121 A2
Wildown Gdns BH6 ...124 A2
Wildown Rd BH6 .....124 A2
Wilfred Rd BH5 .....122 C2

Wilkins Way BH15 ....119 A1
Wilkinson Dr BH8 .....91 A1
Willett Rd BH21 ......59 A1
William Barnes CP Sch
  DT10 ....197 D8
William Cl
  Christchurch BH23 ....94 A1
  Laverstock SP1 ......213 C3
William St **17** BH23 ..126 A4
William Rd BH7 ......122 C4
William St DT4 ......167 C2
William's Ind Pk BH25 ..94 C1
Williams Ave DT1 ....107 C1
Williams' Ave DT4 ...180 B4
Williford La DT2 ....195 C2
Willis Way BH15 .....119 A3
Willis's La TA18 .....192 B4
Willoughby Cl **3** DT2 ..78 A1
Willow Cl
  Bournemouth BH4 ....121 C3
  Salisbury SP1 ....213 C3
  St.Leonards BH24 .....53 C2
  Upton BH16 ....118 B3
Willow Cres
  Holton Heath BH20 ..116 A1
  Overcombe/Preston
    DT3 ....168 A4
Willow Ct BH7 ......123 B3
Willow Dr
  Christchurch BH23 ...124 A3
  Ringwood BH24 ....55 B3
  Wimborne Minster BH21 ..60 B3
Willow Farm **11** DT9 ..194 C5
Willow Gr **6** DT8 ...204 D4
Willow Lodge **1** BH1 .122 B2
Willow Lodge Montessori
  Sch BH16 ....117 A4
Willow Mead BH8 ......90 B2
Willow Pk BH14 ......120 A4
Willow Pl BH23 ......124 B3
Willow Rd BA21 ....27 A3
Willow Tree Rise BH11 ..89 A2
Willow View BH16 ....118 B2
Willow Way
  Bridport DT6 ....100 C4
  Christchurch BH23 ...124 A3
  Ferndown BH22 ....61 B4
  Motcombe SP7 ....12 A4
  Northport BH20 .....142 B3
Willow Wlk BH25 .....127 A4
Willowdene Cl BH25 ...95 B2
Willows The BH25 ...127 A4
Wills Cl BH21 ....86 B2
Wills La DT2 ....207 D4
Wills Rd Poole BH12 .120 C2
  Swanage BH19 ....178 C1
Willwood Cl BH17 ....87 C2
Wilman Way SP2 .....213 A1
Wilmslow Rd DT3 ....166 B3
Wilmur Cres BH15 ...119 C3
Wilson Pk DT11 .....212 C2
Wilson Rd
  Bournemouth BH1 ....122 C3
  Dorchester DT1 ......108 B1
  Poole BH14 ....120 B2
Wilton Cl BH23 ....91 B1
Wilton Dr DT4 ......167 A1
Wilton Gdns BH25 ....94 C2
Wilton Rd
  Bournemouth BH7 ....122 C3
  Salisbury SP2 ....213 A3
  Yeovil BA21 ....28 A4
Wiltshire Ave DT4 ...167 A2
Wiltshire Cl SP8 ......5 C2
Wiltshire Gdns BH23 ..92 C2
Wiltshire Rd
  Bransgore BH23 ....92 C2
  Salisbury SP2 ....213 A1
Wilverley Ave BH8 ....90 C1
Wilverley Rd BH23 ...125 A4
Wilverly Gdns DT11 ..212 C2
Wimborne Fst Sch
  BH21 ....59 A3
Wimborne Minst Model Town
  & Gdns* BH21 ......59 A2
Wimborne Rd
  Blandford Forum DT11 .212 C2
  Bournemouth BH10 ....89 B3
  Broadstone BH21 ......58 C1
  Lytchett Matravers BH16 ..84 C2
  Poole BH15 ....119 B3
  Tarrant Keyneston DT11 .211 E8
  Tarrant Rushton DT11 ..48 A3
  Wimborne Minster BH21 ..59 B3
Wimborne Rd E BH22 ..61 B3
Wimborne Rd W BH21 ..60 B3
Wimborne St BH21 ....40 A4
Wimborne St Giles CE Fst
  Sch BH21 ....201 E7
Wimborough La BA22 .192 F7
Win Gn View SP7 ......13 A2
Winbrook Fold DT2 ...156 C3
Winchelsea Sch BH12 ..88 B1
Winchester Cl DT4 ...166 C2
Winchester Gdns BA21 ..27 C4
Winchester Pl **3** BH15 .119 B1
Winchester Rd BH25 ..95 C2
Winchester St SP1 ...213 B3
Wincombe Bsns Pk
  SP7 ....13 A3
Wincombe Cl BH22 ....61 B2
Wincombe Dr BH22 ....61 B2
Wincombe La SP7 ....12 C2
Wincombe Pk* SP7 ...13 B3
Wind Whistle Farm **1**
  DT11 ....81 C4
Windermere Rd BA20 ..27 A1

Windermere Cres
 DT3 ....167 A3
Windermere Rd BH3 ..122 A4
Windgreen Est BH21 ...86 C4
Windham Mews BH1 ..122 B3
Windham Rd BH1 .....122 B3
Windlesham Rd SP1 ..213 B4
Windmill Barrow★
 BH21 ....84 A4
Windmill Cl
 Shaftesbury SP7 ......12 C2
 St.Leonards BH24 .....54 C2
Windmill La
 St Leonards & St Ives
  BH24 ....55 A2
 St.Leonards BH24 .....54 C2
Windmill Rd DT11 ....212 C2
Windmill Rise 6 TA18 ..191 F5
Windsor Cl
 Bovington Camp BH20 .139 C3
 Hordle SO41 ....95 C2
 1 Mosterton DT8 ....204 A7
 St.Leonards BH24 .....54 A3
Windsor Ct
 5 Christchurch BH23 ..126 A4
 Poole BH14 ....120 A2
Windsor La SP8 ....5 B1
Windsor Rd
 Bournemouth BH5 ....122 C2
 Christchurch BH23 ...123 C4
 Dorchester DT1 ......107 C1
 Poole BH14 ....120 A2
 Radipole DT3 ....152 A2
 12 Salisbury SP2 ....213 A3
Windsor St 11 SP2 ...213 A3
Windsor Way SP6 .....42 B3
Windwhistle Cnr SP7 ..13 C2
Windy Cnr DT11 ......200 C1
Windy Ridge DT8 .....204 C4
Wine St 1 BA20 ......27 B2
Winfrith Cres BH12 ...120 C4
Winfrith Dro
 West Lulworth BH20 ..172 C4
 Winfrith Newburgh DT2 .156 C3
Winfrith Newburgh CE Fst
 Sch DT2 ....156 C3
Winfrith Tech Ctr DT2 .139 A1
Wingate Ave BA21 ....27 C4
Wingfield Ave
 Christchurch BH23 ....93 B1
 Poole BH15 ....119 B3
Wingfield Ct BH1 ....122 B2
Wingfield Rd DT9 .....30 A3
Wingreen Cl 8 DT3 ..168 A4
Winifred Rd BH15 ....119 C3
Winkelbury Hill (Hill Fort)★
 SP7 ....188 C8
Winkton Cl BH23 .....92 B2
Winkton House BH23 ..92 B2
Winnards Cl BH22 ....61 C1
Winniford Cl DT6 .....99 A4
Winsford Cl BH23 .....93 B1
Winsley Ave BH6 ....123 B2
Winslow Rd DT3 .....153 B2
Winspit Cl BH15 .....118 C2
Winspit Rd BH19 ....183 B4
Winston Ave BH12 ...121 A3
Winston Ct
 1 Christchurch BH23 ..124 A4
 20 New Milton BH25 ..95 A1
Winston Dr BA21 .....27 A4
Winston Gdns BH12 ..121 A3
Winston Par 22 BH25 ..95 A1
Winston Pk BH12 ....121 A3
Winston Rd BH9 ......90 A2
Winston Way BH24 ....55 B4
Winter La DT9 ....15 C3
Winter's La DT3 .....150 A4
Winterborne La BH20 ..82 C3
Winterbourne Cl
 BH15 ....119 B2
Winterbourne Copse
 DT4 ....180 B4
Winterbourne Faringdon
 Village★ DT2 ....135 A3
Winterbourne Hospl
 DT1 ....134 C4
Winterbourne Rd
 BH15 ....119 B3

Winterbourne Valley CE Fst
 Sch DT2 ....105 B1
Winterhayes Cl BH17 ..87 C2
Winters Cl 6 DT3 ....150 A4
Winton (Boys) Sch
 BH10 ....89 B1
Winton Prim Sch BH9 ..89 C1
Winton Way
 Bournemouth BH10 ....89 B1
 New Milton BH25 .....95 A3
Winyards View TA18 ..191 F3
Wisbech Way SO41 ...95 C2
Wishart Gdns BH9 ....90 A3
Wishay St 2 DT1 ....107 B1
Wistaria Ho 7 BH10 ..89 C2
Wisteria Cl BA22 .....26 B3
Wisteria Dr BH31 .....45 C2
Witch Cl SP8 ....10 B2
Witch La SP8 ....10 B2
Witcham La DT2 .....205 F5
Witchampton CE Fst Sch
 BH21 ....200 F1
Witchampton La
 Hinton Martell BH21 ...50 A4
 Witchampton BH21 ...201 A1
Witchampton Rd BH18 ..86 C1
Withermoor Rd BH9 ..121 C4
Withies Croft DT5 ...187 B3
Withingham Rd BH13 ..120 C2
Withybed La BA9 .....4 B2
Witley BH14 ....147 B4
Witney Rd BH17 .....87 B1
Wittey's La TA20 ....202 E6
Woburn Rd BA21 .....28 A4
Woking Rd BH14 ....120 B2
Wolfe Cl BH23 ......124 B4
Wolfeton House★
 DT2 ....107 B3
Wollaston Rd
 Bournemouth BH6 ....123 C2
 Dorchester DT1 ......108 A1
Wollaton Cres BH22 ..61 B2
Wollaton Rd BH22 ....61 B2
Wollstonecraft Rd 25
 BH5 ....122 C2
Wolseley Rd BH12 ...120 B3
Wolterton Rd BH12 ..121 A3
Wolverley Ct 16 BH4 ..121 B2
Wolverton Rd BH7 ...122 C3
Wonderholm Par BH11 ..89 A1
Wood Cl La TA17 ....191 A8
Wood Fold View DT2 ..205 B8
Wood La
 Bournemouth BH11 ....88 C3
 Broadwinsdor DT8 ...203 B7
 Hinton St Mary DT10 ..35 A2
 Stalbridge DT10 ......33 B4
 Symondsbury DT6 .....67 B3
Wood Lawn Cl BH25 ..126 C4
Wood Row BH9 ....90 C2
Wood View BH21 .....60 A4
Woodacre Gdns BH22 ..61 C2
Wood's La DT8 ......204 B3
Woodbury BH1 ....122 A1
Woodbury Ave BH8 ...90 C1
Woodbury Cl BH23 ....91 C2
Woodbury Dro DT2 ..137 B3
Woodbury Gdns SP2 ..213 B1
Woodbury Hill (Fort)★
 BH20 ....81 B1
Woodcocks Cres BH7 ..123 A4
Woodcote 2 BA20 ....26 C1
Woodcote Dr BH16 ...118 A3
Woodcutts La BH21 ...50 B4
Woodend Rd BH9 ....121 C4
Woodfield Gdns BH23 ..93 B1
Woodfield Rd BH11 ....89 A3
Woodford Cl BH24 ....55 B4
Woodford Rd BH1 ...122 B2
Woodgreen Dr BH11 ...88 B2
Woodhayes BA8 ......19 A2
Woodhayes Ave BH23 ..93 C1
Woodhenge BA22 ....26 B3
Woodhouse Cross SP8 ..4 C2
Woodhouse La EX13 ..202 A1
Woodhouse Rd EX13 ..202 A1
Woodlake Cl BH17 ....87 B1
Woodland Ave BH5 ..123 A2
Woodland Cl BH31 ....45 A4

Woodland Ct BH7 ....122 C3
Woodland Gr 12 BA20 ..27 B2
Woodland Mans BH14 ..120 A3
Woodland Way BH23 ..125 B4
Woodland Wlk
 Bournemouth BH5 ...123 A2
 Ferndown BH22 .....61 C4
Woodlands DT2 ......136 A1
Woodlands Ave BH15 ..118 C2
Woodlands Cl BH31 ...45 B2
Woodlands Cres BH15 ..118 C2
Woodlands Dr BH20 ..116 A1
Woodlands Manor★
 BA12 ....3 A2
Woodlands Mead DT10 ..20 C2
Woodlands Rd
 Barton on Sea BH25 ..126 C4
 Mere BA12 ....3 A1
Woodlands Way
 New Milton BH25 .....95 A3
 St.Leonards BH24 .....54 A2
Woodleaze Cl BH18 ...87 A3
Woodlinken Cl BH31 ...45 B2
Woodlinken Dr BH31 ..45 B2
Woodlinken Way BH31 ..45 C2
Woodmead Rd DT7 ...96 A3
Woodpecker Cl BH31 ..45 A3
Woodpecker Dr BH17 ..118 C4
Woodpeckers The
 DT3 ....152 B2
Woodrising BH13 ....147 A2
Woodrisings The BH2 .121 B2
Woodroffe Sch DT7 ...96 A3
Woodruff Cl BH23 ...125 B4
Woods View Rd BH9 ..121 B4
Woodsage Dr SP8 .....5 B1
Woodsford Castle★
 DT2 ....110 A1
Woodsford Cl DT2 ...137 B3
Woodsford House Sch
 DT2 ....110 B1
Woodsford La DT2 ...138 A4
Woodsford Rd DT2 ...137 B4
Woodside Cl BH22 ....61 C3
Woodside Rd
 Bournemouth BH5 ...123 A2
 Ferndown BH22 .....52 C2
 Poole BH14 ....120 B2
Woodstock Cl BH14 ..120 A1
Woodstock Ct BH22 ...61 C2
Woodstock La BH24 ...55 B4
Woodstock Rd
 Burton BH23 ....92 B1
 Poole BH14 ....120 A1
 Salisbury SP1 ....213 B3
 Yeovil BA21 ....27 C4
Woodswater La 5 DT8 ..204 D4
Woodvale Gdns BH25 ..95 B2
Woodvill Rd SP1 ....213 C4
Wool Bridge★ BH20 ..140 A2
Wool CE Fst Sch
 BH20 ....140 A1
Wool Rd BH12 ......120 A4
Wool Sta BH20 ......140 A1
Wooland Gdns DT4 ..180 B4
Woolands La SP7 .....12 B2
Woolcombe Rd DT5 ..186 C2
Woolcott La SP8 ......1 B1
Woolmer La BH24 ....47 B1
Woolsbarrow (Fort)★
 BH20 ....114 C3
Woolsbridge Ind Est
 BH21 ....53 B1
Woolsbridge Rd BH24 ..54 A1
Woolslope Cl BH22 ...53 A1
Woolslope Gdns BH22 ..53 A1
Woolslope Rd BH22 ...53 A1
Woolven Cl BH14 ....120 A1
Wooperton St 9 DT4 ..167 B2
Wootton Cross DT6 ...65 B2
Wootton Gdns BH1 ..122 B2
Wootton Gr DT9 .....30 A4
Wootton La DT6 .....65 B2
Wootton Mount BH1 ..122 A2
Wootton Rd BH25 ....95 B4
Wootton Rough BH25 ..95 A4
Wor Barrow (Long Barrow)★
 SP5 ....189 C4

Worbarrow Gdns
 BH12 ....120 B4
Wordsworth Ave BH8 ..90 C1
Wordsworth Rd SP1 ..213 B3
Worgret Hill BH20 ...141 C1
Worgret Rd
 Poole BH15 ....119 B4
 Wareham BH20 ......142 B2
Worrell Dr BH12 ....120 B4
Worthington Cres
 BH14 ....120 A2
Worthy Rd BH25 .....95 A1
Wortley Rd BH23 ....126 A4
Wrackle Cl DT2 .....106 C4
Wraxall Cl BH17 .....87 B1
Wraxall La DT2 .....206 B2
Wraxhill Rd BA20 .....27 A1
Wren Cl
 Christchurch BH23 ...125 A3
 New Milton BH25 .....94 C1
 Ringwood BH24 ......55 C3
Wren Cres BH12 ....121 A3
Wren Gdns SP6 ......42 B3
Wrenscroft 9 SP2 ...213 B1
Wriggle River La DT2 ..194 E1
Writh Rd DT9 ....31 B1
Wroxham Rd BH12 ...120 C3
Wyatt's La BH20 ....142 C2
Wyatts Cl BH21 ......86 B3
Wyatts La BH21 ......86 B3
Wych Hill DT6 ......100 B2
Wych Ridge DT6 ....100 B2
Wychwood Cl BH2 ...121 C2
Wychwood Dr BH2 ..121 C2
Wychwood Grange 1
 BH2 ....121 C2
Wycliffe Rd BH9 ....121 C4
Wyke CP Sch SP8 .....5 B1
Wyke Oliver Rd DT3 ..168 A4
Wyke Rd Gillingham SP8 ..5 C1
 Weymouth DT4 ......167 A1
Wyke Regis CE Jun Sch
 DT4 ....180 B4
Wyke Regis Com & Sports Ctr
 DT4 ....180 B3
Wyke Regis Inf Sch
 DT4 ....180 B4
Wykeham Cl BH17 ...119 C4
Wykeham Lodge
 BH13 ....147 C3
Wynchard Bank 1
 DT11 ....198 E3
Wyncombe Rd BH5 ..123 A3
Wyndham Pk Sch SP1 ..213 B4
Wyndham Rd
 Christchurch BH23 ...94 A1
 Poole BH14 ....120 A2
 Salisbury SP1 ....213 B3
Wyndham St 5 BA20 ..27 C3
Wyndham Terr SP1 ..213 B3
Wyndham View BA21 ..27 C3
Wynford Rd
 Bournemouth BH9 ....90 A2
 Poole BH14 ....120 B2
Wynne Cl BH18 ......86 C2
Wynnes Cl 4 DT9 ....30 A3
Wynnes Rise DT9 ....30 A3
Wynter Cl BH7 .....122 C4
Wytch Pas BH20 ....162 B4
Wyvern Cl
 East Coker BA20 .....26 C1
 Poole BH12 ....120 B4
Wyvern Ct 24 TA18 ..191 F4
Wyvern Rd 1 DT1 ...107 C1

Y

Yalbury La DT2 .....137 B3
Yard La
 Marshwood DT6 .....203 D2
 Rampisham DT2 .....205 E6
Yarde Farm 5 DT11 ..199 D3
Yarmouth Cl BH12 ...121 A3
Yarmouth Rd BH12 ..120 C3
Yarn Barton

10 Beaminster DT8 .....
18 Yeovil BA20 ....
Yarnbarton DT8 ......
Yarrells Cl BH16 ....118 B3
Yarrells Dr BH16 ...118 A4
Yarrells La BH16 ...118 B3
Yarrells Sch BH16 ...118 A4
Yarrow Cl BH23 .....125 A4
Yarrow Ct 1 SP8 ......5 B1
Yarrow Rd BH12 ....120 A4
Yearlings' Dro BH20 ..113 A4
Yeates Rd DT5 .....186 C3
Yeatman Hospl The
 DT9 ....30 A3
Yeatmans Cl SP7 .....12 B2
Yeatmans La SP7 .....12 B2
Yeatminster Rd BH17 ..87 C1
Yellow La DT6 ....69 B1
Yellowham Hill DT2 ..109 B4
Yelverton Rd 38 BH1 ..121 C2
Yenston Hill BA8 .....18 C4
Yeolands Rd 7 DT5 ..186 C2
Yeomans Ind Pk BH8 ..90 C1
Yeomans Rd BH8 ....90 C2
Yeomans Way BH8 ...90 C1
Yeovil Coll BA22 .....26 B4
Yeovil Coll IT Ctr BA20 ..27 C2
Yeovil Golf Club BA21 ..28 A2
Yeovil Junc Sta BA22 ..28 A1
Yeovil Pen Mill Sta
 BA21 ....28 A3
Yeovil Rd
 Crewkerne TA18 .....191 F4
 Halstock BA22 ......193 D3
 Sherborne DT9 ......29 C3
 Yeovil BA20 ....27 A1
Yeovil Ski Activity Ctr
 BA20 ....27 C2
Yeovil Sports Club
 BA21 ....27 A4
Yerville Gdns SO41 ...95 C2
Yetminster Sta DT9 ..194 C5
Yew La BH25 ....95 B2
Yew Tree Cl
 Wimborne Minster BH21 ..59 B3
 Yeovil BA20 ....27 A1
Yew Tree Ct 30 BH25 ..95 A1
Yew Tree Farm DT2 ..205 A8
Yew Tree La DT2 ....106 C3
Yews The BA12 ......3 A3
Yewstock Sch DT10 ...35 A1
York Ave BH25 ......95 A2
York Cl Broadstone BH18 ..87 A1
 Charminster DT2 ....107 C3
 Christchurch BH23 ...123 C4
York Pl
 Bournemouth BH7 ...123 A3
 17 New Milton BH25 ..95 A2
 Yeovil BA20 ....27 B3
York Rd
 Bournemouth BH1 ...122 A2
 Broadstone BH18 ....87 A1
 Dorchester DT1 .....108 A1
 Salisbury SP2 ....213 A3
Youngs Rd BH11 .....89 A2

Z

Zamek Cl BH11 ......89 A3
Zeals Fst Sch BA12 ....2 A2
Zeals Gn Dr BA12 .....2 A2
Zeals Rise BA12 ......1 C2
Zetland Ct BH4 .....121 A1
Zig Zag Hill SP7 .....24 C3
Zinnia Cl BH10 ......89 C1
Zoar La DT10 ......197 B4

NG	NH	NJ	NK	
NM	NN	NO	NP	
NR	NS	NT	NU	
NX	NY	NZ		
SC	SD	SE	TA	
SH	SJ	SK	TF	TG
SM	SN	SO	SP	TL	TM
SR	SS	ST	SU	TQ	TR
SW	SX	SY	SZ	TV	

Any feature in this atlas can be given a unique reference to help you find the same feature on other Ordnance Survey maps of the area, or to help someone else locate you if they do not have a Street Atlas.

The grid squares in this atlas match the Ordnance Survey National Grid and are at 1 kilometre intervals. The small figures at the bottom and sides of every other grid line are the National Grid kilometre values (**00** to **99** km) and are repeated across the country every 100 km (see left).

To give a unique National Grid reference you need to locate where in the country you are. The country is divided into 100 km squares with each square given a unique two-letter reference. Use the administrative map to determine in which 100 km square a particular page of this atlas falls.

The bold letters and numbers between each grid line (**A** to **C**, **1** to **4**) are for use within a specific Street Atlas only, and when used with the page number, are a convenient way of referencing these grid squares.

Example   The railway bridge over DARLEY GREEN RD in grid square A1

Step 1: Identify the two-letter reference, in this example the page is in **SP**

Step 2: Identify the 1 km square in which the railway bridge falls. Use the figures in the southwest corner of this square: Eastings **17**, Northings **74**. This gives a unique reference: **SP 17 74**, accurate to 1 km.

Step 3: To give a more precise reference accurate to 100 m you need to estimate how many tenths along and how many tenths up this 1 km square the feature is. This makes the bridge about **8** tenths along and about **1** tenth up from the southwest corner.

This gives a unique reference: **SP 178 741**, accurate to 100 m.

Eastings (read from left to right along the bottom) come before Northings (read from bottom to top). If you have trouble remembering say to yourself "Along the hall, THEN up the stairs"!

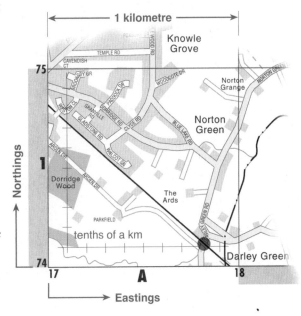

Addresses

Name and Address	Telephone	Page	Grid reference

Name and Address	Telephone	Page	Grid reference

Street Atlases from Philip's

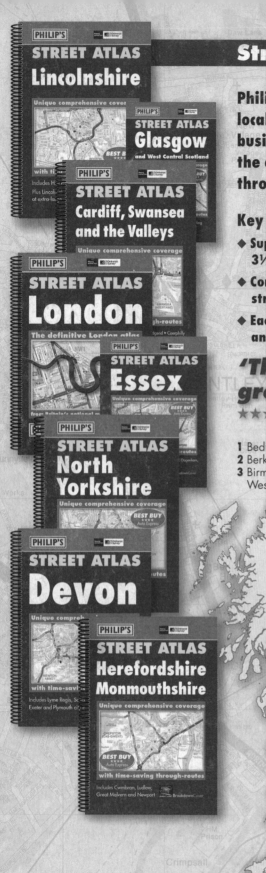

Philip's publish an extensive range of regional and local street atlases which are ideal for motoring, business and leisure use. They are widely used by the emergency services and local authorities throughout Britain.

Key features include:

◆ Superb county-wide mapping at an extra-large scale of 3½ inches to 1 mile, or 2½ inches to 1 mile in pocket editions

◆ Complete urban and rural coverage, detailing every named street in town and country

◆ Each atlas available in two handy sizes – standard spiral and pocket paperback

'The mapping is very clear... great in scope and value'

★★★★ BEST BUY   AUTO EXPRESS

1 Bedfordshire	4 Bristol and Bath	16 Essex
2 Berkshire	5 Buckinghamshire	17 North Essex
3 Birmingham and West Midlands	6 Cambridgeshire	18 South Essex
	7 Cardiff, Swansea and The Valleys	19 Fife and Tayside
	8 Cheshire	20 Glasgow and West Central Scotland
	9 Cornwall	21 Gloucestershire
	10 Cumbria	22 North Hampshire
	11 Derbyshire	23 South Hampshire
	12 Devon	24 Herefordshire and Monmouthshire
	13 Dorset	25 Hertfordshire
	14 County Durham and Teesside	26 East Kent
	15 Edinburgh and East Central Scotland	27 West Kent
		28 Lancashire
		29 Leicestershire and Rutland
		30 Lincolnshire
		31 London
		32 Greater Manchester
		33 Merseyside
		34 Norfolk
		35 Northamptonshire
		36 Nottinghamshire
		37 Oxfordshire
		38 Shropshire
		39 Somerset
		40 Staffordshire
		41 Suffolk
		42 Surrey
		43 East Sussex
		44 West Sussex
		45 Tyne and Wear and Northumberland
		46 Warwickshire
		47 Wiltshire and Swindon
		48 Worcestershire
		49 East Yorkshire and Northern Lincolnshire
		50 North Yorkshire
		51 South Yorkshire
		52 West Yorkshire

How to order

The Philip's range of street atlases is available from good retailers or directly from the publisher by phoning 01903 828503